THE PREACHING OF ISLAM

The Masterpiece Library of ISLAM—5

THE PREACHING OF ISLAM

(A History of the Propagation of the Muslim Faith)

BY

T.W. ARNOLD

ARYAN BOOKS INTERNATIONAL

NEW DELHI

The Preaching of Islam

Published in 1998 By:

ARYAN BOOKS INTERNATIONAL
4378/4B, Pooja Apartments
4B, Ansari Road, Darya Ganj
New Delhi-110002 (India)

ISBN-81-7305-141-0

Printed in India at Print Perfect, New Delhi.

PREFACE TO THE FIRST EDITION

It is with considerable diffidence that I publish these pages; the subject with which they deal is so vast, and I have had to prosecute it under circumstances so disadvantageous, that I can hope but for small measure of success. When I may be better equipped for the task, and after further study has enabled me to fill up the gaps [1] left in the present work, I hope to make it a more worthy contribution to this neglected department of Muhammadan history; and to this end I shall be deeply grateful for the criticisms and corrections of any scholars who may deign to notice the book. To such I would say in the words of St. Augustine: " Qui hæc legens dicit, intelligo quidem quid dictum sit, sed non vere dictum est; asserat ut placet sententiam suam, et redarguat meam, si potest. Quod si cum caritate et veritate fecerit, mihique etiam (si in hac vita maneo) cognoscendum facere curaverit, uberrimum fructum laboris huius mei cepero." [2]

As I can neither claim to be an authority nor a specialist on any of the periods of history dealt with in this book, and as many of the events referred to therein have become matter for controversy, I have given full references to the sources consulted; and here I have thought it better to err on the side of excess rather than that of defect. I have myself suffered so much inconvenience and wasted so much time in hunting up references to books indicated in some obscure or unintelligible manner, that I would desire to spare others a similar annoyance; and while to the general reader I may appear guilty of pedantry, I may perchance save trouble to some scholar who wishes to test the accuracy of a statement or pursue any part of the subject further.

The scheme adopted in this book for the transliteration of Arabic words is that laid down by the Transliteration Committee of the Tenth International Congress of Orientalists, held at Geneva in 1894, with the exception that the last letter of the article is assimilated to the so-called solar

[1] E.g. The spread of Islam in Sicily and the missionary labours of the numerous Muslim saints.

[2] De Trinitate, i. 5. (Migne, tom. xlii, p. 823.)

letters. In the case of geographical names this scheme has not been so rigidly applied—in many instances because I could not discover the original Arabic form of the word, in others (e. g. Mecca, Medina), because usage has almost created for them a prescriptive title.

Though this work is confessedly, as explained in the Introduction, a record of missionary efforts and not a history of persecutions,[1] I have endeavoured to be strictly impartial and to conform to the ideal laid down by the Christian historian [2] who chronicled the successes of the Ottomans and the fall of Constantinople: *οὔτε πρὸς χάριν οὔτε πρὸς φθόνον, ἀλλ' οὐδὲ πρὸς μῖσος ἢ καὶ πρὸς εὔνοιαν συγγράφειν χρεὼν ἐστι τὸν συγγράφοντα, ἀλλ' ἱστορίας μόνον χάριν καὶ τοῦ μὴ λήθης βυθῷ παραδοθῆναι, ἣν ὁ χρόνος οἶδε γεννᾶν, τὴν ἱστορίαν.*

I desire to thank Her Excellency the Princess Barberini; His Excellency the Prince Chigi; the Most Rev. Dr. Paul Goethals, Archbishop of Calcutta; the Right Rev. Fr. Francis Pesci, Bishop of Allahabad; the Rev. S. S. Allnutt, of the Cambridge Mission, Dehli; the Trustees of Dr. Williams's Library, Gordon Square, London, for the liberal use they have allowed me of their respective libraries.

I am under an especial debt of gratitude to James Kennedy, Esq., late of the Bengal Civil Service, who has never ceased to take a kindly interest in my book, though it has almost exemplified the Horatian precept, Nonum prematur in annum; to his profound scholarship and wide reading I have been indebted for much information that would otherwise have remained unknown to me, nor do I owe less to the stimulus of his enthusiastic love of learning and his helpful sympathy. I am also under a debt of gratitude to the kindness of Conte Ugo Balzani, but for whose assistance certain parts of my work would have been impossible to me. To the late Professor Robertson Smith I am indebted for valuable suggestions as to the lines of study on which the history of the North African Church and the condition of the Christians under Muslim rule, should be worked out; the profound regret which all Semitic scholars feel at his loss is to me intensified by the thought that this is the only acknowledgment I am able to make of his generous help and encouragement.

[1] Accordingly the reader will find no account of the recent history of Armenia or Crete, or indeed of any part of the empire of the Turks during the present century—a period singularly barren of missionary enterprise on their part.

[2] Phrantzes, p. 5.

I desire also to acknowledge my obligations to Sir Sayyid Aḥmad K͟hān Bahādur, K.C.S.I., LL.D.; to my learned friend and colleague, Shamsu-l 'Ulamā' Mawlawī Muḥammad Shiblī Nu'mānī, who has assisted me most generously out of the abundance of his knowledge of early Muhammadan history; and to my former pupil, Mawlawī Bahādur 'Alī, M.A.

Lastly, and above all, must I thank my dear wife, but for whom this work would never have emerged out of a chaos of incoherent materials, and whose sympathy and approval are the best reward of my labours.

PREFACE TO THE SECOND EDITION

THE first edition of this book having been out of print for several years and frequent inquiries having been made for copies, this new edition has been prepared and an effort has been made to revise the work in the light of the fresh materials that have accumulated during the last sixteen years; but I can make no claim to have made myself acquainted with the whole of the vast literature on the subject, in upwards of ten different languages, which has been published during this interval. The growing interest in Islam and the various branches of study connected with it, may be estimated from the fact that since 1906 five periodicals have made their appearance devoted to investigations cognate to the subject-matter of the present work, viz. Revue du Monde Musulman, publiée par La Mission Scientifique du Maroc (Paris, 1906–); Der Islam, Zeitschrift für Geschichte und Kultur des islamischen Orients (Strassburg, 1910–); The Moslem World, a quarterly review of current events, literature, and thought among Mohammedans, and the progress of Christian Missions in Moslem lands (London, 1911–); Mir Islama (St. Petersburg, 1912–); and Die Welt des Islams, Zeitschrift der deutschen Gesellschaft für Islamkunde (Berlin, 1913–). The Christian missionary societies are also now devoting increased attention to the subject of Muslim missionary activity and accordingly it takes up a proportionately larger place in their publications than before.

This second edition would have been completed several years ago but for the illiberal policy which closes the Reading Room of the British Museum at 7 o'clock and has thus made it practically inaccessible to me except on Saturdays.[1] I therefore desire to express my grateful thanks to those friends who have facilitated my labours by the loan of books from the Libraries of the University of Leiden and the University of Utrecht (through the kind offices of

[1] The student of the literature of Science or of the Fine Arts finds the libraries at South Kensington open till 10 o'clock on three evenings every week, but the one library in this country that aims at any completeness is available only to such students as are at leisure during the day-time.

Professor Wensinck), and the École des Langues Orientales Vivantes, Paris;—to Mr. J. A. Oldham, editor of The International Review of Missions, I am indebted for the loan of volumes of the Allgemeine Missions-Zeitschrift, a set of which I have been unable to find in London; my thanks are specially due to Dr. F. W. Thomas, who has allowed me to study for lengthy periods (along with other books from the India Office Library) the monumental *Annali dell' Islam* by Leone Caetani, Principe di Teano,—a work of inestimable value for the early history of Islam, but unfortunately placed out of the reach of the average scholar by reason of its great cost.

I am also much indebted for several valuable indications to those scholars who reviewed the book when it first appeared,—above all, to Professor Goldziher, whose sympathetic interest in this work has encouraged me to continue it.

London, 1913.

CONTENTS

CHAPTER IV.

THE SPREAD OF ISLAM AMONG THE CHRISTIAN NATIONS OF AFRICA.

CHAPTER V.

THE SPREAD OF ISLAM AMONG THE CHRISTIANS OF SPAIN.

CHAPTER VI.

THE SPREAD OF ISLAM AMONG THE CHRISTIAN NATIONS IN EUROPE UNDER THE TURKS.

CHAPTER VII.

THE SPREAD OF ISLAM IN PERSIA AND CENTRAL ASIA.

CHAPTER VIII.

THE SPREAD OF ISLAM AMONG THE MONGOLS AND TATARS.

CHAPTER IX.

THE SPREAD OF ISLAM IN INDIA.

CHAPTER X.

THE SPREAD OF ISLAM IN CHINA.

CHAPTER XI.

THE SPREAD OF ISLAM IN AFRICA.

CHAPTER XII.

THE SPREAD OF ISLAM IN THE MALAY ARCHIPELAGO.

CHAPTER XIII.

CONCLUSION.

APPENDIX I.

APPENDIX II.

APPENDIX III.

THE PREACHING OF ISLAM

CHAPTER I.

INTRODUCTION.

EVER since Professor Max Müller delivered his lecture in Westminster Abbey, on the day of intercession for missions, in December, 1873, it has been a literary commonplace, that the six great religions of the world may be divided into missionary and non-missionary; under the latter head fall Judaism, Brahmanism and Zoroastrianism, and under the former Buddhism, Christianity and Islam; and he well defined what the term,—a missionary religion,—should be taken to mean, viz. one "in which the spreading of the truth and the conversion of unbelievers are raised to the rank of a sacred duty by the founder or his immediate successors. . . . It is the spirit of truth in the hearts of believers which cannot rest, unless it manifests itself in thought, word and deed, which is not satisfied till it has carried its message to every human soul, till what it believes to be the truth is accepted as the truth by all members of the human family." [1]

It is such a zeal for the truth of their religion that has inspired the Muhammadans to carry with them the message of Islam to the people of every land into which they penetrate, and that justly claims for their religion a place among those we term missionary. It is the history of the birth of this missionary zeal, its inspiring forces and the modes of its activity that forms the subject of the following pages. The 200 millions of Muhammadans scattered over the

[1] A note on Mr. Lyall's article: "Missionary Religions." *Fortnightly Review*, July, 1874.

world at the present day are evidences of its workings through the length of thirteen centuries.

The doctrines of this faith were first proclaimed to the people of Arabia in the seventh century, by a prophet under whose banner their scattered tribes became a nation; and filled with the pulsations of this new national life, and with a fervour and enthusiasm that imparted an almost invincible strength to their armies, they poured forth over three continents to conquer and subdue. Syria, Palestine, Egypt, North Africa and Persia were the first to fall before them, and pressing westward to Spain and eastward beyond the Indus, the followers of the Prophet found themselves, one hundred years after his death, masters of an empire greater than that of Rome at the zenith of its power.

Although in after years this great empire was split up and the political power of Islam diminished, still its spiritual conquests went on uninterruptedly. When the Mongol hordes sacked Baghdād (A.D. 1258) and drowned in blood the faded glory of the 'Abbāsid dynasty,—when the Muslims were expelled from Cordova by Ferdinand of Leon and Castile (A.D. 1236), and Granada, the last stronghold of Islam in Spain, paid tribute to the Christian king,—Islam had just gained a footing in the island of Sumatra and was just about to commence its triumphant progress through the islands of the Malay Archipelago. In the hours of its political degradation, Islam has achieved some of its most brilliant spiritual conquests: on two great historical occasions, infidel barbarians have set their feet on the necks of the followers of the Prophet,—the Saljūq Turks in the eleventh and the Mongols in the thirteenth century,—and in each case the conquerors have accepted the religion of the conquered. Unaided also by the temporal power, Muslim missionaries have carried their faith into Central Africa, China and the East India Islands.

At the present day the faith of Islam extends from Morocco to Zanzibar, from Sierra Leone to Siberia and China, from Bosnia to New Guinea. Outside the limits of strictly Muhammadan countries and of lands, such as China and Russia, that contain a large Muhammadan population, there are some few small communities of the followers of the Prophet, which bear witness to the faith of Islam in the midst of unbelievers. Such are the Polish-speaking Muslims of Tatar origin in Lithuania, that inhabit the districts of Kovno, Vilno and Grodno;[1] the Dutch-speaking Muslims of Cape Colony; and the Indian coolies that have carried the faith of Islam with them to the West India Islands and to British and Dutch Guiana. In recent years, too, Islam has found adherents in England, in North America, Australia and Japan.

The spread of this faith over so vast a portion of the globe is due to various causes, social, political and religious: but among these, one of the most powerful factors at work in the production of this stupendous result, has been the unremitted labours of Muslim missionaries, who, with the Prophet himself as their great ensample, have spent themselves for the conversion of unbelievers.

The duty of missionary work is no after-thought in the history of Islam, but was enjoined on believers from the beginning, as may be judged from the following passages in the Qur'ān,—which are here quoted in chronological order according to the date of their being delivered.

> "Summon thou to the way of thy Lord with wisdom and with kindly warning: dispute with them in the kindest manner. (xvi. 126.)
>
> "They who have inherited the Book after them (i.e. the Jews and Christians), are in perplexity of doubt concerning it.
>
> "For this cause summon thou (them to the faith), and walk uprightly therein as thou hast been bidden, and follow not their desires: and say: In whatsoever Books God hath sent down do I believe: I am commanded to decide justly between you: God is your Lord and our Lord: we have our works and you have your works: between us and you let there be no strife: God will make us all one: and to Him shall we return." (xlii. 13–14.)

Similar injunctions are found also in the Medinite Sūrahs,

[1] Reclus, vol. v. p. 433; Gasztowtt, p. 320 sqq.

delivered at a time when Muḥammad was at the head of a large army and at the height of his power.

"Say to those who have been given the Book and to the ignorant, Do you accept Islam? Then, if they accept Islam, are they guided aright: but if they turn away, then thy duty is only preaching; and God's eye is on His servants. (iii. 19.)

"Thus God clearly showeth you His signs that perchance ye may be guided;

"And that there may be from among you a people who invite to the Good, and enjoin the Just, and forbid the Wrong; and these are they with whom it shall be well. (iii. 99–100.)

"To every people have We appointed observances which they observe. Therefore let them not dispute the matter with thee, but summon them to thy Lord: Verily thou art guided aright:

"But if they debate with thee, then say: God best knoweth what ye do!" (xxii. 66–67.)

The following passages are taken from what is generally supposed to be the last Sūrah that was delivered.

"If any one of those who join gods with God ask an asylum of thee, grant him an asylum in order that he may hear the word of God; then let him reach his place of safety." (ix. 6.)

With regard to the unbelievers who had broken their plighted word, who "sell the signs of God for a mean price and turn others aside from His way," and "respect not with a believer either ties of blood or good faith," . . . it is said:—

"Yet if they turn to God and observe prayer and give alms, then are they your brothers in the faith: and We make clear the signs for men of knowledge." (ix. 11.)

Thus from its very inception Islam has been a missionary religion, both in theory and in practice, for the life of Muḥammad exemplifies the same teaching, and the Prophet himself stands at the head of a long series of Muslim missionaries who have won an entrance for their faith into the hearts of unbelievers. Moreover it is not in the cruelties of the persecutor or the fury of the fanatic that we should look for the evidences of the missionary spirit of Islam, any more than in the exploits of that mythical personage, the Muslim warrior with sword in one hand and Qur'ān in the other,[1]—but in the quiet, unobtrusive labours of the preacher and the trader who have carried their faith into every quarter of the globe. Such peaceful methods of preaching and persuasion were not adopted, as some would have us believe, only when political circumstances made force and violence impossible or impolitic, but were most strictly enjoined in numerous passages of the Qur'ān, as follows :—

> " And endure what they say with patience, and depart from them with a decorous departure.
>
> " And let Me alone with the gainsayers, rich in the pleasures (of this life) ; and bear thou with them yet a little while. (lxxiii. 10–11.)
>
> " (My) sole (work) is preaching from God and His message. (lxxii. 24.)
>
> " Tell those who have believed to pardon those who hope not for the days of God in which He purposeth to recompense men according to their deserts. (xlv. 13.)
>
> " They who had joined other gods with God say, 'Had He pleased, neither we nor our forefathers had worshipped aught but Him ; nor had we, apart from Him, declared anything unlawful.' Thus acted they who were before them. Yet is the duty of the apostles other than plain-spoken preaching ? (xvi. 37.)

[1] This misinterpretation of the Muslim wars of conquest has arisen from the assumption that wars waged for the extension of Muslim domination over the lands of the unbelievers implied that the aim in view was their conversion. Goldziher has well pointed out this distinction in his *Vorlesungen über den Islam :* " Was Muhammed zünachst in seinem arabischen Umkreise getan, das hinterlässt er als Testament für die Zukunft seiner Gemeinde : Bekämpfung der Ungläubigen, die Ausbreitung nicht so sehr des Glaubens als seiner Machtsphäre, die die Machtsphäre Allahs ist. Es ist dabei den Kämpfern des Islams zunächst nicht so sehr um Bekehrung als um Unterwerfung der Ungläubigen zu tun." (p. 25.)

"Then if they turn their backs, still thy office is only plain-spoken preaching. (xvi. 84.)

"Dispute ye not, unless in kindliest sort, with the people of the Book; save with such of them as have dealt wrongfully (with you): and say ye, 'We believe in what has been sent down to us and hath been sent down to you. Our God and your God is one, and to Him are we self-surrendered.' (xxix. 45.)

"But if they turn aside from thee, yet We have not sent thee to be guardian over them. 'Tis thine but to preach. (xlii. 47.)

"But if thy Lord had pleased, verily all who are in the world would have believed together. Wilt thou then compel men to become believers? (x. 99.)

"And we have not sent thee otherwise than to mankind at large, to announce and to warn." (xxxiv. 27.)

Such precepts are not confined to the Meccan Sūrahs, but are found in abundance also in those delivered at Medina, as follows:—

"Let there be no compulsion in religion. (ii. 257.)

"Obey God and obey the apostle; but if ye turn away, yet is our apostle only charged with plain-spoken preaching. (lxiv. 12.)

"Obey God and obey the apostle: but if ye turn back, still the burden of his duty is on him only, and the burden of your duty rests on you. And if ye obey him, ye shall have guidance: but plain preaching is all that devolves upon the apostle. (xxiv. 53.)

"Say: O men! I am only your plain-spoken (open) warner. (xxii. 48.)

"Verily We have sent thee to be a witness and a herald of good and a warner,

"That ye may believe on God and on His apostle; and may assist Him and honour Him, and praise Him morning and evening. (xlviii. 8–9.)

"Thou wilt not cease to discover the treacherous ones among them, except a few of them. But forgive them and pass it over. Verily, God loveth those who act generously." (v. 16.)

It is the object of the following pages to show how this ideal was realised in history and how these principles of missionary activity were put into practice by the exponents of Islam. And at the outset the reader should clearly understand that this work is not intended to be a history of Muhammadan persecutions but of Muhammadan missions —it does not aim at chronicling the instances of forced conversions which may be found scattered up and down the pages of Muhammadan histories. European writers have taken such care to accentuate these, that there is no fear of their being forgotten, and they do not strictly come within the province of a history of missions. In a history of Christian missions we should naturally expect to hear more of the labours of St. Liudger and St. Willehad among the pagan Saxons than of the baptisms that Charlemagne forced them to undergo at the point of the sword.[1] The true missionaries of Denmark were St. Ansgar and his successors rather than King Cnut, who forcibly rooted out paganism from his dominions.[2] Abbot Gottfried and Bishop Christian, though less successful in converting the pagan Prussians, were more truly representative of Christian missionary work than the Brethren of the Sword and other Crusaders who brought their labours to completion by means of fire and sword. The knights of the "Ordo fratrum militiæ Christi" forced Christianity on the people of Livonia, but it is not to these militant propagandists but to the monks Meinhard and Theodoric that we should point as being the true missionaries of the Christian faith in this country. The violent means sometimes employed by the Jesuit missionaries[3] cannot derogate from the honour due to St. Francis Xavier and other preachers of the same order. Nor is Valentyn any the less the apostle of Amboyna because in 1699 an order was promulgated to the Rajas of this

[1] See Enhardi Fuldensis Annales, A.D. 777. "Saxones post multas cædes et varia bella afflicti, tandem christiani effecti, Francorum dicioni subduntur." G. H. Pertz: Monumenta Germaniæ Historica, vol. i. p. 349. (See also pp. 156, 159.)

[2] "Tum zelo propagandæ fidei succensus, barbara regna iusto certamine aggressus, devictas subditasque nationes christianæ legi subiugavit." (Breviarium Romanum. Iun. 19.)

[3] Mathurin Veyssière de la Croze: Histoire du Christianisme des Indes, pp. 529–531. (The Hague, 1724.)

island that they should have ready a certain number of pagans to be baptised, when the pastor came on his rounds.[1]

In the history of the Christian church missionary activity is seen to be intermittent, and an age of apostolic fervour may be succeeded by a period of apathy and indifference, or persecution and forced conversion may take the place of the preaching of the Word; so likewise does the propaganda of Islam in various epochs of Muhammadan history ebb and flow. But since the zeal of proselytising is a distinct feature of either faith, its missionary history may fittingly be singled out as a separate branch of study, not as excluding other manifestations of the religious life but as concentrating attention on an aspect of it that has special characteristics of its own. Thus the annals of propaganda and persecution may be studied apart from one another, whether in the history of the Christian or the Muslim church, though in both they may be at times commingled. For just as the Christian faith has not always been propagated by the methods adopted in Viken (the southern part of Norway) by King Olaf Trygvesson, who either slew those who refused to accept Christianity, or cut off their hands or feet, or drove them into banishment, and in this manner spread the Christian faith throughout the whole of Viken,[2]—and just as the advice of St. Louis has not been made a principle of Christian missionary work,—"When a layman hears the Christian law ill spoken of, he should not defend that law save with his sword, which he should thrust into the infidel's belly, as far as it will go,"[3]—so there have been Muslim missionaries who have not been guided in their propagandist methods by the savage utterance of Marwān, the last of the 'Umayyad caliphs: "Whosoever among the people of Egypt does not enter into my religion and pray as I pray and follow my tenets, I will slay and crucify him."[4] Nor are al-Mutawak-

[1] Revue de l'Histoire des Religions, vol. xi. p. 89.
[2] Konrad Maurer: Die Bekehrung des norwegischen Stammes zum Christenthume, vol. i. p. 284. (München, 1855.)
[3] Jean, Sire de Joinville: Histoire de Saint Louis, ed. N. de Wailly, p. 30, (§ 53).
[4] Severus, p. 191 (ll. 21–22).

kil, al-Ḥākim and Tīpū Sulṭān to be looked upon as typical missionaries of Islam to the exclusion of such preachers as Mawlānā Ibrāhīm, the apostle of Java, Khwājah Mu'īn al-Dīn Chishtī in India and countless others who won converts to the Muslim faith by peaceful means alone.

But though a clear distinction can be drawn between conversion as the result of persecution and a peaceful propaganda by means of methods of persuasion, it is not so easy to ascertain the motives that have induced the convert to change his faith, or to discover whether the missionary has been wholly animated by a love of souls and by the high ideal set forth in the first paragraph of this chapter. Both in Christianity and Islam there have been at all times earnest souls to whom their religion has been the supreme reality of their lives, and this absorbing interest in matters of the spirit has found expression in that zeal for the communication of cherished truths and for the domination of doctrines and systems they have deemed perfect, which constitutes the vivifying force of missionary movements,—and there have likewise been those without the pale, who have responded to their appeal and have embraced the new faith with a like fervour. But, on the other hand, Islam—like Christianity—has reckoned among its adherents many persons to whom ecclesiastical institutions have been merely instruments of a political policy or forms of social organisation, to be accepted either as disagreeable necessities or as convenient solutions of problems that they do not care to think out for themselves; such persons may likewise be found among the converts of either faith. Thus both Christianity and Islam have added to the number of their followers by methods and under conditions—social, political and economic—which have no connection with such a thirst for souls as animates the true missionary. Moreover, the annals of missionary enterprise frequently record the admission of converts without any attempt to analyse the motives that have led them to change their faith, and especially for the history of Muslim missions there is a remarkable poverty of material in this respect, since Muslim literature is singularly poor in those records of conversions that occupy such a large place in the literature of the Christian church. Accordingly, in the following sketch of the missionary activity of Islam, it has not always been possible to discover whether political, social, economic or purely religious motives have determined conversion, though occasional reference can be made to the operation of one or the other influence.

CHAPTER II.

STUDY OF THE LIFE OF MUHAMMAD CONSIDERED AS A PREACHER OF ISLAM.

It is not proposed in this chapter to add another to the already numerous biographies of Muḥammad, but rather to make a study of his life in one of its aspects only, viz. that in which the Prophet is presented to us as a preacher, as the apostle unto men of a new religion. The life of the founder of Islam and the inaugurator of its propaganda may naturally be expected to exhibit to us the true character of the missionary activity of this religion. If the life of the Prophet serves as the standard of conduct for the ordinary believer, it must do the same for the Muslim missionary. From the pattern, therefore, we may hope to learn something of the spirit that would animate those who sought to copy it, and of the methods they might be expected to adopt. For the missionary spirit of Islam is no after-thought in its history; it interpenetrates the religion from its very commencement, and in the following sketch it is desired to show how this is so, how Muḥammad the Prophet is the type of the missionary of Islam. It is therefore beside the purpose to describe his early history, or the influences under which he grew up to manhood, or to consider him in the light either of a statesman or a general: it is as the preacher alone that he will demand our attention.

When, after long internal conflict and disquietude, Muḥammad was at length convinced of his divine mission, his earliest efforts were directed towards persuading his own family of the truth of the new doctrine. The unity of God, the abomination of idolatry, the duty laid upon man of submission to the will of his Creator,—these were the simple truths to which he claimed their allegiance.

The first convert was his faithful and loving wife, Khadījah,—she who fifteen years before had offered her hand in marriage to the poor kinsman that had so successfully traded with her merchandise as a hired agent,—with the words, "I love thee, my cousin, for thy kinship with me, for the respect with which thy people regard thee, for thy honesty, for the beauty of thy character and for the truthfulness of thy speech." [1] She had lifted him out of poverty, and enabled him to live up to the social position to which he was entitled by right of birth; but this was as nothing to the fidelity and loving devotion with which she shared his mental anxieties, and helped him with tenderest sympathy and encouragement in the hour of his despondency.

Up to her death in A.D. 619 (after a wedded life of five and twenty years) she was always ready with sympathy, consolation and encouragement whenever he suffered from the persecution of his enemies or was tortured by doubts and misgivings. "So Khadījah believed," says the biographer of the Prophet, "and attested the truth of that which came to him from God and aided him in his undertaking. Thus was the Lord minded to lighten the burden of His Prophet; for whenever he heard anything that grieved him touching his rejection by the people, he would return to her and God would comfort him through her, for she reassured him and lightened his burden and declared her trust in him and made it easy for him to bear the scorn of men." [2]

Among the earliest believers were his adopted children Zayd and 'Alī, and his bosom friend Abū Bakr, of whom Muḥammad would often say in after years, "I never invited any to the faith who displayed not hesitation, perplexity and vacillation—excepting only Abū Bakr; who when I told him of Islam tarried not, neither was perplexed." He was a wealthy merchant, much respected by his fellow citizens for the integrity of his character and for his intelligence and ability. After his conversion he expended the greater part of his fortune on the purchase of Muslim slaves who were persecuted by their masters on account of their adherence to the teaching of Muḥammad,

[1] Ibn Isḥāq, p. 120. [2] Id. p. 155.

Through his influence, to a great extent, five of the earliest converts were added to the number of believers, Sa'd b. Abī Waqqāṣ, the future conqueror of the Persians; al-Zubayr b. al-'Awwām, a relative both of the Prophet and his wife; Ṭalḥah, famous as a warrior in after days; a wealthy merchant 'Abd al-Raḥmān b. 'Awf, and 'Uthmān, the third Khalīfah. The last was early exposed to persecution; his uncle seized and bound him, saying, "Dost thou prefer a new religion to that of thy fathers? I swear I will not loose thee until thou givest up this new faith thou art following after." To which 'Uthmān replied, "By the Lord, I will never abandon it!" Whereupon his uncle, seeing the firmness of his attachment to his faith, released him.

With other additions, particularly from among slaves and poor persons, the Prophet succeeded in collecting round him a little band of followers during the first three years of his mission. Encouraged by the success of these private efforts, Muḥammad determined on more active measures and began to preach in public. He called his kinsmen together and invited them to embrace the new faith. "No Arab," he urged, "has offered to his nation more precious advantages than those I bring you. I offer you happiness in this world and in the life to come. Who among you will aid me in this task?" All were silent. Only 'Alī, with boyish enthusiasm, cried out, "Prophet of God, I will aid thee." At this the company broke up with derisive laughter.

Undeterred by the ill-success of this preaching, he repeatedly appealed to them on other occasions, but his message and his warnings received from them nothing but scoffing and contempt.

More than once the Quraysh tried to induce his uncle Abū Ṭālib, as head of the clan of the Banū Hāshim, to which Muḥammad belonged, to restrain him from making such attacks upon their ancestral faith, or otherwise they threatened to resort to more violent measures. Abū Ṭālib accordingly appealed to his nephew not to bring disaster on himself and his family. The Prophet replied: "Were the sun to come down on my right hand and the moon on my left, and the choice were offered me of abandoning my mission until God himself should reveal it, or perishing in the achievement of it, I would not abandon it." Abū Ṭālib was moved and exclaimed, "Go and say whatever thou wilt: by God! I will never give thee up unto thy enemies."

The Quraysh viewed the progress of the new religion with increasing dissatisfaction and hatred. They adopted all possible means, threats and promises, insults and offers of worldly honour and aggrandisement to induce Muḥammad to abandon the part he had taken up. The violent abuse with which he was assailed is said to have been the indirect cause of drawing to his side one important convert in the person of his uncle, Ḥamzah, whose chivalrous soul was so stung to sudden sympathy by a tale of insult inflicted on and patiently borne by his nephew, that he changed at once from a bitter enemy into a staunch adherent. His was not the only instance of sympathy for the sufferings of the Muslims being aroused at the sight of the persecutions they had to endure, and many, no doubt, secretly favoured the new religion who did not declare themselves until the day of its triumph.

The hostility of the Quraysh to the new faith increased in bitterness as they watched the increase in the numbers of its adherents. They realised that the triumph of the new teaching meant the destruction of the national religion and the national worship, and a loss of wealth and power to the guardians of the sacred Ka'bah. Muḥammad himself was safe under the protection of Abū Ṭālib and the Banū Hāshim, who, though they had no sympathy for the doctrines their kinsman taught, yet with the strong clan-feeling peculiar to the Arabs, secured him from any attempt upon his life, though he was still exposed to continual insult and annoyance. But the poor who had no protector, and the slaves, had to endure the cruelest persecution, and were imprisoned and tortured in order to induce them to recant. It was at this time that Abū Bakr purchased the freedom of Bilāl,[1] an African slave, who was called by

[1] He is famous throughout the Muhammadan world as the first mu'a<u>dh</u><u>dh</u>in.

Muḥammad "the first-fruits of Abyssinia." He had been cruelly tortured by being exposed, day after day, to the scorching rays of the sun, stretched out on his back, with an enormous stone on his stomach; here he was told he would have to stay until either he died or renounced Muhammad and worshipped idols, to which he would reply only, "There is but one God, there is but one God." Two persons died under the tortures they had to undergo. The constancy of a few gave way under the trial, but persecution served only to re-kindle the zeal of others. 'Abd Allāh b. Mas'ūd made bold to recite a passage of the Qur'ān within the precincts of the Ka'bah itself,—an act of daring that none of the followers of Muḥammad had ventured upon before. The assembled Quraysh attacked him and smote him on the face, but it was some time before they compelled him to desist. He returned to his companions, prepared to bear witness to his faith in a similar manner on the next day, but they dissuaded him, saying, "This is enough for thee, since thou hast made them listen to what they hated to hear."

The virulence of the opposition of the Quraysh is probably the reason why in the fourth year of his mission Muḥammad took up his residence in the house of al-Arqam, one of the early converts. It was in a central situation, much frequented by pilgrims and strangers, and here peaceably and without interruption he was able to preach the doctrines of Islam to all enquirers that came to him. Muḥammad's stay in this house marks an important epoch in the propagation of Islam in Mecca, and many Muslims dated their conversion from the days when the Prophet preached in the house of al-Arqam.

As Muḥammad was unable to relieve his persecuted followers, he advised them to take refuge in Abyssinia, and in the fifth year of his mission (A.D. 615), eleven men and four women crossed over to Abyssinia, where they received a kind welcome from the Christian king of the country. Among them was a certain Muṣ'ab b. 'Umayr whose history is interesting as of one who had to endure that most bitter trial of the new convert—the hatred of those he loves and who once loved him. He had been led to embrace Islam through the teaching he had listened to in the house of al-Arqam, but he was afraid to let the fact of his conversion become known, because his tribe and his mother, who bore an especial love to him, were bitterly opposed to the new religion; and indeed, when they discovered the fact, seized and imprisoned him. But he succeeded in effecting his escape to Abyssinia.

The hatred of the Quraysh is said to have pursued the fugitives even to Abyssinia, and an embassy was sent to demand their extradition from the king of that country. But when he heard their story from the Muslims, he refused to withdraw from them his protection. In answer to his enquiries as to their religion, they said: "O King, we were plunged in the darkness of ignorance, worshipping idols, and eating carrion; we practised abominations, severed the ties of kinship and maltreated our neighbours; the strong among us devoured the weak; and so we remained until God sent us an apostle, from among ourselves, whose lineage we knew as well as his truth, his trustworthiness and the purity of his life. He called upon us to worship the One God and abandon the stones and idols that our fathers had worshipped in His stead. He bade us be truthful in speech, faithful to our promises, compassionate and kind to our parents and neighbours, and to desist from crime and bloodshed. He forbade to do evil, to lie, to rob the orphan or defame women. He enjoined on us the worship of God alone, with prayer, almsgiving and fasting. And we believed in him and followed the teachings that he brought us from God. But our countrymen rose up against us and persecuted us to make us renounce our faith, and return to the worship of idols and the abominations of our former life. So when they cruelly entreated us, reducing us to bitter straits and came between us and the practice of our religion, we took refuge in your country; putting our trust in your justice, we hope that you will deliver us from the oppression of our enemies." Their prayer was heard and the embassy of the Quraysh returned discomfited.[1] Meanwhile, in Mecca, a fresh attempt

[1] Ibn Isḥāq, p. 219–220. Ṭabarī makes no mention of this mission and Caetani (i. p. 278) accordingly suggests that it is a later invention.

was made to induce the Prophet to abandon his work of preaching by promises of wealth and honour, but in vain.

While the result of the embassy to Abyssinia was being looked for in Mecca with the greatest expectancy, there occurred the conversion of a man, who before had been one of the most bitter enemies of Muḥammad, and had opposed him with the utmost persistence and fanaticism—a man whom the Muslims had every reason then to look on as their most terrible and virulent enemy, though afterwards he shines as one of the noblest figures in the early history of Islam, viz. 'Umar b. al-Khaṭṭāb. One day, in a fit of rage against the Prophet, he set out, sword in hand, to slay him. On the way, one of his relatives met him and asked him where he was going. "I am looking for Muḥammad," he answered, "to kill the renegade who has brought discord among the Quraysh, called them fools, reviled their religion and defamed their gods." "Why dost thou not rather punish those of thy own family, and set them right?" "And who are these of my own family?" answered 'Umar. "Thy brother-in-law Sa'īd and thy sister Fāṭimah, who have become Muslims and followers of Muḥammad." 'Umar at once rushed off to the house of his sister, and found her with her husband and Khabbāb, another of the followers of Muḥammad, who was teaching them to recite a chapter of the Qur'ān. 'Umar burst into the room: "What was that sound I heard?" "It was nothing," they replied. "Nay, but I heard you, and I have learned that you have become followers of Muḥammad." Whereupon he rushed upon Sa'īd and struck him. Fāṭimah threw herself between them, to protect her husband, crying, "Yes, we are Muslims; we believe in God and His Prophet: slay us if you will." In the struggle his sister was wounded, and when 'Umar saw the blood on her face, he was softened and asked to see the paper they had been reading: after some hesitation she handed it to him. It contained the 20th Sūrah of the Qur'ān. When 'Umar read it, he exclaimed, "How beautiful, how sublime it is!" As he read on, conviction suddenly overpowered him and he cried, "Lead me to Muḥammad that I may tell him of my conversion." [1]

[1] Ibn Isḥāq, pp. 225–6.

The conversion of 'Umar is a turning-point in the history of Islam: the Muslims were now able to take up a bolder attitude. Muḥammad left the house of al-Arqam and the believers publicly performed their devotions together round the Ka'bah. The situation might thus be expected to give the aristocracy of Mecca just cause for apprehension. For they had no longer to deal with a band of oppressed and despised outcasts, struggling for a weak and miserable existence. It was rather a powerful faction, adding daily to its strength by the accession of influential citizens and endangering the stability of the existing government by an alliance with a powerful foreign prince.

The Quraysh resolved accordingly to make a determined effort to check the further growth of the new movement in their city. They put the Banū Hāshim, who through ties of kindred protected the Prophet, under a ban, in accordance with which the Quraysh agreed that they would not marry their women, nor give their own in marriage to them; they would sell nothing to them, nor buy aught from them—that dealings with them of every kind should cease. For three years the Banū Hāshim are said to have been confined to one quarter of the city, except during the sacred months, in which all war ceased throughout Arabia and a truce was made in order that pilgrims might visit the sacred Ka'bah, the centre of the national religion.

Muḥammad used to take advantage of such times of pilgrimage to preach to the various tribes that flocked to Mecca and the adjacent fairs. But with no success, for his uncle Abū Lahab used to dog his footsteps, crying with a loud voice, "He is an impostor who wants to draw you away from the faith of your fathers to the false doctrines that he brings, wherefore separate yourselves from him and hear him not." They would taunt him with the words: "Thine own people and kindred should know thee best: wherefore do they not believe and follow thee?" But at length the privations endured by Muḥammad and his kinsmen enlisted the sympathy of a numerous section of the Quraysh and the ban was withdrawn.

In the same year the loss of K͟hadījah, the faithful wife who for twenty-five years had been his counsellor and support, plunged Muḥammad into the utmost grief and despondency; and a little later the death of Abū Ṭālib deprived him of his constant and most powerful protector and exposed him afresh to insult and contumely.

Scorned and rejected by his own townsmen, to whom he had delivered his message with so little success for ten years, he resolved to see if there were not others who might be more ready to listen, among whom the seeds of faith might find a more receptive and fruitful soil. With this hope he set out for Ṭā'if, a city about seventy miles from Mecca. Before an assembly of the chief men of the city, he expounded his doctrine of the unity of God and of the mission he had received as the Prophet of God to proclaim this faith; at the same time he besought their protection against his persecutors in Mecca. The disproportion between his high claims (which moreover were unintelligible to the heathen people of Ṭā'if) and his helpless condition only excited their ridicule and scorn, and pitilessly stoning him with stones they drove him from their city.

On his return from Ṭā'if the prospects of the success of Muḥammad seemed more hopeless than ever, and the agony of his soul gave itself utterance in the words that he puts into the mouth of Noah: "O my Lord, verily I have cried to my people night and day; and my cry only makes them flee from me the more. And verily, so oft as I cry to them, that Thou mayest forgive them, they thrust their fingers into their ears and wrap themselves in their garments, and persist (in their error), and are disdainfully disdainful." (lxxi. 5–6.)

It was the Prophet's habit at the time of the annual pilgrimage to visit the encampments of the various Arab tribes and discourse with them upon religion. By some his words were treated with indifference, by others rejected with scorn. But consolation came to him from an unexpected quarter. He met a little group of six or seven persons whom he recognised as coming from Medina, or, as it was then called, Ya<u>th</u>rib. "Of what tribe are you?" said he, addressing them. "We are of the <u>Kh</u>azraj," they answered. "Friends of the Jews?" "Yes." "Then will you not sit down awhile, that I may talk with you?" "Assuredly," replied they. Then they sat down with him, and he proclaimed unto them the true God and preached Islam and recited to them the Qur'ān. Now so it was, in that God wrought wonderfully for Islam that there were found in their country Jews, who possessed scriptures and wisdom, while they themselves were heathen and idolaters. Now the Jews ofttimes suffered violence at their hands, and when strife was between them had ever said to them, "Soon will a Prophet arise and his time is at hand; him will we follow, and with him slay you with the slaughter of 'Ād and of Iram." When now the apostle of God was speaking with these men and calling on them to believe in God, they said one to another: "Know surely that this is the Prophet, of whom the Jews have warned us; come let us now make haste and be the first to join him." So they embraced Islam, and said to him, "Our countrymen have long been engaged in a most bitter and deadly feud with one another; but now perhaps God will unite them together through thee and thy teaching. Therefore we will preach to them and make known to them this religion, that we have received from thee." So, full of faith, they returned to their own country.[1]

Such is the traditional account of this event which was the turning-point of Muḥammad's mission. He had now met with a people whose antecedents had in some way prepared their minds for the reception of his teaching and whose present circumstances, as afterwards appeared, were favourable to his cause.

The city of Ya<u>th</u>rib had been long occupied by Jews whom some national disaster, possibly the persecution under Hadrian, had driven from their own country, when a party of wandering emigrants, the two Arab clans of <u>Kh</u>azraj and Aws, arrived at Ya<u>th</u>rib and were admitted to a share in the territory. As their numbers increased they encroached more and more on the power of the Jewish rulers, and finally, towards the end of the fifth century, the government of the city passed entirely into their hands.

Some of the Arabs had embraced the Jewish religion, and many of the former masters of the city still dwelt there in

[1] Ibn Isḥāq, pp. 286–7.

the service of their conquerors, so that it contained in Muḥammad's time a considerable Jewish population. The people of Ya<u>th</u>rib were thus familiar with the idea of a Messiah who was to come, and were consequently more capable of understanding the claim of Muḥammad to be accepted as the Prophet of God, than were the idolatrous Meccans to whom such an idea was entirely foreign and especially distasteful to the Quraysh, whose supremacy over the other tribes and whose worldly prosperity arose from the fact that they were the hereditary guardians of the national collection of idols kept in the sacred enclosure of the Ka'bah.

Further, the city of Ya<u>th</u>rib was distracted by incessant civil discord through a long-standing feud between the Banū <u>Kh</u>azraj and the Banū Aws. The citizens lived in uncertainty and suspense, and anything likely to bind the conflicting parties together by a tie of common interest could not but prove a boon to the city. Just as the mediæval republics of Northern Italy chose a stranger to hold the chief post in their cities in order to maintain some balance of power between the rival factions, and prevent, if possible, the civil strife which was so ruinous to commerce and the general welfare, so the Ya<u>th</u>ribites would not look upon the arrival of a stranger with suspicion, even though he was likely to usurp or gain permission to assume the vacant authority.

On the contrary, one of the reasons for the warm welcome which Muḥammad received in Medina would seem to be that the adoption of Islam appeared to the more thoughtful of its citizens to be a remedy for the disorders from which their society was suffering, by its orderly discipline of life and its bringing the unruly passions of men under the discipline of laws enunciated by an authority superior to individual caprice.[1]

These facts go far to explain how eight years after the Hijrah Muḥammad could, at the head of 10,000 followers, enter the city in which he had laboured for ten years with so meagre a result.

But this is anticipating. Muḥammad had proposed to

[1] Caetani, vol. i. pp. 334–5.

accompany his new converts, the Khazrajites, to Yathrib himself, but they dissuaded him therefrom, until a reconciliation could be effected with the Banū Aws. "Let us, we pray thee, return unto our people, if haply the Lord will create peace amongst us; and we will come back again unto thee. Let the season of pilgrimage in the following year be the appointed time." So they returned to their homes, and invited their people to the faith; and many believed, so that there remained hardly a family in which mention was not made of the Prophet.

When the time of pilgrimage again came round, a deputation from Yathrib, ten men of the Banū Khazraj, and two of the Banū Aws, met him at the appointed spot and pledged him their word to obey his teaching. This, the first pledge of 'Aqabah, so called from the secret spot at which they met, ran as follows :—"We will not worship any but the one God; we will not steal, neither will we commit adultery or kill our children; we will abstain from calumny and slander; we will obey the Prophet in every thing that is right." These twelve men now returned to Yathrib as missionaries of Islam, and so well prepared was the ground, and with such zeal did they prosecute their mission, that the new faith spread rapidly from house to house and from tribe to tribe.

They were accompanied on their return by Muṣ'ab b. 'Umayr; though, according to another account he was sent by the Prophet upon a written requisition from Yathrib. This young man had been one of the earliest converts, and had lately returned from Abyssinia; thus he had had much experience, and severe training in the school of persecution had not only sobered his zeal but taught him how to meet persecution and deal with those who were ready to condemn Islam without waiting to learn the true contents of its teaching; accordingly Muḥammad could with the greatest confidence entrust him with the difficult task of directing and instructing the new converts, cherishing the seeds of religious zeal and devotion that had already been sown and bringing them to fruition. Muṣ'ab took up his abode in the house of As'ad b. Zurārah, and gathered the converts together for prayer and the reading of the Qur'ān, sometimes here and sometimes in a house belonging to the Banū Ẓafar, which was situated in a quarter of the town occupied jointly by this family and that of 'Abd al-Ashhal.

The heads of the latter family at that time were Sa'd b. Mu'ādh and Usayd b. Ḥuḍayr. One day it happened that Muṣ'ab was sitting together with As'ad in this house of the Banū Ẓafar, engaged in instructing some new converts, when Sa'd b. Mu'ādh, having come to know of their whereabouts, said to Usayd b. Ḥuḍayr: "Drive out these fellows who have come into our houses to make fools of the weaklings among us; I would spare thee the trouble did not the tie of kinship between me and As'ad prevent my doing him any harm" (for he himself was the cousin of As'ad). Hereupon Usayd took his spear and, bursting in upon As'ad and Muṣ'ab, "What are you doing?" he cried, "leading weak-minded folk astray? If you value your lives, begone hence." "Sit down and listen," Muṣ'ab answered quietly, "if thou art pleased with what thou hearest, accept it; if not, then leave it." Usayd stuck his spear in the ground and sat down to listen, while Muṣ'ab expounded to him the fundamental doctrines of Islam and read several passages of the Qur'ān. After a time Usayd, enraptured, cried, "What must I do to enter this religion?" "Purify thyself with water," answered Muṣ'ab, "and confess that there is no god but God and that Muḥammad is the apostle of God." Usayd at once complied and repeated the profession of faith, adding, "After me you have still another man to convince" (referring to Sa'd b. Mu'ādh). "If he is persuaded, his example will bring after him all his people. I will send him to you forthwith."

With these words he left them, and soon after came Sa'd b. Mu'ādh himself, hot with anger against As'ad for the patronage he had extended to the missionaries of Islam. Muṣ'ab begged him not to condemn the new faith unheard, so Sa'd agreed to listen and soon the words of Muṣ'ab touched him and brought conviction to his heart, and he embraced the faith and became a Muslim. He went back to his people burning with zeal and said to them, "Sons of 'Abd al-Ashhal, say, what am I to you?" "Thou art our lord," they answered, "thou art the wisest and most illustrious among us." "Then I swear," replied Sa'd, "nevermore to speak to any of you until you believe in God and Muḥammad, His apostle." And from that day, all the descendants of 'Abd al-Ashhal embraced Islam.[1]

With such zeal and earnestness was the preaching of the faith pushed forward that within a year there was not a family among the Arabs of Medina that had not given some of its members to swell the number of the faithful, with the exception of one branch of the Banū Aws, which held aloof under the influence of Abū Qays b. al-Aslat, the poet.

The following year, when the time of the annual pilgrimage again came round, a band of converts, amounting to seventy-three in number, accompanied their heathen fellow-countrymen from Yathrib to Mecca. They were commissioned to invite Muḥammad to take refuge in Yathrib from the fury of his enemies, and had come to swear allegiance to him as their prophet and their leader. All the early converts who had before met the Prophet on the two preceding pilgrimages, returned to Mecca on this important occasion, and Muṣ'ab their teacher accompanied them. Immediately on his arrival he hurried to the prophet, and told him of the success that had attended his mission. It is said that his mother, hearing of his arrival, sent a message to him, saying: "Ah, disobedient son, wilt thou enter a city in which thy mother dwelleth, and not first visit her!" "Nay, verily," he replied, "I will never visit the house of any one before the Prophet of God." So, after he had greeted and conferred with Muḥammad, he went to his mother, who thus accosted him: "Then I ween thou art still a renegade." He answered, "I follow the prophet of the Lord and the true faith of Islam." "Art thou then well satisfied with the miserable way thou hast fared in the land of Abyssinia and now again at Yathrib?" Now he perceived that she was meditating his imprisonment, and exclaimed, "What! wilt thou force a man from his religion? If ye seek to confine me, I will assuredly slay the first person that layeth hands upon me." His mother said, "Then depart from my presence," and she began to

[1] Ibn Isḥāq, p. 291 sq.

weep. Muṣ'ab was moved, and said, "Oh, my mother! I give thee loving counsel. Testify that there is no God but the Lord and that Muḥammad is His servant and messenger." But she replied, "By the sparkling stars! I will never make a fool of myself by entering into thy religion. I wash my hands of thee and thy concerns, and cleave steadfastly unto mine own faith."

In order not to excite suspicion and incur the hostility of the Quraysh, a secret meeting was arranged at 'Aqabah, the scene of the former meeting with the converts of the year before. Muḥammad came accompanied only by his uncle 'Abbās, who, though he was still an idolater, had been admitted into the secret. 'Abbās opened the solemn conclave, by recommending his nephew as a scion of one of the noblest families of his clan, which had hitherto afforded the Prophet protection, although rejecting his teachings; but now that he wished to take refuge among the people of Ya<u>th</u>rib, they should bethink themselves well before undertaking such a charge, and resolve not to go back from their promise, if once they undertook the risk. Then Barā b. Ma'rūr, one of the Banū <u>Kh</u>azraj, protesting that they were firm in their resolve to protect the Prophet of God, besought him to declare fully what he wished of them.

Muḥammad began by reciting to them some portions of the Qur'ān, and exhorted them to be true to the faith they had professed in the one God and the Prophet, His apostle; he then asked them to defend him and his companions from all assailants just as they would their own wives and children. Then Barā b. Ma'rūr, taking his hand, cried out, "Yea, by Him who sent thee as His Prophet, and through thee revealed unto us His truth, we will protect thee as we would our own bodies, and we swear allegiance to thee as our leader. We are the sons of battle and men of mail, which we have inherited as worthy sons of worthy forefathers." So they all in turn, taking his hand in theirs, swore allegiance to him.

As soon as the Quraysh gained intelligence of these secret proceedings, the persecution broke out afresh against the Muslims, and Muḥammad advised them to flee out of the city. "Depart unto Yat͟hrib; for the Lord hath verily given you brethren in that city, and a home in which ye may find refuge." So quietly, by twos and threes they escaped to Yat͟hrib, where they were heartily welcomed, their co-religionists in that city vying with one another for the honour of entertaining them, and supplying them with such things as they had need of. Within two months nearly all the Muslims except those who were seized and imprisoned and those who could not escape from captivity had left Mecca, to the number of about 150. There is a story told of one of these Muslims, by name Ṣuhayb, whom Muḥammad called "the first-fruits of Greece" (he had been a Greek slave, and being set free by his master had amassed considerable wealth by successful trading); when he was about to emigrate the Meccans said to him, "Thou camest hither in need and penury; but thy wealth hath increased with us, until thou hast reached thy present prosperity; and now thou art departing, not thyself only, but with all thy property. By the Lord, that shall not be;" and he said, "If I relinquish my property, will ye leave me free to depart?" And they agreed thereto; so he parted with all his goods. And when that was told unto Muḥammad, he said, "Verily, Ṣuhayb hath made a profitable bargain."

Muḥammad delayed his own departure (with the intention, no doubt, of withdrawing attention from his faithful followers) until a determined plot against his life warned him that further delay might be fatal, and he made his escape by means of a stratagem.

His first care after his arrival in Yat͟hrib, or Medina as it was called from this period—Madīnah al-Nabī, the city of the Prophet—was to build a mosque, to serve both as a place of prayer and of general assembly for his followers, who had hitherto met for that purpose in the dwelling-place of one of their number. The worshippers at first used to turn their faces in the direction of Jerusalem—an arrangement most probably adopted with the hope of gaining over the Jews. In many other ways, by constant appeals to their own sacred Scriptures, by according them perfect freedom of worship and political equality, Muḥammad endeavoured to conciliate the Jews, but they met his advances with scorn and derision. When all hopes of amalgamation proved fruitless and it became clear that the Jews would not accept him as their Prophet, Muḥammad bade his followers turn their faces in prayer towards the Ka'bah in Mecca. (ii. 144.) [1]

This change of direction during prayer has a deeper significance than might at first sight appear. It was really the beginning of the National Life of Islam : it established the Ka'bah at Mecca as a religious centre for all the Muslim people, just as from time immemorial it had been a place of pilgrimage for all the tribes of Arabia. Of similar importance was the incorporation of the ancient Arab custom of pilgrimage to Mecca into the circle of the religious ordinances of Islam, a duty that was to be performed by every Muslim at least once in his lifetime.

There are many passages in the Qur'ān that appeal to this germ of national feeling and urge the people of Arabia to realise the privilege that had been granted them of a divine revelation in their own language and by the lips of one of their own countrymen.

"Verily We have made it an Arabic Qur'ān that ye may haply understand. (xliii. 2–3.)

"And thus We have revealed to thee an Arabic Qur'ān, that thou mayest warn the mother of cities and those around it. (xlii. 5.)

"And if We had made it a Qur'ān in a foreign tongue, they had surely said, 'Unless its verses be clearly explained (we will not receive it).' (xli. 44.)

"And verily We have set before men in this Qur'ān every kind of parable that haply they be monished :

"An Arabic Qur'ān, free from tortuous (wording), that haply they may fear (God). (xxxix. 28–29.)

"Verily from the Lord of all creatures hath this (book) come down, . . . in the clear Arabic tongue. (xxvi. 192, 195.)

"And We have only made it (i.e. the Qur'ān) easy, in

[1] The appointment of the fast of Ramaḍān (Qur'ān ii. 179–84), is doubtless another sign of the breaking with the Jews, the fast on the Day of Atonement being thus abolished.

thine own tongue, in order that thou mayest announce glad tidings thereby to the God-fearing, and that thou mayest warn the contentious thereby." (xix. 97.)

But the message of Islam was not for Arabia only; the whole world was to share in it.[1] As there was but one God, so there was to be but one religion into which all men were to be invited. This claim to be universal, to hold sway over all men and all nations, found a practical illustration in the letters which Muḥammad is said to have sent in the year A.D. 688 (A.H. 6) to the great potentates of that time. An invitation to embrace Islam was sent in this year to the Emperor Heraclius, the king of Persia, the governor of Yaman, the governor of Egypt and the king of Abyssinia. The letter to Heraclius is said to have been as follows :—" In the name of God, the Merciful, the Compassionate, Muḥammad, who is the servant of God and His apostle, to Hiraql the Qayṣar of Rūm. Peace be on whoever has gone on the straight road. After this I say, Verily I call you to Islam. Embrace Islam, and God will reward you twofold. If you turn away from the offer of Islam, then on you be the sins of your people. O people of the Book, come towards a creed which is fit both for us and for you. It is this—to worship none but God, and not to associate anything with God, and not to call others God. Therefore, O ye people of the Book, if ye refuse, beware. We are Muslims and our religion is Islam." However absurd this summons may have seemed to those who then received it, succeeding years showed that it was dictated by no empty enthusiasm.[2] These letters only gave a more open and widespread expression to the claim to the universal acceptance which is repeatedly made for Islam in the Qur'ān.

[1] " Aber Gottes Botschaft ist nicht auf die Araber beschränkt. Sein Wille gilt für alle Creatur, es heischt unbedingten Gehorsam von aller Menschheit, und dass Muhammed als sein Bote denselben Gehorsam zu heischen berechtigt und verpflichtet sei, scheint von Anfang an ein integrirender Bestandtheil seines Gedankensystem gewesen zu sein." (Sachau, pp. 293–4.) Goldziher (Vorlesungen über den Islam, p. 25 sqq.) and Nöldeke (WZKM, vol. xxi. pp. 307–8) express a similar opinion.

[2] On the doubtful authenticity of these letters, see Caetani, vol. i. p. 725 sqq.

"Of a truth it (i.e. the Qur'ān) is no other than an admonition to all created beings, and after a time shall ye surely know its message. (xxxviii. 87–88.)

"This (book) is no other than an admonition and a clear Qur'ān, to warn whoever liveth; and that against the unbelievers sentence may be justly given. (xxxvi. 69–70.)

"We have not sent thee save as a mercy to all created beings. (xxi. 107.)

"Blessed is He who hath sent down al-Furqān upon His servant, that he may be a warner unto all created beings. (xxv. 1.)

"And We have not sent thee otherwise than to mankind at large, to announce and to warn. (xxxiv. 27.)

"He it is who hath sent His apostle with guidance and the religion of truth, that He may make it victorious over every other religion, though the polytheists are averse to it." (lxi. 9.)

In the hour of his deepest despair, when the people of Mecca persistently turned a deaf ear to the words of their prophet (xvi, 23, 114, etc.), when the converts he had made were tortured until they recanted (xvi. 108), and others were forced to flee from the country to escape the rage of their persecutors (xvi. 43, 111)—then was delivered the promise, "One day we will raise up a witness out of every nation." (xvi. 86.)[1]

This claim upon the acceptance of all mankind which the Prophet makes in these passages is further prophetically indicated in the words "first-fruits of Abyssinia," used by Muḥammad in reference to Bilāl, and "first-fruits of Greece," to Ṣuhayb; Salmān, the first Persian convert, was a Christian slave in Medina, who embraced the new faith in the first

[1] It seems strange that in the face of these passages, some have denied that Islam was originally intended by its founder to be a universal religion. Thus Sir William Muir says, "That the heritage of Islam is the world, was an afterthought. The idea, spite of much prophetic tradition, had been conceived but dimly, if at all, by Mahomet himself. His world was Arabia, and for it the new dispensation was ordained. From first to last the summons was to Arabs and to none other. . . . The seed of a universal creed had indeed been sown; but that it ever germinated was due to circumstance rather than design." (The Caliphate, pp. 43–4.) Caetani is the latest exponent of this view. (Annali dell' Islām, vol. v. pp. 323–4.)

year of the Hijrah. Thus long before any career of conquest was so much as dreamed of, the Prophet had clearly shown that Islam was not to be confined to the Arab race. The following account of the sending out of missionaries to preach Islam to all nations, points to the same claim to be a universal religion: "The Apostle of God said to his companions, 'Come to me all of you early in the morning.' After the morning prayer he spent some time in praising and supplicating God, as was his wont; then he turned to them and sent forth some in one direction and others in another, and said: 'Be faithful to God in your dealings with His servants (i.e. with men), for whosoever is entrusted with any matter that concerns mankind and is not faithful in his service of them, to him God shuts the gate of Paradise: go forth and be not like the messengers of Jesus, the son of Mary, for they went only to those that lived near and neglected those that dwelt in far countries.' Then each of these messengers came to speak the language of the people to whom he was sent. When this was told to the Prophet he said, 'This is the greatest of the duties that they owe to God with respect to His servants.'" [1]

The proof of the universality of Islam, of its claim on the acceptance of all men, lay in the fact that it was the religion divinely appointed for the whole human race and was now revealed to them anew through Muḥammad, "the seal of the prophets" (xxxiii. 40), as it had been to former generations by other prophets.

"Men were of one religion only: then they disagreed one with another and had not a decree (of respite) previously gone forth from thy Lord, judgment would surely have been given between them in the matter wherein they disagree. (x. 20.)

"I am no apostle of new doctrines. (xlvi. 8.)

"Mankind was but one people: then God raised up prophets to announce glad tidings and to warn: and He sent down with them the Book with the Truth, that it might decide the disputes of men: and none disagreed save those to whom the book had been

[1] Ibn Sa'd, § 10. This story may indeed be apocryphal, but is significant at least of the early realisation of the missionary character of Islam.

given, after the clear tokens had reached them, through mutual jealousy. And God guided those who believed into the truth concerning which they had disagreed, by His will; and God guideth whom He pleaseth into the straight path. (ii. 209.)

"And We revealed to thee, 'follow the religion of Abraham, the sound in faith, for he was not of those who join gods with God.' (xvi. 124.)

"Say: As for me, my Lord hath guided me into a straight path: a true faith, the religion of Abraham, the sound in faith; for he was not of those who join gods with God. (vi. 162.)

"Say: Nay, the religion of Abraham, the sound in faith and not one of those who join gods with God (is our religion). (ii. 129.)

"Say: God speaketh truth. Follow therefore the religion of Abraham, he being a Ḥanīf and not one of those who join other gods with God.

"Verily the first temple that was set up for men was that which is in Bakka, blessed and a guidance for all created beings. (iii. 89, 90.)

"And who hath a better religion than he who resigneth himself to God, who doth what is good and followeth the faith of Abraham, the sound in faith? (iv. 124.)

"He hath elected you, and hath not laid on you any hardship in religion, the faith of your father Abraham. He hath named you the Muslims." (xx. 77.)

But to return to Muḥammad in Medina. In order properly to appreciate his position after the Flight, it is important to remember the peculiar character of Arab society at that time, as far at least as this part of the peninsula was concerned. There was an entire absence of any organised administrative or judicial system such as in modern times we connect with the idea of a government. Each tribe or clan formed a separate and absolutely independent body, and this independence extended itself also to the individual members of the tribe, each of whom recognised the authority, or leadership of his chief only as being the exponent of a public opinion which he himself happened to share; but he was quite at liberty to refuse his conformity to the (even) unanimous resolve of his fellow clansmen. Further, there was no regular transmission of the office of chieftain; but he was generally chosen as being the oldest member of the richest and most powerful family of the clan, and as being personally most qualified to command respect. If such a tribe became too numerous, it would split up into several divisions, each of which continued to enjoy a separate and independent existence, uniting only on some extraordinary occasion for common self-defence or some more than usually important warlike expedition. We can thus understand how Muḥammad could establish himself in Medina at the head of a large and increasing body of adherents who looked up to him as their head and leader and acknowledged no other authority,—without exciting any feeling of insecurity, or any fear of encroachment on recognised authority, such as would have arisen in a city of ancient Greece or any similarly organised community. Muḥammad thus exercised temporal authority over his people just as any other independent chief might have done, the only difference being that in the case of the Muslims a religious bond took the place of family and blood ties.

Islam thus became what, in theory at least, it has always remained—a political as well as a religious system.

"It was Muḥammad's desire to found a new religion, and in this he succeeded; but at the same time he founded a political system of an entirely new and peculiar character. At first his only wish was to convert his fellow-countrymen to the belief in the One God—Allāh; but along with this he brought about the overthrow of the old system of government in his native city, and in place of the tribal aristocracy under which the conduct of public affairs was shared in common by the ruling families, he substituted an absolute theocratic monarchy, with himself at the head as vicar of God upon earth.

"Even before his death almost all Arabia had submitted to him; Arabia that had never before obeyed one prince, suddenly exhibits a political unity and swears allegiance to the will of an absolute ruler. Out of the numerous tribes, big and small, of a hundred different kinds that were incessantly at feud with one another, Muḥammad's word created a nation. The idea of a common religion under one common head bound the different tribes together into one political organism which developed its peculiar characteristics with surprising rapidity. Now only one great idea could have produced this result, viz. the principle of national life in heathen Arabia. The clan-system was thus for the first time, if not entirely crushed—(that would have been impossible)—yet made subordinate to the feeling of religious unity. The great work succeeded, and when Muḥammad died there prevailed over by far the greater part of Arabia a peace of God such as the Arab tribes, with their love of plunder and revenge, had never known; it was the religion of Islam that had brought about this reconciliation." [1]

Even in the case of death, the claims of relationship were set aside and the bond-brother inherited all the property of his deceased companion. But after the battle of Badr, when such an artificial bond was no longer needed to unite his followers, it was abolished; such an arrangement was only necessary so long as the number of the Muslims was still small and the corporate life of Islam a novelty; moreover Muḥammad had lived in Medina for a very short space of time before the rapid increase in the number of his adherents made so communistic a social system almost impracticable.

It was only to be expected that the growth of an independent political body composed of refugees from Mecca, located in a hostile city, should eventually lead to an outbreak of hostilities; and, as is well known, every biography of Muḥammad is largely taken up with the account of a long series of petty encounters and bloody battles between his followers and the Quraysh of Mecca, ending in his triumphal entry into that city in A.D. 630, and of his hostile relations with numerous other tribes, up to the time of his death, A.D. 633.

To give any account of these campaigns is beyond the scope of the present work, but it is important to show that Muḥammad, when he found himself at the head of a band

[1] A. von Kremer (3), pp. 309, 310.

of armed followers, was not transformed at once, as some would have us believe, from a peaceful preacher into a fanatic, sword in hand, forcing his religion on whomsoever he could.[1]

It has been frequently asserted by European writers that from the date of Muḥammad's migration to Medina, and from the altered circumstances of his life there, the Prophet appears in an entirely new character. He is no longer the preacher, the warner, the apostle of God to men, whom he would persuade of the truth of the religion revealed to him, but now he appears rather as the unscrupulous bigot, using all means at his disposal of force and statecraft to assert himself and his opinions.

But it is false to suppose that Muḥammad in Medina laid aside his *rôle* of preacher and missionary of Islam, or that when he had a large army at his command, he ceased to invite unbelievers to accept the faith. Ibn Sa'd gives a number of letters written by the Prophet from Medina to chiefs and other members of different Arabian tribes, in addition to those addressed to potentates living beyond the limits of Arabia, inviting them to embrace Islam; and in the following pages will be found instances of his having sent missionaries to preach the faith to the unconverted members of their tribes, whose very ill-success in some cases is a sign of the genuinely missionary character of their efforts and the absence of an appeal to force. A typical example of such an unsuccessful mission is that sent to preach Islam to the Banū 'Āmir b. Ṣa'ṣa'ah in the year A.H. 4. The chief of this tribe, Abū Barā 'Āmir, visited Muḥammad in Medina, listened to his teaching, but declined to become a convert; he seemed, however, to be favourably disposed towards the new faith and asked the Prophet to send some of his followers to Najd to preach to the people of that country. The Prophet sent a party of forty Muslims, most of them young men of Medina, who were skilled in reciting the Qur'ān, and had been accustomed to meet together at night for study and prayer. But in

[1] This would seem to be acknowledged even by Muir, when speaking of the massacre of the Banū Qurayẓah (A.H. 6): "The ostensible grounds upon which Mahomet proceeded were purely political, for as yet he did not profess to force men to join Islam, or to punish them for not embracing it." (Muir (2), vol. iii. p. 282.)

spite of the safe conduct given them by Abū Barā 'Āmir, they were treacherously murdered and three only of the party escaped with their lives.[1]

The successes of the Muslim arms, however, attracted every day members of various tribes, particularly those in the vicinity of Medina, to swell the ranks of the followers of the Prophet; and " the courteous treatment which the deputations of these various clans experienced from the Prophet, his ready attention to their grievances, the wisdom with which he composed their disputes, and the politic assignments of territory by which he rewarded an early declaration in favour of Islam, made his name to be popular and spread his fame as a great and generous prince throughout the Peninsula." [2]

It not unfrequently happened that one member of a tribe would come to the Prophet in Medina and return home as a missionary of Islam to convert his brethren; we have the following account of such a conversion in the year 5 (A.H.).

The Banū Sa'd b. Bakr sent one of their number, by name Ḍimām b. Tha'labah as their envoy to the Prophet. He came and made his camel kneel down at the gate of the mosque and tied up its fore-leg. Then he went into the mosque, where the Prophet was sitting with his companions. He went up close to them and said, " Which among you is the son of 'Abd al-Muṭṭalib ? " " I am," replied the Prophet. " Art thou Muḥammad ? " " Yes," was the answer. " Then, if thou wilt not take it amiss, I would fain ask thee some weighty questions." " Nay, ask what thou wilt," answered the Prophet. " I adjure thee by Allāh, thy God and the God of those who were before thee and of those who are to come after thee, hath Allāh sent thee as a prophet unto us ? " Muḥammad answered, " Yea, by Allāh." He continued, " I adjure thee by Allāh, thy God and the God of those who were before thee and of those who are to come after thee, hath He commanded thee to

[1] Ibn Isḥāq, p. 648 sq.

[2] Muir (2), vol. iv. pp. 107–8. See also Caetani, vol. i. p. 663. " Assai più che tutte le prediche del Profeta, assai più che tutta la bontà delle dottrine islamiche, siffatti vantaggi militari contribuirono al aumentare il numero dei seguaci. La rapidità della diffusione dell' Islām divenne in special modo sensibile per il contegno et per lo spirito di tolleranza, di libertà, e di opportunismo, che diresse il Profeta nei suoi rapporti con i convertiti."

bid us worship Him alone, and to associate naught else with Him and to abandon these idols that our fathers worshipped?" Muḥammad answered, "Yea, by Allāh." Then he questioned the Prophet concerning all the ordinances of Islam, one after another, prayer and fasting, pilgrimage, etc., solemnly adjuring him as before. At the end he said, "Then I bear witness that there is no God save Allāh and I bear witness that Muḥammad is the Prophet of Allāh, and I will observe these ordinances and shun what thou hast forbidden, adding nothing thereto, and taking nothing away." Then he turned away and loosened his camel and returned unto his own people, and when he had gathered them together, the first words he spoke unto them were: "Vile things are Lāt and 'Uzzā." They cried out, "Hold! Ḍimām, take heed of leprosy or madness!" "Fie on you!" he replied. "By Allāh! they can neither work you weal nor woe, for Allāh has sent a Prophet and revealed to him a book, whereby he delivers you from your evil plight; I bear witness that there is no God save Allāh alone and that Muḥammad is His servant and His Prophet; and I have brought you tidings of what he enjoins and what he forbids." The story goes on that ere nightfall there was not a man or woman in the camp who had not accepted Islam.[1]

Another such missionary was 'Amr b. Murrah, belonging to the tribe of the Banū Juhaynah, who dwelt between Medina and the Red Sea. The date of his conversion was prior to the Flight, in the same year (A.H. 5), and he thus describes it: "We had an idol that we worshipped, and I was the guardian of its shrine. When I heard of the Prophet, I broke it in pieces and set off to Muḥammad, where I accepted Islam and bore witness to the truth, and believed on what Muḥammad declared to be allowed and forbidden. And to this my verses refer: 'I bear witness that God is Truth and that I am the first to abandon the gods of stones, and I have girded up my loins to make my way to you over rough ways and smooth, to join myself to him who in himself and for his ancestry is the noblest of men, the apostle of

[1] Ibn Isḥāq, p. 943–4. (This story rests on somewhat doubtful authority, cf. Caetani, vol. i. p. 610.)

the Lord whose throne is above the clouds.' " He was sent by Muḥammad to preach Islam to his tribe, and his efforts were crowned with such success that there was only one man who refused to listen to his exhortations.[1]

When the truce of Ḥudaybiyyah (A.H. 6) made friendly relations with the people of Mecca possible, many persons of that city, who had had the opportunity of listening to the teaching of Muḥammad in the early days of his mission, and among them some men of great influence, came out to Medina, to embrace the faith of Islam.

The continual warfare carried on with the people of Mecca had hitherto kept the tribes to the south of that city almost entirely outside the influence of the new religion. But this truce now made communications with southern Arabia possible, and a small band from the tribe of the Banū Daws came from the mountains that form the northern boundary of Yaman, and joined themselves to the Prophet in Medina. Even before the appearance of Muḥammad, there were some members of this tribe who had had glimmerings of a higher religion than the idolatry prevailing around them, and argued that the world must have had a creator, though they knew not who he was; and when Muḥammad came forward as the apostle of this creator, one of these men, by name Ṭufayl b. 'Amr, came to Mecca to learn who the creator was.

Though warned by the Quraysh of the dangerous influence that Muḥammad might exercise over him if he entered into conversation with him, he followed the Prophet to his house one day, after watching him at prayer by the Ka'bah. Muḥammad expounded to him the doctrines of Islam, and Ṭufayl left Mecca full of zeal for the new faith. On his return home he succeeded in converting his father and his wife, but found his fellow-tribesmen unwilling to abandon their old idolatrous worship. Disheartened at the ill-success of his mission, he returned to the Prophet and besought him to call down the curse of God on the Banū Daws; but Muḥammad encouraged him to persevere in his efforts, saying, " Return to thy people and summon them to the faith, but deal gently with them." At the

[1] Ibn Sa'd, § 118.

same time he prayed, " Oh God ! guide the Banū Daws in the right way." The success of Ṭufayl's propaganda was such that in the year A.H. 7 he came to Medina with between seventy and eighty families of his tribesmen who had been won over to the faith of Islam, and after the triumphal entry of Muḥammad into Mecca, Ṭufayl set fire to the block of wood that had hitherto been venerated as the idol of the tribe.[1]

In A.H. 7, fifteen more tribes submitted to the Prophet, and after the surrender of Mecca in A.H. 8, the ascendancy of Islam was assured, and those Arabs who had held aloof, saying, " Let Muḥammad and his fellow-tribesmen fight it out; if he is victorious, then is he a genuine prophet,"[2] now hastened to give in their allegiance to the new religion. Among those who came in after the fall of Mecca were some of the most bitter persecutors of Muḥammad in the earlier days of his mission, to whom his noble forbearance and forgiveness now gave a place in the brotherhood of Islam. The following year witnessed the martyrdom of 'Urwah b. Mas'ūd, one of the chiefs of the people of Ṭā'if, which city the Muslims had unsuccessfully attempted to capture. He had been absent at that time in Yaman, and returned from his journey shortly after the raising of the siege. He had met the Prophet two years before at Ḥudaybiyyah, and had conceived a profound veneration for him, and now came to Medina to embrace the new faith. In the ardour of his zeal he offered to go to Ṭā'if to convert his fellow-countrymen, and in spite of the efforts of Muḥammad to dissuade him from so dangerous an undertaking, he returned to his native city, publicly declared that he had renounced idolatry, and called upon the people to follow his example. While he was preaching, he was mortally wounded by an arrow, and died giving thanks to God for having granted him the glory of martyrdom. A more successful missionary effort was made by another follower of the Prophet in Yaman—probably a year later—of which we have the following graphic account : " The apostle of God wrote to al-Ḥārith and Masrūḥ, and Nu'aym b. 'Abd al-Kulāl of Ḥimyar : ' Peace be upon you so long as

[1] Ibn Isḥāq, pp. 252–4.

[2] Caetani, vol. ii. t. i. p. 341.

ye believe on God and His apostle. God is one God, there is no partner with Him. He sent Moses with his signs, and created Jesus with his words. The Jews say, " Ezra is the Son of God," and the Christians say, " God is one of three, and Jesus is the Son of God." ' He sent the letter by 'Ayyāsh b. Abī Rabī'ah al-Makhzūmī, and said: ' When you reach their city, go not in by night, but wait until the morning; then carefully perform your ablutions, and pray with two prostrations, and ask God to bless you with success and a friendly reception, and to keep you safe from harm. Then take my letter in your right hand, and deliver it with your right hand into their right hands, and they will receive it. And recite to them, " The unbelievers among the people of the Book and the polytheists did not waver," etc. (Sūrah 98), to the end of the Sūrah; when you have finished, say, " Muḥammad has believed, and I am the first to believe." And you will be able to meet every objection they bring against you, and every glittering book that they recite to you will lose its light. And when they speak in a foreign tongue, say, " Translate it," and say to them, " God is sufficient for me; I believe in the Book sent down by Him, and I am commanded to do justice among you; God is our Lord and your Lord; to us belong our works, and to you belong your works; there is no strife between us and you; God will unite us, and unto Him we must return." If they now accept Islam, then ask them for their three rods, before which they gather together to pray, one rod of tamarisk that is spotted white and yellow, and one knotted like a cane, and one black like ebony. Bring the rods out and burn them in the market-place.' So I set out," tells 'Ayyāsh, " to do as the Apostle of God had bid me. When I arrived, I found that all the people had decked themselves out for a festival: I walked on to see them, and came at last to three enormous curtains hung in front of three doorways. I lifted the curtain and entered the middle door, and found people collected in the courtyard of the building. I introduced myself to them as the messenger of the Apostle of God, and did as he had bidden me; and they gave heed to my words, and it fell out as he had said." [1]

[1] Ibn Sa'd, § 56.

In A.H. 9 a deputation of thirteen men from the Banū Kilāb, a branch of the Banū 'Āmir b. Ṣa'ṣa'ah, came to the Prophet and informed him that one of his followers, Ḍaḥḥāk b. Sufyān, had come to them, reciting the Qur'ān and teaching the doctrines of Islam, and that his preaching had won over their tribe to the new faith.[1] Another branch of the same tribe, the Banū Ru'ās b. Kilāb, was converted by one of its members, named 'Amr b. Mālik, who had been to Medina and accepted Islam, and then returned to his fellow tribes and persuaded them to follow his example.[2]

In the same year a less successful attempt was made by a new convert, Wāt͟hilah b. al-Asqa', to induce his clan to accept the faith that he himself had embraced after an interview with the Prophet. His father scornfully cast him off, saying, "By God! I will never speak a word to you again," and none were found willing to believe the doctrines he preached with the exception of his sister, who provided him with the means of returning to the Prophet at Medina.[3] This ninth year of the Hijrah has been called the year of the deputations, because of the enormous number of Arab tribes and cities that now sent delegates to the Prophet, to give in their submission. The introduction into Arab society of a new principle of social union in the brotherhood of Islam had already begun to weaken the binding force of the old tribal ideal, which erected the fabric of society on the basis of blood-relationship. The conversion of an individual and his reception into the new society was a breach of one of the most fundamental laws of Arab life, and its frequent occurrence had acted as a powerful solvent on tribal organisation and had left it weak in the face of a national life so enthusiastic and firmly-knit as that of the Muslims had become. The Arab tribes were thus impelled to give in their submission to the Prophet, not merely as the head of the strongest military force in Arabia, but as the exponent of a theory of social life that was making all others weak and ineffective.[4] Muḥammad had succeeded in introducing into the anarchical society of his time a

[1] Ibn Sa'd, § 85. [2] Id. § 86. [3] Id. § 91.
[4] See Sprenger, vol. iii. pp. 360–1.

sentiment of national unity, a consciousness of rights and duties towards one another such as the Arabs had not felt before.[1] In this way, Islam was uniting together clans that hitherto had been continually at feud with one another, and as this great confederacy grew, it more and more attracted to itself the weaker among the tribes of Arabia. In the accounts of the conversion of the Arab tribes, there is continual mention of the promise of security against their enemies, made to them by the Prophet on the occasion of their submission. "Woe is me for Muḥammad!" was the cry of one of the Arab tribes on the news of the death of the Prophet. "So long as he was alive, I lived in peace and in safety from my enemies;" and the cry must have found an echo far and wide throughout Arabia.

How superficial was the adherence of numbers of the Arab tribes to the faith of Islam may be judged from the widespread apostasy that followed immediately on the death of the Prophet. Their acceptance of Islam would seem to have been often dictated more by considerations of political expediency, and was more frequently a bargain struck under pressure of violence than the outcome of any enthusiasm or spiritual awakening. They allowed themselves to be swept into the stream of what had now become a great national movement, and we miss the fervent zeal of the early converts in the cool, calculating attitude of those who came in after the fall of Mecca. But even from among these must have come many to swell the ranks of the true believers animated with a genuine zeal for the faith, and ready, as we have seen, to give their lives in the effort to preach it to their brethren.

"These men were the true moral heirs of the Prophet, the future apostles of Islam, the faithful trustees of all that Muḥammad had revealed unto the men of God. Into these men, through their constant contact with the Prophet and their devotion to him, there had really entered a new mode of thought and feeling, loftier and more civilised than any they had known before; they had really changed for the better from every point of view, and later on as statesmen and generals, in the most difficult moments of the war of

[1] Caetani, vol. ii. p. 433.

conquest they gave magnificent and undeniable proof that the ideas and the doctrines of Muḥammad had been seed cast on fruitful soil, and had produced a body of men of the very highest worth. They were the depositaries of the sacred text of the Qur'ān, which they alone knew by heart; they were the jealous guardians of the memory of every word and bidding of the Prophet, the trustees of the moral heritage of Muḥammad. These men formed the venerable stock of Islam from whom one day was to spring the noble band of the first jurists, theologians and traditionists of Muslim society."[1]

But for such men as these, so vast a movement could not have held together, much less have recovered the shock given it by the death of the founder. For it must not be forgotten how distinctly Islam was a *new* movement in heathen Arabia, and how diametrically opposed were the ideals of the two societies.[2] For the introduction of Islam into Arab society did not imply merely the sweeping away of a few barbarous and inhuman practices, but a complete reversal of the pre-existing ideals of life.

Herein we have the most conclusive proof of the essentially missionary character of the teaching of Muḥammad, who thus comes forward as the exponent of a new scheme of faith and practice. Whatever may have been the conditions favourable to the formation of a new political organisation, Muḥammad certainly did not find the society of his day prepared to receive his religious teaching and waiting only for the voice that would express in speech the inarticulate yearnings of their hearts. But it is just this spirit of expectancy that is wanting among the Arabs—those at least of the Central Arabia towards whom Muḥammad's efforts were at first directed. They were by no means ready to receive the preaching of a new teacher, least of all one who came with the (to them unintelligible) title of apostle of God.

Again, the equality in Islam of all believers and the common brotherhood of all Muslims, which suffered no

[1] Caetani, vol. ii. p. 429.

[2] This has been nowhere more fully and excellently brought out than in the scholarly work of Prof. Ignaz Goldziher (Muhammedanische Studien, vol. i.), from which I have derived the following considerations.

distinctions between Arab and non-Arab, between free and slave, to exist among the faithful, was an idea that ran directly counter to the proud clan-feeling of the Arab, who grounded his claims to personal consideration on the fame of his ancestors, and in the strength of the same carried on the endless blood-feuds in which his soul delighted. Indeed, the fundamental principles in the teaching of Muḥammad were a protest against much that the Arabs had hitherto most highly valued, and the newly-converted Muslim was taught to consider as virtues, qualities which hitherto he had looked down upon with contempt.

To the heathen Arab, friendship and hostility were as a loan which he sought to repay with interest, and he prided himself on returning evil for evil, and looked down on any who acted otherwise as a weak nidering.

> He is the perfect man who late and early plotteth still
> To do a kindness to his friends and work his foes some ill.

To such men the Prophet said, "Recompense evil with that which is better" (xxiii. 98); as they desired the forgiveness of God, they were to pass over and pardon offences (xxiv. 22), and a Paradise, vast as the heavens and the earth, was prepared for those who mastered their anger and forgave others. (iii. 128.)

The very institution of prayer was jeered at by the Arabs to whom Muḥammad first delivered his message, and one of the hardest parts of his task was to induce in them that pious attitude of mind towards the Creator, which Islam inculcates equally with Judaism and Christianity, but which was practically unknown to the heathen Arabs. This self-sufficiency and this lack of the religious spirit, joined with their intense pride of race, little fitted them to receive the teachings of one who maintained that "The most worthy of honour in the sight of God is he that feareth Him most" (xlix. 13). No more could they brook the restrictions that Islam sought to lay upon the licence of their lives; wine, women, and song, were among the things most dear to the Arab's heart in the days of the ignorance, and the Prophet was stern and severe in his injunctions respecting each of them.

Thus, from the very beginning, Islam bears the stamp of a missionary religion that seeks to win the hearts of men, to convert them and persuade them to enter the brotherhood of the faithful; and as it was in the beginning, so has it continued to be up to the present day, as will be the object of the following pages to show.

CHAPTER III.

THE SPREAD OF ISLAM AMONG THE CHRISTIAN NATIONS OF WESTERN ASIA.

AFTER the death of Muḥammad, the army he had intended for Syria was despatched thither by Abū Bakr, in spite of the protestations made by certain Muslims in view of the then disturbed state of Arabia. He silenced their expostulations with the words : " I will not revoke any order given by the Prophet. Medina may become the prey of wild beasts, but the army must carry out the wishes of Muḥammad." This was the first of that wonderful series of campaigns in which the Arabs overran Syria, Persia and Northern Africa—overturning the ancient kingdom of Persia and despoiling the Roman Empire of some of its fairest provinces. It does not fall within the scope of this work to follow the history of these different campaigns, but, in view of the expansion of the Muslim faith that followed the Arab conquests, it is of importance to discover what were the circumstances that made such an expansion possible.

A great historian [1] has well put the problem that meets us here, in the following words : " Was it genuine religious enthusiasm, the new strength of a faith now for the first time blossoming forth in all its purity, that gave the victory in every battle to the arms of the Arabs and in so incredibly short a time founded the greatest empire the world had ever seen ? But evidence is wanting to prove that this was the case. The number was far too small of those who had given their allegiance to the Prophet and his teaching with a free and heartfelt conviction, while on the other hand all the greater was the number of those who had been

[1] Döllinger, pp. 5–6.

brought into the ranks of the Muhammadans only through pressure from without or by the hope of worldly gain. Khālid, 'that sword of the swords of God,' exhibited in a very striking manner that mixture of force and persuasion whereby he and many of the Quraysh had been converted, when he said that God had seized them by the hearts and by the hair and compelled them to follow the Prophet. The proud feeling too of a common nationality had much influence—a feeling which was more alive among the Arabs of that time than (perhaps) among any other people, and which alone determined many thousands to give the preference to their countryman and his religion before foreign teachers. Still more powerful was the attraction offered by the sure prospect of gaining booty in abundance, in fighting for the new religion and of exchanging their bare, stony deserts, which offered them only a miserable subsistence, for the fruitful and luxuriant countries of Persia, Syria and Egypt."

These stupendous conquests which laid the foundations of the Arab empire, were certainly not the outcome of a holy war, waged for the propagation of Islam, but they were followed by such a vast defection from the Christian faith that this result has often been supposed to have been their aim. Thus the sword came to be looked upon by Christian historians as the instrument of Muslim propaganda, and in the light of the success attributed to it the evidences of the genuine missionary activity of Islam were obscured. But the spirit which animated the invading hosts of Arabs who poured over the confines of the Byzantine and Persian empires, was no proselytising zeal for the conversion of souls. On the contrary, religious interests appear to have entered but little into the consciousness of the protagonists of the Arab armies.[1] This expansion of the Arab race is more rightly envisaged as the migration of a vigorous and energetic people driven by hunger and want, to leave their inhospitable deserts and overrun the richer lands of their more fortunate neighbours.[2] Still the unifying

[1] Caetani, Studi di Storia Orientale, I, p. 365 sqq. (Milano, 1911.)

[2] This interpretation of the Arab conquests as the last of the great Semitic migrations has been worked out in a masterly manner by Caetani, vol. ii. pp. 831–61.

principle of the movement was the theocracy established in Medina, and the organisation of the new state proceeded from the devoted companions of Muḥammad, the faithful depositaries of his teaching, whose moral weight and enthusiasm kept Islam alive as the official religion, despite the indifference of those Arabs who gave to it a mere nominal adherence.[1] It is not, therefore, in the annals of the conquering armies that we must look for the reasons which lead to the so rapid spread of the Muslim faith, but rather in the conditions prevailing among the conquered peoples.

The national character of this ethnic movement of migration naturally attracted to the invading Arab hosts the outlying representatives of the Arab race through whom the path of the conquering armies lay. Accordingly it is not surprising to find that many of the Christian Bedouins were swept into the rushing tide of this great movement and that Arab tribes, who for centuries had professed the Christian religion, now abandoned it to embrace the Muslim faith. Among these was the tribe of the Banū Ghassān, who held sway over the desert east of Palestine and southern Syria, of whom it was said that they were "Lords in the days of the ignorance and stars in Islam."[2] After the battle of Qādisiyyah (A.H. 14) in which the Persian army under Rustam had been utterly discomfited, many Christians belonging to the Bedouin tribes on both sides of the Euphrates came to the Muslim general and said: "The tribes that at the first embraced Islam were wiser than we. Now that Rustam hath been slain, we will accept the new belief."[3] Similarly, after the conquest of northern Syria, most of the Bedouin tribes, after hesitating a little, joined themselves to the followers of the Prophet.[4]

That force was not the determining factor in these conversions may be judged from the amicable relations that existed between the Christian and the Muslim Arabs. Muḥammad himself had entered into treaty with several

[1] Caetani, vol. ii. p. 455; vol. v. p. 521. ("In Madīnah si formò un considerevole nucleo religioso, composto d'elementi eterogenei, ma forse in maggioranza madinesi, i quali presero l'Islām molto sul serio e cercarono sinceramente di osservare la nuova dottrina, per la convinzione che, così agendo facevan bene, ed in devoto omaggio alla volontà del Profeta.")

[2] Mas'ūdī, tome iv. p. 238.

[3] Muir's Caliphate, pp. 121–2.

[4] Caetani, vol. iii. p. 814 (§ 323).

Christian tribes, promising them his protection and guaranteeing them the free exercise of their religion and to their clergy undisturbed enjoyment of their old rights and authority.[1] A similar bond of friendship united his followers with their fellow-countrymen of the older faith, many of whom voluntarily came forward to assist the Muslims in their military expeditions in the same spirit of loyalty to the new government as had caused them to hold aloof from the great apostasy that raised the standard of revolt throughout Arabia immediately after the death of the Prophet.[2] It has been suggested that the Christian Arabs who guarded the frontier of the Byzantine empire bordering on the desert threw in their lot with the invading Muslim army, when Heraclius refused any longer to pay them their accustomed subsidy for military service as wardens of the marches.[3]

In the battle of the Bridge (A.H. 13) when a disastrous defeat was imminent and the panic-stricken Arabs were hemmed in between the Euphrates and the Persian host, a Christian chief of the Banū Ṭayy sprang forward like another Spurius Lartius to the side of an Arab Horatius, to assist Mut͟hannah the Muslim general in defending the bridge of boats which could alone afford the means of an orderly retreat. When fresh levies were raised to retrieve this disgrace, among the reinforcements that came pouring in from every direction was a Christian tribe of the Banū Namir, who dwelt within the limits of the Byzantine empire, and in the ensuing battle of Buwayb (A.H. 13), just before the final charge of the Arabs that turned the fortune of battle in their favour, Mut͟hannah rode up to the Christian chief and said: "Ye are of one blood with us; come now, and as I charge, charge ye with me." The Persians fell back before their furious onslaught, and another great victory was added to the glorious roll of Muslim triumphs. One of the most gallant exploits of the day was performed by a youth belonging to another Christian tribe of the desert, who with his companions, a company of Bedouin horse-dealers, had come up just as the Arab army was being

[1] Caetani, vol. ii. pp. 260, 299, 351.
[2] Id. pp. 792–3; vol. iii. p. 253 (§ 8).
[3] Id. pp. 1112–15.

drawn up in battle array. They threw themselves into the fight on the side of their compatriots; and while the conflict was raging most fiercely, this youth, rushing into the centre of the Persians, slew their leader, and leaping on his richly-caparisoned horse, galloped back amidst the plaudits of the Muslim line, crying as he passed in triumph: "I am of the Banū Taghlib. I am he that hath slain the chief."[1]

The tribe to which this young man boasted that he belonged was one of those that elected to remain Christian, while other tribes of Mesopotamia, such as the Banū Namir and the Banū Quḍā'ah, became Muslim. The Banū Taghlib had sent an embassy to the Prophet as early as the year A.H. 9. The heathen members of the deputation embraced Islam and he made a treaty with the Christians according to which they were to retain their old faith but were not to baptise their children. A condition so entirely at variance with the usual tolerant attitude of Muḥammad towards the Christian Arabs, who were allowed to choose between conversion to Islam and the payment of jizyah and never compelled to abandon their faith, has given rise to the conjecture that this condition was suggested by the Christian families of the Banū Taghlib themselves, out of motives of economy.[2] The long survival of Christianity in this tribe shows that this condition was certainly not observed. The caliph 'Umar forbade any pressure to be put upon them, when they showed themselves unwilling to abandon their old faith and ordered that they should be left undisturbed in the practice of it, but that they were not to oppose the conversion of any member of their tribe to Islam nor baptise the children of such as became Muslims.[3] They were called upon to pay the jizyah[4] or tax imposed on the non-Muslim subjects, but they felt it to be humiliating to their pride to pay a tax that was levied in return for

[1] Muir: Caliphate, pp. 90–4.
[2] Caetani, vol. ii. p. 299. Wellhausen, iv. p. 156 (*n.* 5).
[3] Ṭabarī, Prima Series, p. 2482.
[4] For an exhaustive study of the jizyah, with a masterly array and critical examination of all the available historical materials, see Caetani, vol. v. p. 319 sqq.; for Egypt during the first century of Muslim rule, see Bell, p. 167 sqq., and Becker, Beiträge zur Geschichte Aegyptens unter dem Islam, p. 81 sqq.

protection of life and property, and petitioned the caliph to be allowed to make the same kind of contribution as the Muslims did. So in lieu of the jizyah they paid a double Ṣadaqah or alms,[1]—which was a poor tax levied on the fields and cattle, etc., of the Muslims.[2] It especially irked the Muslims that any of the Arabs should remain true to the Christian faith. The majority of the Banū Tanūkh had become Muslim in the year A.H. 12, when with other Christian Arab tribes they submitted to Khālid b. al-Walīd,[3] but some of them appear to have remained true to their old faith for nearly a century and a half, since the caliph al-Mahdī (A.H. 158–169) is said to have seen a number of them who dwelt in the neighbourhood of Aleppo, and learning that they were Christians, in anger ordered them to accept Islam—which they did to the number of 5000, and one of them suffered martyrdom rather than apostatise.[4] But for the most part, details are lacking for any history of the disappearance of Christianity from among the Christian Arab tribes of Northern Arabia; they seem to have become absorbed in the surrounding Muslim community by an almost insensible process of "peaceful penetration"; had attempts been made to convert them by force when they first came under Muhammadan rule, it would not have been possible for Christians to have survived among them up to the times of the 'Abbāsid caliphs.[5]

The people of Ḥīrah had likewise resisted all the efforts made by Khālid to induce them to accept the Muslim faith. This city was one of the most illustrious in the annals of Arabia, and to the mind of the impetuous hero of Islam it seemed that an appeal to their Arab blood would be enough to induce them to enrol themselves with the followers of the Prophet of Arabia. When the besieged citizens sent an embassy to the Muslim general to arrange the terms of the capitulation of their city, Khālid asked them, "Who are

[1] Caetani (vol. iv. p. 227) believes that this story is the invention of a later epoch, to explain the fiscal anomaly of a Christian tribe being treated as if it were Muslim.

[2] The few meagre notices of this tribe in the works of Arabic historians have been admirably summarised by Lammens: Le Chantre des Omiades. (J. A., ix. sér., tome iv. pp. 97–9, 438–59.) See also Caetani, vol. iv. p. 227 sqq.

[3] Caetani, vol. ii. p. 1180.

[4] Barhebræus (3), pp. 134–5.

[5] Caetani, vol. ii. p. 828.

you? are you Arabs or Persians?" Then 'Adī, the spokesman of the deputation, replied, "Nay, we are pure-blooded Arabs, while others among us are naturalised Arabs." Kh. "Had you been what you say you are, you would not have opposed us or hated our cause." 'A. "Our pure Arab speech is the proof of what I say." Kh. "You speak truly. Now choose you one of these three things: either (1) accept our faith, then your rights and obligations will be the same as ours, whether you choose to go into another country or stay in your own land; or (2) pay jizyah; or (3) war and battle. Verily, by God! I have come to you with a people who are more desirous of death than you are of life." 'A. "Nay, we will pay you jizyah." Kh. "Ill-luck to you! Unbelief is a pathless desert and foolish is the Arab who, when two guides meet him wandering therein—the one an Arab and the other not—leaves the first and accepts the guidance of the foreigner." [1]

Due provision was made for the instruction of the new converts, for while whole tribes were being converted to the faith with such rapidity, it was necessary to take precautions against errors, both in respect of creed and ritual, such as might naturally be feared in the case of ill-instructed converts. Accordingly we find that the caliph 'Umar appointed teachers in every country, whose duty it was to instruct the people in the teachings of the Qur'ān and the observances of their new faith. The magistrates were also ordered to see that all, whether old or young, were regular in their attendance at public prayer, especially on Fridays and in the month of Ramaḍān. The importance attached to this work of instructing the new converts may be judged from the fact that in the city of Kūfah it was no less a personage than the state treasurer who was entrusted with this task.[2]

From the examples given above of the toleration extended towards the Christian Arabs by the victorious Muslims of the first century of the Hijrah and continued by succeeding generations, we may surely infer that those Christian tribes that did embrace Islam, did so of their own choice and free

[1] Ṭabarī, i. p. 2041.
[2] Mas'ūdī, tome iv. p. 256.

will.[1] The Christian Arabs of the present day, dwelling in the midst of a Muhammadan population, are a living testimony of this toleration; Layard speaks of having come across an encampment of Christian Arabs at al-Karak, to the east of the Dead Sea, who differed in no way, either in dress or in manners, from the Muslim Arabs.[2] Burckhardt was told by the monks of Mount Sinai that in the last century there still remained several families of Christian Bedouins who had not embraced Islam, and that the last of them, an old woman, died in 1750, and was buried in the garden of the convent.[3]

Many of the Arabs of the renowned tribe of the Banū G͟hassān, Arabs of the purest blood, who embraced Christianity towards the end of the fourth century, still retain the Christian faith, and since their submission to the Church of Rome, about two centuries ago, employ the Arabic language in their religious services.[4]

If we turn from the Bedouins to consider the attitude of the settled inhabitants of the towns and the non-Arab population towards the new religion, we do not find that the Arab conquest was so rapidly followed by conversions to Islam. The Christians of the great cities of the eastern provinces of the Byzantine empire seem for the most part to have remained faithful to their ancestral creed, to which indeed they still in large numbers cling.

In order that we may fully appreciate their condition under the Muslim rule, and estimate the influences that led to occasional conversions, it will be well briefly to sketch their situation under the Christian rule of the Byzantine empire which fell back before the Arab arms.

A hundred years before, Justinian had succeeded in giving some show of unity to the Roman Empire, but after

[1] "Gli Arabi nei primi anni non perseguitarono invece alcuno per ragioni di fede, non si diedero pena alcuna per convertire chicchessia, sicchè sotto l'Islām, dopo le prime conquiste, i cristiani Semiti goderno d'una tolleranza religiosa quale non si era mai vista da varie generazioni." (Caetani, vol. v. p. 4.)

[2] Sir Henry Layard: Early Adventures in Persia, Susiana and Babylonia, vol. i. p. 100. (London, 1887); R. Hartmann: Die Herrschaft von al-Karak. (Der Islam, vol. ii. p. 137.)

[3] Burckhardt (2), p. 564.

[4] W. G. Palgrave: Essays on Eastern Questions, pp. 206–8. (London, 1872.)

his death it rapidly fell asunder, and at this time there was an entire want of common national feeling between the provinces and the seat of government. Heraclius had made some partially successful efforts to attach Syria again to the central government, but unfortunately the general methods of reconciliation which he adopted had served only to increase dissension instead of allaying it. Religious passions were the only existing substitute for national feeling, and he tried, by propounding an exposition of faith, that was intended to serve as an eirenicon, to stop all further disputes between the contending factions and unite the heretics to the Orthodox Church and to the central government. The Council of Chalcedon (451) had maintained that Christ was "to be acknowledged in two natures, without confusion, change, division, or separation; the difference of the natures being in nowise taken away by reason of their union, but rather the properties of each nature being preserved, and concurring into one person and one substance, not as it were divided or separated into two persons, but one and the same Son and only begotten, God the Word." This council was rejected by the Monophysites, who only allowed one nature in the person of Christ, who was said to be a composite person, having all attributes divine and human, but the substance bearing these attributes was no longer a duality, but a composite unity. The controversy between the orthodox party and the Monophysites, who flourished particularly in Egypt and Syria and in countries outside the Byzantine empire, had been hotly contested for nearly two centuries, when Heraclius sought to effect a reconciliation by means of the doctrine of Monotheletism: while conceding the duality of the natures, it secured unity of the person in the actual life of Christ, by the rejection of two series of activities in this one person; the one Christ and Son of God effectuates that which is human and that which is divine by one divine human agency, i.e. there is only one will in the Incarnate Word.[1]

But Heraclius shared the fate of so many would-be

[1] I. A. Dorner: A System of Christian Doctrine, vol. iii. pp. 215–16. (London, 1885.) J. C. Robertson: History of the Christian Church, vol. ii. p. 226. (London, 1875.)

peace-makers: for not only did the controversy blaze up again all the more fiercely, but he himself was stigmatised as a heretic and drew upon himself the wrath of both parties.

Indeed, so bitter was the feeling he aroused that there is strong reason to believe that even a majority of the orthodox subjects of the Roman Empire, in the provinces that were conquered during this emperor's reign, were the well-wishers of the Arabs; they regarded the emperor with aversion as a heretic, and were afraid that he might commence a persecution in order to force upon them his Monotheletic opinions.[1] They therefore readily—and even eagerly—received the new masters who promised them religious toleration, and were willing to compromise their religious position and their national independence if only they could free themselves from the immediately impending danger.

Michael the Elder, Jacobite Patriarch of Antioch, writing in the latter half of the twelfth century, could approve the decision of his co-religionists and see the finger of God in the Arab conquests even after the Eastern churches had had experience of five centuries of Muhammadan rule. After recounting the persecutions of Heraclius, he writes: "This is why the God of vengeance, who alone is all-powerful, and changes the empire of mortals as He will, giving it to whomsoever He will, and uplifting the humble—beholding the wickedness of the Romans who, throughout their dominions, cruelly plundered our churches and our monasteries and condemned us without pity—brought from the region of the south the sons of Ishmael, to deliver us through them from the hands of the Romans. And, if in truth, we have suffered some loss, because the catholic churches, that had been taken away from us and given to the Chalcedonians, remained in their possession; for when the cities submitted to the Arabs, they assigned to each denomination the churches which they found it to be in possession of (and at that time the great church of Emessa

[1] That such fears were not wholly groundless may be judged from the emperor's intolerant behaviour towards many of the Monophysite party in his progress through Syria after the defeat of the Persians in 627. (See Michael the Elder, vol. ii. p. 412, and Caetani, vol. ii. p. 1049.) For the outrages committed by the Byzantine soldiers on their co-religionists in the reign of Constans II (642–668), see Michael the Elder, vol. ii. p. 443.

and that of Harran had been taken away from us); nevertheless it was no slight advantage for us to be delivered from the cruelty of the Romans, their wickedness, their wrath and cruel zeal against us, and to find ourselves at peace." [1]

When the Muslim army reached the valley of the Jordan and Abū 'Ubaydah pitched his camp at Fiḥl, the Christian inhabitants of the country wrote to the Arabs, saying: "O Muslims, we prefer you to the Byzantines, though they are of our own faith, because you keep better faith with us and are more merciful to us and refrain from doing us injustice and your rule over us is better than theirs, for they have robbed us of our goods and our homes." [2] The people of Emessa closed the gates of their city against the army of Heraclius and told the Muslims that they preferred their government and justice to the injustice and oppression of the Greeks.[3]

Such was the state of feeling in Syria during the campaign of 633–639 in which the Arabs gradually drove the Roman army out of the province. And when Damascus, in 637, set the example of making terms with the Arabs, and thus secured immunity from plunder and other favourable conditions, the rest of the cities of Syria were not slow to follow. Emessa, Arethusa, Hieropolis and other towns entered into treaties whereby they became tributary to the Arabs. Even the patriarch of Jerusalem surrendered the city on similar terms. The fear of religious compulsion on the part of the heretical emperor made the promise of Muslim toleration appear more attractive than the connection with the Roman Empire and a Christian government, and after the first terrors caused by the passage of an invading army, there succeeded a profound revulsion of feeling in favour of the Arab conquerors.[4]

[1] Michael the Elder, vol. ii. pp. 412–13. Barhebræus, about a century later, wrote in a similar strain. (Chronicon Ecclesiasticum, ed. J. B. Abbeloos et Lamy, p. 474.)

[2] Azdī, p. 97.

[3] Balādhurī, p. 137.

[4] Caetani, vol. iii. p. 813; vol. v. p. 394. ("Gli abitanti accettarono con non celato favore il mutamento di governo, appena ebbero compreso che gli Arabi avrebbero rispettato i loro diritti individuali, ed avrebbero lasciata completa libertà di coscienza in materia religiosa. In Siria, città ed interi distretti si affrettarono a trattare con gli Arabi anche prima della rotta finale dei Greci. Nel Sawād si lasciarono passivamente sopraffare accettando il nuovo dominio senza pattuire condizioni di sorta; è probabile che anche in Siria questo fosse il caso per molte regioni remote dalle grandi vie di comunicazioni.")

For the provinces of the Byzantine empire that were rapidly acquired by the prowess of the Muslims found themselves in the enjoyment of a toleration such as, on account of their Monophysite and Nestorian opinions, had been unknown to them for many centuries. They were allowed the free and undisturbed exercise of their religion with some few restrictions imposed for the sake of preventing any friction between the adherents of the rival religions, or arousing any fanaticism by the ostentatious exhibition of religious symbols that were so offensive to Muslim feeling.[1] The extent of this toleration—so striking in the history of the seventh century—may be judged from the terms granted to the conquered cities, in which protection of life and property and toleration of religious belief were given in return for submission and the payment of jizyah.[2]

The exact details of these agreements cannot easily be disentangled from the accretions with which they have become overlaid, but whether verbally authentic or not, they are significant as representing the historic tradition accepted by the Muslim historians of the second century of the Hijrah—a tradition that could hardly have become established had there been extant evidence to the contrary. As an example of such an agreement, the conditions [3] may be quoted that are stated to have been drawn up when Jerusalem submitted to the caliph 'Umar b. al-Khaṭṭāb: "In the name of God, the Merciful, the Compassionate! This is the security which 'Umar, the servant of God, the commander of the faithful, grants to the people of Ælia. He grants to all, whether sick or sound, security for their lives, their possessions, their churches and their crosses, and for all that concerns their religion. Their churches shall not be changed into dwelling places, nor destroyed, neither shall they nor their appurtenances be in any way diminished, nor the crosses of the inhabitants nor aught of their possessions, nor shall any constraint be put upon them in the matter of their faith, nor shall any one of them be harmed." [4]

[1] Gottheil has brought together a valuable collection of documentary evidence as to the condition of the protected peoples under Muslim rule in his "Dhimmīs and Moslems in Egypt."

[2] Balādhurī, pp. 74 (*ad fin.*), 116, 121 (*med.*).

[3] For a discussion of this document, see Caetani, vol. iii. p. 952 sqq.

[4] Ṭabarī, i. p. 2405.

Tribute was imposed upon them of five dīnārs for the rich, four for the middle class and three for the poor. In company with the Patriarch, 'Umar visited the holy places, and it is said while they were in the Church of the Resurrection, as it was the appointed hour of prayer, the Patriarch bade the caliph offer his prayers there, but he thoughtfully refused, saying that if he were to do so, his followers might afterwards claim it as a place of Muslim worship.

It is in harmony with the same spirit of kindly consideration for his subjects of another faith, that 'Umar is recorded to have ordered an allowance of money and food to be made to some Christian lepers, apparently out of the public funds.[1] Even in his last testament, in which he enjoins on his successor the duties of his high office, he remembers the dhimmīs (or protected persons of other faiths): "I commend to his care the dhimmīs, who enjoy the protection of God and of the Prophet; let him see to it that the covenant with them is kept, and that no greater burdens than they can bear are laid upon them."[2]

A later generation attributed to 'Umar a number of restrictive regulations which hampered the Christians in the free exercise of their religion, but De Goeje[3] and Caetani[4] have proved without doubt that they are the invention of a later age; as, however, Muslim theologians of less tolerant periods accepted these ordinances as genuine, they are of importance for forming a judgment as to the condition of the Christian Churches under Muslim rule. This so-called ordinance of 'Umar runs as follows:—"In the name of God, the Merciful, the Compassionate! This is a writing to 'Umar b. al-Khaṭṭāb from the Christians of such and such a city. When you marched against us, we asked of you protection for ourselves, our posterity, our possessions and our co-religionists; and we made this stipulation with you, that we will not erect in our city or the suburbs any new monastery, church, cell or hermitage;[5]

[1] Balādhurī, p. 129.
[2] Ibn S'ad, III, i. p. 246.
[3] Mémoire sur la conquête de la Syrie, p. 143 sq.
[4] Annali dell' Islām, vol. iii. p. 957.
[5] Some authorities on Muhammadan law held that this rule did not extend to villages and hamlets, in which the construction of churches was not to be prevented. (Hidāyah, vol. ii. p. 219.)

that we will not repair any of such buildings that may fall into ruins, or renew those that may be situated in the Muslim quarters of the town; that we will not refuse the Muslims entry into our churches either by night or by day; that we will open the gates wide to passengers and travellers; that we will receive any Muslim traveller into our houses and give him food and lodging for three nights; that we will not harbour any spy in our churches or houses, or conceal any enemy of the Muslims; that we will not teach our children the Qur'ān; [1] that we will not make a show of the Christian religion nor invite any one to embrace it; that we will not prevent any of our kinsmen from embracing Islam, if they so desire. That we will honour the Muslims and rise up in our assemblies when they wish to take their seats; that we will not imitate them in our dress, either in the cap, turban, sandals, or parting of the hair; that we will not make use of their expressions of speech,[2] nor adopt their surnames; that we will not ride on saddles, or gird on swords, or take to ourselves arms or wear them, or engrave Arabic inscriptions on our rings; that we will not sell wine; that we will shave the front of our heads; that we will keep to our own style of dress, wherever we may be; that we will wear girdles round our waists; that we will not display the cross upon our churches or display our crosses or our sacred books in the streets of the Muslims, or in their market-places; [3] that we will strike the bells [4] in our churches lightly; that we will not recite our services in a loud voice when a Muslim is present, that we will not carry palm-branches or our images in procession in the streets, that at the burial of our dead we will not chant loudly or carry lighted candles

[1] "The 'Ulamā' are divided in opinion on the question of the teaching of the Qur'ān: the sect of Mālik forbids it: that of Abū Ḥanīfah allows it; and Shāfi'ī has two opinions on the subject: on the one hand, he countenances the study of it, as indicating a leaning towards Islam; and on the other hand, he forbids it, because he fears that the unbeliever who studies the Qur'ān being still impure may read it solely with the object of turning it to ridicule, since he is the enemy of God and the Prophet who wrote the book; now as these two statements are contradictory, Shāfi'ī has no formally stated opinion on this matter." (Belin, p. 508.)

[2] Such as the forms of greeting, etc., that are only to be used by Muslims to one another.

[3] Abū Yūsuf (p. 82) says that Christians were to be allowed to go in procession once a year with crosses, but not with banners; outside the city, not inside where the mosques were.

[4] The nāqūs, lit. an oblong piece of wood, struck with a rod.

in the streets of the Muslims or their market-places; that we will not take any slaves that have already been in the possession of Muslims, nor spy into their houses; and that we will not strike any Muslim. All this we promise to observe, on behalf of ourselves and our co-religionists, and receive protection from you in exchange; and if we violate any of the conditions of this agreement, then we forfeit your protection and you are at liberty to treat us as enemies and rebels." [1]

The earliest mention of this document is made by Ibn Ḥazm, who died in the middle of the fifth century of the Hijrah; its provisions represent the more intolerant practice of a later age, and indeed were regulations that were put into force with no sort of regularity, some outburst of fanaticism being generally needed for any appeal to be made for their application. There is abundant evidence to show that the Christians in the early days of the Muhammadan conquest had little to complain of in the way of religious disabilities. It is true that adherence to their ancient faith rendered them obnoxious to the payment of jizyah—a word which originally denoted tribute of any kind paid by the non-Muslim subjects of the Arab empire, but came later on to be used for the capitation-tax as the fiscal system of the new rulers became fixed; [2] but this jizyah was too moderate to constitute a burden, seeing that it released them from the compulsory military service that was incumbent on their Muslim fellow-subjects. Conversion to Islam was certainly attended by a certain pecuniary advantage, but his former religion could have had but little hold on a convert who abandoned it merely to gain exemption from the jizyah; and now, instead of jizyah, the convert had to pay the legal alms, zakāt, annually levied on most kinds of movable and immovable property.[3]

[1] Gottheil, pp. 382–4, where references are given to the various versions of this document.

[2] There is evidence to show that the Arab conquerors left unchanged the fiscal system that they found prevailing in the lands they conquered from the Byzantines, and that the explanation of jizyah as a capitation-tax is an invention of later jurists, ignorant of the true condition of affairs in the early days of Islam. (Caetani, vol. iv. p. 610 (§ 231); vol. v. p. 449.) H. Lammens: Ziād ibn Abīhi. (Rivista degli Studi Orientali, vol. iv. p. 215.)

[3] Goldziher, vol. i. pp. 50–7, 427–30. Caetani, vol. v. p. 311 sqq.

The pecuniary temptation to escape the incidence of taxation by means of conversion was considerably lessened when financial considerations compelled the Arab government, towards the end of the first century, to insist on the new converts continuing to pay jizyah even after they had been received into the community of the faithful.[1] On the other hand it must be remembered that the non-Muslim sections of the population always ran the risk of becoming the victims of fiscal oppression when the state was in need of revenue.

The rates of jizyah levied by the early conquerors were not uniform,[2] and the great Muslim doctors, Abū Ḥanīfah and Mālik, are not in agreement on some of the less important details;[3] the following facts taken from the Kitāb al-Kharāj, drawn up by Abū Yūsuf at the request of Hārūn al-Rashīd (A.D. 786–809) may be taken as generally representative of Muhammadan procedure under the ʻAbbāsid Caliphate. The rich were to pay forty-eight dirhams[4] a year, the middle classes twenty-four, while from the poor, i. e. the field-labourers and artisans, only twelve dirhams were taken. This tax could be paid in kind if desired; cattle, merchandise, household effects, even needles were to be accepted in lieu of specie, but not pigs, wine, or dead animals. The tax was to be levied only on able-bodied males, and not on women or children.[5] The poor who were dependent for their livelihood on alms and the aged poor who were incapable of work were also specially excepted, as also the blind, the lame, the incurables and the insane, unless they happened to be men of wealth; this same condition applied to priests and monks, who were exempt if dependent on the alms of the rich, but had to pay if they were well-to-do and lived in comfort. The collectors of the jizyah were particularly instructed to show leniency, and refrain from all harsh treatment or the infliction of corporal punishment, in case of non-payment.[6]

This tax was not imposed on the Christians, as some would have us think, as a penalty for their refusal to accept the Muslim faith, but was paid by them in common with the

[1] Caetani, vol. v. pp. 424 (§ 752), 432.
[2] Balādhurī, pp. 124–5.
[3] A. von Kremer (1), vol. i. pp. 60, 436.
[4] A dirham is about fivepence.
[5] Bell, pp. xxv, 173.
[6] Abū Yūsuf, pp. 69–71.

other dhimmīs or non-Muslim subjects of the state whose religion precluded them from serving in the army, in return for the protection secured for them by the arms of the Musalmans. When the people of Hīrah contributed the sum agreed upon, they expressly mentioned that they paid this jizyah on condition that " the Muslims and their leader protect us from those who would oppress us, whether they be Muslims or others." [1] Again, in the treaty made by Khālid with some towns in the neighbourhood of Hīrah, he writes : " If we protect you, then jizyah is due to us ; but if we do not, then it is not due." [2] How clearly this condition was recognised by the Muhammadans may be judged from the following incident in the reign of the Caliph 'Umar. The Emperor Heraclius had raised an enormous army with which to drive back the invading forces of the Muslims, who had in consequence to concentrate all their energies on the impending encounter. The Arab general, Abū 'Ubaydah, accordingly wrote to the governors of the conquered cities of Syria, ordering them to pay back all the jizyah that had been collected from the cities, and wrote to the people, saying, " We give you back the money that we took from you, as we have received news that a strong force is advancing against us. The agreement between u was that we should protect you, and as this is not now in our power, we return you all that we took. But if we are victorious we shall consider ourselves bound to you by the old terms of our agreement." In accordance with this order, enormous sums were paid back out of the state treasury, and the Christians called down blessings on the heads of the Muslims, saying, " May God give you rule over us again and make you victorious over the Romans ; had it been they, they would not have given us back anything, but would have taken all that remained with us." [3]

As stated above, the jizyah was levied on the able-bodied males, in lieu of the military service they would have been called upon to perform had they been Musalmans ; and it is very noticeable that when any Christian people served in the Muslim army, they were exempted from the payment

[1] Ṭabarī, Prima Series, p. 2055. [2] Id. p. 2050.
[3] Abū Yūsuf, p. 81.

of this tax. Such was the case with the tribe of al-Jurājimah, a Christian tribe in the neighbourhood of Antioch, who made peace with the Muslims, promising to be their allies and fight on their side in battle, on condition that they should not be called upon to pay jizyah and should receive their proper share of the booty.[1] When the Arab conquests were pushed to the north of Persia in A.H. 22, a similar agreement was made with a frontier tribe, which was exempted from the payment of jizyah in consideration of military service.[2]

We find similar instances of the remission of jizyah in the case of Christians who served in the army or navy under the Turkish rule. For example, the inhabitants of Megaris, a community of Albanian Christians, were exempted from the payment of this tax on condition that they furnished a body of armed men to guard the passes over Mounts Cithæron and Geranea, which lead to the Isthmus of Corinth; the Christians who served as pioneers of the advance-guard of the Turkish army, repairing the roads and bridges, were likewise exempt from tribute and received grants of land quit of all taxation; [3] and the Christian inhabitants of Hydra paid no direct taxes to the Sultan, but furnished instead a contingent of 250 able-bodied seamen to the Turkish fleet, who were supported out of the local treasury.[4]

The Southern Rumanians, the so-called Armatoli,[5] who constituted so important an element of strength in the Turkish army during the sixteenth and seventeenth centuries, and the Mirdites, a tribe of Albanian Catholics who occupied the mountains to the north of Scutari, were exempt from taxation on condition of supplying an armed contingent in time of war.[6] In the same spirit, in consideration of the services they rendered to the state, the capitation-tax was not imposed upon the Greek Christians who looked after the aqueducts that supplied Constantinople with drinking water,[7] nor on those who had charge of the powder-magazine in that city.[8] On the other hand, when the Egyptian

[1] Balādhurī, p. 159.
[2] Ṭabarī, Prima Series, p. 2665.
[3] Marsigli, vol. i. p. 86 (he calls them "Musellim").
[4] Finlay, vol. vi. pp. 30, 33.
[5] Lazăr, p. 56.
[6] De la Jonquière, p. 14.
[7] Thomas Smith, p. 324.
[8] Dorostamus, p. 326.

peasants, although Muslim in faith, were made exempt from military service, a tax was imposed upon them as on the Christians, in lieu thereof.[1]

Living under this security of life and property and such toleration of religious thought, the Christian community—especially in the towns—enjoyed a flourishing prosperity in the early days of the Caliphate.

Mu'āwiyah (661–680) employed Christians very largely in his service, and other members of the reigning house followed his example.[2] Christians frequently held high posts at court, e. g. a Christian Arab, al-Akhṭal, was court poet, and the father of St. John of Damascus, counsellor to the caliph 'Abd al-Malik (685–705). In the service of the caliph al-Mu'taṣim (833–842), there were two brothers, Christians, who stood very high in the confidence of the Commander of the Faithful: the one, named Salmūyah, seems to have occupied somewhat the position of a modern secretary of state, and no royal documents were valid until countersigned by him, while his brother, Ibrāhīm, was entrusted with the care of the privy seal, and was set over the Bayt al-Māl or Public Treasury, an office that, from the nature of the funds and their disposal, might have been expected to have been put into the hands of a Muslim; so great was the caliph's personal affection for this Ibrāhīm, that he visited him in his sickness, and was overwhelmed with grief at his death, and on the day of the funeral ordered the body to be brought to the palace and the Christian rites performed there with great solemnity.[3]

'Abd al-Malik appointed a certain Athanasius, a Christian scholar of Edessa, tutor to his brother, 'Abd al-'Azīz. Athanasius accompanied his pupil, when he was appointed governor of Egypt, and there amassed great wealth; he is said to have possessed 4000 slaves, villages, houses, gardens, and gold and silver "like stones"; his sons took a dīnār from each of the soldiers when they received their pay, and as there were 30,000 troops then in Egypt, some idea may be formed of the wealth that Athanasius accumulated during

[1] De la Jonquière, p. 265.
[2] Lammens, p. 13.
[3] Ibn Abī Usaybi'ah, vol. i. p. 164.

the twenty-one years that he spent in that country.[1] At the close of the eighth century, a certain Abū Nūḥ al-Anbārī was secretary to Abū Mūsā b. Muṣ'ab, governor of Mosul, and used his powerful influence for the benefit of his Christian co-religionists.[2]

In the reign of al-Mu'tadid (892–902), the governor of Anbār, 'Umar b. Yūsuf, was a Christian, and the caliph approved of the appointment on the ground that if a Christian were found to be competent, a post might well be given to him, as there were better reasons for trusting a Christian than either a Jew, a Muslim or a Zoroastrian.[3] Al-Muwaffaq, who was virtual ruler of the empire during the reign of his brother al-Mu'tamid (870–892), entrusted the administration of the army to a Christian named Israel, and his son, al-Mu'taḍid, had as one of his secretaries another Christian, Malik b. al-Walīd. In a later reign, that of al-Muqtadir (908–932), a Christian was again in charge of the war office.[4]

Naṣr b. Hārūn, the Prime Minister of 'Aḍud al-Dawlah (949–982), of the Buwayhid dynasty of Persia, who ruled over Southern Persia and 'Irāq, was a Christian.[5] For a long time, the government offices, especially in the department of finance, were filled with Christians and Persians;[6] to a much later date was such the case in Egypt, where at times the Christians almost entirely monopolised such posts.[7] Particularly as physicians, the Christians frequently amassed great wealth and were much honoured in the houses of the great. Gabriel, the personal physician of the caliph Hārūn al-Rashīd, was a Nestorian Christian and derived a yearly income of 800,000 dirhams from his private property, in addition to an emolument of 280,000 dirhams a year in return for his attendance on the caliph; the second physician, also a Christian, received 22,000 dirhams a year.[8] In trade and commerce, the Christians also attained considerable affluence: indeed it was frequently their wealth that excited against them the jealous

[1] Michael the Elder, vol. ii. p. 475.
[2] Mārī b. Sulaymān, p. 71 (l. 16). Abū Nūḥ al-Anbārī wrote a refutation of the Qur'ān and other theological works (Wright, p. 191 n. 3).
[3] Mārī b. Sulaymān, p. 84.
[4] Hilāl al-Ṣābī, p. 95.
[5] Ibn al-Athīr, vol. ix. p. 16.
[6] Von Kremer (1), vol. i. pp. 167–8. Lammens, p. 11.
[7] Renaudot, pp. 430, 540.
[8] Von Kremer (1), vol. ii. pp. 180–1.

cupidity of the mob—a feeling that fanatics took advantage of, to persecute and oppress them. Further, the non-Muslim communities enjoyed an almost complete autonomy, for the government placed in their hands the independent management of their internal affairs, and their religious leaders exercised judicial functions in cases that concerned their co-religionists only.[1] Their churches and monasteries were, for the most part, not interfered with, except in the large cities, where some of them were turned into mosques—a measure that could hardly be objected to in view of the enormous increase in the Muslim and corresponding decrease in the Christian population.

Recent historical criticism has demonstrated the impossibility of the legend that when Damascus was taken by the Arabs, the churches were equally divided between the Christians and the conquerors, on the plea that while one Muslim general made his way into the city by the eastern gate at the point of the sword, another at the western gate received the submission of the governor of the city; a similar scrutiny of historical documents as well as of the topography of the building has shown that the great cathedral of St. John could never have been used in the manner described by some Arabic historians as a common place of worship for both Christians and Muslims.[2] But the very fact that these historians should have believed that such an arrangement continued for nearly eighty years, testifies to the early recognition of the liberty granted to the Christians of practising the observances of their religion.

The opinion of the Muhammadan legists is very diverse on this question, from the more liberal Ḥanafī doctrine, which declares that, though it is unlawful to construct churches and synagogues in Muhammadan territory, those already existing can be repaired if they have been destroyed or have fallen into decay, while in villages and hamlets, where the tokens of Islam do not appear, new churches and synagogues may be built—to the intolerant Ḥanbalite view that they may neither be erected nor be restored when damaged or ruined. Some legists held that the privileges varied according to treaty rights: in towns taken by force,

[1] Von Kremer (1), vol. i. p. 183. [2] Caetani, vol. iii. pp. 350 sq., 387 sqq.

no new houses of prayer might be erected by dhimmīs, but if a special treaty had been made, the building of new churches and synagogues was allowed.[1] But like so many of the lucubrations of Muhammadan legists, these prescriptions bore but little relation to actual facts.[2] Schoolmen might agree that the dhimmīs could build no houses of prayer in a city of Muslim foundation, but the civil authority permitted the Copts to erect churches in the new capital of Cairo.[3] In other cities also the Christians were allowed to erect new churches and monasteries. The very fact that 'Umar II (717–720), at the close of the first century of the Hijrah, should have ordered the destruction of all recently constructed churches,[4] and that rather more than a century later, the fanatical al-Mutawakkil (847–861) should have had to repeat the same order, shows how little the prohibition of the building of new churches was put into force.[5] We have numerous instances recorded, both by Christian and Muhammadan historians, of the building of new churches: e. g. in the reign of 'Abd al-Malik (685–705), a wealthy Christian of Edessa, named Athanasius, erected in his native city a fine church dedicated to the Mother of God, and a Baptistery in honour of the picture of Christ that was reputed to have been sent to King Abgar; he also built a number of churches and monasteries in various parts of Egypt, among them two magnificent churches in Fusṭāṭ.[6] Some Christian chamberlains in the service of 'Abd al-'Aziz b. Marwān (brother of 'Abd al-Malik), the governor of Egypt, obtained permission to build a church in Ḥalwān, which was dedicated to St. John,[7] though this town was a Muslim creation. In A.D. 711 a Jacobite church was built at Antioch by order of the caliph al-Walīd (705–715).[8] In the first year of the reign of Yazīd

[1] Gottheil, pp. 360–1. Goldziher: Zur Literatur des Ichtilâf al-maḏâhib, ZDMG., vol. 38, pp. 673–4.

[2] On this theoretical character of much of Muslim legal literature, see Snouck Hurgonje: Mohammedanisches Recht in Theorie und Wirklichkeit.

[3] Gottheil, p. 363.

[4] Gottheil, pp. 358–9, however, doubts whether there is evidence for attributing this intolerance to 'Umar II.

[5] Journal Asiatique, IVme série, tome xviii. (1851), pp. 433, 450. Ṭabarī, III, p. 1419.

[6] Michael the Elder, vol. ii. p. 476. Renaudot, p. 189.

[7] Eutychius, II, p. 41 init. Severus (p. 139) says "two churches."

[8] Von Kremer (1), vol. ii. p. 175.

II (A.D. 720), Mār Elias, the Jacobite Patriarch of Antioch, made a solemn entry into Antioch, accompanied by his clergy and monks, to consecrate a new church which he had caused to be built; and in the following year he consecrated another church in the village of Sarmada, in the district of Antioch, and the only opposition he met with was from the rival Christian sect that accepted the Council of Chalcedon.[1] In the following reign, Khālid al-Qasrī, who was governor of Arabian and Persian 'Irāq from 724 to 738, built a church for his mother, who was a Christian, to worship in.[2] In 759 the building of a church at Nisibis was completed, on which the Nestorian bishop, Cyprian, had expended a sum of 56,000 dīnārs.[3] From the same century dates the church of Abū Sirjah in the ancient Roman fortress in old Cairo.[4] In the reign of al-Mahdī (775–785) a church was erected in Baghdād for the use of the Christian prisoners that had been taken captive during the numerous campaigns against the Byzantine empire.[5] Another church was built in the same city, in the reign of Hārūn al-Rashīd (786–809), by the people of Samālū, who had submitted to the caliph and received protection from him;[6] during the same reign Sergius, the Nestorian Metropolitan of Baṣrah, received permission to build a church in that city,[7] though it was a Muslim foundation, having been created by the caliph 'Umar in the year 638, and a magnificent church was erected in Babylon in which were enshrined the bodies of the prophets Daniel and Ezechiel.[8] When al-Ma'mūn (813–833) was in Egypt he gave permission to two of his chamberlains to erect a church on al-Muqaṭṭam, a hill near Cairo; and by the same caliph's leave, a wealthy Christian, named Bukām, built several fine churches at Būrah in Egypt.[9] The Nestorian Patriarch, Timotheus, who died A.D. 820, erected a church at Takrīt and a monastery at Baghdād.[10] In the tenth century, the beautiful Coptic church of Abū

[1] Michael the Elder, vol. ii. pp. 490, 491.
[2] Ibn Khallikān, vol. i. p. 485.
[3] Elias of Nisibis, p. 128.
[4] A. J. Butler: The Ancient Coptic Churches of Egypt, vol. i. p. 181. (Oxford, 1884.)
[5] Yāqūt, vol. ii. p. 662.
[6] Yāqūt, vol. ii. p. 670.
[7] Mārī b. Sulaymān, p. 73.
[8] Ishok of Romgla, p. 266.
[9] Eutychius, II, p. 58.
[10] Von Kremer (1), vol. ii. pp. 175–6.

Sayfayn was built in Fusṭāṭ.[1] A new church was built at Jiddah in the reign of al-Ẓāhir, the seventh Fāṭimid caliph of Egypt (1020–1035).[2] New churches and monasteries were also built in the reign of the 'Abbāsid, al-Mustaḍī (1170–1180).[3] In 1187 a church was built at Fusṭāṭ and dedicated to Our Lady the Pure Virgin.[4]

Indeed, so far from the development of the Christian Church being hampered by the establishment of Muhammadan rule, the history of the Nestorians exhibits a remarkable outburst of religious life and energy from the time of their becoming subject to the Muslims.[5] Alternately petted and persecuted by the Persian kings, in whose dominions by far the majority of the members of this sect were found, it had passed a rather precarious existence and had been subjected to harsh treatment, when war between Persia and Byzantium exposed it to the suspicion of sympathising with the Christian enemy. But, under the rule of the caliphs, the security they enjoyed at home enabled them to vigorously push forward their missionary enterprises abroad. Missionaries were sent into China and India, both of which were raised to the dignity of metropolitan sees in the eighth century; about the same period they gained a footing in Egypt, and later spread the Christian faith right across Asia, and by the eleventh century had gained many converts from among the Tatars.[6]

If the other Christian sects failed to exhibit the same vigorous life, it was not the fault of the Muhammadans. All were tolerated alike by the supreme government, and furthermore were prevented from persecuting one another.[7] In the fifth century, Barsauma, a Nestorian bishop, had persuaded the Persian king to set on foot a fierce persecution

[1] Butler : Ancient Coptic Churches of Egypt, vol. i. p. 76.
[2] Renaudot, p. 399. [3] Ishok of Romgla, p. 333. [4] Abū Ṣāliḥ, p. 92.
[5] A Dominican monk from Florence, by name Ricoldus de Monte Crucis, who visited the East about the close of the thirteenth and the beginning of the fourteenth century, speaks of the toleration the Nestorians had enjoyed under Muhammadan rule right up to his time : " Et ego inveni per antiquas historias et autenticas aput Saracenos, quod ipsi Nestorini amici fuerunt Machometi et confederati cum eo, et quod ipse Machometus mandauit suis posteris, quod Nestorinos maxime conseruarent. Quod usque hodie diligenter obseruant ipsi Sarraceni." (Laurent, p. 128.)
[6] J. Labourt : De Timotheo I, Nestorianorum Patriarcha, p. 37 sqq. (Paris, 1904.)
[7] E. von Dobschütz, p. 390–1.

of the Orthodox Church, by representing Nestorius as a friend of the Persians and his doctrines as approximating to their own; as many as 7800 of the Orthodox clergy, with an enormous number of laymen, are said to have been butchered during this persecution.[1] Another persecution was instituted against the Orthodox by Khusrau II, after the invasion of Persia by Heraclius, at the instigation of a Jacobite, who persuaded the King that the Orthodox would always be favourably inclined towards the Byzantines.[2] But the principles of Muslim toleration forbade such acts of injustice as these: on the contrary, it seems to have been their endeavour to deal fairly by all their Christian subjects: e.g. after the conquest of Egypt, the Jacobites took advantage of the expulsion of the Byzantine authorities to rob the Orthodox of their churches, but later they were restored by the Muhammadans to their rightful owners when these had made good their claim to possess them.[3]

In view of the toleration thus extended to their Christian subjects in the early period of the Muslim rule, the common hypothesis of the sword as the factor of conversion seems hardly satisfactory, and we are compelled to seek for other motives than that of persecution. But unfortunately very few details are forthcoming and we are obliged to have recourse to conjecture.[4] In an age so prolific of theological speculation, there may well have been some thinkers whose trend of thought had prepared them for the acceptance of the Muhammadan position. Such were those Shahrīghān or landed proprietors in Persia in the eighth century, who were nominally Christians, but maintained that Christ was an ordinary man and that he was as one of the Prophets.[5] They appear at times to have given a good deal of trouble

[1] Michael the Elder, vol. ii. p. 439–40.

[2] Makīn, p. 12. J. Labourt: Le Christianisme sous la dynastie sassanide, p. 139 sq. (Paris, 1904.)

[3] Renaudot, p. 169.

[4] Von Kremer well remarks: "Wir verdanken dem unermüdlichen Sammelfleiss der arabischen Chronisten unsere Kenntniss der politischen und militärischen Geschichte jener Zeiten, welche so genau ist als dies nur immer auf eine Entfernung von zwölf Jahrhunderten der Fall sein kann; allein gerade die innere Geschichte jener denkwürdigen Epoche, die Geschichte des Kampfes einer neuen, rohen Religion gegen die alten hochgebildeten, zum Theile überbildeten Culte ist kaum in ihren allgemeinsten Umrissen bekannt." (Von Kremer (2), pp. 1–2.)

[5] Thomas of Margā, vol. ii. p. 309 sq.

to the Nestorian clergy, who were at great pains to draw them into the paths of orthodoxy;[1] but their theological position was more closely akin to Islam than to Christian doctrine, and they probably went to swell the ranks of the converts after the Arab conquest of the Persian empire.

Many Christian theologians[2] have supposed that the debased condition—moral and spiritual—of the Eastern Church of that period must have alienated the hearts of many and driven them to seek a healthier spiritual atmosphere in the faith of Islam which had come to them in all the vigour of new-born zeal.[3] For example, Dean Milman[4] asks, "What was the state of the Christian world in the provinces exposed to the first invasion of Mohammedanism? Sect opposed to sect, clergy wrangling with clergy upon the most abstruse and metaphysical points of doctrine. The orthodox, the Nestorians, the Eutychians, the Jacobites were persecuting each other with unexhausted animosity; and it is not judging too severely the evils of religious controversy to suppose that many would rejoice in the degradation of their adversaries under the yoke of the unbeliever, rather than make common cause with them in defence of the common Christianity. In how many must this incessant disputation have shaken the foundations of their faith! It had been wonderful if thousands had not, in their weariness and perplexity, sought refuge from these interminable and implacable controversies in the simple, intelligible truth of the Divine Unity, though purchased by the acknowledgment of the prophetic mission of Mohammed." Similarly, Caetani sees in the spread of Islam, among the Christians of the Eastern Churches, a revulsion of feeling from the dogmatic subtleties introduced into Christian theology by the Hellenistic spirit. "For the East, with its love of clear and simple concepts, Hellenic culture was, from the religious point of view, a misfortune, because

[1] Thomas of Margā, vol. ii. pp. 310, 324 sq.

[2] Cf. in addition to the passages quoted below, M'Clintoch & Strong's Cyclopædia, sub art. Mohammedanism, vol. vi. p. 420. James Freeman Clarke: Ten Great Religions, Part ii. p. 75. (London, 1883.)

[3] Thus the Emperor Heraclius is represented by the Muhammadan historian as saying, "Their religion is a new religion which gives them new zeal." (Ṭabarī, p. 2103.)

[4] History of Latin Christianity, vol. ii. pp. 216–17.

it changed the sublime and simple teachings of Christ into a creed bristling with incomprehensible dogmas, full of doubts and uncertainties; these ended with producing a feeling of deep dismay and shook the very foundations of religious belief; so that when at last there appeared, coming out suddenly from the desert, the news of the new revelation, this bastard oriental Christianity, torn asunder by internal discords, wavering in its fundamental dogmas, dismayed by such incertitudes, could no longer resist the temptations of a new faith, which swept away at one single stroke all miserable doubts, and offered, along with simple, clear and undisputed doctrines, great material advantages also. The East then abandoned Christ and threw itself into the arms of the Prophet of Arabia." [1]

Again, Canon Taylor [2] says: "It is easy to understand why this reformed Judaism spread so swiftly over Africa and Asia. The African and Syrian doctors had substituted abstruse metaphysical dogmas for the religion of Christ: they tried to combat the licentiousness of the age by setting forth the celestial merit of celibacy and the angelic excellence of virginity—seclusion from the world was the road of holiness, dirt was the characteristic of monkish sanctity—the people were practically polytheists, worshipping a crowd of martyrs, saints and angels; the upper classes were effeminate and corrupt, the middle classes oppressed by taxation,[3] the slaves without hope for the present or the future. As with the besom of God, Islam swept away this mass of corruption and superstition. It was a revolt against empty theological polemics; it was a masculine protest against the exaltation of celibacy as a crown of piety. It brought out the fundamental dogmas of religion—the unity and greatness of God, that He is merciful and righteous, that He claims obedience to His will, resignation and faith. It proclaimed the responsibility of man, a future life, a day of judgment, and stern retribution to fall upon the wicked; and enforced the duties of prayer, almsgiving, fasting and

[1] Caetani, vol. ii. pp. 1045–6.

[2] A paper read before the Church Congress at Wolverhampton, October 7th, 1887.

[3] For the oppressive fiscal system under the Byzantine empire, see Gfrörer: Byzantinische Geschichten, vol. ii. pp. 337–9, 389–91, 450.

benevolence. It thrust aside the artificial virtues, the religious frauds and follies, the perverted moral sentiments, and the verbal subtleties of theological disputants. It replaced monkishness by manliness. It gave hope to the slave, brotherhood to mankind, and recognition to the fundamental facts of human nature."

Islam has, moreover, been represented as a reaction against that Byzantine ecclesiasticism,[1] which looked upon the emperor and his court as a copy of the Divine Majesty on high, and the emperor himself as not only the supreme earthly ruler of Christendom, but as High-priest also.[2] Under Justinian this system had been hardened into a despotism that pressed like an iron weight upon clergy and laity alike. In 532 the widespread dissatisfaction in Constantinople with both church and state, burst out into a revolt against the government of Justinian, which was only suppressed after a massacre of 35,000 persons. The Greens, as the party of the malcontents was termed, had made open and violent protest in the circus against the oppression of the emperor, crying out, "Justice has vanished from the world and is no more to be found. But we will become Jews, or rather we will return again to Grecian paganism."[3] The lapse of a century had removed none of the grounds for the dissatisfaction that here found such violent expression, but the heavy hand of the Byzantine government prevented the renewal of such an outbreak as that of 532 and compelled the malcontents to dissemble, though in 560 some secret heathens were detected in Constantinople and punished.[4] On the borders of the empire, however, at a distance from the capital, such malcontents were safer, and the persecuted heretics, and others dissatisfied with the

[1] "Der Islam war ein Rückstoss gegen den Missbrauch, welchen Justinian mit der Menschheit, besonders aber mit der christlichen Religion trieb, deren oberstes geistliches und weltliches Haupt er zu sein behauptete. Dass der Araber Mahomed, welcher 571 der christlichen Zeitrechnung, sechs Jahre nach dem Tode Justinians, das Licht der Welt erblickte, mit seiner Lehre unerhörtes Glück machte, verdankte er grossentheils dem Abscheu, welchen die im Umkreise des byzantinischen Reiches angesessenen Völker, wie die benachbarten Nationen, über die von dem Basileus begangenen Greuel empfanden." (Gfrörer: Byzantinische Geschichten, vol. ii. p. 437.)

[2] Id. vol. ii. pp. 296–306, 337.

[3] Id. vol. ii. pp. 442–4.

[4] Id. vol. ii. p. 445.

Byzantine state-church, took refuge in the East, and here the Muslim armies would be welcomed by the spiritual children of those who a hundred years before had desired to exchange the Christian religion for another faith.

Further, the general adoption of the Arabic language throughout the empire of the caliphate, especially in the towns and the great centres of population, and the gradual assimilation in manners and customs that in the course of about two centuries caused the numerous conquered races to be largely merged in the national life of the ruling race, had no doubt a counterpart in the religious and intellectual life of many members of the protected religions. The rationalistic movement that so powerfully influenced Muslim theology from the second to the fifth century of the Hijrah may very possibly have influenced Christian thinkers, and turned them from a religion, the prevailing tone of whose theology seems at this time to have been *Credo quia impossibile.* A Muhammadan writer of the fourth century of the Hijrah has preserved for us a conversation with a Coptic Christian which may safely be taken as characteristic of the general mental attitude of the rest of the Eastern Churches at this period :—

"My proof for the truth of Christianity is, that I find its teachings contradictory and mutually destructive, for they are repugnant to reason and revolting to the intellect, on account of their inconsistency and mutual contrariety. No reflection can strengthen them, no discussion can prove them; and however thoughtfully we may investigate them, neither the intellect nor the senses can provide us with any argument in support of them. Notwithstanding this, I have seen that many nations and mighty kings of learning and sound judgment, have given in their allegiance to the Christian faith; so I conclude that if these have accepted it in spite of all the contradictions referred to, it is because the proofs they have received, in the form of signs and miracles, have compelled them to submit to it." [1]

On the other hand, it should be remembered that those who passed over from Christianity to Islam, under the influence of the rationalistic tendencies of the age, would

[1] Mas'ūdī, vol. ii. p. 387.

find in the Mu'tazilite presentment of Muslim theology, very much that was common to the two faiths, so that as far as the articles of belief and the intellectual attitude towards many theological questions were concerned, the transition was not so violent as might be supposed. To say nothing of the numerous fundamental doctrines, that will at once suggest themselves to those even who have only a slight knowledge of the teachings of the Prophet, there were many other common points of view, that were the direct consequences of the close relationships between the Christian and Muhammadan theologians in Damascus under the Umayyad caliphs as also in later times; for it has been maintained that there is clear evidence of the influence of the Byzantine theologians on the development of the systematic treatment of Muhammadan dogmatics. The very form and arrangement of the oldest rule of faith in the Arabic language suggest a comparison with similar treatises of St. John of Damascus and other Christian fathers.[1] The oldest Arab Ṣūfiism, the trend of which was purely towards the ascetic life (as distinguished from the later pantheistic Ṣūfiism) originated largely under the influence of Christian thought.[2] Such influence is especially traceable in the doctrines of some of the Mu'tazilite sects,[3] who busied themselves with speculations on the attributes of the divine nature quite in the manner of the Byzantine theologians: the Qadariyyah or libertarians of Islam probably borrowed their doctrine of the freedom of the will directly from Christianity, while the Murji'ah in their denial of the doctrine of eternal punishment were in thorough agreement with the teaching of the Eastern Church on this subject as against the generally received opinion of orthodox Muslims.[4] On the other hand, the influence of the more orthodox doctors of Islam in the conversion of unbelievers is attested by the tradition that twenty thousand Christians, Jews and Magians became Muslims when the great Imām Ibn Ḥanbal died.[5] A cele-

[1] Von Kremer (2), p. 8. [2] Id. p. 54 and (3), p. 32. Nicholson, p. 231.

[3] Among the Mu'tazilite philosophers, Muḥammad b. al-Huzayl, the teacher of al-Ma'mūn, is said to have converted more than three thousand persons to Islam. (Aḥmad b. Yaḥyā b. al-Murtaḍā, p. 26, l. 7.)

[4] Von Kremer (2), pp. 3, 7–8. C. H. Becker: Christliche Polemik und islamische Dogmenbildung (Zeitschrift für Assyriologie, xxvi. 1912).

[5] Ibn Khallikān, vol. i. p. 45.

brated doctor of the same sect, Abu'l-Faraj b. al-Jawzī (A.D. 1115–1201), the most learned man of his time, a popular preacher and most prolific writer, is said to have boasted that just the same number of persons accepted the faith of Islam at his hands.[1]

Further, the vast and unparalleled success of the Muslim arms shook the faith of the Christian peoples that came under their rule and saw in these conquests the hand of God.[2] Worldly prosperity they associated with the divine favour and the God of battle (they thought) would surely give the victory only into the hands of his favoured servants. Thus the very success of the Muhammadans seemed to argue the truth of their religion.

The Islamic ideal of the brotherhood of all believers was a powerful attraction towards this creed, and though the Arab pride of birth strove to refuse for several generations the privileges of the ruling race to the new converts, still as " clients " of the various Arab tribes to which at first they used to be affiliated, they received a recognised position in the community, and by the close of the first century of the Hijrah they had vindicated for this ideal its true place in Muslim theology and at least a theoretical recognition in the state.[3]

But the condition of the Christians did not always continue to be so tolerable as under the earlier caliphs. In the interests of the true believers, vexatious conditions were sometimes imposed upon the non-Muslim population (or dhimmīs), with the object of securing for the faithful superior social advantages. Unsuccessful attempts were made by several caliphs to exclude them from the public offices. Decrees to this effect were passed by al-Manṣūr (754–775), al-Mutawakkil (847–861), al-Muqtadir (908–932), and in Egypt by al-Āmir (1101–1130), one of the Fāṭimid caliphs, and by the Mamlūk Sultans in the

[1] Wüstenfeld, p. 103.

[2] Michael the Elder, vol. ii. pp. 412–13. Caetani, vol. v. p. 508. (" Le vittorie sui Greci e sui Persiani non solamente erano il trionfo della razza araba sulle popolazioni delle provincie conquistate, ma nella mente orientale che vede in tutto la mano di Dio, costituivano un trionfo del principio islamico su quello cristiano e mazdeista, ma sovrattutto sul cristiano.")

[3] Goldziher, vol. i. chaps. 3 and 4.

fourteenth century.[1] But the very fact that these decrees excluding the dhimmīs from government posts were so often renewed, is a sign of the want of any continuity or persistency in putting such intolerant measures into practice. In fact they may generally be traced either to popular indignation excited by the harsh and insolent behaviour of Christian officials,[2] or to outbursts of fanaticism which forced upon the government acts of oppression that were contrary to the general spirit of Muslim rule and were consequently allowed to lapse as soon as possible.

The beginning of a harsher treatment of the native Christian population dates from the reign of Hārūn al-Rashīd (786–809) who ordered them to wear a distinctive dress and give up the government posts they held to Muslims. The first of these orders shows how little one at least of the ordinances ascribed to 'Umar was observed, and these decrees were the outcome, not so much of any purely religious feeling, as of the political circumstances of the time. The Christians under Muhammadan rule have often had to suffer for the bad faith kept by foreign Christian powers in their relations with Muhammadan princes, and on this occasion it was the treachery of the Byzantine Emperor, Nicephorus, that caused the Christian name to stink in the nostrils of Hārūn.[3] Many of the persecutions of Christians in Muslim countries can be traced either to distrust of their loyalty, excited by the intrigues and interference of Christian foreigners and the enemies of Islam, or to the bad feeling stirred up by the treacherous or brutal behaviour of the latter towards the Musalmans. Religious fanaticism is, however, responsible for many of such persecutions, as in the reign of the Caliph al-Mutawakkil (847–861), under whom severe measures of oppression were taken against the Christians. This prince took advantage of the strong Orthodox reaction that had set in in Muhammadan theology against the rationalistic and freethinking tendencies that

[1] The last of these was prompted by the discovery of an attempt on the part of the Christians to burn the city of Cairo. (De Guignes, vol. iv. pp. 204–5.) Gottheil, p. 359, Journal Asiatique, IVme série, tome xviii. (1851), pp. 454, 455, 463, 484, 491.

[2] Assemani, tom. iii. pars. 2, p. c. Renaudot, pp. 432, 603, 607.

[3] Muir: The Caliphate, p. 475.

had had free play under former rulers,—and came forward as the champion of the extreme orthodox party, to which the mass of the people as contrasted with the higher classes belonged,[1] and which was eager to exact vengeance for the persecutions it had itself suffered in the two preceding reigns;[2] he sought to curry their favour by persecuting the Mu'tazilites, forbidding all further discussions on the Qur'ān and declaring the doctrine that it was created, to be heretical; he had the followers of 'Alī imprisoned and beaten, pulled down the tomb of Ḥusayn at Karbalā' and forbade pilgrimages to be made to the site. The Christians shared in the sufferings of the other heretics; for al-Mutawakkil put rigorously into force the rules that had been passed in former reigns prescribing a distinction in the dress of d͟himmīs and Muslims, ordered that the Christians should no longer be employed in the public offices, doubled the capitation-tax, forbade them to have Muslim slaves or use the same baths as the Muslims, and harassed them with several other restrictions.

It is noteworthy that the historians of the Nestorian Church—which had to suffer most from this persecution—describe it as something new and individual to al-Mutawakkil, and as ceasing with his death.[3] One of his successors, al-Muqtadir (A.D. 908–932), renewed these regulations, which the lapse of half a century had apparently caused to fall into disuse.

Other outbursts of fanaticism led to the destruction of churches and synagogues,[4] and the terror of such persecution led to the defection of many from the Christian Church.[5] But such oppression was contrary to the tolerant spirit of Islam, and to the teaching traditionally ascribed to the Prophet;[6] and the fanatical party tried in vain to enforce

[1] Von Kremer (3), p. 246. [2] Muir (1), pp. 508, 516–17.
[3] Mārī b. Sulaymān, p. 79 sq. Ṣalībā b. Yuḥannā, p. 71.
[4] Gottheil, p. 364 sqq. [5] Mārī b. Sulaymān, p. 114 (ll. 14–16).
[6] This tradition appears in several forms, e. g. "Whoever wrongs one with whom a compact has been made (i. e. a d͟himmī) and lays on him a burden beyond his strength, I will be his accuser." (Balād͟hurī, p. 162, fin.) (Yaḥyā b. Ādam, p. 54 (fin), adds the words, "till the day of judgment.") "Whoever does violence to a d͟himmī who has paid his jizyah and evidenced his submission—his enemy am I." (Usd al-G͟hāba, quoted by Goldziher, in the Jewish Encyclopædia, vol. vi. p. 655.) The Christian historian al-Makīn (p. 11) gives, "Whoever torments the d͟himmīs, torments me."

the persistent execution of these oppressive measures for the humiliation of the non-Muslim population. "The 'ulama' (i. e. the learned, the clergy) consider this state of things; they weep and groan in silence, while the princes who had the power of putting down these criminal abuses only shut their eyes to them." [1] The rules that a fanatical priesthood may lay down for the repression of unbelievers cannot always be taken as a criterion of the practice of civil governments: it is failure to realise this fact that has rendered possible the highly-coloured pictures of the sufferings of the Christians under Muhammadan rule, drawn by writers who have assumed that the prescriptions of certain Muslim theologians represented an invariable practice. Such outbursts of persecution seem in some cases to have been excited by the alleged abuse of their position by those Christians who held high posts in the service of the government; they aroused considerable hostility of feeling towards themselves by their oppression of the Muslims, it being said that they took advantage of their high position to plunder and annoy the faithful, treating them with great harshness and rudeness and despoiling them of their lands and money. Such complaints were laid before the caliphs al-Manṣūr (754–775), al-Mahdī (775–785), al-Ma'mūn (813–833), al-Mutawakkil (847–861), al-Muqtadir (908–932), and many of their successors.[2] They also incurred the odium of many Muhammadans by acting as the spies of the 'Abbāsid dynasty and hunting down the adherents of the displaced Umayyad family.[3] At a later period, during the time of the Crusades they were accused of treasonable correspondence with the Crusaders [4] and brought on themselves severe restrictive measures which cannot justly be described as religious persecution.

In proportion as the lot of the conquered peoples became harder to bear, the more irresistible was the temptation to free themselves from their miseries, by the words, "There is no god but God: Muḥammad is the Apostle of God."

[1] Journal Asiatique, IVme série, tome xix. p. 109. (Paris, 1852.) See also R. Gottheil: A Fetwa on the appointment of Dhimmīs to office. (Zeitschrift für Assyriologie, vol. xxvi. p. 203 sqq.)

[2] Belin, pp. 435–40, 442, 448, 456, 459–61, 479–80.

[3] Id. p. 435, n. 2. [4] Id. p. 478.

When the state was in need of money—as was increasingly the case—the subject races were more and more burdened with taxes, so that the condition of the non-Muslims was constantly growing more unendurable, and conversions to Islam increased in the same proportion. The dreary record of scandals, with which the pages of the Christian historians of this later period are filled, would suggest that the Christian Churches had failed to develop a moral fibre strong enough to endure the stress of adverse conditions, and when persecution came, the reason for the defection that followed might—as the historian of the Nestorian Church suggests [1]—be sought for in the prevailing negligence in the performance of religious duties and the evil life of the clergy.

Further causes that contributed to the decrease of the Christian population may be found in the fact that the children of the numerous Christian captive women who were carried off to the harems of the Muslims had to be brought up in the religion of their fathers, and in the frequent temptation that was offered to the Christian slave by an indulgent master, of purchasing his freedom at the price of conversion to Islam. But of any organised attempt to force the acceptance of Islam on the non-Muslim population, or of any systematic persecution intended to stamp out the Christian religion, we hear nothing. Had the caliphs chosen to adopt either course of action, they might have swept away Christianity as easily as Ferdinand and Isabella drove Islam out of Spain, or Louis XIV made Protestantism penal in France, or the Jews were kept out of England for 350 years. The Eastern Churches in Asia were entirely cut off from communion with the rest of Christendom, throughout which no one would have been found to lift a finger on their behalf, as heretical communions. So that the very survival of these Churches to the present day is a strong proof of the generally

[1] Mārī b. Sulaymān (p. 115, ll. 1–2) offers this explanation of the defections that followed the persecution towards the close of the tenth century.
واسلم خلق كثير وكان اصل ذلك تجوّز الناس في اديانهم وقبح
سيرة الكهنة في المذبح والبيع وبيوت المقدس

tolerant attitude of the Muhammadan governments towards them.[1]

Of the ancient Churches in Western Asia at the time of the Muhammadan conquest, there still survive about 150,000 Nestorians,[2] and their number would have been larger but for the proselytising efforts of other Christian Churches; the Chaldees who have submitted to the Church of Rome number 70,000, in 1898 the Nestorian Bishop Mār Jonan, with several of the clergy and 15,000 Nestorians were received into the Orthodox Russian Church; and numbers of Nestorians have also become Protestants.[3] The Jacobite Patriarch of Antioch exercises jurisdiction over about 80,000 members of this ancient Church, while 25,000 families of Uniat Jacobites obey the Syrian Catholic Patriarch.[4] Belonging to the Greek Orthodox Church, there are 28,836 families under the Patriarch of Antioch and more than 15,000 persons under the Patriarch of Jerusalem,[5] while the Melchites or Greek-Catholics number about 130,000.[6] The Maronite Church, which has been in union with the Roman Catholic Church since the year 1182, has a following of 300,000.[7]

The marvel is that these isolated and scattered communities should have survived so long, exposed as they have been to the ravages of war, pestilence and famine,[8] living in a country that was for centuries a continual battle-field, overrun by Turks, Mongols and Crusaders,[9] it being

[1] The Caliph of Egypt, al-Ḥākim (A.D. 996–1020), did in fact order all the Jews and Christians to leave Egypt and emigrate into the Byzantine territory, but yielded to their entreaties to revoke his orders. (Maqrīzī (1), p. 91.) It would have been quite possible, however, for him to have enforced its execution as it would have been for the ferocious Salīm I (1512–1520), who with the design of putting an end to all religious differences in his dominions caused 40,000 Shī'ahs to be massacred, to have completed this politic scheme by the extermination of the Christians also. But in allowing himself to be dissuaded from this design, he most certainly acted in accordance with the general policy adopted by Muhammadan rulers towards their Christian subjects. (Finlay, vol. v. pp. 29–30.)

[2] Silbernagl, p. 268. [3] Id. p. 354. [4] Id. pp. 307, 360.

[5] Id. p. 25–6. [6] Id. p. 335. [7] Id. p. 384.

[8] See A. von Kremer (1), vol. ii. pp. 490–2.

[9] The sack of Constantinople by the Crusaders in 1204 may be taken as a type of the treatment that the Eastern Christians met with at the hands of the Latins. Barhebræus complains that the monastery of Harran was sacked and plundered by Count Goscelin, Lord of Emessa, in 1184, just as though he had been a Saracen or a Turk. (Barhebræus (1), vol. ii. pp. 506–8.)

further remembered that they were forbidden by the Muhammadan law to make good this decay of their numbers by proselytising efforts—if indeed they had cared to do so, for they seem (with the exception of the Nestorians) even before the Muhammadan conquest, to have lost that missionary spirit, without which, as history abundantly shows, no healthy life is possible in a Christian Church. It has also been suggested that the monastic ideal of continence so widespread in the East, and the Christian practice of monogamy, together with the sense of insecurity and their servile condition, may have acted as checks on the growth of the Christian population.[1]

Of the details of conversion to Islam we have hardly any information. At the time of the first occupation of their country by the Arabs, the Christians appear to have gone over to Islam in very large numbers. Some idea of the extent of these early conversions in 'Irāq for example may be formed from the fact that the income from taxation in the reign of 'Umar was from 100 to 120 million dirhams, while in the reign of 'Abd al-Malik, about fifty years later, it had sunk to forty millions : while this fall in the revenue is largely attributable to the devastation caused by wars and insurrections, still it was chiefly due to the fact that large numbers of the population had become Muhammadan and consequently could no longer be called upon to pay the capitation-tax.[2]

This same period witnesses the conversion of large numbers of the Christians of Khurāsān, as we learn from a letter of a contemporary ecclesiastic, the Nestorian Patriarch Īshō'-yabh III, addressed to Simeon, the Metropolitan of Rev-Ardashīr and Primate of Persia. We possess so very few Christian documents of the first century of the Hijrah, and this letter bears such striking testimony to the peaceful character of the spread of the new faith, and has moreover been so little noticed by modern historians—that it may well be quoted here at length. " Where are thy sons, O father bereft of sons ? Where is that great people of Merv, who though they beheld neither sword, nor fire or tortures, capti-

[1] H. H. Milman, vol. ii. p. 218.
[2] A. von Kremer (1), vol. i. p. 172.

vated only by love for a moiety of their goods, have turned aside, like fools, from the true path and rushed headlong into the pit of faithlessness—into everlasting destruction, and have utterly been brought to nought, while two priests only (priests at least in name), have, like brands snatched from the burning, escaped the devouring flames of infidelity. Alas, alas! Out of so many thousands who bore the name of Christians, not even one single victim was consecrated unto God by the shedding of his blood for the true faith. Where, too, are the sanctuaries of Kirmān and all Persia? it is not the coming of Satan or the mandates of the kings of the earth or the orders of governors of provinces that have laid them waste and in ruins—but the feeble breath of one contemptible little demon, who was not deemed worthy of the honour of demons by those demons who sent him on his errand, nor was endowed by Satan the seducer with the power of diabolical deceit, that he might display it in your land; but merely by the nod of his command he has thrown down all the churches of your Persia. . . . And the Arabs, to whom God at this time has given the empire of the world, behold, they are among you, as ye know well: and yet they attack not the Christian faith, but, on the contrary, they favour our religion, do honour to our priests and the saints of the Lord, and confer benefits on churches and monasteries. Why then have your people of Merv abandoned their faith for the sake of these Arabs? and that, too, when the Arabs, as the people of Merv themselves declare, have not compelled them to leave their own religion but suffered them to keep it safe and undefiled if they gave up only a moiety of their goods. But forsaking the faith which brings eternal salvation, they clung to a moiety of the goods of this fleeting world: that faith which whole nations have purchased and even to this day do purchase by the shedding of their blood and gain thereby the inheritance of eternal life, your people of Merv were willing to barter for a moiety of their goods—and even less."[1] The reign of the caliph 'Umar II (A.D. 717–720) particularly was marked with very extensive conversions: he organised a zealous missionary movement and offered every kind of inducement to the

[1] Assemani, tom. iii. Pars Prima, pp. 130–1.

conquered peoples to accept Islam, even making them grants of money; on one occasion he is said to have given a Christian military officer the sum of 1000 dīnārs to induce him to accept Islam.[1] He instructed the governors of the provinces to invite the dhimmīs to the Muslim faith, and al-Jarrāḥ b. 'Abd Allāh, governor of Khurāsān, is said to have converted about 4000 persons.[2] He is even said to have written a letter to the Byzantine Emperor, Leo III, urging on him the acceptance of the faith of Islam.[3] He abrogated the decree passed in A.D. 700 for the purpose of arresting the impoverishment of the treasury, according to which the convert to Islam was not released from the capitation-tax, but was compelled to continue to pay it as before; even though the dhimmī apostatised the very day before his yearly payment of the jizyah was due or while his contribution was actually being weighed in the scales, it was to be remitted to the new convert.[4] He no longer exacted the kharāj from the Muhammadan owners of landed property, and imposed upon them the far lighter burden of a tithe. These measures, though financially most ruinous, were eminently successful in the way the pious-minded caliph desired they should be, and enormous numbers hastened to enrol themselves among the Muslims.[5]

It must not, however, be supposed that such worldly considerations were the only influences at work in the conversion of the Christians to Islam. The controversial works of St. John of Damascus, of the same century, give us glimpses of the zealous Muslim striving to undermine by his arguments the foundations of the Christian faith. The very dialogue form into which these treatises are thrown, and the frequent repetition of such phrases as "If the Saracen asks you,"—"If the Saracen says . . . then tell him" . . . —give them an air of *vraisemblance* and make them appear as if they were intended to provide the Christians with ready answers to the numerous objections which their Muslim neighbours brought against the Christian creed.[6] That the aggressive attitude of the Muhammadan disputant is

[1] Ibn Sa'd, Ṭabaqāt, vol. v. p. 258.
[2] Id. p. 285.
[3] Maḥbūb al-Manbijī, p. 358 (ll. 2–3).
[4] Ibn Sa'd, Ṭabaqāt, vol. v. p. 262.
[5] August Müller, vol. i. p. 440.
[6] Migne: Patr. Gr., tom. 96, pp. 1336–48.

most prominently brought forward in these dialogues is only what might be expected, it being no part of this great theologian's purpose to enshrine in his writings an apology for Islam. His pupil, Bishop Theodore Abū Qurrah, also wrote several controversial dialogues [1] with Muhammadans, in which the disputants range over all the points of dispute between the two faiths, the Muslim as before being the first to take up the cudgels, and enabling us to form some slight idea of the activity with which the cause of Islam was prosecuted at this period. "The thoughts of the Agarenes," says the bishop, "and all their zeal, are directed towards the denial of the divinity of God the Word, and they strain every effort to this end." [2] The Nestorian Patriarch, Timotheus, used to hold discussions on religious matters in the presence of the caliphs, al-Hādī and Hārūn al-Rashīd, and embodied them in a work that is now lost.[3] Timotheus had secured his election to the patriarchate in the face of the active opposition of many of the most powerful ecclesiastics of his own Church; among these was Joseph, the metropolitan of Merv, who intrigued against him with the caliph, al-Mahdī (775–785), but was persuaded by the caliph to accept Islam and was rewarded for his apostasy with rich presents and an official appointment in Baṣrah.[4]

These details from the first two centuries of the Hijrah are meagre in the extreme and rather suggest the existence of proselytising efforts than furnish definite facts. The earliest document of a distinctly missionary character which has come down to us, would seem to date from the reign of al-Ma'mūn (813–833), and takes the form of a letter [5] written by a cousin of the caliph to a Christian Arab of noble birth and of considerable distinction at the court, and held in high esteem by al-Ma'mūn himself. In this letter he begs his friend to embrace Islam, in terms of affectionate appeal and in language that strikingly illustrates the tolerant attitude of the Muslims towards the Christian Church at this period. This letter occupies an almost unique place in the early history of the propagation of Islam, and has

[1] Migne: Patr. Gr., tom. 97, pp. 1528–9, 1548–61.
[2] Id. p. 1557. [3] 'Amr b. Mattai, p. 65. [4] Id. p. 72.
[5] Risālah 'Abd Allāh b. Ismā'īl al-Hāshimī ilā 'Abd al-Masīḥ b. Isḥāq al-Kindī, pp. 1–37. (London, 1885.)

on this account been given in full in an appendix.[1] In the same work we have a report of a speech made by the caliph at an assembly of his nobles, in which he speaks in tones of the strongest contempt of those who had become Muhammadans merely out of worldly and selfish motives, and compares them to the Hypocrites who while pretending to be friends of the Prophet, in secret plotted against his life. But just as the Prophet returned good for evil, so the caliph resolves to treat these persons with courtesy and forbearance until God should decide between them.[2] The record of this complaint on the part of the caliph is interesting as indicating that disinterested and genuine conviction was expected and looked for in the new convert to Islam, and that the discovery of self-seeking and unworthy motives drew upon him the severest censure.

Al-Ma'mūn himself was very zealous in his efforts to spread the faith of Islam, and sent invitations to unbelievers even in the most distant parts of his dominions, such as Transoxania and Farghānah.[3] At the same time he did not abuse his royal power, by attempting to force his own faith upon others: when a certain Yazdānbakht, a leader of the Manichæan sect, came on a visit to Baghdād[4] and held a disputation with the Muslim theologians, in which he was utterly silenced, the caliph tried to induce him to embrace Islam. But Yazdānbakht refused, saying, "Commander of the faithful, your advice is heard and your words have been listened to; but you are one of those who do not force men to abandon their religion." So far from resenting the ill-success of his efforts, the caliph furnished him with a bodyguard, that he might not be exposed to insult from the fanatical populace.[5]

[1] Appendix I. For an account of Muslim controversial literature, see Appendix II.

[2] Kindī, pp. 111–13.

[3] Balādhurī, pp. 430.

[4] It is very probable that the occasion of this visit of Yazdānbakht to Baghdād was the summoning of a great assembly of the leaders of all the religious bodies of the period, by al-Ma'mūn, when it had come to his ears that the enemies of Islam declared that it owed its success to the sword and not to the power of argument: in this meeting, the Muslim doctors defended their religion against this imputation, and the unbelievers are said to have acknowledged that the Muslims had satisfactorily proved their point. (Aḥmad b. Yaḥyā b. al-Murtaḍā: Al-munyah wa'l-amal fī sharḥ kitāb al-milal wa'l-niḥal. British Museum, Or. 3937, fol. 53 (b), ll. 9–11.)

[5] Kitāb al-Fihrist, vol. i. p. 338.

Some scanty references are made by Christian historians to cases of ecclesiastical dignitaries who became Muhammadans, e. g. George, Bishop of Baḥrayn, about the middle of the ninth century, having been deposed from his office for some ecclesiastical offence, exchanged the Christian faith for that of Islam,[1] and the conversion of a brother of Gabriel, metropolitan of Fārs about the middle of the tenth century, only receives mention because the fact of his having become a Muslim was alleged as disqualifying Gabriel for election to the patriarchate of the Nestorian church.[2]

In the early part of the same century, Theodore, the Nestorian Bishop of Beth Garmai, became a Muslim, and there is no mention of any force or compulsion by the ecclesiastical historian [3] who records the fact, as there undoubtedly would have been, had such existed. Some years later (between A.D. 962 and 979), Philoxenos, a Jacobite Bishop of Ādharbayjān, also became a Muslim,[4] and in the following century, in 1016, Ignatius,[5] the Jacobite Metropolitan of Takrīt, who had held this office for twenty-five years, set out for Baghdād and embraced Islam in the presence of the caliph al-Qādir, taking the name of Abū Muslim.[6] It would be exceedingly interesting if an Apologia pro Vita Sua had survived to reveal to us the religious development that took place in the mind of either of these converts. The Christian chronicler hints at immorality in the last three cases, but such an accusation uncorroborated by any further evidence is open to suspicion,[7] much as it would be

[1] Barhebræus (1), vol. iii. p. 194.

[2] Mārī b. Sulaymān, p. 101 (ll. 3–4).

[3] Barhebræus (1), vol. iii. p. 230.

[4] Id., (1), vol. iii. p. 248.

[5] All the Jacobite Patriarchs assumed the name of Ignatius; before his consecration he was called Mark bar Qīqī.

[6] Barhebræus (1), vol. iii. pp. 288–90. Elias of Nisibis, pp. 153–4. He returned to the Christian faith, however, before his death, which took place about twenty years later. Two similar cases are recorded in the annals of the Jacobite Patriarchs of Antioch in the sixteenth century: of these one, named Joshua, became a Muhammadan in 1517, but afterwards recanting fled to Cyprus (at that time in the hands of the Venetians), where prostrate at the door of a church in penitential humility he suffered all who went in or out to tread over his body; the other, Ni'mat Allāh (flor. 1560), having abjured Christianity for Islam, sought absolution of Pope Gregory XIII in Rome. (Barhebræus (1), vol. ii. pp. 847–8.)

[7] In fact Elias of Nisibis, the contemporary chronicler of the conversion of the Jacobite Patriarch, makes no mention of such a failing, nor does Mārī b. Sulaymān (pp. 115–16), the historian of the rival Nestorian Church,

if brought forward by a Roman Catholic when recording the conversion of a priest of his own communion to the Protestant faith. It is doubtless owing to their exalted position in the Church that the conversion of these prominent ecclesiastics of two hostile Christian sects has been handed down to us, while that of more obscure individuals has not been recorded. As Barhebræus brings his ecclesiastical chronicle nearer to his own time, he gives fuller details of the career of such converts, e. g. in recording the public lapse of some of the Jacobite bishops, in the middle of the twelfth century he makes particular mention of Aaron, bishop of a town in Khurāsān, as having become a Muhammadan after having been convicted of some moral fault; repenting of this change, he wished to regain his episcopal status, and when this was refused him, went to Constantinople and abjured the Monophysite doctrines of the Jacobite Church; then apparently dissatisfied with the reception he received in Constantinople, he returned to the Jacobite Patriarch, but a second time went over to Islam "without any reason"; then repenting again, he finally ended his days among the Maronites of Mount Lebanon.[1] A contemporary of Barhebræus, in the middle of the thirteenth century—Daniel, Bishop of Khabur—who is said to have been proficient in secular learning, sought to be appointed to the diocese of Aleppo, but disappointed in this ambition, he abandoned the Christian faith and to the grief and shame of all Christian people "became a Muslim; but God (praise be to His grace !) soon consoled his afflicted people and took away the shame from the redeemed, the redeemed of the Lord; for a few months later that unhappy wretch died miserably in a caravanserai; his name perished, he was taken away out of our midst, and no man knoweth his abiding place." [2]

But that these conversions were not merely isolated instances we have the valuable evidence of Jacques de Vitry, Bishop of Acre (1216–1225), who thus speaks of the Eastern Church from his experience of it in the Holy Land :—

---

though he accuses him of plundering the sacred vessels and ornaments of the churches. As Wright (Syriac Literature, p. 192) says of Joseph of Merv, "We need not believe all the evil that Barhebræus tells us of this unhappy man."

[1] Barhebræus (1), vol. ii. p. 518.

[2] Id. vol. ii. p. 712 sq.

" Weakened and lamentably ensnared, nay rather grievously wounded, by the lying persuasions of the false prophet and by the allurements of carnal pleasure, she hath sunk down, and she that was brought up in scarlet, hath embraced dunghills." [1]

So far the Christian Churches that have been described as coming within the sphere of Muhammadan influence, have been the Orthodox Eastern Church and the heretical communions that had sprung out of it. But with the close of the eleventh century a fresh element was added to the Christian population of Syria and Palestine, in the large bodies of Crusaders of the Latin rite who settled in the kingdom of Jerusalem and the other states founded by the Crusaders, which maintained a precarious existence for nearly two centuries. During this period, occasional conversions to Islam were made from among these foreign immigrants. In the first Crusade, for example, a body of Germans and Lombards under the command of a certain knight, named Rainaud, had separated themselves from the main body and were besieged in a castle by the Saljūq Sultan, Arslān; on pretence of making a sortie, Rainaud and his personal followers abandoned their unfortunate companions and went over to the Turks, among whom they embraced Islam.[2]

The history of the ill-fated second Crusade presents us with a very remarkable incident of a similar character. The story, as told by Odo of Deuil, a monk of St. Denis, who, in the capacity of private chaplain to Louis VII, accompanied him on this Crusade and wrote a graphic account of it, runs as follows. While endeavouring to make their way overland through Asia Minor to Jerusalem the Crusaders sustained a disastrous defeat at the hands of the Turks in the mountain-passes of Phrygia (A.D. 1148), and with difficulty reached the seaport town of Attalia. Here, all who could afford to satisfy the exorbitant demands of the Greek merchants, took ship for Antioch; while the sick and wounded and the mass of the pilgrims were left behind at the mercy of their treacherous allies, the Greeks, who received five hundred

[1] Historia Orientalis, C. 15 (p. 45).
[2] De Guignes, tome ii. (Seconde Partie), p. 15.

marks from Louis, on condition that they provided an escort for the pilgrims and took care of the sick until they were strong enough to be sent on after the others. But no sooner had the army left, than the Greeks informed the Turks of the helpless condition of the pilgrims, and quietly looked on while famine, disease and the arrows of the enemy carried havoc and destruction through the camp of these unfortunates. Driven to desperation, a party of three or four thousand attempted to escape, but were surrounded and cut to pieces by the Turks, who now pressed on to the camp to follow up their victory. The situation of the survivors would have been utterly hopeless, had not the sight of their misery melted the hearts of the Muhammadans to pity. They tended the sick and relieved the poor and starving with open-handed liberality. Some even bought up the French money which the Greeks had got out of the pilgrims by force or cunning, and lavishly distributed it among the needy. So great was the contrast between the kind treatment the pilgrims received from the unbelievers and the cruelty of their fellow-Christians, the Greeks, who imposed forced labour upon them, beat them and robbed them of what little they had left, that many of them voluntarily embraced the faith of their deliverers. As the old chronicler says: "Avoiding their co-religionists who had been so cruel to them, they went in safety among the infidels who had compassion upon them, and, as we heard, more than three thousand joined themselves to the Turks when they retired. Oh, kindness more cruel than all treachery! They gave them bread but robbed them of their faith, though it is certain that contented with the services they performed, they compelled no one among them to renounce his religion."[1]

The increasing intercourse between Christians and Muslims, the growing appreciation on the part of the Crusaders of the virtues of their opponents, which so strikingly dis-

[1] Odo de Diogilo. (De Ludovici vii. Itinere. Migne, Patr. Lat., tom. cxcv. p. 1243.) "Vitantes igitur sibi crudeles socios fidei, inter infideles sibi compatientes ibant securi, et sicut audivimus plusquam tria millia iuvenum sunt illis recedentibus sociati. O pietas omni proditione crudelior! Dantes panem fidem tollebant, quamvis certum sit quia, contenti servitio, neminem negare cogebant."

tinguishes the later from the earlier chroniclers of the Crusades,[1] the numerous imitations of Oriental manners and ways of life by the Franks settled in the Holy Land, did not fail to exercise a corresponding influence on religious opinions. One of the most remarkable features of this influence is the tolerant attitude of many of the Christian Knights towards the faith of Islam—an attitude of mind that was most vehemently denounced by the Church. When Usāma b. Munqidh, a Syrian Amīr of the twelfth century, visited Jerusalem, during a period of truce, the Knights Templar, who had occupied the Masjid al-Aqṣā, assigned to him a small chapel adjoining it, for him to say his prayers in, and they strongly resented the interference with the devotions of their guest on the part of a newly-arrived Crusader, who took this new departure in the direction of religious freedom in very bad part.[2] It would indeed have been strange if religious questions had not formed a topic of discussion on the many occasions when the Crusaders and the Muslims met together on a friendly footing, during the frequent truces, especially when it was religion itself that had brought the Crusaders into the Holy Land and set them upon these constant wars. When even Christian theologians were led by their personal intercourse with the Muslims to form a juster estimate of their religion, and contact with new modes of thought was unsettling the minds of men and giving rise to a swarm of heresies, it is not surprising that many should have been drawn into the pale of Islam.[3] The renegades in the twelfth century were in sufficient numbers to be noticed in the statute books of the Crusaders, the so-called Assises of Jerusalem, according to which, in certain cases, their bail was not accepted.[4]

It would be interesting to discover who were the Muslims who busied themselves in winning these converts to Islam, but they seem to have left no record of their labours. We know, however, that they had at their head the great Saladin himself, who is described by his biographer as setting before

[1] Guizot: Histoire de la civilisation en Europe, p. 234. (Paris, 1882.)
[2] Usāma b. Munqidh, p. 99.
[3] Prutz, pp. 266–7.
[4] Assises de la Cour des Bourgeois. (Recueil des historiens des Croisades, Assises de Jérusalem, tome ii. p. 325.)

his Christian guest the beauties of Islam and urging him to embrace it.[1]

The heroic life and character of Saladin seems to have exercised an especial fascination on the minds of the Christians of his time; some even of the Christian knights were so strongly attracted towards him that they abandoned the Christian faith and their own people and joined themselves to the Muslims; such was the case, for example, with a certain English Templar, named Robert of St. Albans, who in A.D. 1185 gave up Christianity for Islam and afterwards married a grand-daughter of Saladin.[2] Two years later, Saladin invaded Palestine and utterly defeated the Christian army in the battle of Ḥiṭṭīn, Guy, king of Jerusalem, being among the prisoners. On the eve of the battle, six of his knights, "possessed with a devilish spirit," deserted the king and escaped into the camp of Saladin, where of their own accord they became Saracens.[3] At the same time Saladin seems to have had an understanding with Raymund III, Count of Tripoli, according to which he was to induce his followers to abandon the Christian faith and go over to the Muslims; but the sudden death of the Count effectually put a stop to the execution of this scheme.[4]

The fall of Jerusalem and the successes of Saladin in the Holy Land stirred up Europe to undertake the third Crusade, the chief incident of which was the siege of Acre (A.D. 1189–1191). The fearful sufferings that the Christian army was exposed to, from famine and disease, drove many of them to desert and seek relief from the cravings of hunger in the Muslim camp. Of these deserters, many made their way back again after some time to the army of the Crusaders; on the other hand, many elected to throw in their lot with the Muslims; some, taking service under their former enemies, still remained true to the Christian faith and (we are told) were well pleased with their new masters, while others embracing Islam became good Muslims.[5] The conversion of these deserters is recorded also by the chronicler who accompanied Richard I upon this Crusade:—"Some

[1] Bahā al-Dīn, p. 25. [2] Roger Hoveden, vol. ii. p. 307.
[3] Benedict of Peterborough, vol. ii. pp. 11–12.
[4] Id., vol. ii. pp. 20–1. Roger Hoveden, vol. ii. pp. 316, 322.
[5] Abū Shāmah, p. 150.

of our men (whose fate cannot be told or heard without grievous sorrow) yielding to the severity of the sore famine, in achieving the salvation of the body, incurred the damnation of their souls. For after the greater part of the affliction was past, they deserted and fled to the Turks: nor did they hesitate to become renegades; in order that they might prolong their temporal life a little space, they purchased eternal death with horrid blasphemies. O baleful trafficking! O shameful deed beyond all punishment! O foolish man likened unto the foolish beasts, while he flees from the death that must inevitably come soon, he shuns not the death unending."[1]

From this time onwards references to renegades are not infrequently to be met with in the writings of those who travelled to the Holy Land and other countries of the East. The terms of the oath which was proposed to St. Louis by his Muhammadan captors when he was called upon to promise to pay the ransom imposed upon him (A.D. 1250), were suggested by certain whilom priests who had become Muslims;[2] and while this business of paying the ransom was still being carried on, another renegade, a Frenchman, born at Provins, came to bring a present to the king: he had accompanied King John of Jerusalem on his expedition against Damietta in 1219 and had remained in Egypt, married a Muhammadan wife and become a great lord in that country.[3] The danger of the pilgrims to the Holy Land becoming converts to Islam was so clearly recognised at this time that in a "Remembrance," written about 1266 by Amaury de la Roche, the master of the Knights Templar in France, he requests the Pope and the legates of France and Sicily to prevent the poor and the aged and those incapable of bearing arms from crossing the sea to Palestine, for such persons either got killed or were taken prisoners by the Saracens or turned renegades.[4] Ludolf de Suchem, who travelled in the Holy Land from 1336 to 1341, speaks of three renegades he found at Hebron; they had come from the diocese of Minden and had been in the service of a

[1] Itinerarium Peregrinorum et Gesta Regis Richardi, p. 131. (Chronicles and Memorials of the reign of Richard I. Edited by William Stubbs.) (London, 1864.)

[2] Joinville, p. 238.

[3] Id. p. 262.

[4] Mas Latrie (1), vol. ii. p. 72.

Westphalian knight, who was held in high honour by the Soldan and other Muhammadan princes.[1]

These scattered notices are no doubt significant of more extensive conversions of Christians to Islam, of which no record has come down to us: e.g. there were said to be about 25,000 renegades in the city of Cairo towards the close of the fifteenth century,[2] and there must have been many also to be found in the cities of the Holy Land after the disappearance of the Latin princedoms of the East. But the Muhammadan historians of this period seem to have been too busily engaged in recording the exploits of princes and the vicissitudes of dynasties, to turn their attention to religious changes in the lives of obscure individuals; and (as far as I have been able to discover) they as little notice the conversions of Christians to Islam as of those of their own co-religionists to Christianity. Consequently, we have to depend for our knowledge of both of these classes of events on Christian writers, who, while they give us detailed and sympathetic accounts of the latter, bear unwilling testimony to the existence of instances of the former and represent the motives of the renegades in the worst light possible. The possibility of any Christian becoming converted to Islam from honest conviction, probably never entered into the head of any of these writers, and even had such an idea occurred to them they would hardly have ventured to expose themselves to the thunders of ecclesiastical censure by giving open expression to it.

As an example of the rare instances of such a conversion being recorded, the account may here be cited which Fürer von Haimendorf, who was in Cairo in 1565, gives of the conversion of a German scholar who had studied in the University of Leipzig. "Sed dum nos hanc moram Cairi nectimus, accidit ut Justus quidam Stevenius Germanus Hamelensis qui in iisdem ædibus nobiscum habitaverat, fide Christianorum abnegata Turcarum religioni se initiandum atque circumcidendum obtulerit. Vir erat doctus, qui diu se Witebergæ ac Lipsiæ studiis operam dedisse sæpe nobis

[1] Ludolf de Suchem, p. 71.

[2] Lionardo Frescobaldi, quoted in the preface of Defrémery and Sanguinetti's edition of Ibn Baṭūṭah, vol. i. p. xl.

narrabat: verum de hoc facto interrogatus, peculiarem nunc sibi Spiritum adesse ajebat, sine cujus instinctu nihil vel facere sibi, vel cogitare fas esset; quæ hominis apostasia nimium quantum animos nostros commovit, et ad fugam quasi excitavit. Eodem quoque die Judæus quidam, qui paucis diebus ante religionem Mahumetanam amplexus fuerat, triumphali pompa per urbem circumducebatur; quod idem cum Stevenio isto futurum esse, Janissarii quidam nobis affirmabant." [1]

From the historical sources quoted above, we have as little information respecting the number of these converts as of the proselytising efforts made to induce them to change their faith. A motive frequently assigned for going over to Islam is the desire to escape the death penalty by means of apostasy. European travellers make frequent mention of such cases. A late example of such an account may be selected, for the picturesqueness of its language, from the report of a Jesuit, who was in Cairo in 1627; he saw a Copt who, having allowed himself to be carried away "partly by passion and partly by the violence of an indiscreet zeal, had killed his brother with his own hand, in detestation of his having in a dastardly manner left Jesus Christ to embrace Mahometanism, in order to deliver himself from the vexation of the Turks. The poor man was at once seized in the heat of his crime, and he boldly confessed that the renegade, unworthy of being his brother, could only wipe out so black a spot by his blood. He was urged to abandon his faith in order to save his life," but he declared that he was resolved to die a Christian; the cruel torments, however, inflicted on him by the executioners, weakened his resolution and he yielded at the last moment. "This disaster changed him in a moment from a confessor into a renegade, from a martyr into an apostate, from a saint into one of the damned, and from an angel into a veritable devil. He made the profession of faith or rather of perfidy, after the manner of the Mahometans . . . he was set at liberty, the liberty not of the sons of God, but of the sons of perdition." Later on, the reproaches of his conscience caused him again to recant

[1] Christophori Füreri ab Haimendorf Itinerarium Ægypti, p. 42. (Norimbergæ, 1620.)

and he was put to death by the Muhammadans for his apostasy.[1]

The monk Burchard,[2] writing about 1283, a few years before the Crusaders were driven out of their last strongholds and the Latin power in the East came utterly to an end—represents the Christian population as largely outnumbering the Muslims throughout the whole of the Muhammadan world, the latter (except in Egypt and Arabia) forming not more than three or four per cent. of the whole population. This language is undoubtedly exaggerated and the good monk was certainly rash in assuming that what he observed in the cities of the Crusaders and of the kingdom of Little Armenia held good in other parts of the East. But his words may be certainly taken to indicate that during the period of the Crusades there had been no widespread conversion to Islam, and that when the Muhammadans resumed their sovereignty over the Holy Land, they extended the same toleration to the Christians as before, suffering them to "purchase peace and quiet" by the payment of the jizyah. The presumption is that the conversions that took place were of individual Christians, who were persuaded in their own minds before they took the final step. Instances have already been given of Christians who took service under Muhammadan masters, in the full enjoyment of their own faith, and the Assises of Jerusalem made a distinction between "those who have denied God

[1] Le Voyage en Ethiopie entrepris par le Père Aymard Guérin. (Rabbath, pp. 17–18.)

[2] "Notandum autem in rei veritate, licet quidam contrarium senciant, qui ea volunt asserere, que non viderunt, quod oriens totus ultra mare Yndiam et Ethiopiam nomen Christi confitetur et predicat, preter solos Sarracenos et quosdam Turcomannos, qui in Cappadocia sedem habent, ita quod pro certo assero, sicut per memet ipsum vidi et ab aliis, quibus notum erat, audivi, quod semper in omni loco et regno preterquam in Egypto et Arabia, ubi plurimum habitant Sarraceni et alii Machometum sequentes, pro uno Sarraceno triginta vel amplius invenies Christianos. Verum tamen, quod Christiani omnes transmarini natione sunt orientales, qui licet sint Christiani, quia tamen usum armorum non habent multum, cum impugnantur a Sarracenis, Tartaris, vel aliis quibuscumque, subiciuntur eis et tributis pacem et quietem emunt, et Sarraceni sive alii, qui eis dominantur, balivos suos et exactores in terris illis ponunt. Et inde contigit, quod regnum illud dicitur esse Sarracenorum, cum tamen in rei veritate sunt omnes Christiani preter ipsos balivos et exactores et aliquos de familia ipsorum, sicut oculis meis vidi in Cilicia et Armenia minori, que est subdita dominio Tartarorum." (Burchardi de Monte Sion Descriptio Terræ Sanctæ, p. 90.)

and follow another law" and "all those who have done armed service to the Saracens and other miscreants against the Christians for more than a year and a day."[1]

The native Christians certainly preferred the rule of the Muhammadans to that of the Crusaders,[2] and when Jerusalem fell finally and for ever into the hands of the Muslims (A.D. 1244), the Christian population of Palestine seems to have welcomed the new masters and to have submitted quietly and contentedly to their rule.[3]

This same sense of security of religious life under Muslim rule led many of the Christians of Asia Minor, also, about the same time, to welcome the advent of the Saljūq Turks as their deliverers from the hated Byzantine government, not only on account of its oppressive system of taxation, but also of the persecuting spirit of the Greek Church, which had with such cruelty crushed the heresies of the Paulicians and the Iconoclasts. In the reign of Michael VIII (1261–1282), the Turks were often invited to take possession of the smaller towns in the interior of Asia Minor by the inhabitants, that they might escape from the tyranny of the empire; and both rich and poor often emigrated into Turkish dominions.[4]

Some account still remains to be given of two other Christian Churches of Western Asia, viz. the Armenian and the Georgian. Of the former it may be said that of all the Eastern Churches that have come under Muhammadan rule, the Armenian Church has probably given fewer of its members (in proportion to the size of the community) to swell the ranks of Islam, than any other. So in spite of the interest that attaches to the story of the struggle of

[1] Recueil des historiens des Croisades. (Assises de Jérusalem, tome i. p. 325.)
[2] Prutz, pp. 146–7, 150.
[3] The prelates of the Holy Land wrote as follows, in 1244, concerning the invasion of the Khwarizmians, whom Sultan Ayyūb had called in to assist him in driving out the Crusaders:—"Per totam terram usque ad partes Nazareth et Saphet libere nullo resistente discurrunt, occupantes eandem, et inter se quasi propriam dividentes, per villas et cazalia Christianorum legatos et bajulos præficiunt, suscipientes a rusticis redditus et tributa, quæ Christianis præstare solebant, qui jam Christianis hostes effecti et rebelles dictis Corosminis universaliter adhæserunt." (Matthei Parisiensis Chronica Majora, ed. H. R. Luard, vol. iv. p. 343.) (London, 1872–83.)
[4] Finlay, vol. iii. pp. 358–9. J. H. Krause: Die Byzantiner des Mittelalters, p. 276. (Halle, 1869.)

this brave nation against overwhelming odds and of the fidelity with which it has clung to the Christian faith—through centuries of warfare and oppression, persecution and exile—it does not come within the scope of the present volume to do more than briefly indicate its connection with the history of the Muhammadans. The Armenian kingdom survived the shock of the Arab conquest, and in the ninth century rose to be a state of some importance and flourished during the decay of the caliphate of Baghdād, but in the eleventh century was overthrown by the Saljūq Turks. A band of fugitives founded the kingdom of Lesser Armenia, but this too disappeared in the fourteenth century. The national life of the Armenian people still survived in spite of the loss of their independence, and, as was the case in Greece under the Turks, their religion and the national church served as the rallying point of their eager, undying patriotism. Though a certain number, under the pressure of cruel persecution, have embraced Islam, yet the bulk of the race has remained true to its ancient faith. As Tavernier [1] rather unsympathetically remarks, " There may be some few Armenians, that embrace Mahometanism for worldly interest, but they are generally the most obstinate persons in the world, and most firm to their superstitious principles."

The Georgian Church (founded in the early part of the fourth century) was an offshoot from the Greek Church, with which she has always remained in communion, although from the middle of the sixth century the Patriarch or Katholikos of the Georgian Church declared himself independent. Torn asunder by internal discords and exposed to the successive attacks of Greeks, Persians, Arabs, Turks and Mongols, the history of this heroic warrior people is one of almost uninterrupted warfare against foreign foes and of fiercely contested feuds between native chiefs : the reigns of one or two powerful monarchs who secured for their subjects brief intervals of peace, serving only to bring out in more striking contrast the normally unsettled state of the country. The fierce independent spirit of the Georgians that could not brook a foreign rule has often exasperated well-

[1] Tavernier (1), p. 174.

nigh to madness the fury of their Muhammadan neighbours, when they failed to impose upon them either their civil authority or their religion. It is this circumstance—that a change of faith implied loss of political independence—which explains in a great measure the fact that the Georgian Church inscribes the names of so many martyrs in her calendar, while the annals of the Greek Church during the same period have no such honoured roll to show.

It was not until after Georgia had been overrun by the devastating armies of the Mongols, leaving ruined churches and monasteries and pyramids of human heads to mark the progress of their destroying hosts, and consequently the spiritual wants of the people had remained long unprovided for, owing to the decline in the numbers and learning of the clergy—that Christianity began to lose ground.[1] Even among those who still remained Christian, some added to the sufferings of the clergy by plundering the property of the Church and appropriating to their own use the revenues of churches and monasteries, and thus hastened the decay of the Christian faith.[2]

In 1400 the invasion of Tīmūr added a crowning horror to the sufferings of Georgia, and though for a brief period the rule of Alexander I (1414–1442) delivered the country from the foreign yoke and drove out all the Muhammadans—after his death it was again broken up into a number of petty princedoms, from which the Turks and the Persians wrested the last shreds of independence. But the Muhammadans always found Georgia to be a turbulent and rebellious possession, ever ready to break out into open revolt at the slightest opportunity. Both Turks and Persians sought to secure the allegiance of these troublesome subjects by means of conversion to Islam. After the fall of Constantinople and the increase of Turkish power in Asia Minor, the inhabitants of Akhaltsikhé and other districts to the west of it became Muhammadans.[3] In 1579 two Georgian princes—brothers—came on an embassy to Constantinople with a large retinue of about two hundred

[1] Joselian, p. 125. All the Abkhazes, Djikhethes, Ossetes, Kabardes and Kisthethes fell away from the Christian faith about this time.

[2] Id. p. 127.

[3] Id. p. 143.

persons: here the younger brother together with his attendants became a Musalman, in the hope (it was said) of thereby supplanting his elder brother.[1] At a rather later date, the conquests of the Turks brought some of the districts in the very centre of Georgia into their power, the inhabitants of which embraced the creed of the conquerors.[2] From this period Samtzkhé, the most western portion of Georgia, recognised the suzerainty of Turkey: its rulers and people were allowed to continue undisturbed in the Christian faith, but from 1625 the ruling dynasty became Muhammadan and many of the chiefs and the aristocracy followed their example.

Christianity retained its hold upon the peasants much longer, but when the clergy of Samtzkhé refused allegiance to the Katholikos of Karthli, there ceased to be regular provision made for supplying the spiritual needs of the people: the nobles, even before their conversion, had taken to plundering the estates of the Church, and after becoming Musalmans they naturally ceased to assist it with their offerings, and the churches and monasteries falling into decay were replaced by mosques.[3]

The rest of Georgia had submitted to Persia, and when Tavernier visited this part of the country, about the middle of the seventeenth century, he found it divided into two kingdoms, which were provinces of the Persian empire, and were governed by native Georgian princes who had to turn Muhammadan before being advanced to this dignity.[4] One of the first of such princes was the Tsarevitch Constantine, son of King Alexander II of Kakheth, who had been brought up at the Persian court and had there embraced Islam, at the beginning of the seventeenth century.[5] The first Muhammadan king of Karthli, the Tsarevitch Rustam (1634–1658), had also been brought up in Persia, and he and his successors to the end of the century were all Muhammadans.[6]

Tavernier describes the Georgians as being very ignorant in matters of religion and the clergy as unlettered and vicious; some of the heads of the Church actually sold the

[1] David Chytræus, p. 49. [2] Joselian, p. 157.
[3] Brosset, IIe partie, Ire livraison, pp. 227–35. Description géographique de la Géorgie par le Tsarévitch Wakhoucht, p. 79. (St. Petersburg, 1842.)
[4] The Six Voyages, p. 123. [5] Joselian, p. 149. [6] Id. pp. 160–1.

Christian boys and girls as slaves to the Turks and Persians.[1] From this period there seems to have been a widespread apostasy, especially among the higher classes and those who sought to win the favour of the Persian court.[2] In 1701 the occupant of the throne of Georgia, Wakhtang VI, was a Christian : for the first seven years of his reign he was a prisoner in Ispahan, where great efforts were made to induce him to become a Muhammadan; when he declared that he preferred to lose his throne rather than purchase it at the price of apostasy, it is said that his younger brother, although he was the Patriarch of Georgia, offered to abandon Christianity and embrace Islam, if the crown were bestowed upon him, but though invested by the Persians with the royal power, the Georgians refused to accept him as their ruler, and drove him out of the kingdom.[3]

Towards the close of the eighteenth century, the king of Georgia placed his people under the protection of the Russian crown. Hitherto their intense patriotic feeling had helped to keep the Christian faith alive among them so long as their foreign invaders had been Musalmans, but now that the foreign power that sought to rob them of their independence was Christian, this same feeling operated in some of the districts north of the Caucasus to the advantage of Islam. In Daghistan a certain Darvīsh Manṣūr endeavoured to unite the different tribes of the Caucasus to oppose the Russians; preaching the faith of Islam he succeeded in converting the princes and nobles of Ubichistan and Daghistan, who have remained faithful to Islam ever since; many of the Circassians, too, were converted by his preaching, and preferred exile to submitting to the Russian rule.[4] But in 1791 he was taken prisoner, and in 1800 Georgia was formally incorporated in the Russian empire.

Darvīsh Manṣūr was not alone in his efforts to convert the Circassians. When the treaty of Kūchak-Qaïnarji in 1774 had recognised the independence of the Crimea and

[1] Tavernier (1), pp. 124, 126. He estimates the number of Muhammadans at about twelve thousand. (Id. p. 123.)

[2] Brosset, IIe partie, Ire livraison, pp. 85, 181.

[3] Documens originaux sur les relations diplomatiques de la Géorgie avec la France vers la fin du regne de Louis XIV, recueillis par M. Brosset jeune. (J. A. 2me série, tome ix. (1832), pp. 197, 451.)

[4] Mackenzie, p. 7. Garnett, p. 194.

opened the Black Sea to Russian vessels, the Turkish government became alarmed at the prospect of a further movement of Russian domination along the eastern coast of the Black Sea and resolved to make an attempt to stir the Circassians to resistance. A Turkish officer, named Faraḥ 'Alī, was sent in 1782 to establish a military colony at Anāpa, near the outlet of the sea of Azov, and to enter into relations with the Circassian tribes. Faraḥ 'Alī's first care was to seek the hand of a daughter of one of the Circassian beys, offering rich presents of arms, horses, etc., to her father; the marriage was celebrated with great pomp and ceremony, and Faraḥ 'Alī encouraged his soldiers to follow his example, by promising to defray the expenses of their nuptials. The result was that a number of Circassian women joined the little colony and accepted the religion of their husbands, and with the zeal of new converts won over to Islam their fathers and brothers. An active movement of proselytism began, and the Circassians who came in contact with the Turkish colony appear readily to have abandoned their pagan beliefs for the religion of the Qur'ān, the mollas were kept busy in instructing the new Muslims, and help had to be sought from Constantinople to deal with the increasing number of conversions.[1] But the work of Faraḥ 'Alī was short-lived; he died in 1785 and his tomb was reverenced as that of a saint, but his work perished with him. Anāpa passed into the hands of the Russians in 1812, and when the resistance of the Circassians was finally overcome in 1864, more than half a million Circassian Muhammadans migrated into Turkish territory.

Under Russian law conversions to any faith other than that of the Orthodox Church were illegal, and the further progress of Islam was stayed until the promulgation of the edict of toleration in 1905. One of the results of this in the Caucasus was a large accession to Islam from among the Abkhazes, who had long been nominal converts to Christianity, but now became Muhammadans in such numbers that the Orthodox clergy became alarmed and founded a special society for the distribution of religious tracts among them, in the hope of combating Muhammadan influences.[2]

[1] Barbier de Meynard, p. 45 sqq. [2] R. du M. M., VII, p. 320 (1909).

CHAPTER IV.

THE SPREAD OF ISLAM AMONG THE CHRISTIAN NATIONS OF AFRICA.

ISLAM was first introduced into Africa by the Arab army that invaded Egypt under the command of 'Amr b. al-'Āṣ in A.D. 640. Three years later the withdrawal of the Byzantine troops abandoned the vast Christian population into the hands of the Muslim conquerors. The rapid success of the Arab invaders was largely due to the welcome they received from the native Christians, who hated the Byzantine rule not only for its oppressive administration, but also—and chiefly—on account of the bitterness of theological rancour. The Jacobites, who formed the majority of the Christian population, had been very roughly handled by the Orthodox adherents of the court and subjected to indignities that have not been forgotten by their children even to the present day.[1] Some were tortured and then thrown into the sea; many followed their Patriarch into exile to escape from the hands of their persecutors, while a large number disguised their real opinions under a pretended acceptance of the Council of Chalcedon.[2] To these Copts, as the Jacobite Christians of Egypt are called, the Muhammadan conquest brought a freedom of religious life such as they had not enjoyed for a century. On payment of the tribute, 'Amr left them in undisturbed possession of their churches and guaranteed to them autonomy in all ecclesiastical matters, thus delivering them from the continual interference that had been so grievous a burden under

[1] Amélineau, p. 3; Caetani, vol. iv. p. 81 sq. Justinian is said to have had 200,000 Copts put to death in the city of Alexandria, and the persecutions of his successors drove many to take refuge in the desert. (Wansleben: The Present State of Egypt, p. 11.) (London, 1678.)

[2] Renaudot, p. 161. Severus, p. 106.

the previous rule; he laid his hands on none of the property of the churches and committed no act of spoliation or pillage.[1] In the early days of the Muhammadan rule then, the condition of the Copts seems to have been fairly tolerable,[2] and there is no evidence of their widespread apostasy to Islam being due to persecution or unjust pressure on the part of their new rulers. Even before the conquest was complete, while the capital, Alexandria, still held out, many of them went over to Islam,[3] and a few years later the example these had set was followed by many others.[4] In the reign of 'Uthmān (A.D. 643–655), the revenue derived from Egypt amounted to twelve millions; a few years later, in the reign of Mu'āwiyah (661–679), it had fallen to five millions owing to the enormous number of conversions: under 'Umar II (717–720) it fell still lower, so that the governor of Egypt[5] proposed that in future the converts should not be exempted from the payment of the capitation-tax, but this the pious caliph refused to allow, saying that God had sent Muḥammad to call men to a knowledge of the truth and not to be a collector of taxes.[6]

But later rulers recognised that for fiscal reasons such a policy was ruinous to the state, and insisted on the converts continuing to pay taxes as before; there was, however, no continuity in such a policy, and individual governors acted in an arbitrary and irregular manner.[7] When Ḥafṣ b. al-Walīd, who was governor of Egypt in A.D. 744, promised that all those who became Muslims would be exempted

[1] John, Jacobite bishop of Nikiu (second half of seventh century), p. 584. Caetani, vol. iv. pp. 515–16.

[2] Bell, p. xxxvii. But the exactions and hardships that, according to Maqrīzī, the Copts had to endure about seventy years after the conquest hardly allow us to extend this period so far as Von Ranke does: "Von Aegypten weiss man durch die bestimmtesten Zeugnisse, dass sich die Einwohner in den nächsten Jahrhunderten unter der arabischen Herrschaft in einem erträglichen Zustand befunden haben." (Weltgeschichte, vol. v. p. 153, 4th ed.)

[3] John of Nikiu, p. 560.

[4] Id. p. 585. "Or beaucoup des Égyptiens, qui étaient de faux chrétiens, renièrent la sainte religion orthodoxe et le baptême qui donne la vie, embrassèrent la religion des Musulmans, les ennemis de Dieu, et acceptèrent la détestable doctrine de ce monstre, c'est-à-dire de Mahomet; ils partagèrent l'égarement de ces idolâtres et prirent les armes contre les chrétiens."

[5] Qurra b. Sharīk (governor of Egypt from 709 to 714), or his predecessor, appears to have insisted on the converts continuing to pay jizyah. (Becker Papyri Schott-Reinhardt, p. 18.)

[6] Ibn Sa'd, Ṭabaqāt, vol. v. p. 283.

[7] Caetani, vol. iv, p. 618; vol. v. pp. 384–5.

from the payment of jizyah, as many as 24,000 Christians are reported to have accepted Islam.[1] A similar proclamation is said to have been made by al-Saffāḥ, the first of the 'Abbāsid caliphs, soon after his accession in A.D. 750, for "he wrote to the whole of his dominions saying that every one who embraced his religion and prayed according to his fashion, should be quit of the jizyah, and many, both rich and poor, denied the faith of Christ by reason of the magnitude of the taxation and the burdens imposed upon them."[2] In fact many of the Christians of Egypt seem to have abandoned Christianity as lightly and as rapidly as, in the beginning of the fourth century, they had embraced it. Prior to that period, a very small section of the population of the valley of the Nile was Christian, but the sufferings of the martyrs in the persecution of Diocletian, the stories of the miracles they performed, the national feeling excited by the sense of their opposition to the dictates of the foreign government,[3] the assurance that a paradise of delights was opened to the martyr who died under the hands of his tormentors,—all these things stirred up an enthusiasm that resulted in an incredibly rapid spread of the Christian faith. "Instead of being converted by preaching, as the other countries of the East were, Egypt embraced Christianity in a fit of wild enthusiasm, without any preaching, or instruction being given, with hardly any knowledge of the new religion beyond the name of Jesus, the Messiah, who bestowed a life of eternal happiness on all who confessed Him."[4]

In the seventh century Christianity had probably very little hold on a great mass of the people of Egypt. The theological catchwords that their leaders made use of, to stir up in them feelings of hatred and opposition to the Byzantine government, could have been intelligible to a very few, and the rapid spread of Islam in the early days of the Arab occupation was probably due less to definite efforts to attract than to the inability of such a Christianity to retain. The theological basis for the existence of the

[1] Severus, pp. 172–3. [2] Id. pp. 205–6.
[3] "Sans aucun doute il y eut dans la multiplicité des martyrs une sorte de résistance nationale contre les gouverneurs étrangers." (Amélineau, p. 58.) [4] Amélineau, pp. 57–8.

Jacobites as a separate sect, the tenets that they had so long and at so great a cost struggled to maintain, were embodied in doctrines of the most abstruse and metaphysical character, and many doubtless turned in utter perplexity and weariness from the interminable controversies that raged around them, to a faith that was summed up in the simple, intelligible truth of the Unity of God and the mission of His Prophet, Muḥammad. Even within the Coptic Church itself at a later period, we find evidence of a movement which, if not distinctly Muslim, was at least closely allied thereto, and in the absence of any separate ecclesiastical organisation in which it might find expression, probably contributed to the increase of the converts to Islam. In the beginning of the twelfth century, there was in the monastery of St. Anthony (near Iṭfīḥ on the Nile), a monk named Balūṭus, " learned in the doctrines of the Christian religion and the duties of the monastic life, and skilled in the rules of the canon-law. But Satan caught him in one of his nets; for he began to hold opinions at variance with those taught by the Three Hundred and Eighteen (of Nicæa); and he corrupted the minds of many of those who had no knowledge or instruction in the Orthodox faith. He announced with his impure mouth, in his wicked discourses, that Christ our Lord—to Whom be glory—was like one of the prophets. He associated with the lowest among the followers of his religion, clothed as he was in the monastic habit. When he was questioned as to his religion and his creed, he professed himself a believer in the Unity of God. His doctrines prevailed during a period which ended in the year 839 of the Righteous Martyrs (A.D. 1123); then he died, and his memory was cut off for ever." [1]

Further, a theory of the Christian life that found its highest expression in asceticism of the grossest type [2] could offer little attraction, in the face of the more human morality of Islam.[3] On account of the large numbers of Copts that

[1] Abū Ṣāliḥ, pp. 163–4. [2] Amélineau, pp. 53–4, 69–70.

[3] Abū Ṣāliḥ gives an account of some monks who embraced the faith of the Prophet, and these are probably representative of a larger number of whom the historian has left no record, as lacking the peculiar circumstances of loss to the monastery or of recantation that made such instances of interest to him (pp. 128, 142).

from time to time have become Muhammadans, they have come to be considered by the followers of the Prophet as much more inclined to the faith of Islam than any other Christian sect, and though they have had to endure the most severe oppression and persecution on many occasions, yet the Copts that have been thus driven to abandon their faith are said to have been few in comparison with those who have changed their religion voluntarily,[1] and even in the nineteenth century, when Egypt was said to be the most tolerant of all Muhammadan countries, there were yearly conversions of the Copts to the Muslim faith.[2] Still, persecution and oppression have undoubtedly played a very large part in the reduction of the numbers of the Copts, and the story of the sufferings of the Jacobite Church of Egypt,—persecuted alike by their fellow Christians [3] and by the followers of the dominant faith, is a very sad one, and many abandoned the religion of their fathers in order to escape from burdensome taxes and unendurable indignities. The vast difference in this respect between their condition and that of the Christians of Syria, Palestine and Spain at the same period finds its explanation in the turbulent character of the Copts themselves. Their long struggle against the civil and theological despotism of Byzantium seems to have welded the zealots into a national party that could as little brook the foreign rule of the Arabs as, before, that of the Greeks. The rising of the Copts against their new masters in 646, when they drove the Arabs for a time out of Alexandria and opened the gates of the city to the Byzantine troops (who, however, treated the unfortunate Copts as enemies,

[1] Lane, pp. 546, 549.

[2] Lüttke (1), vol. i. pp. 30, 35. Dr. Andrew Watson writes: "No year has passed during my residence of forty-four years in the Nile valley without my hearing of several instances of defection. The causes are, chiefly, the hope of worldly gain of various kinds, severe and continued persecution, exposure to the cruelty and rapacity of Moslem neighbours, and personal indignities as well as political disabilities of various kinds." (Islam in Egypt: Mohammedan World, p. 24.)

[3] Severus, pp. 122, 126, 143. One of the very first occasions on which they had to complain of excessive taxation was when Menas, the Christian prefect of Lower Egypt, extorted from the city of Alexandria 32,057 pieces of gold, instead of 22,000 which 'Amr had fixed as the amount to be levied. (John of Nikiu, p. 585.) Renaudot (p. 168) says that after the restoration of the Orthodox hierarchy, about seventy years after the Muhammadan conquest, the Copts suffered as much at its hands as at the hands of the Muhammadans themselves.

not having yet forgotten the welcome they had before given to the Muhammadan invaders), was the first of a long series of risings and insurrections,[1]—excited frequently by excessive taxation,—which exposed them to terrible reprisals, and caused the lot of the Jacobite Christians of Egypt to be harder to bear than that of any other Christian sect in this or other countries under Muhammadan rule. But the history of these events belongs rather to a history of Muhammadan persecution and intolerance than to the scope of the present work. It must not, however, be supposed that the condition of the Copts was invariably that of a persecuted sect; on the contrary there were times when they rose to positions of great affluence and importance in the state. They filled the posts of secretaries and scribes in the government offices,[2] farmed the taxes,[3] and in some cases amassed enormous wealth.[4] The annals of their Church furnish us with many instances of ecclesiastics who were held in high favour and consideration by the reigning princes of the country, under the rule of many of whom the Christians enjoyed the utmost tranquillity.[5] To such a period of the peace of the Church belongs an incident that led to the absorption of many Christians into the body of the faithful.

During the reign of Ṣalāḥ al-Dīn (Saladin) (1169–1193) over Egypt, the condition of the Christians was very happy under the auspices of this tolerant ruler; the taxes that had been imposed upon them were lightened and several swept away altogether; they crowded into the public offices as secretaries, accountants and registrars; and for nearly a century under the successors of Saladin, they enjoyed the same toleration and favour, and had nothing to complain of except the corruption and degeneracy of their own clergy. Simony had become terribly rife among them; the priesthood was sold to ignorant and vicious persons, while postulants for the sacred office who were unable to pay the sums demanded for ordination, were repulsed with scorn, in spite of their

[1] Maqrīzī mentions five other risings of the Copts that had to be crushed by force of arms, within the first century of the Arab domination. (Maqrīzī (2), pp. 76–82.)

[2] Renaudot, pp. 189, 374, 430, 540.

[3] Id. p. 603.

[4] Id. pp. 432, 607. Nāṣir-i-Khusrau: Safar-nāmah, ed. Schefer, pp. 155–6.

[5] Renaudot, pp. 212, 225, 314, 374, 540.

being worthy and fit persons. The consequence was that the spiritual and moral training of the people was utterly neglected and there was a lamentable decay of the Christian life.[1] So corrupt had the Church become that when, on the death of John, the seventy-fourth Patriarch of the Jacobites, in 1216, a successor was to be elected, the contending parties who pushed the claims of rival candidates, kept up a fierce and irreconcilable dispute for nearly twenty years, and all this time cared less for the grievous scandal and the harmful consequences of their shameless quarrels than for the maintenance of their dogged and obstinately factious spirit. On more than one occasion the reigning sultan tried to make peace between the contending parties, refused the enormous bribes of three, five, and even ten thousand gold pieces that were offered in order to induce him to secure the election of one of the candidates by the pressure of official influence, and even offered to remit the fee that it was customary for a newly-elected Patriarch to pay, if only they would put aside their disputes and come to some agreement,—but all to no purpose. Meanwhile many episcopal sees fell vacant and there was no one to take the place of the bishops and priests that died in this interval; in the monastery of St. Macarius alone there were only four priests left as compared with over eighty under the last Patriarch.[2] So utterly neglected were the Christians of the western dioceses, that they all became Muslims.[3] To this bald statement of the historian of the Coptic Church, we unfortunately have no information to add, of the positive efforts made by the Musalmans to bring these Christians over to their faith. That such there were, there can be very little doubt, especially as we know that the Christians held public disputations and engaged in written controversies on the respective merits of the rival creeds.[4] That these

[1] Renaudot, p. 388.
[2] Id. pp. 567, 571, 574–5.
[3] Wansleben, p. 30. Wansleben mentions another instance (under different circumstances) of the decay of the Coptic Church, in the island of Cyprus, which was formerly under the jurisdiction of the Coptic Patriarch : here they were so persecuted by the Orthodox clergy, who enjoyed the protection of the Byzantine emperors, that the Patriarch could not induce priests to go there, and consequently all the Copts on the island either accepted Islam or the Council of Chalcedon, and their churches were all shut up. (Id. p. 31.)
[4] Renaudot, p. 377.

conversions were not due to persecution, we know from direct historical evidence that during this vacancy of the patriarchate, the Christians had full and complete freedom of public worship, were allowed to restore their churches and even to build new ones, were freed from the restrictions that forbade them to ride on horses or mules, and were tried in law-courts of their own, while the monks were exempted from the payment of tribute and granted certain privileges.[1]

How far this incident is a typical case of conversion to Islam among the Copts it is difficult to say; a parallel case of neglect is mentioned by two Capuchin missionaries who travelled up the Nile to Luxor in the seventeenth century, where they found that the Copts of Luxor had no priest, and some of them had not gone to confession or communion for fifty years.[2] Under such circumstances the decay of their numbers can readily be understood.

A similar neglect probably contributed to the decay of the Nubian Church which recognised the primacy of the Jacobite Patriarch of Alexandria, as do the Abyssinians to the present day. The Nubians had been converted to Christianity about the middle of the sixth century, and retained their independence when Egypt was conquered by the Arabs; a treaty was made according to which the Nubians were to send every year three hundred and sixty slaves, with forty more for the governor of Egypt, while the Arabs were to furnish them with corn, oil and raiment.[3] In the reign of al-Muʻtaṣim (833–842), ambassadors were sent by the caliph renewing this treaty, and the king of Nubia visited the capital, where he was received with great magnificence and dismissed with costly presents.[4] In the twelfth century they were still all Christian,[5] and retained their old independence in spite of the frequent expeditions sent against them from Egypt.[6] In 1275 the nephew of the then king of Nubia obtained from the sultan of Egypt a body of troops to assist him in his revolt against his uncle,

[1] Renaudot, p. 575.
[2] Relation du voyage du Sayd ou de la Thebayde fait en 1668, par les PP. Protais et Charles-François d'Orleans, Capuchins Missionaires, p. 3. (Thevenot, vol. ii.)
[3] Caetani, vol. iv. p. 520.
[4] Ishok, of Romgla, pp. 272–3.
[5] Idrīsī, p. 32.
[6] Maqrīzī (2), tome i. 2me partie, p. 131.

whom he by their help succeeded in deposing; in return for this assistance he had to cede the two northernmost provinces of Nubia to the sultan, and as the inhabitants elected to retain their Christian faith, an annual tribute of one dīnār for each male was imposed upon them.[1] But this Muhammadan overlordship was temporary only, and the Nubians of the ceded provinces soon reasserted their independence.[2]

But settlements of Arabs had been established in Nubia for several centuries earlier and the Arabs on the Blue Nile had so increased in number and wealth in the tenth century that they were able to ask permission to build a mosque in Soba,[3] the capital of the Christian kingdom.[4] In the thirteenth and especially from the beginning of the fourteenth century there began a general process of interpenetration through the migration into Nubia of Arabs, especially of the Juhaynah tribe, who intermarried with the women of the land and gradually succeeded in breaking up the power of the Nubian princes.[5] In the latter half of the fourteenth century Ibn Baṭūṭah[6] tells us that the Nubians were still Christians, though the king of their chief city, Dongola,[7] had embraced Islam in the reign of Nāṣir (probably Nāṣir b. Qulāūn, one of the Mamluk sultans of Egypt, who died A.D. 1340); the repeated expeditions of the Muslims so late as the fifteenth century had not succeeded in pushing their conquests south of the first cataract, near which was their last fortified place,[8] while Christianity seems to have extended as far up the Nile as Sennaar.

The Christian Nubian kingdom appears to have come to an end partly through internal dissensions and partly

[1] Maqrīzī, pp. 128–30. [2] Burckhardt (1), p. 494.
[3] About twelve miles above the modern Khartum.
[4] Artin, pp. 62, 144.
[5] Becker, Geschichte des östlichen Sūdān, p. 160.
[6] Vol. iv. p. 396.
[7] Slatin Pasha records a tradition current among the Danagla Arabs that this town was founded by their ancestor, Dangal, who called it after his own name. (This however is impossible, inasmuch as Dongola was in existence in ancient Egyptian times, and is mentioned on the monuments. See Vivien de Saint-Martin, vol. ii. p. 85.) According to their tradition, this Dangal, though a slave, rose to be ruler of Nubia, but paid tribute to Bahnesa, the Coptic bishop of the entire district lying between the present Sarras and Debba. (Fire and Sword in the Sudan, p. 13.) (London, 1896.)
[8] Ibn Salīm al-Aswānī, quoted by Maqrīzī: Kitāb al-Khiṭaṭ, vol. i. p. 190. (Cairo, A.H. 1270.)

through the attacks of Arab and Negro tribes on its borders, and finally by the establishment of the powerful Fūnj empire in the fifteenth century.[1]

But it is probable that the progress of Islam in the country was all this time being promoted by the Muhammadan merchants and others that frequented it. Maqrīzī (writing in the early part of the fifteenth century) quotes one of those missionary anecdotes which occur so rarely in the works of Arabic authors; it is told by Ibn Salīm al-Aswāni, and is of interest as giving us a living picture of the Muslim propagandist at work. Though the convert referred to is neither a Christian nor a Nubian, still the story shows that there was such a thing as conversion to Islam in Nubia in the fifteenth century. Ibn Salīm says that he once met a man at the court of the Nubian chief of Muqurrah, who told him that he came from a city that lay three months' journey from the Nile. When asked about his religion, he replied, "My Creator and thy Creator is God; the Creator of the universe and of all men is One, and his dwelling-place is in Heaven." When there was a dearth of rain, or when pestilence attacked them or their cattle, his fellow-countrymen would climb up a high mountain and there pray to God, who accepted their prayers and supplied their needs before even they came down again. When he acknowledged that God had never sent them a prophet, Ibn Salīm recounted to him the story of the prophets Moses and Jesus and Muḥammad, and how by the help of God they had been enabled to perform many miracles. And he answered, "The truth must indeed have been with them, when they did these things; and if they performed these deeds, I believe in them."[2]

Very slowly and gradually the Nubians seem to have drifted from Christianity into Muhammadanism.[3] The spiritual life of their Church had sunk to the lowest ebb, and as no movement of reform sprang up in their midst, and as they had lost touch with the Christian Churches beyond their borders, it was only natural that they should seek for an expression of their spiritual aspirations in the

[1] Budge, vol. ii. p. 199. Artin, p. 144.
[2] Maqrīzī: Kitāb al-Khiṭaṭ, vol. i. p. 193. [3] Morié, vol. i. pp. 417–18.

religion of Islam, whose followers had so long borne witness to its living power among them, and had already won over some of their countrymen to the acceptance of it. A Portuguese priest, who travelled in Abyssinia from 1520–1527, has preserved for us a picture of the Nubians in this state of transition; he says that they were neither Christians, Jews nor Muhammadans, but had come to be without faith and without laws; but still "they lived with the desire of being Christians." Through the fault of their clergy they had sunk into the grossest ignorance, and now there were no bishops or priests left among them; accordingly they sent an embassy of six men to the king of Abyssinia, praying him to send priests and monks to instruct them, but this the king refused to do without the permission of the Patriarch of Alexandria, and as this could not be obtained, the unfortunate ambassadors returned unsuccessful to their own country.[1] The same writer was informed by a Christian who had travelled in Nubia, that he had found 150 churches there, in each of which were still to be seen the figures of the crucified Christ, of the Virgin Mary, and other saints painted on the walls. In all the fortresses, also, that were scattered throughout the country, there were churches.[2] Before the close of the following century, Christianity had entirely disappeared from Nubia "for want of pastors," but the closed churches were to be found still standing throughout the whole country.[3] The Nubians had yielded to the powerful Muhammadan influences that surrounded them, to which the proselytising efforts of the Muslims who had travelled in Nubia for centuries past no doubt contributed a great deal; on the north were Egypt and the Arab tribes that had made their way up the Nile and extended their authority along the banks of that river;[4] on the south, the Muhammadan state of the Belloos, separating them from Abyssinia.

[1] Lord Stanley of Alderley in his translation of Alvarez' Narrative from the original Portuguese, gives the answer of the king as follows: "He said to them that he had his Abima from the country of the Moors, that is to say from the Patriarch of Alexandria; . . . . how then could he give priests and friars since another gave them" (p. 352). (London, 1881.)

[2] Viaggio nella Ethiopia al Prete Ianni fatto par Don Francesco Alvarez Portughese (1520–1527). (Ramusio, tom. i. pp. 200, 250.)

[3] Wansleben, p. 30. For descriptions of the ruins that still remain, see Budge, vol. ii. p. 299 sqq., and G. S. Nileham, Churches in Lower Nubia. (Philadelphia, 1910.)

[4] Burckhardt (1), p. 133.

These Belloos, in the early part of the sixteenth century, were, in spite of their Muslim faith, tributaries of the Christian king of Abyssinia; [1] and—if they may be identified with the Baliyyūn, who, together with their neighbours, the Bajah (the inhabitants of the so-called island of Meroe), are spoken of by Idrīsī, in the twelfth century, as being Jacobite Christians,[2]—it is probable that they had only a few years before been converted to Islam, at the same time as the Bajah, who had been incorporated into the Muhammadan empire of the Fūnj, when these latter extended their conquests in 1499–1530 from the south up to the borders of Nubia and Abyssinia and founded the powerful state of Sennaar. When the army of Aḥmad Grāñ invaded Abyssinia and made its way right through the country from south to north, it effected a junction about 1534 with the army of the sultan of Maseggia or Mazaga, a province under Muhammadan rule but tributary to Abyssinia, lying between that country and Sennaar; in the army of this sultan there were 15,000 Nubian soldiers who, from the account given of them, appear to have been Musalmans.[3] Fragmentary and insufficient as these data of the conversion of the Nubians are, we may certainly conclude from all we know of the independent character of this people and the tenacity with which they clung to the Christian faith, so long as it was a living force among them, that their change of religion was a gradual one, extending through several centuries.

Let us now pass to the history of Islam among the Abyssinians, who had received Christianity two centuries before the Nubians, and like them belonged to the Jacobite Church.

The tide of Arab emigration does not seem to have set across the Red Sea, the western shores of which formed part of the Abyssinian kingdom, until many centuries after Arabia had accepted the faith of the prophet. Up to the tenth century only a few Muhammadan families were to be found residing in the coast towns of Abyssinia, but at the end of the twelfth century the foundation of an Arab dynasty alienated some of the coast-lands from the Abyssinian kingdom. In 1300 a missionary, named Abū 'Abd Allāh Muḥammad, made his way into Abyssinia, calling

[1] Alvarez, p. 250. [2] Idrīsī, p. 32. [3] 'Arabfaqih, p. 323.

on the people to embrace Islam, and in the following year, having collected around him 200,000 men, he attacked the ruler of Amhara in several engagements.[1] King Saifa Ar'ād (1342–1370) took energetic measures against the Muhammadans in his kingdom, putting to death or driving into exile all those who refused to embrace Christianity.[2] At the close of the same century the disturbed state of the country, owing to the civil wars that distracted it, made it possible for the various Arab settlements along the coast to make themselves masters of the entire seaboard and drive the Abyssinians into the interior, and the king, Ba'eda Māryām (1468–1478), is said to have spent the greater part of his reign in fighting against the Muhammadans on the eastern border of his kingdom.[3] In the early part of the sixteenth century, while the powerful Muhammadan kingdom of Adal, between Abyssinia and the southern extremity of the Red Sea, and some others were bitterly hostile to the Christian power, there were others again that formed peaceful tributaries of "Prester John"; e.g. in Massowah there were Arabs who kept the flocks of the Abyssinian seigniors, wandering about in bands of thirty or forty with their wives and children, each band having its Christian "captain."[4] Some Musalmans are also mentioned as being in the service of the king and being entrusted by him with important posts;[5] while some of these remained faithful to Islam, others embraced the prevailing religion of the country. What was implied in the fact of these Muhammadan communities being tributaries of the king of Abyssinia, it is difficult to determine. The Musalmans of Ḥadya had along with other tribute to give up every year to the king a maiden who had to become a Christian; this custom was in accordance with an ancient treaty, which the king of Abyssinia has always made them observe, "because he was the stronger"; besides this, they were forbidden to carry arms or put on war-apparel, and, if they rode, their horses were not to be saddled; "these orders," they said, "we have always obeyed, so that the

[1] Maqrīzī (2), tome ii. 2me partie, p. 183.
[2] Basset, p. 240. [3] Id., p. 247.
[4] Alvarez. (Ramusio, tom. i. pp. 218, 242, 249.)
[5] 'Arabfaqīh, pp. 83, 191.

king may not put us to death and destroy our mosques. When the king sends his people to fetch the maiden and the tribute, we put her on a bed, wash her and cover her with a cloth, and recite the prayers for the dead over her and give her up to the people of the king; and thus did our fathers and our grandfathers before us." [1]

These Muhammadan tributaries were chiefly to be found in the low-lying countries that formed the northern boundary of Abyssinia, from the Red Sea westward to Sennaar,[2] and on the south and the south-east of the kingdom.[3] What influence these Muhammadans had on the Christian populations with which they were intermingled, and whether they made converts to Islam as in the present century, is matter only of conjecture. Certain it is, however, that when the independent Muhammadan ruler of Adal, Aḥmad Grāñ—himself said to have been the son of a Christian priest of Aijjo, who had left his own country and adopted Islam in that of the Adals [4]—invaded Abyssinia from 1528 to 1543, many Abyssinian chiefs with their followers joined his victorious army and became Musalmans, and though the Christian populations of some districts preferred to pay jizyah,[5] others embraced the religion of the conqueror.[6] But the contemporary Muslim historian himself tells us that in some cases this conversion was the result of fear, and that suspicions were entertained of the genuineness of the allegiance of the new converts.[7] But such apparently was not universally the case, and the widespread character of the conversions in several districts give the impression of a popular movement. The Christian chiefs who went over to Islam made use of their personal influence in inducing their troops to follow their example. They were, as we are told, in some cases very ignorant of their own religion,[8] and thus the change of faith was a less difficult matter. Particularly instrumental in conversions of this kind were those Muhammadan chiefs who had previously entered the service of the king of Abyssinia, and those renegades who took the opportunity of the invasion of the country by a conquering Musalman

[1] 'Arabfaqīh, p. 275–6. [2] Id. pp. 319, 324. [3] Id. pp. 28, 129, 275.
[4] Plowden, p. 36. [5] 'Arabfaqīh, pp. 321, 335, 343.
[6] Id. passim. [7] Id. pp. 175, 195, 248. [8] Id. p. 178.

army to throw off their allegiance at once to Christianity and the Christian king and declare themselves Muhammadans once more.[1]

One of these in 1531 wrote the following letter to Aḥmad Grāñ :—" I was formerly a Muslim and the son of a Muslim, was taken prisoner by the polytheists and made a Christian by force; but in my heart I have always clung to the true faith and now I seek the protection of God and of His Prophet and of thee. If thou wilt accept my repentance and punish me not for what I have done, I will return in penitence to God; and I will devise means whereby the troops of the king, that are with me, may join thee and become Muslims;"—and in fact the greater part of his army elected to follow their general; including the women and children their numbers are said to have amounted to 20,000 souls.[2]

But with the help of the Portuguese, the Abyssinians succeeded in shaking off the yoke of their Muhammadan conquerors and Aḥmad Grāñ himself was slain in 1543. Islam had, however, gained a footing in the country, which the troublous condition of affairs during the remainder of the sixteenth and the following century enabled it to retain, the rival Christian Churches being too busily engaged in contending with one another, to devote much attention to their common enemy. For the successful proselytising of the Jesuits and other Roman Catholic missionaries and the active interference of the Portuguese in all civil and political matters, excited violent opposition in the mass of the Abyssinian Christians;—indeed so bitter was this feeling that some of the chiefs openly declared that they would rather submit to a Muhammadan ruler than continue their alliance with the Portuguese;[3]—and the semi-religious, semi-patriotic movement set on foot thereby, rapidly assumed such vast proportions as to lead (about 1632) to the expulsion of the Portuguese and the exclusion of all foreign Christians from the country. The condition of Abyssinia then speedily became one of terrible confusion and anarchy, of which some tribes of the Galla race took

[1] 'Arabfaqīh, pp. 34–5, 120–1, 182–3, 244, 327.
[2] 'Arabfaqīh, pp. 181–2, 186.
[3] Iobi Ludolfi ad suam Historiam Æthiopicam Commentarius, p. 474. Frankfurt a. M., 1691.)

advantage, to thrust their way right into the very centre of the country, where their settlements remain to the present day.

The progress achieved by Islam during this period may be estimated from the testimony of a traveller of the seventeenth century, who tells us that in his time the adherents of this faith were scattered throughout the whole of Abyssinia and formed a third of the entire population.[1] During the following century the faith of the Prophet seems steadily to have increased by means of the conversion of isolated individuals here and there. The absence of any strong central government in the country favoured the rise of petty independent chieftains, many of whom had strong Muhammadan sympathies, though (in accordance with a fundamental law of the state) all the Abyssinian princes had to belong to the Christian faith; the Muhammadans, too, aspiring to the dignity of the Abyssinian aristocracy, abjured the faith in which they had been born and pretended conversion to Christianity in order to get themselves enrolled in the order of the nobles, and as governors of Christian provinces made use of all their influence towards the spread of Islam.[2] One of the chief reasons of the success of this faith seems to have been the moral superiority of the Muslims as compared with that of the Christian population of Abyssinia. Rüppell says that he frequently noticed in the course of his travels in Abyssinia that when a post had to be filled which required that a thoroughly honest and trustworthy person should be selected, the choice always fell upon a Muhammadan. In comparison with the Christians, he says that they were more active and energetic; that every Muhammadan had his sons taught to read and write, whereas Christian children were only educated when they were intended for the priesthood.[3] This moral superiority of the Muhammadans of

[1] Histoire de la Haute Ethiopie, par le R. P. Manoel d'Almeïda, p. 7. (Thevenot, vol. ii.)

[2] Massaja, vol. ii. pp. 205–6. "Ognuno comprende che movente di queste conversioni essendo la sete di regnare, nel fatto non si riducevano che ad una formalità esterna, restando poi i nuovi convertiti veri mussulmani nei cuori e nei costumi. E perciò accadeva che, elevati alla dignità di Râs, si circondavano di mussulmani, dando ad essi la maggior parte degli impieghi e colmandoli di titoli, ricchezze e favori: e così l'Abissinia cristiana invasa e popolata da questa pessima razza, passò coll' andar del tempo sotto il giogo dell' islamismo." (Id. p. 206.)

[3] Rüppell, vol. i. pp. 328, 366.

Abyssinia over the Christian population goes far to explain the continuous though slow progress made by Islam during the eighteenth and nineteenth centuries; the degradation and apathy of the Abyssinian clergy and the interminable feuds of the Abyssinian chiefs, have left Muhammadan influences free to work undisturbed. Mr. Plowden, who was English consul in Abyssinia from 1844 to 1860, speaking of the Ḥabāb, three Tigrē tribes dwelling between 16° and 17° 30′ lat., to the north-west of Massowah, says that they have become Muhammadan "within the last 100 years, and all, save the latest generation, bear Christian names. They have changed their faith, through the constant influence of the Muhammadans with whom they trade, and through the gradual and now entire abandonment of the country by the Abyssinian chiefs, too much occupied in ceaseless wars with their neighbours." [1] They have a tradition that one of their chiefs named Jāwej rejected Christianity for Islam, in the belief that the latter faith brought good luck and long life; he then said to his priest, "Break in pieces the Tābōt"; [2] the priest answered, "I dare not break in pieces the Tābōt of Mary"; so Jāwej seized the Tābōt with his own hands and cut it in pieces with an axe; the Christian priests then adopted Islam, and all their descendants are shaykhs of the tribe to the present day.[3]

Other sections of the population of the northern districts of the country were similarly converted to Islam during the same period, because the priests had abandoned these districts and the churches had been suffered to fall into ruins,—apparently entirely through neglect, as the Muhammadans here are said to have been by no means fanatical nor to have borne any particular enmity to Christianity.[4] Similar testimony to the progress of Islam in the early part of the nineteenth century is given by other travellers,[5] who found numbers of Christians to be continually passing over to that faith. The Muhammadans were especially favoured by Ras 'Alī, one of the vice-regents of Abyssinia and practically master of the country before the accession

[1] Plowden, p. 15.
[2] Tābōt, the ark of the covenant.
[3] Littmann, pp. 69–70.
[4] Plowden, pp. 8–9.
[5] Beke, pp. 51–2. Isenberg, p. 36.

of King Theodore in 1853. Though himself a Christian, he distributed posts and even the spoils of the churches among the followers of Islam, and during his reign one half of the population of the central provinces of Abyssinia embraced the faith of the Prophet.[1] Such deep roots had this faith now struck in Abyssinia that its followers had in their hands all the commerce as well as all the petty trade of the country, enjoyed vast possessions, were masters of large towns and central markets, and had a firm hold upon the mass of the people. Indeed, a Christian missionary who lived for thirty-five years in this country, rated the success and the zeal of the Muslim propagandists so high as to say that were another Aḥmad Grāñ to arise and unfurl the banner of the Prophet, the whole of Abyssinia would become Muhammadan.[2] Embroilments with the Egyptian government (with which Abyssinia was at war from 1875 to 1882) brought about a revulsion of feeling against Muhammadanism: hatred of the foreign Muslim foe reacted upon their co-religionists within the border. In 1878, King John summoned a Convocation of the Abyssinian clergy, who proclaimed him supreme arbiter in matters of faith and ordained that there should be but one religion throughout the whole kingdom. Christians of all sects other than the Jacobite were given two years in which to become reconciled to the national Church; the Muhammadans were to submit within three, and the heathen within five, years. A few days later the king promulgated an edict that showed how little worth was the three years' grace allowed to the Muhammadans; for not only did he order them to build Christian churches wherever they were needed and to pay tithes to the priests resident in their respective districts, but also gave three months' notice to all Muhammadan officials to either receive baptism or resign their posts. Such compulsory conversion (consisting as it did merely of the rite of baptism and the payment of tithes) was naturally of the most ineffectual character, and while outwardly conforming, the Muslims in secret protested their loyalty to their old faith. Massaja saw some such go straight from the church

[1] Reclus, vol. x. p. 247. Massaja, vol. xi. p. 125.
[2] Massaja, vol. xi. p. 124.

in which they had been baptised to the mosque, in order to have this enforced baptism wiped off by some holy man of their own faith.[1] These mass conversions were rendered the more ineffectual by being confined to the men, for as the royal edict had made no mention of the women they were in no way molested,—a circumstance that probably proved to be of considerable significance in the future history of Islam in Abyssinia, as Massaja bears striking testimony to the important part the Muhammadan women have played in the diffusion of their faith in this country.[2] By 1880 King John is said to have compelled about 50,000 Muhammadans to be baptised, as well as 20,000 members of one of the pagan tribes and half a million of Gallas,[3] but as their conversion went no further than baptism and the payment of tithes, it is not surprising to learn that the only result of these violent measures was to increase the hatred and hostility of both the Muslim and the heathen Abyssinians towards the Christian faith.[4] The king of the petty state of Kafa (which had almost always acknowledged the supremacy of Abyssinia),—Sawo-Teheno,—took advantage of the embarrassment of King John, who was threatened at once by the Italians and the followers of the Mahdī, to assert his independence, and became a Musalman, in order to do so more effectively. He successfully resisted all attacks until 1897, when his state was reconquered and he himself taken prisoner by the Emperor Menelik, the former king of Shoa, who had established his authority over the whole of Abyssinia after the death of King John in 1889. Christianity was re-established as the state religion throughout Kafa and Christian worship renewed in the churches, which had been left uninjured, being either shut up or turned into mosques.[5] But these violent measures taken in the interests of the Christian faith have failed to arrest the growing power of Islam during the nineteenth century. Whole tribes that were once Christian and still bear Christian names, such as Taklēs ("Plant of Jesus"), Hebtēs ("Gift of Jesus")

[1] Massaja, vol. xi. pp. 77–8.
[2] Id. pp. 124, 125.
[3] Oppel, p. 307. Reclus, tome x. p. 247.
[4] Massaja, vol. xi. pp. 79, 81.
[5] Morié, vol. ii. p. 449.

and Temāryām ("Gift of Mary"), have become Muslim. The two Mänsa' tribes which were entirely Christian about the middle of the nineteenth century had become Muslim, for the most part, at the beginning of the twentieth century; the propagandist efforts of the Muslims who converted them appear to have been facilitated through the ignorance of the Christian clergy. A similar Muhammadanising process has been going on for some time among other tribes also.[1]

We must return now to the history of Africa in the seventh century, when the Arabs were pushing their conquests from East to West along the north coast. The comparatively easy conquest of Egypt, where so many of the inhabitants assisted the Arabs in bringing the Byzantine rule to an end, found no parallel in the bloody campaigns and the long-continued resistance that here barred their further progress, and half a century elapsed before the Arabs succeeded in making themselves complete masters of the north coast from Egypt to the Atlantic Ocean. It was not till 698 that the fall of Carthage brought the Roman rule in Africa to an end for ever, and the subjugation of the Berbers made the Arabs supreme in the country.

The details of these campaigns it is no part of our purpose to consider, but rather to attempt to discover in what way Islam was spread among the Christian population. Unfortunately the materials available for such a purpose are lamentably sparse and insufficient. What became of that great African Church that had given such saints and theologians to Christendom? The Church of Tertullian, St. Cyprian and St. Augustine, which had emerged victorious out of so many persecutions, and had so stoutly championed the cause of Christian orthodoxy, seems to have faded away like a mist.

In the absence of definite information, it has been usual to ascribe the disappearance of the Christian population to fanatical persecutions and forced conversions on the part of the Muslim conquerors. But there are many considerations that militate against such a rough and ready settlement of this question. First of all, there is the absence

[1] Littmann, pp. 68–70. K. Cedcrquist: Islam and Christianity in Abyssinia, p. 154 (The Moslem World, vol. ii.).

of definite evidence in support of such an assertion. Massacres, devastation and all the other accompaniments of a bloody and long-protracted war, there were in horrible abundance, but of actual religious persecution we have little mention, and the survival of the native Christian Church for more than eight centuries after the Arab conquest is a testimony to the toleration that alone could have rendered such a survival possible.

The causes that brought about the decay of Christianity in North Africa must be sought for elsewhere than in the bigotry of Muhammadan rulers. But before attempting to enumerate these, it will be well to realise how very small must have been the number of the Christian population at the end of the seventh century—a circumstance that renders its continued existence under Muhammadan rule still more significant of the absence of forced conversion, and leaves such a hypothesis much less plausibility than would have been the case had the Arabs found a large and flourishing Christian Church there when they commenced their conquest of northern Africa.

The Roman provinces of Africa, to which the Christian population was confined, never extended far southwards; the Sahara forms a barrier in this direction, so that the breadth of the coast seldom exceeds 80 or 100 miles.[1] Though there were as many as 500 bishoprics just before the Vandal conquest, this number can serve as no criterion of the number of the faithful, owing to the practice observed in the African Church of appointing bishops to the most inconsiderable towns and very frequently to the most obscure villages,[2] and it is doubtful whether Christianity ever spread far inland among the Berber tribes.[3] When the power of the Roman Empire declined in the fifth century, different tribes of this great race, known to the Romans under the names of Moors, Numidians, Libyans, etc., swarmed up from the south to ravage and destroy the wealthy cities of the coast. These invaders were certainly heathen. The Libyans, whose devastations are so pathetically bewailed

[1] Gibbon, vol. i. p. 161.
[2] Id. vol. ii. p. 212.
[3] C. O. Castiglioni: Recherches sur les Berbères atlantiques, pp. 96–7. (Milan, 1826.)

by Synesius of Cyrene, pillaged and burnt the churches and carried off the sacred vessels for their own idolatrous rites,[1] and this province of Cyrenaica never recovered from their devastations, and Christianity was probably almost extinct here at the time of the Muslim invasion. The Moorish chieftain in the district of Tripolis, who was at war with the Vandal king Thorismund (496–524), but respected the churches and clergy of the orthodox, who had been ill-treated by the Vandals, declared his heathenism when he said, "I do not know who the God of the Christians is, but if he is so powerful as he is represented, he will take vengeance on those who insult him, and succour those who do him honour."[2] There is some probability that the nomads of Mauritania also were very largely heathen.

But whatever may have been the extent of the Christian Church, it received a blow from the Vandal persecutions from which it never recovered. For nearly a century the Arian Vandals persecuted the orthodox with relentless fury; sent their bishops into exile, forbade the public exercise of their religion and cruelly tortured those who refused to conform to the religion of their conquerors.[3] When in 534, Belisarius crushed the power of the Vandals and restored North Africa to the Roman Empire, only 217 bishops met in the Synod of Carthage[4] to resume the direction of the Christian Church. After the fierce and long-continued persecution to which they had been subjected the number of the faithful must have been very much reduced, and during the century that elapsed before the coming of the Muhammadans, the inroads of the barbarian Moors, who shut the Romans up in the cities and other centres of population, and kept the mountains, the desert and the open country for themselves,[5] the prevalent disorder and ill-government, and above all the desolating plagues that signalised the latter half of the sixth century, all combined to carry on the work of destruction. Five millions of Africans are said to have been consumed by the wars and government of the Emperor Justinian. The wealthier

[1] Synesii Catastasis. (Migne: Patr. Gr., tom. lxvi. p. 1569.)
[2] Neander (2), p. 320.
[3] Gibbon, vol. iv. pp. 331–3.
[4] Id. vol. v. p. 115.
[5] Tijānī, p. 201. Gibbon, vol. v. p. 122.

citizens abandoned a country whose commerce and agriculture, once so flourishing, had been irretrievably ruined. "Such was the desolation of Africa, that in many parts a stranger might wander whole days without meeting the face either of a friend or an enemy. The nation of the Vandals had disappeared; they once amounted to an hundred and sixty thousand warriors, without including the children, the women, or the slaves. Their numbers were infinitely surpassed by the number of Moorish families extirpated in a relentless war; the same destruction was retaliated on the Romans and their allies, who perished by the climate, their mutual quarrels, and the rage of the barbarians." [1]

In 646, the year before the victorious Arabs advanced from Egypt to the subjugation of the western province, the African Church that had championed so often the purity of Christian doctrine, was stirred to its depths by the struggle against Monotheletism; but when the bishops of the four ecclesiastical provinces in the archbishopric of Carthage, viz. Mauritania, Numidia, Byzacena and Africa Proconsularis, held councils to condemn Monotheletism, and wrote synodal letters to the Emperor and the Pope, there were only sixty-eight bishops who assembled at Carthage to represent the last-mentioned province, and forty-two for Byzacena. The numbers from the other two dioceses are not given, but the Christian population had undoubtedly suffered much more in these than in the two other dioceses which were nearer to the seat of government.[2] It is exceedingly unlikely that any of the bishops were absent on an occasion that excited so much feeling, when zeal for Christian doctrine and political animosity to the Byzantine court both combined in stimulating this movement, and when Africa took the most prominent part in stirring up the opposition that led to the convening of the great Lateran Council of 648. This diminution in the number of the African bishops certainly points to a vast decrease in the Christian population, and in consideration of the numerous causes contributing to a decay of the population, too great

[1] Gibbon, vol. v. p. 214.

[2] Neander (1), vol. v. pp. 254–5. J. E. T. Wiltsch: Hand-book of the geography and statistics of the Church, vol. i. pp. 433–4. (London, 1859.) J. Bournichon: L'Invasion musulmane en Afrique, pp. 32–3. (Tours, 1890.)

stress even must not be laid upon the number of these, because an episcopal see may continue to be filled long after the diocese has sunk into insignificance.

From the considerations enumerated above, it may certainly be inferred that the Christian population at the time of the Muhammadan invasion was by no means a large one. During the fifty years that elapsed before the Arabs assured their victory, the Christian population was still further reduced by the devastations of this long conflict. The city of Tripolis, after sustaining a siege of six months, was sacked, and of the inhabitants part were put to the sword and the rest carried off captive into Egypt and Arabia.[1] Another city, bordering on the Numidian desert, was defended by a Roman count with a large garrison which bravely endured a blockade of a whole year; when at last it was taken by storm, all the males were put to the sword and the women and children carried off captive.[2] The number of such captives is said to have amounted to several hundreds of thousands.[3] Many of the Christians took refuge in flight,[4] some into Italy and Spain,[5] and it would almost seem that others even wandered as far as Germany, judging from a letter addressed to the diocese of St. Boniface by Pope Gregory II.[6] In fact, many of the great Roman cities were quite depopulated, and remained uninhabited for a long time or were even left to fall to ruins entirely,[7] while in several cases the conquerors chose entirely new sites for their chief towns.[8]

As to the scattered remnants of the once flourishing Christian Church that still remained in Africa at the end

[1] Leo Africanus. (Ramusio, tom. i. p. 70, D.)

[2] "Deusen, una città antichissima edificata da Romani dove confina il regno di Buggia col diserto di Numidia." (Id. p. 75, F.)

[3] Pavy, vol. i. p. iv.

[4] "Tous ceux qui ne se convertirent pas à l'islamisme, ou qui (conservant leur foi) ne voulurent pas s'obliger à payer la capitation, durent prendre la fuite devant les armées musulmanes." (Tijānī, p. 201.)

[5] Leo Africanus. (Ramusio, tom. i. p. 7.)

[6] "Afros passim ad ecclesiasticos ordines (procedentes) prætendentes nulla ratione suscipiat (Bonifacius), quia aliqui eorum Manichæi, aliqui rebaptizati sæpius sunt probati." Epist. iv. (Migne: Patr. Lat., tom. lxxxix, p. 502.)

[7] Leo Africanus. (Ramusio, pp. 65, 66, 68, 69, 76.)

[8] Qayrwān or Cairoan, founded A.H. 50; Fez, founded A.H. 185; al-Mahdiyyah, founded A.H. 303; Masīlah, founded A.H. 315; Marocco, founded A.H. 424. (Abū-l Fidā, tome ii. pp. 198, 186, 200, 191, 187.)

of the seventh century, it can hardly be supposed that persecution is responsible for their final disappearance, in the face of the fact that traces of a native Christian community were to be found even so late as the sixteenth century. Idrīs, the founder of the dynasty in Morocco that bore his name, is indeed said to have compelled by force Christians and Jews to embrace Islam in the year A.D. 789, when he had just begun to carve out a kingdom for himself with the sword,[1] but, as far as I have been able to discover, this incident is without parallel in the history of the native Church of North Africa.[2]

The very slowness of its decay is a testimony to the toleration it must have received. About 300 years after the Muhammadan conquest there were still nearly forty bishoprics left,[3] and when in 1053 Pope Leo IX laments that only five bishops could be found to represent the once flourishing African Church,[4] the cause is most probably to be sought for in the terrible bloodshed and destruction wrought by the Arab hordes that had poured into the country a few years before and filled it with incessant conflict

[1] Ibn Abī Zar', p. 16.

[2] A doubtful case of forced conversion is attributed to 'Abd al-Mu'min, who conquered Tunis in 1159. See De Mas Latrie (2), pp. 77–8. "Deux auteurs arabes, Ibn-al-Athir, contemporain, mais vivant à Damas au milieu de l'exaltation religieuse que provoquaient les victoires de Saladin, l'autre El-Tidjani, visitant l'Afrique orientale au quatorzième siècle, ont écrit que le sultan, maître de Tunis, força les chrétiens et les juifs établis dans cette ville à embrasser l'islamisme, et que les réfractaires furent impitoyablement massacrés. Nous doutons de la réalité de toutes ces mesures. Si l'arrêt fatal fut prononcé dans l'emportement du triomphe et pour satisfaire quelques exigences momentanées, il dut être éludé ou révoqué, tant il était contraire au principe de la liberté religieuse respecté jusque-là par tous les princes maugrebins. Ce qu'il y a de certain, c'est que les chrétiens et les juifs ne tardèrent pas à reparaître à Tunis et qu'on voit les chrétiens avant la fin du règne d'Abd-el-Moumen établis à Tunis et y jouissant comme par le passé de la liberté, de leurs établissements, de leur commerce et de leur religion . . . . 'Accompagné ainsi par Dieu même dans sa marche, dit un ancien auteur maugrebin, il traversa victorieusement les terres du Zab et de l'Ifrikiah, conquérant le pays et les villes, accordant l'aman à ceux qui le demandaient et tuant *les récalcitrants*.' Ces derniers mots confirment notre sentiment sur sa politique à l'égard des chrétiens qui acceptèrent l'arrêt fatal de la destinée."

[3] De Mas Latrie (2), pp. 27–8.

[4] S. Leonis IX. Papæ Epist. lxxxiii. (Migne: Patr. Lat., tom. cxliii. p. 728.) This letter deals with a quarrel for precedence between the bishops of Gummi and Carthage, and it is quite possible that the disordered condition of Africa at the time may have kept the African bishops ignorant of the condition of other sees besides their own and those immediately adjacent, and that accordingly the information supplied to the Pope represented the number of the bishops as being smaller than it really was.

and anarchy.[1] In 1076, the African Church could not provide the three bishops necessary for the consecration of an aspirant to the dignity of the episcopate, in accordance with the demands of canon law, and it was necessary for Pope Gregory VII to consecrate two bishops to act as coadjutors of the Archbishop of Carthage; but the numbers of the faithful were still so large as to demand the creation of fresh bishops to lighten the burden of the work, which was too heavy for these three bishops to perform unaided.[2] In the course of the next two centuries, the Christian Church declined still further, and in 1246 the bishop of Morocco was the sole spiritual leader of the remnant of the native Church.[3] Up to the same period traces of the survival of Christianity were still to be found among the Kabils of Algeria; [4] these tribes had received some slight instruction in the tenets of Islam at an early period, but the new faith had taken very little hold upon them, and as years went by they lost even what little knowledge they had at first possessed, so much so that they even forgot the Muslim formula of prayer. Shut up in their mountain fastnesses and jealous of their independence, they successfully resisted the introduction of the Arab element into their midst, and thus the difficulties in the way of their conversion were very considerable. Some unsuccessful attempts to start a mission among them had been made by the inmates of a monastery belonging to the Qādiriyyah order, Sāqiyah al-ḥamrā', but the honour of winning an entrance among them for the Muslim faith was reserved for a number of Andalusian Moors who were driven out of Spain after the taking of Granada in 1492. They had taken refuge in this monastery and were recognised by the shaykh to be eminently fitted for the arduous task that had previously so completely baffled the efforts of his disciples. Before dismissing them on this pious errand, he thus addressed them: " It is a duty incumbent

[1] A. Müller, vol. ii. pp. 628–9.

[2] S. Gregorii VII. Epistola xix. (Liber tertius). (Migne: Patr. Lat., tom. cxlviii. p. 449.)

[3] De Mas Latrie, p. 226. A number of Spanish Christians, whose ancestors had been deported to Morocco in 1122, were to be found there as late as 1386, when they were allowed to return to Seville through the good offices of the then sultan of Morocco. (Whishaw, pp. 31–4.)

[4] C. Trumelet: Les Saintes de l'Islam, p. xxxiii. (Paris, 1881.)

upon us to bear the torch of Islam into these regions that have lost their inheritance in the blessings of religion; for these unhappy Kabils are wholly unprovided with schools, and have no shaykh to teach their children the laws of morality and the virtues of Islam; so they live like the brute beasts, without God or religion. To do away with this unhappy state of things, I have determined to appeal to your religious zeal and enlightenment. Let not these mountaineers wallow any longer in their pitiable ignorance of the grand truths of our religion; go and breathe upon the dying fire of their faith and re-illumine its smouldering embers; purge them of whatever errors may still cling to them from their former belief in Christianity; make them understand that in the religion of our lord Muḥammad—may God have compassion upon him—dirt is not, as in the Christian religion, looked upon as acceptable in the eyes of God.[1] I will not disguise from you the fact that your task is beset with difficulties, but your irresistible zeal and the ardour of your faith will enable you, by the grace of God, to overcome all obstacles. Go, my children, and bring back again to God and His Prophet these unhappy people who are wallowing in the mire of ignorance and unbelief. Go, my children, bearing the message of salvation, and may God be with you and uphold you."

The missionaries started off in parties of five or six at a time in various directions; they went in rags, staff in hand, and choosing out the wildest and least frequented parts of the mountains, established hermitages in caves and clefts of the rocks. Their austerities and prolonged devotions soon excited the curiosity of the Kabils, who after a short time began to enter into friendly relations with them. Little by little the missionaries gained the influence they desired through their knowledge of medicine, of the mechanical arts, and other advantages of civilisation, and each hermitage became a centre of Muslim teaching.

[1] Compare the articles published by a Junta held at Madrid in 1566, for the reformation of the Moriscoes; one of which runs as follows: "That neither themselves, their women, nor any other persons should be permitted to wash or bathe themselves either at home or elsewhere; and that all their bathing houses should be pulled down and demolished." (J. Morgan, vol. ii. p. 256.)

Students, attracted by the learning of the new-comers, gathered round them and in time became missionaries of Islam to their fellow-countrymen, until their faith spread throughout all the country of the Kabils and the villages of the Algerian Sahara.[1]

The above incident is no doubt illustrative of the manner in which Islam was introduced among such other sections of the independent tribes of the interior as had received any Christian teaching, but whose knowledge of this faith had dwindled down to the observance of a few superstitious rites; [2] for, cut off as they were from the rest of the Christian world and unprovided with spiritual teachers, they could have had little in the way of positive religious belief to oppose to the teachings of the Muslim missionaries.

There is little more to add to these sparse records of the decay of the North African Church. A Muhammadan traveller,[3] who visited al-Jarīd, the southern district of Tunis, in the early part of the fourteenth century, tells us that the Christian churches, although in ruins, were still standing in his day, not having been destroyed by the Arab conquerors, who had contented themselves with building a mosque in front of each of these churches. Ibn Khaldūn (writing towards the close of the fourteenth century), speaks of some villages in the province of Qastīliyyah,[4] with a Christian population whose ancestors had lived there since the time of the Arab conquest.[5] At the end of the following century there was still to be found in the city of Tunis a small community of native Christians, living together in one of the suburbs, quite distinct from that in which the foreign Christian merchants resided; far from being oppressed or persecuted, they were employed as the bodyguard of the Sultan.[6] These were doubtless

[1] C. Trumelet: Les Saints de l'Islam, pp. xxviii–xxxvi.

[2] Leo Africanus says that at the end of the fifteenth century all the mountaineers of Algeria and of Buggia, though Muhammadans, painted black crosses on their cheeks and palms of the hand (Ramusio, i. p. 61); similarly the Banū Mzab to the present day still keep up some religious observances corresponding to excommunication and confession (Oppel, p. 299), and some nomad tribes of the Sahara observe the practice of a kind of baptism and use the cross as a decoration for their stuffs and weapons. (De Mas Latrie (2), p. 8.)

[3] Tijānī, p. 203.

[4] The modern Touzer, in Tunis.

[5] Ta'rīkh al-duwal al-islāmiyyah bi'l maghrib, I. p. 146. (ed. De Slane. Alger, 1847.)

[6] Leo Africanus. (Ramusio, tom. i. p. 67.)

the same persons as were congratulated on their perseverance in the Christian faith by Charles V after the capture of Tunis in 1535.[1]

This is the last we hear of the native Christian Church in North Africa. The very fact of its so long survival would militate against any supposition of forced conversion, even if we had not abundant evidence of the tolerant spirit of the Arab rulers of the various North African kingdoms, who employed Christian soldiers,[2] granted by frequent treaties the free exercise of their religion to Christian merchants and settlers,[3] and to whom Popes [4] recommended the care of the native Christian population, while exhorting the latter to serve their Muhammadan rulers faithfully.[5]

1 Pavy, vol. i. p. vii.
2 De Mas Latrie (2), pp. 61–2, 266–7. L. del Marmol-Caravajal: De l'Afrique, tome ii. p. 54. (Paris, 1667.)
3 De Mas Latrie (2), p. 192.
4 e.g. Innocent III, Gregory VII, Gregory IX and Innocent IV.
5 De Mas Latrie (2), p. 273.

CHAPTER V.

THE SPREAD OF ISLAM AMONG THE CHRISTIANS OF SPAIN.

IN 711 the victorious Arabs introduced Islam into Spain: in 1502 an edict of Ferdinand and Isabella forbade the exercise of the Muhammadan religion throughout the kingdom. During the centuries that elapsed between these two dates, Muslim Spain had written one of the brightest pages in the history of mediæval Europe. Her influence had passed through Provence into the other countries of Europe, bringing into birth a new poetry and a new culture, and it was from her that Christian scholars received what of Greek philosophy and science they had to stimulate their mental activity up to the time of the Renaissance. But these triumphs of the civilised life—art and poetry, science and philosophy—we must pass over here and fix our attention on the religious condition of Spain under the Muslim rule.

When the Muhammadans first brought their religion into Spain they found Catholic Christianity firmly established after its conquest over Arianism. The sixth Council of Toledo had enacted that all kings were to swear that they would not suffer the exercise of any other religion but the Catholic, and would vigorously enforce the law against all dissentients, while a subsequent law forbade any one under pain of confiscation of his property and perpetual imprisonment, to call in question the Holy Catholic and Apostolic Church, the Evangelical Institutions, the definitions of the Fathers, the decrees of the Church, and the Holy Sacraments. The clergy had gained for their order a preponderating influence in the affairs of the state;[1] the bishops and chief

[1] Baudissin, p. 22.

ecclesiastics sat in the national councils, which met to settle the most important business of the realm, ratified the election of the king and claimed the right to depose him if he refused to abide by their decrees. The Christian clergy took advantage of their power to persecute the Jews, who formed a very large community in Spain; edicts of a brutally severe character were passed against such as refused to be baptised;[1] and they consequently hailed the invading Arabs as their deliverers from such cruel oppression, they garrisoned the captured cities on behalf of the conqueror and opened the gates of towns that were being besieged.[2]

The Muhammadans received as warm a welcome from the slaves, whose condition under the Gothic rule was a very miserable one, and whose knowledge of Christianity was too superficial to have any weight when compared with the liberty and numerous advantages they gained, by throwing in their lot with the Muslims.

These down-trodden slaves were the first converts to Islam in Spain. The remnants of the heathen population of which we find mention as late as A.D. 693,[3] probably followed their example. Many of the Christian nobles, also, whether from genuine conviction or from other motives, embraced the new creed.[4] Many converts were won, too, from the lower and middle classes, who may well have embraced Islam, not merely outwardly, but from genuine conviction, turning to it from a religion whose ministers had left them ill-instructed and uncared for, and busied with worldly ambitions had plundered and oppressed their flocks.[5] Having once become Muslims, these Spanish converts showed themselves zealous adherents of their adopted faith, and they and their children joined themselves to the Puritan party of the rigid Muhammadan theologians as against the careless and luxurious life of the Arab aristocracy.[6]

At the time of the Muhammadan conquest the old Gothic virtues are said by Christian historians to have declined

[1] Helfferich, p. 68.
[2] Makkarī, vol. i. pp. 280–2.
[3] Baudissin, p. 7.
[4] Dozy (2), tome ii. pp. 45–6.
[5] A. Müller, vol. ii. p. 463.
[6] Dozy (2), tome ii. pp. 44–6.

and given place to effeminacy and corruption, so that the Muhammadan rule appeared to them to be a punishment sent from God on those who had gone astray into the paths of vice;[1] but such a statement is too frequent a commonplace of the ecclesiastical historian to be accepted in the absence of contemporary evidence.[2]

But certainly as time went on, matters do not seem to have mended themselves; and when Christian bishops took part in the revels of the Muhammadan court, when episcopal sees were put up to auction and persons suspected to be atheists appointed as shepherds of the faithful, and these in their turn bestowed the office of the priesthood on low and unworthy persons,[3] we may well suppose that it was not only in the province of Elvira[4] that Christians turned from a religion, the corrupt lives of whose ministers had brought it into discredit,[5] and sought a more congenial atmosphere for the moral and spiritual life in the pale of Islam.

Had ecclesiastical writers cared to chronicle them, Spain would doubtless be found to offer instances of many a man leaving the Christian Church like Bodo, a deacon at the French court in the reign of Louis the Pious, who in A.D. 838 became a Jew, in order that (as he said), forsaking his sinful life, he might "abide steadfast in the law of the Lord."[6]

[1] So St. Boniface (A.D. 745, Epist. lxii.). "Sicut aliis gentibus Hispaniæ et Provinciæ et Burgundionum populis contigit, quæ sic a Deo recedentes fornicatæ sunt, donec index omnipotens talium criminum ultrices pœnas per ignorantiam legis Dei et per Saracenos venire et sævire permisit." (Migne: Patr. Lat., tom. lxxxix. p. 761.) Eulogius: lib. i. § 30. "In cuius (i.e. gentis Saracenicæ) ditione nostro compellente facinore sceptrum Hispaniæ translatum est." (Migne: Patr. Lat., tom. cxv. p. 761.) Similarly Alvar (2), § 18. "Et probare nostro vitio inlatum intentabo flagellum. Nostra hæc, fratres, nostra desidia peperit mala, nostra impuritas, nostra levitas, nostra morum obscœnitas . . . unde tradidit nos Dominus qui iustitiam diligit, et cuius vultus æquitatem decernit, ipsi bestiæ conrodendos" (pp. 531–2).

[2] Dozy (3), tome i. pp. 15–20. Whishaw, pp. 38, 44.

[3] Samson, pp. 377–8, 381.

[4] Dozy (2), tome ii. p. 210.

[5] Bishop Egila, who was sent to Southern Spain by Pope Hadrian I, towards the end of the eighth century, on a mission to counteract the growing influence of Muslim thought, denounces the Spanish priests who lived in concubinage with married women. (Helfferich, p. 83.)

[6] Alvari Cordubensis, Epist. xix. "Ob meritum æternæ retributionis devovi me sedulum in lege Domini consistere." (Migne: Patr. Lat., tom. cxxi. p. 512.)

It is very possible, too, that the lingering remains of the old Gothic Arianism—of which, indeed, there had been some slight revival in the Spanish Church just before the Arab conquest [1]—may have predisposed men's minds to accept the new faith whose Christology was in such close agreement with Arian doctrine,[2] and a later age may have witnessed parallels to that change of faith which is the earliest recorded instance of conversion to Islam in western Europe and occurred before the Arab invasion of Spain—namely the conversion of a Greek named Theodisclus, who succeeded St. Isidore (ob. A.D. 636) as Archbishop of Seville; he was accused of heresy, for maintaining that Jesus was not one God in unity with the Father and the Holy Spirit, but was rather Son of God by adoption; he was accordingly condemned by an ecclesiastical synod, deprived of his archbishopric and degraded from the priesthood. Whereupon he went over to the Arabs and embraced Islam among them.[3]

Of forced conversion or anything like persecution in the early days of the Arab conquest, we hear nothing. Indeed, it was probably in a great measure their tolerant attitude towards the Christian religion that facilitated their rapid acquisition of the country. The only complaint that the Christians could bring against their new rulers for treating them differently to their non-Christian subjects, was that they had to pay the usual capitation-tax of forty-eight dirhams for the rich, twenty-four for the middle classes, and twelve for those who made their living by manual labour: this, as being in lieu of military service, was levied only on the able-bodied males, for women, children, monks, the halt, and the blind, and the sick, mendicants and slaves were exempted therefrom; [4] it must moreover have appeared

[1] Helfferich, pp. 79–80.

[2] "Bedenkt man nun, wie wichtig gerade die alttestamentliche Idee des Prophetenthums in der Christologie des germanischen Arianismus nachklang und auch nach der Annahme des katholischen Dogmas in dem religiösen Bewusstsein der Westgothen haften blieb, so wird man es sehr erklärlich finden, dass unmittelbar nach dem Einfall der Araber die verwandten Vorstellungen des Mohammedanismus unter den geknechteten Christen auftauchten." (Helfferich, p. 82.)

[3] Lucæ Diaconi Tudensis Chronicon Mundi. (Andreas Schottus: Hispaniæ Illustratæ, tom. iv. p. 53.) (Francofurti, 1603–8.)

[4] Dozy (2), tome ii. p. 41. Whishaw, p. 17.

the less oppressive as being collected by the Christian officials themselves.[1]

Except in the case of offences against the Muslim religious law, the Christians were tried by their own judges and in accordance with their own laws.[2] They were left undisturbed in the exercise of their religion;[3] the sacrifice of the mass was offered, with the swinging of censers, the ringing of the bell, and all the other solemnities of the Catholic ritual; the psalms were chanted in the choir, sermons preached to the people, and the festivals of the Church observed in the usual manner. They do not appear to have been condemned, like their co-religionists in Syria and Egypt, to wear a distinctive dress as sign of their humiliation, and in the ninth century at least, the Christian laity wore the same kind of costume as the Arabs.[4] They were at one time even allowed to build new churches.[5]

We read also of the founding[6] of several fresh monasteries in addition to the numerous convents both for monks and nuns that flourished undisturbed by the Muhammadan rulers. The monks could appear publicly in the woollen robes of their order and the priest had no need to conceal the mark of his sacred office,[7] nor at the same time did their religious profession prevent the Christians from being entrusted with high offices at court,[8] or serving in the Muslim armies.[9]

[1] Dozy (2), tome ii. p. 39.

[2] Baudissin, pp. 11–13, 196.

[3] Eulogius: Mem. Sanct., lib. i. § 30, "inter ipsos sine molestia fidei degimus" (p. 761). Id., ib., lib. i. § 18, "Quos nulla præsidialis violentia fidem suam negare compulit, nec a cultu sanctæ piæque religionis amovit" (p. 751). John of Gorz (who visited Spain about the middle of the tenth century) § 124, "(Christiani), qui in regno eius libere divinis suisque rebus utebantur."

A Spanish bishop thus described the condition of the Christians to John of Gorz. "Peccatis ad hæc devoluti sumus, ut paganorum subiaceamus ditioni. Resistere potestati verbo prohibemur apostoli. Tantum hoc unum relictum est solatii, quod in tantæ calamitatis malo legibus nos propriis uti non prohibent; qui quos diligentes Christianitatis viderint observatores, colunt et amplectuntur, simul ipsorum convictu delectantur. Pro tempore igitur hoc videmur tenere consilii, ut quia religionis nulla infertur iactura, cetera eis obsequamur, iussisque eorum in quantum fidem non impediunt obtemperemus" § 122 (p. 302).

[4] Baudissin, pp. 16–17.

[5] Eulogius, ob. 859 (Mem. Sanct. lib. iii. c 3) speaks of churches recently erected (ecclesias nuper structas). The chronicle falsely ascribed to Luitprand records the erection of a church at Cordova in 895 (p. 1113).

[6] Eulogius: Mem. Sanct., lib. iii. c. 11 (p. 812).

[7] Baudissin, p. 16.

[8] Id. p. 21, and John of Gorz, § 128 (p. 306).

[9] Whishaw, pp. 272, 301.

Certainly those Christians who could reconcile themselves to the loss of political power had little to complain of, and it is very noticeable that during the whole of the eighth century we hear of only one attempt at revolt on their part, namely at Beja, and in this they appear to have followed the lead of an Arab chief.[1] Those who migrated into French territory in order that they might live under a Christian rule, certainly fared no better than the co-religionists they had left behind. In 812 Charlemagne interfered to protect the exiles who had followed him on his retreat from Spain from the exactions of the imperial officers. Three years later Louis the Pious had to issue another edict on their behalf, in spite of which they had soon again to complain against the nobles who robbed them of the lands that had been assigned to them. But the evil was only checked for a little time to break out afresh, and all the edicts passed on their behalf did not avail to make the lot of these unfortunate exiles more tolerable, and in the Cagots (i. e. *canes Gothi*), a despised and ill-treated class of later times, we probably meet again the Spanish colony that fled away from Muslim rule to throw themselves upon the mercy of their Christian co-religionists.[2]

The toleration of the Muhammadan government towards its Christian subjects in Spain and the freedom of intercourse between the adherents of the two religions brought about a certain amount of assimilation in the two communities. Inter-marriages became frequent;[3] Isidore of Beja, who fiercely inveighs against the Muslim conquerors, records the marriage of 'Abd al-'Azīz, the son of Mūsā, with the widow of King Roderic, without a word of blame.[4] Many of the Christians adopted Arab names, and in outward observances imitated to some extent their Muhammadan neighbours, e.g. many were circumcised,[5] and in matters

[1] Dozy (2), tome ii. p. 42.

[2] Baudissin, pp. 96–7.

[3] See the letter of Pope Hadrian I to the Spanish bishops: "Porro diversa capitula quæ ex illis audivimus partibus, id est, quod multi dicentes se catholicos esse, communem vitam gerentes cum Iudæis et non baptizatis paganis, tam in escis quamque in potu et in diversis erroribus nihil pollui se inquiunt: et illud quod inhibitum est, ut nulli liceat iugum ducere cum infidelibus, ipsi enim filias suas cum alio benedicent, et sic populo gentili tradentur." (Migne: Patr. Lat., tome xcviii. p. 385.)

[4] Isidori Pacensis Chronicon, § 42 (p. 1266).

[5] Alvar: Indic. Lum., § 35 (p. 53). John of Gorz, § 123 (p. 303).

of food and drink followed the practice of the "unbaptized pagans." [1]

The very term Muzarabes (i.e. must aribīn or Arabicised) applied to the Spanish Christians living under Arab rule, is significant of the tendencies that were at work. The study of Arabic very rapidly began to displace that of Latin throughout the country,[2] so that the language of Christian theology came gradually to be neglected and forgotten. Even some of the higher clergy rendered themselves ridiculous by their ignorance of correct Latinity.[3] It could hardly be expected that the laity would exhibit more zeal in such a matter than the clergy, and in 854 a Spanish writer brings the following complaint against his Christian fellow-countrymen :—"While we are investigating their (i.e. the Muslim) sacred ordinances and meeting together to study the sects of their philosophers—or rather philo-braggers—not for the purpose of refuting their errors, but for the exquisite charm and for the eloquence and beauty of their language—neglecting the reading of the Scriptures, we are but setting up as an idol the number of the beast. (Apoc. xiii. 18.) Where nowadays can we find any learned layman who, absorbed in the study of the Holy Scriptures, cares to look at the works of any of the Latin Fathers? Who is there with any zeal for the writings of the Evangelists, or the Prophets, or Apostles? Our Christian young men, with their elegant airs and fluent speech, are showy in their dress and carriage, and are famed for the learning of the gentiles; intoxicated with Arab eloquence they greedily handle, eagerly devour and zealously discuss the books of the Chaldeans (i.e. Muhammadans), and make them known by praising them with every flourish of rhetoric, knowing nothing of the beauty of the Church's literature, and looking down with contempt on the streams of the Church that flow forth from Paradise; alas! the Christians are so ignorant

[1] Letter of Hadrian I, p. 385. John of Gorz, § 123 (p. 303).

[2] Some Arabic verses of a Christian poet of the eleventh century are still extant, which exhibit considerable skill in handling the language and metre. (Von Schack, II. 95.)

[3] Abbot Samson gives us specimens of the bad Latin written by some of the ecclesiastics of his time, e.g. "Cum contempti essemus simplicitas christiana," but his correction is hardly much better, "contenti essemus simplicitati christianæ" (pp. 404, 406).

of their own law, the Latins pay so little attention to their own language, that in the whole Christian flock there is hardly one man in a thousand who can write a letter to inquire after a friend's health intelligibly, while you may find a countless rabble of all kinds of them who can learnedly roll out the grandiloquent periods of the Chaldean tongue. They can even make poems, every line ending with the same letter, which display high flights of beauty and more skill in handling metre than the gentiles themselves possess."[1]

In fact the knowledge of Latin so much declined in one part of Spain that it was found necessary to translate the ancient Canons of the Spanish Church and the Bible into Arabic for the use of the Christians.[2]

While the brilliant literature of the Arabs exercised such a fascination and was so zealously studied, those who desired an education in Christian literature had little more than the materials that had been employed in the training of the barbaric Goths, and could with difficulty find teachers to induct them even into this low level of culture. As time went on this want of Christian education increased more and more. In 1125 the Muzarabes wrote to King Alfonso of Aragon: "We and our fathers have up to this time been brought up among the gentiles, and having been baptised, freely observe the Christian ordinances; but we have never had it in our power to be fully instructed in our divine religion; for, subject as we are to the infidels who have long oppressed us, we have never ventured to ask for teachers from Rome or France; and they have never come to us of their own accord on account of the barbarity of the heathen whom we obey."[3]

From such close intercourse with the Muslims and so diligent a study of their literature—when we find even so bigoted an opponent of Islam as Alvar[4] acknowledging that the Qur'ān was composed in such eloquent and beautiful language that even Christians could not help reading and

[1] Alvar: Indic. Lum., § 35 (pp. 554–6).

[2] Von Schack, vol. ii. p. 96.

[3] Orderic Vitalis, p. 928.

[4] Alvar: Ind. Lum., § 29. "Compositionem verborum, et preces omnium eius membrorum quotidie pro eo eleganti facundia, et venusto confectas eloquio, nos hodie per eorum volumina et oculis legimus et plerumque miramur." (Migne: Patr. Lat., tome cxxi. p. 546.)

admiring it—we should naturally expect to find signs of a religious influence : and such indeed is the case. Elipandus, bishop of Toledo (ob. 810), an exponent of the heresy of Adoptionism—according to which the Man Christ Jesus was Son of God by adoption and not by nature—is expressly said to have arrived at these heretical views through his frequent and close intercourse with the Muhammadans.[1] This new doctrine appears to have spread quickly over a great part of Spain, while it was successfully propagated in Septimania, which was under French protection, by Felix, bishop of Urgel in Catalonia.[2] Felix was brought before a council, presided over by Charlemagne, and made to abjure his error, but on his return to Spain he relapsed into his old heresy, doubtless (as was suggested by Pope Leo III at the time) owing to his intercourse with the pagans (meaning thereby the Muhammadans) who held similar views.[3] When prominent churchmen were so profoundly influenced by their contact with Muhammadans, we may judge that the influence of Islam upon the Christians of Spain was very considerable, indeed in A.D. 936 a council was held at Toledo to consider the best means of preventing this intercourse from contaminating the purity of the Christian faith.[4]

It may readily be understood how these influences of Islamic thought and practice—added to definite efforts at conversion [5]—would lead to much more than a mere approximation and would very speedily swell the number of the converts to Islam so that their descendants, the so-called Muwallads—a term denoting those not of Arab blood—soon formed a large and important party in the state, indeed the majority of the population of the country,[6] and as early

[1] Enhueber, § 26, p. 353.

[2] Helfferich, p. 88.

[3] "Postmodum transgressus legem Dei, fugiens ad paganos consentaneos, periuratus effectus est." Frobenii dissertatio de hæresi Elipandi et Felicis, § xxiv. (Migne : Patr. Lat., tome ci. p. 313.)

[4] Pseudo-Luitprandi Chronicon, § 341 (p. 1115). "Basilius Toletanum concilium contrahit; quo providetur, ne Christiani detrimentum acciperent convictu Saracenorum."

[5] There is little record of such, but they seem referred to in the following sentences of Eulogius (Liber Apologeticus Martyrum, § 20), on Muḥammad : "Cuius quidem erroris insaniam, prædicationis deliramenta, et impiæ novitatis præcepta quisquis catholicorum cognoscere cupit, evidentius ab eiusdem sectæ cultoribus perscrutando advertet. Quoniam sacrum se quidpiam tenere et credere autumantes, non modo privatis, sed apertis vocibus vatis sui dogmata prædicant." (Migne : Patr. Lat., tome cxv. p. 862.)

[6] Dozy (2), tome ii. p. 53.

as the beginning of the ninth century we read of attempts made by them to shake off the Arab rule, and on several occasions later they come forward actively as a national party of Spanish Muslims.

We have little or no details of the history of the conversion of these New-Muslims. Instances appeared to have occurred right up to the last days of Muslim rule, for when the army of Ferdinand and Isabella captured Malaga in 1487, it is recorded that all the renegade Christians found in the city were tortured to death with sharp-pointed reeds, and in the capitulation that secured the submission of Purchena two years later, an express promise was made that renegades would not be forced to return to Christianity.[1] Some few apostatised to escape the payment of some penalty inflicted by the law-courts.[2] But the majority of the converts were no doubt won over by the imposing influence of the faith of Islam itself, presented to them as it was with all the glamour of a brilliant civilisation, having a poetry, a philosophy and an art well calculated to attract the reason and dazzle the imagination : while in the lofty chivalry of the Arabs there was free scope for the exhibition of manly prowess and the knightly virtues—a career closed to the conquered Spaniards that remained true to the Christian faith. Again, the learning and literature of the Christians must have appeared very poor and meagre when compared with that of the Muslims, the study of which may well by itself have served as an incentive to the adoption of their religion. Besides, to the devout mind Islam in Spain could offer the attractions of a pious and zealous Puritan party with the orthodox Muslim theologians at its head, which at times had a preponderating influence in the state and struggled earnestly towards a reformation of faith and morals.

Taking into consideration the ardent religious feeling that animated the mass of the Spanish Muslims and the provocation that the Christians gave to the Muhammadan government through their treacherous intrigues with their co-religionists over the border, the history of Spain under Muhammadan rule is singularly free from persecution.

[1] Lea, The Moriscos, pp. 17, 18.

[2] Samson, p. 379.

With the exception of three or four cases of genuine martyrdom, the only approach to anything like persecution during the whole period of the Arab rule is to be found in the severe measures adopted by the Muhammadan government to repress the madness for voluntary martyrdom that broke out in Cordova in the ninth century. At this time a fanatical party came into existence among the Christians in this part of Spain (for apparently the Christian Church in the rest of the country had no sympathy with the movement), which set itself openly and unprovokedly to insult the religion of the Muslims and blaspheme their Prophet, with the deliberate intention of incurring the penalty of death by such misguided assertion of their Christian bigotry.

This strange passion for self-immolation displayed itself mainly among priests, monks and nuns between the years 850 and 860. It would seem that brooding, in the silence of their cloisters, over the decline of Christian influence and the decay of religious zeal, they went forth to win the martyr's crown—of which the toleration of their infidel rulers was robbing them—by means of fierce attacks on Islam and its founder. Thus, for example, a certain monk, by name Isaac, came before the Qāḍī and pretended that he wished to be instructed in the faith of Islam; when the Qāḍī had expounded to him the doctrines of the Prophet, he burst out with the words: "He hath lied unto you (may the curse of God consume him!), who, full of wickedness, hath led so many men into perdition, and doomed them with himself to the pit of hell. Filled with Satan and practising Satanic jugglery, he hath given you a cup of deadly wine to work disease in you, and will expiate his guilt with everlasting damnation. Why do ye not, being endowed with understanding, deliver yourselves from such dangers? Why do ye not, renouncing the ulcer of his pestilential doctrines, seek the eternal salvation of the Gospel of the faith of Christ?"[1] On another occasion two Christians forced their way into a mosque and there reviled the Muhammadan religion, which, they declared, would very speedily bring upon its followers the destruction of hell-fire.[2] Though

[1] Eulogius: Mem. Sanct. Pref., § 2. (Migne, tom. cxv. p. 737.)
[2] Id. c. xiii. (p. 794).

the number of such fanatics was not considerable,[1] the Muhammadan government grew alarmed, fearing that such contempt for their authority and disregard of their laws against blasphemy, argued a widespread disaffection and a possible general insurrection, for in fact, in 853 Muḥammad I had to send an army against the Christians at Toledo, who, incited by Eulogius, the chief apologist of the martyrs, had risen in revolt on the news of the sufferings of their co-religionists.[2] He is said to have ordered a general massacre of the Christians, but when it was pointed out that no men of any intelligence or rank among the Christians had taken part in such doings[3] (for Alvar himself complains that the majority of the Christian priests condemned the martyrs[4]), the king contented himself with putting into force the existing laws against blasphemy with the utmost rigour. The moderate party in the Church seconded the efforts of the government; the bishops anathematised the fanatics, and an ecclesiastical council that was held in 852 to discuss the matter agreed upon methods of repression[5] that eventually quashed the movement. One or two isolated cases of martyrdom are recorded later—the last in 983, after which there was none as long as the Arab rule lasted in Spain.[6]

But under the Berber dynasty of the Almoravids at the

[1] The number of the martyrs is said not to have exceeded forty. (W. H. Prescott: History of the Reign of Ferdinand and Isabella, vol. i. p. 342, n.) (London 1846.)

[2] Dozy (2), tome ii. pp. 161–2.

[3] Eulogius: Mem. Sanct. I, iii. c. vii. (p. 805). "Pro eo quod nullus sapiens, nemo urbanus, nullusque procerum Christianorum huiusce modi rem perpetrasset, idcirco non debere universos perimere asserebant, quos non præit personalis dux ad prælium."

[4] Alvar: Ind. Lum., § 14. "Nonne ipsi qui videbantur columnæ, qui putabantur Ecclesiæ petræ, qui credebantur electi, nullo cogente, nemine provocante, iudicem adierunt, et in præsentia Cynicorum, imo Epicureorum, Dei martyres infamaverunt? Nonne pastores Christi, doctores Ecclesiæ, episcopi, abbates, presbyteri, proceres et magnati, hæreticos eos esse publice clamaverunt? et publica professione sine desquisitione, absque interrogatione, quæ nec imminente mortis sententia erant dicenda, spontanea voluntate, et libero mentis arbitrio, protulerunt?" (Migne: tom. cxxi. p. 529.)

[5] Alvar: Indic. Lum., § 15. "Quid obtendendum est de illis quos ecclesiastice interdiximus, et a quibus ne aliquando ad martyrii surgerent palmam iuramentum extorsimus? quibus errores gentilium infringere vetuimus, et maledictum ne maledictionibus impeterent? Evangelio et cruce educta vi iurare improbiter fecimus, imo feraliter et belluino terrore coegimus, minantes inaudita supplicia, et monstruosa promittentes truncationum membrorum varia et horrenda dictu audituve flagella?" (Migne: tom. cxxi. p. 530.)

[6] Baudissin, p. 199.

beginning of the twelfth century, there was an outburst of fanaticism on the part of the theological zealots of Islam in which the Christians had to suffer along with the Jews and the liberal section of the Muhammadan population—the philosophers, the poets and the men of letters. But such incidents are exceptions to the generally tolerant character of the Muhammadan rulers of Spain towards their Christian subjects.

One of the Spanish Muhammadans who was driven out of his native country in the last expulsion of the Moriscoes in 1610, while protesting against the persecutions of the Inquisition, makes the following vindication of the toleration of his co-religionists: "Did our victorious ancestors ever once attempt to extirpate Christianity out of Spain, when it was in their power? Did they not suffer your forefathers to enjoy the free use of their rites at the same time that they wore their chains? Is not the absolute injunction of our Prophet, that whatever nation is conquered by Musalman steel, should, upon the payment of a moderate annual tribute, be permitted to persevere in their own pristine persuasion, how absurd soever, or to embrace what other belief they themselves best approved of? If there may have been some examples of forced conversions, they are so rare as scarce to deserve mentioning, and only attempted by men who had not the fear of God, and the Prophet, before their eyes, and who, in so doing, have acted directly and diametrically contrary to the holy precepts and ordinances of Islam which cannot, without sacrilege, be violated by any who would be held worthy of the honourable epithet of Musulman. . . . You can never produce, among us, any bloodthirsty, formal tribunal, on account of different persuasions in points of faith, that anywise approaches your execrable Inquisition. Our arms, it is true, are ever open to receive all who are disposed to embrace our religion; but we are not allowed by our sacred Qur'ān to tyrannise over consciences. Our proselytes have all imaginable encouragement, and have no sooner professed God's Unity and His Apostle's mission but they become one of us, without reserve; taking to wife our daughters, and being employed in posts of trust, honour and profit; we contenting ourselves with only obliging them to wear our habit, and to seem true believers in outward appearance, without ever offering to examine their consciences, provided they do not openly revile or profane our religion: if they do that, we indeed punish them as they deserve; since their conversion was voluntarily, and was not by compulsion."[1]

This very spirit of toleration was made one of the main articles in an account of the "Apostacies and Treasons of the Moriscoes," drawn up by the Archbishop of Valencia in 1602 when recommending their expulsion to Philip III, as follows: "That they commended nothing so much as that liberty of conscience, in all matters of religion, which the Turks, and all other Muhammadans, suffer their subjects to enjoy."[2]

What deep roots Islam had struck in the hearts of the Spanish people may be judged from the fact that when the last remnant of the Moriscoes was expelled from Spain in 1610, these unfortunate people still clung to the faith of their fathers, although for more than a century they had been forced to outwardly conform to the Christian religion, and in spite of the emigrations that had taken place since the fall of Granada, nearly 500,000 are said to have been expelled at that time.[3] Whole towns and villages were deserted and the houses fell into ruins, there being no one to rebuild them.[4] These Moriscoes were probably all descendants of the original inhabitants of the country, with little or no admixture of Arab blood; the reasons that may be adduced in support of this statement are too lengthy to be given here; one point only in the evidence may be mentioned, derived from a letter written in 1311, in which it is stated that of the 200,000 Muhammadans then living in the city of Granada, not more than 500 were of Arab descent, all the rest being descendants of converted Spaniards.[5] Finally, it is of interest to note that even up to the last days of its power in Spain, Islam won converts to the faith, for the historian, when writing of events that occurred in the year 1499, seven years after the fall of Granada, draws attention to the fact that among the Moors were a few Christians who had lately embraced the faith of the Prophet.[6]

[1] Morgan, vol. ii. pp. 297–8, 345.
[2] Id. p. 310.
[3] Lea, The Moriscos, p. 259.
[4] Morgan, vol. ii. p. 337.
[5] Id. p. 289.
[6] Stirling-Maxwell, vol. i. p. 115.

CHAPTER VI.

THE SPREAD OF ISLAM AMONG THE CHRISTIAN NATIONS IN EUROPE UNDER THE TURKS.

WE first hear of the Ottoman Turks at the commencement of the thirteenth century, when fleeing before the Mongols, to the number of about 50,000, they came to the help of the Sultan of Iconium, and in return for their services both against the Mongols and the Greeks, had assigned to them a district in the north-west of Asia Minor. This was the nucleus of the future Ottoman empire, which, increasing at first by the absorption of the petty states into which the Saljūq Turks had split up, afterwards crossed over into Europe, annexing kingdom after kingdom, until its victorious growth received a check before the gates of Vienna in 1683.[1]

From the earliest days of the extension of their kingdom in Asia Minor, the Ottomans exercised authority over Christian subjects, but it was not until the ancient capital of the Eastern empire fell into their hands in 1453 that the relations between the Muslim Government and the Christian Church were definitely established on a fixed basis. One of the first steps taken by Muḥammad II, after the capture of Constantinople and the re-establishment of order in that

[1] This is no place to give a history of these territorial acquisitions, which may be briefly summed up thus. In 1353 the Ottoman Turks first passed over into Europe and a few years later Adrianople was made their European capital. Under Bāyazīd (1389–1402), their dominions stretched from the Ægæan to the Danube, embracing all Bulgaria, Macedonia, Thessaly and Thrace, with the exception of Chalkidike and the district just round Constantinople. Murād II (1421–1451) occupied Chalkidike and pushed his conquests to the Adriatic. Muḥammad II (1451–1481) by the overthrow of Constantinople, Albania, Bosnia and Servia, became master of the whole South-Eastern peninsula, with the exception of the parts of the coast held by Venice and Montenegro. Sulaymān II (1520–1566) added Hungary and made the Ægæan an Ottoman sea. In the seventeenth century Crete was won and Podolia ceded by Poland.

city, was to secure the allegiance of the Christians, by proclaiming himself the protector of the Greek Church. Persecution of the Christians was strictly forbidden; a decree was granted to the newly elected patriarch which secured to him and his successors and the bishops under him, the enjoyment of the old privileges, revenues and exemptions enjoyed under the former rule. Gennadios, the first patriarch after the Turkish conquest, received from the hands of the Sultan himself the pastoral staff, which was the sign of his office, together with a purse of a thousand golden ducats and a horse with gorgeous trappings, on which he was privileged to ride with his train through the city.[1] But not only was the head of the Church treated with all the respect he had been accustomed to receive from the Christian emperors, but further he was invested with extensive civil power. The patriarch's court sat to decide all cases between Greek and Greek: it could impose fines, imprison offenders in a prison provided for its own special use, and in some cases even condemn to capital punishment: while the ministers and officials of the government were directed to enforce its judgments. The complete control of spiritual and ecclesiastical matters (in which the Turkish government, unlike the civil power of the Byzantine empire, never interfered), was left entirely in his hands and those of the grand Synod which he could summon whenever he pleased; and hereby he could decide all matters of faith and dogma without fear of interference on the part of the state. As a recognised officer of the imperial government, he could do much for the alleviation of the oppressed, by bringing the acts of unjust governors to the notice of the Sultan. The Greek bishops in the provinces in their turn were treated with great consideration and were entrusted with so much jurisdiction in civil affairs, that up to modern times they have acted in their dioceses almost as if they were Ottoman prefects over the orthodox population, thus taking the place of the old Christian aristocracy which had been exterminated by the conquerors, and we find that the higher clergy were generally more active as Turkish agents than as Greek priests, and they always taught their people that the Sultan

[1] Phrantzes, pp. 305–6.

possessed a divine sanction, as the protector of the Orthodox Church. A charter was subsequently published, securing to the orthodox the use of such churches as had not been confiscated to form mosques, and authorising them to celebrate their religious rites publicly according to their national usages.[1]

Consequently, though the Greeks were numerically superior to the Turks in all the European provinces of the empire, the religious toleration thus granted them, and the protection of life and property they enjoyed, soon reconciled them to the change of masters and led them to prefer the domination of the Sultan to that of any Christian power. Indeed, in many parts of the country, the Ottoman conquerors were welcomed by the Greeks as their deliverers from the rapacious and tyrannous rule of the Franks and the Venetians who had so long disputed with Byzantium for the possession of the Peloponnesos and some of the adjacent parts of Greece; by introducing into Greece the feudal system, these had reduced the people to the miserable condition of serfs, and as aliens in speech, race and creed, were hated by their subjects,[2] to whom a change of rulers, since it could not make their condition worse, would offer a possible chance of improving it, and though their deliverers were likewise aliens, yet the infidel Turk was infinitely to be preferred to the heretical Catholics.[3] The Greeks who lived under the immediate government of the Byzantine court, were equally unlikely to be averse to a change of rulers. The degradation and tyranny that characterised

[1] Finlay, vol. iii. p. 522. Pitzipios, seconde partie, p. 75. M. d'Ohsson, vol. iii. p. 52–4. Arminjon, vol. i. p. 16.

[2] A traveller who visited Cyprus in 1508 draws the following picture of the tyranny of the Venetians in their foreign possessions: "All the inhabitants of Cyprus are slaves to the Venetians, being obliged to pay to the state a third part of all their increase or income, whether the product of their ground or corn, wine, oil, or of their cattle, or any other thing. Besides, every man of them is bound to work for the state two days of the week wherever they shall please to appoint him: and if any shall fail, by reason of some other business of their own, or for indisposition of body, then they are made to pay a fine for as many days as they are absent from their work: and which is more, there is yearly some tax or other imposed on them, with which the poor common people are so flead and pillaged that they hardly have wherewithal to keep soul and body together." (The Travels of Martin Baumgarten, p. 373.) See also the passages quoted by Hackett, History of the Orthodox Church of Cyprus, p. 183.

[3] Finlay, vol. iii. p. 502.

the dynasty of the Palæologi are frightful to contemplate. "A corrupt aristocracy, a tyrannical and innumerable clergy, the oppression of perverted law, the exactions of a despicable government, and still more, its monopolies, its fiscality, its armies of tax and custom collectors, left the degraded people neither rights nor institutions, neither chance of amelioration nor hope of redress."[1] Lest such a judgment appear dictated by a spirit of party bias, a contemporary authority may be appealed to in support of its correctness. The Russian annalists who speak of the fall of Constantinople bring a similar indictment against its government. "Without the fear of the law an empire is like a steed without reins. Constantine and his ancestors allowed their grandees to oppress the people; there was no more justice in their law courts; no more courage in their hearts; the judges amassed treasures from the tears and blood of the innocent; the Greek soldiers were proud only of the magnificence of their dress; the citizens did not blush at being traitors; the soldiers were not ashamed to fly. At length the Lord poured out His thunder on these unworthy rulers, and raised up Muḥammad, whose warriors delight in battle, and whose judges do not betray their trust."[2] This last item of praise[3] may sound strange in the ears of a generation that has constantly been called upon to protest against Turkish injustice; but it is clearly and abundantly borne out by the testimony of contemporary historians. The Byzantine historian who has handed down to us the story of the capture of Constantinople tells us how even the impetuous Bāyazīd was liberal and generous to his Christian subjects, and made himself extremely popular among them by admitting them freely to his society.[4] Murād II distinguished himself by his attention to the administration of justice and by his reforms of the abuses

[1] Urquhart, quoted by Clark: Races of European Turkey, p. 82.
[2] Karamsin, vol. v. p. 437.
[3] Martin Crusius writes in the same spirit: "Et mirum est, inter barbaros, in tanta tantæ urbis colluvie, nullas cædes audiri, vim iniustam non ferri, ius cuivis dici. Ideo Constantinopolin Sultanus, Refugium totius orbis scribit: quod omnes miseri, ibi tutissime latent: quodque omnibus (tam infimis quam summis: tam Christianis quam infidelibus) iustitia administretur." (Turcogræcia, p. 487.) (Basileæ, 1584.)
[4] Phrantzes, p. 81.

prevalent under the Greek emperors, and punished without mercy those of his officials who oppressed any of his subjects.[1] For at least a century after the fall of Constantinople a series of able rulers secured, by a firm and vigorous administration, peace and order throughout their dominions, and an admirable civil and judicial organisation, if it did not provide an absolutely impartial justice for Muslims and Christians alike, yet caused the Greeks to be far better off than they had been before. They were harassed by fewer exactions of forced labour, extraordinary contributions were rarely levied, and the taxes they paid were a trifling burden compared with the endless feudal obligations of the Franks and the countless extortions of the Byzantines. The Turkish dominions were certainly better governed and more prosperous than most parts of Christian Europe, and the mass of the Christian population engaged in the cultivation of the soil enjoyed a larger measure of private liberty and of the fruits of their labour, under the government of the Sultan than their contemporaries did under that of many Christian monarchs.[2] A great impulse, too, was given to the commerical activity of the country, for the early Sultans were always ready to foster trade and commerce among their subjects, and many of the great cities entered upon an era of prosperity when the Turkish conquest had delivered them from the paralysing fiscal oppression of the Byzantine empire, one of the first of them being Nicæa, which capitulated to Urkhān in 1330 under the most favourable terms after a long-protracted siege.[3] Like the ancient Romans, the Ottomans were great makers of roads and bridges, and thereby facilitated trade throughout their empire; and foreign states were compelled to admit the Greek merchants into ports from which they had been excluded in the time of the Byzantine emperors, but now sailing under the Ottoman

[1] Phrantzes, p. 92.

[2] Finlay, vol. v. pp. 5, 123. Adeney, p. 311. Gerlach, writing in the year 1577, says: "Wo Christen oder Juden in den Orten wohnen, da es Kadi oder Richter und Subbassi oder Vögte hat, dass die gemeinen Türcken nicht ihres Gefallens mit ihnen umbgehen dörffen, sind sie viel lieber unter den Türcken, dann unter den Christen. Wann sie Jährlich ihren Tribut geben, sind sie hernach frey. Aber in der Christenheit ist das gantze Jahr des Gebens kein Ende." (Tage-Buch, p. 413.)

[3] Hertzberg, pp. 467, 646, 650.

flag, they assumed the dress and manners of Turks, and thus secured from the nations of Western Europe the respect and consideration which the Catholics had hitherto always refused to the members of the Greek Church.[1]

There is, however, one notable exception to this general good treatment and toleration, viz. the tribute of Christian children, who were forcibly taken from their parents at an early age and enrolled in the famous corps of Janissaries. Instituted by Urkhān in 1330, it formed for centuries the mainstay of the despotic power of the Turkish Sultans, and was kept alive by a regular contribution exacted every four years,[2] when the officers of the Sultan visited the districts on which the tax was imposed, and made a selection from among the children about the age of seven. The Muhammadan legists attempted to apologise for this inhuman tribute by representing these children as the fifth of the spoil which the Qur'ān assigns to the sovereign,[3] and they prescribed that the injunction against forcible conversion [4] should be observed with regard to them also, although the tender age at which they were placed under the instruction of Muslim teachers must have made it practically of none effect.[5] Christian Europe has always expressed its horror at such a barbarous tax, and travellers in the Turkish dominions have painted touching pictures of desolated homes and of parents weeping for the children torn from their arms. But when the corps was first instituted, its numbers were rapidly swelled by voluntary accessions from among the Christians themselves,[6] and the circumstances under which this tribute was first imposed may go far to explain the apathy which the Greeks themselves appear to

[1] Finlay, vol. v. pp. 156–7.

[2] This interval was, however, not a fixed one; at first, the levy took place every seven or five years, but later at more frequent intervals according to the exigencies of the state. (Menzel, p. 52.) Metrophanes Kritopoulos, writing in 1625, states that the collectors came to the cities every seventh year and that each city had to contribute three or four, or at least two boys (p. 205).

[3] Qur'ān, viii. 42.

[4] Id. x. 99. 100.

[5] "On ne forçait cependant pas les jeunes Chrétiens à changer de foi. Les principes du gouvernement s'y opposaient aussi bien que les préceptes du Cour'ann; et si des officiers, mus par leur fanatisme, usaient quelquefois de contrainte, leur conduite à cet égard pouvait bien être tolerée; mais elle n'était jamais autorisée par les chefs." (M. d'Ohsson, tome iii. pp. 397–8.)

[6] Hertzberg, p. 472.

have exhibited. The whole country had been laid waste by war, and families were often in danger of perishing with hunger; the children who were thus adopted were in many cases orphans, who would otherwise have been left to perish; further, the custom so widely prevalent at that time of selling Christians as slaves may have made this tax appear less appalling than might have been expected. This custom has, moreover, been maintained to have been only a continuation of a similar usage that was in force under the Byzantine emperors.[1] It has even been said that there was seldom any necessity of an appeal to force on the part of the officers who collected the appointed number of children, but rather that the parents were often eager to have their children enrolled in a service that secured for them in many cases a brilliant career, and under any circumstances a well-cared-for and comfortable existence, since these little captives were brought up and educated as if they were the Sultan's own children.[2] This institution appears in a less barbarous light if it be true that the parents could often redeem their children by a money payment.[3] Metrophanes Kritopoulos, who was Patriarch of Constantinople and afterwards of Alexandria, writing in 1625, mentions various devices adopted by the Christians for escaping from the burden of this tax, e.g. they purchased Muhammadan boys and represented them to be Christians, or they bribed the collectors to take Christian boys who were of low birth or had been badly brought up or such as "deserved hanging."[4]

[1] "Sed hoc tristissimum est, quod, ut olim Christiani imperatores, ex singulis oppidis, certum numerum liberorum, in quibus egregia indoles præ cæteris elucebat, delegerunt: quos ad publica officia militiæ togatæ et bellicæ in Aula educari curarunt: ita Turci, occupato Græcorum imperio, idem ius eripiendi patribus familias liberos ingeniis eximiis præditos, usurpant." (David Chytræus, pp. 12–14.)

[2] Creasy, p. 99. M. d'Ohsson, tome iii. p. 397. Menzel, p. 53. Thomas Smith, speaking of such parents, says: "Others, to the great shame and dishonour of the Religion, Christians only in name, part with them freely and readily enough, not only because they are rid of the trouble and charge of them, but in hopes they may, when they are grown up, get some considerable command in the government." (An Account of the Greek Church, p. 12. London, 1680.) In the reign of Murād I, Christian troops were employed in collecting this tribute of Christian children. (Finlay, vol. v. p. 45.)

[3] "Verum tamen hos (liberos) pecunia redimere a conquisitoribus sæpe parentibus licet." (David Chytræus, p. 13.) De la Guilletière mentions it in 1669 as one of the privileges of the Athenians. (An Account of a Late Voyage to Athens, p. 272. London, 1676.)

[4] Confessio, p. 205.

Thomas Smith, among others, speaks of the possibility of buying off the children, so impressed: "Some of their parents, out of natural pity and out of a true sense of religion, that they may not be thus robbed of their children, who hereby lie under a necessity of renouncing their Christianity, compound for them at the rate of fifty or a hundred dollars, as they are able, or as they can work upon the covetousness of the Turks more or less." [1] The Christians of certain cities, such as Constantinople, and of towns and islands that had made this stipulation at the time of their submission to the Turks, or had purchased this privilege, were exempted from the operation of this cruel tax.[2] These extenuating circumstances at the outset, and the ease with which men acquiesce in any established usage—though serving in no way as an excuse for so inhuman an institution—may help us to understand what a traveller in the seventeenth century calls the "unaccountable indifference" [3] with which the Greeks seem to have fallen in with this demand of the new government, which so materially improved their condition.

Further, the Christian subjects of the Turkish empire had to pay the capitation-tax, in return for protection and in lieu of military service. The rates fixed by the Ottoman law were 2½, 5 and 10 piastres a head for every full-grown male, according to his income,[4] women and the clergy being exempt.[5] In the nineteenth century the rates were 15, 30 and 60 piastres, according to income.[6] Christian writers of the sixteenth and seventeenth centuries generally speak of this tax as being a ducat a head,[7] but it

[1] An Account of the Greek Church, p. 12. (London, 1680.)

[2] Menzel, p. 52. Thomas Smith: De Moribus ac Institutis Turcarum, p. 81. (Oxonii, 1672.)

[3] Hill, p. 174.

[4] Joseph von Hammer (2), vol. ii. p. 151. Hans Schiltberger, who was captured by the Turks in 1396 and returned home to Munich after thirty-two years' captivity, states that the tax the Christians had to pay did not amount to more than two pfennig a month. (Reisebuch, p. 92.)

[5] Soli Sacerdotes, quasi in honorem sacri illius, quo funguntur, Deo ita ordinante, ministerii hoc factum sit, una cum fœminis, ab hoc tributo pendendo immunes habentur. (De Græcæ Hodierno Statu Epistola, authore Thoma Smitho, p. 12.) (Trajecti ad Rhenum, 1698.)

[6] Silbernagl, p. 60.

[7] Martin Crusius, p. 487; Sansovino, p. 67; Georgieviz, p. 98–9; Scheffler, § 56; Hertzberg, p. 648; De la Jonquière, p. 267. A work published in London in 1595, entitled "The Estate of Christians living

is also variously described as amounting to 3, 5 or $5\frac{7}{8}$ crowns or dollars.[1] The fluctuating exchange value of the Turkish coinage in the seventeenth century is the probable explanation of the latter variations. To estimate with any exactitude how far this tax was a burden to those who had to pay it, would require a lengthened disquisition on the purchasing value of money at that period and a comparison with other items of expenditure.[2] But by itself it could hardly have formed a valid excuse for a change of faith, as Tournefort points out, when writing in 1700 of the conversion of the Candiots: "It must be confessed, these Wretches sell their Souls a Pennyworth: all they get in exchange for their Religion, is a Vest, and the Privilege of being exempt from the Capitation-Tax, which is not above five Crowns a year."[3] Scheffler also, who is anxious to represent the condition of the Christians under Turkish rule in as black colours as possible, admits that the one ducat a head was a trifling matter, and has to lay stress on the extraordinary taxes, war contributions, etc., that they were called upon to pay.[4] The land taxes were the

---

under the subjection of the Turke," states the capitation-tax for male children to have been eight shillings (p. 2). Michel Baudin says one sequin a head for every male. (Histoire du Serrail, p. 7. Paris, 1662.)

[1] Georgirenes, p. 9; Tournefort, vol. i. p. 91; Tavernier (3), p. 11.

[2] In a work published by Joseph Georgirenes, Archbishop of Samos, in 1678, during a visit to London, he gives us an account of the income of his own see, the details of which are not likely to have been considered extortionate, as they were here set down for the benefit of English readers: in comparing the sums here mentioned, it should be borne in mind that he speaks of the capitation-tax as being three crowns or dollars (pp. 8–9). "At his (i.e. the Archbishop's) first coming, the Papas or Parish Priest of the Church of his Residence presents him fifteen or twenty dollers, they of the other Churches according to their Abilities. The first year of his coming, every Parish Priest pays him four dollers, and the following year two. Every Layman pays him forty-eight aspers"—(In the commercial treaty with England, concluded in the year 1675, the value of the dollar was fixed at eighty aspers (Finlay, v. 28))—"and the following years twenty-four. The Samians pay one Doller for a Licence; all Strangers two; but he that comes after first marriage for a Licence for a second or third, pays three or four" (pp. 33–4).

[3] Tournefort, vol. i. p. 91.

[4] Scheffler, § 56. "Was aber auch den Ducaten anbelangt, so werdet ihr mit demselben in eurem Sinn ebener massen greulich betrogen. Denn es ist zwar wahr, dass der Türckische Käyser ordentlich nicht mehr nimt als vom Haupt einen Ducaten: aber wo bleiben die Zölle und ausserordentliche Anlagen? nehmen dann seine Königliche Verweser und Hauptleute nichts? muss man zu Kriegen nichts ausser ordentlich geben? . . . Was aber die ausser ordentliche Anlagen betrifft; die steigen und fallen nach den bösen Zeiten, und müssen von den Türckischen Unterthanen so wohl gegeben werden als bey uns."

same both for Christians and Musalmans,[1] for the old distinction between lands on which tithe was paid by the Muhammadan proprietor, and those on which kharāj was paid by the non-Muhammadan proprietor, was not recognised by the Ottomans.[2] Whatever sufferings the Christians had to endure proceeded from the tyranny of individuals, who took advantage of their official position to extort money from those under their jurisdiction. Such acts of oppression were not only contrary to the Muhammadan law, but were rare before the central government had grown weak and suffered the corruption and injustice of local authorities to go unpunished.[3] There is a very marked difference between the accounts we have of the condition of the Christians during the first two centuries of the Turkish rule in Europe and those of a later date, when the period of decadence had fully set in. But it is noticeable that in those very times in which the condition of the Christians had been most intolerable there is least record of conversion to Islam. In the eighteenth century, when the condition of the Christians was worse than at any other period, we find hardly any mention of conversions at all, and the Turks themselves are represented as utterly indifferent to the progress of their religion and considerably infected with scepticism and unbelief.[4] A further proof that their sufferings have been due to misgovernment rather than to religious persecution is the fact that Muslims and Christians suffered alike.[5]

[1] Finlay, vol. v. pp. 24–5. H. von Moltke: Brief über Zustände und Begebenheiten in der Türkei aus den Jahren 1835 bis 1839, pp. 274, 354. (5th ed., Berlin, 1891.) [2] Hammer (2), vol. i. p. 346.

[3] "The hard lot of the Christian subjects of the Sultan has at all times arisen from the fact that the central authority at Constantinople has but little real authority throughout the Empire of Turkey. It is the petty tyranny of the village officials, sharpened by personal hatred, which has instigated those acts of atrocity to which, both in former times, and still more at the present day, the Christians in Turkey are subjected. In the days of a nation's greatness justice and even magnanimity towards a subject race are possible; these, however, are rarely found to exist in the time of a nation's decay." (Rev. W. Denton: Servia and the Servians, p. 15. London, 1862.) Gerlach, pp. 49, 52.

[4] Businello, pp. 43–4.

[5] "The central government of the Sultan has generally treated its Mussulman subjects with as much cruelty and injustice as the conquered Christians. The sufferings of the Greeks were caused by the insolence and oppression of the ruling class and the corruption that reigned in the Othoman administration, rather than by the direct exercise of the Sultan's power. In his private affairs, a Greek had a better chance of obtaining justice from

The Christians would, however, naturally be more exposed to extortion and ill-treatment owing to the difficulties that lay in the way of obtaining redress at law, and some of the poorest may thus have sought a relief from their sufferings in a change of faith.

But if we except the tribute of the children, to which the conquered Greeks seem to have submitted with so little show of resistance, and which owed its abolition, not to any revolt or insurrection against its continuance, but to the increase of the Turkish population and of the number of the renegades who were constantly entering the Sultan's service,[1]—the treatment of their Christian subjects by the Ottoman emperors—at least for two centuries after their conquest of Greece—exhibits a toleration such as was at that time quite unknown in the rest of Europe. The Calvinists of Hungary and Transylvania, and the Unitarians of the latter country, long preferred to submit to the Turks rather than fall into the hands of the fanatical house of Hapsburg;[2]

---

his bishop and the elders of his district than a Turk from the cadi or the voivode." (Finlay, vol. vi. pp. 4–5.)

"It would be a mistake to suppose that the Christians are the only part of the population that is oppressed and miserable. Turkish misgovernment is uniform, and falls with a heavy hand upon all alike. In some parts of the kingdom the poverty of the Mussulmans may be actually worse than the poverty of the Christians, and it is *their* condition which most excites the pity of the traveller." (William Forsyth: The Slavonic Provinces South of the Danube, pp. 157–8. London, 1876.)

"All this oppression and misery (i.e. in the north of Asia Minor) falls upon the Mohammedan population equally with the Christian." (James Bryce: Transcaucasia and Ararat, p. 381.)

"L'Europe s'imagine que les chrétiens seuls sont soumis, en Turquie, à l'arbitraire, aux souffrances, aux avilissements de toute nature, qui naissent de l'oppression; il n'en est rien! Les musulmans, précisément parce que nulle puissance étrangère ne s'intéresse à eux, sont peut-être plus indignement spoliés, plus courbés sous le joug que ceux qui méconnaissent le prophète." (De la Jonquière, p. 507.)

"To judge from what we have already observed, the lowest order of Christians are not in a worse condition in Asia Minor than the same class of Turks; and if the Christians of European Turkey have some advantages arising from the effects of the superiority of their numbers over the Turks, those of Asia have the satisfaction of seeing that the Turks are as much oppressed by the men in power as they are themselves; and they have to deal with a race of Mussulmans generally milder, more religious, and better principled than those of Europe." (W. M. Leake: Journal of a Tour in Asia Minor, p. 7. London, 1824.)

Cf. also Laurence Oliphant: The Land of Gilead, pp. 320–3, 446. (London, 1880.)

[1] It was in the sixteenth century that the tribute of children fell into desuetude, and the last recorded example of its exaction was in the year 1676.

[2] De la Jonquière, p. 333. Scheffler, § 45–6. Gasztowtt, p. 51.

and the Protestants of Silesia looked with longing eyes towards Turkey, and would gladly have purchased religious freedom at the price of submission to the Muslim rule.[1] It was to Turkey that the persecuted Spanish Jews fled for refuge in enormous numbers at the end of the fifteenth century,[2] and the Cossacks who belonged to the sect of the Old Believers and were persecuted by the Russian State Church, found in the dominions of the Sultan the toleration which their Christian brethren denied them.[3] Well might Macarius, Patriarch of Antioch in the seventeenth century, congratulate himself when he saw the fearful atrocities that the Catholic Poles inflicted on the Russians of the Orthodox Eastern Church: "We all wept much over the thousands of martyrs who were killed by those impious wretches, the enemies of the faith, in these forty or fifty years. The number probably amounted to seventy or eighty thousand souls. O you infidels! O you monsters of impurity! O you hearts of stone! What had the nuns and women done? What the girls and boys and infant children, that you should murder them? . . . And why do I pronounce them (the Poles) accursed? Because they have shown themselves more debased and wicked than the corrupt worshippers of idols, by their cruel treatment of Christians, thinking to abolish the very name of Orthodox. God perpetuate the empire of the Turks for ever and ever! For they take their

[1] "Denn ich höre mit grosser Verwunderung und Bestürtzung, dass nicht allein unter den gemeinen Pövel Reden im Schwange gehn, es sey unter dem Türcken auch gut wohnen: wann man einen Ducaten von Haupt gebe, so wäre man frey; Item er liesse die Religion frey; man würde die Kirchen wieder bekommen; und was vergleichen: sondern dass auch andre, die es wol besser verstehen sollten, sich dessen erfreuen, und über ihr eigen Unglück frolocken! welches nicht allein Halssbrüchige, sondern auch Gottlose Vermessenheiten seynd, die aus keinem andrem Grunde, als aus dem Geist der Ketzerey, der zum Auffruhr und gäntzlicher Ausreitung des Christenthumbs geneigt ist, herkommen." (Scheffler, § 48.)

[2] Hertzberg, p. 650.

[3] De la Jonquière, p. 34. A similar contrast was made in 1605 by Richard Staper, an English merchant who had been in Turkey as early as 1578: "And notwithstanding that the Turks in general be a most wicked people, walking in the works of darkness . . . yet notwithstanding do they permit all Christians, both Greeks and Latins, to live in their religion and freely to use to their conscience, allowing them churches for their divine service, both in Constantinople and very many other places, whereas to the contrary by proof of twelve years' residence in Spain I can truly affirm, we are not only forced to observe their popish ceremonies, but in danger of life and goods" (M. Epstein: The Early History of the Levant Company, p. 57. London, 1908.)

impost, and enter into no account of religion, be their subjects Christians or Nazarenes, Jews or Samarians: whereas these accursed Poles were not content with taxes and tithes from the brethren of Christ, though willing to serve them; but they subjected them to the authority of the enemies of Christ, the tyrannical Jews, who did not even permit them to build churches, nor leave them any priests that knew the mysteries of their faith."[1] Even in Italy there were men who turned longing eyes towards the Turks in the hope that as their subjects they might enjoy the freedom and the toleration they despaired of enjoying under a Christian government.[2] It would seem, then, that Islam was not spread by force in the dominion of the Sultan of Turkey, and though the want of even-handed justice and the oppression of unscrupulous officials in the days of the empire's decline, may have driven some Christians to attempt to better their condition by a change of faith, such cases were rare in the first two centuries of the Turkish rule in Europe, to which period the mass of conversions belong. It would have been wonderful indeed if the ardour of proselytising that animated the Ottomans at this time had never carried them beyond the bounds of toleration established by their own laws. Yet it has been said by one who was a captive among them for twenty-two years that the Turks "compelled no one to renounce his faith."[3] Similar testimony is borne by others: an English gentleman who visited Turkey in the early part of the seventeenth century, tells us that "There is seldom any compulsion of conscience, and then not by death, where no criminal offence gives

[1] Macarius, vol. i. pp. 183, 165. Cf. the memorial presented by Polish refugees from Russia to the Sublime Porte, in 1853. (Gasztowtt, p. 217.)

[2] "Alii speciem sibi quandam confixerunt stultam libertatis . . . quod quum sub Christiano consequuturos se desperent, ideo vel Turcam mallent: quasi is benignior sit in largienda libertate hac, quam Christianus." (Ioannis Ludovici Vivis De Conditione Vitæ Christianorum sub Turca, pp. 220, 225.) (Basileæ, 1538.) "Quidam obganniunt, liberam esse sub Turca fidem." (Othonis Brunfelsii ad Principes et Christianos omnes Oratio, p. 133.) (Basileæ, 1538.) Ubertus Folieta, a noble of Genoa, writing about 1577, says, "Sæpe mecum quaesivi . . . qua re fiat, ut tot de nostris hominibus ad illos continenter transfugiant, Christianaque religione eiurata Mahumetanæ sectæ nomina dent." (De Causis Magnitudinis Turcarum Imperii, col. 1209.) (Thesaurus Antiquitatum et Historiarum Italiæ, curâ Joannis Georgii Grævii, tom. i. Lugduni Batavorum, 1725.)

[3] Turchicæ Spurcitiæ Suggillatio, fol. xvii. (a).

occasion." [1] Writing about thirty years later (in 1663), the author [2] of a Türcken-Schrifft says: "Meanwhile he (i.e. the Turk) wins (converts) by craft more than by force, and snatches away Christ by fraud out of the hearts of men. For the Turk, it is true, at the present time compels no country by violence to apostatise; but he uses other means whereby imperceptibly he roots out Christianity. . . . What then has become of the Christians? They are not expelled from the country, neither are they forced to embrace the Turkish faith: then they must of themselves have been converted into Turks."

The Turks considered that the greatest kindness they could show a man was to bring him into the salvation of the faith of Islam,[3] and to this end they left no method of persuasion untried: a Dutch traveller of the sixteenth century, tells us that while he was admiring the great mosque of Santa Sophia, some Turks even tried to work upon his religious feelings through his æsthetic sense, saying to him, "If you become a Musalman, you will be able to come here every day of your life." About a century later, an English traveller [4] had a similar experience: "Sometimes, out of an excess of zeal, they will ask a Christian civilly enough, as I have been asked myself in the Portico of Sancta Sophia, why will you not turn Musalman, and be as one of us?" The public rejoicings that hailed the accession of a new convert to the faith, testify to the ardent love for souls which made these men such zealous proselytisers. The new Muslim was set upon a horse and led in triumph through the streets of the city. If he was known to be genuinely honest in his change of faith and had voluntarily entered the pale of Islam, or if he was a person of good position, he was received with high honour and some provision made for his support.[5] There was certainly abundant evidence for saying that "The Turks are preposterously zealous in praying for the conversion, or perversion rather, of Christians to their irreligious religion: they pray heartily, and every day in their Temples, that Christians may imbrace the

[1] Blount, vol. i. p. 548. [2] Scheffler, §§ 51, 53.
[3] Dousa, p. 38. Busbecq, p. 190. [4] Thomas Smith, p. 32.
[5] Thomas Smith, p. 42. Blount, vol. i. p. 548. Georgieviz, p. 20. Schiltberger, pp. 83–4. Baudier, pp. 149, 313.

Alcoran, and become their Proselytes, in effecting of which they leave no means unassaied by fear and flattery, by punishments and rewards." [1]

These zealous efforts for winning converts were rendered the more effective by certain conditions of Christian society itself. Foremost among these was the degraded condition of the Greek Church. Side by side with the civil despotism of the Byzantine empire, had arisen an ecclesiastical despotism which had crushed all energy of intellectual life under the weight of a dogmatism that interdicted all discussion in matters of morals and religion. The only thing that disturbed this lethargy was the fierce controversial war waged against the Latin Church with all the bitterness of theological polemics and race hatred. The religion of the people had degenerated into a scrupulous observance of outward forms, and the intense fervour of their devotion found an outlet in the worship of the Virgin and the saints, of pictures and relics. There were many who turned from a Church whose spiritual life had sunk so low, and weary of interminable discussions on such subtle points of doctrine as the Double Procession of the Holy Spirit, and such trivialities as the use of leavened and unleavened bread in the Blessed Sacrament, gladly accepted the clear and intelligible theistic teaching of Islam. We are told [2] of large numbers of persons being converted, not only from among the simple folk, but also learned men of every class, rank and condition; of how the Turks made a better provision for those monks and priests who embraced the Muslim creed, in order that their example might lead others to be converted. While Adrianople was still the Turkish capital (e. g. before

[1] Alexander Ross, p. ix. Baudier, p. 317. Cf. also Rycaut, vol. i. p. 276. " On croit meriter beaucoup que de faire un Proselyte, il n'y a personne assez riche pour avoir un esclave qui n'en veüille un jeune, qui soit capable de recevoir sans peine toutes sortes d'impressions, et qu'il puisse appeller son converti, afin de meriter l'honneur d'avoir augmenté le nombre des fidèles." Thomas Smith relates how the old man who showed him the tomb of Urkhān at Brusa " ingenti cum fervore, oculis ad Cælum elevatis, Deum precatus est ut nos ad fidem Musulmannicam suo tempore tandem convertere dignaretur : Hoc nimirum est summum erga nos affectus testimonium, qui ex isto falso et imperitissimo zelo solet profluere." (Epistolæ duae, quarum altera De Moribus ac Institutis Turcarum agit, p. 20.) (Oxonii, 1672.)

[2] By an anonymous writer who was a captive in Turkey from 1436 to 1458. Turchicæ Spurcitiæ Suggillatio, fol. xvii. (a).

1453) the court was thronged with renegades, and they are said to have formed the majority of the magnates there.[1] Byzantine princes and others often passed over to the side of the Muhammadans, and received a ready welcome among them: one of the earliest of such cases dates from 1140 when a nephew of the emperor John Comnenes embraced Islam and married a daughter of Mas'ūd, the Sultan of Iconium.[2] After the fall of Constantinople, the upper classes of Christian society showed much more readiness to embrace Islam than the mass of the Greeks; among the converts we meet with several bearing the name of the late imperial family of the Palæologi, and the learned George Amiroutzes of Trebizond abandoned Christianity in his declining years, and the names of many other such individuals have found a record.[3] The new religion only demanded assent to its simple creed, "There is no god but God: Muḥammad is the apostle of God"; as the above-mentioned writer[4] says, "The whole difficulty lies in this profession of faith. For if only a man can persuade himself that he is a worshipper of the One God, the poison of his error easily infects him under the guise of religion. This is the rock of offence on which many have struck and fallen into the snare that has brought perdition on their souls. This is the mill-stone that hung about the necks of many has plunged them into the pit of despair. For when these fools hear the Turks execrate idolatry and express their horror of every image and picture as though it were the fire of hell, and so continually profess and preach the worship of One God, there no longer remains any room for suspicion in their minds."

The faith of Islam would now be the natural refuge for

[1] Turchicæ Spurcitiæ Suggillatio, fol. xi. (b). Lionardo of Scio, Archbishop of Mitylene, who was present at the taking of Constantinople, speaks of the large number of renegades in the besieging army: "Chi circondò la città, e chi insegnò a' turchi l'ordine, se non i pessimi christiani? Io son testimonio, che i Greci, ch' i Latini, che i Tedeschi, che gli Ungari, e che ogni altra generation di christiani, mescolati co' turchi impararono l'opere e la fede loro, i quali domenticatisi della fede christiana, espugnavano la città. O empij che rinegasti Christo. O settatori di antichristo, dannati alle pene infernali, questo è hora il vostro tempo." (Sansovino, p. 258.)

[2] J. H. Krause: Die Byzantiner des Mittelalters, pp. 385–6. (Halle, 1869.)

[3] Hertzberg, p. 616. Finlay, vol. v. p. 118.

[4] Turchicæ Spurcitiæ Suggillatio, fol. xix. (a).

those members of the Eastern Church who felt such yearnings after a purer and simpler form of doctrine as had given rise to the Paulician heresy so fiercely suppressed a few centuries before. This movement had been very largely a protest against the superstitions of the Orthodox Church, against the worship of images, relics and saints, and an effort after simplicity of faith and the devout life. As some adherents of this heresy were to be found in Bulgaria even so late as the seventeenth century,[1] the Muhammadan conquerors doubtless found many who were dissatisfied with the doctrine and practice of the Greek Church; and as all the conditions were unfavourable to the formation of any such Protestant Churches as arose in the West, such dissentient spirits would doubtless find a more congenial atmosphere in the religion of Islam. There is every reason to think that such was the result of the unsuccessful attempt to Protestantise the Greek Church in the beginning of the seventeenth century. The guiding spirit of this movement was Cyril Lucaris, five times Patriarch of Constantinople, from 1621 to 1638; as a young man he had visited the Universities of Wittenberg and Geneva, for the purpose of studying theology in the seats of Protestant learning, and on his return he kept up a correspondence with doctors of the reformed faith in Geneva, Holland and England. But neither the doctrines of the Church of England nor of the Lutherans attracted his sympathies so warmly as the teachings of John Calvin,[2] which he strove to introduce into the Greek Church; his efforts in this direction were warmly supported by the Calvinists of Geneva, who sent a learned young theologian, named Leger, to assist the work by translating into Greek the writings of Calvinist theologians.[3] Cyril also found warm friends in the Protestant embassies at Constantinople, the Dutch and English ambassadors especially assisting him liberally with funds; the Jesuits, on the other hand, supported by the Catholic ambassadors, tried in every way to thwart this attempt to Calvinise the Greek Church, and actively seconded the intrigues of the party of opposition among the Greek clergy, who finally compassed the death

[1] Rycaut, vol. i. pp. 710–11. Bizzi, fol. 49 (b).
[2] Pichler, pp. 164, 172.
[3] Id. p. 143.

of the Patriarch. In 1629 Cyril published a Confession of Faith, the main object of which seems to have been to present the doctrines of the Orthodox Church in their opposition to Roman Catholicism in such a way as to imply a necessary accord with Protestant teaching.[1] From Calvin he borrows the doctrines of Predestination and salvation by faith alone, he denies the infallibility of the Church, rejects the authority of the Church in the interpretation of Holy Scripture, and condemns the adoration of pictures: in his account of the will and in many other questions, he inclines rather to Calvinism than to the teachings of the Orthodox Church.[2] The promulgation of this Confession of Faith as representing the teaching of the whole Church of which he was the spiritual head, excited violent opposition among the mass of the Greek clergy, and a few weeks after Cyril's death a synod was held to condemn his opinions and pronounce him to be Anathema; in 1642 a second synod was held at Constantinople for the same purpose, which after refuting each article of Cyril's Confession in detail, as the first had done, thus fulminated its curse upon him and his followers:—"With one consent and in unqualified terms, we condemn this whole Confession as full of heresies and utterly opposed to our orthodoxy, and likewise declare that its compiler has nothing in common with our faith, but in calumnious fashion has falsely charged his own Calvinism on us. All those who read and keep it as true and blameless, and defend it by written word or speech, we thrust out of the community of the faithful as followers and partakers of his heresy and corruptors of the Christian Church, and command that whatever be their rank and station, they be treated as heathen and publicans. Let them be laid under an anathema for ever and cut off from the Father, the Son and the Holy Ghost in this life and in the life to come, accursed, excommunicated, be lost after death, and be partakers of everlasting punishment."[3] In 1672 a third synod met at Jerusalem to repudiate the heretical articles of this Confession of Faith and vindicate the orthodoxy of the Greek Church against those

[1] Pichler, p. 148. It is doubtful, however, whether Cyril was really the author of this document bearing his name. (Kyriakos, p. 100.)

[2] Id. pp. 183–9.

[3] Id. p. 226.

who represented her as infected with Calvinism. The attempt to Protestantise the Greek Church thus completely failed to achieve success: the doctrines of Calvin were diametrically opposed to her teachings, and indeed inculcated many articles of faith that were more in harmony with the tenets of Muslim theologians than with those of the Orthodox Church, and which moreover she had often attacked in her controversies with her Muhammadan adversaries. It is this approximation to Islamic thought which gives this movement towards Calvinism a place in a history of the spread of Islam: a man who inveighed against the adoration of pictures, decried the authority and the very institution of the priesthood, maintained the doctrines of absolute Predestination, denied freedom to the human will and was in sympathy with the stern spirit of Calvinism that had more in common with the Old than the New Testament —would certainly find a more congenial atmosphere in Islam than in the Greek Church of the seventeenth century, and there can be little doubt that among the numerous converts of Islam during that century were to be found men who had been alienated from the Church of their fathers through their leanings towards Calvinism.[1] We have no definite information as to the number of the followers of Cyril Lucaris and the extent of Calvinistic influences in the Greek Church; the clergy, jealous of the reputation of their Church, whose orthodoxy and immunity from heresy were so boastfully vindicated by her children, and had thus been impugned through the suspicion of Calvinism, wished to represent the heretical patriarch as standing alone in his opinions.[2] But a following he undoubtedly had: his Confession of Faith had received the sanction of a synod composed of his followers;[3] those who sympathised with his heresies were anathematised both by the second synod of Constantinople (1642) and by the synod of Jerusalem (1672)[4]—surely a meaningless repetition, had no such persons existed; moreover the names of some few of these

[1] As regards the Christian captives the Protestants certainly had the reputation among the Turks of showing a greater inclination towards conversion than the Catholics. (Gmelin, p. 21.)

[2] Pichler, pp. 211, 227.

[3] Id. pp. 181, 228.

[4] Id. pp. 222, 226.

have come down to us: Sophronius, Metropolitan of Athens, was a warm supporter of the Reformation;[1] a monk named Nicodemus Metaras, who had brought a printing-press from London and issued heretical treatises therefrom, was rewarded with a metropolitan see by Cyril in return for his services;[2] the philosopher Corydaleus, a friend of Cyril, opened a Calvinistic school in Constantinople, and another Greek, Gerganos, published a Catechism so as to introduce the teachings of Calvin among his fellow-countrymen;[3] and Neophytus II, who was made Patriarch in 1636, while Cyril was in exile in the island of Rhodes, was his disciple and adopted son; he recalled his master from banishment and resigned the patriarchal chair in his favour.[4] In a letter to the University of Geneva (dated July, 1636), Cyril writes that Leger had gained a large number of converts to Calvinism by his writings and preaching;[5] in another letter addressed to Leger, he describes how he had made his influence felt in Candia.[6] His successor[7] in the patriarchal chair was banished to Carthage and there strangled by the adherents of Lucaris in 1639.[8] The Calvinists are said to have entertained hopes of Parthenius I (the successor of Cyril II), but his untimely end (whether by poison or banishment is uncertain) disappointed their expectations.[9] Parthenius II, who was Patriarch of Constantinople from 1644 to 1646, was at heart a thorough Calvinist, and though he did not venture openly to teach the doctrines of Calvin, still his known sympathy with them caused him to be deposed, sent into exile and strangled.[10] Thus the influence of Calvinism was undoubtedly more widespread than the enemies of Cyril Lucaris were willing to admit, and as stated above, those who refused to bow to the anathemas of the synods that condemned their leader, had certainly more in common with their Muhammadan neighbours than with the Orthodox clergy who cast them out of their midst. There is no actual evidence, it is true, of Calvinistic influences in Turkey

[1] Pichler, p. 173.
[2] Id. pp. 128, 132, 143.
[3] Id. p. 143.
[4] Le Quien, tom. i. col. 334.
[5] Pichler, p. 172.
[6] Hefele, vol. i. p. 473.
[7] Cyril II of Berrhœa.
[8] Le Quien, tom. i. col. 335.
[9] Id. tom. i. col. 336.
[10] Id. tom. i. col. 337.

facilitating conversion to Islam,[1] but in the absence of any other explanation it certainly seems a very plausible conjecture that such were among the factors that so enormously increased the number of the Greek renegades towards the middle of the seventeenth century—a period during which the number of renegades from among the middle and lower orders of society is said to have been more considerable than at any other time.[2] Frequent mention is made of cases of apostasy from among the clergy, and even among the highest dignitaries of the Church, such as a former Metropolitan of Rhodes.[3] In 1676 it is said that in Corinth some Christian people went over every day to "the Turkish abomination," and that three priests had become Musalmans the year before;[4] in 1679 is recorded the death of a renegade monk.[5] On the occasion of the circumcision of Muṣṭafā, son of Muḥammad IV, in 1675, there were at least two hundred proselytes made during the thirteen days of public rejoicing,[6] and numerous other instances may be found in writings of this period. A contemporary writer (1663) has well described the mental attitude of such converts. "When you mix with the Turks in the ordinary intercourse of life and see that they pray and sing even the Psalms of David; that they give alms and do other good works; that they think highly of Christ, hold the Bible in great honour, and the like; that, besides, any ass may become parish priest who plies the Bassa with presents, and he will

[1] However, in an earlier attempt made by the Protestant theologians of Tübingen (1573–77) to introduce the doctrines of the Reformed Church into the Eastern Church, the Vaivode Quarquar of Samtskheth in Georgia embraced the Confession of Augsburg, but in 1580 became a Muslim. (Joselian, p. 140.)

[2] Scheffler, §§ 53–6. Finlay, vol. v. pp. 118–19.

[3] Hammer (1), vol. vi. p. 94.

[4] Spon, vol. ii. p. 57.

[5] Hammer (1), vol. vi. p. 364.

[6] Early Voyages and Travels in the Levant, edited by J. Theodore Bent, p. 210. (London, 1893.) Similarly, Michel Baudier concludes his description of the festivities in Constantinople on the occasion of the circumcision of Muḥammad III in the latter part of the sixteenth century, with an account of the conversion of a large number of Christians. "During the spectacles of this solemnity, the wretched Grecians ran by troupes in this place to make themselves Mahometans; Some abandoned Christianitie to avoid the oppression of the Turkes, others for the hope of private profit. . . . The number of these cast-awayes was found to be above foure thousand soules." (The History of the Serrail, and of the Court of the Grand Seigneur Emperour of the Turkes, pp. 93–4. (London, 1635.) Histoire generale du Serrail, et de la Cour du Grand Seigneur, Empereur des Turcs, pp. 89–90. (Paris, 1631.))

not urge Christianity on you very much; so you will come to think that they are good people and will very probably be saved; and so you will come to believe that you too may be saved, if you likewise become Turks. Herewith will the Holy Trinity and the crucified Son of God, with many other mysteries of the faith, which seem quite absurd to the unenlightened reason, easily pass out of your thoughts, and imperceptibly Christianity will quite die out in you, and you will think that it is all the same whether you be Christians or Turks." [1]

Thomas Smith, who was in Constantinople in 1669, speaks of the number of Christian converts about this period, but assigns baser motives. "'Tis sad to consider the great number of wretched people, who turn Turks; some out of meer desperation; being not able to support the burthen of slavery, and to avoid the revilings and insultings of the Infidels; some out of a wanton light humour, to put themselves into a condition of domineering and insulting over others . . . some to avoid the penalties and inflictions due to their heinous crimes, and to enjoy the brutish liberties, that Mahomet consecrated by his own example, and recommended to his followers. These are the great and tempting arguments and motives of their apostasy, meer considerations of ease, pleasure and prosperity, or else of vanity and guilt; for it cannot be presumed, that any through conviction of mind should be wrought upon to embrace the dotages and impostures of Turcisme." [2] Records of conversions after this period are rare, but Motraye gives an account of several renegades, who became Muhammadans in Constantinople in 1703; among them was a French priest and some other French Catholics, and some priests from Smyrna.[3]

Another feature in the condition of the Greek Church that contributed to the decay of its numbers, was the corruption and degradation of its pastors, particularly the higher clergy. The sees of bishops and archbishops were put up to auction to the highest bidders, and the purchasers sought to recoup

[1] Scheffler, § 55.

[2] Thomas Smith: An Account of the Greek Church, pp. 15–16. (London, 1680.)

[3] A. de la Motraye: Voyages en Europe, Asie et Afrique, vol. i. pp. 306, 308. (La Haye, 1727.)

themselves by exacting levies of all kinds from their flocks; they burdened the unfortunate Christians with taxes ordinary and extraordinary, made them purchase all the sacraments at exorbitant rates, baptism, confession, holy communion, indulgences, and the right of Christian burial. Some of the clergy even formed an unholy alliance with the Janissaries, and several bishops had their names and those of their households inscribed on the list of one of their Ortas or regiments, the better to secure an immunity for their excesses and escape the punishment of their crimes under the protection of this corporation which the weakness of the Ottoman rulers had allowed to assume such a powerful position in the state.[1] The evidence of contemporary eye-witnesses to the oppressive behaviour of the Greek clergy presents a terrible picture of the sufferings of the Christians. Tournefort in 1700, after describing the election of a new Patriarch, says: "We need not at all doubt but the new Patriarch makes the best of his time. Tyranny succeeds to Simony: the first thing he does is to signify the Sultan's order to all the Archbishops and Bishops of his clergy: his greatest study is to know exactly the revenues of each Prelate; he imposes a tax upon them, and enjoins them very strictly by a second letter to send the sum demanded, otherwise their dioceses are adjudg'd to the highest bidder. The Prelates being used to this trade, never spare their Suffragans; these latter torment the Papas: the Papas flea the Parishioners and hardly sprinkle the least drop of Holy Water, but what they are paid for beforehand. If afterwards the Patriarch has occasion for money, he farms out the gathering of it to the highest bidder among the Turks: he that gives most for it, goes into Greece to cite the Prelates. Usually for twenty thousand crowns that the clergy is tax'd at, the Turk extorts two and twenty; so that he has the two thousand crowns for his pains, besides having his charges borne in every diocese. In virtue of the agreement he has made with the Patriarch, he deprives and interdicts from all ecclesiastical functions, those prelates who refuse to pay their tax."[2] The Christian

[1] Pitzipios, Seconde Partie, pp. 83–7. Pichler, p. 29.
[2] Tournefort, vol. i. p. 107. Spon uses much the same language, vol. i. p. 56.

clergy are even said to have carried off the children of the parishioners and sold them as slaves, to get money for their simoniacal designs.[1]

The extortions practised in the seventeenth have found their counterpart in the nineteenth century, and the sufferings of the Christians of the Greek Church in Bosnia, before the Austrian occupation, exactly illustrate the words of Tournefort. The Metropolitan of Serajevo used to wring as much as £10,000 a year from his miserable flock—a sum exactly double the salary of the Turkish Governor himself—and to raise this enormous sum the unfortunate parishioners were squeezed in every possible way, and the Turkish authorities had orders to assist the clergy in levying their exactions; and whole Christian villages suffered the fate of sacked cities, for refusing, or often being unable, to comply with the exorbitant demands of Christian Prelates.[2] Such unbearable oppression on the part of the spiritual leaders who should protect the Christian population, has often stirred it up to open revolt, whenever a favourable opportunity has offered itself.[3] It is not surprising then to learn that many of the Christians went over to Islam, to deliver themselves from such tyranny.[4]

Ecclesiastical oppression of a rather different character is said to have been responsible for the conversion of the ancestors of a small community of about 4000 Southern Rumanians, at Noanta in the Meglen district of the vilayet of Salonika; they have a tradition that in the eighteenth century the Patriarch of Constantinople persuaded the reigning Sultan that only the Christians who spoke Greek could be loyal subjects of the Turkish empire; the Sultan

[1] Gaultier de Leslie, p. 137.

[2] A. J. Evans, p. 267. Similarly Mackenzie and Irby say: "In most parts of Old Serbia the idea we found associated with a bishop, was that of a person who carried off what few paras the Turks had left" (p. 258). A similar account of the clergy of the Greek Church is given by a writer in the *Revue des Deux Mondes* (tome 97, p. 336), who narrates the following story: "Au début de ce siècle, à Tirnova, un certain pope du nom de Joachim, adoré de ses ouailles, détesté de son évêque, reçut l'ordre, un jour, de faire la corvée du fumier dans l'écurie episcopale. Il se rebiffa: aussitôt la valetaille l'assaillit à coups de fourche. Mais notre homme était vigoureux: il se débattit, et, laissant sa tunique en gage, s'en fut tout chaud chez le cadi. Le soleil n'était pas couché qu'il devenait bon Musulman."

[3] Pitzipios, Seconde Partie, p. 87.

[4] Id. Seconde Partie, p. 87. Pichler, p. 29.

thereupon forbade the Christians to speak anything but Greek, on pain of having their tongues cut out; when the news of this reached Noanta, a part of the population fled into the woods and founded fresh villages, but those who were left behind went over to Islam, with their bishop at their head, in order thereby to retain their mother-tongue.[1]

Though the mass of the parish clergy were innocent of the charges brought against their superiors,[2] still they were very ignorant and illiterate. At the end of the seventeenth century, there were said to be hardly twelve persons in the whole Turkish dominions thoroughly skilled in the knowledge of the ancient Greek language; it was considered a great merit in the clergy to be able to read, while they were quite ignorant of the meaning of the words of their service-books.[3]

While there was so much in the Christian society of the time to repel, there was much in the character and life of the Turks to attract, and the superiority of the early Ottomans as compared with the degradation of the guides and teachers of the Christian Church would naturally impress devout minds that revolted from the selfish ambition, simony and corruption of the Greek ecclesiastics. Christian writers constantly praise these Turks for the earnestness and intensity of their religious life; their zeal in the performance of the observances prescribed by their faith; the outward decency and modesty displayed in their apparel and mode of living; the absence of ostentatious display and the simplicity of life observable even in the great and powerful.[4] The annalist of the embassy from the Emperor Leopold I to the Ottoman Porte in 1665–1666, especially eulogises the devoutness and regularity of the Turks in prayer, and he even goes so far as to say, " Nous devons dire à la confusion des Chrêtiens, que les Turcs têmoignent beaucoup plus de soin et de zèle à l'exercice de leur Religion : que les Crêtiens n'en font paroître à la pratique de la leur. . . . Mais ce qui passe tout ce que nous experimentons de dévot entre les Chrêtiens : c'est que pendant le tems de la prière, vous ne

[1] Lazăr, p. 223. [2] Finlay, vol. iv. pp. 153–4.
[3] Tournefort, vol. i. p. 104. Cf. Pichler, pp. 29, 31. Spon, vol. i. p. 44.
[4] Turchicæ Spurcitiæ Suggillatio, fol. xiii. (b); fol. xv. (b); fol. xvii. (b); fol. xx. (a). Veniero, pp. 32, 36. Busbecq, p. 174.

voyez pas une personne distraite de ses yeux : vous n'en voyez pas une qui ne soit attachée à l'objet de sa prière : et pas une qui n'ait toute la révérence extérieure pour son Créateur, qu'on peut exiger de la Créature." [1]

Even the behaviour of the soldiery receives its meed of praise. During the march of an army the inhabitants of the country, we are told by the secretary to the Embassy sent by Charles II to the Sultan, had no complaints to make of being plundered or of their women being maltreated. All the taverns along the line of march were shut up and sealed two or three days before the arrival of the army, and no wine was allowed to be sold to the soldiers under pain of death.[2]

Many a tribute of praise is given to the virtues of the Turks even by Christian writers who bore them no love; one such who had a very poor opinion of their religion,[3] speaks of them as follows :—" Even in the dirt of the Alcoran you shall find some jewels of Christian Virtues; and indeed if Christians will but diligently read and observe the Laws and Histories of the Mahometans, they may blush to see how zealous they are in the works of devotion, piety, and charity, how devout, cleanly, and reverend in their Mosques, how obedient to their Priest, that even the great Turk himself will attempt nothing without consulting his Mufti; how careful are they to observe their hours of prayer five times a day wherever they are, or however employed ? how constantly do they observe their Fasts from morning till night a whole month together; how loving and charitable the Muslemans are to each other, and how careful of strangers may be seen by their Hospitals, both for the Poor and for Travellers; if we observe their Justice, Temperance, and other moral Vertues, we may truly blush at our own coldness, both in devotion and charity, at our injustice, intemperance, and oppression; doubtless these Men will rise up in judgment against us; and surely their devotion, piety,

[1] Gaultier de Leslie, pp. 180, 182.

[2] Rycaut, vol. i. p. 689. See also Georgieviz, pp. 53–4, and Menavino, p. 73.

[3] Alexander Ross, p. ix.; he calls the Qur'ān a " gallimaufry of Errors (a Brat as deformed as the Parent, and as full of Heresies, as his scald head was of scurf),"—" a hodg podge made up of these four Ingredients. 1. Of Contradictions. 2. Of Blasphemy. 3. Of ridiculous Fables. 4. Of Lyes."

and works of mercy are main causes of the growth of Mahometism."

The same conclusion is drawn by a modern historian,[1] who writes :—" We find that many Greeks of high talent and moral character were so sensible of the superiority of the Mohammedans, that even when they escaped being drafted into the Sultan's household as tribute-children, they voluntarily embraced the faith of Mahomet. The moral superiority of Othoman society must be allowed to have had as much weight in causing these conversions, which were numerous in the fifteenth century, as the personal ambition of individuals."

A generation that has watched the decay of the Turkish power in Europe and the successive curtailment of its territorial possessions, and is accustomed to hearing it spoken of as the " sick man," destined to a speedy dissolution, must find it difficult to realise the feelings which the Ottoman empire inspired in the early days of its rise in Europe. The rapid and widespread success of the Turkish arms filled men's minds with terror and amazement. One Christian kingdom after another fell into their hands: Bulgaria, Servia, Bosnia, and Hungary yielded up their independence as Christian states. The proud Republic of Venice saw one possession after another wrested from it, until the Lion of St. Mark held sway on the shores of the Adriatic alone. Even the safety of the Eternal City itself was menaced by the capture of Otranto. Christian literature of the latter half of the fifteenth and of the sixteenth centuries is full of direful forebodings of the fate that threatened Christian Europe unless the victorious progress of the Turk was arrested; he is represented as a scourge in the hand of God for the punishment of the sins and backslidings of His people,[2] or on the other hand as the unloosed power of the Devil working for the destruction of Christianity under the hypocritical guise of religion. But—what is most important to notice here—some men began to ask themselves, " Is it possible that God would allow the Muhammadans to increase in such countless numbers without good reason ? Is it conceivable that so many thousands

[1] Finlay, vol. v. p. 29. [2] Schiltberger, p. 96.

are to be damned like one man? How can such multitudes be opposed to the true faith? since truth is stronger than error and is more loved and desired by all men, it is not possible for so many men to be fighting against it. How could they prevail against truth, since God always helps and upholds the truth? How could their religion so marvellously increase, if built upon the rotten foundation of error?"[1] Such thoughts, we are told, appealed strongly to the Christian peoples that lived under the Turkish rule, and with especial force to the unhappy Christian captives who watched the years drag wearily on without hope of release or respite from their misery. Can we be surprised when we find such a one asking himself? "Surely if God were pleased with the faith to which you have clung, He would not have thus abandoned you, but would have helped you to gain your freedom and return to it again. But as He has closed every avenue of freedom to you, perchance it is His pleasure that you should leave it and join this sect and be saved therein."[2]

The Christian slave who thus describes the doubts that arose in his mind as the slow-passing years brought no relief, doubtless gives expression here to thoughts that suggested themselves to many a hapless Christian captive with overwhelming persistency, until at last he broke away from the ties of his old faith and embraced Islam. Many who would have been ready to die as martyrs for the Christian religion if the mythical choice between the Qur'ān and the sword had been offered them, felt more and more strongly, after long years of captivity, the influence of Muhammadan thought and practice, and humanity won converts where violence would have failed.[3] For though the lot of many of the Christian captives was a very pitiable one, others who held positions in the households of private individuals, were often no worse off than domestic servants in the rest of Europe.

[1] Turchicæ Spurcitiæ Suggillatio, fol. xii. (b), xiii. (a).

[2] Id. fol. xxvii. (a).

[3] "Dum corpora exterius fovendo sub pietatis specie non occidit: interius fidem auferendo animas sua diabolica astutia occidere intendit. Huius rei testimonium innumerabilis multitudo fidelium esse potest. Quorum multi promptissimi essent pro fide Christi et suarum animarum salute in fide Christi mori: quos tamen conservando a morte corporali: et ductos in captivitatem per successum temporis suo infectos veneno fidem Christi turpiter negare facit." Turchicæ Spurctiæ Suggillatio, fol. i.; cf. fol. vi. (a).

As organised by the Muhammadan Law, slavery was robbed of many of its harshest features, nor in Turkey at least does it seem to have been accompanied by such barbarities and atrocities as in the pirate states of Northern Africa. The slaves, like other citizens, had their rights, and it is even said that a slave might summon his master before the Qāḍī for ill usage, and that if he alleged that their tempers were so opposite, that it was impossible for them to agree, the Qāḍī could oblige his master to sell him.[1] The condition of the Christian captives naturally varied with circumstances and their own capabilities of adapting themselves to a life of hardship; the aged, the priests and monks, and those of noble birth suffered most, while the physician and the handicraftsman received more considerate treatment from their masters, as being servants that best repaid the money spent upon them.[2] The galley-slaves naturally suffered most of all, indeed the kindest treatment could have but little relieved the hardships incident to such an occupation.[3] Further, the lot of the slaves who were state property was more pitiable than that of those who had been purchased by private individuals.[4] As a rule they were allowed the free exercise of their religion; in the state-prisons at Constantinople, they had their own priests and chapels, and the clergy were allowed to administer the consolations of religion to the galley-slaves.[5] The number of the Christian slaves who embraced Islam was enormous; some few cases have been recorded of their being threatened

[1] Menavino, p. 96. John Harris: Navigantium atque Itinerantium Bibliotheca, vol. ii. p. 819. (London, 1764.)

[2] "Dieses muss man den Türken nachsagen, dass sie die Diener und Sclaven, durch deren Fleiss und Bemühung sie sich einen Nutzen schaffen können, sehr wol und oft besser, als die Christian die ihrige, halten . . . und wann ein Knecht in einer Kunst erfahren ist, gehet ihm nichts anders als die Freyheit ab, ausser welche er alles andere hat, was ein freyer Mensch sich nur wünschen kan." (G. C. von den Driesch, p. 132.)

[3] Sir William Stirling-Maxwell says of these: "The poor wretches who tugged at the oar on board a Turkish ship of war lived a life neither more nor less miserable than the galley-slaves under the sign of the Cross. Hard work, hard fare, and hard knocks were the lot of both. Ashore, a Turkish or Algerine prison was, perhaps, more noisome in its filth and darkness than a prison at Naples or Barcelona; but at sea, if there were degrees of misery, the Christian in Turkish chains probably had the advantage; for in the Sultan's vessels the oar-gang was often the property of the captain, and the owner's natural tenderness for his own was sometimes supposed to interfere with the discharge of his duty." (Vol. i. pp. 102–3.)

[4] Gmelin, p. 16.

[5] Id. p. 23.

and ill-treated for the very purpose of inducing them to recant, but as a rule the masters seldom forced them to renounce their faith,[1] and put the greatest pressure upon them during the first years of their captivity, after which they let them alone to follow their own faith.[2] The majority of the converted slaves therefore changed their religion of their own free choice; and when the Christian embassies were never sure from day to day that some of their fellow-countrymen that had accompanied them to Constantinople as domestic servants, might not turn Turk,[3] it can easily be understood that slaves who had lost all hope of return to their native country, and found little in their surroundings to strengthen and continue the teachings of their earlier years, would yield to the influences that beset them and would feel few restraints to hinder them from entering a new society and a new religion. An English traveller [4] of the seventeenth century has said of them: "Few ever return to their native country; and fewer have the courage and constancy of retaining the Christian Faith, in which they were educated; their education being but mean, and their knowledge but slight in the principles and grounds of it; whereof some are frightened into Turcism by their impatience

[1] John Harris: Navigantium atque Itinerantium Bibliotheca, vol. ii. p. 810.

[2] "Die ersten Jahre sind für solche unglückliche Leute am beschwehrlichsten, absonderlich wenn sie noch jung, weil die Türken selbige entweder mit Schmeicheln, oder, wann dieses nichts verfangen will, mit der Schärfe zu ihren Glauben zu bringen suchen; wann aber dieser Sturm überwunden, wird man finden, dass die Gefangenschaft nirgend erträglicher als bey den Türken seye." (G. C. von den Driesch, p. 132.) Moreover Georgieviz says that those who persevered in the Christian faith were set free after a certain fixed period. "Si in Christiana fide perseveraverint, statuitur certum tempus serviendi, quo elapso liberi fiunt . . . Verum illis qui nostram religionem abiurarunt, nec certum tempus est serviendi, ned ullum ius in patriam redeundi, spes libertatis solummodo pendet a domini arbitrio" (p. 87). Similarly Menavino, p. 65. Cantacuzenos gives this period as seven years:—"Grata è la compagnia che essi fanno a gli schiavi loro, percioche Maumetto gli ha fra l'altre cose comandato che egli non si possa tener in servitù uno schiavo più che sette anni, et perciò nessuno o raro è colui che a tal comandamento voglia contrafare" (p. 128).

[3] "Fromme Christen, die nach der Türkei oder in andere muhamedanische Länder kamen, hatten Anlass genug zur Trauer über die Häufigkeit des Abfalls ihrer Glaubensgenossen, und besonders die Schriften der Ordensgeistlichen sind voll von solchen Klagen. Bei den Sclaven konnte sich immer noch ein Gefühl des Mitleids dem der Missbilligung beimischen, aber oft genug musste man die bittersten Erfahrungen auch an freien Landsleuten machen. Die christlichen Gesandten waren keinen Tag sicher, ob ihnen nicht Leute von ihrem Gefolge davon liefen, und man that gut daran, den Tag nicht vor dem Abend zu loben." (Gmelin, p. 22.) Cf. Von den Driesch, p. 161.

[4] Thomas Smith, pp. 144–5.

and too deep resentments of the hardships of the servitude; others are enticed by the blandishments and flatteries of pleasure the Mahometan Law allows, and the allurements they have of making their condition better and more easy by a change of their Religion; having no hope left of being redeemed, they renounce their Saviour and their Christianity, and soon forget their original country, and are no longer looked upon as strangers, but pass for natives."

Much of course depended upon the individual character of the different Christian slaves themselves. The anonymous writer, so often quoted above, whose long captivity made him so competent to speak on their condition, divides them into three classes:—first, those who passed their days in all simplicity, not caring to trouble themselves to learn anything about the religion of their masters; for them it was enough to know that the Turks were infidels, and so, as far as their captive condition and their yoke of slavery allowed, they avoided having anything to do with them and their religious worship, fearing lest they should be led astray by their errors, and striving to observe the Christian faith as far as their knowledge and power went. The second class consisted of those whose curiosity led them to study and investigate the doings of the Turks: if, by the help of God, they had time enough to dive into their secrets, and understanding enough for the investigation of them and light of reason to find the interpretation thereof, they not only came out of the trial unscathed, but had their own faith strengthened. The third class includes those who, examining the Muslim religion without due caution, fail to dive into its depths and find the interpretation of it and so are deceived; believing the errors of the Turks to be the truth, they lose their own faith and embrace the false religion of the Muslims, hereby not only compassing their own destruction, but setting a bad example to others: of such men the number is infinite.[1]

Conversion to Islam did not, as some writers have affirmed, release the slave from his captivity and make him a free man,[2]

[1] Turchicæ Spurcitiæ Suggillatio, fol. xxxv. (a).

[2] M. d'Ohsson, vol. iii. p. 133. Georgieviz, p. 87 (quoted above). Menavino, p. 95.

for emancipation was solely at the discretion of the master; who indeed often promised to set any slave free, without the payment of ransom, if only he would embrace Islam;[1] but, on the other hand, would also freely emancipate the Christian slave, even though he had persevered in his religion, provided he had proved himself a faithful servant, and would make provision for his old age.[2]

There were many others who, like the Christian slaves, separated from early surroundings and associations, found themselves cut loose from old ties and thrown into the midst of a society animated by social and religious ideals of an entirely novel character. The crowds of Christian workmen that came wandering from the conquered countries in the fifteenth century to Adrianople and other Turkish cities in search of employment, were easily persuaded to settle there and adopt the faith of Islam.[3] Similarly the Christian families that Muḥammad II transported from conquered provinces in Europe into Asia Minor,[4] may well have become merged into the mass of the Muslim population by almost imperceptible degrees, as was the case with the Armenians carried away into Persia by Shāh 'Abbās I (1587–1629), most of whom appear to have passed over to Islam in the second generation.[5]

During the eighteenth and nineteenth centuries there would seem to have been a decay of the missionary spirit among the Turks, but the latter years of the reign of Sultan 'Abd al-Ḥamīd witnessed a renewed interest in Muslim propaganda, and Turkish newspapers began to record instances of conversion. Among the most noteworthy of such converts were some eighteen amīrs of the princely family of Shihāb in Mount Lebanon, which had been Christian for about a century; they are said to claim descent from the Quraysh, and the Turks made every effort to bring them back to the fold of Islam; those who became

[1] Von den Driesch, p. 250.
[2] Id. p. 131–2.
[3] Turchicæ Spurcitiæ Suggillatio, fol. xi.
[4] Hertzberg, p. 621.
[5] "The old People dying, the young ones generally turn Mahumetans: so that now (1655) you can hardly meet with two Christian Armenians in all those fair Plains, which their fathers were sent to manure." Tavernier (I), p. 16.

Muslims were appointed to lucrative posts in the Turkish civil service.[1]

In the following pages it is proposed to give a more detailed and particular account of the spread of Islam among the Christian populations of Albania, Servia, Bosnia and Crete, as the history of each of these countries after its conquest by the Ottomans presents some special features of interest in the history of the propagation of Islam.

The Albanians, with the exception of some settlements in Greece,[2] inhabit the mountainous country that stretches along the east shore of the Adriatic from Montenegro to the Gulf of Arta. They form one of the oldest and purest-blooded races in Europe and are said to belong to the Pelasgic branch of the Aryan stock.

Their country was first invaded by the Turks in 1387, but the Turkish forces soon had to withdraw, and the authority of the Sultan was recognised for the first time in 1423. For a short period Albania regained its independence under George Kastriota, who is better known under his Muhammadan name of Scanderbeg or Sikandarbeg. Recent investigations have established the falsity of the romantic fictions that had gathered round the story of his early days—how that as a boy he had been surrendered as a hostage to the Turks, had been brought up among them as a Muslim and had won the special favour of the Sultan. The truth is, that the days of his youth were passed in his native mountains and his warfare with the Turks began with the victory gained over them in 1444; for more than twenty years he maintained a vigorous and successful resistance to their invading forces, but after his death in 1467, the Turks began again to take possession of Albania. Krūya, the capital of the Kastriot dynasty, fell into their hands eleven years later, and from this date there appears to have been no organised resistance of the whole country, though revolts were frequent and the subjection of the country was never complete. Some of the sea-port towns held out much longer; Durazzo was captured in 1501, while Antivari, the northernmost point of the sea-coast of Albania, did not

[1] H. H. Jessup: Fifty-three Years in Syria, vol. ii. p. 658. (New York, 1910.)
[2] For a list of these, see Finlay, vol. vi. pp. 28–9.

surrender until 1571. The terms of capitulation were that the city should retain its old laws and magistrature, that there should be free and public exercise of the Christian religion, that the churches and chapels should remain uninjured and might be rebuilt if they fell into decay; that the citizens should retain all their movable and immovable property and should not be burdened by any additional taxation.

The Albanians under Turkish rule appear always to have maintained a kind of semi-autonomy, and the several tribes and clans remained as essentially independent as they were before the conquest. Though vassals of the Sultans, they would not brook the interference of Turkish officials in their internal administration, and there is reason to believe that the Turkish Government has never been able to appoint or confirm any provincial governor who was not a native of Albania, and had not already established his influence by his arms, policy or connections.[1] Their racial pride is intense, and to the present day, the Albanian, if asked what he is, will call himself a Skipetar,[2] before saying whether he is a Christian or a Muhammadan—a very remarkable instance of national feeling obliterating the fierce distinction between these two religions that so forcibly obtrudes itself in the rest of the Ottoman empire. The Christian and Muhammadan Albanians alike, just as they speak the same language, so do they cherish the same traditions, and observe the same manners and customs; and pride in their common nationality has been too strong a bond to allow differences of religious belief to split the nation into separate communities on this basis.[3] Side by side they served in the

[1] Leake, p. 250.

[2] The name by which the Albanians always call themselves, lit. rock-dwellers.

[3] One of themselves, an Albanian Christian, speaking of the enmity existing between the Christians and Muhammadans of Bulgaria, says: "Aber für Albanien liegen die Dachen ganz anders. Die Muselmänner sind Albanesen, wie die Christen; sie sprechen dieselbe Sprache, sie haben dieselben Sitten, sie folgen denselben Gebräuchen, sie haben dieselben Traditionen; sie und die Christen haben sich niemals gehasst, zwischen ihnen herrscht keine Jahrhunderte alte Feindschaft. Der Unterschied der Religion war niemals ein zu einer systematischen Trennung treibendes Motiv; Muselmänner und Christen haben stets, mit wenigen Ausnahmen, auf gleichem Fusse gelebt, sich der gleichen Rechte erfreuend, dieselben Pflichten erfüllend." (Wassa Effendi: Albanien und die Albanesen, p. 59.) (Berlin, 1879.)

irregular troops, which soon after the Turkish conquest became the main dependence of the government in all its internal administration, and both classes found the same ready employment in the service of the local pashas, being accounted the bravest soldiers in the empire. Christian Albanians served in the Ottoman army in the Crimean War,[1] and though they have perhaps been a little more quiet and agricultural than their Muslim fellow-countrymen, still the difference has been small: they have always retained their arms and military habits, have always displayed the same fierce, proud, untameable spirit, and been animated with the same intense national feeling as their brethren who had embraced the creed of the Prophet.[2]

The consideration of these facts is of importance in tracing the spread of Islam in Albania, for it appears to have been propagated very gradually by the people of the country themselves, and not under pressure of foreign influences. The details that we possess of this movement are very meagre, as the history of Albania from the close of the fifteenth century to the rise of 'Alī Pasha three hundred years later, is almost a blank; what knowledge we have, therefore, of the slow but continuous accession of converts to Islam during this period, is derived from the ecclesiastical chronicles of the various dioceses,[3] and the reports sent in from time to time to the Pope and the Congregatio de Propaganda Fide.[4] But it goes without saying that the very nature of these sources gives the information derived from them the stamp of imperfection—especially in the matter of the motives assigned for conversion. For an ecclesiastic of those times to have even entertained the possibility of a conversion to Islam from genuine conviction —much less have openly expressed such an opinion in writing to his superiors—is well-nigh inconceivable.

[1] Finlay, vol. v. p. 46.

[2] Clark, pp. 175–7. The Mirdites, who are very fanatical Roman Catholics (in the diocese of Alessio), will not suffer a Muhammadan to live in their mountains, and no member of their tribe has ever abjured his faith; were any Mirdite to attempt to do so, he would certainly be put to death, unless he succeeded in making good his escape from Albania. (Hecquard: Histoire de la Haute Albanie, p. 224.)

[3] Published in Farlati's Illyricum Sacrum.

[4] Alessandro Comuleo, 1593. Bizzi, 1610. Marco Crisio, 1651. Fra Bonaventura di S. Antonio, 1652. Zmaievich, 1703.

During the sixteenth century, Islam appears to have made but little progress, though the tide of conversion had already set in. In 1610 the Christian population exceeded the Muhammadan in the proportion of ten to one,[1] and as most of the villages were inhabited by Christians, with a very small admixture of Muhammadans,[2] the conversions appear to have been more frequent in the large towns. In Antivari, for example, while many Christians elected to emigrate into the neighbouring Christian countries, the majority of those who remained, both high-born and low, went over gradually to the Muslim faith, so that the Christian population grew less and less day by day.[3] As the number of accessions to Islam increased, churches were converted into mosques—a measure which, though contrary to the terms of the capitulation, seems justified by the change in the religion of the people.[4] In 1610 two collegiate churches only remained in the hands of the Latin Christians, but these appear to have sufficed for the needs of the community;[5] what this amounted to can only roughly be guessed from the words of Marco Bizzi: "There are about 600 houses inhabited indiscriminately by Muhammadans and Christians—both Latin and Schismatics (i.e. of the Orthodox Greek Church): the number of the Muhammadans is a little in excess of the Christians, and that of the Latins in excess of the Schismatics."

In the accounts we have of the social relations between the Christians and the Muslims, and in the absence of any sharp line of demarcation between the two communities, we find some clue to the manner in which Muhammadan influences gradually gained converts from among the Christian population in proportion as the vigour and the spiritual life of the Church declined.

[1] Bizzi, fol. 60, b. [2] Bizzi, fol. 35, a. [3] Farlati, vol. vii. pp. 104, 107.

[4] It is also complained that the Archbishop's palace was appropriated by the Muhammadans, but it had been left unoccupied for eight years, as Archbishop Ambrosius (flor. 1579–1598) had found it prudent to go into exile, having attacked Islam "with more fervour than caution, inveighing against Muḥammad and damning his Satanic doctrines." (Farlati, vol. vii. p. 107.)

[5] Bizzi, fol. 9. where he says, "E comunicai quella mattina quasi tutta la Christianità latina." From a comparison with statistics given by Zmaievich (fol. 227) I would hazard the conjecture that the Latin Christian community at this time amounted to rather over a thousand souls.

It had become very common for Christian parents to give their daughters in marriage to Muhammadans, and for Christian women to make no objection to such unions.[1] The male children born of these mixed marriages were brought up as Musalmans, but the girls were allowed to follow the religion of their mother.[2] Such permission was rendered practically ineffective by the action of the Christian ecclesiastics, who ordered the mothers to be excluded from the churches and from participation in the sacraments;[3] and consequently (though the parish priests often disregarded the commands of their superiors) many of these women embraced the faith of their husbands. But even then they kept up a superstitious observance of the rite of baptism, which was supposed to be a sovereign specific against leprosy, witches and wolves,[4] and Christian priests were found ready to pander to this superstition for any Muhammadan woman who wished to have her children baptised.[5] This good feeling between the members of the two religions[6] is similarly illustrated by the attendance of Muhammadans at the festivals of Christian saints; e.g. Marco Bizzi says that on the feast-day of St. Elias (for whom the Albanians appear to have had a special devotion) there were as many Muhammadans present in the church as Christians.[7] Even to the present day we are told that Albanian Muhammadans revere the Virgin Mary and the Christian saints, and make pilgrimages to their shrines,

[1] Bizzi, fol. 27, b; 38, b.

[2] Veniero, fol. 34. This was also the custom in some villages of Albania as late as the beginning of the nineteenth century; see W. M. Leake: Travels in Northern Greece, vol. i. p. 49. (London, 1835): "In some villages, Mahometans are married to Greek women, the sons are educated as Turks, and the daughters as Christians; and pork and mutton are eaten at the same table."

[3] Bizzi, fol. 38, b. Farlati, tom. vii. p. 158.

[4] Bizzi, fol. 10, b. Veniero, fol. 34.

[5] Shortly after Marco Bizzi's arrival at Antivari a Muhammadan lady of high rank wished to have her child baptised by the Archbishop himself, who tells us that she complained bitterly to one of the leading Christians of the city that "io non mi fossi degnato di far a lei questo piacere, il qual quotidianamente vien fatto dai miei preti a richiesta di qualsivoglia plebeo" (fol. 10, b).

[6] For modern instances of the harmonious relations subsisting between the followers of the two faiths living together in the same village, see Hyacinthe Hecquard: Histoire et description de la Haute Albanie (pp. 153, 162, 200). (Paris, 1858.)

[7] Bizzi, fol. 38, a.

while Christians on the other hand resort to the tombs of Muslim saints for the cure of ailments or in fulfilment of vows.[1] In the town of Calevacci, where there were sixty Christian and ten Muhammadan households, the followers of the Prophet contributed towards the support of the parish priest, as the majority of them had Christian wives.[2] Under such circumstances it is hardly surprising to learn that many openly professed Islam, while satisfying their consciences by saying that they professed Christianity in their hearts.[3] Marco Bizzi has three explanations to offer for such a lapse—the attraction of worldly advantage, the desire to avoid the payment of tribute, and the want of a sufficiently large number of intelligent clergy to supply the spiritual needs of the country.[4] Conversions are frequently ascribed to the pressure of the burden of taxation imposed upon the Christians, and whole villages are said to have apostatised to avoid payment of the tribute. As no details are given, it is impossible to judge whether there was really sufficient ground for the complaint, or whether this was not the apology for their conduct alleged by the renegades in order to make some kind of excuse to their former co-religionists—or indeed an exaggeration on the part of ecclesiastics to whom a genuine conversion to Islam on rational grounds seemed an absolute impossibility. A century later (in 1703) the capitation-tax was six reals a head for each male and this (with the exception of a tax, termed sciataraccio, of three reals a year) was the only burden imposed on the Christians exclusively.[5] Men must have had very little attachment to their religion to abandon it merely in order to be quit of so slight a penalty, and with no other motive; and the very existence of so large a body of Christians in Albania at the present time shows that the burden could not have been so heavy as to force them into apostasy without any other alternative.

If only we had something more than vague general complaints against the "Turkish tyranny," we should be better able to determine how far this could have had such a

[1] Garnett, p. 267.
[2] Bizzi, fol. 36, b.
[3] Id. fol. 38, b.; 37, a.
[4] Bizzi, fol. 38, b; 61, a; 37, a; 33, b.
[5] Zmaievich, fol. 5. The Venetian real in the eighteenth century was equal to a Turkish piastre. (Businello, p. 94.)

preponderating influence as is ascribed to it : but the evidence alleged seems hardly to warrant such a conclusion. The vicious practice followed by the Ottoman Court of selling posts in the provinces to the highest bidder and the uncertainty of the tenure of such posts, often resulted in the occupants trying to amass as large a fortune as possible by extortions of every kind. But such burdens are said to have weighed as heavily on Muhammadans as Christians.[1] Though certainly an avaricious and unjust official may have found it easier to oppress the Christians than the Muslims, especially when the former were convicted of treasonable correspondence with the Venetians and other Christian states and were suspected of a wish to revolt.

However this may have been, there can be little doubt of the influence exerted by the zealous activity and vigorous life of Islam in the face of the apathetic and ignorant Christian clergy. If Islam in Albania had many such exponents as the Mullā, whose sincerity, courtesy and friendliness are praised by Marco Bizzi, with whom he used to discuss religious questions, it may well have made its way.[2] The majority of the Christian clergy appear to have been wholly unlettered : most of them, though they could read a little, did not know how to write, and were so ignorant of the duties of their sacred calling that they could not even repeat the formula of absolution by heart.[3] Though they had to recite the mass and other services in Latin, there were very few who could understand any of it, as they were ignorant of any language but their mother tongue, and they had only a vague, traditionary knowledge of the truths of their religion.[4] Marco Bizzi considered the inadequate episcopate of the country responsible for these evils, as for the small numbers of the clergy, and their ignorance of their sacred calling, and for the large number of Christians who grew old and even died without being confirmed, and apostatised almost everywhere ;[5] and unless this were

[1] Bizzi, fol. 12–13. Zmaievich, fol. 5.
[2] Bizzi, fol. 10–11.
[3] Id. fol. 31, b.
[4] Id. fol. 60, b.
[5] Id. fol. 33, b. " Qui deriva il puoco numero de Sacerdoti in quelle parti e la puoca loro intelligenza in quel mestiero ; il gran numero de' Christiani, che invecchiano, et anco morono senza il sacramento della Confermatione et apostatano della fede quasi per tutto."

remedied he prophesied a rapid decay of Christianity in the country.[1] Several priests were also accused of keeping concubines, and of drunkenness.[2]

It may here be observed that the Albanian priests were not the repositories of the national aspirations and ideals, as were the clergy of the Orthodox Church in other provinces of the Turkish empire, who in spite of their ignorance kept alive among their people that devotion to the Christian faith which formed the nucleus of the national life of the Greeks.[3] On the contrary, the Albanians cherished a national feeling that was quite apart from religious belief, and with regard to the Turks, considered, in true feudal spirit, that as they were the masters of the country they ought to be obeyed whatever commands they gave.[4]

There is a curious story of conversion which is said to have taken place owing to a want of amicable relations between a Christian priest and his people, as follows: "Many years since, when all the country was Christian, there stood in the city of Scutari a beautiful image of the Virgin Mary, to whose shrine thousands flocked every year from all parts of the country to offer their gifts, perform their devotions, and be healed of their infirmities. For some cause or other, however, it fell out that there was dissension between the priest and the people, and one day the latter came to the church in great crowds, declaring that unless the priest yielded to them they would then and there abjure the faith of Christ and embrace in its stead that of Muḥammad. The priest, whether right or wrong, still remaining firm, his congregation tore the rosaries and crosses from their necks, trampled them under their feet, and going to the nearest mosque, were received by the Mollah into the fold of the True Believers." [5]

Through the negligence and apathy of the Christian clergy

1 "Se l'Albania non riceverà qualche maggior agiuto in meno di anni anderà a male quasi tutta quella Christianità per il puoco numero dei Vescovi e dei Sacerdoti di qualche intelligenza." (Id. fol. 61, a.)

2 Id. fol. 36, a. Id. fol. 64, b.

3 Finlay, vol. v. pp. 153–4. Clark, p. 290.

4 "E quei miseri hanno fermata la conscientia in creder di non peccar per simil coniuntioni (i.e. the giving of Christian girls in marriage to Muhammadans) per esser i turchi signori del paese, e che però non si possa, nè devea far altro che obbedirli quando comandano qualsivoglia cosa." (Bizzi, fol. 38, b.)

5 Garnett, p. 268.

many abuses and irregularities had been allowed to creep into the Christian society; in one of which, namely the practice of contracting marriages without the sanction of the Church or any religious ceremony, we find an approximation to the Muhammadan law, which makes marriage a civil contract. In order to remedy this evil, the husband and wife were to be excluded from the Church, until they had conformed to the ecclesiastical law and gone through the service in the regular manner.[1]

In the course of the seventeenth century, the social conditions and other factors, indicated above, bore fruit abundantly, and the numbers of the Christian population began rapidly to decline. In the brief space of thirty years, between 1620 and 1650, about 300,000 Albanians are said to have gone over to Islam.[2] In 1624 there were only 2000 Catholics in the whole diocese of Antivari, and in the city itself only one church; at the close of the century, even this church was no longer used for Christian worship, as there were only two families of Roman Catholics left.[3] In the whole country generally, the majority of the Christian community in 1651 was composed of women, as the male population had apostatised in such large numbers to Islam.[4] Matters were still worse at the close of the century, the Catholics being then fewer in number than the Muhammadans, the proportions being about 1 to $1\frac{1}{3}$,[5] whereas less than a hundred years before, they had outnumbered the Muhammadans in the proportion of 10 to 1;[6] in the Archbishopric of Durazzo the Christian population had decreased by about half in twenty years,[7] in another town (in the diocese of Kroia) the entire population passed from Christianity to Islam in the course of thirty years.[8] In spite of the frequent protests and regulations made by their ecclesiastical superiors, the parish priests continued to countenance the open profession of Islam along with a secret adherence to Christianity, on the part of many male members of their flocks, by administering to them the Blessed Sacrament; the result of which was that the children

[1] Bizzi, fol. 38, b; 63, a.
[2] Kyriakos, p. 12.
[3] Farlati, tom. vii. pp. 124, 141.
[4] Marco Crisio, p. 202.
[5] Zmaievich, fol. 227.
[6] Bizzi, fol. 60, b.
[7] Zmaievich, fol. 137.
[8] Zmaievich, fol. 157.

of such persons, being brought up as Muhammadans, were for ever lost to the Christian Church.[1] Similarly, Christian parents still gave their daughters in marriage to Muhammadans, the parish priests countenancing such unions by administering the sacrament to such women,[2] in spite of the fulminations of the higher clergy against such indulgence.[3] Such action on the part of the lower clergy can hardly, however, be taken as indicating any great zeal on behalf of the spiritual welfare of their flocks, in the face of the accusations brought against them; the majority of them are accused of being scandalous livers, who very seldom went to confession and held drunken revels in their parsonages on festival days; they sold the property of the Church, frequently absented themselves from their parishes, and when censured, succeeded in getting off by putting themselves under the protection of the Turks.[4] The Reformed Franciscans and the Observants who had been sent to minister to the spiritual wants of the people did nothing but quarrel and go to law with one another; much to the scandal of the laity and the neglect of the mission.[5] In the middle of the seventeenth century five out of the twelve Albanian sees were vacant; the diocese of Pullati had not been visited by a bishop for thirty years, and there were only two priests to 6348 souls.[6] In some parishes in the interior of the country, there had been no priests for more than forty years; and this was in no way due to the oppression of the "Turkish tyrant," for when at last four Franciscan missionaries were sent, they reported that they could go through the country and exercise their sacred office without any hindrance whatever.[7] The bishop of Sappa, to the great prejudice of his diocese, had been long resident in Venice, where he is said to have lived a vicious life, and had appointed as his vicar an ignorant priest who was a notorious evil-liver: this man had 12,400 souls under his charge, and, says the ecclesiastical visitor, "through the absence of the bishop there is danger of his losing his own

[1] Zmaievich, fol. 11, 159.
[2] Zmaievich, fol. 13.
[3] Bizzi, fol. 38, b. Farlati, vol. vii. p. 158.
[4] Zmaievich, fol. 13–14.
[5] Informatione circa la missione d'Albania, fol. 196.
[6] Crisio, fol. 204.
[7] Fra Bonaventura, fol. 201

soul and compassing the destruction of the souls under him and of the property of the Church." [1] The bishop of Scutari was looked upon as a tyrant by his clergy and people, and only succeeded in keeping his post through the aid of the Turks; [2] and Zmaievich complains of the bishops generally that they burdened the parishes in their diocese with forced contributions.[3] It appears that Christian ecclesiastics were authorised by the Sultan to levy contributions on their flocks. Thus the Archbishop of Antivari (1599–1607) was allowed to "exact and receive" two aspers from each Christian family, twelve for every first marriage (and double the amount for a second, and quadruple for a third marriage), and one gold piece from each parish annually, and it seems to have been possible to obtain the assistance of the Turkish authorities in levying these contributions.[4]

Throughout the whole of Albania there was not a single Christian school,[5] and the priests were profoundly ignorant: some were sent to study in Italy, but Marco Crisio condemns this practice, as such priests were in danger of finding life in Italy so pleasant that they refused to return to their native country. With a priesthood so ignorant and so careless of their sacred duties, it is not surprising to learn that the common people had no knowledge even of the rudiments of their faith, and that numerous abuses and corruptions sprang up among them, which "wrought the utmost desolation to this vineyard of the Lord." [6] Many Christians lived in open concubinage for years, still, however, being admitted to the sacraments,[7] while others had a plurality of wives.[8] In this latter practice we notice an assimilation between the habits of the two communities—the Christian and the Muslim—which is further illustrated by the admission of Muhammadans as sponsors at the baptism of Christian children, while the old superstitious custom of baptising Muhammadan children was still sanctioned by the priests.[9]

1 Marco Crisio, fol. 202, 205.
2 Id. fol. 205.
3 Zmaievich, fol. 13.
4 Farlati, tom. vii. p. 109. Bizzi, fol. 19, b.
5 Marco Crisio, fol. 205.
6 Zmaievich, fol. 11.
7 Id. fol. 32.
8 Crisio, fol. 204.
9 Zmaievich, fol. 11. Farlati, vol. vii. p. 151.

Such being the state of the Christian Church in Albania in the latter half of the seventeenth century, some very trifling incentive would have been enough to bring about a widespread apostasy; and the punishment inflicted on the rebellious Catholics in the latter half of the century was a determining factor more than sufficient to consummate the tendencies that had been drawing them towards Islam and to cause large numbers of them to fall away from the Christian Church. The rebellious movement referred to seems to have been instigated by George, the thirty-ninth Archbishop of Antivari (1635–1644), who through the bishops of Durazzo, Scodra and Alessio tried to induce the leaders of the Christian community to conspire against the Turkish rule and hand over the country to the neighbouring Christian power, the Republic of Venice. As in his time Venice was at peace with the Turks a fitting opportunity for the hatching of this plot did not occur, but in 1645 war broke out between Turkey and the Republic, and the Venetians made an unsuccessful attempt to capture the city of Antivari, which before the Turkish conquest had been in their possession for more than three centuries (1262–1571). The Albanian Catholics who had sided with the enemy and secretly given them assistance were severely punished and deprived of their privileges, while the Greek Christians (who had everything to fear in the event of the restoration of the Venetian rule and had remained faithful to the Turkish government) were liberally rewarded and were lauded as the saviours of their country. Many of the Catholics either became Muhammadans or joined the Greek Church. The latter fact is very significant as showing that there was no persecution of the Christians *as such*, nor any attempt to *force* the acceptance of Islam upon them. The Catholics who became Muhammadans did so to avoid the odium of their position after the failure of their plot, and could have gained the same end and have at the same time retained their Christian faith by joining the Greek Church, which was not only officially recognised by the Turkish government but in high favour in Antivari at this time: so that those who neglected to do so, could have had very little attachment to the Christian religion. The same remark holds good of the numerous conversions to Islam in the succeeding years: Zmaievich attributes them in some cases to the desire to avoid the payment of tribute, but, from what has been said above, it is very unlikely that this was the sole determining motive.

In 1649 a still more widespread insurrection broke out, an Archbishop of Antivari, Joseph Maria Bonaldo (1646–1654), being again the main instigator of the movement; and the leading citizens of Antivari, Scodra and other towns conspired to throw open their gates to the army of the Venetian Republic. But this plot also failed and the insurrection was forcibly crushed by the Turkish troops, aided by the dissensions that arose among the Christians themselves. Many Albanians whose influence was feared were transported from their own country into the interior of the Turkish dominions; a body of 3000 men crossed the border into Venetian territory; those who remained were overawed by the erection of fortresses and the marching of troops through the disaffected districts, while heavy fines were imposed upon the malcontents.[1]

Unfortunately the Christian writers who complain of the "unjust tributes and vexations" with which the Turks oppressed the Albanians, so that they apostatised to Islam,[2] make use only of general expressions, and give us no details to enable us to judge whether or not such complaints were justified by the facts. Zmaievich prefaces his account of the apostasy of 2000 persons with an enumeration of the taxes and other burdens the Christians had to bear, but all these, he says, were common also to the Muhammadans, with the exception of the capitation-tax of six reals a year for each male, and another tax, termed sciataraccio, of three reals a year.[3] He concludes with the words: "The nation, wounded by these taxes in its weakest part, namely, worldly interest, to the consideration of which it has a singular leaning either by nature or by necessity, has given just cause for lamenting the deplorable loss of about 2000 souls who apostatised from the true faith so as not to be subject to the tribute."[4] There is nothing in his report to show that

[1] Farlati, vol. vii. pp. 126–32. Zmaievich, fol. 4–5, fol. 20.
[2] "Plerique, ut se iniquis tributis et vexationibus eximerent, paullatim a Christiana religione deficere coeperunt." (Farlati, tom. vii. p. 311.)
[3] Zmaievich fol. 5. [4] Id. fol. 5.

the taxes the Catholics had to pay constituted so intolerable a burden as to force them to renounce their creed, and though he attributes many conversions to Islam to the desire of escaping the tribute, he says expressly that these apostasies from the Christian faith are mainly to be ascribed to the extreme ignorance of the clergy,[1] in great measure also to their practice of admitting to the sacraments those who openly professed Islam while in secret adhering to the Christian faith: [2] in another place he says, speaking of the clergy who were not fit to be parish priests and their practice of administering the sacraments to apostates and secret Christians: "These are precisely the two causes from which have come all the losses that the Christian Church has sustained in Albania." [3] There is very little doubt that the widespread apostasy at this time was the result of a long series of influences similar to those mentioned in the preceding pages, and that the deliverance from the payment of the tribute was the last link in the chain.

What active efforts Muhammadans themselves were making to gain over the Christians to Islam, we can hardly expect to learn from the report of an ecclesiastical visitor. But we find mention of a district, the inhabitants of which, from their intercourse with the Turks, had "contracted the vices of these infidels," and one of the chief causes of their falling away from the Christian faith was their contracting marriages with Turkish women.[4] There were no doubt strong Muhammadan influences at work here, as also in the two parishes of Biscascia and Basia, whose joint population of nearly a thousand souls was "exposed to the obvious risk of apostatising through lack of any pastor," and were "much tempted in their faith, and needed to be strengthened in it by wise and zealous pastors." [5]

Zmaievich speaks of one of the old noble Christian families in the neighbourhood of Antivari which was represented at that time by two brothers; the elder of these had been "wheedled" by the prominent Muhammadans of the place, who were closely related to him, into denying his

[1] Zmaievich, fol. 15, 197.
[2] Id. fol. 11.
[3] Id. fol. 137.
[4] Id. fol. 149.
[5] Id. fol. 143–4.

faith; the younger wished to study for the priesthood, in which office " he would be of much assistance to the Christian Church through the high esteem in which the Turks held his family; which though poor was universally respected."[1] This indeed is another indication of the fact that the Muhammadans did not ill-treat the Christians, merely as such, but only when they showed themselves to be politically disaffected. Zmaievich, who was himself an Albanian, and took up his residence in his diocese instead of in Venetian territory, as many of the Archbishops of Antivari seem to have done,[2] was received with " extraordinary honours " and with " marvellous courtesy," not only by the Turkish officials generally, but also by the Supreme Pasha of Albania himself, who gave him the place of honour in his Divan, always accompanying him to the door on his departure and receiving him there on his arrival.[3] This " barbarian " who " showed himself more like a generous-hearted Christian than a Turk," gave more substantial marks of good feeling towards the Christians by remitting—at the Archbishop's request—the tribute due for the ensuing year from four separate towns.[4] If any of the Christian clergy were roughly treated by the Turks, it seems generally to have been due to the suspicion of treasonable correspondence with the enemies of the Turks; ecclesiastical visits to Italy seem also to have excited—and in many cases, justly—such suspicions. Otherwise the Christian clergy seem to have had no reason to complain of the treatment they received from the Muslims; Zmaievich even speaks of one parish priest being " much beloved by the principal Turks,"[5] and doubtless there were parallels in Albania to the case of a priest in the diocese of Trebinje in Herzegovina, who in the early part of the eighteenth century was suspected, on account of his familiar intercourse with Muhammadans, of having formed an intention to embrace Islam, and was accordingly sent by his bishop to Rome under safe custody.[6]

No subsequent period of Albanian history appears to

[1] Zmaievich, fol. 22.
[2] Farlati, tom. vii. p. 141.
[3] Zmaievich, fol. 7, 17.
[4] Id. fol. 9.
[5] Id. fol. 141.
[6] Farlati, vol. vi. p. 317.

have witnessed such widespread apostasy as the seventeenth century, but there have been occasional accessions to Islam up to more recent times. In Southern Albania, the country of the Tosks, the preponderance of the Muhammadan population placed the Christians at a disadvantage, and a story is told of the Karamurtads, inhabitants of thirty-six villages near Pogoniani, that up to the close of the eighteenth century they were Christians, but finding themselves unable to repel the continual attacks of the neighbouring Muhammadan population of Leskoviki, they met in a church and prayed that the saints might work some miracle on their behalf; they swore to fast till Easter in expectation of the divine assistance; but Easter came and no miracle was wrought, so the whole population embraced Islam; soon afterwards they obtained the arms they required and massacred their old enemies in Leskoviki and took possession of their lands.[1] Community of faith in Albania is never allowed to stand in the way of a tribal feud. Even up to the nineteenth century Albanian tribes and villages have changed their religion for very trivial reasons; part of one Christian tribe is said to have turned Muhammadan because their priest, who served several villages and visited them first, insisted on saying mass at an unreasonably early hour.[2]

At the present day the Muhammadans in Albania are said to number about 1,000,000 and the Christians 480,000, but the accuracy of these figures is not certain. The Mirdites are entirely Christian; they submitted to the Sultan on condition that no Muslim would be allowed to settle in their territory, but adherents of both the rival creeds are found in almost all the other tribes. Central Albania is said to be almost entirely Muhammadan, and the followers of Islam form about sixty per cent. of the population of Northern Albania; the Christian population attains its largest proportion in Southern Albania, especially in the districts bordering upon Greece.

The kingdom of Servia first paid tribute to the Ottomans in 1375 and lost its independence after the disastrous defeat of Kossovo (1389), where both the king of Servia and the

[1] Eliot, p. 401. [2] Id. p. 392.

Turkish sultan were left dead upon the field. The successors of the two sovereigns entered into a friendly compact, the young Servian prince, Stephen, acknowledged the suzerainty of Turkey, gave his sister in marriage to the new sultan, Bāyazīd, and formed with him a league of brotherhood. At the battle of Nikopolis (1394), which gave to the Turks assured possession of the whole Balkan peninsula, except the district surrounding Constantinople, the Servian contingent turned the wavering fortune of the battle and gave the victory to the Turks. On the field of Angora (1402), when the Turkish power was annihilated and Bāyazīd himself taken prisoner by Tīmūr, Stephen was present with his Servian troops and fought bravely for his brother-in-law, and instead of taking this opportunity of securing his independence, remained faithful to his engagement, and stood by the sons of Bāyazīd until they recovered their father's throne. Under the successor of Stephen, George Brankovich, Servia enjoyed a semi-independence, but when in 1438 he raised the standard of revolt, his country was again overrun by the Turks. Then for a time Servia had to acknowledge the suzerainty of Hungary, but the defeat of John Hunyady at Varna in 1444 brought her once more under tribute, and in 1459 she finally became a Turkish province.

It is not impossible that the Servians who had embraced Islam after the battle of Kossovo had knowledge of the fate of the little Muslim community that had been rooted out of Hungary about a century before, and therefore preferred the domination of the Turks to that of the Hungarians. Yāqūt gives the following account of his meeting, about the year 1228, with some members of this group of followers of the Prophet in mediæval Europe, who had owed their conversion to Muslims who had settled among them. "In the city of Aleppo, I met a large number of persons called Bashkirs, with reddish hair and reddish faces. They were studying law according to the school of Abū Ḥanīfah (may God be well pleased with him!) I asked one of them who seemed to be an intelligent fellow for information concerning their country and their condition. He told me, 'Our country is situated on the other side of Constantinople, in a kingdom of a people of the Franks called the Hungarians.

We are Muslims, subjects of their king, and live on the border of his territory, occupying about thirty villages, which are almost like small towns. But the king of the Hungarians does not allow us to build walls round any of them, lest we should revolt against him. We are situated in the midst of Christian countries, having the land of the Slavs on the north, on the south, that of the Pope, i. e. Rome (now the Pope is the head of the Franks, the vicar of the Messiah in their eyes, like the commander of the faithful in the eyes of the Muslims; his authority extends over all matters connected with religion among the whole of them); on the west, Andalusia; on the east, the land of the Greeks, Constantinople and its provinces.' He added, 'Our language is the language of the Franks, we dress after their fashion, we serve with them in the army, and we join them in attacking all their enemies, because they only go to war with the enemies of Islam.' I then asked him how it was they had adopted Islam in spite of their dwelling in the midst of the unbelievers. He answered, 'I have heard several of our forefathers say that a long time ago seven Muslims came from Bulgaria and settled among us. In kindly fashion they pointed out to us our errors and directed us into the right way, the faith of Islam. Then God guided us and (praise be to God!) we all became Muslims and God opened our hearts to the faith. We have come to this country to study law; when we return to our own land, the people will do us honour and put us in charge of their religious affairs.'"[1] Islam kept its ground among the Bashkirs of Hungary until 1340, when King Charles Robert compelled all his subjects that were not yet Christians to embrace the Christian faith or quit the country.[2]

The Servian Muslims may, therefore, well have been pleased to escape from the rule of Hungary, like their Christian fellow-countrymen, for when these were given the choice between the Roman Catholic rule of Hungary and the Muslim rule of the Turks, the devotion of the Servians to the Greek Church led them to prefer the tolerance of the Muhammadans to the uncompromising proselytising

[1] Yāqūt, vol. i. p. 469 sq.
[2] Géographie d'Aboulféda, traduite par M. Reinaud, tome ii. pp 294–5.

spirit of the Latins. An old legend thus represents their feelings at this time :—The Turks and the Hungarians were at war; George Brankovich sought out John Hunyady and asked him, "If you are victorious, what will you do?" "Establish the Roman Catholic faith," was the answer. Then he sought out the sultan and asked him, "If you come out victorious, what will you do with our religion?" "By the side of every mosque shall stand a church, and every man shall be free to pray in whichever he chooses." [1] The treachery of some Servian priests forced the garrison of Belgrade to capitulate to the Turks; [2] similarly the Servians of Semendria, on the Danube, welcomed the Turkish troops who in 1600 delivered them from the rule of their Catholic neighbours.[3]

The spread of Islam among the Servians began immediately after the battle of Kossovo, when a large part of the old feudal nobility, such as still remained alive and did not take refuge in neighbouring Christian countries, went over voluntarily to the faith of the Prophet, in order to keep their old privileges undisturbed.[4] In these converted nobles the sultans found the most zealous propagandists of the new faith.[5] But the majority of the Servian people clung firmly to their old religion through all their troubles and sufferings, and only in Stara Serbia or Old Servia,[6] which now forms the north-eastern portion of modern Albania, has there been any very considerable number of conversions. Even here the spread of Muhammadanism proceeded very slowly until the seventeenth century, when the Austrians induced the Servians to rise in revolt and, after the ill-success of this rising, the then Patriarch, Arsenius III Tsernoïevich, in 1690 emigrated with 40,000 Servian families across the border into Hungary; another exodus in 1739 of 15,000 families under the leadership of Arsenius IV Jovanovich, well nigh denuded this part of the country of its original Servian population.[7]

1 Enrique Dupuy de Lôme: Los Esclavos y Turquía, pp. 17–18. (Madrid, 1877.)

2 De la Jonquière, p. 215.

3 Id. p. 290.

4 Kanitz, p. 37.

5 Id. pp. 37–8.

6 A map of this country is given by Mackenzie and Irby (p. 243): it contains Prizren, the old Servian capital, Ipek, the seat of the Servian Patriarch, and the battle-field of Kossovo.

7 Kanitz, p. 37.

Albanian colonists from the south pressed into the country vacated by the fugitives: these Albanians at the time of their arrival were Roman Catholics for the most part, but after they settled in Old Servia they gradually adopted Islam and at the present time the remnant of Roman Catholic Albanians is but small, though from time to time it is recruited by fresh arrivals from the mountains: the new-comers, however, usually follow the example of their predecessors, and after a while become Muhammadans.[1]

After this Albanian immigration, Islam began to spread more rapidly among the remnant of the Servian population. The Servian clergy were very ignorant and unlettered, they could only manage with difficulty to read their service-books and hardly any had learned to write; they neither preached to the people nor taught them the catechism, consequently in whole villages scarcely a man could be found who knew the Lord's Prayer or how many commandments there were; even the priests themselves were quite as ignorant.[2] After the insurrection of 1689, the Patriarch of Ipek, the ecclesiastical capital of Servia, was appointed by the Porte, but in 1737, as the result of another rebellion, the Servian Patriarchate was entirely suppressed and the Servian Church made dependent upon the Greek Patriarch of Constantinople. The churches were filled with Greek bishops, who made common cause with the Turkish Beys and Pashas in bleeding the unfortunate Christians: their national language was proscribed and the Old Slavonic service-books, etc., were collected and sent off to Constantinople.[3] With such a clergy it is not surprising that the Christian faith should decline: e. g. in the commune of Gora (in the district of Prizren), which had begun to become Muhammadanised soon after the great exodus of 1690, the Servians that still clung to the Christian faith, appealed again and again to the Greek bishop of Prizren to send them priests, at least occasionally, but all in vain; their children remained unbaptised, weddings and burials were conducted without the blessing of the Church, and the consecrated buildings fell into decay.[4] In the neighbouring district

[1] Mackenzie and Irby, pp. 250–1. [2] Farlati, vol. vii. pp. 127–8.
[3] Mackenzie and Irby, pp. 374–5. Kanitz, p. 39. [4] Id. pp. 39–40.

of Opolje, similarly, the present Muslim population of 9500 souls is probably for the most part descended from the original Slav inhabitants of the place.[1] At the beginning of the seventeenth century, Bizzi found in the city of Jagnevo, 120 Roman Catholic households, 200 Greek and 180 Muhammadan;[2] less than a hundred years later, every house in the city was looked upon as Muhammadan, as the head of each family professed this faith and the women only, with some of the children, were Christian.[3] About the middle of the eighteenth century, the village of Ljurs was entirely Catholic; in 1863 there were 90 Muslim and 23 Christian families, but at the present day this village, together with the surrounding villages, has wholly given up Christianity.[4] Until recently some lingering survivals of their old Christian faith, such as the burning of the Yule-log at Christmas, etc., were still to be met with in certain villages, but such customs are now fast dying out.

After the battle of Kossovo and the downfall of the Servian empire, the wild highlands of Montenegro afforded a refuge to those Servians who would not submit to the Turks but were determined to maintain their independence. It is not the place here to relate the history of the heroic struggles of this brave people against overwhelming odds, how through centuries of continual warfare, under the rule of their prince-bishops,[5] they have kept alive a free Christian state when all their brethren of the same race had been compelled to submit to Muhammadan rule. While the very basis of their separate existence as a nation was their firm adherence to the Christian faith it could hardly have been expected that Islam would have made its way among them, but in the seventeenth century many Montenegrins in the frontier districts became Muhammadans and took service with the neighbouring Pashas. But in 1703, Daniel Petrovich, the then reigning bishop, called the tribes together and told them that the only hope for their country and their faith lay in the destruction of the Muhammadans living among them. Accordingly, on Christmas Eve, all

[1] Kanitz, p. 38.
[2] Bizzi, fol. 48, b.
[3] Zmaievich, fol. 182.
[4] Kanitz, p. 38.
[5] Montenegro was ruled by bishops from 1516 to 1852.

the converted Montenegrins who would not forswear Islam and embrace Christianity were massacred in cold blood.[1]

To pass now to Bosnia :—in this country the religious and social conditions of the people, before the Turkish conquest, merit especial attention. The majority of the population belonged to a heretical Christian sect, called Bogomiles, who from the thirteenth century had been exposed to the persecution of the Roman Catholics and against whom Popes had on several occasions preached a Crusade.[2] In 1325, Pope John XXII wrote thus to the king of Bosnia : "To our beloved son and nobleman, Stephen, Prince of Bosnia,—knowing that thou art a faithful son of the Church, we therefore charge thee to exterminate the heretics in thy dominion, and to render aid and assistance to Fabian, our Inquisitor, forasmuch as a large multitude of heretics from many and divers parts collected hath flowed together into the principality of Bosnia, trusting there to sow their obscene errors and dwell there in safety. These men, imbued with the cunning of the Old Fiend, and armed with the venom of their falseness, corrupt the minds of Catholics by outward show of simplicity and the sham assumption of the name of Christians ; their speech crawleth like a crab, and they creep in with humility, but in secret they kill, and are wolves in sheep's clothing, covering their bestial fury as a means to deceive the simple sheep of Christ." In the fifteenth century, the sufferings of the Bogomiles became so intolerable that they appealed to the Turks to deliver them from their unhappy condition, for the king of Bosnia and the priests were pushing the persecution of the Bogomiles to an extreme which perhaps it had never reached before ; as many as forty thousand of them fled from Bosnia and took refuge in neighbouring countries ; others who did not succeed in making their escape, were sent in chains to Rome. But even these violent measures did little to diminish the strength of the Bogomiles in Bosnia, as in 1462 we are told that heresy was as powerful as ever in this country. The following year, when Bosnia was invaded by Muḥammad II, the Catholic

[1] E. L. Clark, pp. 362–3.

[2] Honorius III in 1221, Gregory IX in 1238, Innocent IV in 1246, Benedict XII in 1337. The Inquisition was established in 1291.

king found himself deserted by his subjects : the keys of the principal fortress, the royal city of Bobovatz, were handed over to the Turks by the Bogomile governor; the other fortresses and towns hastened to follow this example, and within a week seventy cities passed into the hands of the Sultan, and Muḥammad II added Bosnia to the number of his numerous conquests.[1]

From this time forth we hear but little of the Bogomiles; they seem to have willingly embraced Islam in large numbers immediately after the Turkish conquest, and the rest seem to have gradually followed later, while the Bosnian Roman Catholics emigrated into the neighbouring territories of Hungary and Austria. It has been supposed by some[2] that a large proportion of the Bogomiles, at least in the earlier period of the conquest, embraced Islam with the intention of returning to their faith when a favourable opportunity presented itself; as, being constantly persecuted they may have learnt to deny their faith for the time being; but that, when this favourable opportunity never arrived, this intention must have gradually been lost sight of and at length have been entirely forgotten by their descendants. Such a supposition is, however, a pure conjecture and has no direct evidence to support it. We may rather find the reason for the willingness of the Bogomiles to allow themselves to be merged in the general mass of the Musalman believers, in the numerous points of likeness between their peculiar beliefs and the tenets of Islam. They rejected the worship of the Virgin Mary, the institution of Baptism and every form of priesthood.[3] They abominated the cross as a religious symbol, and considered it idolatry to bow down before religious pictures and the images and relics of the saints. Their houses of prayer were very simple and unadorned, in contrast to the gaudily decorated Roman Catholic churches, and they shared the Muhammadan dislike of bells, which they styled " the devil's trumpets." They believed that

[1] Asboth, pp. 42–95. Evans, pp. xxxvi–xlii.

[2] Asboth, pp. 96–7.

[3] " They revile the ceremonies of the church and all church dignitaries, and they call orthodox priests blind Pharisees, and bay at them as dogs at horses. As to the Lord's Supper, they assert that it is not kept according to God's commandment, and that it is not the body of God, but ordinary bread." (Kosmas, quoted by Evans, pp. xxx–xxxi.)

Christ was not himself crucified but that some phantom was substituted in his place: in this respect agreeing partially with the teaching of the Qur'ān.[1] Their condemnation of wine and the general austerity of their mode of life and the stern severity of their outward demeanour would serve as further links to bind them to Islam,[2] for it was said of them: "You will see heretics quiet and peaceful as lambs without, silent, and wan with hypocritical fasting, who do not speak much nor laugh loud, who let their beard grow, and leave their person incompt."[3] They prayed five times a day and five times a night, repeating the Lord's Prayer with frequent kneelings,[4] and would thus find it very little change to join in the services of the mosque. I have brought together here the many points of likeness to the teachings of Islam, which we find in this Bogomilian heresy, but there were, of course, some doctrines of a distinctly Christian character which an orthodox Muslim could not hold; still, with so much in common, it can easily be understood how the Bogomiles may gradually have been persuaded to give up those doctrines that were repugnant to the Muslim faith. Their Manichæan dualism was equally irreconcilable with Muslim theology, but Islam has always shown itself tolerant of such theological speculations provided that they did not issue in a schism and that a general assent and consent were given to the main principles of its theory and practice.

The Turks, as was their usual custom, offered every advantage to induce the Bosnians to accept their creed. All who embraced Islam were allowed to retain their lands and possessions, and their fiefs were exempt from all taxation,[5] and it is probable that many rightful heirs of ancient houses who had been dispossessed for heretical opinions by the Catholic faction among the nobility, now embraced the opportunity of regaining their old position by submission to the dominant creed. The Bosnian Muhammadans

[1] Sūrah iv. 156.

[2] Cf. the admiration of the Turks for Charles XII of Sweden. "Son opiniâtreté à s'abstenir du vin, et sa régularité à assister deux fois par jour aux prières publiques, leur fesaient dire: C'est un vrai musulman." (Œuvres de Voltaire, tome 23, p. 200.) (Paris, 1785.)

[3] Kosmas, quoted by Evans, p. xxxi.

[4] Asboth, p. 36. Wetzer und Welte, vol. ii. p. 975.

[5] Olivier, pp. 17–18.

retained their nationality and still for the most part bear Serb names and speak only their national tongue;[1] at the same time they have always evinced a lively zeal for their new faith, and by their military prowess, their devotion to Islam and the powerful influence they exercised, the Bosnian nobility rapidly rose into high favour in Constantinople and many were entrusted with important offices of state, e. g. between the years 1544 and 1611 nine statesmen of Bosnian origin filled the post of Grand Vizier.

The latest territorial acquisition of the Ottoman conquests was the island of Crete, which in 1669 was wrested from the hands of the Venetian Republic by the capture of the city of Candia after a long and desperate siege of nearly three years, which closed a struggle of twenty-five years between these rival powers for the possession of the island.

This was not the first time that Crete had come under Muslim rule. Early in the ninth century the island was suddenly seized by a band of Saracen adventurers from Spain, and it remained in their power for nearly a century and a half (A.D. 825–961).[2] During this period well nigh the whole population of the island had become Muslim, and the churches had either fallen into ruins or been turned into mosques; but when the authority of the Byzantine empire was once re-established here, the people were converted again to their ancient faith through the skilful preaching of an Armenian monk, and the Christian religion became the only one professed on the island.[3] In the beginning of the thirteenth century, the Venetians purchased the island from Boniface, Duke of Montserrat, to whose lot it had fallen after the partition of the Byzantine empire, and they ruled it with a heavy hand, apparently looking upon it only in the light of a purchase that was to be exploited for the benefit of the home government and its colonists. Their administration was so oppressive and tyrannical as to excite several revolts, which were crushed with pitiless severity; on one of these occasions whole cantons in the provinces of Sfakia and Lassiti were depopulated, and it was forbidden under pain of death to sow any corn there, so that these districts remained barren

[1] Olivier, p. 113.
[2] Amari, vol. i. p. 163; vol. ii. p. 260.
[3] Cornaro, vol. i. pp. 205–8.

and uncultivated for nearly a century.[1] The terrific cruelty with which the Venetian senate suppressed the last of these attempts at the beginning of the sixteenth century added a crowning horror to the miserable condition of the unhappy Cretans. How terrible was their lot at this time we learn from the reports of the commissioners sent by the Venetian senate in the latter part of the same century, in order to inquire into the condition of the islanders. The peasants were said to be crushed down by the cruelest oppression and tyranny on the part of the Venetian nobles, their feudal lords, being reduced to a worse condition than that of slaves, so that they never dared even to complain of any injustice. Each peasant had to do twelve days' forced labour for his feudal lord every year without payment, and could then be compelled to go on working for as long as his lord required his services at the nominal rate of a penny a day; his vineyards were mulcted in a full third of their produce, but fraud and force combined generally succeeded in appropriating as much as two-thirds; his oxen and mules could be seized for the service of the lord, who had a thousand other devices for squeezing the unfortunate peasant.[2] The protests of these commissioners proved ineffectual to induce the Venetian senate to alleviate the unhappy condition of the Cretans and put a stop to the cruelty and tyranny of the nobles: it preferred to listen to the advice of Fra Paolo Sarpi who in 1615 thus addressed the Republic on the subject of its Greek colonies: "If the gentlemen of these Colonies do tyrannize over the villages of their dominion, the best way is not to seem to see it, that there may be no kindness between them and their subjects."[3]

It is not surprising to learn from the same sources that the Cretans longed for a change of rulers, and that "they would not much stick at submitting to the Turk, having the example of all the rest of their nation before their eyes." Indeed, many at this time fled into Turkey to escape the intolerable burden of taxation, following in the footsteps of countless others, who from time to time had taken refuge

[1] Perrot, p. 151.
[2] Pashley, vol. i. p. 30; vol. ii. pp. 284, 291–2.
[3] Id. vol. ii. p. 298.

there.[1] Large numbers of them also emigrated to Egypt, where many embraced Islam.[2] Especially galling to the Cretans were the exactions of the Latin clergy who appropriated the endowments that belonged of right to the Greek ecclesiastics, and did everything they could to insult the Christians of the Greek rite, who constituted nine-tenths of the population of the island.[3] The Turks, on the other hand, conciliated their good-will by restoring the Greek hierarchy. This, according to a Venetian writer, was brought about in the following manner: "A certain papas or priest of Canea went to Cusseim the Turkish general, and told him that if he desired to gain the good-will of the Cretan people, and bring detestation upon the name of Venice, it was necessary for him to bear in mind that the staunchest of the links which keep civilised society from falling asunder is religion. It would be needful for him to act in a way different from the line followed by the Venetians. These did their utmost to root out the Greek faith and establish that of Rome in its place, with which interest they had made an injunction that there should be no Greek bishops in the island. By thus removing these venerated and authoritative shepherds, they thought the more easily to gain control over the scattered flocks. This prohibition had caused such distress in the minds of the Cretans that they were ready to welcome with joy and obedience any sovereignty that would lend its will to the re-institution of this order in their hierarchy—an order so essential for the proper exercise of their divine worship. He added, that it would be a further means of conciliating the people if they were assured that they would not only be confirmed in the old privileges of their religion, but that new privileges would be granted them. These arguments seemed to Cusseim so plausible that he wrote at once to Constantinople with a statement of them. Here they were approved, and the Greek Patriarch was bidden to institute an archbishop who should be metropole of the Province of Candia. Under the metropolitan seven other bishops were also to be nominated." [4]

[1] Pashley, vol. ii. p. 285.
[2] Id. vol. i. p. 319.
[3] Perrot, p. 151.
[4] Charles Edwardes: Letters from Crete, pp. 90–2. (London, 1887.)

The Turkish conquest seems to have been very rapidly followed by the conversion of large numbers of the Cretans to Islam. It is not improbable that the same patriotism as made them cling to their old faith under the foreign domination of the Venetians who kept them at arm's length and regarded any attempt at assimilation as an unpardonable indignity,[1] and always tried to impress on their subjects a sense of their inferiority—may have led them to accept the religion of their new masters, which at once raised them from the position of subjects to that of equals and gave them a share in the political life and government of their country. Whatever may have been the causes of the widespread conversion of the Cretans, it seems almost incredible that violence should have changed the religion of a people who had for centuries before clung firmly to their old faith despite the persecution of a hostile and a foreign creed. Whatever may have been the means by which the ranks of Islam were filled, thirty years after the conquest we are told that the majority of the Muslims were renegades or the children of renegades,[2] and in little more than a century half the population of Crete had become Muhammadan. From one end of the island to the other, not only in the towns but also in the villages, in the inland districts and in the very heart of the mountains, were (and are still) found Cretan Muslims who in figure, habits and speech are thoroughly Greek. There never has been, and to the present day there is not, any other language spoken on the island of Crete except Greek; even the few Turks to be found here had to adopt the language of the country and all the firmans of the Porte and decrees of the Pashas were read and published in Greek.[3] The bitter feelings between the Christians and Muhammadans of Crete that have made the history of this island during the nineteenth century so sad a one, was by no means so virulent before the outbreak of the Greek revolution, in days when the Cretan Muslims were very generally in the habit of taking as their wives Christian maidens, the children of their Christian friends.[4] The social communication between the two communities was further signified by their common dress,

[1] Pashley, vol. ii. pp. 151–2.
[2] Id. vol. i. p. 9.
[3] Perrot, p. 159.
[4] Pashley, vol. i. pp. 10, 195.

as the Cretans of both creeds dressed so much alike that the distinction was often not even recognised by residents of long standing or by Greeks of the neighbouring islands.[1]

Recent political events have brought about a considerable diminution in the Muhammadan population of Crete. In 1881 the number of Muhammadans in the island was 73,234; in 1909, in consequence of continual emigrations, it had been reduced to 33,496.[2]

[1] T. A. B. Spratt: Travels and Researches in Crete, vol. i. p. 47. (London, 1865.)

[2] R. du M. M. vii. p. 99.

CHAPTER VII.

THE SPREAD OF ISLAM IN PERSIA AND CENTRAL ASIA.

In order to follow the course of the spread of Islam westward into Central Asia, we must retrace our steps to the period of the first Arab conquests. By the middle of the seventh century, the great dynasty of the Sāsānids had fallen, and the vast empire of Persia that for four centuries had withstood the might of Rome and Byzantium, now became the heritage of the Muslims. When the armies of the state had been routed, the mass of the people offered little resistance; the reigns of the last representatives of the Sāsānid dynasty had been marked by terrible anarchy, and the sympathies of the people had been further alienated from their rulers on account of the support they gave to the persecuting policy of the state religion of Zoroastrianism. The Zoroastrian priests had acquired an enormous influence in the state; they were well-nigh all-powerful in the councils of the king and arrogated to themselves a very large share in the civil administration. They took advantage of their position to persecute all those religious bodies—(and they were many)—that dissented from them. Besides the numerous adherents of older forms of the Persian religion, there were Christians, Jews, Sabæans and numerous sects in which the speculations of Gnostics, Manichæans and Buddhists found expression. In all of these, persecution had stirred up feelings of bitter hatred against the established religion and the dynasty that supported its oppressions, and so caused the Arab conquest to appear in the light of a deliverance.[1] The followers of all these varied forms of faith could breathe again under a rule that granted them religious freedom and exemption from military service, on

[1] Caetani, vol. ii. pp. 910–11. A. de Gobineau (1), pp. 55–6.

payment of a light tribute. For the Muslim law granted toleration and the right of paying jizyah not only to the Christians and Jews, but to Zoroastrians and Sabæans, to worshippers of idols, of fire and of stone.[1] It was said that the Prophet himself had distinctly given directions that the Zoroastrians were to be treated exactly like "the people of the book," i. e. the Jews and Christians, and that jizyah might also be taken from them in return for protection,[2] —a tradition that probably arose in the second century of the Hijrah, when apostolic sanction was sought for the toleration that had been extended to all the followers of the various faiths that Arabs had found in the countries they had conquered, whether such non-Muslims came under the category Ahl al-Kitāb or not.[3]

To the distracted Christian Church in Persia the change of government brought relief from the oppression of the Sāsānid kings, who had fomented the bitter struggles of Jacobites and Nestorians and added to the confusion of warring sects. Some reference has already[4] been made to earlier persecutions, and even during the expiring agony of the Sāsānid dynasty, Khusrau II, exasperated at the defeat he had suffered at the hands of the Christian emperor, Heraclius, ordered a fresh persecution of the Christians within his dominions, a persecution from which all the various Christian sects alike had to suffer. These terrible conditions may well have prepared men's minds for that revulsion of feeling that facilitates a change of faith. "Side by side with the political chaos in the state was the moral confusion that filled the minds of the Christians; distracted by such an accumulation of disasters and by the moral agony wrought by the furious conflict of so many warring doctrines among them, they tended towards that peculiar frame of mind in which a new doctrine finds it easy to take root, making a clean sweep of such a bewildering babel and striving to reconstruct faith and society on a new basis. In other words the people of Persia, and especially the Semitic races, were just in the very mental condition calculated to make them

[1] Abū Yūsuf: Kitāb al-Kharāj, p. 73.
[2] Id. p. 74 and Balādhurī, pp. 71 (fin.), 79, 80.
[3] Caetani, vol. v. pp. 361 (§ 611 n. 1), 394–5, 457.
[4] pp. 68–9.

welcome the Islamic revolution and urge them on to enthusiastically embrace the new and rugged creed, which with its complete and virile simplicity swept away at one stroke all those dark mists, opened the soul to new, alluring and tangible hopes, and promised immediate release from a miserable state of servitude." [1]

But the Muslim creed was most eagerly welcomed by the townsfolk, the industrial classes and the artisans, whose occupations made them impure according to the Zoroastrian creed, because in the pursuance of their trade or occupations they defiled fire, earth or water, and who thus, outcasts in the eyes of the law and treated with scant consideration in consequence, embraced with eagerness a creed that made them at once free men, and equal in a brotherhood of faith.[2] Nor were the conversions from Zoroastrianism itself less striking: the fabric of the National Church had fallen with a crash in the general ruin of the dynasty that had before upheld it; having no other centre round which to rally, the followers of this creed would find the transition to Islam a simple and easy one, owing to the numerous points of similarity in the old creed and the new. For the Persian could find in the Qur'ān many of the fundamental doctrines of his old faith, though in a rather different form: he would meet again Ahuramazda and Ahriman under the names of Allāh and Iblīs; the creation of the world in six periods; the angels and the demons; the story of the primitive innocence of man; the resurrection of the body and the doctrine of heaven and hell.[3] Even in the details of daily worship there were similarities to be found and the followers of Zoroaster when they adopted Islam were enjoined by their new faith to pray five times a day just as they had been by the Avesta.[4] Those tribes in the north of Persia that had stubbornly resisted the ecclesiastical organisation of the state religion, on the ground that each man was a priest in his own household and had no need of any other, and believing in a supreme being and the immortality of the soul, taught that a man should love his neighbour, conquer his passions, and strive patiently after a better life—such

[1] Caetani, vol. ii. p. 910.
[2] A de Gobineau (2), pp. 306–10.
[3] Dozy (1), p. 157.
[4] Haneberg, p. 5.

men could have needed very little persuasion to induce them to accept the faith of the Prophet.[1] Islam had still more points of contact with some of the heretical sects of Persia, that had come under the influence of Christianity.

In addition to the causes above enumerated of the rapid spread of Islam in Persia, it should be remembered that the political and national sympathies of the conquered race were also enlisted on behalf of the new religion through the marriage of Ḥusayn, the son of 'Alī with Shāhbānū, one of the daughters of Yazdagird, the last monarch of the Sāsānid dynasty. In the descendants of Shāhbānū and Ḥusayn the Persians saw the heirs of their ancient kings and the inheritors of their national traditions, and in this patriotic feeling may be found the explanation of the intense devotion of the Persians to the 'Alid faction and the first beginnings of Shī'ism as a separate sect.[2]

That this widespread conversion was not due to force or violence is evidenced by the toleration extended to those who still clung to their ancient faith. Even to the present day there are some small communities of fire-worshippers to be found in certain districts of Persia, and though these have in later years often had to suffer persecution,[3] their ancestors in the early centuries of the Hijrah enjoyed a remarkable degree of toleration, their fire-temples were respected, and we even read of a Muhammadan general (in the reign of al-Mu'taṣim, A.D. 833–842), who ordered an imām and a mu'adhdhin to be flogged because they had destroyed a fire-temple in Sughd and built a mosque in its place.[4] In the tenth century, three centuries after the conquest of the country, fire-temples were to be found in 'Irāq, Fārs, Kirmān, Sijistān, Khurāsān, Jibāl, Ādharbayjān and Arrān, i. e. in almost every province of Persia.[5] In Fārs

[1] Dozy (1), p. 191. A. de Gobineau (1), p. 55.

[2] Les croyances Mazdéennes dans la religion Chiite, par Ahmed-Bey Agaeff. (Transactions of the Ninth International Congress of Orientalists, vol. ii. pp. 509–11. London, 1893.) For other points of contact, see Goldziher: Islamisme et Parsisme. (Revue de l'Histoire des Religions, xliii. p. 1. sqq.)

[3] Dosabhai Framji Karaka: History of the Parsis, vol. i. pp. 56–9, 62–7. (London, 1884.) Nicolas de Khanikoff says that there were 12,000 families of fire-worshippers in Kirmān at the end of the 18th century. (Mémoire sur la partie méridionale de l'Asie centrale, p. 193. Paris, 1861.)

[4] Chwolsohn, vol. i. p. 287.

[5] Mas'ūdī, vol. iv. p. 86.

itself there were hardly any cities or districts in which fire-temples and Magians were not to be found.[1] Al-Sharastānī also (writing as late as the twelfth century), makes mention of a fire-temple at Isfīniyā, in the neighbourhood of Baghdād itself.[2]

In the face of such facts, it is surely impossible to attribute the decay of Zoroastrianism entirely to violent conversions made by the Muslim conquerors. The number of Persians who embraced Islam in the early days of the Arab rule was probably very large from the various reasons given above, but the late survival of their ancient faith and the occasional record of conversions in the course of successive centuries, render it probable that the acceptance of Islam was both peaceful and voluntary. About the close of the eighth century, Sāmān, a noble of Balkh, having received assistance from Asad b. 'Abd-Allāh, the governor of Khurāsān, renounced Zoroastrianism, embraced Islam and named his son Asad after his protector: it is from this convert that dynasty of the Sāmānids (A.D. 874–999) took its name. About the beginning of the ninth century, Karīm b. Shahriyār was the first king of the Qābūsiyyah dynasty who became a Musalman, and in 873 a large number of fire-worshippers were converted to Islam in Daylam through the influence of Nāṣir al-Ḥaqq Abū Muḥammad. In the following century, about A.D. 912, Ḥasan b. 'Alī, of the 'Alid dynasty on the southern shore of the Caspian Sea, who is said to have been a man of learning and intelligence and well acquainted with the religious opinions of different sects, invited the inhabitants of Ṭabaristān and Daylam, who were partly idolaters and partly Magians, to accept Islam; many of them responded to his call, while others persisted in their former state of unbelief.[3] In the year A.H. 394 (A.D. 1003–1004), a famous poet, Abu'l Ḥasan Mihyār, a native of Daylam, who had been a fire-worshipper, was converted to Islam by a still more famous poet, the Sharīf al-Riḍā, who was his master in the poetic art.[4]

It was probably about the same period that the grand-

[1] Iṣṭakhrī, pp. 100, 118. Ibn Ḥawqal, pp. 189–190.
[2] Kitāb al-milal wa'l-niḥal, edited by Cureton, part i. p. 198.
[3] Mas'ūdī, vol. viii. p. 279; vol. ix. pp. 4–5.
[4] Ibn Khallikān, vol. iii. p. 517.

father of the great geographer, Ibn Khūrdādbih, was converted through the influence of one of the Barmecides,[1] whose ancestor had been likewise a Magian and high priest of the great Fire Temple of Nawbahār at Balkh.

Scanty as these notices of conversion are, they appear to have been voluntary, and the Zoroastrians would seem to have enjoyed on the whole toleration for the exercise of their religion up to the close of the 'Abbasid period. With the Mongol invasion a darker period in their history begins, and the miseries which the Persian Muslims themselves suffered seems to have generated in them a spirit of fanatical intolerance which exposed the Zoroastrians at times to cruel sufferings.[2]

In the middle of the eighth century, Persia gave birth to a movement that is of interest in the missionary history of Islam, viz. the sect of the Ismā'īlians. This is not the place to enter into a history of this sect or of the theological position taken up by its followers, or of the social and political factors that lent it strength, but it demands attention here on account of the marvellous missionary organisation whereby it was propagated. The founder of this organisation—which rivals that of the Jesuits for the keen insight into human nature it displays and the consummate skill with which the doctrines of the sect were accommodated to varying capacities and prejudices—was a certain 'Abd Allāh b. Maymūn, who early in the ninth century infused new life into the Ismā'īlians. He sent out his missionaries in all directions under various guises, very frequently as ṣūfīs but also as merchants and traders and the like; they were instructed to be all things to all men and to win over different classes of men to allegiance to the grandmaster of their sect, by speaking to each man, as it were, in his own language, and accommodating their teaching to the varying capacities and opinions of their hearers. They captivated the ignorant multitude by the performance of marvels that were taken for miracles and by mysterious utterances that excited their curiosity. To the devout they appeared as

[1] Kitāb al-Fihrist, ed. Flügel, p. 149 (l. 2).

[2] For a comprehensive sketch of their condition under Muslim rule, see D. Menant: Les Zoroastriens de Perse. (R. du M. M. iii. pp. 193 sqq., p. 421 sqq.)

models of virtue and religious zeal; to the mystics they revealed the hidden meaning of popular teachings and initiated them into various grades of occultism according to their capacity. Taking advantage of the eager looking-forward to a deliverer that was common to so many faiths of the time, they declared to the Musalmans the approaching advent of the Imām Mahdī, to the Jews that of the Messiah, and to the Christians that of the Comforter, but taught that the aspirations of each could alone be realised in the coming of 'Alī as the great deliverer. With the Shī'ah, the Ismā'īlian missionary was to put himself forward as the zealous partisan of all the Shī'ah doctrine, was to dwell upon the cruelty and injustice of the Sunnīs towards 'Alī and his sons, and liberally abuse the Sunnī Khalīfahs; having thus prepared the way, he was to insinuate, as the necessary completion of the Shī'ah system of faith, the more esoteric doctrines of the Ismā'īlian sect. In dealing with the Jew, he was to speak with contempt of both Christians and Muslims and agree with his intended convert in still looking forward to a promised Messiah, but gradually lead him to believe that this promised Messiah could be none other than 'Alī, the great Messiah of the Ismā'īlian system. If he sought to win over the Christian, he was to dwell upon the obstinacy of the Jews and the ignorance of the Muslims, to profess reverence for the chief articles of the Christian creed, but gently hint that they were symbolic and pointed to a deeper meaning, to which the Ismā'īlian system alone could supply the key; he was also cautiously to suggest that the Christians had somewhat misinterpreted the doctrine of the Paraclete and that it was in 'Alī that the true Paraclete was to be found. Similarly the Ismā'īlian missionaries who made their way into India endeavoured to make their doctrines acceptable to the Hindus, by representing 'Alī as the promised tenth Avatār of Viṣṇu who was to come from the West, i. e. (they averred) from Alamūt. They also wrote a Mahdī Purāṇa and composed hymns in imitation of those of the Vāmācārins or left-hand Śāktas, whose mysticism already predisposed their minds to the acceptance of the esoteric doctrines of the Ismā'īlians.[1]

[1] Khojā Vrittānt, pp. 141–8. For a further account of Ismā'īlian missionaries in India, see chap. ix.

By such means as these an enormous number of persons of different faiths were united together to push forward an enterprise, the real aim of which was known to very few. The aspirations of ʻAbd Allāh b. Maymūn seem to have been entirely political, but as the means he adopted were religious and the one common bond—if any—that bound his followers together was the devout expectation of the coming of the Imām Mahdī, the missionary activity connected with the history of this sect deserves this brief mention in these pages.[1]

The history of the spread of Islam in the countries of Central Asia to the north of Persia presents little in the way of missionary activity. When Qutaybah b. Muslim went to Samarqand, he found many idols there, whose worshippers maintained that any man who dared outrage them would perish; the Muslim conqueror, undeterred by such superstitious fears, set fire to the idols; whereupon a number of persons embraced Islam.[2] There is, however, but scanty record of such conversions in the early history of the Muslim advance into Central Asia; moreover the people of this country seem often to have pretended to embrace Islam for a time and then to have thrown off the mask and renounced their allegiance to the caliph as soon as the conquering armies were withdrawn,[3] and it was not until Qutaybah had forcibly occupied Bukhārā for the fourth time that he succeeded in compelling the inhabitants to conform to the faith of their conquerors.

In Bukhārā and Samarqand the opposition to the new faith was so violent and obstinate that none but those who had embraced Islam were allowed to carry arms, and for many years the Muslims dared not appear unarmed in the mosques or other public places, while spies had to be set to keep a watch on the new converts. The conquerors made various efforts to gain proselytes, and even tried to encourage attendance at the Friday prayers in the mosques by rewards of money, and allowed the Qur'ān to be recited in Persian instead of in Arabic, in order that it might be intelligible to all.[4]

[1] Le Bon Silvestre De Sacy : Exposé de la Religion des Druzes, tome i, pp. lxvii–lxxvi, cxlviii–clxii.

[2] Balādhurī, p. 421.

[3] Narshakhī, p. 46.

[4] Id. p. 47.

The progress of Islam in Transoxania was certainly very slow: some of the inhabitants accepted the invitation of 'Umar II (A.D. 717–720) to embrace Islam,[1] and large numbers were converted through the preaching of a certain Abū Ṣaydā who commenced this mission in Samarqand in the reign of Hishām (724–743),[2] but it was not until the reign of Al-Mu'taṣim (A.D. 833–842) that Islam was generally adopted there,[3] one of the reason probably being the more intimate relations established at this time with the then capital of the Muhammadan world, Baghdād, through the enormous numbers of Turks that had flocked in thousands to join the army of the caliph.[4] Islam having thus gained a footing among the Turkish tribes seems to have made but slow progress until the middle of the tenth century, when the conversion of some of their chieftains to Islam, like that of Clovis and other barbarian kings of Northern Europe to Christianity, led their clansmen to follow their example in a body.

Pious legends have grown up to supply the lack of sober historical record of such conversions. The city of Khīva reveres as its national saint a Muslim wrestler—Pahlavān—who was in the service of a heathen king of Khwārizm. The king of India, hearing of the fame of this Pahlavān, sent his own court wrestler with a challenge to the king of Khwārizm. A day was fixed for the trial of strength and the nobles and people of Khīva were summoned to view the spectacle; the vanquished man was to have his head cut off. On the day before, the saintly Pahlavān was praying in the mosque when he overheard the prayer of an old woman: "O God, suffer not my son to be beaten by this invincible Pahlavān, for I have no other child." Touched with compassion for the mother, Pahlavān lets the Indian wrestler win the day; the enraged king orders his head to be cut off, but at that very moment the horse on which the king is sitting, bolts, carrying his master straight towards a dangerous precipice. Pahlavān springs forward, catches the horse and rescues the king from a horrible death. In gratitude the king embraces the true faith, and the saintly

[1] Balādhurī, p. 426.
[2] Ṭabarī, ii. pp. 1507 sqq.
[3] Balādhurī, p. 431.
[4] August Müller, vol. i. p. 520.

wrestler, full of joy, goes away into the desert and becomes a hermit.[1]

A strange legend is told of the conversion of Sātūq Bughrā Khān, the founder of the Muhammadan dynasty of the Īlik-Khāns of Kāshgar, about the middle of the tenth century. A prince of the Sāmānid house, Khwājah Abu'l-Naṣr Sāmānī, a man of great piety and humility of character, finding no scope for the exercise of his talent for administration, resolved to become a merchant, with the purpose of spreading the true faith in the lands of the unbelievers. Instead of trying to acquire a fortune by his commercial enterprises, he devoted all his gains to the furtherance of his proselytising efforts. One night the Prophet appeared to him in a dream, saying: "Arise, and go into Turkistan where the prince Sātūq Bughrā Khān only awaits your coming to be converted to Islam." The young prince had in a similar manner been warned in a vision to expect the arrival of an instructor in the faith, and when some days later he met Abu'l-Naṣr Sāmānī he was prepared to accept his teaching and become a Musalman. This legend would appear to have been based on the historic fact that Islam made its way from the Sāmānid kingdom into the neighbouring country of Turkistan, and the example of the ruler seems to have been followed by his subjects, for in A.D. 960 as many as 200,000 tents of the Turks, i. e. probably the greater part of the Turkish population of Bughrā Khān's kingdom, professed the faith of Islam.[2] Legend credits him with miraculous powers in his wars against the heathen, when a devouring flame would issue from his mouth and the sword that he brandished would become forty feet long. By the time he had reached the age of ninety-six, the terror of his sword is said to have converted the unbelievers from the banks of the Oxus in the south to Qurāquram in the north, and just before his death he is said to have led his victorious army into China, and spread Islam as far as Turfan.[3] This picturesque account of

[1] Cahun, p. 150.

[2] Ibn al-Athīr, vol. viii. p. 396 (ll. 19–20.) Grenard, pp. 7 sq., 42–3.

[3] Grenard, pp. 9–10. "D'une guerre d'ambition [la tradition] fait une guerre sainte, elle attribue à Satoḳ Boghra Khân une conquête qui a été accomplie réellement par son douzième successeur; par une confusion absurde, elle donne le nom de ce dernier à l'oncle infidèle de Satoḳ. Non contente de réduire deux personnages en un seul, elle prête au même prince

a dynastic struggle with the Buddhist kingdom of Khotan credits the hero with a measure of success which was not really achieved until the fourteenth century. How limited the success of Sātūq Bug̲h̲rā K̲h̲ān really was, may be judged from the fact that when his successors among the Īlik-K̲h̲āns sought in 1026 to contract matrimonial alliances with princesses of the house of Maḥmūd of Ghazna, Maḥmūd replied that he was a Musalman, while they were unbelievers, and that it was not the custom to give the sisters and daughters of Musalmans in marriage to unbelievers, but that, if they would embrace Islam, the matter would be considered.[1] A few years later, in 1041–1042, a number of Turks who were still heathen and living in Tibetan territory sought permission from Arslān K̲h̲ān b. Qadr K̲h̲ān to settle in his dominions, having heard of the justice and mildness of his rule; when they arrived in the neighbourhood of Bālāsāg̲h̲ūn [2] he sent a message to them urging them to accept Islam; but they refused, and as he found them to be peaceable and obedient subjects, he left them alone. There is no record of their conversion, which probably ensued in course of time; but they can hardly be identified with the group of ten thousand tents of infidel Turks who embraced Islam in the following year, as these latter are expressly stated to have harried and plundered the Musalmans before their conversion.[3] The invasion of the Qarā K̲h̲itāy into Turkistan [4] dealt a severe blow to the power of Islam, and as late as the thirteenth century the reports of European travellers show that there were still important groups of Buddhists, Manichæans and Christians in these parts.[5]

Of supreme importance to Islam was the conversion of the Saljūq Turks, but no record of their conversion remains beyond the statement that in A.D. 956 Saljūq migrated from Turkistan with his clan to the province of Buk̲h̲ārā, where he and his people enthusiastically embraced Islam.[6] This

une marche sur Tourfân, c'est-à-dire contre les Ouigour, qui est en effet l'œuvre d'un troisième." (Id. p. 50.)

[1] Raverty, p. 905.

[2] This was the capital of the K̲h̲āns of Turkistan during the tenth and eleventh centuries, but the exact site is uncertain.

[3] Narshak̲h̲ī, pp. 234–5.

[4] Raverty, pp. 925–7.

[5] Grenard, p. 76.

[6] Raverty, p. 117.

was the origin of the famous Saljūq Turks, whose wars and conquests revived the fading glory of the Muhammadan arms and united into one empire the Muslim kingdoms of Western Asia.

When at the close of the twelfth century, the Saljūq empire had lost all power except in Asia Minor, and when Muḥammad Ghūrī was extending his empire from Khurāsān eastward across the north of India, there was a great revival of the Muslim faith among the Afghāns and their country was overrun by Arab preachers and converts from India, who set about the task of proselytising with remarkable energy and boldness.[1] The traditions of the Afghāns represent Islam as having been peaceably introduced among them. They say that in the first century of the Hijrah they occupied the Ghūr country to the east of Herāt, and that Khālid b. Walīd came to them there with the tidings of Islam and invited them to join the standard of the Prophet; he returned to Muḥammad accompanied by a deputation of six or seven representative men of the Afghan people, with their followers, and these, when they went back to their own country, set to work to convert their fellow-tribesmen.[2] This tradition is, however, devoid of any historical foundation, and the earliest authentic record of conversion to Islam from among the Afghans seems to be that of a king of Kābul in the reign of al-Ma'mūn.[3] His successors, however, seem to have relapsed to Buddhism, for when Ya'qūb b. Layth, the founder of the Ṣaffārid dynasty, extended his conquests as far as Kābul in 871, he found the ruler of the land to be an "idolater," and Kābul now became really Muhammadan for the first time, the Afghans probably being quite willing to take service in the army of so redoubtable a conqueror as Ya'qūb b. Layth,[4] but it was not until after the conquests of Sabaktigīn and Maḥmūd of Ghazna that Islam became established throughout Afghanistan.

Of the further history of Islam in Persia and Central Asia some details will be found in the following chapter.

[1] Bellew, p. 96.
[2] Id. pp. 15–16.
[3] Balādhurī, p. 402.
[4] August Müller, vol. ii. p. 29.

CHAPTER VIII.

THE SPREAD OF ISLAM AMONG THE MONGOLS AND TATARS.

THERE is no event in the history of Islam that for terror and desolation can be compared to the Mongol conquest. Like an avalanche, the hosts of Chingīz Khān swept over the centres of Muslim culture and civilisation, leaving behind them bare deserts and shapeless ruins where before had stood the palaces of stately cities, girt about with gardens and fruitful corn-land. When the Mongol army had marched out of the city of Herāt, a miserable remnant of forty persons crept out of their hiding-places and gazed horror-stricken on the ruins of their beautiful city—all that were left out of a population of over 100,000. In Bukhārā, so famed for its men of piety and learning, the Mongols stabled their horses in the sacred precincts of the mosques and tore up the Qur'āns to serve as litter; those of the inhabitants who were not butchered were carried away into captivity and their city reduced to ashes. Such too was the fate of Samarqand, Balkh and many another city of Central Asia, which had been the glories of Islamic civilisation and the dwelling-places of holy men and the seats of sound learning —such too the fate of Baghdād that for centuries had been the capital of the 'Abbāsid dynasty.

Well might the Muhammadan historian shudder to relate such horrors; when Ibn al-Athīr comes to describe the inroads of the Mongols into the countries of Islam, " for many years," he tells us, " I shrank from giving a recital of these events on account of their magnitude and my abhorrence. Even now I come reluctant to the task, for who would deem it a light thing to sing the death-song of Islam and of the Muslims, or find it easy to tell this tale? O that my mother had not given me birth! 'Oh, would that I had died ere this, and been a thing forgotten, forgotten quite!'[1] Many friends have urged me and still I stood irresolute; but I saw that it was of no profit to forego the task and so I thus resume. I shall have to describe events so terrible and calamities so stupendous that neither day nor night have ever brought forth the like; they fell on all nations, but on the Muslims more than all; and were one to say that since God created Adam the world has not seen the like, he would but tell the truth, for history has nothing to relate that at all approaches it. Among the greatest calamities in history is the slaughter that Nebuchadnezzar wrought among the children of Israel and his destruction of the Temple; but what is Jerusalem in comparison to the countries that these accursed ones laid waste, every town of which was far greater than Jerusalem, and what were the children of Israel in comparison to those they slew, since the inhabitants of one of the cities they destroyed were greater in numbers than all the children of Israel? Let us hope that the world may never see the like again."[2] But Islam was to rise again from the ashes of its former grandeur and through its preachers win over these savage conquerors to the acceptance of the faith. This was a task for the missionary energies of Islam that was rendered more difficult from the fact that there were two powerful competitors in the field. The spectacle of Buddhism, Christianity and Islam emulously striving to win the allegiance of the fierce conquerors that had set their feet on the necks of adherents of these great missionary religions, is one that is without parallel in the history of the world.

Before entering on a recital of this struggle, it will be well in order to the comprehension of what is to follow briefly to glance at the partition of the Mongol empire after the death of Chingīz Khān, when it was split up into four sections and divided among his sons. His third son, Ogotāy, succeeded his father as Khāqān and received as his share the eastern portion of the empire, in which Qūbīlāy afterwards included the whole of China. Chaghatāy the second son took the middle kingdom. Bātū, the son of

[1] Qur'ān, xix. 23. [2] Ibn al-Athīr, vol. xii. pp. 233–4.

his first-born Jūjī, ruled the western portion as Khān of the Golden Horde; Tulūy the fourth son took Persia, to which Hūlāgū, who founded the dynasty of the Īlkhāns, added a great part of Asia Minor.

The primitive religion of the Mongols was Shamanism, which while recognising a supreme God, offered no prayers to Him, but worshipped a number of inferior divinities, especially the evil spirits whose powers for harm had to be deprecated by means of sacrifices, and the souls of ancestors who were considered to exercise an influence on the lives of their descendants. To propitiate these powers of the heaven and of the lower world, recourse was had to the Shamans, wizards or medicine-men, who were credited with possessing mysterious influence over the elements and the spirits of the departed. Their religion was not one that was calculated to withstand long the efforts of a proselytising faith, possessed of a systematic theology capable of satisfying the demands of the reason and an organised body of religious teachers, when once the Mongols had been brought into contact with civilised races, had responded to their civilising influences and begun to pass out of their nomadic barbarism. It so happened that the civilised races with which the conquest of the Mongols brought them in contact comprised large numbers of Buddhists, Christians and Muhammadans, and the adherents of these three great missionary faiths entered into rivalry with one another for the conversion of their conquerors. When not carried away by the furious madness for destruction and insult that usually characterised their campaigns, the Shamanist Mongols showed themselves remarkably tolerant of other religions, whose priests were exempted from taxation and allowed perfect freedom of worship. Buddhist priests held controversies with the Shamans in the presence of Chingīz Khān; and at the courts of Mangū Khān and Qūbīlāy the Buddhist and Christian priests and the Muslim Imāms alike enjoyed the patronage of the Mongol prince.[1] In the reign of the latter monarch the Mongols in China began to yield to the powerful influences of the surrounding Buddhism, and by the beginning of the fourteenth century

[1] William of Rubruck, pp. 182, 191. C. d'Ohsson, tome ii. p. 488.

the Buddhist faith seems to have gained a complete ascendancy over them.[1] It was the Lamas of Tibet who showed themselves most zealous in this work of conversion, and the people of Mongolia to the present day cling to the same faith, as do the Kalmuks who migrated to Russia in the seventeenth century.

Although Buddhism made itself finally supreme in the eastern part of the empire, at first the influence of the Christian Church was by no means inconsiderable and great hopes were entertained of the conversion of the Mongols. The Nestorian missionaries in the seventh century had carried the knowledge of the Christian faith from west to east across Asia as far as the north of China, and scattered communities were still to be found in the thirteenth century. The famous Prester John, around whose name cluster so many legends of the Middle Ages, is supposed to have been the chief of the Karaïts, a Christian Tartar tribe living to the south of Lake Baikal. When this tribe was conquered by Chingīz Khān, he married one of the daughters of the then chief of the tribe, while his son Ogotāy took a wife from the same family. Ogotāy's son, Kuyūk, although he did not himself become a Christian, showed great favour towards this faith, to which his chief minister and one of his secretaries belonged. The Nestorian priests were held in high favour at his court and he received an embassy from Pope Innocent IV.[2] The Christian powers both of the East and the West looked to the Mongols to assist them in their wars against the Musalmans. It was Hayton, the Christian King of Armenia, who was mainly instrumental in persuading Mangū Khān to despatch the expedition that sacked Baghdād under the leadership of Hūlāgū,[3] the influence of whose Christian wife led him to show much favour to the Christians, and especially to the Nestorians. Many of the Mongols who occupied the countries of Armenia and Georgia were converted by the Christians of these countries and received baptism.[4] The marvellous tales of the greatness and magnificence of Prester John, that fired the imagination of mediæval Europe, had given rise

[1] De Guignes, tome iii. pp. 200, 203.
[2] Id. vol. iii. p. 115.
[3] Id. p. 125. Cahun, p. 391.
[4] Klaproth, p. 204.

to a belief that the Mongols were Christians—a belief which was further strengthened by the false reports that reached Europe of the conversion of various Mongol princes and their zeal for the Christian cause. It was under this delusion that St. Louis sent an ambassador, William of Rubruck, to exhort the great Khāqān to persevere in his supposed efforts for the spread of the Christian faith. But these reports were soon discovered to be without any foundation in fact, though William of Rubruck found that the Christian religion was freely tolerated at the court of Mangū Khān, and the adhesion of some few Mongols to this faith made the Christian priests hopeful of still further conquests. But so long as Latins, Greeks, Nestorians and Armenians carried their theological differences into the very midst of the Mongol camp, there was very little hope of much progress being made, and it is probably this very want of union among the preachers of Christianity that caused their efforts to meet with so little success among the Mongols; so that while they were fighting among one another, Buddhism and Islam were gaining a firm footing for themselves. The haughty pretensions of the Roman Pontiff soon caused the proud conquerors of half the world to withdraw from his emissaries what little favour they might at first have been inclined to show, and many other circumstances contributed to the failure of the Roman mission.[1]

As for the Nestorians, who had been first in the field, they appear to have been too degraded and apathetic to take much advantage of their opportunities. Of the Nestorians in China, William of Rubruck[2] says that they were very ignorant and could not even understand their service books, which were written in Syriac. He accuses them of drunkenness, polygamy and covetousness, and makes an unfavourable comparison between their lives and those of the Buddhist priests. Their bishop paid them very rare visits—sometimes only once in fifty years:

[1] C. d'Ohsson, tome ii. pp. 226–7. Cahun, p. 408 sq.

[2] Of this writer Yule says, "He gives an unfavourable account of the literature and morals of their clergy, which deserves more weight than such statements regarding those looked upon as schismatics generally do; for the narrative of Rubruquis gives one the impression of being written by a thoroughly honest and intelligent person." (Cathay and the Way Thither, vol. i. p. xcviii.)

on such occasions he would ordain all the male children, even the babies in their cradles. The priests were eaten up with simony, made a traffic of the sacred rites of their Church and concerned themselves more with money-making than with the propagation of the faith.[1]

In the western parts of the Mongol empire, where the Christians looked to the newly-risen power to help them in their wars with the Musalmans and to secure for them the possession of the Holy Land, the alliance between the Christians and the Īlkhāns of Persia was short-lived, as the victories of Baybars, the Mamlūk Sultan of Egypt (1260–1277) and his alliance with Baraka Khān, gave the Īlkhāns quite enough to do to look after their own interests. The excesses that the Christians of Damascus and other cities committed during the brief period in which they enjoyed the favour of this Mongol dynasty of Persia, did much to discredit the Christian name in Western Asia.[2]

In the course of the struggle, the adherents of either faith were at times guilty of much brutality. One example may be taken from the middle of the thirteenth century as told by al-Jūzjānī, who claims to have heard the story, while in Delhi, from the lips of a certain Sayyid Ashraf al-Dīn who had come there from Samarqand. "The eminent Sayyid thus related, that one of the Christians of Samarqand attained unto the felicity of Islam, and the Musalmans of Samarqand, who are staunch in their faith, paid him great honour and reverence, and conferred great benefits upon him. Unexpectedly, one of the haughty Mongol infidels of China, who possessed power and influence, and the inclinations of which accursed one were towards the Christian faith, arrived at Samarqand. The Christians of that city repaired to that Mongol, and complained saying: 'The Musalmans are enjoining our children to turn away from the Christian faith and from serving Jesus—on whom be peace—and calling upon them to follow the religion of Muṣṭafā [3]—on whom be peace—and, in case that gate becomes unclosed, the whole of our dependents will turn away from the Christian faith. By

[1] William of Rubruck, pp. 158–9.
[2] Maqrīzī (2), tome i. 1re partie, pp. 98, 106.
[3] The Chosen One—Muḥammad.

thy power and authority devise a settlement of our case.' The Mongol commanded that the youth, who had turned Musalman, should be produced, and they tried with blandishment and kindness, and money and wealth to induce the newly-converted Musalman to recant, but he refused to recant, and put not off from his heart and spirit that garment of freshness—the Muslim faith. The Mongol ruler then turned over a leaf in his temper, and began to speak of severe punishment; and every punishment, which it was in his power to inflict, or his severity to devise, he inflicted upon the youth, who, from his great zeal for the faith of Islam, did not recant, and did not in any way cast away from his hand the sweet draught of religion through the blow of infidel perverseness. As the youth continued firm in the true faith, and paid no heed to the promises and threats of that depraved company, the accursed Mongol commanded that they should bring the youth to public punishment; and he departed from the world in the felicity of religion—may God reward and requite him!—and the Musalman community in Samarqand were overcome with despondency and consternation in consequence. A petition was got up, and was attested with the testimony of the chief men and credible persons of the Musalman religion dwelling at Samarqand, and we proceeded with that petition to the camp of Baraka Khān, and presented to him an account of the proceedings and disposition of the Christians of that city. Zeal for the Muslim religion was manifested in the mind of that monarch of exemplary faith, and the defence of the truth became predominant in his disposition. After some days, he showed honour to this Sayyid, appointed a body of Turks and confidential persons among the chief Musalmans, and commanded that they should slaughter the Christian company who had committed that dire oppression, and despatch them to hell. When that mandate had been obtained, it was preserved until that wretched sect had assembled in the church, then they seized them all together, and despatched the whole of them to hell, and reduced the church again to bricks."[1]

[1] Jūzjānī, pp. 448–50. Raverty, pp. 1288–90.

For Islam to enter into competition with such powerful rivals as Buddhism and Christianity were at the outset of the period of Mongol rule, must have appeared a well-nigh hopeless undertaking. For the Muslims had suffered more from the storm of the Mongol invasions than the others. Those cities that had hitherto been the rallying points of spiritual organisation and learning for Islam in Asia, had been for the most part laid in ashes : the theologians and pious doctors of the faith, either slain or carried away into captivity.[1] Among the Mongol rulers—usually so tolerant towards all religions—there were some who exhibited varying degrees of hatred towards the Muslim faith. Chingīz Khān ordered all those who killed animals in the Muhammadan fashion to be put to death, and this ordinance was revived by Qūbīlāy, who by offering rewards to informers set on foot a sharp persecution that lasted for seven years, as many poor persons took advantage of this ready means of gaining wealth, and slaves accused their masters in order to gain their freedom.[2] During the reign of Kuyūk (1246–1248), who left the conduct of affairs entirely to his two Christian ministers and whose court was filled with Christian monks, the Muhammadans were made to suffer great severities.[3]

A contemporary historian, al-Jūzjānī, gives the following account of the kind of treatment to which a Muhammadan theologian might be exposed at the court of Kuyūk. " Trustworthy persons have related that Kuyūk was constantly being incited by the Buddhist priests to acts of oppression towards the Musalmans and the persecution of the faithful. There was an Imām in that country, one of the men of learning among the Muslims . . . named Nūr-al-Dīn, al-Khwārazmī. A number of Christian laymen and priests and a band of idol-worshipping Buddhist priests made a request to Kuyūk, asking him to summon that

[1] So notoriously brutal was the treatment they received that even the Chinese showmen in their exhibitions of shadow figures exultingly brought forward the figure of an old man with a white beard dragged by the neck at the tail of a horse, as showing how the Mongol horsemen behaved towards the Musalmans. (Howorth, vol. i. p. 159.)

[2] Raverty, p. 1146. Howorth, vol. i. pp. 112, 273. This edict was only withdrawn when it was found that it prevented Muhammadan merchants from visiting the court and that trade suffered in consequence.

[3] Howorth, vol. i. p. 165.

Imām of the Musalmans that they might hold a controversy with him and get him to prove the superiority of the faith of Muḥammad and his prophetic mission—otherwise, he should be put to death. The Khān agreed, the Imām was sent for, and a discussion ensued upon the claim of Muḥammad to be a prophet and the manner of his life as compared with that of other prophets. At length, as the arguments of those accursed ones were weak and devoid of the force of truth, they withdrew their hand from contradiction and drew the mark of oppression and outrage on the pages of the business and asked Kuyūk Khān to tell the Imām to perform two genuflexions in prayer, according to the rites and ordinances of the Muhammadan law, in order that his unbecoming movements in the performance of this act of worship might become manifest to them and to the Khān." Kuyūk gave the order accordingly, and the Imām and another Musalman who was with him performed the ritual of the prayer according to the prescribed forms. "When the godly Imām and the other Musalman who was with him, had placed their foreheads on the ground in the act of prostration, some infidels whom Kuyūk had summoned, greatly annoyed them and knocked their heads with force upon the ground, and committed other abominable acts against them. But that godly Imām endured all this oppression and annoyance and performed all the required forms and ceremonies of the prayer and in no way curtailed it. When he had repeated the salutation, he lifted up his face towards heaven and observed the form of 'Invoke your Lord with humility and in secret,' and having asked permission to depart, he returned unto his own house." [1]

Arghūn (1284–1291) the fourth Īlkhān persecuted the Musalmans and took away from them all posts in the departments of justice and finance, and forbade them to appear at his court.[2]

In spite of all difficulties, however, the Mongols and the savage tribes that followed in their wake [3] were at length

[1] Jūzjānī, pp. 404–5. Raverty, p. 1160 sqq.
[2] De Guignes, vol. iii. p. 265.
[3] In the thirteenth century, three-fourths of the Mongol hosts were Turks. (Cahun, p. 279.)

brought to submit to the faith of those Muslim peoples whom they had crushed beneath their feet. Unfortunately history sheds little light on the progress of this missionary movement and only a few details relating to the conversion of the more prominent converts have been preserved to us. Scattered up and down throughout the length and breadth of the Mongol empire, there must have been many of the followers of the Prophet who laboured successfully and unknown, to win unbelievers to the faith. In the reign of Ogotāy (1229–1241), we read of a certain Buddhist governor of Persia, named Kurguz, who in his later years abjured Buddhism and became a Musalman.[1] In the reign of Tīmūr Khān (1323–1328), Ānanda, a grandson of Qūbīlāy and viceroy of Kan-Su, was a zealous Musalman and had converted a great many persons in Tangut and won over a large number of the troops under his command to the same faith. He was summoned to court and efforts were made to induce him to conform to Buddhism, and on his refusing to abandon his faith he was cast into prison. But he was shortly after set at liberty, for fear of an insurrection among the inhabitants of Tangut, who were much attached to him.[2]

The author of the Muntakhab al-Tawārīkh asserts that Ānanda built four mosques in Khānbāligh (the modern Peking), which provided accommodation for 1,000,000 men at the time of the Friday prayer; but no credence can be given to this or to his other statements regarding the spread of Islam in China, in view of the fact that he represents Ānanda to have been the successor of Tīmūr Khān on the imperial throne and gives an entirely fictitious account of his descendants, several of whom are represented as having professed Islam, though none of the five had any existence except in the imagination of the writer.[3]

The first Mongol ruling prince who professed Islam was Baraka Khān, who was chief of the Golden Horde from 1256 to 1267.[4] According to Abu'l-Ghāzī he was converted

[1] C. d'Ohsson, vol. iii. p. 121.
[2] Rashīd al-Dīn, pp. 600–2.
[3] Blochet, pp. 74–7.
[4] It is of interest to note that Najm al-Dīn Mukhtār al-Zāhidī in 1260 compiled for Baraka Khān a treatise which gave the proofs of the divine mission of the Prophet, a refutation of those who denied it, and an account

after he had come to the throne. He is said one day to have fallen in with a caravan coming from Bukhārā, and taking two of the merchants aside, to have questioned them on the doctrines of Islam, and they expounded to him their faith so persuasively that he became converted in all sincerity. He first revealed his change of faith to his youngest brother, whom he induced to follow his example, and then made open profession of his new belief.[1] But, according to al-Jūzjānī, Baraka Khān was brought up as a Musalman from infancy, and, as soon as he was old enough to learn, was taught the Qur'ān by one of the 'Ulamā of the city of Khujand.[2] The same author (who compiled his history during the lifetime of Baraka Khān), states that the whole of his army was Musalman. "Trustworthy persons have also related that, throughout his whole army, it is the etiquette for every horseman to have a prayer-carpet with him, so that, when the time for prayer arrives, they may occupy themselves in their devotions. Not a person in his whole army takes any intoxicating drink whatever; and great 'Ulamā, consisting of commentators, traditionists, jurists, and disputants, are in his society. He has a great number of religious books, and most of his receptions and debates are with 'Ulamā. In his place of audience debates on ecclesiastical law constantly take place; and, in his faith, as a Musalman, he is exceedingly strict and orthodox."[3] Baraka Khān entered into a close alliance with the Mamlūk Sultan of Egypt, Rukn al-Dīn Baybars. The initiative came from the latter, who had given a hospitable reception to a body of troops, two hundred in number, belonging to the Golden Horde; these men, observing the growing enmity between their Khān and Hūlāgū, the conqueror of Baghdād, in whose army they were serving, took flight into Syria, whence they were honourably conducted to Cairo to the court of Baybars, who persuaded them to embrace Islam.[4] Baybars himself was at war with Hūlāgū, whom he had recently defeated and driven out of Syria. He sent

of the controversies between Christians and Muslims. (Steinschneider, pp. 63–4.)

[1] Abu'l-Ghāzī, tome ii. p. 181.

[2] Jūzjānī, p. 447. Raverty, pp. 1283–4.

[3] Jūzjānī, p. 447. Raverty, pp. 1285–6.

[4] Maqrīzī (2), tome i. pp. 180–1, 187.

two of the Mongol fugitives, with some other envoys, to bear a letter to Baraka Khān. On their return these envoys reported that each princess and amīr at the court of Baraka Khān had an imām and a mu'adhdhin, and the children were taught the Qur'ān in the schools.[1] These friendly relations between Baybars and Baraka Khān brought many of the Mongols of the Golden Horde into Egypt, where they were prevailed upon to become Musalmans.[2]

In Persia, where Hūlāgū founded the dynasty of the Īlkhāns, the progress of Islam among the Mongols was much slower. In order to strengthen himself against the attacks of Baraka Khān and the Sultan of Egypt, Hūlāgū accepted the alliance of the Christian powers of the East, such as the king of Armenia and the Crusaders. His favourite wife was a Christian and favourably disposed the mind of her husband towards her co-religionists, and his son Abāqā Khān married the daughter of the Emperor of Constantinople. Though Abāqā Khān did not himself become a Christian, his court was filled with Christian priests, and he sent envoys to several of the princes of Europe—St. Louis of France, King Charles of Sicily and King James of Aragon—to solicit their alliance against the Muhammadans; to the same end also, an embassy of sixteen Mongols was sent to the Council of Lyons in 1274, where the spokesman of this embassy embraced Christianity and was baptised with some of his companions. Great hopes were entertained of the conversion of Abāqā, but they proved fruitless. His brother Takūdār,[3] who succeeded him, was the first of the Īlkhāns who embraced Islam. He had been brought up as a Christian, for (as a contemporary Christian writer [4] tells us), "he was baptised when young and called by the name of Nicholas. But when he was grown up, through his intercourse with Saracens of whom he was very fond, he became a base Saracen, and, renouncing the Christian faith, wished to be called Muḥammad Khān, and strove with all his might that the

[1] Maqrīzī (2), tome i. p. 215. [2] Id. p. 222.
[3] Waṣṣāf calls him Nikūdār before, and Aḥmad after, his conversion.
[4] Hayton. (Ramusio, tome ii. p. 60, c.)

Tartars should be converted to the faith and sect of Muḥammad, and when they proved obstinate, not daring to force them, he brought about their conversion by giving them honours and favours and gifts, so that in his time many Tartars were converted to the faith of the Saracens." This prince sent the news of his conversion to the Sultan of Egypt in the following letter:—" By the power of God Almighty, the mandate of Aḥmad to the Sultan of Egypt. God Almighty (praised be His name!) by His grace preventing us and by the light of His guidance, hath guided us in our early youth and vigour into the true path of the knowledge of His deity and the confession of His unity, to bear witness that Muḥammad (on whom rest the highest blessings!) is the Prophet of God, and to reverence His saints and His pious servants. 'Whom God shall please to guide, that man's breast will He open to Islam.'[1] We ceased not to incline our heart to the promotion of the faith and the improvement of the condition of Islam and the Muslims, up to the time when the succession to the empire came to us from our illustrious father and brother, and God spread over us the glory of His grace and kindness, so that in the abundance of His favours our hopes were realised, and He revealed to us the bride of the kingdom, and she was brought forth to us a noble spouse. A Qūriltāy or general assembly was convened, wherein our brothers, our sons, great nobles, generals of the army and captains of the forces, met to hold council; and they were all agreed on carrying out the order of our elder brother, viz. to summon here a vast levy of our troops whose numbers would make the earth, despite its vastness, appear too narrow, whose fury and fierce onset would fill the hearts of men with fear, being animated with a courage before which the mountain peaks bow down, and a firm purpose that makes the hardest rocks grow soft. We reflected on this their resolution which expressed the wish of all, and we concluded that it ran counter to the aim we had in view—to promote the common weal, i. e. to strengthen the ordinance of Islam; never, as far as lies in our power, to issue any order that will not tend to prevent bloodshed, remove the ills of men,

[1] Qur'ān, vi. 125.

and cause the breeze of peace and prosperity to blow on all lands, and the kings of other countries to rest upon the couch of affection and benevolence, whereby the commands of God will be honoured and mercy be shown to the people of God. Herein, God inspired us to quench this fire and put an end to these terrible calamities, and make known to those who advanced this proposal (of a levy) what it is that God has put into our hearts to do, namely, to employ all possible means for the healing of all the sickness of the world, and putting off what should only be appealed to as the last remedy. For we desire not to hasten to appeal to arms, until we have first declared the right path, and will permit it only after setting forth the truth and establishing it with proofs. Our resolve to carry out whatever appears to us good and advantageous has been strengthened by the counsels of the Shaykh al-Islām, the model of divines, who has given us much assistance in religious matters. We have appointed our chief justice, Qutb al-Dīn and the Atābak, Bahā al-Dīn, both trustworthy persons of this flourishing kingdom, to make known to you our course of action and bear witness to our good intentions for the common weal of the Muslims; and to make it known that God has enlightened us, and that Islam annuls all that has gone before it, and that God Almighty has put it into our hearts to follow the truth and those who practice it. . . . If some convincing proof be required, let men observe our actions. By the grace of God, we have raised aloft the standards of the faith, and borne witness to it in all our orders and our practice, so that the ordinances of the law of Muḥammad may be brought to the fore and firmly established in accordance with the principles of justice laid down by Aḥmad. Whereby we have filled the hearts of the people with joy, have granted free pardon to all offenders, and shown them indulgences, saying, 'May God pardon the past!' We have reformed all matters concerning the pious endowments of Muslims given for mosques, colleges, charitable institutions, and the rebuilding of caravanserais; we have restored their incomes to those to whom they were due according to the terms laid down by the donors. . . . We have ordered the pilgrims to be treated with respect, provision to be made for their caravans and for securing their safety on the pilgrim routes; we have given perfect freedom to merchants, travelling from one country to another, that they may go wherever they please; and we have strictly prohibited our soldiers and police from interfering with them in their comings or goings." He seeks the alliance of the Sultan of Egypt "so that these countries and cities may again be populated, these terrible calamities be put down, the sword be returned to the scabbard; that all peoples may dwell in peace and quietness, and the necks of the Muslims be freed from the ills of humiliation and disgrace." [1]

To the student of the history of the Mongols it is a relief to pass from the recital of nameless horrors and continual bloodshed to a document emanating from a Mongol prince and giving expression to such humane and benevolent sentiments, which sound strange indeed coming from such lips.

This conversion of their chief and the persecutions that he inflicted on the Christians gave great offence to the Mongols, who, although not Christians themselves, had been long accustomed to intercourse with the Christians, and they denounced their chief to Qūbīlāy K͟hān as one who had abandoned the footsteps of his forefathers. A revolt broke out against him, headed by his nephew Arghūn, who compassed his death and succeeded him on the throne. During his brief reign (1284–1291), the Christians were once more restored to favour, while the Musalmans had to suffer persecution in their turn, were dismissed from their posts and driven away from the court.[2]

The successors of Takūdār were all heathen, until, in 1295, G͟hāzān, the seventh and greatest of the Īlk͟hāns, became a Musalman and made Islam the ruling religion of Persia. During the last three reigns the Christians had entertained great hopes of the conversion of the ruling family of Persia, who had shown them such distinguished favour and entrusted them with so many important offices of state. His immediate predecessor, the insurgent Baydū K͟hān, who occupied the throne for a few months only in

[1] Waṣṣāf, pp. 231–4. [2] De Guignes, vol. iii. pp. 263–5.

1295, carried his predilection for Christianity so far as to try to put a stop to the spread of Islam among the Mongols, and accordingly forbade any one to preach the doctrines of this faith among them.[1]

Ghāzān himself before his conversion had been brought up as a Buddhist and had erected several Buddhist temples in Khurāsān, and took great pleasure in the company of the priests of this faith, who had come into Persia in large numbers since the establishment of the Mongol supremacy over that country.[2] He appears to have been naturally of a religious turn of mind, for he studied the creeds of the different religions of his time, and used to hold discussions with the learned doctors of each faith.[3] Rashīd al-Dīn, his learned minister and the historian of his reign, maintained the genuineness of his conversion to Islam, the religious observances of which he zealously kept throughout his whole reign, though his contemporaries (and later writers have often re-echoed the imputation) represented him as having only yielded to the solicitations of some Amīrs and Shaykhs.[4] "Besides, what interested motive," asks his apologist, "could have led so powerful a sovereign to change his faith: much less, a prince whose pagan ancestors had conquered the world?" His conversion, however, certainly won over to his side the hearts of the Persians, when he was contending with Baydū for the throne, and the Muhammadan Mongols in the army of his rival deserted to support the cause of their co-religionist. These were the very considerations that were urged upon Ghāzān by Nawrūz, a Muhammadan Amīr who had espoused his cause and who hailed him as the prince who, according to a prophecy, was to appear about this time to protect the faith of Islam and restore it to its former splendour: if he embraced Islam, he could become the ruler of Persia: the Musalmans, delivered from the grievous yoke of the Pagan Mongols, would espouse his cause, and God, recognising in him the saviour of the true faith from utter destruction, would bless his arms with victory.[5] After hesitating a little, Ghāzān

[1] C. d'Ohsson, tome iv. pp. 141–2.
[2] Id. ib. p. 148.
[3] Id. ib. p. 365.
[4] Id. ib. pp. 148, 354. Cahun, p. 434.
[5] C. d'Ohsson, tome iv. pp. 128, 132.

made a public profession of the faith, and his officers and soldiers followed his example: he distributed alms to men of piety and learning and visited the mosques and tombs of the saints and in every way showed himself an exemplary Muslim ruler. His brother, Uljāytū, who succeeded him in 1304, under the name of Muḥammad Khudābandah, had been brought up as a Christian in the faith of his mother and had been baptised under the name of Nicholas, but after his mother's death, while he was still a young man, he became a convert to Islam through the persuasions of his wife.[1] Ibn Baṭūṭah says that his example exercised a great influence on the Mongols.[2] From this time forward Islam became the paramount faith in the kingdom of the Īlkhāns.

The details that we possess of the progress of Islam in the Middle Kingdom, which fell to the lot of Chaghatāy and his descendants, are still more meagre. Several of the princes of this line had a Muhammadan minister in their service, but they showed themselves unsympathetic to the faith of Islam. Chaghatāy harassed his Muhammadan subjects by regulations that restricted their ritual observances in respect of the killing of animals for food and of ceremonial washings. Al-Jūzjānī says that he was the bitterest enemy of the Muslims among all the Mongol rulers and did not wish any one to utter the word Musalman before him except with evil purpose.[3] Orghana, the wife of his grandson and successor, Qarā-Hūlāgū, brought up

[1] Hammer-Purgstall: Geschichte der Ilchanen, vol. ii. p. 182. It is not improbable that the captive Muslim women took a considerable part in the conversion of the Mongols to Islam. Women appear to have occupied an honoured position among the Mongols, and many instances might be given of their having taken a prominent part in political affairs, just as already several cases have been mentioned of the influence they exercised on their husbands in religious matters. William of Rubruck tells us how he found the influence of a Muslim wife an obstacle in the way of his proselytising labours: "On the day of Pentecost a certain Saracen came to us, and while in conversation with us, we began expounding the faith, and when he heard of the blessings of God to man in the incarnation, the resurrection of the dead, the last judgment, and the washing away of sins in baptism, he said he wished to be baptised; but while we were making ready to baptise him, he suddenly jumped on his horse saying he had to go home to consult with his wife. And the next day talking with us he said he could not possibly venture to receive baptism, for then he could not drink *cosmos*" (mare's milk). (Rubruck, pp. 90–1.)

[2] Ibn Baṭūṭah, vol. ii. p. 57.

[3] Jūzjānī, pp. 381, 397. Raverty, pp. 1110, 1145–6.

her son as a Musalman, and under the name of Mubārak Shāh he came forward in 1264 as one of the claimants of the disputed succession to the Chaghatāy Khānate; but he was soon driven from the throne by his cousin Burāq Khān, and appears to have exercised no influence on behalf of his faith, indeed judging from their names it would not appear that any of his own children even adopted the religion of their father.[1] Burāq Khān is said to have "had the blessedness of receiving the light of the faith" a few days before his death in 1270, and to have taken the name of Sulṭān Ghiyāth al-Dīn,[2] but he was buried according to the ancient funeral rites of the Mongols, and not as a Musalman, and those who had been converted during his reign relapsed into their former heathenism. It was not until the next century that the conversion of Ṭarmāshīrīn Khān, about 1326, caused Islam to be at all generally adopted by the Chaghatāy Mongols, who when they followed the example of their chief this time remained true to their new faith. But even now the ascendancy of Islam was not assured, for Būzun who was Khān in the next decade—the chronology is uncertain—drove Ṭarmāshīrīn from his throne, and persecuted the Muslims,[3] and it was not until some years later that we hear of the first Musalman king of Kāshgar, which the break-up of the Chaghatāy dynasty had erected into a separate kingdom. This prince, Tūqluq Tīmūr Khān (1347–1363), is said to have owed his conversion to a holy man from Bukhārā, by name Shaykh Jamāl al-Dīn. This Shaykh, in company with a number of travellers, had unwittingly trespassed on the game-preserves of the prince, who ordered them to be bound hand and foot and brought before him. In reply to his angry question, how they had dared interfere with his hunting, the Shaykh pleaded that they were strangers and were quite unaware that they were trespassing on forbidden ground. Learning that they were Persians, the prince said that a dog was worth more than a Persian. "Yes," replied the Shaykh, "if we had not the true faith, we should indeed be worse than the dogs." Struck with his reply, the Khān ordered

[1] Rashīd al-Dīn, pp. 173–4, 188. [2] Abu'l-Ghāzī, tome ii. p. 159.
[3] Ibn Baṭūṭah, tome iii. p. 47.

this bold Persian to be brought before him on his return from hunting, and taking him aside asked him to explain what he meant by these words and what was "faith." The Shaykh then set before him the doctrines of Islam with such fervour and zeal that the heart of the Khān that before had been hard as a stone was melted like wax, and so terrible a picture did the holy man draw of the state of unbelief, that the prince was convinced of the blindness of his own errors, but said, "Were I now to make profession of the faith of Islam, I should not be able to lead my subjects into the true path. But bear with me a little; and when I have entered into the possession of the kingdom of my forefathers, come to me again." For the empire of Chaghatāy had by this time been broken up into a number of petty princedoms, and it was many years before Tūqluq Tīmūr succeeded in uniting under his sway the whole empire as before. Meanwhile Shaykh Jamāl al-Dīn had returned to his home, where he fell dangerously ill: when at the point of death, he said to his son Rashīd al-Dīn, "Tūqluq Tīmūr will one day become a great monarch; fail not to go and salute him in my name and fearlessly remind him of the promise he made me." Some years later, when Tūqluq Tīmūr had re-won the empire of his fathers, Rashīd al-Dīn made his way to the camp of the Khān to fulfil the last wishes of his father, but in spite of all his efforts he could not gain an audience of the Khān. At length he devised the following expedient: one day in the early morning, he began to chant the call to prayers, close to the Khān's tent. Enraged at having his slumbers disturbed in this way, the prince ordered him to be brought into his presence, whereupon Rashīd al-Dīn delivered his father's message. Tūqluq Khān was not unmindful of his promise, and said: "Ever since I ascended the throne I have had it on my mind that I made that promise, but the person to whom I gave the pledge never came. Now you are welcome." He then repeated the profession of faith and became a Muslim. "On that morn the sun of bounty rose out of the east of divine favour and effaced the dark night of unbelief. . . . They then decided that for the propagation of Islam they should interview the princes one by one, and it should be well for those who accepted the faith, but those who refused should be slain as heathens and idolaters." The first to be examined was a noble named Amīr Tūlik. The Khān asked him, "Will you embrace Islam?" Amir Tūlik burst into tears and said: "Three years ago I was converted by some holy men at Kāshgar and became a Musalman, but from fear of you I did not openly declare it." Then Tūqluq Khān rose up and embraced him, and the three sat down again together. In this manner they examined the princes one by one, and they all accepted Islam, with the exception of one named Jarās, who suggested a trial of strength between the Shaykh and his servant, an infidel who was above the ordinary stature of man and so strong that he could lift a two-year-old camel. The Shaykh accepted the challenge, saying: "If I do not throw him, I will not require you to become a Musalman. If it is God's wish that the Mongols become honoured with the blessed state of Islam, He will doubtless give me sufficient power to overcome this man." Tūqluq Khān and those who had become Musalmans with him tried to dissuade the holy man, but he persisted in his purpose. "A large crowd assembled, the infidel was brought in, and he and the Shaykh advanced towards one another. The infidel, proud of his own strength, advanced with a conceited air. The Shaykh looked very small and weak beside him. When they came to blows, the Shaykh struck the infidel full in the chest, and he fell senseless. After a little he came to again, and having raised himself, fell again at the feet of the Shaykh, crying out and uttering words of belief. The people raised loud shouts of applause, and on that day 160,000 persons cut off the hair of their heads and became Musalmans. The Khān was circumcised, and the lights of Islam dispelled the shades of unbelief." From that time Islam became the established faith in the settled countries under the rule of the descendants of Chaghatāy.[1] But many of the nomad Mongols appear to have remained outside the pale of Islam up to the early part of the fifteenth century, judging from the violent methods adopted for their conversion by Muḥammad Khān, who was Khān of

[1] Abu' l-Ghāzī, tome ii. pp. 166–8. Muḥammad Ḥaydar, pp. 13–15.

Mughalistān [1] about 1416. "Muḥammad Khān was a wealthy prince and a good Musalman. He persisted in following the road of justice and equity, and was so unremitting in his exertions, that during his blessed reign most of the tribes of the Mongols became Musalmans. It is well known what severe measures he had recourse to, in bringing the Mongols to be believers in Islam. If, for instance, a Mongol did not wear a turban, a horseshoe nail was driven into his head: and treatment of this kind was common. May God recompense him with good." [2]

Even such drastic measures were ineffectual in bringing about a general acceptance of Islam, for as late as at the close of the following century,[3] a dervish named Isḥāq Walī found scope for his proselytising activities in Kāshgar, Yārkand and Khotan, where he spent twelve years in spreading the faith; [4] he also worked among the Kirghiz and Kazaks, from among whom he made 180 converts and destroyed eighteen temples of idols.[5]

In the preceding pages some attempt has been made to indicate some of the steps by which the Muslims won over to their faith the savage hordes who had destroyed their centres of culture. By slow degrees, Islam thus began to emerge out of the ruins of its former ascendancy and take its place again as a dominant faith, after more than a century of depression. In the course of the struggle between the followers of rival creeds for the adherence of the Mongols, considerations of political expediency undoubtedly operated in favour of the Muslim party, and the intrigues of Western Christendom caused the Christians to become suspect, as agents of a foreign power; but at the beginning such of the Mongols as were Nestorians could put forward a better claim to be the national party and could attack the Musalmans as adherents of a foreign faith. Aḥmad Takūdār

[1] When the power of the Chaghatāy Khāns declined, a portion of the eastern division of their realm became practically independent under the name of Mughalistān, a pastoral country suited to the habits of nomad herdsmen, in what is now known as Chinese Turkistan.

[2] Muḥammad Ḥaydar, pp. 57–8.

[3] In the reign of 'Abd al-Karīm, who was Khān of Kāshgar from A.H. 983 to 1003 (A.D. 1575–1594).

[4] Martin Hartmann: Der Islamische Orient, vol. i. p. 203. (Berlin, 1899.)

[5] Id. p. 202.

was denounced by Arghūn as a traitor to the law of his fathers, in that he had followed the way of the Arabs which none of his ancestors had known.[1] The insurrection that caused Ṭarmāshīrīn to be driven into exile, gained strength from the complaint that this monarch had disregarded the Yassāq or ancient code of Mongol institutes.[2] But though the issue of the struggle long remained doubtful, Islam gradually gained ground in the lands of which it had been dispossessed. The means whereby this success was achieved are obscure, and the scanty details set forth above leave much of the tale untold, but enough has been recorded to indicate some of the proselytising agencies that led to individual conversions. Ānanda drank in Islam with his foster-mother's milk;[3] and the remnant of the faithful, especially the older families of Muhammadan Turks, exercised an almost insensible influence on the Mongols who settled down in their midst. But of special importance among the proselytising agencies at work was the influence of the pīr and his spiritual disciples. In the midst of the profound discouragement which filled the Musalmans after the flood of the Mongol conquest had poured over them, their first refuge was in mysticism, and the pīr, or spiritual guide, and religious orders—such as the Naqshbandī, which in the fourteenth century entered on a new period of its development—breathed new life into the Muslim community and inspired it with fresh fervour. "In the hands of the pīr and his monks, the Musalman in Asia came to be an agent, at first passive and unconscious, later on the adherent of a party—the party of the national faith, in opposition to the rule of the Mongols, which was at once foreign, barbaric and secular."[4]

Let us now return to the history of Islam in the Golden Horde. The chief camping ground of this section of the Mongols was the grassy plain watered by the Volga, on the bank of which they founded their capital city Serai, whither the Russian princes sent their tribute to the k͟hān. The conversion of Baraka K͟hān, of which mention has been made above, and the close intercourse with Egypt that

[1] Assemani, tome iii. pars. ii. p. cxvi.
[2] Ibn Baṭūṭah, vol. iii. p. 40.
[3] Rashīd al-Dīn, p. 600, l. 1.
[4] Cahun, p. 410.

subsequently sprang up, contributed considerably to the progress of Islam, and his example seems to have been gradually followed by those of the aristocracy and leaders of the Golden Horde that were of Mongol descent. But many tribes of the Golden Horde appear to have resented the introduction of Islam into their midst, and when the conversion of Baraka Khān was openly proclaimed, they sent to offer the crown, of which they considered him now unworthy, to his rival Hūlāgū. Indeed, so strong was this opposition, that it seems to have largely contributed to the formation of the Nogais as a separate tribe. They took their name from Nogāy, who was the chief commander of the Mongol forces under Baraka Khān. When the other princes of the Golden Horde became Musalmans, Nogāy remained a Shamanist and thus became a rallying point for those who refused to abandon the old religion of the Mongols. His daughter, however, who was married to a Shamanist, became converted to Islam some time after her marriage and had to endure the ill-treatment and contempt of her husband in consequence.[1]

To Ūzbek Khān, who was leader of the Golden Horde from 1313 to 1340, and who distinguished himself by his proselytising zeal, it was said, "Content yourself with our obedience, what matters our religion to you? Why should we abandon the faith of Chingīz Khān for that of the Arabs?" But in spite of the strong opposition to his efforts, Ūzbek Khān succeeded in winning many converts to the faith of which he was so ardent a follower and which owed to his efforts its firm establishment in the country under his sway.[2] A further sign of his influence is found in the tribes of the Ūzbeks of Central Asia, who take their name from him and were probably converted during his reign. He is said to have formed the design of spreading the faith of Islam throughout the whole of Russia,[3] but here he met with no success. Indeed, though the Mongols were paramount in Russia for two centuries, they appear to have exercised very little influence on the people of that country, and least of all in the matter of

[1] Howorth, vol ii. p. 1015.
[2] Abū-l Ghāzī, tome ii. p. 184.
[3] De Guignes, vol. iii. p. 351.

religion. It is noticeable, moreover, that in spite of his zeal for the spread of his own faith, Ūzbek Khān was very tolerant towards his Christian subjects, who were left undisturbed in the exercise of their religion and even allowed to pursue their missionary labours in his territory. One of the most remarkable documents of Muhammadan toleration is the charter that Ūzbek Khān granted to the Metropolitan Peter in 1313:—"By the will and power, the greatness and mercy of the most High! Ūzbek to all our princes, great and small, etc., etc. Let no man insult the metropolitan church of which Peter is the head, or his servants or his churchmen; let no man seize their property, goods or people, let no man meddle with the affairs of the metropolitan church, since they are divine. Whoever shall meddle therein and transgress our edict, will be guilty before God and feel His wrath and be punished by us with death. Let the metropolitan dwell in the path of safety and rejoice, with a just and upright heart let him (or his deputy) decide and regulate all ecclesiastical matters. We solemnly declare that neither we nor our children nor the princes of our realm nor the governors of our provinces will in any way interfere with the affairs of the church and the metropolitan, or in their towns, districts, villages, chases and fisheries, their hives, lands, meadows, forests, towns and places under their bailiffs, their vineyards, mills, winter quarters for cattle, or any of the properties and goods of the church. Let the mind of the metropolitan be always at peace and free from trouble, with uprightness of heart let him pray to God for us, our children and our nation. Whoever, shall lay hands on anything that is sacred, shall be held guilty, he shall incur the wrath of God and the penalty of death, that others may be dismayed at his fate. When the tribute or other dues, such as custom duties, plough-tax, tolls or relays are levied, or when we wish to raise troops among our subjects, let nothing be exacted from the cathedral churches under the metropolitan Peter, or from any of his clergy: . . . whatever may be exacted from the clergy, shall be returned threefold. . . Their laws, their churches, their monasteries and chapels shall be respected; whoever condemns or blames this religion, shall not be allowed to excuse himself under any pretext, but shall be punished with death. The brothers and sons of priests and deacons, living at the same table and in the same house, shall enjoy the same privileges." [1]

That these were no empty words and that the toleration here promised became a reality, may be judged from a letter sent to the Khān by Pope John XXII in 1318, in which he thanks the Muslim prince for the favour he showed to his Christian subjects and the kind treatment they received at his hands.[2] The successors of Ūzbek Khān do not appear to have been animated by the same zeal for the spread of Islam as he had shown, and could not be expected to succeed where he failed. So long as the Russians paid their taxes, they were left free to worship according to their own desires, and the Christian religion had become too closely intertwined with the life of the people to be disturbed, even had efforts been made to turn them from the faith of their fathers; for Christianity had been the national religion of the Russian people for well-nigh three centuries before the Mongols established themselves in Russian territory.

Another race many years before had tried to win the Russians to Islam but had likewise failed, viz. the Muslim Bulgarians who were found in the tenth century on the banks of the Volga, and who probably owed their conversion to the Muslim merchants, trading in furs and other commodities of the North; their conversion must have taken place some time before A.D. 921, when the caliph al-Muqtadir sent an envoy to confirm them in the faith and instruct them in the tenets and ordinances of Islam.[3]

These Bulgarians attempted the conversion of Vladimir, the then sovereign of Russia, who (the Russian chronicler tells us) had found it necessary to choose some religion better than his pagan creed, but they failed to overcome his objections to the rite of circumcision and to the prohibition of

[1] Karamzin, vol. iv. pp. 391–4.

[2] Hammer-Purgstall: Geschichte der Goldenen Horde in Kiptschak, p. 290.

[3] De Baschkiris quae memoriae prodita sunt ab Ibn-Foszlano et Jakuto, interprete C. N. Fraehnio. (Mémoires de l'Académie Impériale des Sciences de St. Pétersbourg, tome viii. p. 626. 1822.)

wine, the use of which, he declared, the Russians could never give up, as it was the very joy of their life. Equally unsuccessful were the Jews who came from the country of the Khazars on the Caspian Sea and had won over the king of that people to the Mosaic faith.[1] After listening to their arguments, Vladimir asked them where their country was. "Jerusalem," they replied, "but God in His anger has scattered us over the whole world." "Then you are cursed of God," cried the king, "and yet want to teach others: begone! we have no wish, like you, to be without a country." The most favourable impression was made by a Greek priest who, after a brief criticism of the other religions, set forth the whole scheme of Christian teaching beginning with the creation of the world and the story of the fall of man and ending with the seven œcumenical councils accepted by the Greek Church; then he showed the prince a picture of the Last Judgment with the righteous entering paradise and the wicked being thrust down into hell, and promised him the heritage of heaven, if he would be baptised. But Vladimir was unwilling to make a rash choice of a substitute for his pagan religion, so he called his boyards together and having told them of the accounts he had received of the various religions, asked them for their advice. "Prince," they replied "every man praises his own religion, and if you would make choice of the best, send wise men into the different countries to discover which of all the nations honours God in the manner most worthy of Him." So the prince chose out for this purpose ten men who were eminent for their wisdom. These ambassadors found among the Bulgarians mean-looking places of worship, gloomy prayers and solemn faces; among the German Catholics religious ceremonies that lacked both grandeur and magnificence. At length they reached Constantinople: "Let them see the glory of our God," said the Emperor. So they were taken to the church of Santa Sophia, where the Patriarch, clad in his pontifical robes, was celebrating mass. The magnificence of the building, the rich vestments of the priests, the ornaments of the altars, the sweet odour of

[1] Abū 'Ubayd al-Bakrī, pp. 470–1.

the incense, the reverent silence of the people, and the mysterious solemnity of the ceremonial filled the savage Russians with wonder and amazement. It seemed to them that this church must be the dwelling of the Most High, and that He manifested His glory therein to mortals. On their return to Kief, the ambassadors gave the prince an account of their mission; they spoke with contempt of the religion of the Prophet and had little to say for the Roman Catholic faith, but were enthusiastic in their eulogies of the Greek Church. "Every man," they said, "who has put his lips to a sweet draught, henceforth abhors anything bitter; wherefore we having come to the knowledge of the faith of the Greek Church desire none other." Vladimir once more consulted his boyards, who said unto him, "Had not the Greek faith been best of all, Olga, your grandmother, the wisest of mortals, would never have embraced it." Whereupon Vladimir hesitated no longer and in A.D. 988 declared himself a Christian. On the day after his baptism he threw down the idols his forefathers had worshipped, and issued an edict that all the Russians, masters and slaves, rich and poor, should submit to be baptised into the Christian faith.[1]

Thus Christianity became the national religion of the Russian people, and after the Mongol conquest, the distinctive national characteristics of Russians and Tatars that have kept the two races apart to the present day, the bitter hatred of the Tatar yoke, the devotion of the Russians to their own faith and the want of religious zeal on the part of the Tatars, kept the conquered race from adopting the religion of the conqueror. Especially has the prohibition of spirituous liquors by the laws of Islam been supposed to have stood in the way of the adoption of this religion by the Russian people.

It would appear that not until after the promulgation of the edict of religious toleration in 1905 throughout the Russian empire and the active Muslim propaganda that followed it, were cases observed of Russians being converted to Islam, and those that have occurred are ascribed to the strong attraction of the material help offered by the Tatars

[1] Karamsin, tome i. pp. 259–71.

to such converts and the influence of the moral strength of the Muslims themselves.[1]

Not that the Tatars in Russia had been altogether inoperative in promoting the spread of Islam during the preceding centuries. The distinctly Hellenic type of face that is to be found among the so-called Tatars of the Crimea has led to the conjecture that these Muhammadans have absorbed into their community the Greek and Italian populations that they found settled on the Crimean peninsula, and that we find among them the Muhammadanised descendants of the indigenous inhabitants, and of the Genoese colonists.[2] A traveller of the seventeenth century tells us that the Tatars of the Crimea tried to induce their slaves to become Muhammadans, and won over many of them to this faith by promising them their liberty if they would be persuaded.[3] Conversions to Islam from among the Tatars of the Crimea are also reported after the proclamation of religious liberty in 1905.[4]

A brief reference may here be made to the Tatars in Lithuania, where small groups of them have been settled since the early part of the fifteenth century; these Muslim immigrants, dwelling in the midst of a Christian population, have preserved their old faith, but (probably for political reasons) do not appear to have attempted to proselytise. But they have been in the habit of marrying Lithuanian and Polish women, whose children were always brought up as Muslims, whereas no Muhammadan girl was permitted to marry a Christian. The grand dukes of Lithuania in the fifteenth century encouraged the marriage of Christian women with their Tatar troops, on whom they bestowed grants of land and other privileges.[5]

One of the most curious incidents in the missionary history of Islam is the conversion of the Kirghiz of Central Asia by Tatar mullās, who preached Islam among them in the eighteenth century, as emissaries of the Russian government. The Kirghiz began to come under Russian rule

[1] Bobrovnikoff, p. 13.
[2] Reclus, tome v. p. 831. R. du M. M., tome iii. pp. 76, 78.
[3] Relation des Tartares, par Jean de Luca, p. 17. (Thevenot, tome i.)
[4] Islam and Missions, p. 257.
[5] Gasztowtt, pp. 321–3. R. du M. M., xi. (1910), pp. 287 sqq.

about 1731, and for 120 years all diplomatic correspondence was carried on with them in the Tatar language under the delusion that they were ethnographically the same as the Tatars of the Volga. Another misunderstanding on the part of the Russian government was that the Kirghiz were Musalmans, whereas in the eighteenth century they were nearly all Shamanists, as a large number of them were still up to the middle of the nineteenth century. At the time of the annexation of their country to the Russian empire only a few of their K͟hāns and Sulṭāns had any knowledge of the faith of Islam—and that very confused and vague. Not a single mosque was to be found throughout the whole of the Kirghiz Steppes, or a single religious teacher of the faith of the Prophet, and the Kirghiz owed their conversion to Islam to the fact that the Russians, taking them for Muhammadans, insisted on treating them as such. Large sums of money were given for the building of mosques, and mullās were sent to open schools and instruct the young in the tenets of the Muslim faith: the Kirghiz scholars were to receive every day a small sum to support themselves on, and the fathers were to be induced to send their children to the schools by presents and other means of persuasion. An incontrovertible proof that the Musalman propaganda made its way into the Kirghiz Steppes from the side of Russia, is the circumstance that it was especially those Kirghiz who were more contiguous to Europe that first became Musalmans, and the old Shamanism lingered up to the nineteenth century among those who wandered in the neighbourhood of Khiva, Buk͟hārā and Khokand, though these for centuries had been Muhammadan countries.[1]

This is probably the only instance of a Christian government co-operating in the promulgation of Islam, and is the more remarkable inasmuch as the Russian government of this period was attempting to force Christianity on its Muslim subjects in Europe, in continuation of the efforts

[1] The Russian Policy regarding Central Asia. An historical sketch. By Prof. V. Grigorief. (Eugene Schuyler: Turkistan, vol. ii. pp. 405–6. 5th ed. London, 1876); Franz von Schwarz: Turkestan, p. 58. (Freiburg, 1910.)

made in the sixteenth century soon after the conquest of the Khanate of Kazan.

At the beginning of the nineteenth century many of the Kirghiz dwelling in the vast plains stretching southwards from the district of Tobolsk towards Turkistan were still heathen, and the Russian government was approached for permission for a Christian mission to be established among them. But this request was not granted, on the ground that "these people were as yet too wild and savage to be accessible to the Gospel. But soon after other missionaries, not depending on the good-will of any government, and having more zeal and understanding, occupied this field and won the whole of the Kirghis tribe to the faith of Islam."[1]

After the conquest of Kazan by the Russians in the sixteenth century, the occupation of the former Tatar Khanate was followed up by an official Christian missionary movement, and a number of the heathen population of the Khanate were baptised, the labours of the clergy being actively seconded by the police and the civil authorities, but as the Russian priests did not understand the language of their converts and soon neglected them, it had to be admitted that the new converts "shamelessly retain many horrid Tartar customs, and neither hold nor know the Christian faith." When spiritual exhortations failed, the government ordered its officials to "pacify, imprison, put in irons, and thereby unteach and frighten from the Tartar faith those who, though baptised, do not obey the admonitions of the Metropolitan."

In the eighteenth century the Russian government made fresh efforts to convert the heathen tribes and the relapsed Tatars, and held out many inducements to them to become baptised. Catherine II in 1778 ordered that all the new converts should sign a written promise to the effect that "they would completely forsake their infidel errors, and, avoiding all intercourse with unbelievers, would hold firmly and unwaveringly the Christian faith and its dogmas." But in spite of all, these so-called "baptised Tartars" were Christians only in name, and soon began to try to escape

[1] Islam and Missions, pp. 251–2, 255.

from the propagandist efforts of the Orthodox Church and abandoned Christianity for Islam, their so-called conversion merely serving as a stepping-stone to their entrance into the faith of the Prophet.

They may, indeed, have been inscribed in the official registers as Christians, but they resolutely stood out against any efforts that were made to Christianise them. In a semi-official article, published in 1872, the writer says: "It is a fact worthy of attention that a long series of evident apostasies coincides with the beginning of measures to confirm the converts in the Christian faith. There must be, therefore, some collateral cause producing those cases of apostasy precisely at the moment when the contrary might be expected." The fact seems to be that these Tatars having all the time remained Muhammadan at heart, resisted the active measures taken to make their nominal profession of Christianity in any way a reality.[1] But in the latter part of the nineteenth century efforts were made to Christianise these heathen and Muslim tribes by means of schools established in their midst. In this way it was hoped to win the younger generation, since otherwise it seemed impossible to gain an entrance for Christianity among the Tatars, for, as a Russian professor said, "The citizens of Kazan are hard to win, but we get some little folk from the villages on the steppe, and train them in the fear of God. Once they are with us they can never turn back."[2] For the Russian criminal code used to contain severe enactments against those who fell away from the Orthodox Church,[3] and sentenced any person convicted of converting a Christian to Islam to the loss of all civil rights and to imprisonment with hard labour for a term varying from eight to ten years. In spite, however, of the edicts of the government, Muslim propagandism succeeded in winning over whole villages

[1] D. Mackenzie Wallace: Russia, vol. i. pp. 242–4. (London, 1877, 4th ed.) R. du M. M., vol. ix. (1909), p. 249. Bobrovnikoff, p. 5 sqq.

[2] W. Hepworth Dixon: Free Russia, vol. ii. p. 284. (London, 1870.)

[3] E. g. "En 1883, des paysans Tatars du village d'Apozof étaient poursuivis, devant le tribunal de Kazan, pour avoir abandonné l'orthodoxie. Les accusés déclaraient avoir toujours été musalmans; sept d'entre eux n'en furent pas moins condamnés, comme apostats, aux travaux forcés. . . . Beaucoup de ces relaps ont été déportés en Sibérie." Anatole Leroy-Beaulieu: L'Empire des Tsars et les Russes, tome iii. p. 645. (Paris, 1889–93.)

to the faith of Islam, especially among the tribes of north-eastern Russia.[1]

The town of Kazan is the chief centre of this missionary activity; a large number of Muslim publications are printed here every year, and mullās go forth from the University to convert the pagans in the villages and bring back to Islam the Tatars who have allowed themselves to be baptised. The increasing number of these Christian Tatars, who have gone to swell the ranks of Islam, has alarmed the clergy of the Orthodox Church, but their efforts have failed to check the success of the mullās.[2] Especially since the edict of toleration in 1905, mass conversions have been reported, e.g. in 1909, ninety-one families in the village of Atomva are said to have become Muhammadan,[3] and as many as 53,000 persons between 1906 and 1910.[4] This propaganda is said to owe much of its success to the higher moral level of life in Muslim society, as well as to the stronger feeling of solidarity that prevails in it;[5] moreover, the methods adopted by the Russian clergy, supported by the government, to make the so-called Christian Tatars more orthodox, have caused the Christian faith to become unpopular among them.[6] On the other hand, the propaganda of Islam is very zealously carried forward; "every simple, untaught Moslem is a missionary of his religion, and the poor, dark, untaught heathen or half-heathen tribes cannot resist their force. In many villages of baptised aborigines the men go away for the winter to work as tailors in Moslem villages. There they are converted to Islam, and they return to their villages as fanatics bringing with them Moslem ideas with which to influence their homes."[7]

The tribes that have chiefly come under the influence of this missionary movement are the Votiaks, the greater part of whom are baptised Christians, but many became Muslims in the eighteenth and the beginning of the nineteenth centuries; and the influence of Islam is continually growing both among those that are Christian and among the small

[1] D. Mackenzie Wallace: Russia, vol. i. p. 245.
[2] Palmieri, pp. 85–6. R. du M. M., i. (1907), pp. 162 sq.
[3] R. du M. M., ix. (1909), p. 294.
[4] Id. x. (1910), p. 413. Id. i. (1907), p. 273.
[5] Id. ix. p. 252.
[6] Id. p. 249.
[7] Bobrovnikoff, p. 12.

remnant that is still heathen. The Cheremiss, like the Votiaks, are a Finnish tribe, about a quarter of whom are still heathen, but many have already embraced Islam and it is probable that most of them will soon adopt the same religion. The movement of the Cheremiss towards Islam made itself manifest in the nineteenth century and though many of them were nominally Christian, whole villages of them became Muhammadan despite the laws forbidding conversion except to the Orthodox Church.[1] They became Muhammadan through their immediate contact with the Bashkirs and Tatars, whose family and social customs were very similar to their own. The process sometimes began with intermarriages with Muhammadans—e. g. in one village a Cheremiss family intermarried with some Bashkirs and adopted their faith; the converts being persecuted as " circumcised dogs " in their own village, moved away and founded a new settlement some miles off, some wealthy Bashkirs helping them with money; but as they were officially registered as heathen, they could not get permission for the building of a mosque, so a few Bashkir families in the neighbourhood moved into the new settlement, in order to make up the number requisite for obtaining the necessary official permission.[2] A similar process has several times occurred in other villages in which Muhammadans have come to settle and have intermarried with Cheremiss.[3] In other cases there has been a definite missionary movement—e. g. in the beginning of the nineteenth century the village of Karakul was inhabited by Christian Cheremiss, but shortly after the middle of the century some families were converted to Islam by a Cheremiss who had become a mullā; on his death he was succeeded by a Bashkir from another village. Later on, the converts moved away to Tatar and Bashkir villages, their place being taken by Tatars, until the whole village became practically Tatar, few of the younger generation retaining any knowledge of the Cheremiss language, and intermarriages taking place only with Tatars.[4] Apart from this proselytising activity, there has been a very distinct spread of

[1] Reclus, tome v. pp. 746, 748.
[2] Eruslanov, pp. 3, 6.
[3] Id. pp. 7–8.
[4] Id. pp. 5–6.

Tatar influence in speech and manners among the Cheremiss. The Tatar language has spread among them, bringing with it the moral and religious ideas of Islam; the adoption of the Tatar dress is held to be a sign of superior culture, and if a Cheremiss does not dress like a Tatar he runs the risk of being laughed at by the first Tatar he meets or by his fellow Cheremiss; all this cultural movement tends to the ultimate adoption of the Tatar religion.[1] After their conversion, the Cheremiss are said to be very zealous in the propagation of their new faith and receive the assistance of wealthy Tatars;[2] on the other hand, the Russians despise the Cheremiss as an inferior race and apply opprobrious epithets even to those among them who are Christians.[3] About one-fourth of the Cheremiss are still heathen, but Muslim influences are so powerful among them that it is probable that in course of time they will for the most part become Muhammadans.[4] The Chuvash, who number about 1,000,000, have nearly all been baptised; there are about 20,000 of them that are still heathen but these are gradually being absorbed by Islam, while some of the Christian Chuvash have become Muhammadans and the rest are coming under Muslim influences. The extent of their zeal for their converts may be judged from the instance of a Christian Chuvash village, the priest of which had spent several years in collecting the 300 roubles necessary for the repair of the church; eight Chuvash families became Muhammadan and in the course of a few months 2000 roubles were collected for the building of a mosque.[5] Such ready activity is characteristic of the Muslim propaganda now being carried among the aboriginal tribes. Each family that accepts Islam receives help either in money or in kind: a house is built for one; a field, cattle, etc., are purchased for another; when several families in a village are converted, a mosque is built for them and a school established for their children.[6]

Of the spread of Islam among the Tatars of Siberia, we have a few particulars. It was not until the latter half of

[1] Eruslanov, pp. 9, 13.
[2] Id. pp. 17, 20, 36.
[3] Id. pp. 38–9.
[4] Bobrovnikoff, p. 22.
[5] Id. pp. 21–2, 31.
[6] Id. p. 13. Islam and Missions, p. 257.

the sixteenth century that it gained a footing in this country, but even before this period Muhammadan missionaries had from time to time made their way into Siberia with the hope of winning the heathen population over to the acceptance of their faith, but the majority of them met with a martyr's death. When Siberia came under Muhammadan rule, in the reign of Kūchum Khān, the graves of seven of these missionaries were discovered by an aged Shaykh who came from Bukhārā to search them out, being anxious that some memorial should be kept of the devotion of these martyrs to the faith : he was able to give the names of this number, and up to the last century their memory was still revered by the Tatars of Siberia.[1] When Kūchum Khān (who was descended from Jūjī Khān, the eldest son of Chingīz Khān) became Khān of Siberia (about the year 1570), either by right of conquest or (according to another account) at the invitation of the people whose Khān had died without issue,[2] he made every effort for the conversion of his subjects, and sent to Bukhārā asking for missionaries to assist him in this pious undertaking. One of the missionaries who was sent from Bukhārā has left us an account of how he set out with a companion to the capital of Kūchum Khān, on the bank of the Irtish. Here, after two years, his companion died, and, for some reasons that the writer does not mention, he went back again; but soon afterwards returned to the scene of his labours, bringing with him another coadjutor, when Kūchum Khān had appealed for help once more to Bukhārā.[3] Missionaries also came to Siberia from Kazan. But the advancing tide of Russian conquest soon brought the proselytising efforts of Kūchum Khān to an end before much had been accomplished, especially as many of the tribes under his rule offered a strong opposition to all attempts made to convert them.

But though interrupted by the Russian conquest, the progress of Islam was by no means stopped. Mullās from Bukhārā and other cities of Central Asia and merchants from Kazan were continually active as missionaries of Islam in Siberia. In 1745 an entrance was first effected among

[1] G. F. Müller : Sammlung Russischer Geschichte, vol. vii. p. 191.
[2] Id. vol. vii. pp. 183–4.
[3] Radloff, vol. i. p. 147.

the Baraba Tatars (between the Irtish and the Ob), and though at the beginning of the nineteenth century many were still heathen, they have now all become Musalmans.[1] The conversion of the Kirghiz has already been spoken of above: the history of most of the other Muslim tribes of Siberia is very obscure, but their conversion is probably of a recent date. Among the instruments of Muhammadan propaganda at the present time, it is interesting to note the large place taken by the folk-songs of the Kirghiz, in which, interwoven with tale and legend, the main truths of Islam make their way into the hearts of the common people.[2]

[1] Jadrinzew, p. 138. Radloff, vol. i. p. 241.
[2] Radloff, vol. i. pp. 472, 497.

CHAPTER IX.

THE SPREAD OF ISLAM IN INDIA.

THE Muhammadan invasions of India and the foundation and growth of the Muhammadan power in that country, have found many historians, both among contemporary and later writers. But hitherto no one has attempted to write a history of the spread of Islam in India, considered apart from the military successes and administrative achievements of its adherents. Indeed, to many, such a task must appear impossible. For India has often been picked out as a typical instance of a country in which Islam owes its existence and continuance in existence to the settlement in it of foreign, conquering Muhammadan races, who have transmitted their faith to their descendants, and only succeeded in spreading it beyond their own circle by means of persecution and forced conversions. Thus the missionary spirit of Islam is supposed to show itself in its true light in the brutal massacres of Brahmans by Maḥmūd of Ghaznā, in the persecutions of Aurangzeb, the forcible circumcisions effected by Ḥaydar 'Alī, Tīpū Sulṭān and the like.

But among the sixty-six millions of Indian Musalmans there are vast numbers of converts or descendants of converts, in whose conversion force played no part and the only influences at work were the teaching and persuasion of peaceful missionaries. This class of converts forms a very distinct group by itself which can be distinguished from that of the forcibly converted and the other heterogeneous elements of which Muslim India is made up. The entire community may be roughly divided into those of foreign race who brought their faith into the country along with them, and those who have been converted from one of the previous religions of the country under various inducements and at many different periods of history. The foreign settlement consists of three main bodies : first, and numerically the most important, are the immigrants from across the north-west frontier, who are found chiefly in Sind and the Panjāb; next come the descendants of the court and armies of the various Muhammadan dynasties, mainly in Upper India and to a much smaller extent in the Deccan; lastly, all along the west coast are settlements probably of Arab descent, whose original founders came to India by sea.[1] But the number of families of foreign origin that actually settled in India is nowhere great except in the Panjāb and its neighbourhood. More than half the Muslim population of India has indeed assumed appellations of distinctly foreign races, such as Shaykh, Beg, Khān, and even Sayyid, but the greater portion of them are local converts or descendants of converts, who have taken the title of the person of highest rank amongst those by whom they were converted or have affiliated themselves to the aristocracy of Islam on even less plausible grounds.[2] Of this latter section of the community—the converted natives of the country—part no doubt owed their change of religion to force and official pressure, but by far the majority of them entered the pale of Islam of their own free will. The history of the proselytising movements and the social influences that brought about their conversion has hitherto received very little attention, and most of the commonly accessible histories of the Muhammadans in India, whether written by European or by native authors, are mere chronicles of wars, campaigns and the achievements of princes, in which little mention of the religious life of the time finds a place, unless it has taken the form of fanaticism or intolerance. From the biographies of the Muslim saints, however, and from local traditions, something may be learned of the missionary work that was carried on quite independently of the political life of the country. But before dealing with these it is proposed to give an account of the official propagation of Islam and of the part played by the Muhammadan rulers in the spread of their faith.

[1] Census of India, 1891. General Report by J. A. Baines, p. 167 (London, 1893.)
[2] Id. pp. 126, 207.

From the fifteenth year after the death of the Prophet, when an Arab expedition was sent into Sind, up to the eighteenth century, a series of Muhammadan invaders, some founders of great empires, others mere adventurers, poured into India from the north-west. While some came only to plunder and retired laden with spoils, others remained to found kingdoms that have had a lasting influence to the present day. But of none of these do we learn that they were accompanied by any missionaries or preachers. Not that they were indifferent to their religion. To many of them, their invasion of India appeared in the light of a holy war. Such was evidently the thought in the minds of Maḥmūd of G͟haznā and Tīmūr. The latter, after his capture of Dehli, writes as follows in his autobiography:—"I had been at Dehli fifteen days, which time I passed in pleasure and enjoyment, holding royal Courts and giving great feasts. I then reflected that I had come to Hindustān to war against infidels, and my enterprise had been so blessed that wherever I had gone I had been victorious. I had triumphed over my adversaries, I had put to death some lacs of infidels and idolaters, and I had stained my proselyting sword with the blood of the enemies of the faith. Now this crowning victory had been won, and I felt that I ought not to indulge in ease, but rather to exert myself in warring against the infidels of Hindustān."[1] Though he speaks much of his "proselyting sword," it seems, however, to have served no other purpose than that of sending infidels to hell. Most of the Muslim invaders seem to have acted in a very similar way; in the name of Allāh, idols were thrown down, their priests put to the sword, and their temples destroyed; while mosques were often erected in their place. It is true that the offer of Islam was generally made to the unbelieving Hindus before any attack was made upon them.[2] Fear occasionally dictated a timely acceptance of such offers and led to conversions which, in the earlier days of the Muhammadan invasion at least, were generally short-lived and ceased to be effective after the retreat of the invader. An

[1] Elliot, vol. ii. p. 448.

[2] Muḥammad b. Qāsim invited the Hindu princes to embrace Islam, and the invaders who followed him were probably equally observant of the religious law. (Elliot, vol. i. pp. 175, 207.)

illustration in point is furnished by the story of Hardatta, a rā'īs of Bulandshahr, whose submission to Maḥmūd of Ghaznā is thus related in the history of that conqueror's campaigns written by his secretary. "At length (about A.D. 1019) he (i. e. Maḥmūd) arrived at the fort of Barba,[1] in the country of Hardat, who was one of the rā'īs, that is "kings," in the Hindī language. When Hardat heard of this invasion by the protected warriors of God, who advanced like the waves of the sea, with the angels around them on all sides, he became greatly agitated, his steps trembled, and he feared for his life, which was forfeited under the law of God. So he reflected that his safety would best be secured by conforming to the religion of Islam, since God's sword was drawn from the scabbard, and the whip of punishment was uplifted. He came forth, therefore, with ten thousand men, who all proclaimed their anxiety for conversion and their rejection of idols."[2]

These new converts probably took the earliest opportunity of apostatising presented to them by the retreat of the conqueror—a kind of action which we find the early Muhammadan historians of India continually complaining of. For when Quṭb al-Dīn Ībak attacked Baran in 1193, he was stoutly opposed by Chandrasen, the then Rājā, who was a lineal descendant of Hardatta and whose very name betrays his Hindu faith: nor do we hear of there being any Musalmans remaining under his rule.[3]

But these conquerors would appear to have had very little of that "love for souls" which animates the true missionary and which has achieved such great conquests for Islam. The Khiljīs (1290–1320), the Tughlaqs (1320–1412), and the Lodīs (1451–1526) were generally too busily engaged in fighting to pay much regard to the interests of religion, or else thought more of the exaction of tribute than of the work of conversion.[4] Not that they were entirely lacking

[1] Or Baran, the old name of Bulandshahr. [2] Elliot, vol. ii. pp. 42–3.
[3] Gazetteer of the N.W.P., vol. iii. part ii. p. 85.
[4] "The military adventurers, who founded dynasties in Northern India and carved out kingdoms in the Dekhan, cared little for things spiritual; most of them had indeed no time for proselytism, being continually engaged in conquest or in civil war. They were usually rough Tartars or Moghals; themselves ill-grounded in the faith of Mahomed, and untouched by the true Semitic enthusiasm which inspired the first Arab standard bearers of

in religious zeal: e.g. the Ghakkars, a barbarous people in the mountainous districts of the North of the Panjāb, who gave the early invaders much trouble, are said to have been converted through the influence of Muḥammad Ghorī at the end of the twelfth century. Their chieftain had been taken prisoner by the Muhammadan monarch, who induced him to become a Musalman, and then confirming him in his title of chief of this tribe, sent him back to convert his followers, many of whom having little religion of their own were easily prevailed upon to embrace Islam.[1] According to Ibn Baṭūṭah, the Khiljīs offered some encouragement to conversion by making it a custom to have the new convert presented to the sultan, who clad him in a robe of honour and gave him a collar and bracelets of gold, of a value proportionate to his rank.[2] But the monarchs of the earlier Muhammadan dynasties as a rule evinced very little proselytising zeal, and it would be hard to find a parallel in their history to the following passage from the autobiography of Fīrūz Shāh Tughlaq (1351–1388): "I encouraged my infidel subjects to embrace the religion of the Prophet, and I proclaimed that every one who repeated the creed and became a Musalman should be exempt from the jizyah, or poll tax. Information of this came to the ears of the people at large and great numbers of Hindus presented themselves, and were admitted to the honour of Islam. Thus they came forward day by day from every quarter, and, adopting the faith, were exonerated from the jizyah, and were favoured with presents and honours."[3]

As the Muhammadan power became consolidated, and particularly under the Mughal dynasty, the religious influences of Islam naturally became more permanent and persistent. These influences are certainly apparent in the Hindu

---

Islam. The empire which they set up was purely military, and it was kept in that state by the half success of their conquests and the comparative failure of their spiritual invasion. They were strong enough to prevent anything like religious amalgamation among the Hindus, and to check the gathering of tribes into nations; but so far were they from converting India, that among the Mahommedans themselves their own faith never acquired an entire and exclusive monopoly of the high offices of administration." (Sir Alfred C. Lyall: Asiatic Studies, p. 289.) (London, 1882.)

[1] Firishtah, vol. i. p. 184.

[2] Ibn Baṭūṭah, tome iii. p. 197.

[3] Elliot, vol. iii. p. 386.

theistic movements that arose in the fifteenth and sixteenth centuries, and Bishop Lefroy has conjectured that the positive character of Muslim teaching attracted minds that were dissatisfied with the vagueness and subjectivity of a Pantheistic system of thought. "When Mohammedanism, with its strong grasp of the reality of the Divine existence and, as flowing from this, of the absolutely fixed and objective character of truth, came into conflict with the haziness of Pantheistic thought and the subjectivity of its belief, it necessarily followed, not only that it triumphed in the struggle, but also that it came as a veritable tonic to the life and thought of Upper India, quickening into a fresh and more vigorous life many minds which never accepted for themselves its intellectual sway." [1]

A powerful incentive to conversion was offered, when adherence to an idolatrous system stood in the way of advancement at the Muhammadan courts; and though a spirit of tolerance, which reached its culmination under the eclectic Akbar, was very often shown towards Hinduism, and respected even, for the most part, the state endowments of that religion;[2] and though the dread of unpopularity and the desire of conciliation dictated a policy of non-interference and deprecated such deeds of violence and such outbursts of fanaticism as had characterised the earlier period of invasion and triumph, still such motives of self-interest gained many converts from Hinduism to the Muhammadan faith. Many Rajputs became converts in this way, and their descendants are to this day to be found among the landed aristocracy. The most important perhaps among these is the Musalman branch of the great Bachgoti clan, the head of which is the premier Muhammadan noble of Oudh. According to one tradition, their ancestor Tilok Chand was taken prisoner by the Emperor Bābar, and to regain his liberty adopted the faith of Islam; [3] but another legend places his conversion in the reign of Humāyūn. This prince having heard of the marvellous beauty of Tilok Chand's wife, had her carried off while she was at a fair. No sooner, however, was she

[1] Mankind and the Church, p. 286. (London, 1907.)
[2] Sir Richard Temple: India in 1880, p. 164. (London, 1881.) Punjab States Gazetteers, vol. xxxvi A, Bahawalpur, p. 183.
[3] Manual of Titles for Oudh, p. 78. (Allahabad, 1889.)

brought to him than his conscience smote him and he sent for her husband. Tilok Chand had despaired of ever seeing her again, and in gratitude he and his wife embraced the faith "which taught such generous purity."[1] These converted Rajputs are very zealous in the practice of their religion, yet often betray their Hindu origin in a very striking manner. In the district of Bulandshahr, for example, a large Musalman family, which is known as the Lālkhānī Paṭhāns, still (with some exceptions) retains its old Hindu titles and family customs of marriage, while Hindu branches of the same clan still exist side by side with it.[2] In the Mirzapur district, the Gaharwār Rajputs, who are now Muslim, still retain in all domestic matters Hindu laws and customs and prefix a Hindu honorific title to their Muhammadan names.[3]

Official pressure is said never to have been more persistently brought to bear upon the Hindus than in the reign of Aurangzeb. In the eastern districts of the Panjāb, there are many cases in which the ancestor of the Musalman branch of the village community is said to have changed his religion in the reign of this zealot, "in order to save the land of the village." In Gurgaon, near Dehli, there is a Hindu family of Banyās who still bear the title of Shaykh (which is commonly adopted by converted Hindus), because one of the members of the family, whose line is now extinct, became a convert in order to save the family property from confiscation.[4] Many Rajput landowners, in the Cawnpore district, were compelled to embrace Islam for the same reason.[5] In

[1] Gazetteer of the Province of Oudh, vol. i. p. 466.

[2] Gazetteer of the N.W.P., vol. iii. part ii. p. 46.

[3] Gazetteer of the N.W.P., vol. xiv. part ii. p. 119. In the Cawnpore district, the Musalman branch of the Dikhit family observes Muhammadan customs at births, marriages, and deaths, and, though they cannot, as a rule, recite the prayers (namāz), they perform the orthodox obeisances (sijdah). But at the same time they worship Chachak Devī to avert small-pox, and keep up their friendly intercourse with their old caste brethren, the Thakurs, in domestic occurrences, and are generally called by common Hindu names. (Gazetteer of the N.W.P., vol. vi. p. 64.)

[4] Ibbetson, p. 163.

[5] Gazetteer of the N.W.P., vol. vi. p. 64. Compare also id. vol. xiv. part iii. p. 47. "Muhammadan cultivators are not numerous; they are usually Nau-Muslims. Most of them assign the date of their conversion to the reign of Aurangzeb, and represent it as the result sometimes of persecution and sometimes as made to enable them to retain their rights when unable to pay revenue."

other cases the ancestor is said to have been carried as a prisoner or hostage to Dehli, and there forcibly circumcised and converted.[1] It should be noted that the only authority for these forced conversions is family or local tradition, and no mention of such (as far as I have been able to discover) is made in the historical accounts of Aurangzeb's reign.[2] It is established without doubt that forced conversions have been made by Muhammadan rulers, and it seems probable that Aurangzeb's well-known zeal on behalf of his faith has caused many families of Northern India (the history of whose conversion has been forgotten) to attribute their change of faith to this, the most easily assignable cause. Similarly in the Deccan, Aurangzeb shares with Ḥaydar 'Alī and Tīpū Sulṭān (these being the best known of modern Muhammadan rulers) the reputation of having forcibly converted sundry families and sections of the population, whose conversion undoubtedly dates from a much earlier period, from which no historical record of the circumstances of the case has come down.[3]

Tīpū Sulṭān is probably the Muhammadan monarch who most systematically engaged in the work of forcible conversion. In 1788 he issued the following proclamation to the people of Malabar : " From the period of the conquest until this day, during twenty-four years, you have been a turbulent and refractory people, and in the wars waged during your rainy season, you have caused numbers of our warriors to taste the draught of martyrdom. Be it so. What is past is past. Hereafter you must proceed in an opposite manner, dwell quietly and pay your dues like good subjects ; and since it is the practice with you for one woman to associate with ten men, and you leave your mothers and sisters unconstrained in their obscene practices, and are thence all born in adultery, and are more shameless in your connections than the beasts of the field, I hereby require you to forsake these sinful practices and to be like the rest of mankind ;

[1] Ibbetson, p. 163.

[2] Indeed Firishtah distinctly says : " Zealous for the faith of Mahommed, he rewarded proselytes with a liberal hand, though he did not choose to persecute those of different persuasions in matters of religion." (The History of Hindostan, translated from the Persian, by Alexander Dow, vol. iii. p. 361.) (London, 1812.)

[3] The Bombay Gazetteer, vol. xxii. p. 222 ; vol. xxiii. p. 282.

and if you are disobedient to these commands, I have made repeated vows to honour the whole of you with Islam and to march all the chief persons to the seat of Government." This proclamation stirred up a general revolt in Malabar, and early in 1789 Tīpū Sulṭān prepared to enforce his proclamation with an army of more than twenty thousand men, and issued general orders that "every being in the district without distinction should be honoured with Islam, that the houses of such as fled to avoid that honour should be burned, that they should be traced to their lurking places, and that all means of truth and falsehood, force or fraud should be employed to effect their universal conversion." Thousands of Hindus were accordingly circumcised and made to eat beef; but by the end of 1790 the British army had destroyed the last remnant of Tīpū Sulṭān's power in Malabar, and this monarch himself perished early in 1799 at the capture of Seringapatam. Most of the Brahmans and Nayars who had been forcibly converted, subsequently disowned their new religion.[1]

How little was effected towards the spread of Islam by violence on the part of the Muhammadan rulers may be judged from the fact that even in the centres of the Muhammadan power, such as Dehli and Agra, the Muhammadans in modern times in the former district hardly exceeded one-tenth, and in the latter they did not form one-fourth of the population.[2] A remarkable example of the worthlessness of forced conversion is exhibited in the case of Bodh Mal, Raja of Majhauli, in the district of Gorakhpur; he was arrested by Akbar in default of revenue, carried to Dehli, and there converted to Islam, receiving the name of Muḥammad Salīm. But on his return his wife refused to let him into the ancestral castle, and, as apparently she had the sympathy of his subjects on her side, she governed his territories during the minority of his son Bhawāni Mal, so that the Hindu succession remained undisturbed.[3] Until recently there were some strange survivals of a similarly futile false conversion, noticeable in certain customs of a

[1] Innes, pp. 72–3, 190.
[2] Sir W. W. Hunter: The Religions of India. (*The Times*, February 25th, 1888.)
[3] Gazetteer of the N.W.P., vol. vi. p. 518.

Hindu sect called the Bishnois, the principal tenet of whose faith is the renunciation of all Hindu deities, except Viṣṇu. They used recently to bury their dead, instead of burning them, to adopt Ghulām Muḥammad and other Muhammadan names, and use the Muslim form of salutation. They explained their adoption of these Muhammadan customs by saying that having once slain a Qāḍī, who had interfered with their rite of widow-burning, they had compounded for the offence by embracing Islam. They have now, however, renounced these practices in favour of Hindu customs.[1]

But though some Muhammadan rulers may have been more successful in forcing an acceptance of Islam on certain of their Hindu subjects than in the last-mentioned cases, and whatever truth there may be in the assertion[2] that "it is impossible even to approach the religious side of the Mahomedan position in India without surveying first its political aspect," we undoubtedly find that Islam has gained its greatest and most lasting missionary triumphs in times and places in which its political power has been weakest, as in Southern India and Eastern Bengal. Of such missionary movements it is now proposed to essay some account, commencing with Southern India and the Deccan, then after reviewing the history of Sind, Cutch and Gujarāt, passing to Bengal, and finally noticing some missionaries whose work lay outside the above geographical limits. Of several of the missionaries to be referred to, little is recorded beyond their names and the sphere of their labours; accordingly, in view of the general dearth of such missionary annals, any available details have been given at length.

The first advent of Islam in South India dates as far back as the eighth century, when a band of refugees, to whom the Mappillas trace their descent, came from 'Irāq and settled in the country.[3] The trade in spices, ivory, gems, etc., between India and Europe, which for many hundred years was conducted by the Arabs and Persians, caused a continual stream of Muhammadan influence to flow in upon the west coast of Southern India. From this constant influx

[1] Gazetteer of the N.W.P., vol. v. part i. pp. 302–3.

[2] Sir Alfred C. Lyall: Asiatic Studies, p. 236.

[3] A tomb in the cemetery of Pantalāyini Kollam bears an inscription with the date A.H. 166. (Innes, p. 436.)

of foreigners there resulted a mixed population, half Hindu and half Arab or Persian, in the trading centres along the coast. Very friendly relations appear to have existed between these Muslim traders and the Hindu rulers, who extended to them their protection and patronage in consideration of the increased commercial activity and consequent prosperity of the country, that resulted from their presence in it,[1] and no obstacles were placed in the way of proselytising, the native converts receiving the same consideration and respect as the foreign merchants, even though before their conversion they had belonged to the lowest grades of society.[2]

The traditionary account of the introduction of Islam into Malabar, as given by a Muhammadan historian of the sixteenth century, represents the first missionaries to have been a party of pilgrims on their way to visit the foot-print of Adam in Ceylon; on their arrival at Cranganore the Raja sent for them and the leader of the party, Shaykh Sharaf b. Mālik, who was accompanied by his brother, Mālik b. Dīnār, and his nephew, Mālik b. Ḥabīb, took the opportunity of expounding to him the faith of Islam and the mission of Muḥammad, "and God caused the truth of the Prophet's teaching to enter into the king's heart and he believed therein; and his heart became filled with love for the Prophet and he bade the Shaykh and companions come back to him again on their return from their pilgrimage to Adam's foot-print."[3] On the return of the pilgrims from Ceylon, the king secretly departed with them in a ship bound for the coast of Arabia, leaving his kingdom in the hand of viceroys. Here he remained for some time, and was just about to return to his own country, with the intention of erecting mosques there and spreading the faith of Islam, when he fell sick and died. On his death-bed he solemnly enjoined on his companions not to abandon their proposed missionary journey to Malabar, and to assist them in their labours, he gave them letters of recommendation to his viceroys, at the same time bidding them conceal the fact of his death. Armed with these letters, Sharaf b. Mālik

[1] Zayn al-Dīn, pp. 34–5.
[2] Id. p. 36 (init.).
[3] Id. p. 21.

and his companions sailed for Cranganore, where the king's letter secured for them a kindly welcome and a grant of land, on which they built a mosque. Mālik b. Dīnār decided to settle there, but Mālik b. Ḥabīb set out on a missionary tour with the object of building mosques throughout Malabar. "So Mālik b. Ḥabīb set out for Quilon with his worldly goods and his wife and some of his children, and he built a mosque there; then leaving his wife there, he went on to Hīlī Mārāwī,[1] where he built a mosque"; and so the narrative continues, giving a list of seven other places at which the missionary erected mosques, finally returning to Cranganore. Later on, he visited all these places again to pray in the mosque at each of them, and came back "praising and giving thanks to God for the manifestation of the faith of Islam in a land filled with unbelievers."[2]

In spite of the circumstantial character of this narrative, there is no evidence of its historicity. Popular belief puts the date of the events recorded as far back as the lifetime of the Prophet; with a mild scepticism Zayn al-Dīn thought that they could not have been earlier than the third century of the Hijrah;[3] but there is no more authority for the one date than for the other, or for the common Mappilla tradition of the existence of the tomb of a Hindu king at Zafār, on the coast of Arabia, bearing the inscription, "'Abd al-Raḥmān al-Sāmirī, arrived A.H. 212, died A.H. 216";[4] and the mosque at Madāyi, said to have been founded by Mālik b. Dīnār, bears an inscription commemorating its erection in A.D. 1124.[5]

But the legend certainly bears witness to the peaceful character of the proselytising influences that were at work on the Malabar coast for centuries. The agents in this work were chiefly Arab merchants, but Ibn Baṭūṭah makes mention of several professed theologians from Arabia and elsewhere, whom he met in various towns on the Malabar coast.[6] The Zamorin of Calicut, who was one of the chief patrons of Arab trade, is said to have encouraged conversion to Islam, in order to man the Arab ships on which he depended for his aggrandisement, and to have ordered that in every

[1] The modern Madāyi.
[2] Zayn al-Dīn, pp. 23–4.
[3] Id. p. 25.
[4] Innes, p. 41.
[5] Id. p. 398.
[6] Ibn Baṭūṭah, tome iv. pp. 82, 88, etc.

family of fishermen in his dominion one or more of the male members should be brought up as Muhammadans.[1] At the beginning of the sixteenth century the Mappillas were estimated to have formed one-fifth of the population of Malabar, spoke the same language as the Hindus, and were only distinguished from them by their long beards and peculiar head-dress. But for the arrival of the Portuguese, the whole of this coast would have become Muhammadan, because of the frequent conversions that took place and the powerful influence exercised by the Muslim merchants from other parts of India, such as Gujarāt and the Deccan, and from Arabia and Persia.[2]

But there would appear to be no record of the individuals who took part in the propaganda, except in the case of the historian 'Abd al-Razzāq, who has himself left an account of his unsuccessful mission to the court of the Zamorin of Calicut. He was sent on this mission in the year 1441 by the Tīmūrid Shāh Rukh Bahādur, in response to an appeal made by an ambassador who had been sent by the Zamorin of Calicut to this monarch. The ambassador was himself a Musalman and represented to the Sultan how excellent and meritorious an action it would be to send a special envoy to the Zamorin, "to invite him to accept Islam in accordance with the injunction 'Summon thou to the ways of thy Lord with wisdom and with kindly warning,'[3] and open the bolt of darkness and error that locked his benighted heart, and let the splendour of the light of the faith and the brightness of the sun of knowledge shine into the window of his soul." 'Abd al-Razzāq was chosen for this task and after

[1] Innes, p. 190.
[2] Oboardo Barbosa, p. 310.
Similarly it has been conjectured that but for the arrival of the Portuguese, Ceylon might have become a Muhammadan kingdom. For before the Portuguese armaments appeared in the Indian seas, the Arab merchants were undisputed masters of the trade of this island (where indeed they had formed commercial establishments centuries before the birth of the Prophet), and were to be found in every sea-port and city, while the facilities for commerce attracted large numbers of fresh arrivals from their settlements in Malabar. Here as elsewhere the Muslim traders intermarried with the natives of the country and spread their religion along the coast. But no very active proselytising movement would seem to have been carried on, or else the Singhalese showed themselves unwilling to embrace Islam, as the Muhammadans of Ceylon at the present day appear mostly to be of Arab descent. (Sir James Emerson Tennent: Ceylon, vol. i. pp. 631–3.) (5th ed., London, 1860.)
[3] Qur'ān, xvi. 126.

an adventurous journey reached Calicut, but appears to have met with a cold reception, and after remaining there for about six months abandoned his original purposes and made his way back to Khurāsān, which he reached after an absence of three years.[1]

Another community of Musalmans in Southern India, the Ravuttans,[2] ascribe their conversion to the preaching of missionaries whose tombs are held in veneration by them to the present day. The most famous of these was Sayyid Nathar Shāh[3] (A.D. 969–1039) who after many wanderings in Arabia, Persia and Northern India, settled down in Trichinopoly, where he spent the remaining years of his life in prayer and works of charity, and converted a large number of Hindus to the faith of Islam; his tomb is much resorted to as a place of pilgrimage and the Muhammadans re-named Trichinopoly Natharnagar, after the name of their saint.[4] Sayyid Ibrāhīm Shahīd (said to have been born about the middle of the twelfth century), whose tomb is at Ervadi, was a militant hero who led an expedition into the Pandyan kingdom, occupied the country for about twelve years, but was at length slain; his son's life was, however, spared in consideration of the beneficent rule of his father, and a grant of land given to him, which his descendants enjoy to the present day. The latest of these saints, Shāh al-Ḥamīd (1532–1600), was born at Manikpur in Northern India, and spent most of his life in visiting the holy shrines of Islam and in missionary tours chiefly throughout Southern India; he finally settled in Nagore, where the descendants of his adopted son are still in charge of his tomb.[5]

Another group of Muhammadans in Southern India, the Dudekulas, who live by cotton cleaning (as their name denotes) and by weaving coarse fabrics, attribute their conversion to Bābā Fakhr al-Dīn, whose tomb they revere

[1] 'Abd al-Razzāq: Maṭla' al-sa'dayn, fol. 173.

[2] They are found chiefly in the Tamil-speaking districts of Madura, Tinnevelly, Coimbatore, North Arcot and the Nilgiris.

[3] The Imperial Gazetteer of India (vol. xxiv. p. 47) spells his name Nādir Shāh; Qādir Ḥusayn Khān calls him Nathad Vali.

[4] Madras District Gazetteers. Trichinopoly, vol. i. p. 338. (Madras, 1907.) Qādir Ḥusayn Khān: South Indian Musalmans, p. 36. (Madras, 1910.)

[5] Qādir Ḥusayn Khān, pp. 36–8.

at Penukonda. Legend says that he was originally a king of Sīstān, who abdicated his throne in favour of his brother and became a religious mendicant. After making the pilgrimage to Mecca and Medina, he was bidden by the Prophet in a dream to go to India; here he met Nathar Shah, of Trichinopoly, and became his disciple and was sent by him in company with 200 religious mendicants on a proselytising mission. The legend goes on to say that they finally settled at Penukonda in the vicinity of a Hindu temple, where their presence was unwelcome to the Raja of the place, but instead of appealing to force he applied several tests to discover whether the Muhammadan saint or his own priest was the better qualified by sanctity to possess the temple. As a final test, he had them both tied up in sacks filled with lime and thrown into tanks. The Hindu priest never re-appeared, but Bābā Fakhr al-Dīn asserted the superiority of his faith by being miraculously transported to a hill outside the town. The Raja hereupon became a Musalman, and his example was followed by a large number of the inhabitants of the neighbourhood, and the temple was turned into a mosque.[1]

The history of Islam in Southern India by no means always continued to be of so peaceful a character, but it does not appear that the forcible conversions of the Hindus and others to Islam which were perpetrated when the Muhammadan power became paramount under Ḥaydar 'Alī (1767–1782) and Tīpū Sulṭān (1782–1799), can be paralleled in the earlier history of this part of India. However this may be, there is no reason to doubt that constant conversions by peaceful methods were made to Islam from among the lower castes,[2] as is the case at the present day when accessions to Islam from time to time occur from among the Tiyans, who are said to form one of the most progressive communities in India, the Mukkuvans or fisherman caste, as well as from the Cherumans or agricultural labourers, and other serf castes, to whom Islam brings deliverance from the disabilities attaching to the outcasts

[1] Qādir Ḥusayn Khān, *op. cit.* pp. 39-42. Madras District Gazetteers. Anantapur, vol. i. pp. 193–4. (Madras, 1905.)
[2] Zayn al-Dīn, pp. 33 (l. 4), 36 (l. 1).

of the Hindu social system; occasionally, also, converts are drawn from among the Nayars and the native Christians. In Ponnani, the residence of the spiritual head of the majority of the Muhammadans of Malabar, there is an association entitled Minnat al-Islām Sabhā, where converts are instructed in the tenets of their new faith and material assistance rendered to those under instruction; the average number of converts received in this institution in the course of the first three years of the twentieth century, was 750.[1] So numerous have these conversions from Hinduism been, that the tendency of the Muhammadans of the west as well as the east coast of Southern India has been to reversion to the Hindu or aboriginal type, and, except in the case of some of the nobler families, they now in great part present all the characteristics of an aboriginal people, with very little of the original foreign blood in them.[2] In the western coast districts the tyranny of caste intolerance is peculiarly oppressive; to give but one instance, in Travancore certain of the lower castes may not come nearer than seventy-four paces to a Brahman, and have to make a grunting noise as they pass along the road, in order to give warning of their approach. Similar instances might be abundantly multiplied. What wonder, then, that the Musalman population is fast increasing through conversion from these lower castes, who thereby free themselves from such degrading oppression, and raise themselves and their descendants in the social scale?

In fact the Mappilas on the west coast are said to be increasing so considerably through accessions from the lower classes of Hindus, as to render it possible that in a few years the whole of the lower races of the west coast may become Muhammadans.[3]

It was most probably from Malabar that Islam crossed over to the Laccadive and Maldive Islands, the population of which is now entirely Muslim. The inhabitants of these islands owed their conversion to the Arab and Persian merchants, who established themselves in the country,

[1] Innes, p. 190. Census of India, 1911. Vol. xii. Part. I. p. 54.

[2] Report on the Census of the Madras Presidency, 1871, by W. R. Cornish, pp. 71, 72, 109. (Madras, 1874.)

[3] Report of the Second Decennial Missionary Conference held at Calcutta 1882–3 (pp. 228, 233, 248). (Calcutta, 1883.)

intermarrying with the natives, and thus smoothing the way for the work of active proselytism. The date of the conversion of the first Muhammadan Sultan of the Maldive Islands, Aḥmad Shanūrāzah,[1] has been conjectured to have occurred about A.D. 1200, but it is very possible that the Muhammadan merchants had introduced their religion into the island as much as three centuries before, and the process of conversion must undoubtedly have been a gradual one.[2] No details, however, have come down to us.

At Mālē, the seat of government, is found the tomb of Shaykh Yūsuf Shams al-Dīn, a native of Tabrīz, in Persia, who is said to have been a successful missionary of Islam in these islands. His tomb is still held in great veneration, and always kept in good repair, and in the same part of the island are buried some of his countrymen who came in search of him, and remained in the Maldives until their death.[3]

The introduction of Islam into the neighbouring Laccadive Islands is attributed to an Arab preacher, known to the islanders by the name of Mumba Mulyaka; his tomb is still shown at Androth and as the present qāḍī of that place claims to be twenty-sixth in descent from him, he probably reached these islands some time in the twelfth century.[4]

The Deccan also was the scene of the successful labours of many Muslim missionaries. It has already been pointed out that from very early times Arab traders had visited the towns on the west coast; in the tenth century we are told that the Arabs were settled in large numbers in the towns of the Konkan, having intermarried with the women of the country and living under their own laws and religion.[5] Under the Muhammadan dynasties of the Bahmanid (1347–1490) and Bījāpūr (1489–1686) kings, a fresh impulse was given to Arab immigration, and with the trader and the soldier of fortune came the missionaries seeking to make

[1] Ibn Baṭūṭah, tome iv. p. 128. Ibn Baṭūṭah resided in the Maldive Islands during the years 1343–4 and married "the daughter of a Vizier who was grandson of the Sulṭān Dā'ūd, who was a grandson of the Sulṭān Aḥmad Shanūrāzah" (tome iv. p. 154); from this statement the date A.D. 1200 has been conjectured.

[2] H. C. P. Bell: The Maldive Islands, pp. 23–5, 57–8, 71. (Colombo, 1883.)

[3] Memoir on the Inhabitants of the Maldive Islands. By J. A. Young and W. Christopher. (Transactions of the Bombay Geographical Society from 1836 to 1838, p. 74. Bombay, 1844.)

[4] Innes, pp. 485, 492.

[5] Mas'ūdī, tome ii. pp. 85–6.

spiritual conquests in the cause of Islam, and win over the unbelieving people of the country by their preaching and example, for of forcible conversions we have no record under the early Deccan dynasties, whose rule was characterised by a striking toleration.[1]

One of these Arab preachers, Pīr Mahābīr Khamdāyat, came as a missionary to the Deccan as early as A.D. 1304, and among the cultivating classes of Bījāpūr are to be found descendants of the Jains who were converted by him.[2] About the close of the same century a celebrated saint of Gulbarga, Sayyid Muḥammad Gīsūdarāz,[3] converted a number of Hindus of the Poona district, and twenty years later his labours were crowned with a like success in Belgaum.[4] At Dahanu still reside the descendants of a relative of one of the greatest saints of Islam, Sayyid 'Abd al-Qādir Jīlānī of Ba<u>gh</u>dād; he came to Western India about the fifteenth century, and after making many converts in the Konkan, died and was buried at Dahanu.[5] In the district of Dharwar, there are large numbers of weavers whose ancestors were converted by Hāshim Pīr Gujarātī, the religious teacher of the Bījāpūr king, Ibrāhīm 'Ādil Shāh II, about the close of the sixteenth century. These men still regard the saint with special reverence and pay great respect to his descendants.[6] The descendants of another saint, Shāh Muḥammad Ṣādiq Sarmast Ḥusaynī, are still found in Nasik; he is said to have been the most successful of Muhammadan missionaries; having come from Medina in 1568, he travelled over the greater part of Western India and finally settled at Nasik—in which district another very successful Muslim missionary, <u>Kh</u>wājah Khunmir Ḥusaynī, had begun to labour about fifty years before.[7] Two other Arab missionaries may be mentioned, the scene of whose proselytising efforts was laid in the district of Belgaum, namely Sayyid Muḥammad b. Sayyid 'Alī and Sayyid 'Umar 'Aydrūs Basheban.[8]

[1] The Bombay Gazetteer, vol. x. p 132; vol. xvi. p. 75.
[2] Id. vol. xxiii. p. 282.
[3] Sometimes called Sayyid Ma<u>kh</u>dūm Gīsūdarāz.
[4] The Bombay Gazetteer, vol. xviii. p. 501; vol. xxi. pp. 218, 223.
[5] Id. vol. xiii. part i. p. 231.
[6] Id. vol. xxii. p. 242.
[7] Id. vol. xvi. pp. 75–6.
[8] Id. vol. xxi. p. 203.

Another missionary movement may be said roughly to centre round the city of Multan.[1] This in the early days of the Arab conquest was one of the outposts of Islam, when Muḥammad b. Qāsim had established Muhammadan supremacy over Sind (A.D. 714). During the three centuries of Arab rule there were naturally many accessions to the faith of the conquerors. Several Sindian princes responded to the invitation of the Caliph 'Umar b. 'Abd al-'Azīz to embrace Islam.[2] The people of Sāwandari—who submitted to Muḥammad b. Qāsim and had peace granted to them on the condition that they would entertain the Musalmans and furnish guides—are spoken of by al-Balā<u>dh</u>urī (writing about a hundred years later) as professing Islam in his time; and the despatches of the conqueror frequently refer to the conversion of the unbelievers.

That these conversions were in the main voluntary, may be judged from the toleration that the Arabs, after the first violence of their onslaught, showed towards their idolatrous subjects. The people of Brahmanābād, for example, whose city had been taken by storm, were allowed to repair their temple, which was a means of livelihood to the Brahmans, and nobody was to be forbidden or prevented from following his own religion,[3] and generally, where submission was made, quarter was readily given, and the people were permitted the exercise of their own creeds and laws.

During the troubles that befell the caliphate in the latter half of the ninth century, Sind, neglected by the central government, came to be divided among several petty princes, the most powerful of whom were the Amīrs of Multan and Mansūra. Such disunion naturally weakened the political power of the Musalmans, which had in fact begun to decline earlier in the century. For in the reign of al-Mu'taṣim (A.D. 833–842), the Indians of Sindān[4] declared themselves independent, but they spared the mosque, in which the Musalmans were allowed to perform their devotions undisturbed.[5] The Muhammadans of Multan

[1] At the time of the Arab conquest the dominions of the Hindu ruler of Sind extended as far north as this city, which is now no longer included in this province. [2] Balā<u>dh</u>urī, p. 441 (fin.) [3] Elliot, vol. i. pp. 185–6.

[4] Probably the Sindān in Abrāsa, the southern district of Cutch.

[5] Balā<u>dh</u>urī, p. 446.

succeeded in maintaining their political independence, and kept themselves from being conquered by the neighbouring Hindu princes, by threatening, if attacked, to destroy an idol which was held in great veneration by the Hindus and was visited by pilgrims from the most distant parts.[1] But in the hour of its political decay, Islam was still achieving missionary successes. Al-Balādhurī [2] tells the following story of the conversion of a king of 'Usayfān, a country between Kashmir and Multan and Kabul. The people of this country worshipped an idol for which they had built a temple. The son of the king fell sick, and he desired the priests of the temple to pray to the idol for the recovery of his son. They retired for a short time, and then returned saying: "We have prayed and our supplications have been accepted." But no long time passed before the youth died. Then the king attacked the temple, destroyed and broke in pieces the idol, and slew the priests. He afterwards invited a party of Muhammadan traders, who made known to him the unity of God; whereupon he believed in the unity and became a Muslim. A similar missionary influence was doubtless exercised by the numerous communities of Muslim merchants who carried their religion with them into the infidel cities of Hindustan. Arab geographers of the tenth and twelfth centuries mention the names of many such cities, both on the coast and inland, where the Musalmans built their mosques, and were safe under the protection of the native princes, who even granted them the privilege of living under their own laws.[3] The Arab merchants at this time formed the medium of commercial communication between Sind and the neighbouring countries of India and the outside world. They brought the produce of China and Ceylon to the sea-ports of Sind and from there conveyed them by way of Multan to Turkistan and Khurāsān.[4]

It would be strange if these traders, scattered about in the cities of the unbelievers, failed to exhibit the same proselytising zeal as we find in the Muhammadan trader elsewhere. To the influence of such trading communities

[1] Iṣṭakhrī, pp. 173–4.
[2] Balādhurī, p. 446.
[3] Iṣṭakhrī, loc. cit. Ibn Ḥawqal, p. 230 sq. Idrīsī (Géographie d'Édrisi, traduite par P. A. Jaubert, vol. i. p. 175 sqq.).
[4] Mas'ūdī, vol. i. p. 207.

was most probably due the conversion of the Sammas, who ruled over Sind from A.D. 1351 to 1521. While the reign of Nanda b. Bābiniyyah of this dynasty is specially mentioned as one of such "peace and security, that never was this prince called upon to ride forth to battle, and never did a foe take the field against him,"[1] it is at the same time described as being "remarkable for its justice and an increase of Islam." This increase could thus only have been brought about by peaceful missionary methods. One of the most famous of these missionaries was the celebrated saint, Sayyid Yūsuf al-Dīn, a descendant of 'Abd al-Qādir Jīlānī, who was bidden in a dream to leave Baghdād for India and convert its inhabitants to Islam. He came to Sind in 1422 and after labouring there for ten years, he succeeded in winning over to Islam 700 families of the Lohāna caste, who followed the example of two of their number, by name Sundarjī and Hansrāj; these men embraced Islam, after seeing some miracles performed by the saint, and on their conversion received the names of Adamjī and Tāj Muḥammad respectively. Under the leadership of the grandson of the former, these people afterwards migrated to Cutch, where their numbers were increased by converts from among the Cutch Lohānas.[2]

Sind was also the scene of the labours of Pīr Ṣadr al-Dīn, an Ismā'īlī missionary, who was head of the Khojah sect about the year 1430. In accordance with the principles of accommodation practised by this sect, he took a Hindu name and made certain concessions to the religious beliefs of the Hindus whose conversion he sought to achieve, and introduced among them a book entitled Dasavatār in which 'Alī was made out to be the tenth Avatār or incarnation of Viṣṇu; this book has been from the beginning the accepted scripture of the Khojah sect, and it is always read by the bedside of the dying and periodically at many festivals; it assumes the nine incarnations of Viṣṇu to be true as far as they go, but to fall short of the perfect truth, and supplements this imperfect Vaiṣṇav system by the cardinal doctrine of the Ismā'īlians, the incarnation and coming manifestation of 'Alī. Further, he made

[1] Elliot, vol. i. p. 273. [2] Bombay Gazetteer, vol. i. p. 93.

out Brahmā to be Muḥammad, Viṣṇu to be 'Alī and Adam Siva. The first of Pīr Ṣadr al-Dīn's converts were won in the villages and towns of Upper Sind: he preached also in Cutch and from these parts the doctrines of this sect spread southwards through Gujarāt to Bombay; and at the present day Khojah communities are to be found in almost all the large trading towns of Western India and on the seaboard of the Indian Ocean.[1]

Pīr Ṣadr al-Dīn was not however the first of the Ismā'īlian missionaries who came into India. He was preceded by 'Abd Allāh, a missionary sent from Yaman about 1067; he is said to have been a man of great learning, and is credited with the performance of many miracles, whereby he convinced a large number of Hindus of the truth of his religion.[2] The second Ismā'īlī missionary, Nūr al-Dīn, generally known by the Hindu name he adopted, Nūr Satāgar, was sent into India from Alamūt, the stronghold of the Grand Master of the Ismā'īlīs, and reached Gujarāt in the reign of the Hindu king, Siddhā Rāj (A.D. 1094–1143).[3] He adopted a Hindu name but told the Muhammadans that his real name was Sayyid Sa'ādat; he is said to have converted the Kanbīs, Khārwās and Korīs, low castes of Gujarāt.[4]

As Nūr Satāgar is revered as the first missionary of the Khojahs, so is 'Abd Allāh believed by some to have been the founder of the sect of the Bohras, a large and important community of Shī'ahs, mainly of Hindu origin, who are found in considerable numbers in the chief commercial centres of the Bombay Presidency. But others ascribe the honour of being the first Bohra missionary to Mullā 'Alī, of whose proselytising methods the following account is given by a Shī'ah historian: "As the people of Gujarāt in those days were infidels and accepted as their religious leader an old man whose teaching they

[1] Khojā Vṛttānt, p. 208. Sir Bartle Frere: The Khojas: the Disciples of the Old Man of the Mountain. Macmillan's Magazine, vol. xxxiv. pp. 431, 433–4. (London, 1876.)

[2] Bombay Gazetteer, vol. ix. part ii. p. 26.

[3] K. B. Fazalullah Lutfullah conjectures that Nūr Satāgar came to India rather later, in the reign of Bhīma II (A.D. 1179–1242.) (Bombay Gazetteer, vol. ix. part ii. p. 38.)

[4] Khojā Vṛttānt, p. 154–8.

blindly followed, Mullā 'Alī saw no alternative but to go to the old man and ask to become his disciple, intending to set before him such convincing arguments that he would become a Musalman, and afterwards to attempt the conversion of others. He accordingly spent some years in the service of the old man, and having learned the language of the people of the country, read their books and acquired a knowledge of their sciences. Step by step he unfolded to the enlightened mind of the old man the truth of the faith of Islam and persuaded him to become a Musalman. After his conversion, some of his disciples followed the old man's example. Finally, the chief minister of the king of that country became aware of the old man's conversion to Islam, and going to see him submitted to his spiritual guidance and likewise became a Musalman. For a long time, the old man, the minister and the rest of the converts to Islam, kept the fact of their conversion concealed and through fear of the king always took care to prevent it coming to his knowledge; but at length the king received a report of the minister's having adopted Islam and began to make inquiries. One day, without giving previous notice, he went to the minister's house and found him bowing his head in prayer and was vexed with him. The minister recognised the purpose of the king's visit, and realised that his displeasure had been excited by suspicions aroused by his prayer, with its bowing and prostrations; but the guidance of God and divine grace befitting the occasion, he said that he was making these movements because he was watching a serpent in the corner of the room. When the king turned towards the corner of the room, by divine providence he saw a snake there, and accepted the minister's excuse and his mind was cleared of all suspicions. In the end the king also secretly became a Musalman, but for reasons of state concealed his change of mind; when however, the hour of his death drew near, he gave orders that his body was not to be burnt, as is the custom of the infidels. Subsequently to his decease, when Sulṭān Ẓafar, one of the trusty nobles of Sulṭān Fīrūz Shāh, king of Dehlī, conquered Gujarāt, some of the Sunnī nobles who accompanied him used arguments to make the people join the Sunnī sect of the Muslim faith;

so some of the Bohras are Sunnīs, but the greater part remain true to their original faith." [1]

Several small groups of Musalmans in Cutch and Gujarāt trace their conversion to Imām Shāh of Pīrāna,[2] who was actively engaged in missionary work during the latter half of the fifteenth century. He is said to have converted a large body of Hindu cultivators, by bringing about a fall of rain after two seasons of scarcity. On another occasion meeting a band of Hindu pilgrims passing through Pīrāna on their way to Benares, he offered to take them there; they agreed and in a moment were in the holy city, where they bathed in the Ganges and paid their vows; they then awoke to find themselves still in Pīrāna and adopted the faith of the saint who could perform such a miracle. He died in 1512 and his tomb in Pīrāna is still an object of pilgrimage for Hindus as well as for Muhammadans.[3]

Many of the Cutch Musalmans that are of Hindu descent reverence as their spiritual leader Dāwal Shāh Pīr, whose real name was Malik 'Abd al-Laṭīf,[4] the son of one of the nobles of Maḥmūd Bīgarah (1459–1511), the famous monarch of the Muhammadan dynasty of Gujarāt, to whose reign popular tradition assigns the date of the conversion of many Hindus.[5]

It is in Bengal, however, that the Muhammadan missionaries in India have achieved their greatest success, as far as numbers are concerned. A Muhammadan kingdom was first founded here at the end of the twelfth century by Muḥammad Ba<u>kh</u>tiyār Khiljī, who conquered Bihar and Bengal and made Gaur the capital of the latter province. The long continuance of the Muhammadan rule would naturally assist the spread of Islam, and though the Hindu rule was restored for ten years under the tolerant Rājā Kāns, whose rule is said to have been popular with his Muhammadan subjects,[6] his son, Jatmall, renounced the Hindu religion and became a Musalman. After his father's death in 1414 he called

[1] Nūr Allāh al-Shūshtarī: Majālis al-Mu'minīn, fol. 65. (India Office MS. No. 1400.)

[2] A town ten miles south-west of Ahmadabad.

[3] Bombay Gazetteer, vol. ix. part ii. pp. 66, 76.

[4] Bombay Gazetteer, vol. v. p. 89.

[5] Id. vol. ii. p. 378; vol. iii. pp. 36–7.

[6] So Firishtah, but see H. Blochmann: Contributions to the Geography and History of Bengal. (J. A. S. B., vol. xlii. No. 1, pp. 264–6. 1873.)

together all the officers of the state and announced his intention of embracing Islam, and proclaimed that if the chiefs would not permit him to ascend the throne, he was ready to give it up to his brother; whereupon they declared that they would accept him as their king, whatever religion he might adopt. Accordingly, several learned men of the Muslim faith were summoned to witness the Raja renounce the Hindu religion and publicly profess his acceptance of Islam : he took the name of Jalāl al-Dīn Muḥammad Shāh, and according to tradition numerous conversions were made during his reign.[1] Many of these were however due to force, for his reign is signalised as being the only one in which any wholesale persecution of the subject Hindus is recorded, during the five centuries and a half of Muhammadan rule in Eastern Bengal.[2]

Conversions, however, often took place at other times under pressure from the Muhammadan government. The Rajas of Kharagpur were originally Hindus, and became Muhammadans because, having been defeated by one of Akbar's generals, they were only allowed to retain the family estates on the condition that they embraced Islam. The Hindu ancestor of the family of Asad 'Alī Khān, in Chittagong, was deprived of his caste by being forced to smell beef and had perforce to become a Muhammadan, and several other instances of the same kind might be quoted.[3]

Murshid Qulī Kh̲ān (son of a converted Brahman), who was made governor of Bengal by the Emperor Aurangzeb at the beginning of the eighteenth century, enforced a law that any official or landord, who failed to pay the revenue that was due or was unable to make good the loss, should with his wife and children be compelled to become Muhammadans. Further, it was the common law that any Hindu who forfeited his caste by a breach of regulations could only be reinstated by the Muhammadan government; if the government refused to interfere, the outcast had no means of regaining his position in the social system of the Hindus, and would probably find no resource but to become a Musalman.[4]

[1] J. H. Ravenshaw : Gaur : its ruins and inscriptions, p. 99. (London, 1878.) Firishtah, vol. iv. p. 337.

[2] Wise, p. 29.

[3] Census of India, 1901, vol. vi. part i. p. 170.

[4] Id. p. 30.

The Afghān adventurers who settled in this province also appear to have been active in the work of proselytising, for besides the children that they had by Hindu women, they used to purchase a number of boys in times of scarcity, and educate them in the tenets of Islam.[1] But it is not in the ancient centres of the Muhammadan government that the Musalmans of Bengal are found in large numbers, but in the country districts, in districts where there are no traces of settlers from the West, and in places where low-caste Hindus and outcasts most abound.[2] The similarity of manners between these low-caste Hindus and the followers of the Prophet, and the caste distinctions which they still retain, as well as their physical likeness, all bear the same testimony and identify the Bengal Musalmans with the aboriginal tribes of the country. Here Islam met with no consolidated religious system to bar its progress, as in the north-west of India, where the Muhammadan invaders found Brahmanism full of fresh life and vigour after its triumphant struggle with Buddhism; where, in spite of persecutions, its influence was an inspiring force in the opposition offered by the Hindus, and retained its hold on them in the hour of their deepest distress and degradation. But in Bengal the Muslim missionaries were welcomed with open arms by the aborigines and the low castes on the very outskirts of Hinduism, despised and condemned by their proud Aryan rulers. "To these poor people, fishermen, hunters, pirates, and low-caste tillers of the soil, Islam came as a revelation from on high. It was the creed of the ruling race, its missionaries were men of zeal who brought the Gospel of the unity of God and the equality of men in its sight to a despised and neglected population. The initiatory rite rendered relapse impossible, and made the proselyte and his posterity true believers for ever. In this way Islam settled down on the richest alluvial province of India, the province which was capable of supporting the most rapid and densest increase of population. Compulsory conversions are occasionally recorded. But it was not to force that Islam owed

[1] Charles Stewart: The History of Bengal, p. 176. (London, 1813.) H. Blochmann: Contributions to the Geography and History of Bengal. (J. A. S. B., vol. xlii. No. 1, p. 220. 1873.)

[2] The Indian Evangelical Review, p. 278. (January 1883.)

its permanent success in Lower Bengal. It appealed to the people, and it derived the great mass of its converts from the poor. It brought in a higher conception of God, and a nobler idea of the brotherhood of man. It offered to the teeming low castes of Bengal, who had sat for ages abject on the outermost pale of the Hindu community, a free entrance into a new social organisation."[1]

The existence in Bengal of definite missionary efforts is said to be attested by certain legends of the zeal of private individuals on behalf of their religion, and the graves of some of these missionaries are still honoured, and are annually visited by hundreds of pilgrims.[2] One of the earliest of these was Shaykh Jalāl al-Dīn Tabrīzī, who died in A.D. 1244. He was a pupil of the great saint, Shihāb al-Dīn Suhrawardī. In the course of his missionary journeys he visited Bengal, where a shrine to which is attached a rich endowment was erected in his honour, the real site of his tomb being unknown. Many miracles are ascribed to him; among others, that he converted a Hindu milkman to Islam by a single look.[3]

In the nineteenth century there was a remarkable revival of the Muhammadan religion in Bengal, and several sects that owe their origin to the influence of the Wahhābī reformation, have sent their missionaries through the province purging out the remnants of Hindu superstitions, awakening religious zeal and spreading the faith among unbelievers.[4]

Some account still remains to be given of Muslim missionaries who have laboured in parts of India other than those mentioned above. One of the earliest of these is Shaykh Ismā'īl, one of the most famous of the Sayyids of Bukhārā, distinguished alike for his secular and religious learning; he is said to have been the first Muslim missionary who preached the faith of Islam in the city of Lahore, whither he came in the year A.D. 1005. Crowds flocked to listen to his sermons, and the number of his converts swelled rapidly day by day, and it is said that no unbeliever ever came

[1] Sir W. W. Hunter: The Religions of India. (*The Times*, February 25, 1888.) See also Wise, p. 32.

[2] Wise, p. 37.

[3] Blochmann, op. cit. p. 260.

[4] Wise, pp. 48–55.

into personal contact with him without being converted to the faith of Islam.[1]

The conversion of the inhabitants of the western plains of the Panjāb is said to have been effected through the preaching of Bahā al-Ḥaqq of Multan [2] and Bābā Farīd al-Dīn of Pakpattan, who flourished about the end of the thirteenth and beginning of the fourteenth centuries.[3] A biographer of the latter saint gives a list of sixteen tribes who were won over to Islam through his preaching, but unfortunately provides us with no details of this work of conversion.[4]

One of the most famous of the Muslim saints of India and a pioneer of Islam in Rajputana was Khwājah Mu'īn al-Dīn Chishtī, who died in Ajmīr in A.D. 1234. He was a native of Sajistān to the east of Persia, and is said to have received his call to preach Islam to the unbelievers in India while on a pilgrimage to Medina. Here the Prophet appeared to him in a dream and thus addressed him: "The Almighty has entrusted the country of India to thee. Go thither and settle in Ajmīr. By God's help, the faith of Islam shall, through thy piety and that of thy followers, be spread in that land." He obeyed the call and made his way to Ajmīr which was then under Hindu rule and idolatry prevailed throughout the land. Among the first of his converts here was a Yogī, who was the spiritual preceptor of the Raja himself: gradually he gathered around him a large body of disciples whom his teachings had won from the ranks of infidelity, and his fame as a religious leader became very widespread and attracted to Ajmīr great numbers of Hindus whom he persuaded to embrace Islam.[5] On his way to Ajmīr he is said to have converted as many as 700 persons in the city of Dehli.

Of immense importance in the history of Islam in India was the arrival in that country of Sayyid Jalāl al-Dīn, who is said to have been born at Bukhārā in 1199. He settled in Uch, now in the Bahawalpur territory, in 1244, and converted numbers of persons in the neighbourhood to

[1] Ghulām Sarwar: Khazīnat al-Aṣfīyā, vol. ii. p. 230.
[2] Otherwise known as Shaykh Bahā al-Dīn Zakariyyā.
[3] Ibbetson, p. 163.
[4] Aṣghar 'Alī: Jawāhir-i-Farīdī (A.H. 1033), p. 395. (Lahore, 1884.)
[5] Elliot, vol. ii. p. 548.

Islam; he died in 1291, and his descendants, many of whom are also revered as saints, have remained as guardians of his shrine up to the present day and form the centre of a widespread religious influence. His grandson, Sayyid Aḥmad Kabīr, known as Makhdūm-i-Jahāniyān, is credited with having effected the conversion of several tribes in the Punjab.[1] About a mile to the east of Uch is situated the shrine of Ḥasan Kabīr al-Dīn, son of Sayyid Ṣadr al-Dīn, who was a contemporary of Jalāl-al-Dīn; both father and son are said to have made many converts, and such was the influence attributed to Ḥasan Kabīr al-Dīn that it was said as soon as his glance fell upon any Hindu, the latter would accept Islam.[2]

Rather later in the same century, a native of Persian 'Irāq, by name Abū 'Alī Qalandar, came into India and took up his residence at Panipat, where he died at the ripe age of 100, in A.D. 1324. The Muslim Rajputs of this city, numbering about 300 males, are descended from a certain Amīr Singh who was converted by this saint. His tomb is still held in honour and is visited by many pilgrims.

Another such was Shaykh Jalāl al-Dīn, a Persian who came into India about the latter half of the fourteenth century and settled down at Silhaṭ, in Lower Assam, in order to convert the people of these parts to Islam. He achieved a great reputation as a holy man, and his proselytising labours were crowned with eminent success.[3]

In more recent years there have been abundant witnesses for Islam seeking to spread this faith in India—and with very considerable success; the second half of the nineteenth century especially witnessed a great revival of missionary activity, the number of annual conversions being variously estimated at ten, fifty, one hundred and six hundred thousand.[4] But it is difficult to obtain accurate information on account of the peculiarly individualistic character of Muslim missionary work and the absence of any central

[1] Punjab States Gazetteers, vol. xxxvi A. Bahawalpur State. (Lahore, 1908), p. 160 sqq. The names of some of the tribes who ascribe their conversion to Makhdūm-i-Jahāniyān are given on p. 162.

[2] Id. p. 171. [3] Ibn Baṭūṭah, tome iv. p. 217. Yule, p. 515.

[4] The Indian Evangelical Review, vol. xvi, pp. 52–3. (Calcutta, 1889–90.) The Contemporary Review, February 1889, p. 170. The Spectator, October 15, 1887, p. 1382.

organisation or of anything in the way of missionary reports, and the success that attends the labours of Muslim preachers is sometimes much exaggerated, e. g. in the Panjāb a certain Ḥājī Muḥammad is said to have converted as many as 200,000 Hindus,[1] and a mawlavī in Bangalore boasted that in five years he had made as many as 1000 converts in this city and its suburbs. But that there are Muslim missionaries engaged in active and successful propagandist labours is undoubted, and the following examples are typical of the period referred to.

Mawlavī Baqā Ḥusayn Khān, an itinerant preacher, in the course of several years converted 228 persons, residents of Bombay, Cawnpore, Ajmīr, and other cities. Mawlavī Ḥasan 'Alī converted twenty-five persons, twelve in Poona, the rest in Ḥaydarabad and other parts of India.[2] In the district of Khandesh, in the Bombay Presidency, the preaching of the Qāḍī of Nasirabad, Sayyid Safdar 'Alī, won over to Islam a large body of artisans, who follow the trade of

[1] Garcin de Tassy : La Langue et la Littérature Hindoustanies de 1850 à 1869, p. 343. (Paris, 1874.)

[2] Mawlavī Ḥasan 'Alī furnished me with these figures some years before his death in 1896. In an obituary notice published in "The Moslem Chronicle" (April 4, 1896), the following quaint account is given of his life : "In private and school life, he was marked as a very intelligent lad and made considerable progress in his scholastic career within a short time. He passed Entrance at a very early age and received scholarship with which he went up to the First Art, but shortly after his innate anxiety to seek truth prompted him to go abroad the world, and abandoning his studies he mixed with persons of different persuasions, Fakirs, Pandits, and Christians, entered churches, and roamed over wilderness and forests and cities with nothing to help him on except his sincere hopes and absolute reliance on the mercy of the Great Lord; for one year he wandered in various regions of religion until in 1874 he accepted the post of a head master in a Patna school. . . . As he was born to become a missionary of the Moslem faith, he felt an imperceptible craving to quit his post, from which he used to get Rs. 100 per mensem. He tendered his resignation, much to the reluctance of his friends, and maintained himself for some time by publishing a monthly journal, 'Noorul Islam.' He gave several lectures on Islam at Patna, and then went to Calcutta, where he delivered his lecture in English, which produced such effect on the audience that several European clergymen vouchsafed the truth of Islam, and a notable gentleman, Babu Bepin Chandra Pal, was about to become Musalman. He was invited by the people at Dacca, where his preachings and lectures left his name imbedded in the hearts of the citizens. His various books and pamphlets and successive lectures in Urdu and in English in the different cities and towns in India gave him a historic name in the world. Some one hundred men become Musalmans on hearing his lectures and reading his books." His missionary zeal manifested itself up to the last hour of his life, when he was overheard to say, "Abjure your religion and become a Musalman." On being questioned, he said he was talking to a Christian.

armourers or blacksmiths.[1] A number of persons of the same trade, who form a small community of about 200 souls in the district of Nasik, were converted in a curious way about 1870. The Presbyterian missionaries of Nasik had for a long time been trying to convert them from Hinduism, and they were in a state of hesitation as to whether or not to embrace Christianity when a Muhammadan faqīr from Bombay, who was well acquainted with their habits of thought, expounded to them the doctrines of Islam and succeeded in winning them over to that faith.[2]

In Patiala, Mawlavī 'Ubayd Allāh, a converted Brahman of great learning, proved himself to be a zealous preacher of Islam, and in spite of the obstacles that were at first thrown in his way by his relatives, achieved so great a success that his converts almost filled an entire ward of the city. He wrote controversial works, which have passed through several editions, directed against the Christian and Hindu religions. In one of these books he thus speaks of his own conversion: "I, Muḥammad 'Ubayd Allāh, the son of Munshi Koṭā Mal, resident of Payal, in the Patiala State, declare that this poor man in his childhood and during the lifetime of his father was held in the bondage of idol-worship, but the mercy of God caught me by the hand and drew me towards Islam, i. e. I came to know the excellence of Islam and the deficiencies of Hinduism, and I accepted Islam heart and soul and counted myself one of the servants of the Prophet of God (peace be upon him !). At that time intelligence, which is the gift of God, suggested to me that it was mere folly and laziness to blindly follow the customs of one's forefathers and be misled by them and not make researches into matters of religion and faith, whereon depend our eternal bliss or misery. With these thoughts I began to study the current faiths and investigated each of them impartially. I thoroughly explored the Hindu religion and conversed with learned Paṇḍits, gained a thorough knowledge of the Christian faith, read the books of Islam and conversed with learned men. In all of them I found errors and fallacies, with the exception of Islam, the excellence of which became

[1] Bombay Gazetteer, vol. xii. p. 126.
[2] Id. vol. xvi. p. 81.

clearly manifest to me; its leader, Muḥammad the Prophet, possesses such moral excellences that no tongue can describe them, and he alone who knows the beliefs and the liturgy, and the moral teachings and practice of this faith, can fully realise them. Praise be to God! So excellent is this religion that everything in it leads the soul to God. In short, by the grace of God, the distinction between truth and falsehood became as clear to me as night and day, darkness and light. But although my heart had long been enlightened by the brightness of Islam and my mouth fragrant with the profession of faith, yet my evil passions and Satan had bound me with the fetters of the luxury and ease of this fleeting world, and I was in evil case because of the outward observances of idolatry. At length, the grace of God thus admonished me: 'How long wilt thou keep this priceless pearl hidden within the shell and this refreshing perfume shut up in the casket? thou shouldest wear this pearl about thy neck and profit by this perfume.' Moreover the learned have declared that to conceal one's faith in Islam and retain the dress and habits of infidels brings a man to Hell. So (God be praised!) on the 'Īd al-Fiṭr 1264 the sun of my conversion emerged from its screen of clouds, and I performed my devotions in public with my Muslim brethren."[1]

Many Muhammadan preachers have adopted the methods of Christian missionaries, such as street preaching, tract distribution, and other agencies. In many of the large cities of India, Muslim preachers may be found daily expounding the teachings of Islam in some principal thoroughfare. In Bangalore this practice is very general, and one of these preachers, who was the imām of the mosque about the year 1890, was so popular that he was even sometimes invited to preach by Hindus: he preached in the market-place, and in the course of seven or eight years gained forty-two converts. In Bombay a Muhammadan missionary preaches almost daily near the chief market of the city, and in Calcutta there are several preaching-stations that are kept constantly supplied. Among the converts are occasionally to be found some Europeans, mostly persons in

[1] Tuḥfat al-Hind, p. 3. (Dehli, A.H. 1309.)

indigent circumstances; the mass, however, are Hindus.[1] Some of the numerous Anjumans that have of recent years sprung up in the chief centres of Musalman life in India, include among their objects the sending of missionaries to preach in the bazars; such are the Anjuman Ḥimāyat-i-Islām of Lahore, and the Anjuman Ḥāmī Islām of Ajmīr. These particular Anjumans appoint paid agents, but much of the work of preaching in the bazaars is performed by persons who are engaged in some trade or business during the working hours of the day and devote their leisure time in the evenings to this pious work.

Much of the missionary zeal of the Indian Musalmans is directed towards counteracting the anti-Islamic tendencies of the instruction given by Christian missionaries and the preachers of the Ārya Samāj, and the efforts made are thus defensive rather than directly proselytising. Some preachers too turn their attention rather to the strengthening of the foundation already laid, and endeavour to rid their ignorant co-religionists of their Hindu superstitions, and instil in them a purer form of faith, such efforts being in many cases the continuation of earlier missionary activity. The work of conversion has indeed been often very imperfect. Of many, nominally Muslims, it may be said that they are half Hindus: they observe caste rules, they join in Hindu festivals and practise numerous idolatrous ceremonies. In certain districts also, e. g. in Mewāt and Gurgaon, large numbers of Muhammadans may be found who know nothing of their religion but its name; they have no mosques, nor do they observe the hours of prayer. This is especially the case among the Muhammadans of the villages or in parts of the country where they are isolated from the mass of believers; but in the towns the presence of learned religious men tends, in great measure, to counteract the influence of former superstitions, and makes for a purer and more intelligent form of religious life. In recent years, however, there has been, speaking generally, a movement noticeable among the Indian Muslims towards

[1] The Indian Evangelical Review, 1884, p. 128. Garcin de Tassy: La Langue et la Littérature Hindoustanies de 1850 à 1869, p. 485. (Paris, 1874.) Garcin de Tassy: La Langue et la Littérature Hindoustanies en 1871, p. 12. (Paris, 1872.)

a religious life more strictly in accordance with the laws of Islam. The influence of the Christian mission schools has also been very great in stimulating among some Muhammadans of the younger generation a study of their own religion and in bringing about a consequent awakening of religious zeal. Indeed, the spread of education generally, has led to a more intelligent grasp of religious principles and to an increase of religious teachers in outlying and hitherto neglected districts. This missionary movement of reform (from whatever cause it may originate), may be observed in very different parts of India. In the eastern districts of the Panjāb, for example, after the Mutiny, a great religious revival took place. Preachers travelled far and wide through the country, calling upon believers to abandon their idolatrous practices and expounding the true tenets of the faith. Now, in consequence, most villages, in which Muhammadans own any considerable portion, have a mosque, while the grosser and more open idolatries are being discontinued.[1] In Rajputana also, the Hindu tribes who have been from time to time converted to Islam in the rural districts, are now becoming more orthodox and regular in their religious observances, and are abandoning the ancient customs which hitherto they had observed in common with their idolatrous neighbours. The Merāts, for example, now follow the orthodox Muhammadan form of marriage instead of the Hindu ritual they formerly observed, and have abjured the flesh of the wild boar.[2] A similar revival in Bengal has already been spoken of above.

Such movements and the efforts of individual missionaries are, however, quite inadequate to explain the rapid increase of the Muhammadans of India, and one is naturally led to inquire what are the causes other than the normal increase of population,[3] which add so enormously to their numbers. The answer is to be found in the social conditions of life among Hindus. The insults and contempt heaped upon the lower castes of Hindus by their co-religionists, and the impassable obstacles placed in the way of any member of

[1] Ibbetson, p. 184.
[2] The Rajputana Gazetteer, vol. i. p. 90; vol. ii. p. 47. (Calcutta, 1879.)
[3] On these as they affect the Muhammadans, see the Census of India, 1901. Vol. vi. p. 172.

these castes desiring to better his condition, show up in striking contrast the benefits of a religious system which has no outcasts, and gives free scope for the indulgence of any ambition. In Bengal, for example, the weavers of cotton piece-goods, who are looked upon as vile by their Hindu co-religionists, embrace Islam in large numbers to escape from the low position to which they are otherwise degraded.[1] A very remarkable instance of a similar kind occurs in the history of the north-eastern part of the same province. Here in the year 1550 the aboriginal tribe of the Kocch established a dynasty under their great leader, Haju; in the reign of his grandson, when the higher classes in the state were received into the pale of Hinduism,[2] the mass of the people finding themselves despised as outcasts, became Muhammadans.[3]

The escape that Islam offers to Hindus from the oppression of the higher castes was strikingly illustrated in Tinnevelli at the close of the nineteenth century. A very low caste, the Shanars, had in recent years become prosperous and many of them had built fine houses; they asserted that they had the right to worship in temples, from which they had hitherto been excluded. A riot ensued, in the course of which the Shanars suffered badly at the hands of Hindus of a higher caste, and they took refuge in the pale of Islam. Six hundred Shanars in one village became Muslims in one day, and their example was quickly followed in other places.[4]

Similar instances might be given from other parts of India. A Hindu who has in any way lost caste and been in consequence repudiated by his relations and by the society of which he has been accustomed to move, would naturally be attracted towards a religion that receives all without distinction, and offers to him a grade of society equal in the social scale to that from which he has been banished. Such a change of religion might well be accompanied with sincere conviction, but men also who might be profoundly indifferent to the number or names of the

[1] E. T. Dalton, p. 324.

[2] For an account of such Hinduising of the aboriginal tribes see Sir Alfred Lyall: Asiatic Studies, pp. 102–4.

[3] E. T. Dalton, p. 89.

[4] The Missionary Review of the World, N. S. vol. xiii, pp. 72–3. (New York, 1900.)

deities they were called upon to worship, would feel very keenly the social ostracism entailed by their loss of caste, and become Muhammadan without any religious feelings at all. The influence of the study of Muhammadan literature also, and the habitual contact with Muhammadan society, must often make itself insensibly felt. Among the Rajput princes of the nineteenth century in Rajputana and Bundelkhand, such tendencies towards Islamism were to be observed,[1] tendencies which, had the Mughal empire lasted, would probably have led to their ultimate conversion. They not only respected Muhammadan saints, but had Muhammadan tutors for their sons; they also had their food killed in accordance with the regulations laid down by the Muhammadan law, and joined in the Muhammadan festivals dressed as faqīrs, and praying like true believers. On the other hand, it has been conjectured that the present position of affairs, under a government perfectly impartial in matters religious, is much more likely to promote conversions among the Hindus generally than was the case under the rule of the Muhammadan kingdoms, when Hinduism gained union and strength from the constant struggle with an aggressive enemy.[2] Hindus, too, often flock in large numbers to the tombs of Muslim saints on the day appointed to commemorate them, and a childless father, with the feeling that prompts a polytheist to leave no God unaddressed, will present his petition to the God of the Muhammadans, and if children are born to him, apparently in answer to this prayer, the whole family will in such a case (and examples are not infrequent) embrace Islam.[3]

[1] Sir Alfred Lyall (Asiatic Studies, p. 29) speaks of the perceptible proclivity towards the faith of Islam occasionally exhibited by some of the Hindu chiefs.

[2] Gazetteer of the Province of Oudh, vol. i. p. xix.

[3] To give one instance only : in Ghātampur, in the district of Cawnpore, one branch of a large family is Muslim in obedience to the vow of their ancestor, Ghātam Deo Bais, who while praying for a son at the shrine of a Muhammadan saint, Madār Shāh, promised that if his prayer were granted, half his descendants should be brought up as Muslims. (Gazetteer of the N.W.P. vol. vi. pp. 64, 238.)

The worship of Muhammadan saints is so common among certain low-caste Hindus that in the Census of 1891, in the North-Western Provinces and Oudh alone, 2,333,643 Hindus (or 5·78 per cent. of the total Hindu population of these provinces) returned themselves as worshippers of Muhammadan saints. (Census of India, 1891, vol. xvi. part i. pp. 217, 244). (Allahabad, 1894.)

Love for a Muhammadan woman is occasionally the cause of the conversion of a Hindu, since the marriage of a Muslim woman to an unbeliever is absolutely forbidden by the Muslim law. Hindu children, if adopted by wealthy Musalmans, would be brought up in the religion of their new parents; and a Hindu wife, married to a follower of the Prophet, would be likely to adopt the faith of her husband.[1] As the contrary process can rarely take place, the number of Muhammadans is bound to increase in proportion to that of the Hindus. Hindus, who for some reason or other have been driven out of their caste; the poor who have become the recipients of Muhammadan charity, or women and children who have been protected when their parents have died or deserted them—(such cases would naturally be frequent in times of famine)—form a continuous though small stream of additions from the Hindus.[2] There are often local circumstances favourable to the growth of Islam; for example, it has been pointed out [3] that in the villages of the Terai, in which the number of Hindus and Muhammadans happen to be equally balanced, any increase in the predominance of the Muhammadans is invariably followed by disputes about the killing of cows and other practices offensive to Hindu feeling. The Hindus gradually move away from the village, leaving behind of their creed only the Chamār ploughman in the service of the Muhammadan peasants. These latter eventually adopt the religion of their masters, not from any conviction of its truth, but from the inconvenience their isolation entails.

Some striking instances of conversions from the lower castes of Hindus are also found in the agricultural districts of Oudh. Although the Muhammadans of this province form only one-tenth of the whole population, still the small groups of Muhammadan cultivators form "scattered centres of revolt against the degrading oppression to which their religion hopelessly consigns these lower castes." [4] The advantages Islam holds out to such classes as the Korīs

[1] Instances of such causes of conversion are given in the Census of India, 1901. Vol. vi. Bengal, part. i, Appendix II.

[2] Report on the Census of the N.W.P. and Oudh, 1881, by Edward White, p. 62. (Allahabad, 1882.)

[3] Id. p. 63.

[4] Gazetteer of the Province of Oudh, vol. i. p. xix.

and Chamārs, who stand at the lowest level of Hindu society, and the deliverance which conversion to Islam brings them, may be best understood from the following passage descriptive of their social condition as Hindus.[1] " The lowest depth of misery and degradation is reached by the Korīs and Chamārs, the weavers and leather-cutters to the rest. Many of these in the northern districts are actually bond-slaves, having hardly ever the spirit to avail themselves of the remedy offered by our courts, and descend with their children from generation to generation as the value of an old purchase. They hold the plough for the Brahman or Chhattri master, whose pride of caste forbids him to touch it, and live with the pigs, less unclean than themselves, in separate quarters apart from the rest of the village. Always on the verge of starvation, their lean, black, and ill-formed figures, their stupid faces, and their repulsively filthy habits reflect the wretched destiny which condemns them to be lower than the beast among their fellow-men, and yet that they are far from incapable of improvement is proved by the active and useful stable servants drawn from among them, who receive good pay and live well under European masters. A change of religion is the only means of escape open to them, and they have little reason to be faithful to their present creed."

It is this absence of class prejudices which constitutes the real strength of Islam in India, and enables it to win so many converts from Hinduism.

To complete this survey of Islam in India, some account still remains to be given of the spread of this faith in Kashmīr and thence beyond the borders of India into Tibet. Of all the provinces and states of India (with the exception of Sind) Kashmīr contains the largest number of Muhammadans (namely 70 per cent.) in proportion to the whole population; but unfortunately historical facts that should explain the existence in this state of so many Musalmans, almost entirely of Hindu or Tibetan origin, are very scanty. But all the evidence leads us to attribute it on the whole to a long-continued missionary movement inaugurated and carried out mainly by faqīrs and dervishes, among whom were Ismā'īlian preachers sent from Alamūt.[2]

[1] Gazetteer of the Province of Oudh, vol. i. pp. xxiii–xxiv.
[2] Khojā Vṛttānt, p. 141.

It is difficult to say when this Islamising influence first made itself felt in the country. The first Muhammadan king of Kashmīr, Ṣadr al-Dīn,[1] is said to have owed his conversion to a certain Darwesh Bulbul Shāh in the early part of the fourteenth century. This saint was the only religious teacher who could satisfy his craving for religious truth when, dissatisfied with his own Hindu faith, he looked for a more acceptable form of doctrine. Towards the end of the same century (in 1388) the progress of Islam was most materially furthered by the advent of Sayyid ʿAlī Hamadānī, a fugitive from his native city of Hamadān in Persia, where he had incurred the wrath of Tīmūr. He was accompanied by 700 Sayyids, who established hermitages all over the country and by their influence appear to have assured the acceptance of the new religion. Their advent appears, however, to have also stirred up considerable fanaticism, as Sultan Sikandar (1393–1417) acquired the name of Butshikan from his destruction of Hindu idols and temples, and his prime minister, a converted Hindu, set on foot a fierce persecution of the adherents of his old faith, but on his death toleration was again made the rule of the kingdom.[2] Towards the close of the fifteenth century, a missionary, by name Mīr Shams al-Dīn, belonging to a Shīʿah sect, came from ʿIrāq, and, with the aid of his disciples, won over a large number of converts in Kashmīr.

When under Akbar, Kashmīr became a province of the Mughal empire, the Muhammadan influence was naturally strengthened and many men of learning came into the country. In the reign of Aurangzeb, the Rajput Raja of Kishtwar was converted by the miracles of a certain Sayyid Shāh Farīd al-Dīn and his conversion seems to have been followed by that of the majority of his subjects, and along the route which the Mughal emperors took on their progresses into Kashmīr we still find Rajas who are the descendants of Muhammadanised Rajputs.[3]

To the north and north-east of Kashmīr, the provinces of Baltistan and Ladakh are inhabited by a mixed Tibetan

[1] Or Shams al-Dīn, according to another account, see Muḥammad Haydar, p. 433 (n. 2).

[2] Firishtah, vol. iv. pp. 464, 469.

[3] F. Drew: The Jummoo and Kashmir Territories, pp. 58, 155. (London, 1875.)

race, among whom Islam has been firmly established for several centuries, but the date and manner of its introduction is unknown. The Muhammadans of Baltistan tell of four brothers who came from Khurasan and brought about a revival of the faith, but appear to have no tradition regarding the earliest propagandists.[1] Up to the middle of the nineteenth century Islam appeared to be making progress, but this tendency was counteracted by the encouragement which Maharaja Ranbir Singh gave to the followers of the Buddhist faith. In Ladakh there are a number of half-castes, called Arghons,[2] born of Tibetan mothers and Muhammadan fathers, traders who have come to Leh and persuaded the Tibetan women they marry to accept Islam. These Arghons are all Musalmans and, like their fathers, marry Tibetan wives; they are said to be increasing in numbers more rapidly than the pure Tibetan stock.[3] Islam has also been carried into Tibet Proper by Kashmiri merchants. Settlements of such merchants are to be found in all the chief cities of Tibet; they marry Tibetan wives, who often adopt the religion of their husbands; and there are now said to be as many as 2000 Muhammadan families in Lhasa.[4] Islam has made its way into Tibet also from Yunnan,[5] and at Su-ching, on the border of the Sze-chwan province and Tibet, converts are being won from among the Tibetan inhabitants.[6] Muhammadan influences are also said to have come from Persia[7] and from Turkestan.[8]

[1] Drew, op. cit. p. 359.
[2] On this word see Yule's Marco Polo, vol. i. p. 290.
[3] Aḥmad Shāh : Four years in Tibet, pp. 45, 74. (Benares, 1906.)
[4] Broomhall, p. 206. Tu Wen-siu, the leader of the Panthay rebellion from 1856 to 1873, who for sixteen years was practically Sultan of half the province of Yunnan, issued a proclamation in Lhasa itself, at the outset of his revolt, in order to gain Muhammadan recruits. (Id. p. 132.)
[5] Mission d'Ollone, pp. 207, 226, 233.
[6] Broomhall, p. 206.
[7] A. Bastian : Die Geschichte der Indochinesen, p. 159. (Leipzig, 1866.)
[8] R. du M. M., tome i, p. 275. (1907.)

CHAPTER X.

THE SPREAD OF ISLAM IN CHINA.

TRADITION ascribes to Muḥammad the saying, " Seek for knowledge, even unto China." [1] Though there is no historical evidence for these words having ever been uttered by the Prophet, it is not impossible that the name of this country may have been known to him, for commercial relations between Arabia and China had been established long before his birth. It was through Arabia, in great measure, that Syria and the ports of the Levant received the produce of the East. In the sixth century, there was a considerable trade between China and Arabia by way of Ceylon, and at the beginning of the seventh century the commerce between China, Persia and Arabia was still further extended, the town of Sīrāf on the Persian Gulf being the chief emporium for the Chinese traders. It was at this period, at the commencement of the T'ang dynasty (618–907) that mention is first made of the Arabs in the Chinese Annals; [2] they note the rise of the Muslim power in Medina and briefly describe the religious observances of the new faith.

The Annals of Kwangtung thus record the coming of the first Muslims into China :—" At the beginning of the T'ang dynasty there came to Canton a large number of strangers, from the kingdoms of Annam, Cambodia, Medina and several other countries. These strangers worshipped heaven (i. e. God) and had neither statue, idol nor image in their temples. The kingdom of Medina is close to that of India, and it is in this kingdom that the religion of these strangers, which is different to that of Buddha, originated. They do not eat pork or drink wine, and they regard as unclean the flesh of any animal not killed by themselves. They are nowadays

[1] Kanz al-'Ummāl, vol. v. p. 202. [2] Bretschneider (2), p. 6.

called Hui Hui.[1] . . . Having asked and obtained from the emperor permission to reside in Canton, they built magnificent houses of a style different to that of our country. They were very rich and obeyed a chief chosen by themselves."[2] Though direct historical evidence is lacking,[3] it is most probable that Islam was first introduced into China by merchants who followed the old-established sea route. But the earliest record we can trust refers to diplomatic relations carried on by land, through Persia. When Yazdagird, the last Sāsānid king of Persia, had perished, his son, Fīrūz, appealed to China for help against the Arab invaders;[4] but the emperor replied that Persia was too far distant for him to send the required troops. But he is said to have despatched an ambassador to the Arab court to plead the cause of the fugitive prince—probably also with instructions to ascertain the extent and power of the new kingdom that had arisen in the West, and the caliph 'U͟thmān is said to have sent one of the Arab generals to accompany the Chinese ambassador on his return in 651, and this first Muslim envoy was honourably received by the emperor. In the reign of Walīd (705–715), the famous Arab general, Qutaybah b. Muslim, having been appointed governor of K͟hurāsān, crossed the Oxus and began a series of successful campaigns, in which he successively subjugated Buk͟hārā, Samarqand and other cities, and carried his conquests up to the eastern frontier of the Chinese empire. In 713 he sent envoys to the emperor, who (according to Arab accounts) dismissed them with valuable presents. A few years later, the Chinese Annals make mention of an ambassador, named Sulaymān, who came from the caliph Hishām in 726 to the Emperor Hsuan Tsung. These diplomatic relations between the Arab and the Chinese empires assumed a new importance at the close of this emperor's reign, when, driven from his throne by a

[1] On the origin of this name, see Devéria, p. 311; Mission d'Ollone, p. 420 sqq.

[2] De Thiersant, vol. i. pp. 19–20.

[3] D'Ollone gives the following warning as to the uncertainty of our knowledge of Islam in China :—" Or rien n'est moins connu que l'Islam chinois. On ne sait exactement ni comment il s'est propagé dans l'Empire, ni combien d'adeptes il a réunis, ni si sa doctrine est pure, ni quelle est son organisation, ni s'il possède des relations avec le reste du monde musulman." (Mission d'Ollone, p. 1.) The references to China in Arabic and Persian writers have been collected by Schefer, " Notice sur les relations des peuples musulmans avec les Chinois."

[4] Chavannes, p. 172.

usurper, he abdicated in favour of his son, Su Tsung (A.D. 756). The latter sought the help of the 'Abbāsīd caliph, al-Manṣūr, who responded to this appeal by sending a body of Arab troops, and with their assistance the emperor succeeded in recovering his two capitals, Si-ngan-fu and Ho-nan-fu, from the rebels. At the end of the war, these Arab troops did not return to their own country, but married and settled in China. Various reasons are assigned for this action on their part; one account represents them as having returned to their native land but, being refused permission to remain on the ground that they had been so long in a land where pork was eaten, they went back again to China; according to another account they were prepared to embark for Arabia, at Canton, when they were taunted with having eaten pork during their campaign, and in consequence they refused to return home and run the risk of similar taunts from their own people; when the governor of Canton tried to compel them, they joined with the Arab and Persian merchants, their co-religionists, and pillaged the principal commercial houses in the city; the governor saved himself by taking refuge on the city wall, and was only able to return after he had obtained from the emperor permission for these Arab troops to remain in the country; houses and lands were assigned to them in different cities, where they settled down and intermarried with the women of the country.[1]

The Chinese Muhammadans have a legend that their faith was first preached in China by a maternal uncle of the Prophet, and his reputed tomb at Canton is highly venerated by them. But there is not the slightest historical base for this legend, and it appears to be of late growth.[2] It doubtless arose from a desire to connect the history of the faith in their own land as closely as possible with apostolic times—a fruitful source of legends in countries far removed from the centres of Muslim history.[3] But of the existence of Muslims in China, especially of merchants in the port

[1] De Thiersant, vol. i. pp. 70–1.

[2] This legend has been exhaustively discussed by Broomhall: Islam in China, cap. iv, vii.

[3] Thus the people of Khotan claim that Islam was first brought to their land by Ja'far, a cousin of the Prophet (Grenard: Mission Dutreuil de Rhins, t. iii. p. 2), and the Chams of Cambodia ascribe their conversion to one of the fathers-in-law of Muḥammad. (R. du M. M., vol. ii. p. 138.)

towns, during the T'ang dynasty there is clear evidence. The Chinese annalist of this period (A.D. 713–742) says that "the barbarians of the West came into the Middle Kingdom in crowds, like a deluge, from a distance of at least 1000 leagues and from more than 100 kingdoms, bringing as tribute their sacred books, which were received and deposited in the hall set apart for translations of sacred and canonical books, in the imperial palace: from this period the religious doctrines of these different countries were thus diffused and openly practised in the empire of T'ang."[1] An Arab geographer, writing about the year 851, describes these settlements and the mosques which these merchants were allowed to build for their religious exercises;[2] he states that he knew of no Chinaman having embraced Islam, but as he makes the same remark of the people of India, it may be that he was as ill-informed in the one case as the other.[3]

But there is certainly no distinct evidence of any proselytising activity on the part of the Muslims in China, and indeed very little information about them at all until the period of Mongol conquests, in the thirteenth century. These conquests resulted in a vast immigration of Musalmans of various nationalities, Arabs, Persians, Turks and others into the Chinese empire.[4] Some came as merchants, artisans, soldiers or colonists, others were brought in as prisoners of war. A large number of them settled permanently in the country and developed into a populous and flourishing community, which gradually lost its original racial peculiarities through intermarriage with Chinese women. Several Muhammadans occupied high posts under the Mongol rulers, e. g. 'Abd al-Raḥmān, who in 1244 was appointed head of the Imperial finances and allowed to farm the taxes imposed upon China,[5] and 'Umar Shams al-Dīn, commonly known as Sayyid Ajall, a native of Bukhārā, to

[1] De Thiersant, vol. i. p. 153.

[2] Reinaud: Relation des Voyages faits par les Arabes et les Persans dans l'Inde et à la Chine, i. pp. 13, 64. (Paris, 1845.)

[3] Id. p. 58.

[4] That there was some migration westward also of Chinese into the conquered countries of Islam, where they would come within the sphere of its religious influence, we learn from the diary of a Chinese monk who travelled through Central Asia to Persia in the years 1221–4; speaking of Samarqand, he says, "Chinese workmen are living everywhere." (Bretschneider (1), vol. i. p. 78.)

[5] Howorth, vol. i. p. 161.

whom Qūbīlāy Khān, on his accession in 1259, entrusted the management of the Imperial finances; he was subsequently governor of Yunnan, after this province had been conquered and added to the Chinese empire.[1] Sayyid Ajall died in 1270, leaving behind him a reputation as an enlightened and upright administrator; he built Confucian temples as well as mosques in Yunnan city.[2]

The descendants of Sayyid Ajall played a great part in the establishing of Islam in China; it was his grandson who in 1335 obtained from the emperor the recognition of Islam as the "True and Pure Religion"—a name which it has kept to the present day,—and another descendant of Sayyid Ajall was authorised by the emperor in 1420 to build mosques in the capitals, Si-ngan-fu and Nan-kin.[3]

The Chinese historians of the reign of Qūbīlāy Khān make it a ground of complaint against this monarch that he did not employ Chinese officials in place of the immigrant Turks and Persians.[4] The exalted position occupied by Sayyid Ajall and the facilities of communication between China and the West established by Mongol conquest, attracted a number of such persons into the north of China, and it was probably as a result of these immigrations that those scattered Muhammadan communities began to be formed, which have grown to large proportions in most of the provinces of China. Marco Polo, who enjoyed the favour of Qūbīlāy Khān and lived in China from 1275 to 1292, notes the presence of Muhammadans in various parts of Yunnan.[5] At the beginning of the fourteenth century, all the inhabitants of Talifu, the capital of Yunnan, are said by a contemporary historian to have been Musalmans;[6] and Ibn Baṭūṭah, who visited several coast towns in China towards the middle of the fourteenth century, speaks of the hearty welcome he received from his co-religionists,[7] and reports that "In every town there is a special quarter for the Muslims, inhabited solely by them, where they have their mosques; they are honoured and respected by the Chinese."[8]

[1] For Chinese biographies of Sayyid Ajall, see R. du M. M., viii. p. 344, sqq. and xi. p. 3 sqq.; Mission d'Ollone, p. 25 sqq.
[2] Broomhall, p. 127.
[3] Mission d'Ollone, pp. 435–6.
[4] Howorth, vol. i. p. 257.
[5] Marco Polo, vol. i. pp. 219, 274; vol. ii. p. 66.
[6] Rashīd al-Dīn (Yule's Cathay, p. 9).
[7] Vol. iv. pp. 270, 283.
[8] Id. p. 258.

Up to this period the Muhammadans appear to have been looked upon as a foreign community in China, but after the expulsion of the Mongol dynasty in the latter part of the fourteenth century they received no fresh addition to their numbers from abroad, in consequence of the policy of isolation which the Chinese government now adopted; and being thus cut off from communication with their co-religionists in other countries, they tended, in most parts of the empire, gradually to become merged into the mass of the native population, through their marriages with Chinese women and their adoption of Chinese habits and manners. The founder of the new Ming dynasty, the emperor Hung-wu, extended to them many privileges, and their flourishing condition during the period that this dynasty lasted (1368–1644) is shown by the large number of mosques erected.

The emperors of this dynasty cultivated friendly relations with the Muhammadan princes on their western frontier, and there was a frequent interchange of embassies between them and the Tīmūrid princes. One of these is of interest in the missionary history of Islam, inasmuch as Shāh Rukh Bahādur in 1412 took advantage of the arrival of a Chinese embassy at his court in Samarqand, to include in his answer an invitation to the emperor to embrace Islam. He sent with his envoy, who accompanied the Chinese ambassadors on their return, two letters, the first of which, written in Arabic, was to the following effect :—" In the name of God, the Merciful, the Compassionate. There is no god save God: Muḥammad is the Apostle of God. The Apostle of God, Muḥammad (peace be on him !) said : ' There shall not cease to be in my church a people abiding in the commandments of God; whosoever fails to help them or opposes them, shall never prosper, until the commandment of the Lord cometh.' When the Most High God purposed to create Adam and his race, he said ' I was a hidden treasure, but it was my pleasure to become known; I therefore created man that I might be known '; It is manifest from hence that the divine purpose (great is His power and exalted is His word !) in the creation of man was to make Himself known and uplift the banners of right guidance and faith. Wherefore He sent His Apostle with guidance and the religion of truth that it might prevail over all other faiths, though the polytheists turn away from it, that he might make known the laws and the ordinances and the observances of what is lawful and unlawful, and He gave him the holy Qur'ān miraculously that thereby he might put to silence the unbelievers and stop their mouths when they discussed and disputed with him, and by His perfect grace and His all-pervading guidance He has caused it to remain even unto the day of judgment. By His power He hath established in all ages and times and in all parts of the world, in east and west, and in China, a mighty monarch, lord of great armies and authority, to administer justice and mercy and spread the wings of peace and security over the heads of men; to enjoin upon them righteousness and warn them against evil and disobedience and lift up among them the banners of the noble religion; and he drives away idolatry and infidelity from among them through belief in the unity of God. The Most High God thus disposeth our hearts by His past mercies and His ensuing grace to strive for the stablishing of the laws of pure religion and the continuance of the ordinances of the shining path. He also bids us administer justice to our subjects in all suits and cases in accordance with the religion of the Prophet and the ordinances of the Chosen One, and build mosques and colleges and monasteries and hermitages and places of worship, that the teaching of the sciences and the schools of learning may not cease nor the memorials and injunctions of religion be swept away. Seeing that the continuance of worldly prosperity and dominion, and the permanence of authority and rule depend upon the assistance given to truth and righteousness and the extirpation of the evils caused by idolatry and unbelief from the earth, in the expectation of blessing and reward, we, therefore, hope that your Majesty and the nobles of your realm will agree with us in these matters and join us in strengthening the foundations of the established law." The other letter, written in Persian, makes a more direct appeal, without the rhetorical embellishments of the Arabic:—"The Most High God, having in the depth of His wisdom and the perfection of His power created Adam (peace be upon him!), made some of his sons prophets and apostles and sent them among men to summon them to the truth. To certain of these prophets, such as Abraham, Moses, David and Muḥammad (peace be upon them !) He gave a book and taught a law, and He bade the people of their time follow the law and the religion of each of them. All these apostles invited men to faith in the unity and to the worship of God and forbade the adoration of the sun, moon and stars, of kings and idols; and though each one of these apostles had a separate law, yet they were all agreed in the doctrine of the unity of the Most High God. At length, when the apostolic and prophetic office devolved on the Apostle Muḥammad Muṣṭafā (the peace and blessing of God be upon him !) all other systems of law were abrogated. He was the apostle and the prophet of the latter age, and it behoves the whole world—lords and kings and ministers, rich and poor, small and great,—to observe his law and forsake all past creeds and laws. This is the true and perfect faith and is called Islam. Some years ago, Chingīz Khān took up arms and sent his sons into various countries and kingdoms—Jūjī Khān to the confines of Sarāy, Qrim and Dasht Qafchāq, where some monarchs, such as Ūzbek Khān, Chānī Khān and Urus Khān, became Musalmans and observed the law of Muḥammad (peace be upon him !). Hūlāgū Khān was set over Khurāsān, 'Irāq and the neighbouring countries, and some of his sons who succeeded him received into their hearts the light of the law of Muḥammad (peace be upon him !), and in like manner became Musalmans, and honoured with the blessedness of Islam passed into the other world, such as the truthful king, Ghāzān, and Uljāytū Sulṭān and the fortunate king, Abū Sa'īd Bahādur, until my honoured father, Amīr Tīmūr Gūrgān, succeeded to the throne. He too observed the law of Muḥammad (peace be upon him !) in all the countries under his rule, and throughout his reign the followers of the faith of Islam enjoyed complete prosperity. Now that by the goodness and favour of God this Kingdom of Khurāsān, 'Irāq, Mā-warā'-al-nahr, etc., has passed into my hands, the administration is carried on throughout the whole kingdom in accordance with the pure law of the Prophet; righteousness is enjoined and wrong forbidden, and the Yarghū and the institutes of Chingīz Khān have been abolished.

Since, then, it is sure and certain that salvation and deliverance in the day of judgment, and sovereignty and felicity in the present world, depend upon true faith and Islam, and the favour of the Most High God, it is incumbent upon us to treat our subjects with justice and equity. I hope that by the bounty and benevolence of God you too will observe the law of Muḥammad, the Apostle of God (peace be upon him !) and strengthen the religion of Islam, so that you may exchange the transitory sovereignty of this world for the sovereignty of the world to come." [1]

It is not improbable that these letters gave rise to the later legend of one of the Chinese emperors having become a convert to Islam.[2] This legend is referred to, among others, by a Muhammadan merchant, Sayyid 'Alī Akbar, who spent some years in Peking at the end of the fifteenth and the beginning of the sixteenth century; he speaks of the large number of Musalmans who had settled in China; in the city of Kenjanfu there were as many as 30,000 Muslim families; they paid no taxes and enjoyed the favour of the emperor, who gave them grants of land; they enjoyed complete toleration for the exercise of their religion, which was favourably viewed by the Chinese, and conversions were freely permitted; in the capital itself there were four great mosques and about ninety more in other provinces of the empire,—all erected at the cost of the emperor.[3]

Up to the establishment of the Manchu dynasty in 1644 there is no record of any Muhammadan uprising, and the followers of Islam appear to have been entirely content with the religious liberty they enjoyed; but difficulties arose soon after the advent of the new ruling power, and an insurrection in the province of Kansu in 1648 was the first occasion on which any Muhammadans rose in arms against the Chinese government, though it was not until the nineteenth century that any such revolt entailed very disastrous consequences, or seriously interrupted the amicable relations that had subsisted from the beginning between the Chinese Muslims

[1] 'Abd al-Razzāq al-Samarqandī: Maṭla' al-sa'dayn, foll. 60–1. (Blochet, pp. 249–52.)

[2] Zenker, pp. 798–9. Mélanges Orientaux, p. 65. (Publications de l'École des Langues Orientales Vivantes, Sér. ii. t. 9.) (Paris, 1883.)

[3] Schefer, pp. 29–30. Zenker, p. 796.

and their rulers. The official view of the Chinese Government of these relations is set forth in an edict published by the emperor Yung Chen in 1731 :—" In every province of the empire, for many centuries past, have been found a large number of Muhammadans who form part of the people whom I regard as my own children just as I do my other subjects. I make no distinction between them and those who do not belong to their religion. I have received from certain officials secret complaints against the Muhammadans on the ground that their religion differs from that of the other Chinese, that they do not speak the same language, and wear a different dress to the rest of the people. They are accused of disobedience, haughtiness, and rebellious feelings, and I have been asked to employ severe measures against them. After examining these complaints and accusations, I have discovered that there is no foundation for them. In fact, the religion followed by the Musalmans is that of their ancestors; it is true their language is not the same as that of the rest of the Chinese, but what a multitude of different dialects there are in China. As to their temples, dress and manner of writing, which differ from those of the other Chinese—these are matters of absolutely no importance. These are mere matters of custom. They bear as good a character as my other subjects, and there is nothing to show that they intend to rebel. It is my wish, therefore, that they should be left in the free exercise of their religion, whose object is to teach men the observance of a moral life, and the fulfilment of social and civil duties. This religion respects the fundamental basis of Government, and what more can be asked for ? If then the Muhammadans continue to conduct themselves as good and loyal subjects, my favour will be extended towards them just as much as towards my other children. From among them have come many civil and military officers, who have risen to the very highest ranks. This is the best proof that they have adopted our habits and customs, and have learned to conform themselves to the precepts of our sacred books. They pass their examinations in literature just like every one else, and perform the sacrifices enjoined by law. In a word, they are true members of the great Chinese family and endeavour always to fulfil their religious, civil and political duties. When the magistrates have a civil case brought before them, they should not concern themselves with the religion of the litigants. There is but one single law for all my subjects. Those who do good shall be rewarded, and those who do evil shall be punished." [1]

About thirty years later, his successor, the Emperor K'ien Lung, showed distinguished marks of his favour towards the Muhammadans by ennobling two Turkī Begs who had materially helped in suppressing a revolt in the north-west and Kashgar, and building palaces for them in Peking; he also erected a mosque for the use of the Turkī Begs who visited the Imperial court and for the prisoners of war who had been brought to the capital from Kāshgar. Among these prisoners was a beautiful girl who became a favourite concubine of the emperor, and it is stated that for love of her he built this mosque immediately opposite his own palace and erected a pavilion within the palace grounds, from which the concubine could watch her fellow-countrymen at prayer and could join in their devotions. This mosque was built in the years 1763–1764 and contains an inscription in four languages, the Chinese text of which was written by the emperor himself.[2]

After crushing the revolt in Zungaria, this same emperor K'ien Lung, in 1770 transported thither from other parts of China ten thousand military colonists, who were followed by their families and other persons, to re-people the country, and they are all said to have embraced the religion of the surrounding Muhammadan population.[3] Whether such mass conversions occurred in other parts of the empire also, we have no means of telling, but the existence of a considerable Muhammadan population in every province of China can hardly be explained merely by reference to foreign immigration and the natural growth of population,[4] though the numbers are larger in those provinces in which foreign

[1] De Thiersant, tome i. pp. 154–6.
[2] Broomhall, p. 92 sqq. Devéria: Musulmans et Manichéens chinois. (J. A. 9me Sér., tome x. p. 447 sqq.)
[3] De Thiersant, tome i. pp. 163–4.
[4] The Muhammadans are said to be more prolific than the ordinary Chinese, and the Chinese census, which counts according to families, estimates six for a Muhammadan family and five for the ordinary Chinese. (Broomhall, pp. 197, 203.)

Muhammadans have settled.[1] It is unlikely that the Muhammadans in China during the many centuries of their residence in this country, in the enjoyment of religious freedom and the liberal patronage of several of the emperors, should have been entirely devoid of that proselytising zeal which modern observers have noted in their descendants at the present day.[2] To such direct proselytising efforts must have been due the conversion of Chinese Jews to Islam; their establishment in this country dates from an early period, they held employments under the Government and were in possession of large estates; but by the close of the seventeenth century a great part of them had been converted to Islam.[3] Such propaganda must have been quite quiet and unobtrusive, and indeed more public methods might have excited suspicions on the part of the Government, as is shown by an interesting report which was sent to the Emperor K'ien Lung in 1783 by a governor of the province of Khwang-Se. It runs as follows: "I have the honour respectfully to inform your Majesty that an adventurer named Han-Fo-Yun, of the province of Khwang-Se, has been arrested on a charge of vagrancy. This adventurer when interrogated as to his occupation, confessed that for the last ten years he had been travelling through the different provinces of the Empire in order to obtain information about his religion. In one of his boxes were found thirty books, some of which had been written by himself, while others were in a language that no one here understands. These books praise in an extravagant and ridiculous manner a Western king, called Muḥammad. The above-mentioned Han-Fo-Yun, when put to the torture, at last confessed that the real object of his journey was to propagate the false religion taught in these books, and that he remained in the province of Shen-Si for a longer time than anywhere else. I have examined these books myself. Some are certainly written in a foreign language; for I have not been able to understand them: the others that are written in Chinese

[1] Broomhall, in chap. xii. of his Islam in China, gives the total as between five and ten millions. D'Ollone puts it as low as four millions (p. 430).

[2] Vide infra, pp. 309–310.

[3] Clark Abel: Narrative of a journey in the interior of China, p. 361. (London, 1818.)

are very bad, I may add, even ridiculous on account of the exaggerated praise given in them to persons who certainly do not deserve it, because I have never even heard of them. Perhaps the above-mentioned Han-Fo-Yun is a rebel from Kan-Su. His conduct is certainly suspicious, for what was he going to do in the provinces through which he has been travelling for the last ten years? I intend to make a serious inquiry into the matter. Meanwhile, I would request your Majesty to order the stereotyped plates, that are in the possession of his family, to be burnt, and the engravers to be arrested, as well as the authors of the books, which I have sent to your Majesty desiring to know your pleasure in the matter." [1]

This report bears testimony to the activity of at least one Muhammadan missionary in the eighteenth century, and the growth of Islam, which the Jesuit missionaries [2] noted in the eighteenth century, was probably not so little connected with direct proselytism as some of them supposed. Du Halde, in one of the few passages he devotes to the Muhammadans in his great work,[3] attributes the increase in their numbers largely to their habit of purchasing children in times of famine. "The Mahometans have been settled for more than six hundred years in various provinces, where they live quite quietly, because they do not make any great efforts to spread their doctrines and gain proselytes, and because in former times they only increased in numbers by the alliances and marriages they contracted. But for several years past they have continued to make very considerable progress by means of their wealth. They buy up heathen children everywhere; and the parents, being often unable to provide them with food, have no scruples in selling them. During a famine that devastated the Province of Chantong, they bought more than 10,000 of them. They marry them, and either purchase or build for them separate quarters in a town, or even whole villages; gradually in several places

[1] De Thiersant, tome ii. pp. 361–3.

[2] One missionary, writing from Peking in 1721, says, "Le secte des Mahométans s'étend de plus en plus." (Lettres édifiantes et curieuses, tome xix. p. 140.)

[3] J. B. du Halde: Description géographique, historique, chronologique, politique et physique de l'Empire de la Chine, tome iii. p. 64. (Paris, 1735.)

they gain such influence that they do not let any one live among them who does not go to the mosque. By such means they have multiplied exceedingly during the last century."

Similarly, in the famine that devastated the province of Kwangtung in 1790, as many as ten thousand children are said to have been purchased by the Muhammadans from parents who, too poor to support them, were willing to part with them to save them from starvation; these were all brought up in the faith of Islam.[1] A Chinese Musalman, from Yunnan, named Sayyid Sulaymān, who visited Cairo in 1894 and was there interviewed by the representative of an Arabic journal,[2] declared that the number of accessions to Islam gained in this way every year was beyond counting. Similar testimony is given by M. d'Ollone, who reports that this practice of buying children in times of famine prevails among the Muhammadans throughout the whole of China to the present day; in the same way, they purchased the children of Christian parents who were massacred by the Boxers in 1900, and brought them up as Musalmans.[3]

The Muhammadans in China tend to live together in separate villages and towns or to form separate Muhammadan quarters in the towns, where they will not allow any person to dwell among them who does not go to the mosque.[4] Though they thus in some measure hold themselves apart, they are careful to avoid the open exhibition of any specially distinguishing features of the religious observances of their faith, which may offend their neighbours, and they have been careful to make concessions to the prejudices of their Chinese fellow-countrymen. In their ordinary life they are completely in touch with the customs and habits that prevail around them; they wear the pigtail and the ordinary dress of the Chinese, and put on a turban, as a rule, only in the mosque. To avoid offending against a superstitious prejudice on the part of the Chinese, they also refrain from building tall minarets, wherever they build them at all.[5] But for the most part, their mosques conform to the Chinese

[1] Anderson, p. 151. Grosier, tome iv. p. 507.
[2] Thamarāt al-Funūn, 17th Shawwāl, p. 3. (Bayrūt, A.H. 1311.)
[3] Mission d'Ollone, p. 279. R. du M.M., tome ix. pp. 577, 578.
[4] Broomhall, p. 226. Grosier, tome iv. p. 508. [5] Vasil'ev, p. 15.

type of architecture, often with nothing to distinguish them from an ordinary temple or dwelling.[1] Every mosque is obliged by law to have a tablet to the emperor, with the inscription on it, " The emperor, the immortal, may he live for ever," and the Muhammadans prostrate themselves before it in accordance with the regular Chinese custom, though with various expedients to satisfy their consciences and avoid the imputation of idolatry.[2] Even in Chinese Tartary, where the special privilege is allowed to the Musalman soldiers, of remaining unmixed, and of forming a separate body, the higher Muhammadan officials wear the dress prescribed to their rank, long moustaches and the pigtail, and on holidays they perform the usual homage demanded from officials, to a portrait of the emperor, by touching the ground three times with their forehead.[3] Similarly all Muhammadan mandarins and other officials in other provinces perform the rites prescribed to their official position, in the temples of Confucius on festival days; in fact every precaution is taken by the Muslims to prevent their faith from appearing to be in opposition to the state religion, and hereby they have succeeded in avoiding the odium with which the adherents of foreign religions, such as Judaism and Christianity are regarded. They even represent their religion to their Chinese fellow-countrymen as being in agreement with the teachings of Confucius, with only this difference, that they follow the traditions of their ancestors with regard to marriages, funerals, the prohibition of pork, wine, tobacco, and games of chance, and the washing of the hands before meals.[4] Similarly the writings of the Chinese Muhammadans treat the works of Confucius and other Chinese classics with great respect, and where possible, point out the harmony between the teachings contained therein and the doctrines of Islam.[5]

The Chinese government, in its turn, has always given to its Muhammadan subjects (except when in revolt) the same privileges and advantages as are enjoyed by the rest of the population. No office of state is closed to them; and as

[1] Broomhall, p. 237. [2] Id. pp. 186, 228.
[3] Arminius Vambéry: Travels in Central Asia, p. 404. (London, 1864.)
[4] Vasil'ev, p. 16. [5] De Thiersant, tome ii. pp. 367, 372.

governors of provinces, generals, magistrates and ministers of state they enjoy the confidence and respect both of the rulers and the people. Not only do Muhammadan names appear in the Chinese annals as those of famous officers of state, whether military or civil, but they have also distinguished themselves in the mechanical arts and in sciences such as mathematics and astronomy.[1]

The Chinese Muhammadans are also said to be keen men of business and successful traders; they monopolise the beef trade and carry on other trades with great success.[2] They are thus in touch with every section of the national life and have every opportunity for carrying on a propaganda, but the few Christian missionaries who have concerned themselves with this matter are of opinion that they are not animated with any particular proselytising zeal.[3] Still, many recent converts are to be met with, and the fact that a large number of Chinese Muslims can cite the name of the particular ancestor who first embraced Islam points to a continuous process of conversion.[4] Apparently the Muslims are not allowed to preach their faith in the streets, as Protestant missionaries do,[5] but (as we have seen above)[6] they do not fail to make use of such opportunities as present themselves for adding to the number of their sect. One of their religious text-books, "A Guide to the Rites of the True Religion" (published in Canton in 1668), commends the work of proselytising and makes reference to such as may have recently become converts from among the heathen.[7] The fundamental doctrines of Islam are taught to the new converts by means of metrical primers,[8] and to the influence of the religious books of the Chinese Muslims, Sayyid Sulaymān attributes many of the conversions made in recent years.[9] The Muslim seminary at Hochow in Kansu is said to train theological students who return to their several provinces, at the completion of their studies, to promulgate their faith there,[10] and in upwards of ten provinces centres are said to

[1] De Thiersant, tome i. p. 247. T͟hamarāt al-Funūn, 28th Sha'bān, p. 3.
[2] Broomhall, p. 224.
[3] Du Halde, loc. cit. Broomhall, p. 282.
[4] Mission d'Ollone, pp. 210, 431.
[5] Broomhall, pp. 274, 282.
[6] p. 307.
[7] Broomhall, pp. 231–2.
[8] W. J. Smith, p. 175. Mission d'Ollone, p. 407 sqq.
[9] T͟hamarāt al-Funūn, loc. cit.
[10] Broomhall, p. 240.

have been started where mullās are to be trained for Muslim propaganda.[1] Military officers convert many of the soldiers serving under them, to Islam, and Muslim mandarins take advantage of the authority they enjoy, to win converts, but as they are frequently transferred from one place to another, they are not able to exercise so much influence as Muslim military officers.[2] Conversions may also occasionally occur, which are not the result of a direct propagandist appeal, e. g. a Turkish traveller who visited Peking in 1895 reported that he found thirty mosques there, among them one that had originally been a temple; this had been the family temple of a wealthy Chinaman, whose life had been saved during the Boxer insurrection by the Mufti Wa-Ahonad ('Abd al-Raḥmān); as a token of his gratitude, he embraced the faith of his deliverer.[3]

Turkish and other Muslim missionaries have in recent years been visiting China and endeavouring to stir up among the Chinese Muslims a more thorough knowledge of their faith and to awaken their zeal, but their efforts seem so far to have borne but little fruit.[4]

In 1867 a Russian writer,[5] in a remarkable work on Islam in China, expressed the opinion that it was destined to become the national faith of the Chinese empire and thereby entirely change the political conditions of the Eastern world. Nearly half a century has elapsed since this note of alarm was sounded, but nothing has occurred since to verify these prognostications. On the contrary, it would appear that Islam has been losing rather than gaining ground during the last century, since the wholesale massacres that accompanied the suppression of the Panthay risings in Yunnan from 1855 to 1873 and the Tungan rebellion in Shen-si and Kan-su in 1864–1877 and 1895–1896, reduced the Muhammadan population by millions.[6] The establishment of the new Republic has given to the Chinese Muslims a freedom of activity unknown under any preceding government, but it is too early yet to discover how far they are likely to avail themselves of the

[1] The Missionary Review of the World, vol. xxv. p. 786 (1912).
[2] Mission d'Ollone, p. 431.
[3] R. du M. M., iii. p. 124 (1907).
[4] Broomhall, pp. 242, 286, 292 sqq.
[5] Vasil'ev, pp. 3, 5, 14, 17.
[6] For a longer list of Muhammadan insurrections, see Mission d'Ollone, p. 436.

opportunities offered by the altered conditions of life. The proselytism that still goes on, restricted as its sphere may be, indicates a still cherished hope of expansion. Though four centuries have elapsed since a Muslim traveller [1] in China could discuss the possibility of the conversion of the emperor being followed by that of his subjects, it was still possible for a Chinese Muslim of the present generation to state that his co-religionists in that country looked forward with confidence to the day when Islam would be triumphant throughout the length and breadth of the Chinese empire.[2]

[1] Sayyid 'Alī Akbar: Khiṭāy Nāmah, p. 83. "If the emperor of China embraces Islam, his subjects must inevitably become Muslims too, because they all worship him to such an extent that they accept whatever he says, and when that light coming from the West grows in strength, the unbelievers of the East will come flocking into Islam without showing any contention, because they are free from all fanaticism in matters of religion."

[2] Thamarāt al-Funūn, 26th Shawwāl, p. 3. (A.H. 1311.)

CHAPTER XI.

THE SPREAD OF ISLAM IN AFRICA.

THE history of Islam in Africa, covering as it does a period of well-nigh thirteen centuries and embracing two-thirds of this vast continent, with its numerous and diverse tribes and races, presents especial difficulties in the way of systematic treatment, as it is impossible to give a simultaneous account in chronological order of the spread of this faith in all the different parts of the continent. Its relations to the Christian Churches of Egypt and the rest of North Africa, of Nubia and Abyssinia have already been dealt with in a former chapter; in the present chapter it is proposed to trace its progress first among the heathen population of North Africa, then throughout the Suđan and along the West coast, and lastly along the East coast and in Cape Colony.[1]

The information we possess of the spread of Islam among the heathen population of North Africa is hardly less meagre than the few facts recorded above regarding the disappearance of the Christian Church. The Berbers offered a vigorous resistance to the progress of the Arab arms, and force seems to have had more influence than persuasion in their conversion. Whenever opportunity presented itself, they rebelled against the religion as well as the rule of their conquerors, and Arab historians declare that they apostasised as many as twelve times.[2] In the annals of the long struggle a few scanty references to conversions are to be found. These would appear sometimes to have been prompted by the recognition of the fact that further resistance to the

[1] An excellent map of the extent of Islam in Africa is to be found in "The International Review of Missions," vol. i. p. 652.

[2] Fournel, vol. i. p. 271.

Arab arms was useless. When in 703 the Berbers made their last stand against the invaders, their intrepid leader and prophetess, al-Kāhinah,[1] foreseeing that the fortune of battle was to turn against them, sent her sons into the camp of the Muslim general with instructions that they were to embrace Islam and make common cause with the enemy; she herself elected to fall fighting with her countrymen in the great battle that crushed the political power of the Berbers and gave Northern Africa into the hands of the Arabs. Peace was made on condition that the Berbers would furnish 12,000 combatants to the ranks of the Arab troops, and of these men two army-corps were formed, each of which was placed under the command of one of the sons of al-Kāhinah.[2] By this device of enlisting the Berbers in their armies, the Arab generals hoped to win them to their own religion by the hope of booty.

The army of seven thousand Berbers that sailed from Africa in 711 under the command of Ṭāriq (himself a Berber) to the conquest of Spain, was composed of recent converts to Islam, and their conversion is expressly said to have been sincere: learned Arabs and theologians were appointed, "to read and explain to them the sacred words of the Qur'ān, and instruct them in all and every one of the duties enjoined by their new religion."[3] Mūsā, the great conqueror of Africa, showed his zeal for the progress of Islam by devoting the large sums of money granted him by the caliph 'Abd al-Malik to the purchase of such captives as gave promise of showing themselves worthy children of the faith: "for whenever after a victory there was a number of slaves put up for sale, he used to buy all those whom he thought would willingly embrace Islam, who were of noble origin, and who looked, besides, as if they were active young men. To these he first proposed the embracing of Islam, and if, after cleansing their understanding and making them fit to receive its sublime truths, they were converted to the best of religions, and their conversion was a sincere one, he then would, by way of putting their abilities to trial, employ them. If they evinced good disposition and talents

[1] i.e. the diviner or priestess; her real name is unknown.
[2] Fournel, vol. i. p. 224.
[3] Makkarī, vol. i. p. 253.

he would instantly grant them liberty, appoint them to high commands in his army, and promote them according to their merits; if, on the contrary, they showed no aptitude for their appointments, he would send them back to the common depôt of captives belonging to the army, to be again disposed of according to the general custom of drawing out the spoil by arrows." [1]

How superficial the conversion of the Berbers was may be judged from the fact that when the pious 'Umar b. 'Abd al-'Azīz in A.H. 100 (A.D. 718) appointed Ismā'īl b. 'Abd Allāh governor of North Africa, ten learned theologians were sent with him to instruct the Muslim Berbers in the ordinances of their faith, since up to that time they do not seem to have recognised that their new religion forbade to them indulgence in wine. The new governor is said to have shown great zeal in inviting the Berbers to accept Islam, but the statement that his efforts were crowned with such success that not a single Berber remained unconverted is certainly not correct.[2] For the conversion of the Berbers was undoubtedly the work of several centuries; even to the present day they retain many of their primitive institutions which are in opposition to Muslim law.[3] Islam took no firm root among them until it assumed the form of a national movement and became connected with the establishment of native dynasties, under which many Berbers came within the pale of Islam who before had looked upon the acceptance of this faith as a sign of loss of political independence. Of these various changes of political condition it is not the place to speak here, but in a history of Muslim propaganda the rise of the Almoravids deserves special mention as a great national movement that attracted a great many of the Berber tribes to join the Muslim community. In the early part of the eleventh century, Yaḥyā b. Ibrāhīm, a chief of the Ṣanhāja, one of the Berber tribes of the Sahara, on his return from a pilgrimage to Mecca, sought in the religious centres of Northern Africa for a learned and pious teacher, who should accompany him as a missionary of Islam to his

[1] Makkarī, vol. i. p. lxv.

[2] Fournel, vol. i. p. 270.

[3] For these and the heretical movements that reveal survivals of the earlier Berber faith, see Goldziher, Materialen zur Kenntniss der Almohadenbewegung in Nordafrika (Z D M G, vol. xli, p. 37 sqq.).

benighted and ignorant tribesmen: at first he found it difficult to find a man willing to leave his scholarly retreat and brave the dangers of the Sahara, but at length he met in 'Abd Allāh b. Yāsīn the fit person, bold enough to undertake so difficult a mission, pious and austere in his life, and learned in theology, law and other sciences. So far back as the ninth century the preachers of Islam had made their way among the Berbers of the Sahara and established among them the religion of the Prophet, but this faith had found very little acceptance there, and 'Abd Allāh b. Yāsīn found even the professed Muslims to be very lax in their religious observances and given up to all kinds of vicious practices. He ardently threw himself into the task of converting them to the right path and instructing them in the duties of religion; but the sternness with which he rebuked their vices and sought to reform their conduct, alienated their sympathies from him, and the ill-success of his mission almost drove him to abandon this stiff-necked people and devote his efforts to the conversion of the Sudan. Being persuaded, however, not to desert the work he had once undertaken, he retired with such disciples as his preaching had gathered around him, to an island in the river Senegal, where they founded a monastery and gave themselves up unceasingly to devotional exercises. The more devout-minded among the Berbers, stung to repentance by the thought of the wickedness that had driven their holy teacher from their midst, came humbly to his island to implore his forgiveness and receive his instructions in the saving truths of religion. Thus day by day there gathered around him an increasing band of disciples, especially from among the Lamtūna, a branch of the Ṣanhāja clan, whose numbers swelled at length to about a thousand. 'Abd Allāh b. Yāsīn then recognised that the time had come for launching out upon a wider sphere of action, and he called upon his followers to show their gratitude to God for the revelation he had vouchsafed them, by communicating the knowledge of it to others: "Go to your fellow-tribesmen, teach them the law of God and threaten them with His chastisement. If they repent, amend their ways and accept the truth, leave them in peace: if they refuse and persist in their errors and evil lives, invoke the aid of God against them, and let us make war upon them until God decide between us." Hereupon each man went to his own tribe and began to exhort them to repent and believe, but without success: equally unsuccessful were the efforts of ʻAbd Allāh b. Yāsīn himself, who left his monastery in the hope of finding the Berber chiefs more willing now to listen to his preaching. At length in 1042 he put himself at the head of his followers, to whom he had given the name of al-Murābiṭīn (the so-called Almoravids)—a name derived from the same root as the ribāṭ [1] or monastery on his island in the Senegal,—and attacked the neighbouring tribes and forced the acceptance of Islam upon them. The success that attended his warlike expeditions appeared to the tribes of the Sahara a more persuasive argument than all his preaching, and they very soon came forward voluntarily to embrace a faith that secured such brilliant successes to the arms of its adherents. ʻAbd Allāh b. Yāsīn died in 1059, but the movement he had initiated lived after him and many heathen tribes of Berbers came to swell the numbers of their Muslim fellow-countrymen, embracing their religion at the same time as the cause they championed, and poured out of the Sahara over North Africa and later on made themselves masters of Spain also.[2]

It is not improbable that the other great national movement that originated among the Berber tribes, viz. the rise of the Almohads at the beginning of the twelfth century, may have attracted into the Muslim community some of the tribes that had up to that time still stood aloof. Their founder, Ibn Tūmart, popularised the sternly Unitarian tenets of this sect by means of works in the Berber language which expounded from his own point of view the fundamental doctrines of Islam, and he made a still further concession to the nationalist spirit of the Berbers by ordering the call to prayer to be made in their own language.[3]

Some of the Berber tribes, however, remained heathen up

[1] On this word, see Doutté, Notes sur l'Islam maghribin. (Revue de l'histoire des religions, tom. xli. p. 24–6.)
[2] Ibn abī Zarʻ, pp. 168–73. A. Müller, vol. ii. pp. 611–13.
[3] Ibn abī Zarʻ, p. 250. Goldziher, *op. laud.*, p. 71.

to the close of the fifteenth century,[1] but the general tendency was naturally towards an absorption of these smaller communities into the larger.

The sixteenth century witnessed the birth of a movement of active proselytising in the Maghrib, which has been traced to the reaction excited by the successes of the Christian powers in Spain and North Africa. This gave an immense impulse to the institution of the "marabouts," [2] and large numbers of them set out from the monastic settlements in the south of Morocco to carry a peaceful missionary campaign throughout the Maghrib, renewing the faith of the lukewarm adherents of Islam and converting their heathen neighbours.[3] To this proselytising movement the Muslim refugees from Spain contributed their part, as has been shown above (p. 127), coming to the aid of the Shurafā' or descendants of Idrīs b. 'Abd Allāh, who had fled to Morocco to escape the wrath of Hārūn al-Rashīd.[4]

From the Sahara the knowledge of Islam first spread among the Negroes of the Sudan. The early history of this movement is wrapped in obscurity, but there seems little doubt that it was the Berbers who first introduced Islam into the lands watered by the Senegal and the Niger; here they came in contact with pagan kingdoms, some of them (e. g. Ghāna and Songhay) of great antiquity.[5] The two Berber tribes, the Lamṭūna and the Jadāla, belonging to the Ṣanhāja clan, especially distinguished themselves by their religious zeal in the work of conversion,[6] and through their agency the Almoravid movement reacted on the pagan tribes of the Sudan. The reign of Yūsuf b. Tāshfīn, the founder of Morocco (A.D. 1062) and the second amīr of the Almoravid dynasty, was very fruitful in conversions, and many Negroes under his rule came to know of the doctrines of Muḥammad.[7] In 1076 the Berbers who

[1] Leo Africanus. (Ramusio, tom. i. p. 11.) [2] مرابط.
[3] Doutté, xl. p. 354; xli. pp. 26–7. [4] Depont et Coppolani, p. 127 sq.
[5] It is not the place here to deal with the rise and political history of the various kingdoms of the Western Sudan; this has been done most fully for the English reader by Lady Lugard in her work entitled, "A Tropical Dependency. An Outline of the Ancient History of the Western Sudan, with an Account of the Modern Settlement of Northern Nigeria." (London, 1905.) See also H. F. Helmolt: The World's History, vol. iii. chap. ix. (London, 1903.) [6] Blau, p. 322.
[7] Leo Africanus. (Ramusio, tom. i. pp. 7, 77.)

had been spreading Islam in the kingdom of Ghāna for some time, drove out the reigning dynasty, which was probably Fulbe, and this ancient kingdom became throughout Muhammadan; at the beginning of the thirteenth century it lost its independence and was conquered by the Mandingos.[1]

Of the introduction of Islam into the ancient kingdom of Songhay, which is said to have been in existence as early as A.D. 700, we have only the record that the first Muhammadan king was named Zā-kassi, the fifteenth monarch of the Zā dynasty; his conversion took place in the year A.H. 400 (A.D. 1009–1010), and in the Songhay language he was styled Muslim-dam, which implied that he had adopted Islam of his own free will and not by compulsion, but there is no mention of the influences to which he owed his conversion.[2]

In the same century there were founded on the Upper Niger two cities, destined in succeeding centuries to exercise an immense influence on the development of Islam in the Western Sudan,—Jenne,[3] founded in A.H. 435 (A.D. 1043–1044),[4] and destined to become an important trading centre, and Timbuktu, the great emporium for the caravan trade with the north, founded about the year A.D. 1100. The king of Jenne, Kunburu, became a Muslim towards the end of the sixth century of the Hijrah (i. e. about A.D. 1200) and his example was followed by the inhabitants of the city; when he had made up his mind to embrace Islam, he is said to have collected together all the 'ulamā' in his kingdom, to the number of 4200—(however exaggerated this number may be, the story would seem to imply that Islam had already made considerable progress in his dominions)—and publicly in their presence declared himself a Muslim and exhorted them to pray for the prosperity of his city; he then had his palace pulled down and built a great mosque[5] in its place.[6] Timbuktu, on the other hand, was a Muham-

[1] Meyer, p. 91.

[2] Ta'rīkh al-Sūdān, p. 3.

[3] Jinnī or Dienné.

[4] So Meyer following Barth; the Ta'rīkh al-Sūdān (p. 12) places the date about three centuries earlier.

[5] Félix Dubois gives a plan and reconstruction of this mosque, which was destroyed by order of Shaykhu Aḥmadu about 1830, in "Tombouctou la Mystérieuse," chap. ix.

[6] Ta'rīkh al-Sūdān, pp. 12–13.

madan city from the beginning; "never did the worship of idols defile it, never did any man prostrate himself on its soil except in prayer to God the Merciful."[1] In later years it became influential as a seat of Muhammadan learning and piety, and students and divines flocked there in large numbers, attracted by the encouragement and patronage they received. Ibn Baṭūṭah, who travelled through this country in the middle of the fourteenth century, praises the Negroes for their zeal in the performance of their devotions and in the study of the Qur'ān: unless one went very early to the mosque on Friday, he tells us, it was impossible to find a place, so crowded was the attendance.[2] In his time, the most powerful state of the Western Sudan was that of Melle or Māllī, which had risen to importance about a century before, after the conquest of Ghāna by the Mandingos, one of the finest races of Africa: Leo Africanus[3] calls them the most civilised, the most intellectual and most respected of all the Negroes, and modern travellers praise them for their industry, cleverness and trustworthiness.[4] These Mandingos have been among the most active missionaries of Islam, which has been spread by them among the neighbouring peoples.[5]

According to the Kano Chronicle it was the Mandingos who brought the knowledge of Islam to the Hausa people; the date is uncertain,[6] as are most dates connected with the history of the Hausa states, because the Fulbe, who conquered them at the beginning of the nineteenth century, destroyed most of their historical records. But the importance of the adoption of Islam by the Hausas cannot be exaggerated; they are an energetic and intelligent people, and their remarkable aptitude for trade has won for them

[1] Ta'rīkh al-Sūdān, p. 21.
[2] Ibn Baṭūṭah, tome iv. pp. 421–2.
[3] Ramusio, tom. i. p. 78.
[4] Winwood Reade describes them as "a tall, handsome, light-coloured race, Moslems in religion, possessing horses and large herds of cattle, but also cultivating cotton, ground-nuts, and various kinds of corn. I was much pleased with their kind and hospitable manners, the grave and decorous aspect of their women, the cleanliness and silence of their villages." (W. Winwood Reade: African Sketchbook, vol. i. p. 303.)
[5] Waitz, II[er] Theil, pp. 18–19.
[6] Palmer (p. 59) places its introduction into Kano between A.D. 1349 and 1385, another Hausa chronicle makes the reign of the first Muhammadan king of Zozo begin about 1456. (Journal of the African Society, vol. ix. p. 161.)

an immense influence among the various peoples with whom they have come in contact; their language has become the language of commerce for the Western Sudan, and wherever the Hausa traders go—and they are found from the coast of Guinea to Cairo—they carry the faith of Islam with them. References to their missionary activity will be found in the following pages. But of their own adoption of the faith, as well as of the rise of the seven Hausa states and their dependencies,[1] historical evidence is almost entirely wanting;[2] one of the missionaries of Islam to Kano and Katsena would certainly seem to have been a learned and pious teacher from Tlemsen, Muḥammad b. 'Abd al-Karīm b. Muḥammad al-Majīlī, who flourished about the year 1500;[3] possibly they were affected by the great wave of Muhammadan influence which moved southward from Egypt in the twelfth century.[4] The merchants of Kordofan and in the Eastern Sudan generally, boast that they are descended from Arabs who made their way thither after the fall of the Fāṭimid caliphate of Egypt in 1171. But there were probably still earlier instances of Muslim influence coming into Central Africa from the north-east. It was from Egypt that Islam spread into Kanem, a kingdom on the N. and N.E. of Lake Chad, which shortly after the adoption of Islam rose to be a state of considerable importance and extended its sway over the tribes of the Eastern Sudan to the borders of Egypt and Nubia; the first Muhammadan king of Kanem is said to have reigned either towards the close of the eleventh or in the first half of the twelfth century.[5] But the details we possess of the spread of Islam from the north-east are even more scanty than those already given for the history of the states of the Western Sudan. The mere dates of the

[1] For the various enumerations of these, see Meyer, p. 27.

[2] As in other parts of the Muslim world, tradition places the first introduction of Islam in the lifetime of the founder and gives the name of al-Fazāzī, a reputed companion of the Prophet, as the apostle of the Hausa people. (J. Lippert: Sudanica. MSOS, iii. part 3, p. 204. (Berlin, 1900.)

[3] Mischlich and Lippert, pp. 138–9.

[4] Meyer, loc. cit. Artin Pasha (p. 62) puts the beginning of this infiltration of Muslim Arabs as early as the eighth century.

[5] Becker, Geschichte des östlichen Sūdān, p. 162–3. Blau, p. 322. Oppel, p. 289. At the close of the fourteenth century 'Umar b. Idrīs moved his capital to the west of Lake Chad in the territory of Bornu, by which name the kingdom of Kanem became henceforth known.

conversion of kings and the establishment of Muhammadan dynasties tell us very little; but one fact stands out clearly from this meagre record, namely the extreme slowness of the process. The survival of considerable groups of fetish-worshippers in the midst of territories which for centuries were under Muhammadan rule, would seem to indicate that the influence of Islam was long confined to the towns and only by degrees made its way among the pagan population, if indeed it did not meet with such stubborn resistance as has kept the Bambara pagan, though (dwelling between the Upper Senegal and the Upper Niger) they have been hemmed in by a Muhammadan population for centuries.

An unsuccessful attempt to convert the Bambara was made by a marabout, named ‘Umaru Kaba, early in the twentieth century. This man had founded a new religious confraternity, connected with the Qādiriyyah, and having failed to attract his co-religionists to it, he turned his attention to the pagan Bambara, and endeavoured to convert them to Islam and enrol them in his order. He seemed to be on the road to success and had already converted a pagan village in the province of Sansanding, when the chief of the province drove the missionary across the frontier and ordered the newly-converted Bambara to return to their old religious observances.[1]

Where intermarriages with such races as Arabs and Berbers have been frequent, a steady process of infiltration has gone on, and this, added to the propagandist activities of those races—Fulbe, Hausa and Mandingo—who have distinguished themselves for their zeal on behalf of their religion, would have contributed to the more rapid growth of a Muhammadan population, had it not been for the internecine wars that caused one Muhammadan state to work the destruction of another. Melle rose on the ruins of Ghāna in the thirteenth century, to be crushed at the beginning of the sixteenth by Songhay, which in its turn was desolated by the Moors a century later. As these Muhammadan empires declined, with the wholesale massacres characteristic of warfare in the Sudan, fetishism regained much of the ground it had lost; and as in the

[1] Maurice Delafosse, p. 87.

Christian, so in the Muhammadan world, there have been periods when missionary zeal has sunk to a low ebb, and Muhammadans in some parts of the Sudan have been content to leave the paganism that surrounded them untouched by any proselytising efforts.

In the fourteenth century the Tunjar Arabs, emigrating south from Tunis, made their way through Bornu and Wadai to Darfur; others came in later from the east;[1] one of their number named Aḥmad met with a kind reception from the heathen king of Darfur, who took a fancy to him, made him director of his household and consulted him on all occasions. His experience of more civilised methods of government enabled him to introduce a number of reforms both into the economy of the king's household and the government of the state. By judicious management, he is said to have brought the unruly chieftains into subjection, and by portioning out the land among the poorer inhabitants to have put an end to the constant internal raids, thereby introducing a feeling of security and contentment before unknown. The king having no male heir gave Aḥmad his daughter in marriage and appointed him his successor,—a choice that was ratified by the acclamation of the people, and the Muhammadan dynasty thus instituted has continued down to the present century. The civilising influences exercised by this chief and his descendants were doubtless accompanied by some work of proselytism, but these Arab immigrants seem to have done very little for the spread of their religion among their heathen neighbours. Darfur only definitely became Muhammadan through the efforts of one of its kings named Sulaymān who began to reign in 1596,[2] and it was not until the sixteenth century that Islam gained a footing in the other kingdoms lying between Kordofan and Lake Chad, such as Wadai and Baghirmi. The first Muhammadan king of Baghirmi was Sultan 'Abd Allāh, who reigned from 1568 to 1608, but the chief centre of Muhammadan influence at this time was the kingdom of Wadai, which was founded by 'Abd al-Karīm about A.D. 1612, and it was not until the latter part of the eighteenth

[1] Becker: Geschichte des östlichen Sūdān, pp. 161–2.

[2] R. C. Slatin Pasha: Fire and Sword in the Sudan, pp. 38, 40–2. (London, 1896.)

century that the mass of the people of Baghirmi were converted to Islam.[1]

But the history of the Muhammadan propaganda in Africa during the seventeenth and eighteenth centuries is very slight and wholly insignificant when compared with the remarkable revival of missionary activity during the present century. Some powerful influence was needed to arouse the dormant energies of the African Muslims, whose condition during the eighteenth century seems to have been almost one of religious indifference. Their spiritual awakening owed itself to the influence of the Wahhābī reformation at the close of the eighteenth century; whence it comes that in modern times we meet with some accounts of proselytising movements among the Negroes that are not quite so forbiddingly meagre as those just recounted, but present us with ample details of the rise and progress of several important missionary enterprises.

Towards the end of the eighteenth century, a remarkable man, Shaykh 'Uthmān Danfodio,[2] arose from among the Fulbe[3] as a religious reformer and warrior-missionary. From the Sudan he made the pilgrimage to Mecca, whence he returned full of zeal and enthusiasm for the reformation and propagation of Islam. Influenced by the doctrines of the Wahhābīs, who were growing powerful at the time of his visit to Mecca, he denounced the practice of prayers for the dead and the honour paid to departed saints, and deprecated the excessive veneration of Muḥammad himself; at the same time he attacked the two prevailing sins of the Sudan, drunkenness and immorality.

Up to that time the Fulbe had consisted of a number of small scattered clans living a pastoral life; they had early embraced Islam, and hitherto had contented themselves with forming colonies of shepherds and planters in different parts of the Sudan. The accounts we have of them in the early part of the eighteenth century, represent them to be a peaceful and industrious people; one[4] who visited their

[1] Westermann, p. 628.
[2] Oppel, p. 292. Meyer, pp. 36–7. Westermann, pp. 629–30.
[3] Fulbe (sing. Pul) is the name by which these people call themselves; upwards of a hundred variants are applied to them by their neighbours, the commonest of which are Fulah and Fulani. (Meyer, p. 28.)
[4] Francis Moore, pp. 75–7.

settlements on the Gambia in 1731 speaks of them thus: "In every kingdom and country on each side of the river are people of a tawny colour, called Pholeys (i.e. Fulbe), who resemble the Arabs, whose language most of them speak; for it is taught in their schools, and the Koran, which is also their law, is in that language. They are more generally learned in the Arabic, than the people of Europe are in Latin; for they can most of them speak it; though they have a vulgar tongue called Pholey. They live in hordes or clans, build towns, and are not subject to any of the kings of the country, tho' they live in their territories; for if they are used ill in one nation they break up their towns and remove to another. They have chiefs of their own, who rule with such moderation, that every act of government seems rather an act of the people than of one man. This form of government is easily administered, because the people are of a good and quiet disposition, and so well instructed in what is just and right, that a man who does ill is the abomination of all. . . . They are very industrious and frugal, and raise much more corn and cotton than they consume, which they sell at reasonable rates, and are so remarkable for their hospitality that the natives esteem it a blessing to have a Pholey town in their neighbourhood; besides, their behaviour has gained them such reputation that it is esteemed infamous for any one to treat them in an inhospitable manner. Though their humanity extends to all, they are doubly kind to people of their own race; and if they know of any of their body being made a slave, all the Pholeys will unite to redeem him. As they have plenty of food they never suffer any of their own people to want; but support the old, the blind, and the lame, equally with the others. They are seldom angry, and I never heard them abuse one another; yet this mildness does not proceed from want of courage, for they are as brave as any people of Africa, and are very expert in the use of their arms, which are the assagay, short cutlasses, bows and arrows and even guns upon occasion. . . . They are strict Mahometans; and scarcely any of them will drink brandy, or anything stronger than water."

Danfodio united into one powerful organisation these

separate communities, scattered throughout the various Hausa states. The first outbreak occurred in the year 1802, in the still pagan kingdom of Gober, which had gained ascendancy over the northernmost of the Hausa states; the attempt of the king of Gober to check the growing power of the Fulbe in his dominions caused Danfodio to raise the standard of revolt; he soon found himself at the head of a powerful army, which attacked not only the pagan tribes, forcing upon them the faith of the Prophet, but also the Muhammadan Hausa states. These fell one after another and the whole of Hausaland came under the rule of Danfodio before his death in 1816. His grave in Sokoto is still an object of reverence to large numbers of pilgrims. He divided his kingdom among his two sons, who still further extended the boundary of Fulbe rule; Adamaua, founded in 1837 on the ruins of several pagan kingdoms, marks the limit of their conquests to the south-east; and the city of Ilorin, in the Yoruba country, founded in the lifetime of Danfodio, was the bulwark of the Pul empire to the south-west. With varying fortunes the dominant power remained throughout the nineteenth century in the hands of the Fulbe, who showed themselves cruel and fanatical propagandists of Islam, until British administration was established in Nigeria in 1900.

The introduction of law and order into Southern Nigeria has favoured the propaganda of Islam as in other parts of Africa that have come under European rule. The Hausa Muslims, some of whom belong to the Tijāniyyah order, have been able to move freely about the country and to penetrate among pagan tribes which had hitherto kept all Muhammadan influences rigidly at bay. In the Yoruba country particularly Islam is said to be rapidly gaining ground. There is a legend of an unsuccessful attempt made by a Muslim missionary as early as the eleventh or twelfth century; he was a Hausa who came to Ife, the religious capital of the pagan Yoruba country, and used to call the people together and read them passages from the Qur'ān; he could only speak the Yoruba language imperfectly, and with a foreign accent he would repeat to his listeners, " Let us worship Allāh : He created the mountain, He created the lowland, He created everything, He created us." He did this from time to time without succeeding in winning a single convert, and died a few months after his arrival in Ife. After his death his Qur'ān was found hanging on a peg in the wall of his room, and it came to be worshipped as a fetish.[1] Where this early apostle of the faith failed, his modern co-religionists have achieved a remarkable success. During the period of anarchy before the British occupation, the Muslims were for the most part congregated in large, walled towns, but under the new conditions of security they are able to reside permanently in villages, and near the scenes of their agricultural labours, and Muhammadan influences have thus become more widely extended over the country. As in German East Africa, the presence of Muhammadans among the native troops has been found to be favourable to the extension of their faith, and the pagan recruits often adopt Islam in order to escape ridicule and gain in self-respect.[2] In the Ijebu country also, in Southern Nigeria, a quite recent propagandist movement has been observed; Islam was only introduced into this part of the country in 1893, and in 1908 there was one town with twenty, and another with twelve mosques.[3] This rapid spread of the Muslim faith is particularly noticeable along the banks of the river Niger in Southern Nigeria; a Christian missionary reports: "When I came out in 1898 there were few Mohammedans to be seen below Iddah.[4] Now they are everywhere, excepting below Abo, and at the present rate of progress there will scarcely be a heathen village on the river-banks by 1910." [5]

There has thus been much missionary work done for Islam in this part of Africa by men who have never taken up the sword to further their end,—the conversion of the heathen. Such have been the members of some of the great Muhammadan religious orders, which form such a prominent feature of the religious life of Northern Africa. Their efforts have achieved great results during the nineteenth century,

[1] R. E. Dennett: Nigerian Studies, pp. 12, 75. (London, 1910.)
[2] Islam and Missions, pp. 71–3. The Moslem World, pp. 296–7, 351.
[3] Church Missionary Review (1908), p. 640.
[4] A town on the Niger, just south of the northern boundary of Southern Nigeria.
[5] Church Missionary Society Intelligencer (1902), p. 353.

and though doubtless much of their work has never been recorded, still we have accounts of some of the movements initiated by them.

Of these one of the earliest owed its inception to Sī Aḥmad b. Idrīs,[1] who enjoyed a wide reputation as a religious teacher in Mecca from 1797 to 1833, and was the spiritual chief of the Khaḍriyyah; before his death in 1835 he sent one of his disciples, by name Muḥammad 'Uthmān al-Amīr Ghanī, on a proselytising expedition into Africa. Crossing the Red Sea to Kossayr, he made his way inland to the Nile; here, among a Muslim population, his efforts were mainly confined to enrolling members of the order to which he belonged, but in his journey up the river he did not meet with much success until he reached Aṣwān; from this point up to Dongola, his journey became quite a triumphant progress; the Nubians hastened to join his order, and the royal pomp with which he was surrounded produced an impressive effect on this people, and at the same time the fame of his miracles attracted to him large numbers of followers. At Dongola Muḥammad 'Uthmān left the valley of the Nile to go to Kordofan, where he made a long stay, and it was here that his missionary work among unbelievers began. Many tribes in this country and about Sennaar were still pagan, and among these the preaching of Muḥammad 'Uthmān achieved a very remarkable success, and he sought to make his influence permanent by contracting several marriages, the issue of which, after his death in 1853, carried on the work of the order he founded—called after his name the Amīrghaniyyah.[2]

A few years before this missionary tour of Muḥammad 'Uthmān, the troops of Muḥammad 'Alī, the founder of the present dynasty of Egypt, had begun to extend their conquests into the Eastern Sudan, and the emissaries of the various religious orders in Egypt were encouraged by the Egyptian government, in the hope that their labours would assist in the pacification of the country, to carry on a propaganda in this newly-acquired territory, where they laboured with so much success, that the recent insurrection

[1] Rinn, pp. 403–4. [2] Le Chatelier (1), pp. 231–3.

in the Sudan under the Mahdī has been attributed to the religious fervour their preaching excited.[1]

In the West of Africa two orders have been especially instrumental in the spread of Islam, the Qādiriyyah and the Tijāniyyah. The former, the most widespread of the religious orders of Islam, was founded in the twelfth century by ʻAbd al-Qādir al-Jīlānī, said to be the most popular and most universally revered of all the saints of Islam,[2]—and was introduced into Western Africa in the fifteenth century, by emigrants from Tuat, one of the oases in the western half of the Sahara; they made Walata the first centre of their organisation, but later on their descendants were driven away from this town, and took refuge in Timbuktu, further to the east. In the beginning of the nineteenth century the great spiritual revival that was so profoundly influencing the Muhammadan world, stirred up the Qādiriyyah of the Sahara and the Western Sudan to renewed life and energy, and before long, learned theologians or small colonies of persons affiliated to the order were to be found scattered throughout the Western Sudan from the Senegal to the mouth of the Niger. The chief centres of their missionary organisation are in Kanka, Timbo (Futah-Jallon) and Musardu (in the Mandingo country).[3] These initiates formed centres of Islamic influence in the midst of a pagan population, among whom they received a welcome as public scribes, legists, writers of amulets, and schoolmasters: gradually they would acquire influence over their new surroundings, and isolated cases of conversion would soon grow into a little band of converts, the most promising of whom would often be sent to complete their studies at the chief centres of the order, or even to the schools of Kairwan or Tripoli, or to the universities of Fez and al-Azhar in Cairo.[4] Here they might remain for several years, until they had perfected their theological studies, and would then return to their native place, fully equipped for the work of spreading the faith among their fellow-countrymen. In this way a leaven has been introduced into the midst of fetish-worshippers and idolaters, which has gradually

[1] Le Chatelier (2), pp. 89–91.
[2] Rinn, p. 175.
[3] Bonet-Maury, p. 239.
[4] Id. p. 230.

spread the faith of Islam surely and steadily, though by almost imperceptible degrees. Up to the middle of the nineteenth century most of the schools in the Sudan were founded and conducted by teachers trained under the auspices of the Qādiriyyah and their organisation provided for a regular and continuous system of propaganda among the heathen tribes. The missionary work of this order has been entirely of a peaceful character, and has relied wholly on personal example and precept, on the influence of the teacher over his pupils, and on the spread of education.[1] In this way the Qādiriyyah missionaries of the Sudan have shown themselves true to the principles of their founder and the universal tradition of their order. For the guiding principles that governed the life of 'Abd al-Qādir were love of his neighbour and toleration: though kings and men of wealth showered their gifts upon him, his boundless charity kept him always poor, and in none of his books or precepts are to be found any expressions of ill-will or enmity towards the Christians; whenever he spoke of the people of the Book, it was only to express his sorrow for their religious errors, and to pray that God might enlighten them. This tolerant attitude he bequeathed as a legacy to his disciples, and it has been a striking characteristic of his followers in all ages.[2]

The Tijāniyyah, belonging to an order founded in Algiers towards the end of the eighteenth century, have, since their establishment in the Sudan about the middle of the nineteenth century, pursued the same missionary methods as the Qādiriyyah, and their numerous schools have contributed largely to the propagation of the faith; but, unlike the former, they have not refrained from appealing to the sword to assist in the furtherance of their scheme of conversion, and, unfortunately for a true estimate of the missionary work of Islam in Western Africa, the fame of their Jihāds or religious wars has thrown into the shade the successes of the peaceful propagandist, though the labours of the latter have been more effectual towards the spread of Islam than the creation of petty, short-lived dynasties. The records of campaigns, especially when they have interfered with the

[1] Le Chatelier (2), pp. 100–9.

[2] Rinn, p. 174.

commercial projects or schemes of conquest of the white men, have naturally attracted the attention of Europeans more than the unobtrusive labours of the Muhammadan preacher and schoolmaster. But the history of such movements possesses this importance, that—as has often happened in the case of Christian missions also—conquest has opened out new fields for missionary activity, and forcibly impressed on the minds of the faithful the existence of large tracts of country whose inhabitants still remained unconverted.

The first of these militant propagandist movements on the part of the members of the Tijāniyyah order owes its inception to al-Ḥājj 'Umar, who had been initiated into this order by a leader of the sect whose acquaintance he made in Mecca. He was born in 1797, near Podor on the Lower Senegal, and appears to have been a man of considerable endowments and personal influence, and of a commanding presence. He was the son of a marabout and received a careful religious education; he was already famed for his learning and piety when he set out on the pilgrimage to Mecca in 1827. He did not return to his own country until 1833, when he commenced an active propaganda of the teaching of the Tijāniyyah order, fiercely attacking his co-religionists for their ignorance and their lukewarmness, especially the adepts of the Qādiriyyah order, whose toleration particularly excited his wrath. He traversed the Central Sudan, winning many adherents and receiving honour as a new prophet, until about 1841 he reached Futah-Jallon, where he armed his followers and commenced a series of proselytising expeditions against those tribes that still remained pagan about the Upper Niger and the Senegal. It was in one of these expeditions that he met his death in 1865. His son, Aḥmadu Shaykhu, succeeded in holding together the various provinces of his father's kingdom for a few years only; internal conflicts and the advance of the French broke up the Tijāniyyah empire, and their territories passed under the rule of France.[1]

Some mention has already been made of the introduction of Islam into this part of Africa. The seed planted here

[1] Oppel, pp. 292–3. Blyden, p. 10. Le Chatelier (3), p. 167 sqq.

by 'Abd Allāh b. Yāsīn and his companions, was fructified by continual contact with Muhammadan merchants and teachers, and with the Arabs of the oasis of al-Ḥawḍ and others. A traveller of the fifteenth century tells how the Arabs strove to teach the Negro chiefs the law of Muḥammad, pointing out how shameful a thing it was for them, being chiefs, to live without any of God's laws, and to do as the base folk did who lived without any law at all. From which it would appear that these early missionaries took advantage of the imposing character of the Muslim religion and constitution to impress the minds of these uncivilised savages.[1]

We have ampler details of a more recent movement of the same kind, which had been set on foot in the south of Senegambia by a Mandingo, named Ṣamudu, commonly known by the name Samory, a pagan soldier of fortune born about 1846, who became a Muhammadan early in the course of his career and founded an empire, south of Senegambia, in the country watered by the upper basin of the Niger and its tributaries. An Arabic account of the career of Samory, written by a native chronicler, gives us some interesting details of his achievements. It begins as follows: "This is an account of the Jihād of the Imām Aḥmadu Ṣamudu, a Mandingo. . . . God conferred upon him His help continually after he began the work of visiting the idolatrous pagans, who dwell between the sea and the country of Wasulu, with a view of inviting them to follow the religion of God, which is Islam. Know all ye who read this—that the first effort of the Imām Ṣamudu was a town named Fulindiyah. Following the Book and the Law and the Traditions, he sent messengers to the king at that town, Sindidu by name, inviting him to submit to his government, abandon the worship of idols and worship one God, the Exalted, the True, whose service is profitable to His people in this world and in the next; but they refused to submit. Then he imposed a tribute upon them, as the Qur'ān commands on this subject; but they persisted in their blindness and deafness. The Imām then collected a small force of about five hundred men, brave and

[1] Delle Navigationi di Messer Alvise da Ca da Mosto. (A.D. 1454.) Ramusio, tome i. p. 101.

valiant, for the Jihād, and he fought against the town, and the Lord helped him against them and gave him the victory over them, and he pursued them with his horses until they submitted. Nor will they return to their idolatry, for now all their children are in schools being taught the Qur'ān, and a knowledge of religion and civilisation. Praise be to God for this."[1] It is not possible here to trace the course of his conquests, which were marked by wholesale massacres and devastation.[2] He reached the height of his power about 1881, shortly after which he came in conflict with the French, who took him prisoner in 1898 after a series of harassing campaigns. He died in 1900. Though the effect of his conquests was the destruction of large numbers of pagans who were massacred by his ruthless armies, while others were terrified into a nominal acceptance of Islam, he does not appear to have put before him the same distinctly religious aim as al-Ḥājj 'Umar did.[3] He left to the Qādiriyyah marabouts the task of propaganda, and they with their accustomed traditions of toleration are said to have done much to mitigate the savagery of his proceedings.[4] They opened schools in the conquered towns, established there the organisation of their order, and both instructed the new converts and sought to win fresh ones.

With regard to these militant movements of Muhammadan propagandism, it is important to notice that it is not the military successes and territorial conquests that have most contributed to the progress of Islam in these parts; for it has been pointed out that, outside the limits of those fragments of the empire of al-Ḥājj 'Umar that have definitively remained in the hands of his successors, the forced conversions that he made have quickly been forgotten, and in spite of the momentary grandeur of his successes and the enthusiasm of his armies, very few traces remain of this armed propaganda.[5] The real importance of these

[1] Blyden, pp. 357–60.
[2] This has been set forth in detail by Le Chatelier (3), p. 225 sqq.
[3] Le Chatelier (3), p. 237. "Samory n'intervint pas directement dans la question religieuse." L. G. Binger arrived at the same conclusion, as the result of personal acquaintance with Samory. (Le Péril de l'Islam, p. 20.) (Paris, 1906.)
[4] Le Chatelier (3), pp. 238–40.
[5] Le Chatelier (2), p. 112. R. du M. M., vol. xii. p. 22.

movements in the missionary history of Islam in Western Africa is the religious enthusiasm they stirred up, which exhibited itself in a widespread missionary activity of a purely peaceful character among the heathen populations. These Jihād̲s, rightly looked upon, are but incidents in the modern Islamic revival and are by no means characteristic of the forces and activities that have been really operative in the promulgation of Islam in Africa: indeed, unless followed up by distinctly missionary efforts they would have proved almost wholly ineffectual in the creation of a true Muslim community. In fact, the devastating wars and cruel violence of conquerors such as al-Ḥājj 'Umar and Samory and especially the emissaries of the Tijāniyyah have caused the faith of Islam to be bitterly hated by the pagan tribes of the Sudan in the countries watered by the Senegal and the Niger. Hostility to the Muslim faith has almost assumed with them the form of a national movement, but still this Muhammadan propaganda has spread the faith of the Prophet in many parts of Guinea and Senegambia, to which the Fulbe [1] and merchants from the Hausa country in their frequent trading expeditions have brought the knowledge of their religion, and have succeeded during the last and the present century in winning large numbers of converts. Especially noteworthy is the activity of those Qādiriyyah preachers and Muslim traders who have won fresh converts to their faith since the French occupation has brought peace to the country; this peaceful penetration has been facilitated in the French Sudan, as in other parts of Africa that have recently come under the sway of European powers, by the consideration shown by French officials to the educated classes, who are of course all Muhammadans, and by the open contempt with which the degraded habits and superstitions of the pagan fetish-worshippers are regarded.[2]

But the proselytising work of the order that is now to be described has never in any way been connected with violence or war and has employed in the service of religion only the

[1] "The Fulanis are all fervent Mohammedans. Wherever there are Fulanis there will be found a mosque." (Haywood, p. 200.)

[2] Le Chatelier (3), pp. 231, 273, 303. Westermann, pp. 632–3.

arts of peace and persuasion. In 1837 a religious society was founded by an Algerian jurisconsult, named Sīdī Muḥammad b. 'Alī al-Sanūsī, with the object of reforming Islam and spreading the faith; before his death in 1859, he had succeeded in establishing, by the sheer force of his genius and without the shedding of blood, a theocratic state, to which his followers render devoted allegiance and the limits of which are every day being extended by his successors.[1] The members of this sect are bound by rigid rules to carry out to the full the precepts of the Qur'ān in accordance with the most strictly monotheistic principles, whereby worship is to be given to God alone, and prayers to saints and pilgrimages to their tombs are absolutely interdicted. They must abstain from coffee and tobacco, avoid all intercourse with Jews or Christians, contribute a certain portion of their income to the funds of the society, if they do not give themselves up entirely to its service, and devote all their energies to the advancement of Islam, resisting at the same time any concessions to European influences. This sect is spread over the whole of North Africa, having religious houses scattered about the country from Egypt to Morocco, and far into the interior, in the oases of the Sahara and the Sudan. The centre of its organisation was in the oasis of Jag͟habūb[2] in the Libyan desert between Egypt and Tripoli, where every year hundreds of missionaries were trained and sent out as preachers of Islam to all parts of northern Africa. It is to the religious house in this village that all the branch establishments (said to be 121 in number) looked for counsel and instruction in all matters concerning the management and extension of this vast theocracy, which embraced in a marvellous organisation thousands of persons of numerous races and nations, otherwise separated from one another by vast differences of geographical situation and worldly interests. For the success that has been achieved by the zealous and energetic emissaries

[1] Muḥammad b. 'Ut͟hmān al Ḥashā'ishī, p. 84 sqq.

[2] In 1895 Sīdī al-Mahdī, the son and successor of Sīdī Muḥammad al-Sanūsī, migrated to Kufra, as being more central than Jag͟habūb (Muḥammad b. 'Ut͟hmān al-Ḥashā'ishī, pp. 111–15), but later went further south to the region of Borku and Tibesti, where he died in 1902. The head of the order in 1908 was Sīdī Aḥmad, a relative of the founder. (J. C. E. Falls: Drei Jahre in der Libyschen Wüste, p. 274.) (Freiburg, 1911.)

of this association is enormous; convents of the order are to be found not only all over the north of Africa from Egypt to Morocco, throughout the Sudan, in Senegambia and Somaliland, but members of the order are to be found also in Arabia, Mesopotamia and the islands of the Malay Archipelago.[1] Though primarily a movement of reform in the midst of Islam itself, the Sanūsiyyah sect is also actively proselytising, and several African tribes that were previously pagan or merely nominally Muslim, have since the advent of the emissaries of this sect in their midst, become zealous adherents of the faith of the Prophet. Thus, for example, the Sanūsī missionaries laboured to convert that portion of the Baele (a tribe inhabiting the hill country of Ennedi, E. of Borku) which was still heathen, and communicated their own religious zeal to such other sections of the tribe as had only a very superficial knowledge of Islam, and were Muhammadan only in name; [2] the Tedas of Tu or Tibesti, in the Sahara, S. of Fezzan, who were likewise Muhammadans only in name when the Sanūsiyyah came among them, also bear witness to the success of their efforts.[3] The missionaries of this sect also carry on an active propaganda in the Galla country and fresh workers are sent thither every year from Harar, where the Sanūsiyyah are very strong and include among their numbers all the chiefs in the court of the Amīr almost without exception.[4] In the furtherance of their proselytising efforts these missionaries open schools, form settlements in the oases of the desert, and—noticeably in the case of the Wadai—they have gained large accessions to their numbers by the purchase of slaves, who have been educated at Jaghabūb and when deemed sufficiently well instructed in the tenets of the sect, enfranchised and then sent back to their native country to convert their brethren.[5] It would appear, however, that the influence of this order is now on the decline.[6]

[1] Riedel (1), pp. 7, 59, 162.
[2] G. Nachtigal: Sahara und Sudan, vol. ii. p. 175. (Berlin, 1879–81.)
[3] Duveyrier, p. 45.
[4] Paulitschke, p. 214.
[5] H. Duveyrier: La Confrérie musulmane de Sîdi Mohammed Ben 'Alî Es-Senousî, passim. (Paris, 1886.) Louis Rinn: Marabouts et Khouans, pp. 481–513. N. Slousch: Les Senoussiya en Tripolitaine. (R. du M. M., vol. i. p. 169 sqq.). For a bibliography of the Sanūsiyyah movement, see Der Islam, iii. pp. 141–2, 312.
[6] R. du M. M., vol. i. p. 181; vol. viii. pp. 64–5.

Slight as these records are of the missionary labours of the Muslims among the pagan tribes of the Sudan, they are of importance in view of the general dearth of information regarding the spread of Islam in this part of Africa. But while documentary evidence is wanting, the Muhammadan communities dwelling in the midst of fetish-worshippers and idolaters, as representatives of a higher faith and civilisation, are a living testimony to the proselytising labours of the Muhammadan missionaries, and (especially on the south-western borderland of Islamic influence) present a striking contrast to the pagan tribes demoralised by the European gin traffic. This contrast has been well indicated by a modern traveller,[1] in speaking of the degraded condition of the tribes of the Lower Niger: "In steaming up the river (i. e. the Niger), I saw little in the first 200 miles to alter my views, for there luxuriated in congenial union fetishism, cannibalism and the gin trade. But as I left behind me the low-lying coast region, and found myself near the southern boundary of what is called the Central Sudan, I observed an ever-increasing improvement in the appearance of the character of the native; cannibalism disappeared, fetishism followed in its wake, the gin trade largely disappeared, while on the other hand, clothes became more voluminous and decent, cleanliness the rule, while their outward more dignified bearing still further betokened a moral regeneration. Everything indicated a leavening of some higher element, an element that was clearly taking a deep hold on the negro nature and making him a new man. That element you will perhaps be surprised to learn is Mahommedanism. On passing Lokoja at the confluence of the Benué with the Niger, I left behind me the missionary outposts of Islam, and entering the Central Sudan, I found myself in a comparatively well-governed empire, teeming with a busy populace of keen traders, expert manufacturers of cloth, brass work and leather; a people, in fact, who have made enormous advances towards civilisation."

In order to form a just estimate of the missionary activity of Islam in Nigritia, it must be borne in mind that, while on

[1] Joseph Thomson (2), p. 185.

the coast and along the southern boundary of the sphere of Islamic influence, the Muhammadan missionary is the pioneer of his religion, there is still left behind him a vast field for Muslim propaganda in the inland countries that stretch away to the north and the east, though it is long since Islam took firm root in this soil. Some sections of the Fūnj, the predominant Negro race of Sennaar, are partly Muhammadan and partly heathen, and Muhammadan merchants from Nubia are attempting the conversion of the latter.[1]

The pagan tribe of the Jukun,[2] whose once powerful kingdom disappeared before the victorious development of the Fulbe, has withstood the advancing influence of Muhammadanism, though the foreign minister of their king has always been a Muslim and colonies of Hausas and other Muhammadans have settled among them; but these Muslim settlers do not succeed in making any converts from among the Jukun, whose traditions of their past greatness make them cling to the national faith whose spiritual headship is vested in their king.[3]

It would be easy also to enumerate many sections of the population of the Sudan and Senegambia, that still retain their heathen habits and beliefs, or cover these only with a slight veneer of Muhammadan observance even though they have been (in most cases) surrounded for centuries by the followers of the Prophet. The Konnohs, an offshoot of the great tribe of the Mandingos, are still largely pagan, and it is only in recent years that Islam has been making progress among them.[4] Consequently, the remarkable zeal for missionary work that has displayed itself among the Muhammadans of these parts during the present century, has not far to go in order to find abundant scope for its activity. Hence the importance, in the missionary history of Islam in this continent, of the movements of reform in the Muslim religion itself and the revivals of religious life, to which attention has been drawn above.

The West Coast is another field for Muhammadan mis-

[1] Oppel, p. 303. [2] In the Muri Province of Northern Nigeria.
[3] Journal of the African Society, vol. vii. pp. 379–81.
[4] Haywood, p. 33.

sionary enterprise where Islam finds itself confronted with a vast population still unconverted, in spite of the progress it has made on the Guinea Coast, in Sierra Leone and Liberia, in which last there are more Muhammadans than heathen. One of the earliest notices of Muslim missionary activity in the neighbourhood of Sierra Leone is to be found in a petition for the dissolution of the Sierra Leone Company, ordered to be printed by the House of Commons, on the 25th May, 1802. "Not more than seventy years ago, a small number of Mahomedans established themselves in a country about forty miles to the northward of Sierra Leone, called from them the Mandingo Country. As is the practice of the professors of that religion they formed schools, in which the Arabic language and the doctrines of Mahomet were taught, and the customs of Mahomedans, particularly that of not selling any of their own religion as slaves, were adopted. Laws founded on the Koran were introduced. Those practices which chiefly contribute to depopulate the coast were eradicated, and in spite of many intestine convulsions, a great comparative degree of civilisation, union and security were introduced. Population, in consequence, rapidly increased and the whole power of that part of the country in which they are settled has gradually fallen into their hands. Those who have been taught in their schools are succeeding to wealth and power in the neighbouring countries, and carry with them a considerable portion of their religion and laws. Other chiefs are adopting the name assumed by these Mahomedans, on account of the respect which attends it; and the religion of Islam seems likely to diffuse itself peaceably over the whole district in which the colony is situated, carrying with it those advantages which seem ever to have attended its victory over Negro superstition." [1] In the Mendi country, about one hundred miles south of Sierra Leone, Islam appears to have found an entrance only in the present century, but to be now making steady progress. "The propagandism is not conducted by any special order of priests set apart for the purpose, but

[1] Claude George: The Rise of British West Africa, pp. 120–1. (London, 1902.)

every Musalman is an active missionary. Some half a dozen of them, more or less, meeting in a town, where they intend to reside for any length of time, soon run up a mosque and begin work. They first approach the chief of the town and obtain his consent to their intended act, and perhaps his promise to become an adherent. They teach him their prayers in Arabic, or as much as he can, or cares to, commit to memory. They put him through the forms and ceremonies used in praying, forbid him the use of alcoholic beverages—a restriction as often observed as not—and lo! the man is a convert." [1] On the Guinea Coast, Muslim influences are spread chiefly by Hausa traders who are to be found in all the commercial towns on this coast; whenever they form a settlement, they at once build a mosque and by their devout behaviour, and their superior culture, they impress the heathen inhabitants; whole tribes of fetish-worshippers pass over to Islam as the result of their imitation of what they recognise to be a higher civilisation than their own, without any particular efforts being necessary for persuading them.[2]

In Ashanti there was a nucleus of a Muhammadan population to be found as early as 1750 and the missionaries of Islam have laboured there ever since with slow but sure success,[3] as they find a ready welcome in the country and have gained for themselves considerable influence at the court; by means of their schools they get a hold on the minds of the younger generation, and there are said to be significant signs that Islam will become the predominant religion in Ashanti, as already many of the chiefs have adopted it.[4] In Dahomey and the Gold Coast, Islam is daily making fresh progress, and even when the heathen chieftains do not themselves embrace it, they very frequently allow themselves to come under the influence of its missionaries, who know how to take advantage of this ascendancy in their labours among the common people.[5] Dahomey and Ashanti are the most important kingdoms in this part of the

[1] Islam and Missions, pp. 73–4.
[2] Lippert: Über die Bedeutung der Haussanation für unsere Togo- und Kamerunkolonie, p. 200. MSOS, Band x. (1907), Abteilung III.
[3] Waïtz: IIer Theil, p. 250.
[4] C. S. Salmon, p. 891.
[5] Pierre Bouche, p. 256.

continent that are still subject to pagan rulers, and their conversion is said to be a question of a short time only.[1] In Lagos there are well-nigh 10,000 Muslims, and all the trading stations of the West Coast include in their populations numbers of Musalmans belonging to the superior Negro tribes, such as the Fulbe, the Mandingos and the Hausa. When these men come down to the cities of the coast, as they do in considerable numbers, either as traders or to serve as troops in the armies of the European powers, they cannot fail to impress by their bold and independent bearing the Negro of the coast-land; he sees that the believers in the Qur'ān are everywhere respected by European governors, officials and merchants; they are not so far removed from him in race, appearance, dress or manners as to make admission into their brotherhood impossible to him, and to him too is offered a share in their privileges on condition of conversion to their faith.[2] As soon as the pagan Negro, however obscure or degraded, shows himself willing to accept the teachings of the Prophet, he is at once admitted as an equal into their society, and admission into the brotherhood of Islam is not a privilege grudgingly granted, but one freely offered by zealous and eager proselytisers. For, from the mouth of the Senegal to Lagos, over two thousand miles, there is said to be hardly any town of importance on the seaboard in which there is not at least one mosque, with active propagandists of Islam, often working side by side with the teachers of Christianity.[3]

We must now turn to the history of the spread of Islam on the other side of the continent of Africa, the inhabitants of which were in closer proximity to the land where this faith had its birth. The facts recorded respecting the early settlements of the Arabs on the East Coast are very meagre; according to an Arabic chronicle which the Portuguese found in Kiloa[4] when that town was sacked by Don Francisco d'Almeïda in 1505, the first settlers were a body of Arabs who were driven into exile because they followed the heretical teachings of a

[1] Blyden, p. 357. [2] C. S. Salmon, p. 887.
[3] Blyden, p. 202. Westermann, pp. 633–4.
[4] Situated on an island about 2° S. of Zanzibar.

certain Zayd,[1] a descendant of the Prophet, after whom they were called Emozaydij (probably أُمّة زيديّة or people of Zayd). The Zayd here referred to is probably Zayd b. 'Alī, a grandson of Ḥusayn and so great-grandson of 'Alī, the nephew of Muḥammad: in the reign of the caliph Hishām he claimed to be the Imām Mahdī and stirred up a revolt among the Shī'ah faction, but was defeated and put to death in A.H. 122 (A.D. 740).[2]

They seem to have lived in considerable dread of the original pagan inhabitants of the country, but succeeded gradually in extending their settlements along the coast, until the arrival of another band of fugitives who came from the Arabian side of the Persian Gulf, not far from the island of Bahrayn. These came in three ships under the leadership of seven brothers, in order to escape from the persecution of the king of Lasah,[3] a city hard by the dwelling-place of their tribe. The first town they built was Magadaxo,[4] which afterwards rose to such power as to assume lordship over all the Arabs of the coast. But the original settlers, the Emozaydij, belonging as they did to a different Muhammadan sect, being Shī'ahs, while the new-comers were Sunnis, were unwilling to submit to the authority of the rulers of Magadaxo, and retired into the interior, where they became merged into the native population, intermarrying with them and adopting their manners and customs.[5]

Magadaxo was founded about the middle of the tenth century and remained the most powerful city on this coast for more than seventy years, when the arrival of another expedition from the Persian Gulf led to the establishment of a rival settlement further south. The leader of this expedition was named 'Alī, one of the seven sons of a certain Sultan Ḥasan of Shiraz: because his mother was an Abyssinian, he was looked down upon with contempt by his brothers, whose cruel treatment of him after the death of their father, determined him to leave his native

[1] "Hum Mouro chamado Zaide, que foi neto de Hocem filho de Ale o sobrinho de Mahamed." (De Barros, Dec. i. Liv. viii. cap. iv. p. 211.)
[2] Ibn Khaldūn, vol. iii. pp. 98–100.
[3] Possibly a mistake for al-Ḥasā. See Ibn Baṭūṭah, tome ii. pp. 247–8.
[4] Or (to give it its Arabic name) Maqdishū.
[5] J. de Barros: Dec. i. Liv. viii. cap. iv. pp. 211–12.

land and seek a home elsewhere. Accordingly, with his wife and children and a small body of followers, he set sail from the island of Ormuz, and avoiding Magadaxo, whose inhabitants belonged to a different sect, and having heard that gold was to be found on the Zanzibar coast, he pushed on to the south and founded the city of Kiloa, where he could maintain a position of independence and be free from the interference of his predecessors further north.[1]

In this way a number of Arab towns sprang up along the east coast from the Gulf of Aden to the Tropic of Capricorn, on the fringe of what was called by the mediæval Arab geographers the country of the Zanj. Whatever efforts may have been made by the Muhammadan settlers to convert the Zanj, no record of them seems to have survived. There is a curious story preserved in an old collection of travels written probably in the early part of the tenth century, which represents Islam as having been introduced among one of these tribes by the king of it himself. An Arab trading vessel was driven out of its course by a tempest in the year A.D. 922 and carried to the country of the man-eating Zanj, where the crew expected certain death. On the contrary, the king of the place received them kindly and entertained them hospitably for several months, while they disposed of their merchandise on advantageous terms; but the merchants repaid his kindness with foul treachery, by seizing him and his attendants when they came on board to bid them farewell, and then carrying them off as slaves to Omam. Some years later the same merchants were driven by a storm to the same port, where they were recognised by the natives who surrounded them in their canoes; giving themselves up for lost this time, they repeated for one another the prayers for the dead. They were taken before the king, whom they discovered to their surprise and confusion to be the same they had so shamefully treated some years before. Instead, however, of taking vengeance upon them for their treacherous conduct, he spared their lives and allowed them to sell their goods, but rejected with scorn the rich presents they offered. Before they left, one of the

[1] De Barros, id. pp. 224–5. See also Justus Strandes: Die Portugiesenzeit von Deutsch- und Englisch-Ostafrika, p. 81 sqq. (Berlin, 1899.)

party ventured to ask the king to tell the story of his escape. He described how he had been taken as a slave to Baṣrah and thence to Baghdād, where he was converted to Islam and instructed in the faith; escaping from his master, he joined a caravan of pilgrims going to Mecca, and after performing the prescribed rites, reached Cairo and made his way up the Nile in the direction of his own country, which he reached at length after encountering many dangers and having been more than once enslaved. Restored once again to his kingdom, he taught his people the faith of Islam; "and now I rejoice in that God hath given to me and to my people the knowledge of Islam and the true faith; to no other in the land of the Zanj hath this grace been vouchsafed; and it is because you have been the cause of my conversion, that I pardon you. Tell the Muslims that they may come to our country, and that we—Muslims like themselves—will treat them as brothers." [1]

From the same source we learn that even at this early period, this coast-land was frequented by large numbers of Arab traders, yet in spite of centuries of intercourse with the followers of Islam, the original inhabitants of this coast (with the exception of the Somalis) have been remarkably little influenced by this religion. Even before the Portuguese conquests of the sixteenth century, what few conversions had been made, seem to have been wholly confined to the sea-border, and even after the decline of Portuguese influence in this part of the world, and the restoration of Arab rule under the Sayyids of Omam, hardly any efforts were made until the twentieth century to spread the knowledge of Islam among the tribes of the interior, with the exception of the Galla and Somali. As a modern traveller has said: "During the three expeditions which I conducted in East Central Africa I saw nothing to suggest Mohammedanism as a civilising power. Whatever living force might be in the religion remained latent. The Arabs, or their descendants, in these parts were not propagandists. There were no missionaries to preach Islam, and the natives of Muscat were content that their slaves should conform, to

[1] Kitāb 'ajā'ib al-Hind ou Livre des Merveilles de l'Inde, publié par P. A. van der Lith. pp. 51–60. (Leiden, 1883.)

a certain extent, to the forms of the religion. They left the East African tribes, who indeed, in their gross darkness, were evidently content to remain in happy ignorance. Their inaptitude for civilisation was strikingly shown in the strange fact that five hundred years of contact with semi-civilised people had left them without the faintest reflection of the higher traits which characterised their neighbours—not a single good seed during all these years had struck root and flourished." [1] Given up wholly to the pursuits of commerce or to slave-hunting, the Arabs in Eastern Africa exhibited a lukewarmness in promoting the interests of their faith, which is in striking contrast to the missionary zeal displayed by their co-religionists in other parts of Africa.

A notable exception is the propagandist activity of the Arab traders who were admitted into Uganda in the first half of the nineteenth century; they probably recognised that the sturdy independence of the Baganda made slave-raiding among them impossible, so they sought to gain their confidence by winning them over to their own faith. Many of the Baganda became Muhammadans during the reign of King Mutesa, but Stanley's visit to this monarch in 1875 led to the introduction of Christian missions in the following year, and the power of the Muhammadans in the state declined with the rapid increase in the numbers of the Christian converts and the establishment of a British Protectorate.[2] But a number of Muhammadans still hold important positions in Uganda, and it is stated that there is a possibility of the Eastern Province becoming Muslim. In the rich tributary country of Busoga, to the north of Uganda, a large number of those in authority were said, in 1906, to be Muhammadans.[3] But with this exception Islam in East Equatorial Africa was up to the latter part of the nineteenth century confined to the coast-lands and the immediately adjoining country. The explanation would appear to be that it was not to the interests of the

[1] Mohammedanism in Central Africa, by Joseph Thomson, p. 877.

[2] Roscoe, p. 229 sq.

[3] Zwemer, p. 236. Gairdner (p. 26) gives the number of Muhammadans as 200,000 out of a population of four millions, but he does not state from what source he derives these figures. Roscoe (p. 6) gives the total population of Uganda as about one million only.

slave-dealers to spread Islam among the heathen tribes from among whom they obtained their unhappy victims; for, once converted to Islam, the native tribes would enter into the brotherhood of the faith and could not be raided and carried off as slaves.[1]

The suppression of the slave-trade, with the extension of European rule over East Equatorial Africa, was followed by a remarkable expansion of Muslim missionary activity; peace and order were established in the interior, railways and high roads were made, and the peaceful Muslim trader could now make his way into districts hitherto closed to him. The administration selected its officials from among the more cultivated Muhammadan section of the population; thousands of posts were created by the government of German East Africa and given to Muhammadan officials, whose influence was used to bring over whole villages to Islam.[2] The teachers of the state schools were likewise Muhammadans, and as early as the last decades of the nineteenth century Swahili schoolmasters were observed to be carrying on a lively and successful mission work among the people of Bondëi and the Wadigo (who dwell a little inland from the coast) in German East Africa.[3] But it was in the beginning of the twentieth century, especially after the suppression of the insurrection of 1905 in German East Africa, that the activity of this new missionary movement became strikingly noticeable in the interior.[4] This movement of expansion has especially followed the railroads and the great trade routes, and has spread right across German East Africa to its western boundary on Lake Tanganyika, northward from Usambara to the Kilimanjaro district, and southward to Lake Nyasa.[5] The workers in this propaganda are merchants, especially Swahilis from the coast, soldiers and government officials.[6] The acceptance of Islam is looked upon as a sign of an elevation to a higher civilisation and social status, and the ridicule with which the pagans are regarded by the Muhammadans is said often

[1] Richter, pp. 146–7, 154. Merensky, p. 156. Klamroth, p. 4.
[2] R. du M. M., vol. ix. (1909), p. 322.
[3] Oscar Baumann: Usambara und seine Nachbargebiete, pp. 141, 153. (Berlin, 1891.)
[4] Becker, Islam in Deutsch-Ostafrika, p. 10.
[5] Id. p. 13 sqq. Klamroth, pp. 14–28.
[6] Id. p. 53.

to be a determining factor in their conversion.[1] An instance of the operation of this feeling may be taken from West Usambara, which was said in 1891 to be still closed to Islam; the feeling of both chiefs and people was hostile to the Muhammadans, who were hated and feared as slave-dealers; but when the days of the slave-trade were over and an ordered administration was established, the first native officials appointed were almost entirely Muhammadans; they impressed upon the chiefs and other notables who came in touch with them that it was the correct thing for those who moved in official circles to be Muhammadans, and thereby achieved the conversion of some of the greater chiefs, who afterwards exercised a similar influence on chiefs of an inferior degree.[2] There seems to be little evidence of the activity of professional missionaries or of any of the religious orders, but there are not wanting evidences of systematic efforts, such as those of a Muslim teacher, who is reported to have regularly visited a district in the Kilimanjaro country every week for five months, preaching the faith of Islam; his ministrations were welcomed by the people, whom he entertained with feasts of rice, etc.[3] In this zealous propaganda it is noticeable that the preachers of Islam do not confine their attention to pagans only, but seek also to win converts from among the native Christians.[4]

Islam made its way into Nyasaland also from the East Coast, having been introduced by the slave-raiding Arabs and their allies the Yaos, whose ancestors came from near the East Coast where they had long since accepted Islam. It is said that an Arab is now seldom seen in Nyasaland, but the Yaos constitute one of the most powerful native tribes in Nyasaland, and look upon Islam as their national faith. Though there appears to be no organised propaganda, Islam has spread very rapidly during the first decade of the twentieth century, and that among some of the most intelligent tribes in the country.[5]

Islam has achieved a similar success among the Galla and the Somali. Mention has already been made of the Galla

[1] Klamroth, pp. 21, 25, 54.
[2] Id. pp. 23–4.
[3] Id. p. 26.
[4] Id. p. 67.
[5] Becker: Islam in Deutsch-Ostafrika, p. 14. The Moslem World, vol. ii. p. 3 sqq.

settlements in Abyssinia; these immigrants, who are divided into seven principal clans, with the generic name of Wollo-Galla, were probably all heathen at the time of their incursion into the country,[1] and a large part of them remain so to the present day. After settling in Abyssinia they soon became naturalised there, and in many instances adopted the language, manners and customs of the original inhabitants of the country.[2]

The story of their conversion is obscure: while some of them are said to have been forcibly baptised into the Christian faith, the absence of any political power in the hands of the Muhammadans precludes the possibility of any converts to Islam having been made in a similar fashion. In the eighteenth century, those in the south were said to be mostly Muhammadans, those to the east and west chiefly pagans.[3] More recent information points to a further increase in the number of the followers of the Prophet, and in 1867 Munzinger prophesied that in a short time all the Galla tribes would be Muhammadan,[4] and as they were said to be "very fanatical," we may presume that they were by no means half-hearted or lukewarm in their adherence to this religion.[5]

The Galla freedman whom Doughty met at Khaybar certainly exhibited a remarkable degree of zeal for his own faith. He had been carried off from his home when a child and sold as a slave in Jiddah; when Doughty asked him whether no anger was left in his heart against those who had stolen him and sold his life to servitude in the ends of the earth, "Yet one thing," he answered, "has recompensed me,—that I remained not in ignorance with the heathen!—Oh, the wonderful providence of Ullah! whereby

[1] A contemporary Ethiopic account of these tribes,—Geschichte der Galla. Bericht eines abessinischen Mönches über die Invasion der Galla in sechzehnten Jahrhundert. Text und Übersetzung hrsg. von A. W. Schleichler (Berlin, 1893),—seems certainly to represent them as heathen, though no detailed account is given of their religion. Reclus (tome x. p. 330), however, supposes them to have been Muhammadan at the time of their invasion.

[2] Henry Salt: A Voyage to Abyssinia, p. 299. (London, 1814.)

[3] James Bruce: Travels to discover the source of the Nile, 2nd ed. vol. iii. p. 243. (Edinburgh, 1805.)

[4] Munzinger, p. 408.

[5] I. L. Krapf: Reisen in Ost-Africa, ausgeführt in den Jahren 1837–55, vol. i. p. 106. (Kornthal, 1858.)

I am come to this country of the Apostle, and to the knowledge of the religion!"[1] "Oh! what sweetness is there in believing! Trust me, dear comrade, it is a thing above that which any heart may speak; and would God thou wert come to this (heavenly) knowledge; but the Lord will surely have a care of thee, that thou shouldst not perish without the religion. Ay, how good a thing it were to see thee a Moslem, and become one with us; but I know that the time is in God's hand: the Lord's will be done."[2]

Among the Galla tribes of the true Galla country, the population is partly Muhammadan (some tribes having been converted about 1500)[3] and partly heathen, with the exception of those tribes immediately bordering on Abyssinia who in the latter part of the nineteenth century were forced by the king of that country to accept Christianity.[4] Among the mountains, the Muhammadans are in a minority, but on the plains the missionaries of Islam have met with striking success, and their teaching found a rapidly increasing acceptance during the last century. Antonio Cecchi, who visited the petty kingdom of Limmu in 1878, gives an account of the conversion of Abba Baghibò,[5] the father of the then reigning chieftain, by Muhammadans who for some years had been pushing their proselytising efforts in this country in the guise of traders. His example was followed by the chiefs of the neighbouring Galla kingdoms and by the officers of their courts; part of the common people also were won over to the new faith, and it continued to make progress among them, but the greater part cling firmly to their ancient cult.[6] These traders received a ready welcome at the courts of the Galla chiefs, inasmuch as they found them a market for the commercial products of the country and imported objects of foreign manufacture in exchange. As they made their journeys to the coast once a year only, or

[1] Arabia Deserta, vol. ii. p. 168. [2] Id., vol. ii. p. 109.
[3] Morié, vol. ii. p. 248.
[4] Reclus, tome. x. p. 309. Basset, pp. 270–1.
[5] When the Roman Catholics opened a mission among the Gallas in 1846, Abba Baghibò said to them: "Had you come thirty years ago, not only I, but all my countrymen might have embraced your religion; but now it is impossible." (Massaja, vol. iv. p. 103.)
[6] Da Zeila alle frontiere del Caffa, vol. ii. p. 160. (Rome, 1886–7.) Massaja, vol. iv. p. 103; vol. vi. p. 10.

even once in two years, and lived all the rest of the time in the Galla country, they had plenty of opportunities, which they knew well how to avail themselves of, for the work of propagating Islam, and wherever they set their foot they were sure in a short space of time to gain a large number of proselytes.[1] Islam here came in conflict with Christian missionaries from Europe, whose efforts, though winning for Christianity a few converts, have been crowned with very little success,[2]—even the converts of Cardinal Massaja (after he was expelled from these parts) either embraced Islam or ended by believing neither in Christ nor in Allāh,[3]—whereas the Muslim missionaries achieved a continuous success, and pushed their way far to the south, and crossed the Wābi river.[4] The majority of the Galla tribes dwelling in the west of the Galla country were still heathen towards the end of the nineteenth century, but among the most westerly of them, viz. the Lega,[5] the old nature worship appeared to be on the decline and the growing influence of the Muslim missionaries made it probable that within a few years the Lega would all have entered into the pale of Islam.[6]

The North-East Africa of the present day presents indeed the spectacle of a remarkably energetic and zealous missionary activity on the part of the Muhammadans. Several hundreds of missionaries come from Arabia every year, and they have been even more successful in their labours among the Somali than among the Galla.[7] The close proximity of the Somali country to Arabia must have caused it very early to have been the scene of Muhammadan missionary labours, but of these unfortunately little record seems to have survived. The people of Zayla' were said by Ibn Ḥawqal[8] in the second half the ninth century to be Christians, but in the first half of the fourteenth century

[1] Massaja, vol. iv. p. 102.

[2] Speaking of the failure of Christian missions, Cecchi says: "di ciò si deve ricercare la causa nello espandersi che fece quaggiù in questi ultimi anni l' islamismo, portato da centinaja di preti e mercanti musulmani, cui non facevano difetto i mezzi, l' astuzia e la piena conoscenza della lingua." (Op. cit. vol. ii. p. 342.)

[3] Id., p. 343.

[4] Reclus, tome xiii. p. 834.

[5] The Lega are found in long. 9° to 9° 30′ and lat. E. 34° 35′ to 35°.

[6] Reclus, tome x. p. 350.

[7] Paulitschke, pp. 330–1.

[8] Ibn Ḥawqal, p. 41.

Abu'l-Fidā speaks of them as being Musalmans.[1] The new faith was probably brought across the sea by Arab merchants or refugees. The Somalis of the north have a tradition of a certain Arab of noble birth who, compelled to flee his own country, crossed the sea to Adel, where he preached the faith of Islam among their forefathers.[2] In the fifteenth century a band of forty-four Arabs came as missionaries from Ḥaḍramawt, landing at Berberah on the Red Sea, and thence dispersed over the Somali country to preach Islam. One of them, Shaykh Ibrāhīm Abū Zarbay, made his way to the city of Harar about A.D. 1430, and gained many converts there, and his tomb is still honoured in that city. A hill near Berberah is still called the Mount of Saints in memory of these missionaries, who are said to have sat there in solemn conclave before scattering far and wide to the work of conversion.[3] Islam gradually became predominant throughout the whole of North-East Africa, but the growing power of the Emperor Menelik and his occupation of Harar in 1886 resulted in a certain number of conversions to Christianity.[4]

In order to complete this survey of Islam in Africa, it remains only to draw attention to the fact that this religion has also made its entrance into the extreme south of this continent, viz. in Cape Colony. These Muhammadans of the Cape are descendants of Malays, who were brought here by the Dutch[5] either in the seventeenth or eighteenth century;[6] they speak a corrupt form of the Boer dialect, with a considerable admixture of Arabic, and some English and Malay words. A curious little book published in this

[1] Abu'l-Fidā, tome ii. 1re partie, pp. 231–2.

[2] Documents sur l'histoire, la géographie et le commerce de l'Afrique Orientale, recueillis par M. Guillain. Deuxième partie, tome i. p. 399. (Paris, 1856.)

[3] R. F. Burton: First Footprints in East Africa, pp. 76, 404. (London, 1856.)

[4] R. du M. M., vi. p. 288. (1908.)

[5] The Cape of Good Hope was in the possession of the Dutch from 1652 to 1795; restored to them after the Peace of Amiens in 1802, it was re-occupied by the British as soon as war broke out again.

[6] Among these was Shaykh Yūsuf, a religious teacher of great influence in Java and the last champion of the independence of Bantam; in 1694 he was removed by the Dutch to Cape Colony as a prisoner of state, together with his family and numerous attendants; his tomb is still regarded as a holy place. (G. M. Theal: History and Ethnography of Africa south of the Zambesi, vol. ii. p. 263.) (London, 1909.)

dialect and written in Arabic characters was published in Constantinople in 1877 by the Turkish minister of education, to serve as a handbook of the principles of the Muslim faith.[1] The thoroughly Dutch names that some of them bear, and the type of face observable in many of them, point to the probability that they have at some time received into their community some persons of Dutch birth, or at least that they have in their veins a considerable admixture of Dutch blood. They have also gained some converts from among the Hottentots. Very little notice has been taken of them by European travellers,[2] or even by their co-religionists until recently. In 1819 Colebrooke had drawn attention to the growth of Islam in some interesting notes he wrote on the Cape Colony: " Mohammedanism is said to be gaining ground among the slaves and free people of colour at the Cape; that is to say, more converts among negroes and blacks of every description are made from Paganism to the Musleman, than to the Christian religion, notwithstanding the zealous exertions of pious missionaries. One cause of this perversion is asserted to be a marked disinclination of slave owners to allow their slaves to be baptized; arising from some erroneous notions or over-charged apprehensions of the rights which a baptized slave acquires. Slaves are certainly impressed with the idea that such a disinclination subsists, and it is not an unfrequent answer of a slave, when asked his motives for turning Musleman, that 'some religion he must have, and he is not allowed to turn Christian.' Prejudices in this respect are wearing away; and less discouragement is now given to the conversion of slaves than heretofore. Masters, it is affirmed, begin to find that their slaves serve not the worse for instruction received in religious duties. Missionaries who devote themselves especially to the religious instruction of slaves (and there is one in each of the principal towns) have increasing congregations, and hope that their labours are not unfruitful. But the

[1] M. J. de Goeje: Mohammedaansche Propaganda, pp. 2, 6. (Overgedrukt uit de Nederlandsche Spectator, No. 51, 1881.)

[2] Attention was drawn to them in 1814 by a Mr. Campbell. See William Adams: The Modern Voyager and Traveller, vol. i. p. 93. (London, 1834.)

Musleman priest, with less exertion, has a greater flock."[1] During the last fifty years the Muhammadans in Cape Colony have been visited by some zealous co-religionists from other countries, and more attention is now paid by them to education, and a deeper religious life has been stirred up among them, and they are said to carry on a zealous propaganda, especially among the coloured people at the Cape and to achieve a certain success.[2] This proselytising movement is especially strong in the western part of Cape Colony. It is said that there is a movement on foot for the founding of a college at Claremont, in the vicinity of Cape Town, which shall become a centre for the propagation of Islam. One of the methods at present employed is the adoption of neglected or abandoned children, who are brought up in the Muslim faith.[3] Every year some of them make the pilgrimage to Mecca, where a special Shaykh has been appointed to look after them.[4] The Indian coolies that come to work in the diamond fields of South Africa are also said to be propagandists of Islam.[5]

On account of its isolated position, 220 to 540 miles from the mainland, the island of Madagascar calls for separate mention. The only tribe that has adopted Islam is that of the Antaimorona, occupying a part of the south-east coast; they undoubtedly owed their conversion to missionaries from Arabia, but the date at which this change of faith took place is entirely unknown; tradition would carry it back to the very days of Muḥammad himself, but it is not until the sixteenth century that we get, in the works of Italian and Portuguese geographers, authentic mention of Muhammadans on the island.[6]

From the historical sketch given above it may be seen that peaceful methods have largely characterised the Muhammadan missionary movement in Africa, and though Islam

[1] Sir T. E. Colebrooke: The Life of H. T. Colebrooke, p. 335. (London, 1873.)
[2] F. Coillard: Au Cap de Bonne Espérance. (Journal des missions évangéliques, avril 1899, p. 265.)
[3] Kumm, p. 233.
[4] C. Snouck Hurgronje (3), vol. ii. pp. 296–7.
[5] Jacques Bonzon: Les Missionaires de l'Islam en Afrique. (Revue Chrétienne, tome xiii. p. 295.) (Paris, 1893.)
[6] G. Ferrand, Les Musulmans à Madagascar, pp. 19, 50 sqq., 138. (Paris, 1891.) Id. Les Migrations musulmanes et juives à Madagascar. (Revue de l'Histoire des Religions, vol. lii. p. 381 sqq.)

has often taken the sword as an instrument to further its spiritual conquests, such an appeal to violence and bloodshed has in most cases been preceded by the peaceful efforts of the missionary, and the preacher has followed the conqueror to complete the imperfect work of conversion. It is true that the success of Islam has been very largely facilitated in many parts of Africa by the worldly successes of Muhammadan adventurers, and the erection of Muhammadan states on the ruins of pagan kingdoms, and fire and bloodshed have often marked the course of a Jihād, projected for the extermination of the infidel. The words of the young Arab from Bornu whom Captain Burton [1] met in the palace of the King of Abeokuta doubtless express the aspirations of many an African Muhammadan: "Give those guns and powder to us, and we will soon Islamise these dogs": and they find an echo in the message that Mungo Park [2] gives us as having been sent by the Muslim King of Futah Toro to his pagan neighbour: "With this knife Abdulkader will condescend to shave the head of Damel, if Damel will embrace the Mahommedan faith; and with this other knife Abdulkader will cut the throat of Damel, if Damel refuses to embrace it; take your choice."

But much as Islam may have owed to the martial prowess of such fanatics as these, there is the overwhelming testimony of travellers and others to the peaceful missionary preaching, and quiet and persistent labours of the Muslim propagandist, which have done more for the rapid spread of Islam in modern Africa than any violent measures: by the latter its opponents may indeed have been exterminated, but by the former chiefly, have its converts been made, and the work of conversion may still be observed in progress in many regions of the coast and the interior.[3] Wherever Islam has made its way, there is the Muhammadan missionary to be found bearing witness to its doctrines,—the trader, be he Arab, Pul or Mandingo, who combines proselytism with the sale of his merchandise, and whose very profession brings him into close and immediate contact with those he would convert,

[1] Richard F. Burton (1), vol. i. p. 256.
[2] Travels in the Interior of Africa, chap. xxv. ad fin.
[3] D. J. East, pp. 118–20. W. Winwood Reade, vol. i. p. 312. Blyden, pp. 13, 202.

and disarms any possible suspicion of sinister motives; such a man when he enters a pagan village soon attracts attention by his frequent ablutions and regularly recurring times of prayer and prostration, in which he appears to be conversing with some invisible being, and by his very assumption of intellectual and moral superiority, commands the respect and confidence of the heathen people, to whom at the same time he shows himself ready and willing to communicate his high privileges and knowledge;—the ḥājī or pilgrim who has returned from Mecca full of enthusiasm for the spread of the faith, to which he devotes his whole energies, wandering about from place to place, supported by the alms of the faithful who bear witness to the truth in the midst of their pagan neighbours;—the student who, in consequence of his knowledge of Islamic theology and law, receives honour as a man of learning: sometimes, too, he practises medicine, or at least he is in great requisition as a writer of charms, texts from the Qur'ān, which are sewn up in pieces of leather or cloth and tied on the arms, or round the neck, and which he can turn to account as a means of adding to the number of his converts: for instance, when childless women or those who have lost their children in infancy, apply for these charms, as a condition of success the obligation is always imposed upon them of bringing up their future children as Muhammadans.[1] These religious teachers, or marabouts, or alūfas as they are variously termed, are held in the highest estimation. In some tribes of Western Africa every village contains a lodge for their reception, and they are treated with the utmost deference and respect: in Darfur they hold the highest rank after those who fill the offices of government: among the Mandingos they rank still higher, and receive honour next to the king, the subordinate chiefs being regarded as their inferiors in point of dignity: in those states in which the Qur'ān is made the rule of government in all civil matters, their services are in great demand, in order to interpret its meaning. So sacred are the persons of these teachers esteemed, that they pass without molestation through the countries of chiefs, not

[1] Bishop Crowther on Islam in Western Africa. (Church Missionary Intelligencer, p. 254, April 1888.)

only hostile to each other, but engaged in actual warfare. Such deference is not only paid to them in Muhammadan countries, but also in the pagan villages in which they establish their schools, where the people respect them as the instructors of their children, and look upon them as the medium between themselves and Heaven, either for securing a supply of their necessities, or for warding off or removing calamities.[1] Many of these teachers have studied in the mosques of Qayrwān, Fas, Tripoli [2] and other centres of Muslim learning; but especially in the mosque of al-Azhar in Cairo. Students flock to it from all parts of the Muslim world, and among them is often to be found a contingent from Negro Africa,—students from Darfur, Wadai and Bornu, and some who even make their way on foot from the far distant West Coast; when they have finished their courses of study in Muslim theology and jurisprudence, there are many of them who become missionaries among the heathen population of their native land. Schools are established by these missionaries in the towns they visit, which are frequented by the pagan as well as the Muslim children. They are taught to read the Qur'ān, and instructed in the doctrines and ceremonies of Islam. Having thus gained a footing, the Muhammadan missionary, by his superior knowledge and attainments, is not slow to obtain great influence over the people among whom he has come to live. In this he is aided by the fact that his habits and manner of life are similar in many respects to their own, nor is he looked upon with suspicion, inasmuch as the trader has already prepared the way for him; and by intermarriage with the natives, being thus received into their social system, his influence becomes firmly rooted and permanent, and so in the most natural manner he gradually causes the knowledge of Islam to spread among them.

His propagandist efforts are further facilitated by the fact that the deism which forms the background of the religious consciousness of many fetish-worshippers may pass by an easy transition into the theism of Islam, together with some

[1] D. J. East, pp. 112–13. Blyden, p. 202.

[2] It is said that over a thousand missionaries of Islam leave Tripoli every year to work in the Sudan. (Paulitschke, p. 331.)

other aspects of their theology, while their general outlook upon life and several of their religious institutions are capable of taking on a Muslim colouring and of being transferred to the new system of faith without undergoing much modification.[1]

The arrival of the Muhammadan in a pagan country is also the beginning of the opening up of a more extensive trade, and of communication with great Muhammadan trading centres such as Jenne, Segu or Kano, and a share in the advantages of this material civilisation is offered, together with the religion of the Prophet. Thus "among the uncivilised negro tribes the missionary may be always sure of a ready audience: he can not only give them many truths regarding God and man which make their way to the heart and elevate the intellect, but he can at once communicate the Shibboleth of admission to a social and political communion, which is a passport for protection and assistance from the Atlantic to the Wall of China. Wherever a Moslem house can be found there the negro convert who can repeat the dozen syllables of his creed, is sure of shelter, sustenance and advice, and in his own country he finds himself at once a member of an influential, if not of a dominant caste. This seems the real secret of the success of the Moslem missionaries in West Africa. It is great and rapid as regards numbers, for the simple reason that the Moslem missionary, from the very first profession of the convert's belief, acts practically on those principles regarding the equality and brotherhood of all believers before God, which Islam shares with Christianity; and he does this, as a general rule, more speedily and decidedly than the Christian missionary, who generally feels bound to require good evidence of a converted heart before he gives the right hand of Christian fellowship, and who has always to contend with race prejudices not likely to die out in a single generation where the white Christian has for generations been known as master, and the black heathen as slave."[2]

It is important, too, to note that neither his colour nor

[1] For a detailed examination of these points of contact, see Forget, p. 28 sqq. Merensky, p. 155.
[2] Sir Bartle Frere (1), pp. 18–19.

his race in any way prejudice the Negro in the eyes of his new co-religionists. The progress of Islam in Negritia has no doubt been materially advanced by this absence of any feeling of repulsion towards the Negro—indeed Islam seems never to have treated the Negro as an inferior, as has been unhappily too often the case in Christendom.[1]

This consideration goes partly to explain the success of Muslim as contrasted with Christian missions among the Negro peoples. It has frequently been pointed out that the Negro convert to Christianity is apt to feel that his European co-religionists belong to a stratum of civilisation alien to his own habits of life, whereas he feels himself to be more at home in a Muslim society. This has been well stated by a modern observer, in the following passage:— "Islam, despite its shortcomings, does not, from the Nigerian point of view, demand race suicide of the Nigerian as an accompaniment of conversion. It does not stipulate revolutionary changes in social life, impossible at the present stage of Nigerian development; nor does it undermine family or communal authority. Between the converter and converted there is no abyss. Both are equal, not in theory, but in practice, before God. Both are African; sons of the soil. The doctrine of the brotherhood of man is carried out in practice. Conversion does not mean for the converted

[1] E. W. Blyden, pp. 18–24. E. Allégret, p. 200. Westermann, pp. 644–5. In a very interesting, but now forgotten, debate before the Anthropological Society of London, on the Efforts of Missionaries among Savages, a case was mentioned of a Christian missionary in Africa who married a negress: the feeling against him in consequence was so strong that he had to leave the colony. The Muslim missionary labours under no such disadvantage. (Journal of the Anthropological Society of London, vol. iii. 1865.)

The contrast between the way in which Christianity and Islam present themselves to the African is well brought out by one who is himself a Negro, in the following passage:—"Tandis que les missions renvoient à une époque indéfinie l'établissement du pastorat indigène, les prêtres musulmans pénètrent dans l'intérieur de l'Afrique, trouvent un accès facile chez les païens et les convertissent à l'islam. De sorte qu'aujourd'hui les nègres regardent l'islam comme la religion des noirs, et le christianisme comme la religion des blancs. Le christianisme, pensent-ils, appelle le nègre au salut, mais lui assigne une place tellement basse que, découragé, il se dit: 'Je n'ai ni part ni portion dans cette affaire.' L'islam appelle le nègre au salut et lui dit: 'Il ne dépend que de toi pour arriver aussi haut que possible.' Alors, le negre enthousiasmé se livre corps et âme au service de cette religion." L'islam et le christianisme en Afrique d'après un Africain. (Journal des Missions Évangiliques. 63e année, p. 207.) (Paris, 1888.)

a break with his interests, his family, his social life, his respect for the authority of his natural rulers. . . . No one can fail to be impressed with the carriage, the dignity of the Nigerian—indeed of the West African—Mohammedan; the whole bearing of the man suggests a consciousness of citizenship, a pride of race which seems to say: 'We are different, thou and I, but we are *men*.' The spread of Islam in Southern Nigeria which we are witnessing to-day is mainly social in its action. It brings to those with whom it comes in contact a higher status, a loftier conception of man's place in the universe around him, release from the thraldom of a thousand superstitious fears."[1]

According to Muhammadan tradition Moses was a black man, as may be seen from the following passages in the Qur'ān. "Now draw thy hand close to thy side: it shall come forth white, but unhurt:—another sign!" (xx. 23). "Then drew he forth his hand, and lo! it was white to the beholders. The nobles of Pharaoh's people said: 'Verily this is an expert enchanter'" (vii. 105–6). The following story also, handed down to us from the golden period of the 'Abbāsid dynasty, is interesting as evidence of Muhammadan feeling with regard to the Negro. Ibrāhīm, a brother of Hārūn al-Rashīd and the son of a negress, had proclaimed himself Caliph at Baghdād, but was defeated and forgiven by al-Ma'mūn, who was then reigning (A.D. 819). He thus describes his interview with the Caliph:—"Al-Ma'mūn said to me on my going to see him after having obtained pardon: 'Is it thou who art the Negro khalīfah?' to which I replied:—'Commander of the faithful! I am he whom thou hast deigned to pardon; and it has been said by the slave of Banu'l-Ḥasḥās:—"When men extol their worth, the slave of the family of Ḥasḥās can supply, by his verses, the defect of birth and fortune." Though I be a slave, my soul, through its noble nature, is free; though my body be dark, my mind is fair.' To this al-Ma'mūn replied: 'Uncle! a jest of mine has put you in a serious mood.' He then repeated these verses: 'Blackness of skin cannot degrade an ingenious mind, or lessen the

[1] E. D. Morel: Nigeria, its people and its problems, pp. 216–17. (London, 1911.)

worth of the scholar and the wit. Let darkness claim the colour of your body: I claim as mine your fair and candid soul.' "[1]

Thus, the converted Negro at once takes an equal place in the brotherhood of believers, neither his colour nor his race nor any associations of the past standing in the way. It is doubtless the ready admission they receive, that makes the pagan Negroes willing to enter into a religious society whose higher civilisation demands that they should give up many of their old barbarous habits and customs; at the same time the very fact that the acceptance of Islam does imply an advance in civilisation and is a very distinct step in the intellectual, moral and material progress of a Negro tribe, helps very largely to explain the success of this faith. The forces arrayed on its side are so powerful and ascendant, that the barbarism, ignorance and superstition which it seeks to sweep away have little chance of making a lengthened resistance. What the civilisation of Muslim Africa imples to the Negro convert, is admirably expressed in the following words: "The worst evils which, there is reason to believe, prevailed at one time over the whole of Africa, and which are still to be found in many parts of it, and those, too, not far from the Gold Coast and from our own settlements—cannibalism and human sacrifice and the burial of living infants—disappear at once and for ever. Natives who have hitherto lived in a state of nakedness, or nearly so, begin to dress, and that neatly; natives who have never washed before begin to wash, and that frequently; for ablutions are commanded in the Sacred Law, and it is an ordinance which does not involve too severe a strain on their natural instincts. The tribal organisation tends to give place to something which has a wider basis. In other words, tribes coalesce into nations, and, with the increase of energy and intelligence, nations into empires. Many such instances could be adduced from the history of the Soudan and the adjoining countries during the last hundred years. If the warlike spirit is thus stimulated, the centres from which war springs are fewer in number and further apart. War is better organised, and is under some form of

[1] Ibn Khallikān, vol. i. p. 18.

restraint; quarrels are not picked for nothing; there is less indiscriminate plundering and greater security for property and life. Elementary schools,[1] like those described by Mungo Park a century ago, spring up, and even if they only teach their scholars to recite the Koran, they are worth something in themselves, and may be a step to much more. The well-built and neatly-kept mosque, with its call to prayer repeated five times a day, its Mecca-pointing niche, its Imam and its weekly service, becomes the centre of the village, instead of the ghastly fetish or Juju house. The worship of one God, omnipotent, omnipresent, omniscient, and compassionate, is an immeasurable advance upon anything which the native has been taught to worship before. The Arabic language, in which the Mussulman scriptures are always written, is a language of extraordinary copiousness and beauty; once learned it becomes a *lingua franca* to the tribes of half the continent, and serves as an introduction to literature, or rather, it is a literature in itself. It substitutes moreover, a written code of law for the arbitrary caprice of a chieftain—a change which is, in itself, an immense advance in civilisation. Manufactures and commerce spring up, not the dumb trading or the elementary bartering of raw products which we know from Herodotus to have existed from the earliest times in Africa, nor the cowrie shells, or gunpowder, or tobacco, or rum, which still serve as a chief medium of exchange all along the coast, but manufactures involving considerable skill, and a commerce

[1] "Extracts from the Koran form the earliest reading lessons of children, and the commentaries and other works founded upon it furnish the principal subjects of the advanced studies. Schools of different grades have existed for centuries in various interior negro countries, and under the provision of law, in which even the poor are educated at the public expense, and in which the deserving are carried on many years through long courses of regular instruction. Nor is the system always confined to the Arabic language, or to the works of Arabic writers. A number of native languages have been reduced to writing, books have been translated from the Arabic and original works have been written in them. Schools also have been kept in which native languages are taught." Condition and Character of Negroes in Africa. By Theodore Dwight. (Methodist Quarterly Review, January 1869.)

Dr. Blyden (pp. 206–7) mentions the following books as read by Muslims in Western Africa: Maqāmāt of Ḥarīrī, portions of Aristotle and Plato translated into Arabic, an Arabic version of Hippocrates, and the Arabic New Testament and Psalms issued by the American Bible Society. For the literature of the Muslims in East Africa, see Becker: Islam in Deutsch Ostafrika, p. 18 sqq.

which is elaborately organised; and under their influence, and that of the more settled government which Islam brings in its train, there have arisen those great cities of Negroland whose very existence, when first they were described by European travellers, could not but be half discredited. I am far from saying that the religion is the sole cause of all this comparative prosperity. I only say it is consistent with it, and it encourages it. Climatic conditions and various other influences co-operate towards the result; but what has Pagan Africa, even where the conditions are very similar, to compare with it? As regards the individual, it is admitted on all hands that Islam gives to its new Negro converts an energy, a dignity, a self-reliance, and a self-respect which is all too rarely found in their Pagan or their Christian fellow-countrymen."[1]

The words above quoted were written before the partition of the greater part of Africa among the governments of Christian Europe—England, France and Germany—but the imposing character of Muslim civilisation has not ceased to impress the Negro mind, or to operate as one of the influences favourable to the conversion of the African fetish-worshippers. Brought suddenly into contact with European culture, these have received an impulse to advance in the path of civilisation, but being unable to bridge over the gulf that separates them from their foreign rulers, they find in Islam a culture corresponding to their needs and capable of understanding their requirements and aspirations.[2] So far, therefore, from the extension of European domination tending to hamper the activities of Muhammadan propagandists, it has to a very remarkable degree contributed towards the progress of Islam. The bringing of peace to countries formerly harassed by wars of extermination or the raids of slave-hunters, the establishment of ordered methods of government and administration, and the increased facilities of communication by the making of roads and the building of railways, have given a great stimulus to trade and have enabled that active propagandist,

[1] Mohammedanism in Africa, by R. Bosworth Smith. (The Nineteenth Century, December 1887, pp. 798–800.)

[2] Le Chatelier, (3), p. 348.

the Muslim trader, to extend his influence in districts previously untrodden, and traverse familiar ground with greater security. Further, the suppression of the slave-trade has removed one of the great obstacles to the spread of Islam in pagan Africa, because it was to the interest of the Arab and other Muhammadan slave-dealers not to narrow the field of their operations by admitting their possible victims into the brotherhood of Islam.[1] Converts are now won from pagan tribes which in the days of the slave-trade were untouched by missionary effort. To this result the European governments have contributed by employing Muhammadans to fill the subordinate posts in the civil administration (since among the Muhammadans alone were educated persons to be found) and distributing them throughout pagan districts, by employing Muhammadan teachers in the Government schools, and by recruiting their armies from among Muhammadan tribes; they have thus added to the prestige of Islam in the eyes of the pagan Africans—a circumstance that the Muslims have not been slow to make use of, to the advantage of their own faith.[2]

So little truth is there in the statement that Islam makes progress only by force of arms,[3] that on the contrary the partition of Africa among the European powers, who have wrested the sword from the hands of the Muslim chiefs now under their control, has initiated a propaganda which seems likely to succeed where centuries of Muhammadan domination have failed.

[1] Forget, p. 95. Merensky, p. 156. (" Den Vertretern des Islam aber stand ihr Vorteil, der Gewinn, den die Unterdrückung der Eingebornen bringt, höher als die Ausbreitung ihres Glaubens. Hätte man die Völker Afrikas durch die Macht geistiger Waffen unter gütigem Entgegenkommen zu Mohammedanern gemacht, so waren sie Glaubensgenossen, gleichberechtige Brüder, die man nicht mehr berauben, zu Sklaven machen, oder als Sklaven nur Arbeit ausnutzen konnte.")

[2] Westermann, p. 643. L. de Contenson, p. 244. Kumm, p. 122.

[3] Thus Merensky, discussing the failure of Islam to dominate the whole of Africa after centuries of occupation says :—" Wir sehen die Ursache für diese merkwürdige Erscheinung in den Beziehungen, in denen bei den Mohammedanern die äussere Gewalt zum Islam und zur Ausbreitung des Islam steht. Beides steht und fällt miteinander, dringt miteinander vor und geht miteinander auch wieder zurück." (p. 156.)

CHAPTER XII.

THE SPREAD OF ISLAM IN THE MALAY ARCHIPELAGO.

THE history of the Malay Archipelago during the last 600 years furnishes us with one of the most interesting chapters in the story of the spread of Islam by missionary efforts. During the whole of this period we find evidences of a continuous activity on the part of the Muhammadan missionaries, in one or other at least of the East India islands. In every instance, in the beginning, their work had to be carried on without any patronage or assistance from the rulers of the country, but solely by the force of persuasion, and in many cases in the face of severe opposition, especially on the part of the Spaniards. But in spite of all difficulties, and with varying success, they have prosecuted their efforts with untiring energy, perfecting their work (more especially in the present day) wherever it has been partial or insufficient.

It is impossible to fix the precise date of the first introduction of Islam into the Malay Archipelago. It may have been carried thither by the Arab traders in the early centuries of the Hijrah, long before we have any historical notices of such influences being at work. This supposition is rendered the more probable by the knowledge we have of the extensive commerce with the East carried on by the Arabs from very early times. In the second century B.C. the trade with Ceylon was wholly in their hands. At the beginning of the seventh century of the Christian era, the trade with China, through Ceylon, received a great impulse, so that in the middle of the eighth century Arab traders were to be found in great numbers in Canton; while from the tenth to the fifteenth century, until the arrival of the Portuguese, they were undisputed masters of the trade with the East.[1] We may therefore conjecture with tolerable certainty that they must have established their commercial settlements on some of the islands of the Malay Archipelago, as they did elsewhere, at a very early period: though no mention is made of these islands in the works of the Arab geographers earlier than the ninth century,[2] yet in the Chinese annals, under the date A.D. 674, an account is given of an Arab chief, who from later notices is conjectured to have been the head of an Arab settlement on the west coast of Sumatra.[3]

Missionaries must also, however, have come to the Malay Archipelago from the south of India, judging from certain peculiarities of Muhammadan theology adopted by the islanders. Most of the Musalmans of the Archipelago belong to the Shāfi'iyyah sect, which is at the present day predominant on the Coromandel and Malabar coasts, as was the case also about the middle of the fourteenth century when Ibn Baṭūṭah visited these parts.[4] So when we consider that the Muhammadans of the neighbouring countries belong to the Ḥanafiyyah sect, we can only explain the prevalence of Shāfi'iyyah teachings by assuming them to have been brought thither from the Malabar coast, the ports of which were frequented by merchants from Java, as well as from China, Yaman and Persia.[5] From India, too, or from Persia, must have come the Shī'ism, of which traces are still found in Java and Sumatra. From Ibn Baṭūṭah we learn that the Muhammadan Sultan of Samudra had entered into friendly relations with the court of Dehli, and among the learned doctors of the law whom this devout prince especially favoured, there were two of Persian origin, the one coming from Shiraz and the other from Ispahan.[6] But long before this time merchants from the Deccan, through whose hands passed the trade between the Musalman states of India and the Malay Archipelago, had established themselves in large numbers in the trading

[1] Niemann, p. 337.
[2] Reinaud: Géographie d'Aboulféda, tome i. p. cccxxxix.
[3] Groeneveldt, pp. 14, 15.
[4] Ibn Baṭūṭah, tome iv. pp. 66, 80.
[5] Veth (3), vol. i. p. 231. Ibn Baṭūṭah, tome iv. p. 89.
[6] Ibn Baṭūṭah, tome iv. pp. 230, 234.

ports of these islands, where they sowed the seed of the new religion.[1]

It is to the proselytising efforts of these Arab and Indian merchants that the native Muhammadan population, which we find already in the earliest historical notices of Islam in these parts, owes its existence. Settling in the centres of commerce, they intermarried with the people of the land, and these heathen wives and the slaves of their households thus formed the nucleus of a Muslim community which its members made every effort in their power to increase. The following description of the methods adopted by these merchant missionaries in the Philippine Islands, gives a picture of what was no doubt the practice of many preceding generations of Muhammadan traders :—" The better to introduce their religion into the country, the Muhammadans adopted the language and many of the customs of the natives, married their women, purchased slaves in order to increase their personal importance, and succeeded finally in incorporating themselves among the chiefs who held the foremost rank in the state. Since they worked together with greater ability and harmony than the natives, they gradually increased their power more and more, as having numbers of slaves in their possession, they formed a kind of confederacy among themselves and established a sort of monarchy, which they made hereditary in one family. Though such a confederacy gave them great power, yet they felt the necessity of keeping on friendly terms with the old aristocracy, and of ensuring their freedom to those classes whose support they could not afford to dispense with." [2] It must have been in some such way as this that the different Muhammadan settlements in the Malay Archipelago laid a firm political and social basis for their proselytising efforts. They did not come as conquerors, like the Spanish in the sixteenth century, or use the sword as an instrument of conversion; nor did they arrogate to themselves the privileges of a superior and dominant race so as to degrade and oppress the original inhabitants, but coming simply in the guise of traders they employed all

[1] Snouck Hurgronje (1), pp. 8–9.
[2] Padre Gainza, quoted by C. Semper, p. 67.

their superior intelligence and civilisation in the service of their religion, rather than as a means towards their personal aggrandisement and the amassing of wealth.[1] With this general statement of the subsidiary means adopted by them, let us follow in detail their proselytising efforts through the various islands in turn.

Tradition represents Islam as having been introduced into Sumatra from Arabia. But there is no sound historical basis for such a belief, and all the evidence seems to point to India as the source from which the people of Sumatra derived their knowledge of the new faith. Active commercial relations had existed for centuries between India and the Malay Archipelago, and the first missionaries to Sumatra were probably Indian traders.[2] There is, however, no historical record of their labours, and the Malay chronicles ascribe the honour of being the first missionary to Atjeh, in the north-west of Sumatra, to an Arab named 'Abd Allāh 'Ārif, who is said to have visited the island about the middle of the twelfth century; one of his disciples, Burhān al-Dīn, is said to have carried the knowledge of the faith down the west coast as far as Priaman.[3] Untrustworthy as this record is, it may yet possibly indicate the existence of some proselytising activity about this period; for the Malay chronicle of Atjeh gives 1205 as the date of the accession of Jūhan Shāh, the traditionary founder of the Muhammadan dynasty. He is said to have been a stranger from the West,[4] and to have come to these shores to preach the faith of the Prophet; he made many proselytes, married a wife from among the people of the country, and was hailed by them as their king, under the half-Sanskrit, half-Arabic title of Srī Padūka Sulṭān. For some time the new faith would in all probability have been confined to the ports at which Muhammadan merchants touched, and its progress inland would be slower, as here

[1] Crawfurd (2), vol. ii. p. 265.
[2] Snouck Hurgronje: L'Arabie et les Indes Néerlandaises. (Revue de l'Histoire des Religions, vol. lvii. p. 69 sqq.)
[3] De Hollander, vol. i. p. 581. Veth (1), p. 60.
[4] This vague reference would fit either Arabia, Persia or India; but if such a person as Jūhan Shāh ever existed, he probably came from the Coromandel or Malabar coast. (Chronique du Royaume d'Atcheh, traduite du Malay par Ed. Dulaurier, p. 7.)

it would come up against the strong Hindu influences that had their centre in the kingdom of Menangkabau.

Marco Polo, who spent five months on the north coast of Sumatra in 1292, speaks of all the inhabitants being idolaters, except in the petty kingdom of Parlāk on the north-east corner of the island, where, too, only the townspeople were Muhammadans, for " this kingdom, you must know, is so much frequented by the Saracen merchants that they have converted the natives to the Law of Mahommet," but the hill-people were all idolaters and cannibals.[1] Further, one of the Malay chronicles says that it was Sultan 'Alī Mughāyat Shāh, who reigned over Atjeh from 1507 to 1522, who first set the example of embracing Islam, in which he was followed by his subjects.[2] But it is not improbable that the honour of being the first Muslim ruler of the state has been here attributed as an added glory to the monarch who founded the greatness of Atjeh and began to extend its sway over the neighbouring country, and that he rather effected a revival of, or imparted a fresh impulse to, the religious life of his subjects than gave to them their first knowledge of the faith of the Prophet. For Islam had certainly set firm foot in Sumatra long before his time. According to the traditionary account of the city of Samudra, the Sharīf of Mecca sent a mission to convert the people of Sumatra. The leader of the party was a certain Shaykh Ismā'īl : the first place on the island at which they touched, after leaving Malabar, was Pasuri (probably situated a little way down the west coast), the people of which were persuaded by their preaching to embrace Islam. They then proceeded northward to Lambri and then coasted round to the other side of the island and sailed as far down the east coast as Aru, nearly opposite Malacca, and in both of these places their efforts were crowned with a like success. At Aru they made inquiries for Samudra, a city on the north coast of the island, which seems to have been the special object of their mission, and found that they had passed it. Accordingly they retraced their course to Parlāk, where Marco Polo had found a Muhammadan community a few years before, and having gained fresh

[1] Marco Polo, vol. ii. p. 284. [2] Veth (1), p. 61.

converts here also, they went on to Samudra. This city and the kingdom of the same name had lately been founded by a certain Mara Silu, who was persuaded by Shaykh Ismā'īl to embrace Islam, and took the name of al-Malik al-Ṣāliḥ. He married the daughter of the king of Parlāk, by whom he had two sons, and in order to have a principality to leave to each, he founded the Muhammadan city and kingdom of Pasei, also on the north coast.[1]

The king, al-Malik al-Ẓāhir, whom Ibn Baṭūṭah found reigning in Samudra when he visited the island in 1345, was probably the elder of these two sons. This prince displayed all the state of Muhammadan royalty, and his dominions extended for many days' journey along the coast; he was a zealous and orthodox Muslim, fond of holding discussions with jurisconsults and theologians, and his court was frequented by poets and men of learning. Ibn Baṭūṭah gives us the names of two jurisconsults who had come thither from Persia and also of a noble who had gone on an embassy to Dehli on behalf of the king—which shows that Sumatra was already in touch with several parts of the Muhammadan world. Al-Malik al-Ẓāhir was also a great general, and made war on the heathen of the surrounding country until they submitted to his rule and paid tribute.[2]

Islam had undoubtedly by this time made great progress in Sumatra, and after having established itself along the coast, began to make its way inland. The mission of Shaykh Ismā'īl and his party had borne fruit abundantly, for a Chinese traveller who visited the island in 1413, speaks of Lambri as having a population of 1000 families, all of whom were Muslims "and very good people," while the king and people of the kingdom of Aru were all of the same faith.[3] It was either about the close of the same century or in the fifteenth century, that the religion of the Prophet found adherents in the great kingdom of Menangkabau, whose territory at one time extended from one shore to another, and over a great part of the island, north and south of the equator.[4] Though its power had by this time much

[1] Yule's Marco Polo, vol. ii. pp. 294, 303.
[2] Ibn Baṭūṭah, tome iv. pp. 230-6. [3] Groeneveldt, p. 94.
[4] At the height of its power, it stretched from 2° N. to 2° S. on the west coast, and from 1° N. to 2° S. on the east coast, but in the sixteenth century it had lost its control over the east coast. (De Hollander, vol. i. p. 3.)

declined, still as an ancient stronghold of Hinduism it presented great obstacles in the way of the progress of the new religion. Despite this fact, Islam eventually took firmer root among the subjects of this kingdom than among the majority of the inhabitants of the interior of the island.[1] It is very remarkable that this, the most central people of the island, should have been more thoroughly converted than the inhabitants of so many other districts that were more accessible to foreign influences. To the present day the inhabitants of the Batak country are still, for the most part, heathen; but Islam has gained a footing among them, e.g. some living on the borders of Atjeh have been converted, by their Muhammadan neighbours,[2] others dwelling in the mountains of the Rau country on the equator have likewise become Musalmans;[3] on the east coast also conversions of Bataks, who come much in contact with Malays, are not uncommon.[4]

The fanatical Padris (p. 372) made strenuous efforts, in vain, to force Islam upon the Bataks at the point of the sword, laying waste their country and putting many to death; but these violent methods did not win converts. When, however, the Dutch Government suppressed the Padri rising and annexed the southern part of the Batak country, Islam began to spread by peaceful means, chiefly through the zealous efforts of the native subordinate officials of the new régime, who were all Muhammadan Malays,[5] but also through the influence of the traders who wandered through the country, whose proselytising activity was followed up by the ḥājīs and other recognised teachers of the faith. It is a remarkable fact that the Bataks, who for centuries had offered a pertinacious resistance to the entrance of Islam into their midst, though they were hemmed in between two fanatical Muhammadan populations, the Achinese on the north and the Malays on the south, have in recent years responded with enthusiasm to the

[1] Marsden, p. 343.
[2] J. H. Moor. (Appendix, p. 1.)
[3] Marsden, p. 355.
[4] Godsdienstige verschijnselen en toestanden in Oost-Indië. (Uit de Koloniale Verslagen van 1886 en 1887.) Med. Ned. Zendelinggen, vol. xxxii. pp. 175–6. (1888.) In 1909, out of a total of 500,000 Bataks, 300,000 were still pagan, but 125,000 were Muslim and 80,000 Christian. (R. du M. M., vol. viii. p. 183.)
[5] J. Warneck: Die Religion der Batak, p. 122. (Leipzig, 1909.)

peaceful efforts made for their conversion. An explanation would appear to be found in the breaking down of their exclusive national characteristics through the Dutch occupation and the conquest opening up their country to foreign influences, which implied the commencement of a new era in their cultural development, as well as in the skilful procedure of the exponents of the new faith, who knew how to accommodate their teachings to the existing beliefs of the Bataks and their deep-rooted superstitions.[1] A considerable impulse seems to have been given to Muslim propaganda by the establishment of Christian missions among the Bataks in 1897, and they appear even to have paved the way for its success. Two Batak villages, the entire population of which had been baptised, are said to have gone over in a body to Islam shortly afterwards.[2]

In Central Sumatra there is still a large heathen population, though the majority of the inhabitants are Muslims; but these latter are very ignorant of their religion, with the exception of a few ḥājīs and religious teachers: even among the people of Korintji, who are for the most part zealous adherents of the faith, there are certain sections of the population who still worship the gods of their pagan ancestors.[3] Efforts are, however, being made towards a religious revival, and the Muslim missionaries are making fresh conquests from among the heathen, especially along the west coast.[4] In the district of Sipirok a religious teacher attached to the mosque in the town of the same name, in a quarter of a century, converted the whole population of this district to Islam, with the exception of the Christians who were to be found there, mostly descendants of former slaves,[5] and a later missionary movement in the first decade of the twentieth century succeeded in winning over to Islam many of the Christians of this district, even

[1] G. R. Simon: Die Propaganda des Halbmondes. Ein Beitrag zur Skizzierung des Islam unter den Batakken, pp. 425, 429–430. (Allgemeine Missions-Zeitschrift, vol. xxvii. 1900.)

[2] R. du M. M., vol. viii. (1909), p. 183.

[3] A. L. van Hassalt, pp. 55, 68.

[4] Med. Ned. Zendelinggen, id. p. 173. (Koloniaal Verslag van 1911, p. 26; 1912, p. 17.)

[5] Uit het Koloniaal Verslag van 1889. (Med. Ned. Zendelinggen, vol. xxxiv. p. 168.) (1890.)

some living in the centre of the sphere of influence of the Christian mission.[1]

Islam is traditionally represented to have been introduced into Palembang about 1440 by Raden Raḥmat, of whose propagandist activity an account will be given below (p. 381). But Hindu influences appear to have been firmly rooted here, and the progress of the new faith was slow. Even up to the nineteenth century the Muslims of Palembang were said to know little of their religion except the external observances of it, with the exception of the inhabitants of the capital who come into daily contact with Arabs;[2] but in the first decade of the twentieth century there would appear to have been a revival of the religious life and a growing propaganda, as the Colonial Reports of the Dutch Government draw attention to the continual spread of Islam among the heathen population of various districts of Palembang.[3]

It was from Java that Islam was first brought into the Lampong districts which form the southern extremity of Sumatra, by a chieftain of these districts, named Minak Kamala Bumi. About the end of the fifteenth century he crossed over the Strait of Sunda to the kingdom of Bantam on the west coast of Java, which had accepted the teachings of the Muslim missionaries a few years before the date of his visit; here he, too, embraced Islam, and after making the pilgrimage to Mecca, spread the knowledge of his newly adopted faith among his fellow-countrymen.[4] This religion has made considerable progress among the Lampongs, and most of the villages have mosques in them, but the old superstitions still linger on in parts of the interior.[5]

In the early part of the nineteenth century a religious revival was set on foot in Sumatra, which was not without its influence in promoting the further propagation of Islam. In 1803 three Sumatran ḥājīs returned from Mecca to their native country: during their stay in the holy city they had

[1] Koloniaal Verslag van 1910, p. 30.
[2] De Hollander, vol. i. p. 703.
[3] Koloniaal Verslag van 1904, p. 80; 1905, p. 46; 1909, p, 47; 1910, p. 33; 1911, p. 29; 1912, p. 21.
[4] Canne, p. 510.
[5] Marsden, p. 301.

been profoundly influenced by the Wahhābī movement for the reformation of Islam, and were now eager to introduce the same reforms among their fellow-countrymen and to stir up in them a purer and more zealous religious life. Accordingly they began to preach the strict monotheism of the Wahhābī sect, forbade prayers to saints, drinking and gambling and all other practices contrary to the law of the Qur'ān. They made a number of proselytes both from among their co-religionists and the heathen population. They later declared a Jihād against the Bataks, and in the hands of unscrupulous and ambitious men the movement lost its original character and degenerated into a savage and bloody war of conquest. In 1821 these so-called Padris came into conflict with the Dutch Government and it was not until 1838 that their last stronghold was taken and their power broken.[1]

All the civilised Malays of the Malay Peninsula trace their origin to migrations from Sumatra, especially from Menangkabau, the famous kingdom mentioned above, which is said at one time to have been the most powerful on the island; some of the chiefs of the interior states of the southern part of the Malay Peninsula still receive their investiture from this place. At what period these colonies from the heart of Sumatra settled in the interior of the Peninsula, is matter of conjecture, but Singapore and the southern extremity of the Peninsula seem to have received a colony in the middle of the twelfth century, by the descendants of which Malacca was founded about a century later.[2] From its advantageous situation, in the highway of eastern commerce it soon became a large and flourishing city, and there is little doubt but that Islam was introduced by the Muhammadan merchants who settled here.[3] The Malay chronicle of Malacca assigns the conversion of this kingdom to the reign of a certain Sulṭān Muḥammad Shāh who came to the throne in 1276. He is said to have been reigning

[1] Niemann, pp. 356–9.

[2] J. H. Moor, p. 255.

[3] " Depois que estes de induzidos por os Mouros Parseos, e Guzarates (que alli vieram residir por causa do commercio), de Gentios os convertêram á secta de Mahamed. Da qual conversão por alli concorrerem varias nações, começou laurar esta inferna peste pela virzinhança de Malaca." (De Barros, Dec. ii. Liv. vi. cap. i. p. 15.)

some years before a ship commanded by Sīdī 'Abd al-'Azīz came to Malacca from Jiddah, and the king was persuaded by the new-comers to change his faith and to give up his Malay name for one containing the name of the Prophet.[1] But the general character of this document makes its trustworthiness exceedingly doubtful,[2] in spite of the likelihood that the date of so important an event would have been exactly noted (as was done in many parts of the Archipelago) by a people who, proud of the event, would look upon it as opening a new epoch in their history. A Portuguese historian gives a much later date, namely 1384, in which year, he says, a Qāḍī came from Arabia and having converted the king, gave him the name of Muḥammad after the Prophet, adding Shāh to it.[3]

In the annals of Queda, one of the northernmost of the states of the Malay Peninsula, we have a curious account of the introduction of Islam into this kingdom, about A.D. 1501,[4] which (divested of certain miraculous incidents) is as follows: A learned Arab, by name Shaykh 'Abd Allāh, having come to Queda, visited the Raja and inquired what was the religion of the country. "My religion," replied the Raja, "and that of all my subjects is that which has been handed down to us by the people of old. We all worship idols." "Then has your highness never heard of Islam, and of the Qur'ān which descended from God to Muḥammad, and has superseded all other religions, leaving them in the possession of the devil?" "I pray you then, if this be true," said the Raja, "to instruct and enlighten us in this new faith." In a transport of holy fervour at this request, Shaykh 'Abd Allāh embraced the Raja and then instructed him in the creed. Persuaded by his teaching, the Raja sent for all his jars of spirits (to which he was much addicted), and with his own hands emptied them on the ground. After this he had all the idols of the palace brought out; the idols of gold, and silver, and clay, and

[1] Aristide Marre: Malâka. Histoire des rois malays de Malâka. Traduit et extrait du Livre des Annales malayses, intitulé en arabe Selâlet al Selâtyn, p. 8. (Paris, 1874.)

[2] Crawfurd (1), pp. 241–2.

[3] De Barros, Dec. iv. Liv. ii. cap. 1.

[4] Barbosa, writing in 1516, speaks of the numerous Muhammadan merchants that frequented the port of Queda. (Ramusio, tom. i. p. 317.)

wood were all heaped up in his presence, and were all broken and cut to pieces by Shaykh 'Abd Allāh with his sword and with an axe, and the fragments consumed in the fire. The Shaykh asked the Raja to assemble all his women of the fort and palace. When they had all come into the presence of the Raja and the Shaykh, they were initiated into the doctrines of Islam. The Shaykh was mild and courteous in his demeanour, persuasive and soft in his language, so that he gained the hearts of the inmates of the palace. The Raja soon after sent for his four aged ministers, who, on entering the hall, were surprised at seeing a Shaykh seated near the Raja. The Raja explained to them the object of the Shaykh's coming; whereupon the four chiefs expressed their readiness to follow the example of his highness, saying, "We hope that Shaykh 'Abd Allāh will instruct us also." The latter hearing these words, embraced the four ministers and said that he hoped that, to prove their sincerity, they would send for all the people to come to the audience hall, bringing with them all the idols that they were wont to worship and the idols that had been handed down by the men of former days. The request was complied with and all the idols kept by the people were at that very time brought down and there destroyed and burnt to dust; no one was sorry at this demolition of their false gods, all were glad to enter the pale of Islam. Shaykh 'Abd Allāh after this said to the four ministers, "What is the name of your prince?" They replied, "His name is Pra Ong Mahāwāngsā." "Let us change it for one in the language of Islam," said the Shaykh. After some consultation, the name of the Raja was changed at his request to Sultan Muzlaf al-Shāh, because, the Shaykh averred, it is a celebrated name and is found in the Qur'ān.[1]

The Raja now built mosques wherever the population was considerable, and directed that to each there should be attached forty-four of the inhabitants at least as a settled congregation, for a smaller number would have been few for the duties of religion. So mosques were erected and great

[1] The form مزلف does not actually occur in the Qur'ān; reference is probably made to some such passage as xxvi. 90: وَأُزْلِفَتِ ٱلْجَنَّةُ لِلْمُتَّقِينَ "And paradise shall be brought near the pious."

drums were attached to them to be beaten to call the people to prayer on Fridays. Shaykh 'Abd Allāh continued for some time to instruct the people in the religion of Islam; they flocked to him from all the coasts and districts of Queda and its vicinity, and were initiated by him into its forms and ceremonies.

The news of the conversion of the inhabitants of Queda by Shaykh 'Abd Allāh reached Atjeh, and the Sultan of that country and a certain Shaykh Nūr al-Dīn, an Arab missionary, who had come from Mecca, sent some books and a letter, which ran as follows :—" This letter is from the Sultan of Atjeh and Nūr al-Dīn to our brother the Sultan of Queda and Shaykh 'Abd Allāh of Yaman, now in Queda. We have sent two religious books, in order that the faith of Islam may be firmly established and the people fully instructed in their duties and in the rites of the faith." A letter was sent in reply by the Raja and Shaykh 'Abd Allāh, thanking the donors. So Shaykh 'Abd Allāh redoubled his efforts, and erected additional small mosques in all the different villages for general convenience, and instructed the people in all the rules and observances of the faith. The Raja and his wife were constantly with the Shaykh, learning to read the Qur'ān. The royal pair searched also for some maiden of the lineage of the Rajas of the country, to be the Shaykh's wife. But no one could be found who was willing to give his daughter thus in marriage because the holy man was about to return to Baghdād, and only waited until he had sufficiently instructed some person to supply his place. Now at this time the Sultan had three sons, Raja Mu'azzam Shāh, Raja Muḥammad Shāh, and Raja Sulaymān Shāh. These names had been borrowed from the Qur'ān by Shaykh 'Abd Allāh and bestowed upon the princes, whom he exhorted to be patient and slow to anger in their intercourse with their slaves and the lower orders, and to regard with pity all the servants of God, and the poor and needy.[1]

It must not be supposed that the labours of Shaykh 'Abd Allāh were crowned with complete success, for we learn

[1] A translation of the Keddah Annals, by Lieut.-Col. James Low, vol. iii. pp. 474–7.

from the annals of Atjeh that a Sultan of this country who conquered Queda in 1649, set himself to "more firmly establish the faith and destroy the houses of the Liar" or temples of idols.[1] Thus a century and a half elapsed before idolatry was completely rooted out.

We possess no other details of the history of the conversion of the Malays of the Peninsula, but in many places the graves of the Arab missionaries who first preached the faith to them are honoured by these people.[2] Their long intercourse with the Arabs and the Muslims of the east coast of India has made them very rigid observers of their religious duties, and they have the reputation of being the most exemplary Muhammadans of the Archipelago; at the same time their constant contact with the Hindus, Buddhists, Christians and pagans of their own country has made them liberal and tolerant. They are very strict in the keeping of the fast of Ramaḍān and in performing the pilgrimage to Mecca. The religious interests of the people are always considered at the same time as their temporal welfare; and when a village is found to contain more than forty houses and is considered to be of a size that necessitates its organisation and the appointment of the regular village officers, a public preacher is always included among the number and a mosque is formally built and instituted.[3]

In the north, where the Malay states border on Siam, Islam has exercised considerable influence on the Siamese Buddhists; those who have here been converted are called Samsams and speak a language that is a mixed jargon of the languages of the two people.[4] Converts are also made from among the wild tribes of the Peninsula.[5]

The history of the spread of Islam in Indo-China is obscure; Arab and Persian merchants probably introduced their religion into the sea-port towns from the tenth century onwards, but its most important expansion was due to the immigrations of Malays which began at the close of the fourteenth century.[6]

[1] A translation of the Keddah Annals, by Lieut.-Col. James Low, vol. iii. p. 480.

[2] Newbold, vol. i. p. 252.

[3] McNair, pp. 226–9.

[4] J. H. Moor, p. 242.

[5] Newbold, vol. ii. pp. 106, 396.

[6] R. du M. M., tome ii (1907), pp. 137–8.

We must now go back several centuries in order to follow out the history of the conversion of Java. The preaching and promulgation of the doctrines of Islam in this island were undoubtedly for a long time entirely the result of the labours of individual merchants or of the leaders of small colonies, for in Java there was no central Muhammadan power to throw in its influence on the side of the new religion or enforce the acceptance of it by warlike means. On the contrary, the Muslim missionaries came in contact with a Hindu civilisation, that had thrust its roots deep into the life of the country and had raised the Javanese to a high level of culture and progress—expressing itself moreover in institutions and laws radically different to those of Arabia. Even up to the present day, the Muhammadan law has failed to establish itself absolutely, even where the authority of Islam is generally predominant, and there is still a constant struggle between the adherents of the old Malayan usages and the Ḥājīs, who having made the pilgrimage to Mecca, return enthusiastic for a strict observance of Muslim Law. Consequently the work of conversion must have proceeded very slowly, and we can say with tolerable certainty that while part of the history of this proselytising movement may be disentangled from legends and traditions, much of it must remain wholly unknown to us. In the Malay Chronicle, which purports to give us an account of the first preachers of the faith, what was undoubtedly the work of many generations and must have been carried on through many centuries, is compressed within the compass of a few years; and, as frequently happens in popular histories, a few well-known names gain the fame and credit that belongs of right to the patient labours of their unknown predecessors.[1] Further, the quiet, unobtrusive labours of many of these missionaries would not be likely to attract the notice of the chronicler, whose attention would naturally be fixed rather on the doings of kings and princes, and of those who came in close relationship to them. But failing such larger knowledge, we must fain be content with the facts that have been handed down to us.

[1] Snouck Hurgronje (1), p. 9.

In the following pages, therefore, it is proposed to give a brief sketch of the establishment of the Muhammadan religion in this island, as presented in the native chronicle, which, though full of contradictions and fables, has undoubtedly a historical foundation, as is attested by the inscriptions on the tombs of the chief personages mentioned and the remains of ancient cities, etc. The following account therefore may, in the want of any other authorities, be accepted as substantially correct, with the caution above mentioned against ascribing too much efficacy to the proselytising efforts of individuals.

The first attempt to introduce Islam into Java was made by a native of the island about the close of the twelfth century. The first king of Pajajaran, a state in the western part of the island, left two sons; of these, the elder chose to follow the profession of a merchant and undertook a trading expedition to India, leaving the kingdom to his younger brother, who succeeded to the throne in the year 1190 with the title of Prabu Munding Sari. In the course of his wanderings, the elder brother fell in with some Arab merchants, and was by them converted to Islam, taking the name of Ḥājī Purwa.

On his return to his native country, he tried with the help of an Arab missionary to convert his brother and the royal family to his new faith; but, his efforts proving unsuccessful, he fled into the jungle for fear of the king and his unbelieving subjects, and we hear no more of him.[1]

In the latter half of the fourteenth century, a missionary movement, which was attended with greater success, was instituted by a certain Mawlānā Malik Ibrāhīm, who landed on the east coast of Java with some of his co-religionists, and established himself near the town of Gresik, opposite the island of Madura. He is said to have traced his descent to Zayn al-ʿĀbidīn, a great-grandson of the Prophet, and to have been cousin of the Raja of Chermen.[2] Here he occupied himself successfully in the work of conversion, and speedily gathered a small band of believers around him.

[1] Veth (3), vol. i. p. 215. Raffles (ed. of 1830), vol. ii. pp. 103, 104, 183.
[2] The situation of Chermen is not certain. Veth (3), vol. i. p. 230, conjectures that it may have been in India, but Rouffaer (p. 115[n]) gives good reasons for placing it in Sumatra.

Later on, he was joined by his cousin, the Raja of Chermen, who came in the hope of converting the Raja of the Hindu Kingdom of Majapahit, and of forming an alliance with him by offering his daughter in marriage. On his arrival he sent his son, Ṣādiq Muḥammad, to Majapahit to arrange an interview, while he busied himself in the building of a mosque and the conversion of the inhabitants. A meeting of the two princes took place accordingly, but before the favourable impression then produced could be followed up, a sickness broke out among the people of the Raja of Chermen, which carried off his daughter, three of his nephews who had accompanied him, and a great part of his retinue; whereupon he himself returned to his own kingdom. These misfortunes prejudiced the mind of the Raja of Majapahit against the new faith, which he said should have better protected its votaries: and the mission accordingly failed. Mawlānā Ibrāhīm, however, remained behind, in charge of the tombs [1] of his kinsfolk and co-religionists, and himself died twenty-one years later, in 1419, and was buried at Gresik, where his tomb is still venerated as that of the first apostle of Islam to Java.

A Chinese Musalman, who accompanied the envoy of the Emperor of China to Java in the capacity of interpreter, six years before the death of Mawlānā Ibrāhīm, i. e. in 1413, mentions the presence of his co-religionists in this island in his " General Account of the Shores of the Ocean," where he says, " In this country there are three kinds of people. First the Muhammadans, who have come from the west, and have established themselves here; their dress and food is clean and proper; second, the Chinese who have run away and settled here; what they eat and use is also very fine, and many of them have adopted the Muhammadan religion and observe its precepts. The third kind are the natives, who are very ugly and uncouth, they go about with uncombed heads and naked feet, and believe devoutly in devils, theirs being one of the countries called devil-countries in Buddhist books." [2]

[1] A description of the present condition of these tombs, on one of which traces of an inscription in Arabic characters are still visible, is given by J. F. G. Brumund, p. 185.

[2] Groeneveldt, pp. vii. 49–50.

We now approach the period in which the rule of the Muhammadans became predominant in the island, after their religion had been introduced into it for nearly a century; and here it will be necessary to enter a little more closely into the details of the history in order to show that this was not the result of any fanatical movement stirred up by the Arabs, but rather of a revolution carried out by the natives of the country themselves,[1] who (though they naturally gained strength from the bond of a common faith) were stirred up to unite in order to wrest the supreme power from the hands of their heathen fellow-countrymen, not by the preaching of a religious war, but through the exhortations of an ambitious aspirant to the throne who had a wrong to avenge.[2]

The political condition of the island may be described as follows:—The central and eastern provinces of the island, which were the most wealthy and populous and the furthest advanced in civilisation, were under the sway of the Hindu kingdom of Majapahit. Further west were Cheribon and several other petty, independent princedoms; while the rest of the island, including all the districts at its western extremity, was subject to the King of Pajajaran.

The King of Majapahit had married a daughter of the prince of Champa, a small state in Cambodia, east of the Gulf of Siam.[3] She being jealous of a favourite concubine of the King, he sent this concubine away to his son Arya Damar, governor of Palembang in Sumatra, where she gave birth to a son, Raden Patah, who was brought up as one of the governor's own children. This child (as we shall see) was destined in after years to work a terrible vengeance for the cruel treatment of his mother. Another daughter of the prince of Champa had married an Arab who had come to Champa to preach the faith of Islam.[4] From this union was born Raden Raḥmat, who was carefully brought up by his father in the Muhammadan religion and is still

[1] Kern, p. 21.
[2] Veth (3), vol. i. pp. 233–42. Raffles, vol. ii. pp. 113–33.
[3] Rouffaer, however, places this Champa, not in Cambodia, but on the north coast of Atjeh and identifies it with the modern Djeumpa. (Encyclopaedie van N.-I., vol. iv. p. 206.)
[4] Remains of minarets and Muhammadan tombs are still to be found in Champa. (Bastian, vol. i. pp. 498–9.)

venerated by the Javanese as the chief apostle of Islam to their country.[1]

When he reached the age of twenty, his parents sent him with letters and presents to his uncle, the King of Majapahit. On his way, he stayed for two months at Palembang, as the guest of Arya Damar, whom he almost persuaded to become a Musalman, only he dared not openly profess Islam for fear of the people who were strongly attached to their ancient superstitions. Continuing his journey Raden Raḥmat came to Gresik, where an Arab missionary, Shaykh Mawlānā Jumāda 'l-Kubrā, hailed him as the promised Apostle of Islam to East Java, and foretold that the fall of paganism was at hand, and that his labours would be crowned by the conversion of many to the faith. At Majapahit he was very kindly received by the King and the princess of Chamba. Although the King was unwilling himself to become a convert to Islam, yet he conceived such an attachment and respect for Raden Raḥmat, that he made him governor over 3000 families at Ampel, on the east coast, a little south of Gresik, allowed him the free exercise of his religion and gave him permission to make converts. Here after some time he gained over most of those placed under him, to Islam.

Ampel was now the chief seat of Islam in Java, and the fame of the ruler who was so zealously working for the propagation of his religion, spread far and wide. Hereupon

[1] This genealogical table will make clear these relationships, as well as others referred to later in the text :—

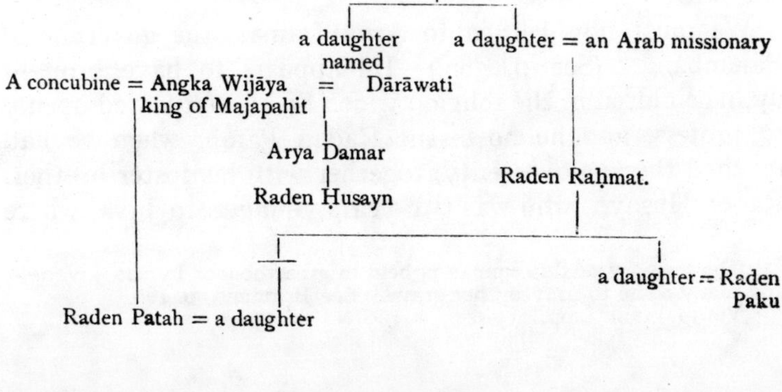

a certain Mawlānā Isḥāq came to Ampel to assist him in the work of conversion, and was assigned the task of spreading the faith in the kingdom of Balambangan, in the extreme eastern extremity of the island. Here he cured the daughter of the King, who was grievously sick, and the grateful father gave her to him in marriage. She ardently embraced the faith of Islam and her father allowed himself to receive instruction in the same, but when the Mawlānā urged him to openly profess it, as he had promised to do, if his daughter were cured, he drove him from his kingdom, and gave orders that the child that was soon to be born of his daughter, should be killed. But the mother secretly sent the infant away to Gresik to a rich Muhammadan widow [1] who brought him up with all a mother's care and educated him until he was twelve years old, when she entrusted him to Raden Raḥmat. He, after learning the history of the child, gave him the name of Raden Paku, and in course of time gave him also his daughter in marriage. Raden Paku afterwards built a mosque at Giri, to the south-west of Gresik, where he converted thousands to the faith; his influence became so great, that after the death of Raden Raḥmat, the King of Majapahit made him governor of Ampel and Gresik.[2] Meanwhile several missions were instituted from Gresik. Two sons of Raden Raḥmat established themselves at different parts of the north-east coast and made themselves famous by their religious zeal and the conversion of many of the inhabitants of those parts. Raden Raḥmat also sent a missionary, by name Shaykh Khalīfah Ḥusayn, across to the neighbouring island of Madura, where he built a mosque and won over many to the faith.

We must now return to Arya Damar, the governor of Palembang. (See p. 380.) He appears to have brought up his children in the religion which he himself feared openly to profess, and he now sent Raden Patah, when he had reached the age of twenty, together with his foster-brother, Raden Ḥusayn, who was two years younger, to Java, where

[1] The memory of this woman is held in great honour by the Javanese, and many come to pray by her grave. See Brumund, p. 186.
[2] Veth (3), vol. i. pp. 235–6.

they landed at Gresik. Raden Patah, aware of his extraction and enraged at the cruel treatment his mother had received, refused to accompany his foster-brother to Majapahit, but stayed with Raden Raḥmat at Ampel while Raden Ḥusayn went on to the capital, where he was well received and placed in charge of a district and afterwards made general of the army.

Meanwhile Raden Patah married a granddaughter of Raden Raḥmat, and formed an establishment in a place of great natural strength called Bintara, in the centre of a marshy country, to the west of Gresik. As soon as the King of Majapahit heard of this new settlement, he sent Raden Ḥusayn to persuade his brother to come to the capital and pay homage. This Raden Ḥusayn prevailed upon him to do, and he went to the court, where his likeness to the king was at once recognised, and where he was kindly received and formally appointed governor of Bintara. Still burning for revenge and bent on the destruction of his father's kingdom, he returned to Ampel, where he revealed his plans to Raden Raḥmat. The latter endeavoured to moderate his anger, reminding him that he had never received anything but kindness at the hands of the king of Majapahit, his father, and that while the prince was so just and so beloved, his religion forbade him to make war upon or in any way to injure him. However, unpersuaded by these exhortations (as the sequel shows), Raden Patah returned to Bintara, which was now daily increasing in importance and population, while great numbers of people in the surrounding country were being converted to Islam. He had formed a plan of building a great mosque, but shortly after the work had been commenced, news arrived of the severe illness of Raden Raḥmat. He hastened to Ampel, where he found the chief missionaries of Islam gathered round the bed of him they looked upon as their leader. Among them were the two sons of Raden Raḥmat mentioned above (p. 382), Raden Paku of Giri, and five others. A few days afterwards Raden Raḥmat breathed his last, and the only remaining obstacle to Raden Patah's revengeful schemes was thus removed. The eight chiefs accompanied him back to Bintara, where they assisted in the completion of the mosque,[1] and bound themselves by a solemn oath to assist him in his attempt against Majapahit. All the Muhammadan princes joined this confederacy, with the exception of Raden Ḥusayn, who with all his followers remained true to his master, and refused to throw in his lot with his rebellious co-religionists.

A lengthy campaign followed, into the details of which we need not enter, but in 1478,[2] after a desperate battle which lasted seven days, Majapahit fell and the Hindu supremacy in eastern Java was replaced by a Muhammadan power. A short time after, Raden Ḥusayn was besieged with his followers in a fortified place, compelled to surrender and brought to Ampel, where he was kindly received by his brother. A large number of those who remained faithful to the old Hindu religion fled in 1481 to the island of Bali, where the worship of Siva is still the prevailing religion.[3] Others seem to have formed small kingdoms, under the leadership of princes of the house of Majapahit, which remained heathen for some time after the fall of the great Hindu capital.

Even under Muslim chiefs the population of central Java long remained heathen, and the progress of Islam southward from the early centres of missionary effort on the north coast was the work of centuries; even to the present day the influence of their old Hindu faith is strikingly

[1] This mosque is still standing and is looked upon by the Javanese as one of the most sacred objects in their island.

[2] There seems little doubt that this date is too early. A study of the Portuguese authorities points to the conclusion that Majapahit did not fall until forty years later. (Rouffaer, p. 144.)

[3] The people of the Bali to the present day have resisted the most zealous efforts of the Muhammadans to induce them to accept the faith of Islam, though from time to time conversions have been made and a small native Muhammadan community has been formed, numbering about 3000 souls out of a population of over 862,000. The favourable situation of the island for purposes of trade has always attracted a number of foreigners to its shores, who have in many cases taken up a permanent residence in the island. While some of these settlers have always held themselves aloof from the natives of the country, others have formed matrimonial alliances with them and have consequently become merged into the mass of the population. It is owing to the efforts of the latter that Islam has made this very slow but sure progress, and the Muhammadans of Bali are said to form an energetic and flourishing community, full of zeal for the promotion of their faith, which at least impresses their pagan neighbours, though not successful in persuading them to deny their favourite food of swine's flesh for the sake of the worship of Allāh. (Liefrinck, pp. 241–3.)

manifest in the religious notions of the Muslim population of central Java. One remarkable evidence of the deep roots that Hinduism had struck in this part of the island is the fact that it was not until 1768 that the authority of the Hindu law-books, particularly the code of Manu, gave way before a code of laws more in accordance with the spirit of Muslim legislation.[1]

Islam was introduced into the eastern parts of the island some years later, probably in the beginning of the following century, through the missionary activity of Shaykh Nūr al-Dīn Ibrāhīm of Cheribon. He won for himself a great reputation by curing a woman afflicted with leprosy, with the result that thousands came to him to be instructed in the tenets of the new faith. At first the neighbouring chiefs tried to set themselves against the movement, but finding that their opposition was of no avail, they suffered themselves to be carried along with the tide and many of them became converts to Islam.[2] Shaykh Nūr al-Dīn Ibrāhīm of Cheribon sent his son, Mawlānā Ḥasan al-Dīn, to preach the faith of Islam in Bantam, the most westerly province of the island, and a dependency of the heathen kingdom of Pajajaran. Here his efforts were attended with considerable success, among the converts being a body of ascetics, 800 in number. It is especially mentioned in the annals of this part of the country that the young prince won over those whom he converted to Islam, solely by the gentle means of persuasion, and not by the sword.[3] He afterwards went with his father on a pilgrimage to Mecca, and on his return extended his power over the neighbouring coast of Sumatra, without ever having to draw the sword, and winning converts to the faith by peaceful methods alone.[4]

But the progress of Islam in the west of Java seems to have been much slower than in the east; a long struggle ensued between the worshippers of Siva and the followers of the Prophet, and it was probably not until the middle of the sixteenth century that the Hindu kingdom of Pajajaran, which at one period of the history of Java seems

[1] Encyclopaedie van N.-I., vol. ii. p. 523.
[2] Veth (3), vol. i. pp. 245, 284.
[3] Raffles, vol. ii. p. 316.
[4] Veth (3), vol. i. pp. 285–6.

to have exercised suzerainty over the princedoms in the western part of the island, came to an end,[1] while other smaller heathen communities survived to a much later period,[2]—some even to the present day. The history of one of these—the so-called Baduwis—is of especial interest; they are the descendants of the adherents of the old religion, who after the fall of Pajajaran fled into the woods and the recesses of the mountains, where they might uninterruptedly carry out the observances of their ancestral faith. In later times, when they submitted to the rule of the Musalman Sultan of Bantam, they were allowed to continue in the exercise of their religion, on condition that no increase should be allowed in the numbers of those who professed this idolatrous faith; [3] and strange to say, they still observe this custom, although the Dutch rule has been so long established in Java and sets them free from the necessity of obedience to this ancient agreement. They strictly limit their number to forty households, and when the community increases beyond this limit, one family or more has to leave this inner circle and settle among the Muhammadan population in one of the surrounding villages.[4]

But, though the work of conversion in the west of Java proceeded more slowly than in the other parts of the island, yet, owing largely to the fact that Hinduism had not taken such deep root among the people here as in the centre of the island, the victory of Islam over the heathen worship which it supplanted was more complete than in the districts which came more immediately under the rule of the Rajas of Majapahit. The Muhammadan law is here a living force and the civilisation brought into the country from Arabia has interwoven itself with the government and the life of the people; and it has been remarked that at the present day the Muhammadans of the west of Java, who study their religion at all or have performed the pilgrimage to Mecca, form as a rule the most intelligent and prosperous part of the population.[5]

[1] Veth (3), vol. i. pp. 305, 318–9.

[2] A traveller in Java in 1596 mentions two or three heathen kingdoms with a large heathen population. (Niemann, p. 342.)

[3] Raffles, vol. ii. pp. 132–3.

[4] Metzger, p. 279.

[5] L. W. C. van den Berg (1), pp. 35–6. C. Poensen, pp. 3–8.

We have already seen that large sections of the Javanese remained heathen for centuries after the establishment of Muhammadan kingdoms in the island; at the present day the whole population of Java, with some trifling exceptions, is Muhammadan, and though many superstitions and customs have survived among them from the days of their pagan ancestors, still the tendency is continually in the direction of the guidance of thought and conduct in accordance with the teaching of Islam. This long work of conversion has proceeded peacefully and gradually, and the growth of Muslim states in this island belongs rather to its political than to its religious history, since the progress of the religion has been achieved by the work rather of missionaries than of princes.

While the Musalmans of Java were plotting against the Hindu Government and taking the rule of the country into their own hands by force, a revolution of a wholly peaceful character was being carried on in other parts of the Archipelago through the preaching of the Muslim missionaries who were slowly but surely achieving success in their proselytising efforts. Let us first turn our attention to the history of this propagandist movement in the Molucca islands.

The trade in cloves must have brought the Moluccas into contact with the islanders of the western half of the Archipelago from very early times, and the converted Javanese and other Malays who came into these islands to trade, spread their faith among the inhabitants of the coast.[1] The companions of Magellan brought back a curious story of the way in which these men introduced their religious doctrines among the Muluccans. "The kings of these islands [2] a few years before the arrival of the Spaniards

[1] De Barros, Dec. iii. Liv. v. Cap. v. pp. 579–80. Argensola, p. 11 B.

[2] At this period, the Moluccas were for the most part under the rule of four princes, viz. those of Ternate, Tidor, Gilolo and Batjan. The first was by far the most powerful: his territory extended over Ternate and the neighbouring small islands, a portion of Halemahera, a considerable part of Celebes, Amboina and the Banda islands. The Sultan of Tidor ruled over Tidor and some small neighbouring islands, a portion of Halemahera, the islands lying between it and New Guinea, together with the west coast of the latter and a part of Ceram. The territory of the Sultan of Gilolo seems to have been confined to the central part of Halemahera and to a part of the north coast of Ceram; while the Sultan of Batjan ruled chiefly over the Batjan and Obi groups. (De Hollander, vol. i. p. 5.)

began to believe in the immortality of the soul, induced by no other argument but that they had seen a very beautiful little bird, that never settled on the earth nor on anything that was of the earth, and the Mahometans, who traded as merchants in those islands, told them that this little bird was born in paradise, and that paradise is the place where rest the souls of those that are dead. And for this reason these seignors joined the sect of Mahomet, because it promises many marvellous things of this place of the souls." [1]

Islam seems first to have begun to make progress here in the fifteenth century. A heathen king of Tidor yielded to the persuasions of an Arab, named Shaykh Manṣūr, and embraced Islam together with many of his subjects. The heathen name of the king, Tjireli Lijatu, was changed to that of Jamāl al-Dīn, while his eldest son was called Manṣūr after their Arab teacher.[2] It was the latter prince who entertained the Spanish expedition that reached Tidor in 1521, shortly after the ill-fated death of Magellan. Pigafetta, the historian of this expedition, calls him Raia Sultan Mauzor, and says that he was more than fifty-five years old, and that not fifty years had passed since the Muhammadans came to live in these islands.[3]

Islam seems to have gained a footing on the neighbouring island of Ternate a little earlier. The Portuguese, who came to this island the same year as the Spaniards reached Tidor, were informed by the inhabitants that it had been introduced a little more than eighty years.[4]

According to the Portuguese account [5] also the Sultan of Ternate was the first of the Muluccan chieftains who became a Muslim. The legend of the introduction of Islam into this island tells how a merchant, named Daṭu Mullā Ḥusayn, excited the curiosity of the people by reading the Qur'ān aloud in their presence; they tried to imitate the characters written in the book, but could not read them, so they asked the merchant how it was that he could read them, while

[1] Massimiliano Transilvano. (Ramusio, tom. i. p. 351 D.)

[2] P. J. B. C. Robidé van der Aa, p. 18.

[3] Pigafetta, tome i. pp. 365, 368.

[4] " Segundo a conta que elles dam, ao tempo que os nossos descubriram aquellas Ilhas, haveria pouco mais de oitenta annos, que nellas tinha entrada esta peste." (J. de Barros : Da Asia, Dec. iii. Liv. v. Cap. v. p. 580.)

[5] De Barros, id. ib.

they could not; he replied that they must first believe in God and His Apostle; whereupon they expressed their willingness to accept his teaching, and became converted to the faith.[1] The Sultan of Ternate, who occupied the foremost place among the independent rulers in these islands, is said to have made a journey to Gresik, in Java, in order to embrace the Muhammadan faith there, in 1495.[2] He was assisted in his propagandist efforts by a certain Pati Putah, who had made the journey from Hitu in Amboina to Java in order to learn the doctrines of the new faith, and on his return spread the knowledge of Islam among the people of Amboina.[3] Islam, however, seems at first to have made but slow progress, and to have met with considerable opposition from those islanders who clung zealously to their old superstitions and mythology, so that the old idolatry continued for some time crudely mixed up with the teachings of the Qur'ān, and keeping the minds of the people in a perpetual state of incertitude.[4] The Portuguese conquest also made the progress of Islam slower than it would otherwise have been. They drove out the Qāḍī, whom they found instructing the people in the doctrines of Muḥammad, and spread Christianity among the heathen population with some considerable, though short-lived success.[5] For when the Muluccans took advantage of the attention of the Portuguese being occupied with their own domestic troubles, in the latter half of the sixteenth century, to try to shake off their power, they instituted a fierce persecution against the Christians, many of whom suffered martyrdom, and others recanted, so that Christianity lost all the ground it had gained,[6] and from this time onwards, the opposition to the political domination of the Christians secured a readier welcome for the Muslim teachers who came in increasing numbers from the west.[7] The Dutch

[1] Simon, p. 13. [2] Bokemeyer, p. 39. [3] Simon, p. 13.
[4] Argensola, pp. 3–4. [5] Id. p. 15 B. [6] Id. pp. 97, 98.
[7] Id. pp. 155 and 158, where he calls Ternate " este receptaculo de setas, donde tienen escuela todas las apostasias; y particularmente los torpes sequazes de Mahoma. Y desde el anno de mil y quinientos y ochenta y cinco, en que los Holandeses tentaron aquellos mares, hasta este tiempo no han cessado de traer sectarios, y capitanes pyratas. Estos llevan las riquezas de Assia, y en su lugar dexan aquella falsa dotrina, con que hazen infrutuosa la conversion de tantas almas."

completed the destruction of Christianity in the Moluccas by driving out the Spanish and Portuguese from these islands in the seventeenth century, whereupon the Jesuit fathers carried off the few remaining Christians of Ternate with them to the Philippines.[1]

From these islands Islam spread into the rest of the Moluccas; though for some time the conversions were confined to the inhabitants of the coast.[2] Most of the converts came from among the Malays, who compose the whole population of the smaller islands, but inhabit the coast-lands only of the larger ones, the interior being inhabited by Alfurs. But converts in later times were drawn from among the latter also.[3] Even so early as 1521, there was a Muhammadan king of Gilolo, a kingdom on the western side of the northern limb of the island of Halemahera.[4] In modern times the existence of certain regulations, devised for the benefit of the state-religion, has facilitated to some extent the progress of the Muhammadan religion among the Alfurs of the mainland, e.g. if any one of them is discovered to have had illicit intercourse with a Muhammadan girl, he must marry her and become a Muslim; any of the Alfur women who marry Muhammadans must embrace the faith of their husbands; offences against the law may be atoned for by conversion to Islam; and in filling up any vacancy that may happen to occur among the chiefs, less regard is paid to the lawful claims of a candidate than to his readiness to become a Musalman.[5]

Similarly, Islam in Borneo is mostly confined to the coast, although it had gained a footing in the island as early as the beginning of the sixteenth century. About this time, it was adopted by the people of Banjarmasin, a kingdom on the southern side, which had been tributary to the Hindu kingdom of Majapahit, until its overthrow in 1478;[6] they owed their conversion to one of the Muhammadan states that rose on the ruins of the latter.[7] The story is that the

[1] Their descendants are still to be found in the province of Cavité in the island of Luzon. (Crawfurd (1), p. 85.)

[2] W. F. Andriessen, p. 222.

[3] T. Forrest, p. 68.

[4] Pigafetta. (Ramusio, vol. i. p. 366.)

[5] Campen, p. 346. Koloniaal Verslag van 1910, p. 56; 1911, p. 52.

[6] Dulaurier, p. 528.

[7] Damak, on the north coast of Java, opposite the south of Borneo.

people of Banjarmasin asked for assistance towards the suppression of a revolt, and that it was given on condition that they adopted the new religion; whereupon a number of Muhammadans came over from Java, suppressed the revolt and effected the work of conversion.[1] On the north-west coast, the Spaniards found a Muhammadan king at Brunai, when they reached this place in 1521.[2] A little later, 1550, it was introduced into the kingdom of Sukadana,[3] in the western part of the island, by Arabs coming from Palembang in Sumatra.[4] The reigning king refused to abandon the faith of his fathers, but during the forty years that elapsed before his death (in 1590), the new religion appears to have made considerable progress. His successor became a Musalman and married the daughter of a prince of a neighbouring island, in which apparently Islam had been long established;[5] during his reign, a traveller,[6] who visited the island in 1600, speaks of Muhammadanism as being a common religion along the coast. The inhabitants of the interior, however, he tells us, were all idolaters—as indeed they remain for the most part to the present day. The progress of Islam in the kingdom of Sukadana seems now to have drawn the attention of the centre of the Muhammadan world to this distant spot, and in the reign of the next prince, a certain Shaykh Shams al-Dīn came from Mecca bringing with him a present of a copy of the Qur'ān and a large hyacinth ring, together with a letter in which this defender of the faith received the honourable title of Sultan Muḥammad Ṣafī al-Dīn.[7]

In the latter part of the eighteenth century one of the inland tribes, called the Idaans, dwelling in the interior of north Borneo, is said to have looked upon the Muhammadans of

[1] Hageman, pp. 236–9.

[2] Pigafetta. (Ramusio, tom. i. pp. 363–4.)

[3] This kingdom had been founded by a colony from the Hindu kingdom of Majapahit (De Hollander, vol. ii. p. 67), and would naturally have come under Muslim influence after the conversion of the Javanese.

[4] Dozy (1), p. 386.

[5] Veth (2), vol. i. p. 193.

[6] Olivier de Noort. (Histoire générale des voyages, vol. xiv. p. 225.) (The Hague, 1756.)

[7] i.e. Pure in Religion; he died about 1677; his father does not seem to have taken a Muhammadan name, at least he is only known by his heathen name of Panembahan Giri-Kusuma. (Netscher, pp. 14–15.)

the coast with very great respect, as having a religion which they themselves had not yet got.[1] Dalrymple, who obtained his information on the Idaans of Borneo during his visit to Sulu from 1761 to 1764, tells us that they " entertain a just regret of their own ignorance, and a mean idea of themselves on that account; for, when they come into the houses, or vessels, of the Mahometans, they pay them the utmost veneration, as superior intelligences, who know their Creator; they will not sit down where the Mahometans sleep, nor will they put their fingers into the same chunam, or betel box, but receive a portion with the utmost humility, and in every instance denote, with the most abject attitudes and gesture, the veneration they entertain for a God unknown, in the respect they pay to those who have a knowledge of Him." [2] These people appear since that time to have embraced the Muhammadan faith,[3] one of the numerous instances of the powerful impression that Islam produces upon tribes that are low down in the scale of civilisation. From time to time other accessions have been gained in the persons of the numerous colonists, Arabs, Bugis and Malays, as well as Chinese (who have had settlements here since the seventh century),[4] and of the slaves introduced into the island from different countries; so that at the present day the Muhammadans of Borneo are a very mixed race.[5] Many of these foreigners were still heathen when they first came to Borneo, and of a higher civilisation than the Dyaks whom they conquered or drove into the interior, where they mostly still remain heathen, except in the western part of the island, in which from time to time small tribes of Dyaks embrace Islam.[6] When the pagan Dyaks change their faith, it is more commonly the case that they yield to the persuasions of the Muhammadan rather than to those of the Christian missionary, or, having first embraced Christianity they then pass over to Islam, and the Muhammadans are making zealous efforts to win converts both from among the heathen and the Christian Dyaks.[7]

In the island of Celebes we find a similar slow growth of

[1] Thomas Forrest, p. 371. [2] Essay towards an account of Sulu, p. 557.
[3] B. Panciera, p. 161. [4] J. Hageman, p. 224.
[5] Veth (2), vol. i. p. 179. [6] De Hollander, vol. ii. p. 61.
[7] Coolsma, p. 556. Koloniaal Verslag van 1911, pp. 38, 41; 1912, p. 30.

the Muhammadan religion, taking its rise among the people of the coast and slowly making its way into the interior. Only the more civilised portion of the inhabitants has, however, adopted Islam; this is mainly divided into two tribes, the Macassars and the Bugis, who inhabit the south-west peninsula, the latter, however, also forming a large proportion of the coast population on the other peninsulas. The interior of the island, except in the south-west peninsula where nearly all the inhabitants are Muhammadan, is still heathen and is populated chiefly by the Alfurs, a race low in the scale of civilisation, who also form the majority of the inhabitants of the north, the east and the south-east peninsulas; at the extremity of the first of these peninsulas, in Minahassa, they have in large numbers been converted to Christianity; the Muhammadans did not make their way hither until after the Portuguese had gained a firm footing in this part of the island, and the Alfurs whom they converted to Roman Catholicism were turned into Protestants by the Dutch, whose missionaries have laboured in Minahassa with very considerable success. But Islam is slowly making its way among the heathen tribes of Alfurs in different parts of the island, both in the districts directly administered by the Dutch Government, and those under the rule of native chiefs.[1]

When the Portuguese first visited the island about 1540, they found only a few Muhammadan strangers in Gowa, the capital of the Macassar kingdom, the natives being still unconverted, and it was not until the beginning of the seventeenth century that Islam began to be generally adopted among them. The history of the movement is especially interesting, as we have here one of the few cases in which Christianity and Islam have been competing for the allegiance of heathen people. One of the incidents in this contest is thus admirably told by an old compiler: "The discovery of so considerable a country was looked upon by the Portuguese as a Matter of Great Consequence, and Measures were taken to secure the Affections of those whom it was not found easy to conquer; but, on the other hand, capable of being obliged, or rendered useful, as their allies, by good usage.

[1] Med. Ned. Zendelinggen, vol. xxxii. p. 177; vol. xxxiv. p. 170.

The People were much braver, and withal had much better Sense than most of the Indians; and therefore, after a little Conversation with the Europeans, they began, in general, to discern that there was no Sense or Meaning in their own Religion; and the few of them who had been made Christians by the care of Don Antonio Galvano (Governor of the Moluccas), were not so thoroughly instructed themselves as to be able to teach them a new Faith. The whole People, in general, however, disclaimed their old Superstitions, and became Deists at once; but, not satisfied with this, they determined to send, at the same time, to Malacca and to Achin,[1] to desire from the one, Christian Priests; and from the other, Doctors of the Mohammedan Law; resolving to embrace the Religion of those Teachers who came first among them. The Portugeze have hitherto been esteemed zealous enough for their Religion; but it seems that Don Ruis Perera, who was then Governor of Malacca, was a little deficient in his Concern for the Faith, since he made a great and very unnecessary delay in sending the Priests that were desired. On the other hand, the Queen of Achin being a furious Mohammedan no sooner received an Account of this Disposition in the people of the Island of Celebes than she immediately dispatched a vessel full of Doctors of the Law, who in a short time, established their Religion effectually among the Inhabitants. Some time after came the Christian Priests, and inveighed bitterly against the Law of Mohammed but to no Purpose; the People of Celebes had made their Choice, and there was no Possibility of bringing them to alter it. One of the Kings of the Island, indeed, who had before embraced Christianity, persisted in the Faith, and most of his Subjects were converted to it; but still, the Bulk of the People of Celebes continued Mohammedans, and are so to this Day, and the greatest Zealots for their Religion of any in the Indies."[2]

This event is said to have occurred in the year 1603.[3]

[1] i. e. Atjeh.

[2] A Compleat History of the Rise and Progress of the Portugeze Empire in the East Indies. Collected chiefly from their own Writers. John Harris: Navigantium atque Itinerantium Bibliotheca, vol. i. p. 682. (London, 1764.)

[3] Crawfurd (1), p. 91. The Encyclopaedie van N.-I. (vol. i. p. 216) gives 1606 as the date.

The frequent references to it in contemporary literature make it impossible to doubt the genuineness of the story.[1] In the little principality of Tallo, to the north of Gowa, with which it has always been confederated, is still to be seen the tomb of one of the most famous missionaries to the Macassars, by name K͟haṭīb Tungal. The prince of this state, after his conversion proved himself a most zealous champion of the new faith, and it was through his influence that it was generally adopted by all the tribes speaking the Macassar language. The sequel of the movement is not of so peaceful a character. The Macassars were carried away by their zeal for their newly adopted faith, to make an attempt to force it on their neighbours the Bugis. The king of Gowa made an offer to the king of Boni to consider him in all respects as an equal if he would worship the one true God. The latter consulted his people on the matter, who said, "We have not yet fought, we have not yet been conquered." They tried the issue of a battle and were defeated. The king accordingly became a Muhammadan and began on his own account to attempt by force to impose his own belief on his subjects and on the smaller states, his neighbours. Strange to say, the people applied for help to the king of Macassar, who sent ambassadors to demand from the king of Boni an answer to the following questions,—Whether the king, in his persecution, was instigated by a particular revelation from the Prophet?—or whether he paid obedience to some ancient custom?—or followed his own personal pleasure? If for the first reason, the king of Gowa requested information; if for the second, he would lend his cordial co-operation; if for the third, the king of Boni must desist, for those whom he presumed to oppress were the friends of Gowa. The king of Boni made no reply and the Macassars having marched a great army into the country defeated him in three successive battles, forced him to fly the country, and reduced Boni into a province. After thirty years of sub-

[1] Fernandez Navarette, a Spanish priest, who went to the Philippine Islands in 1646. (Collection of Voyages and Travels, p. 236. London, 1752.)
Tavernier, who visited Macassar in 1648. (Travels in India, p. 193.) (London, 1678.)
Itinerarium Orientale R. P. F. Philippi à SSma. Trinitate Carmelitae Discalceati ab ipso conscriptum, p. 267. (Lugduni, 1649.)

jection, the people of Boni, with the assistance of the Dutch, revolted against the Macassars, and assumed the headship of the tribes of Celebes, in the place of their former masters.[1] The propagation of Islam certainly seems to have been gradual and slow among the Bugis,[2] but when they had once adopted the new religion, it seems to have stirred them up to action, as it did the Arabs (though this newly-awakened energy in either case turned in rather different directions),—and to have made them what they are now, at once the bravest men and the most enterprising merchants and navigators of the Archipelago.[3] In their trading vessels they make their way to all parts of the Archipelago, from the coast of New Guinea to Singapore, and their numerous settlements, in the establishment of which the Bugis have particularly distinguished themselves, have introduced Islam into many a heathen island: e.g. one of their colonies is to be found in a state that extends over a considerable part of the south coast of Flores, where, intermingling with the native population, which formerly consisted partly of Roman Catholics, they have succeeded in converting all the inhabitants of this state to Islam.[4]

In their native island of Celebes also the Bugis have combined proselytising efforts with their commercial enterprises, and in the little kingdom of Bolaäng-Mongondou in the northern peninsula[5] they have succeeded, in the course of the present century, in winning over to Islam a Christian population whose conversion dates from the end of the seventeenth century. The first Christian king of Bolaäng-Mongondou was Jacobus Manopo (1689–1709), in whose reign Christianity spread rapidly, through the influence of

[1] Crawfurd, vol. ii. pp. 385–9.

[2] "No extraordinary exertion seems for a long time to have been made on behalf of the new religion. An abhorrence of innovation and a most pertinacious and religious adherence to ancient custom, distinguish the people of Celebes beyond all the other tribes of the Eastern isles; and these would, at first, prove the most serious obstacles to the dissemination of Mahometanism. It was this, probably, which deferred the adoption of the new religion for so long a period, and till it had recommended itself by wearing the garb of antiquity." (Crawfurd (2), vol. ii. p. 387.)

[3] Crawfurd (1), p. 75. De Hollander, vol. ii. p. 212.

[4] Id. vol. ii. p. 666. Riedel (2), p. 67.

[5] To the east of Minahassa, between long. 124° 45′ and 123° 20′, with a population that has been variously estimated at 35,000 and 50,000. (De Hollander, vol. ii. p. 247.)

the Dutch East India Company and the preaching of the Dutch clergy.[1] His successors were all Christian until 1844, when the reigning Raja, Jacobus Manuel Manopo, embraced Islam. His conversion was the crown of a series of proselytising efforts that had been in progress since the beginning of the century, for it was about this time that the zealous efforts of some Muhammadan traders—Bugis and others—won over some converts to Islam in one of the coast towns of the southern kingdom, Mongondou; from this same town two trader missionaries, Ḥakīm Bagus and Imām Tuwéko by name, set out to spread their faith throughout the rest of this kingdom. They made a beginning with the conversion of some slaves and native women whom they married, and these little by little persuaded their friends and relatives to embrace the new faith. From Mongondou Islam spread into the northern kingdom Bolaäng; here, in 1830, the whole population was either Christian or heathen, with the exception of two or three Muhammadan settlers; but the zealous preachers of Islam, the Bugis, and the Arabs who assisted them in their missionary labours, soon achieved a wide-spread success. The Christians, whose knowledge of the doctrines of their religion was very slight and whose faith was weak, were ill prepared with the weapons of controversy to meet the attacks of the rival creed; despised by the Dutch Government, neglected and well-nigh abandoned by the authorities of the Church, they began to look on these foreigners, some of whom married and settled among them, as their friends. As the work of conversion progressed, the visits of these Bugis and Arabs,—at first rare,—became more frequent, and their influence in the country very greatly increased, so much so that about 1832 an Arab married a daughter of the king, Cornelius Manopo, who was himself a Christian; many of the chiefs, and some of the most powerful among them, about the same time, abandoned Christianity and embraced Islam. In this way Islam had gained a firm footing in his kingdom before Raja Jacobus Manuel Manopo became a Muslim in 1844; this prince had made repeated applications to the Dutch authorities at Manado to appoint a successor to the Christian

[1] Wilken (1), pp. 42–4.

schoolmaster, Jacobus Bastiaan,—whose death had been a great loss to the Christian community—but to no purpose, and learning from the resident at Manado that the Dutch Government was quite indifferent as to whether the people of his state were Christians or Muhammadans, so long as they were loyal, openly declared himself a Musalman and tried every means to bring his subjects over to the same faith. An Arab missionary took advantage of the occurrence of a terrible earthquake in the following year, to prophecy the destruction of Bolaäng-Mongondou, unless the people speedily became converted to Islam. Many in their terror hastened to follow this advice, and the Raja and his nobles lent their support to the missionaries and Arab merchants, whose methods of dealing with the dilatory were not always of the gentlest. Nearly half the population, however, still remains heathen, but the progress of Islam among them, though slow, is continuous and sure.[1]

The neighbouring island of Sambawa likewise probably received its knowledge of this faith from Celebes, through the preaching of missionaries from Macassar between 1540 and 1550. All the more civilised inhabitants are true believers and are said to be stricter in the performance of their religious duties than any of the neighbouring Muhammadan peoples. This is largely due to a revivalist movement set on foot by a certain Ḥājī ʻAli after the disastrous eruption of Mount Tambora in 1815, the fearful suffering that ensued thereon being made use of to stir up the people to a more strict observance of the precepts of their religion and the leading of a more devout life.[2] At the present time Islam still continues to win over fresh converts in this island.[3]

The Sasaks of the neighbouring island of Lombok also owed their conversion to the preaching of the Bugis, who form a large colony here, having either crossed over the strait from Sambawa or come directly from Celebes: at any rate the conversion appears to have taken place in a peaceable manner.[4] The population of Lombok falls into two distinct divisions, the Sasaks and the Balinese;

[1] Wilken (2), pp. 276–9. Koloniaal Verslag van 1910, p. 52; 1911, p. 47.
[2] Zollinger (2), pp. 126, 169.
[3] Med. Ned. Zendelinggen, xxxii. p. 177; xxxiv. p. 170.
[4] Zollinger (1), p. 527.

the first of these, consisting of the Muhammadan Sasaks, the original inhabitants of the island, far outnumbers the second, but about the middle of the eighteenth century they came under the rule of the Balinese and soon found their island overrun by swarms of the Hindu neighbours.[1] The rule of the Balinese was very oppressive, and they made efforts—though with little success—to bring their Muslim subjects over to Hinduism; the Sasaks tried in vain to shake off the yoke of their oppressors, and more than once appealed to the Dutch Government, before the expedition of 1894 brought peace to the island and established an orderly administration under Dutch rule. The new government brought with it a large number of native Muhammadan officials, who throw in their influence on the side of their own faith, and it is thus expected that one of the results of the Dutch conquest of Lombok will be to give a great impetus to Islam in this island.[2]

In the Philippine Islands we find a struggle between Christianity and Islam for the allegiance of the inhabitants, somewhat similar in character to that in Celebes, but more stern and enduring, entangling the Spaniards and the Muslims in a fierce and bloody conflict, even up to the nineteenth century. It is uncertain when Islam first reached these islands.[3] The traditionary annals of Mindanao represent Islam as having been introduced from Johore, in the Malay Peninsula, by a certain Sharīf Kabungsuwan, who settled with a number of followers in the island and married there. He is said to have refused to land until the men who came to meet him on his arrival promised to embrace Islam, and these early records give the impression that the landing of Kabungsuwan and the conversion of the people of Mindanao at first proceeded quite peacefully; but after he had estab-

[1] De Hollander (in 1882) gave the numbers as 20,000 Balinese and 380,000 Sasaks. (Vol. i. p. 489.)

[2] Encyclopaedie van N.-I. vol. ii. pp. 432–4, 524.

W. Cool: With the Dutch in the East. An outline of the military operations in Lombok, 1894. (London, 1897.)

[3] Captain Thomas Forrest, writing in 1775, says that Arabs came to the island of Mindanao 300 years before and that the tomb of the first Arab, a Sharīf from Mecca, was still shown—" a rude heap of coral rock stones" (pp. 201, 313).

lished his power, he began to conquer the neighbouring chiefs and tribes, and they accepted his religion in submitting to his authority.[1] The Spaniards who discovered them in 1521, found the population of the northern islands to be rude and simple pagans, while Mindanao and the Sulu Islands were occupied by more civilised Muhammadan tribes.[2] The latter up to the close of the nineteenth century successfully resisted for the most part all the efforts of the Christians towards conquest and conversion, so that the Spanish missionaries despaired of ever effecting their conversion.[3] The success of Islam as compared with Christianity has been due in a great measure to the different form under which these two faiths were presented to the natives. The adoption of the latter implied the loss of all political freedom and national independence, and hence came to be regarded as a badge of slavery. The methods adopted by the Spaniards for the propagation of their religion were calculated to make it unpopular from the beginning; their violence and intolerance were in strong contrast to the conciliatory behaviour of the Muhammadan missionaries, who learned the language of the people, adopted their customs, intermarried with them, and melting into the mass of the people, neither arrogated to themselves the exclusive rights of a privileged race nor condemned the natives to the level of a degraded caste. The Spaniards, on the other hand, were ignorant of the language, habits and manners of the natives; their intemperance and above all their avarice and rapacity brought their religion into odium; while its propagation was intended to serve as an instrument of their political advancement.[4] It is not difficult therefore to understand the opposition offered by the natives to the introduction of Christianity, which indeed only became the religion of the

[1] N. N. Saleeby: Studies in Moro History, Law and Religion, pp. 24–5, 53–5. (Manila, 1905.)

[2] Relatione di Ivan Gaetan del discoprimento dell' Isole Molucche. (Ramusio, tom. i. p. 375 E.)

[3] "Se muestran tan obstinados á la gracia de Dios y tan aferrados á sus creencias, que es casi moralmente imposible su conversion al cristianismo." (Cartas de los PP. de la Compañia de Jesús de la Missión de Filipinas, 1879, quoted by Montero y Vidal, tom. i. p. 21.)

[4] Crawfurd (2), vol. ii. pp. 274–280.

people in those parts in which the inhabitants were weak enough, or the island small enough, to enable the Spaniards to effect a total subjugation; the native Christians after their conversion had to be forced to perform their religious duties through fear of punishment, and were treated exactly like school-children.[1] Up to the time of the American occupation of the Philippine Islands the independent Muhammadan kingdom of Mindanao was a refuge for those who wished to escape from the hated Christian government;[2] the island of Sulu, also, though nominally a Spanish possession since 1878, formed another centre of Muhammadan opposition to Christianity, Spanish-knowing renegades even being found here.[3]

We have no certain historical evidence as to how long the inhabitants of the Sulu Islands had been Muhammadan, before the arrival of the Spaniards. The annals of Sulu give the name of Sharīf Karīm al-Makhdūm as the first missionary of Islam in these islands. He is said to have been an Arab who went to Malacca about the middle of the fourteenth century and converted Sulṭān Muḥammad Shāh and the people of Malacca to Islam. Continuing his journey eastward, he reached Sulu about the year 1380 and settled in Bwansa,[4] the old capital of Sulu, where the people built a mosque for him and many of the chiefs accepted his teachings. He is said to have visited almost every island of the Archipelago and to have made converts in many places; his grave is said to be on the island of Sibutu.[5] The next missionary is said to have been Abū Bakr, who is also stated to have been an Arab, and to have commenced his missionary labours in Malacca and to have

[1] "Ils sont peu soigneux de satisfaire au devoir du Christianisme qu'ils ont receu, et il les y faut contraindre par la crainte du chastiment, et gouverner comme des enfans à l'escole." Relation des Isles Philippines, Faite par un Religieux, p. 7. (Thevenot, vol. i.)

[2] "A Mindanao, les Tagal de l'Est, fuyant le joug abhorré de leurs maîtres catholiques, se groupent chaque jour davantage autour des chefs des dynasties nationales. Plus de 360,000 sectateurs du coran y reconnaissent un sultan indépendant. Aux jésuites chassés de l'île, aux représentants du culte officiel, se substituent comme maîtres religieux et éducateurs de la population, les missionnaires musulmans de la Chine et de l'Inde, qui rénovent ainsi la propagande, commencée par les invasions arabes." (A. le Chatelier (2), p. 45.)

[3] Montero y Vidal, vol. i. p. 86.

[4] Situated three miles west of Jolo, the present capital.

[5] N. M. Saleeby: The History of Sulu, pp. 150, 158–9. (Manila, 1908.)

made his way to Palembang and Brunei, and reached Sulu about 1450; he built mosques and carried on a successful propaganda. The Muslim king of Bwansa, Raja Baginda, gave him his daughter in marriage, and appointed him his heir, and Abū Bakr is credited with having organised the government and legislation of Sulu on orthodox Muslim lines as far as local custom would allow.[1] Though so long converted, the people of Sulu are far from being rigid Muhammadans, indeed, the influence of the numerous Christian slaves that they carried off from the Philippines in their predatory excursions used to be so great that it was even asserted[2] that "they would long ere this have become professed Christians but from the prescience that such a change, by investing a predominating influence in the priesthood, would inevitably undermine their own authority, and pave the way to the transfer of their dominions to the Spanish yoke, an occurrence which fatal experience has too forcibly instructed all the surrounding nations that unwarily embrace the Christian persuasion." Further, the aggressive behaviour of the Spanish priests who established a mission in Sulu created in the mind of the people a violent antipathy to the foreign religion.[3]

Since the American occupation of the Philippines, the influence of Islam has been considerably restricted, and is now confined to the island of Palawan, the south coast of Mindanao and the archipelago of Sulu.[4] But it is said to be seeking to extend its propaganda among the northern islands, and to have made a beginning of missionary activity even in Manila. Certain conditions are said to favour its success, especially the fact that the Filipinos are prejudiced against Christianity on account of the abuses that led them to take up arms against the Spanish friars.[5]

As has been already mentioned, Islam has been most favourably received by the more civilised races of the Malay Archipelago, and has taken but little root among the lower races. Such are the Papuans of New Guinea, and the islands to the north-west of it, viz. Waigyu, Misool, Waigama

[1] N. M. Saleeby: The History of Sulu, pp. 150, 162–3.
[2] J. H. Moor. (Appendix, p. 37.) [3] Dalrymple, p. 549.
[4] R. du M. M., vii. pp. 115–16. (1909.)
[5] The Missionary Review of the World, N.S., vol. xiv. p. 877. (New York, 1901.)

and Salawatti. These islands, together with the peninsula of Onin, on the north-west of New Guinea, were in the sixteenth century subject to the Sultan of Batjan,[1] one of the kings of the Moluccas. Through the influence of the Muhammadan rulers of Batjan, the Papuan chiefs of these islands adopted Islam,[2] and though the mass of the people in the interior have remained heathen up to the present day, the inhabitants of the coast are Muhammadans largely no doubt owing to the influence of settlers from the Moluccas.[3] In New Guinea itself, very few of the Papuans seem to have become Muhammadans. Islam was introduced into the west coast (probably in the peninsula of Onin) by Muhammadan merchants, who propagated their religion among the inhabitants, as early as 1606.[4] But it appears to have made very little progress during the centuries that have elapsed since then,[5] and the Papuans have shown as much reluctance to become Muhammadans as to accept the teachings of the Christian missionaries, who have laboured among them without much success since 1855. The Muhammadans of the neighbouring islands have been accused of holding the Papuans in too great contempt to make efforts to spread Islam among them.[6] The name of one missionary,

[1] The first prince of Batjan who became a Muhammadan was a certain Zayn al-'Ābidīn, who was reigning in 1521 when the Portuguese first came to the Moluccas.

[2] Robidé van der Aa, pp. 350, 352–3.

[3] Id. p. 147 (Misool), "De strandbewoners zijn allen Mahomedanen. . . . De bergbewoners zijn heidenen." Id. p. 53 (Salawatti), "Een klein deel der bevolking van het eiland belijdt de leer van Mahamed. Het grootste deel bestaat echter uit Papoesche heidenen, einige tot het Mahomedaansche geloof zijn overgegangen, althans den schijn daarvan aannemen." Id. p. 290 (Waigyu).

Some of the Papuans of the island of Gebi, between Waigyu and Halemahera, have been converted by the Muhammadan settlers from the Moluccas. (Crawfurd (1), p. 143.)

[4] Robidé van der Aa, p. 352.

[5] Captain Forrest, however, in 1775, tells us that "Many of the Papuas turn Musselmen." (Voyage to New Guinea, p. 68.)

[6] Robidé van der Aa, p. 71. "De Papoe is te woest van aard, om behoefte aan godsdienst te gevoelen. Evenmin als de Christelijke leer tot nog toe ingang bij hem heeft kunnen vinden, zou de Mahomedaansche godsdienst slagen, wanneer daartoe bij deze volkstammen poging gedaan werd. Voorzoover mij is gebleken op vijf reizen naar dit land, hebben noch Tidoreezen, noch Cerammers of anderen ooit ernstige pogingen gedaan, om de leer van Mahomed hier in te voeren. . . . Slechts zeer weinige hoofden, zooals de Radja Ampat van Waigeoe, Salawatti, Misool en Waigama, mogen als belijders van die leer aangemerkt worden; zij en eenige hunner bloedverwanten vervullen sommige geloofsvormen, doordien zij meermalen te Tidor geweest zijn en daar niet gaarne als gewone Papoes beschouwd

however, is found, a certain Imām Dikir (? Dhikr), who came from one of the islands on the south-east of Ceram about 1856 and introduced Islam into the little island of Adi, south of the peninsula of Onin; after fulfilling his mission he returned to his own home, resisting the importunities of the inhabitants to settle among them.[1] Muhammadan traders from Ceram and Goram are reported to have made a number of converts from among the heathen during the first decade of the twentieth century.[2] Similar efforts are being made to convert the Papuans of the neighbouring Kei Islands. In the middle of the nineteenth century there were said to be hardly any Muhammadans on these islands, with the exception of the descendants of immigrants from the Banda Islands; some time before, missionaries from Ceram had succeeded in making some converts, but the precepts of the Qur'ān were very little observed, both forbidden meats and intoxicating liquors being indulged in. The women, however, were said to be stricter in their adherence to their faith than the men, so that when their husbands wished to indulge in swine's flesh, they had to do so in secret, their wives not allowing it to be brought into the house.[3] But in 1887 it was noted that there had been a revival of religious life among the Kei islanders, and the number of Muhammadans was daily increasing. Arab merchants from Madura, Java, and Bali proved themselves zealous propagandists of Islam and left no means untried to win converts, sometimes enforcing their arguments by threats and violence, and at other times by bribes: as a rule new converts were said to get 200 florins' worth of presents, while chiefs received as much as a thousand florins.[4] At the close of the nineteenth century about 8000 of the Kei islanders were said to be Muhammadan out of a total population of 23,000.[5]

The above sketch of the spread of Islam from west to east through the Malay Archipelago comprises but a small part

---

worden. Onder de eigenlijke bevolking is nooit gepoogd, den Islam intevoeren, misschien wel uit eerbied voor dien godsdienst, die te verheven is voor de Papoes."

[1] Robidé van der Aa, p. 319.

[2] Koloniaal Verslag van 1906, p. 70; 1911, p. 52.

[3] The Journal of the Indian Archipelago, vol. vii. pp. 64, 71. (Singapore, 1853.)

[4] G. W. W. C. Baron von Hoëvell, p. 120. Krieger, p. 436.

[5] Encyclopaedie van N.-I., vol. ii. p. 210.

of the history of the missionary work of Islam in these islands. Many of the facts of this history are wholly unrecorded, and what can be gleaned from native chronicles and the works of European travellers, officials and missionaries is necessarily fragmentary and incomplete. But there is evidence enough to show the existence of peaceful missionary efforts to spread the faith of Islam during the last six hundred years: sometimes indeed the sword has been drawn in support of the cause of religion, but preaching and persuasion rather than force and violence have been the main characteristics of this missionary movement. The marvellous success that has been achieved has been largely the work of traders, who won their way to the hearts of the natives, by learning their language, adopting their manners and customs, and began quietly and gradually to spread the knowledge of their religion by first converting the native women they married and the persons associated with them in their business relations. Instead of holding themselves apart in proud isolation, they gradually melted into the mass of the population, employing all their superiority of intelligence and civilisation for the work of conversion and making such skilful compromises in the doctrines and practices of their faith as were needed to recommend it to the people they wished to attract.[1] In fact, as Buckle said of them, "The Mahometan missionaries are very judicious."[2]

Beside the traders, there have been numbers of what may be called professional missionaries—theologians, preachers, jurisconsults and pilgrims. The latter have, in recent years, been especially active in the work of proselytising, in stirring up a more vigorous and consistent religious life among their fellow-countrymen, and in purging away the lingering remains of heathen habits and beliefs. The number of those who make the pilgrimage to Mecca from all parts of the Archipelago is constantly on the increase, and there is in consequence a proportionate growth of Muhammadan influence and Muhammadan thought. Up to the middle of the nineteenth century the Dutch Government tried to put obstacles in the way of the pilgrims and passed an order that

[1] Crawfurd (2), pp. 275, 307.
[2] Buckle's Miscellaneous and Posthumous Works, edited by Helen Taylor, vol. i. p. 594. (London, 1872.)

no one should be allowed to make the pilgrimage to the holy city without a passport, for which he had to pay 110 florins; and any one who evaded this order was on his return compelled to pay a fine of double that amount.[1] Accordingly it is not surprising to find that in 1852 the number of pilgrims was so low as seventy, but in the same year this order was rescinded, and since then, there has been a steady increase.

The average number of pilgrims during the last decade of the nineteenth century was 7000—during the first decade of the twentieth, 7300; [2] but the numbers vary considerably from year to year, the largest recorded number from the Dutch Indies being 14,234 in 1910.[3]

Such an increase is no doubt largely due to the increased facilities of communication between Mecca and the Malay Archipelago, but, as a Christian missionary has observed, this by no means "diminishes the importance of the fact, especially as the Hadjis, whose numbers have grown so rapidly, have by no means lost in quality what they gained in quantity; on the contrary, there are now amongst them many more thoroughly acquainted with the doctrines of Islam, and wholly imbued with Moslem fanaticism and hatred against the unbelievers, than there formerly were." [4] The reports of the Dutch Government and of Christian missionaries bear unanimous testimony to the influence and the proselytising zeal of these pilgrims who return to their homes as at once reformers and missionaries.[5] Beside the pilgrims who content themselves with merely visiting the sacred places and performing the due ceremonies, and those who make a longer stay in order to complete their theological studies, there is a large colony of Malays in Mecca at the present time, who have taken up their residence permanently in the sacred city. These are in constant communication with their fellow-countrymen in their native land, and their efforts have been largely effectual in purging Muhammadanism in the Malay Archipelago from the contamination of

[1] Neimann, pp. 406–7.
[2] C. Snouck Hurgronje: De hadji-politiek der Indische Regeering, p. 12. (Overdruk uit Onze Eeuw, 1909.)
[3] Id.: Notes sur le mouvement du pèlerinage de la Mecque aux Indes Néerlandaises. (R. du M. M., vol. xv. pp. 409, 412.)
[4] Report of Centenary Conference on Protestant Missions, vol. i. p. 21. Niemann, p. 407.
[5] Med. Ned. Zendelinggen, vols. xxxii., xxxiv. passim.

heathen customs and modes of thought that have survived from an earlier period. A large number of religious books is also printed in Mecca in the various languages spoken by the Malay Muhammadans and carried to all parts of the Archipelago. Indeed Mecca has been well said to have more influence on the religious life of these islands than on Turkey, India or Bukhārā.[1]

As might be anticipated from a consideration of these facts, there has been of recent years a very great awakening of missionary activity in the Malay Archipelago, and the returned pilgrims, whether as merchants or religious teachers, become preachers of Islam wherever they come in contact with a heathen population. The religious orders moreover have extended their organisation to the Malay Archipelago,[2] even the youngest of them—the Sanūsiyyah—finding adherents in the most distant islands,[3] one of the signs of its influence being the adoption of the name Sanūsī by many Malays, when in Mecca they change their native for Arabic names.[4]

The Dutch Government has been accused by Christian missionaries of favouring the spread of Islam; however this may have been, it is certain that the work of the Muslim missionaries is facilitated by the fact that Malay, which is spoken by hardly any but Muhammadans, has been adopted as the official language of the Dutch Government, except in Java; and as the Dutch civil servants are everywhere attended by a crowd of Muhammadan subordinate officials, political agents, clerks, interpreters and traders, they carry Islam with them into every place they visit. All persons that have to do business with the Government are obliged to learn the Malay language, and they seldom learn it without at the same time becoming Musalmans. In this way the most influential people embrace Islam, and the rest soon follow their example.[5] Thus Islam is at the present time rapidly driving out heathenism from the Malay Archipelago.

[1] Snouck Hurgronje (3), vol. ii. pp. xv. 339–393. Encyclopaedie van N.-I., vol. ii. pp. 576–9.

[2] e. g. the Qādiriyyah, Naqshbandiyyah and Sammāniyyah. (C. Snouck Hurgronje (2), p. 186.) Id. (3) vol. ii. p. 372, etc.

[3] J. G. F. Riedel (1), pp. 7, 59, 162.

[4] Snouck Hurgronje (3), vol. ii. p. 323.

[5] Hauri, p. 313. Encyclopaedie van N.-I., vol. ii. p. 524.

CHAPTER XIII.

CONCLUSION.

To the modern Christian world, missionary work implies missionary societies, paid agents, subscriptions, reports and journals; and missionary enterprise without a regularly constituted and continuous organisation seems a misnomer. The ecclesiastical constitution of the Christian Church has, from the very beginning of its history, made provision for the propagation of Christian teaching among unbelievers; its missionaries have been in most cases, regularly ordained priests or monks; the monastic orders (from the Benedictines downwards) and the missionary societies of more modern times have devoted themselves with special and concentrated attention to the furthering of a department of Christian work that, from the first, has been recognised to be one of the prime duties of the Church. But in Islam the absence of any kind of priesthood or any ecclesiastical organisation whatever has caused the missionary energy of the Muslims to exhibit itself in forms very different to those that appear in the history of Christian missions: there are no missionary societies,[1] no specially trained agents, very little continuity of effort. The only exception appears to be found in the religious orders of Islam, whose organisation resembles to some extent that of the monastic orders of Christendom. But even here the absence of the priestly ideal, of any theory of the separateness of the religious teacher from the common body of believers or of the necessity of a special consecration and authorisation for the performance of religious functions, makes the fundamental difference in the two systems stand out as clearly as elsewhere.

[1] Organisations based on the model of Christian missionary societies do not begin to make their appearance until the twentieth century; some account of these is given in Appendix III.

Whatever disadvantages may be entailed by this want of a priestly class, specially set apart for the work of propagating the faith, are compensated for by the consequent feeling of responsibility resting on the individual believer. There being no intermediary between the Muslim and his God, the responsibility of his personal salvation rests upon himself alone: consequently he becomes as a rule much more strict and careful in the performance of his religious duties, he takes more trouble to learn the doctrines and observances of his faith, and thus becoming deeply impressed with the importance of them to himself, is more likely to become an exponent of the missionary character of his creed in the presence of the unbeliever. The would-be proselytiser has not to refer his convert to some authorised religious teacher of his creed who may formally receive the neophyte into the body of the Church, nor need he dread ecclesiastical censure for committing the sin of Korah. Accordingly, however great an exaggeration it may be to say, as has been said so often,[1] that every Muhammadan is a missionary, still it is true that every Muhammadan may be one, and few truly devout Muslims, living in daily contact with unbelievers, neglect the precept of their Prophet: "Summon them to the way of thy Lord with wisdom and with kindly warning."[2] Thus it is that, side by side with the professional propagandists,—the religious teachers who have devoted all their time and energies to missionary work,—the annals of the propagation of the Muslim faith contain the record of men and women of all ranks of society, from the sovereign[3] to the peasant, and of all trades and professions, who have laboured for the spread of their faith,—the Muslim trader, unlike his Christian brother, showing himself especially active in such work. In a list of Indian missionaries published in the

[1] "À tout musulman, quelque mondain qu'il soit, le prosélytisme semble être en quelque sorte inné." (Snouck Hurgronje, Revue de l'Histoire des Religions, vol. lvii. p. 66.) "Der Muslim ist von Natur Missionär . . . Er treibt Mission auf eigne Faust und Kosten." (Munzinger, p. 411.) Snouck Hurgronje (1), p. 8; Lüttke (2), p. 30; Julius Richter, p. 152; Merensky, p. 154.

[2] Qur'ān, xvi. 126.

[3] See the interesting letter addressed by Mawlā'ī Ismā'īl, Sharīf of Morocco, in 1698 to King James II, inviting him to embrace Islam. (Revue de l'Histoire des Religions, vol. xlvii. p. 174 sqq.)

journal of a religious and philanthropic society of Lahore [1] we find the names of schoolmasters, Government clerks in the Canal and Opium Departments, traders (including a dealer in camel-carts), an editor of a newspaper, a book-binder and a workman in a printing establishment. These men devote the hours of leisure left them after the completion of the day's labour, to the preaching of their religion in the streets and bazaars of Indian cities, seeking to win converts both from among Christians and Hindus, whose religious beliefs they controvert and attack.

It is interesting to note that the propagation of Islam has not been the work of men only, but that Muslim women have also taken their part in this pious task. Several of the Mongol princes owed their conversion to the influence of a Muslim wife, and the same was probably the case with many of the pagan Turks when they had carried their raids into Muhammadan countries. The Sanūsiyyah missionaries who came to work among the Tūbū, to the north of Lake Chad, opened schools for girls, and took advantage of the powerful influence exercised by the women among these tribes (as among their neighbours, the Berbers), in their efforts to win them over to Islam.[2] In German East Africa, the pagan natives who leave their homes for six months or more, to work on the railways or plantations, are converted by the Muhammadan women with whom they contract temporary alliances; these women refuse to have anything to do with an uncircumcised kāfir, and to escape the disgrace attaching to such an appellation, their husbands become circumcised and thus receive an entry into Muslim society.[3] The progress of Islam in Abyssinia during the first half of the last century has been said to be in large measure due to the efforts of Muhammadan women, especially the wives of Christian princes, who had to pretend a conversion to Christianity on the occasion of their marriage, but brought up their children in the tenets of Islam and worked in every possible way for the advancement of that faith.[4] On the western frontier of Abyssinia, there is a pagan tribe

[1] Anjuman Ḥimāyat-i-Islām kā māhwārī risālah, pp. 5–13. (Lahore October 1889.)
[2] Duveyrier, p. 17.
[3] Klamroth, p. 12.
[4] Massaja, vol. xi. pp. 124–5.

called the Boruns; some of these men who had enlisted in a negro regiment, under the Anglo-Egyptian government of the Sudan, were converted to Islam by the wives of the black soldiers while the battalion was returning to Khartum.[1] The Tatar women of Kazan are said to be especially zealous as propagandists of Islam.[2] The professed devotee, because she happens to be a woman, is not thereby debarred from taking her place with the male saint in the company of the preachers of the faith. The legend of the holy women, descended from 'Alī, who are said to have flown through the air from Karbalā' to Lahore, and there by the influence of their devout lives of prayer and fasting to have won the first converts from Hinduism to Islam,[3] could hardly have originated if the influence of such holy women were a thing quite unknown. One of the most venerated tombs in Cairo is that of Nafīsah, the great-granddaughter of Ḥasan (the martyred son of 'Alī), whose theological learning excited the admiration even of her great contemporary, Imām al-Shāfi'ī, and whose piety and austerities raised her to the dignity of a saint: it is related of her that when she settled in Egypt, she happened to have as her neighbours a family of dhimmīs whose daughter was so grievously afflicted that she could not move her limbs but had to lie on her back all day. The parents of the poor girl had to go one day to the market and asked their pious Muslim neighbour to look after their daughter during their absence. Nafīsah, filled with love and pity, undertook this work of mercy; and when the parents of the sick girl were gone, she lifted up her soul in prayer to God on behalf of the helpless invalid. Scarcely was her prayer ended than the sick girl regained the use of her limbs and was able to go to meet her parents on their return. Filled with gratitude, the whole family became converts to the religion of their benefactor.[4]

Even the Muslim prisoner will on occasion embrace the opportunity of preaching his faith to his captors or to his fellow-prisoners. The first introduction of Islam into

[1] Artin, p. 119. [2] R. du M. M., ix. (1909), p. 252.
[3] Ghulām Sarwar: Khazīnat al-Aṣfiyā, vol. ii. p. 407–8.
[4] Goldziher, vol. ii. pp. 303–4.

Eastern Europe was the work of a Muslim jurisconsult who was taken prisoner, probably in one of the wars between the Byzantine empire and its Muhammadan neighbours, and was brought to the country of the Pechenegs[1] in the beginning of the eleventh century. He set before many of them the teachings of Islam and they embraced the faith with sincerity, so that it began to be spread among this people. But the other Pechenegs who had not accepted the Muslim religion, took umbrage at the conduct of their fellow-countrymen and finally came to blows with them. The Muslims, who numbered about twelve thousand, successfully withstood the attack of the unbelievers, though they were more than double their number, and the remnant of the defeated party embraced the religion of the victors. Before the close of the eleventh century the whole nation had become Muhammadan and had among them men learned in Muslim theology and jurisprudence.[2] In the reign of the Emperor Jahāngīr (1605–1628) there was a certain Sunnī theologian, named Shaykh Aḥmad Mujaddid, who especially distinguished himself by the energy with which he controverted the doctrines of the Shī'ahs: the latter, being at this time in favour at court, succeeded in having him imprisoned on some frivolous charge; during the two years that he was kept in prison he converted to Islam several hundred idolaters who were his companions in the same prison.[3] In more recent times, an Indian mawlavī, who had been sentenced to transportation for life to the Andaman Islands by the British Government, because he had taken an active part in the Wahhābī conspiracy of 1864, converted many of the convicts before his death. In Central Africa, an Arab chief condemned to death by the Belgians, spent his last hours in trying to convert to Islam the Christian missionary who had been sent to bring him the consolations of religion.[4]

Such being the missionary zeal of the Muslims, that they

[1] The Pechenegs at that time occupied the country between the lower Danube and the Don, to which they had migrated from the banks of the Ural at the end of the ninth century. (Karamsin, vol. i. pp. 180–1.)

[2] Abū 'Ubayd al-Bakrī (died 1094), pp. 467–8.

[3] Ghulām Sarwar: Khazīnat al-Aṣfiyā, vol. i. p. 613.

[4] D. Crawford: Thinking Black, p. 202. (London, 1913.)

are ready to speak in season and out of season,—as Doughty, with fine insight, says, " Their talk is continually (without hypocrisy) of religion, which is of genial devout remembrance to them," [1]—let us now consider some of the causes that have contributed to their success.

Foremost among these is the simplicity [2] of the Muslim creed, There is no god but God; Muḥammad is the Apostle of God. Assent to these two simple doctrines is all that is demanded of the convert, and the whole history of Muslim dogmatics fails to present any attempt on the part of ecclesiastical assemblies to force on the mass of believers any symbol couched in more elaborate and complex terms. This simple creed demands no great trial of faith, arouses as a rule no particular intellectual difficulties and is within the compass of the meanest intelligence. Unencumbered with theological subtleties, it may be expounded by any, even the most unversed in theological expression. The first half of it enunciates a doctrine that is almost universally accepted by men as a necessary postulate, while the second half is based on a theory of man's relationship to God that is almost equally wide-spread, viz. that at intervals in the world's history God grants some revelation of Himself to men through the mouthpiece of inspired prophets. This, the rationalistic character of the Muslim creed, and the advantage it reaps therefrom in its missionary efforts, have nowhere been more admirably brought out than in the following sentences of Professor Montet :—

" Islam is a religion that is essentially rationalistic in the widest sense of this term considered etymologically and historically. The definition of rationalism as a system that bases religious beliefs on principles furnished by the reason, applies to it exactly. It is true that Muḥammad, who was an enthusiast and possessed, too, the ardour of faith and the fire of conviction, that precious quality he transmitted to so many of his disciples,—brought forward his reform as a

[1] Doughty, vol. ii. p. 39.

[2] This was emphasised by Marracci in the seventeenth century. " Si ethnicus mysteria humani intellectus captum excedentia, vel naturali conditioni et imbecillitati difficillima, si non impossibilia, cum Alcoranica doctrina comparaverit, statim ab his refugiet, et ad illa obviis ulnis accurret." (Alcorani textus . . . translatus, p. 9. Patavii, 1698.)

revelation: but this kind of revelation is only one form of exposition and his religion has all the marks of a collection of doctrines founded on the data of reason. To believers, the Muhammadan creed is summed up in belief in the unity of God and in the mission of His Prophet, and to ourselves who coldly analyse his doctrines, to belief in God and a future life; these two dogmas, the minimum of religious belief, statements that to the religious man rest on the firm basis of reason, sum up the whole doctrinal teaching of the Qur'ān. The simplicity and the clearness of this teaching are certainly among the most obvious forces at work in the religion and the missionary activity of Islam. It cannot be denied that many doctrines and systems of theology and also many superstitions, from the worship of saints to the use of rosaries and amulets, have become grafted on to the main trunk of the Muslim creed. But in spite of the rich development, in every sense of the term, of the teachings of the Prophet, the Qur'ān has invariably kept its place as the fundamental starting-point, and the dogma of the unity of God has always been proclaimed therein with a grandeur, a majesty, an invariable purity and with a note of sure conviction, which it is hard to find surpassed outside the pale of Islam. This fidelity to the fundamental dogma of the religion, the elemental simplicity of the formula in which it is enunciated, the proof that it gains from the fervid conviction of the missionaries who propagate it, are so many causes to explain the success of Muhammadan missionary efforts. A creed so precise, so stripped of all theological complexities and consequently so accessible to the ordinary understanding, might be expected to possess and does indeed possess a marvellous power of winning its way into the consciences of men." [1]

Bishop Lefroy considers that the "secret of the extraordinary power for conquest and advance which Islam has in its best ages evinced" is to be found in its recognition of the Existence of God rather than the Unity of God. "Not so much that God is one as that God *IS*—that His existence is the ultimate fact of the universe—that His will is supreme

[1] Edouard Montet: La propagande chrétienne et ses adversaires musulmans, pp. 17–18. (Paris, 1890.)

—His sovereignty absolute—His power limitless . . . the conviction that, amidst all the chaos and confusion and disorders of the world which so fearfully obscure it, there is nevertheless, an ultimate Will, resistless, supreme, and that man is called to be a minister of that Will, to promulgate it, to compel—if necessary by very simple and elementary means indeed—obedience to that Will—this it was which welded the Mohammedan hosts into so invincible an engine of conquest, which inspired them with a spirit of military subordination and discipline, as well as with a contempt of death, such as has probably never been surpassed in any system—this it is which, so far as it is still in any true sense operative amongst Mohammadans, gives at once that backbone of character, that firmness of determination and strength of will, and also that uncomplaining patience and submission in the presence of the bitterest misfortune, which characterise and adorn the best adherents of the creed." [1]

When the convert has accepted and learned this simple creed, he has then to be instructed in the five practical duties of his religion : (1) recital of the creed, (2) observance of the five appointed times of prayer, (3) payment of the legal alms, (4) fasting during the month of Ramaḍān, and (5) the pilgrimage to Mecca.

The observance of this last duty has often been objected to as a strange survival of idolatry in the midst of the monotheism of the Prophet's teaching, but it must be borne in mind that to him it connected itself with Abraham, whose religion it was his mission to restore.[2] But above all—and herein is its supreme importance in the missionary history of Islam—it ordains a yearly gathering of believers, of all nations and languages, brought together from all parts of the world, to pray in that sacred place towards which their faces are set in every hour of private worship in their distant homes. No fetch of religious genius could have conceived a better expedient for impressing on the minds of the faithful a sense of their common life and of their brotherhood in the bonds of faith. Here, in a supreme act of common worship,

[1] Mankind and the Church, p. 283–4. (London, 1907.)
[2] Qur'ān, ii. 118–26.

the Negro of the west coast of Africa meets the Chinaman from the distant east; the courtly and polished Ottoman recognises his brother Muslim in the wild islander from the farthest end of the Malayan Sea. At the same time throughout the whole Muhammadan world the hearts of believers are lifted up in sympathy with their more fortunate brethren gathered together in the sacred city, as in their own homes they celebrate the festival of 'Īd al-Aḍḥā or (as it is called in Turkey and Egypt) the feast of Bayrām. Their visit to the sacred city has been to many Muslims the experience that has stirred them up to "strive in the path of God," and in the preceding pages constant reference has been made to the active part taken by the ḥājīs in missionary work.

Besides the institution of the pilgrimage, the payment of the legal alms is another duty that continually reminds the Muslim that "the faithful are brothers"[1]—a religious theory that is very strikingly realised in Muhammadan society and seldom fails to express itself in acts of kindness towards the new convert. Whatever be his race, colour or antecedents he is received into the brotherhood of believers and takes his place as an equal among equals.

It is not, however, true, as some European writers have maintained, that if an unbeliever is the slave of a Muslim his conversion to Islam procures for him his manumission, for, according to Muhammadan law, the conversion of a slave does not affect the prior state of bondage;[2] and the condition of the Muslim slave has varied much according to the character of his master. But freedom is in many instances the reward of conversion, and devout minds have even recognised in enslavement God's guidance to the true faith, as the negroes from the Upper Nile countries, whom Doughty met in Arabia. "In those Africans there is no resentment that they have been made slaves . . . even though cruel men-stealers rent them from their parentage. The patrons who paid their price have adopted them into their households, the males are circumcised and—that which enfranchises their souls, even in the long passion of

[1] Qur'ān, xlix. 10.
[2] W. H. Macnaghten: Principles and Precedents of Moohummudan Law, p. 312. (Madras, 1882.)

home-sickness—God has visited them in their mishap; they can say '*it was His grace,*' since they be thereby entered into the saving religion. This, therefore, they think is the better country, where they are the Lord's free men, a land of more civil life, the soil of the two Sanctuaries, the land of Mohammed :—for such they do give God thanks that their bodies were sometime sold into slavery!"[1]

Very effective also, both in winning and retaining, is the ordinance of the daily prayers five times a day. Montesquieu[2] has well said, "Une religion chargée de beaucoup de pratiques attache plus à elle qu'une autre qui l'est moins; on tient beaucoup aux choses dont on est continuellement occupé." The religion of the Muslim is continually present with him and in the daily prayer manifests itself in a solemn and impressive ritual, which cannot leave either the worshipper or the spectator unaffected. Sa'īd b. Ḥasan, an Alexandrian Jew, who embraced Islam in the year 1298, speaks of the sight of the Friday prayer in a mosque as a determining factor in his own conversion. During a severe illness he had had a vision in which a voice bade him declare himself a Muslim. "And when I entered the mosque" (he goes on) "and saw the Muslims standing in rows like angels, I heard a voice speaking within me, 'This is the community whose coming was announced by the prophets (on whom be blessings and peace!)'; and when the preacher came forth clad in his black robe, a deep feeling of awe fell upon me . . . and when he closed his sermon with the words, 'Verily God enjoineth justice and kindness and the giving of gifts to kinsfolk, and He forbiddeth wickedness and wrong and oppression. He warneth you; haply ye will be mindful.'[3] And when the prayer began, I was mightily uplifted, for the rows of the Muslims appeared to me like rows of angels, to whose prostrations and genuflections God Almighty was revealing Himself, and I heard a voice within me saying, 'If God spake twice unto the people of Israel throughout the ages, verily He speaketh unto this community in every time of

[1] Arabia Deserta, vol. i. pp. 554–5.
[2] De l'Esprit des Lois, livre xxv. chap. 2.
[3] Qur., chap. xvi. v. 92.

prayer,' and I was convinced in my mind that I had been created to be a Muslim."[1]

If Renan could say, "Je ne suis jamais entré dans une mosquée sans une vive émotion, le dirai-je ? sans un certain regret de n'être pas musulman,"[2] it can be readily understood how the sight of the Muslim trader at prayer, his frequent prostrations, his absorbed and silent worship of the Unseen, would impress the heathen African, endued with that strong sense of the mysterious such as generally accompanies a low stage of civilisation. Curiosity would naturally prompt inquiry, and the knowledge of Islam thus imparted might sometimes win over a convert who might have turned aside had it been offered unsought, as a free gift. Of the fast during the month of Ramaḍān, it need only be said that it is a piece of standing evidence against the theory that Islam is a religious system that attracts by pandering to the self-indulgence of men. As Carlyle has said, "His religion is not an easy one : with rigorous fasts, lavations, strict complex formulas, prayers five times a day, and abstinence from wine, it did not succeed by being an easy religion."

Bound up with these and other ritual observances, but not encumbered or obscured by them, the articles of the Muslim creed are incessantly finding outward manifestation in the life of the believer, and thus, becoming inextricably interwoven with the routine of his daily life, make the individual Musalman an exponent and teacher of his creed

[1] Goldziher, Sa'īd b. Ḥasan d'Alexandrie. (Revue des Études Juives, tome xxx. pp. 17–18.) (Paris, 1895).

[2] Ernest Renan : L'Islamisme et la Science, p. 19. (Paris, 1883.)

This has been emphasised by many observers, but it will be enough here to quote the words of an eminent Christian bishop. "No one who comes in contact for the first time with Mohammedans can fail to be struck by this aspect of their faith. . . . Wherever one may be, in open street, in railway station, in the field, it is the most ordinary thing to see a man, without the slightest touch of Pharisaism or parade, quietly and humbly leaving whatever pursuit he may be at the moment engaged in, in order to say his prayers at the appointed hour. On a larger scale, no one who has ever seen the courtyard of the Great Mosque at Delhi on the last Friday in the fast-month (Ramazan) filled to overflowing with, perhaps, 15,000 worshippers, all wholly absorbed in prayer, and manifesting the profoundest reverence and humility in every gesture, can fail to be deeply impressed by the sight, or to get a glimpse of the power which underlies such a system; while the very regularity of the daily call to prayer, as it rings out at earliest dawn, before light commences, or amid all the noise and bustle of the business hours, or again as the evening closes in, is fraught with the same message." (Dr. G. A. Lefroy: Mankind and the Church, pp. 287–8. (London, 1907.))

far more than is the case with the adherents of most other religions.[1] Couched in such short and simple language, his creed makes but little demand upon the intellect, and the definiteness, positiveness, and minuteness of the ritual leave the believer in no doubt as to what he has to do, and these duties performed, he has the satisfaction of feeling that he has fulfiled all the precepts of the Law. In this union of rationalism and ritualism, we may find, to a great extent, the secret of the power that Islam has exercised over the minds of men. "If you would win the great masses give them the truth in rounded form, neat and clear, in visible and tangible guise."[2]

Many other circumstances might be adduced that have contributed towards the missionary success of Islam—circumstances peculiar to particular times and countries. Among these may be mentioned the advantage that Muhammadan missionary work derives from the fact of its being so largely in the hands of traders, especially in Africa and other uncivilised countries where the people are naturally suspicious of the foreigner. For, in the case of the trader, his well-known and harmless avocation secures to him an immunity from any such feelings of suspicion, while his knowledge of men and manners, his commercial savoir-faire, gain for him a ready reception, and remove that feeling of constraint which might naturally arise in the presence of the stranger. He labours under no such disadvantages as hamper the professed missionary, who is liable to be suspected of some sinister motive, not only by people whose range of experience and mental horizon are limited and to whom the idea of any man enduring the perils of a long journey and laying aside every mundane occupation for the sole purpose of gaining proselytes, is inexplicable, but also by more civilised men of the world who are very prone to doubt the sincerity of the paid missionary agent.

The circumstances are very different when Islam has not to appear as a suppliant in a foreign country, but stands forth proudly as the religion of the ruling race. In the

[1] "One may notice and admire the kind of chivalrous pride which the average Mohammedan takes in his faith." (Bishop Lefroy: Mankind and the Church, p. 289.)

[2] A. Kuenen: National Religions and Universal Religions, p. 35. (London, 1882.)

preceding pages it has been shown that the theory of the Muslim faith enjoins toleration and freedom of religious life for all those followers of other faiths who pay tribute in return for protection, and though the pages of Muhammadan history are stained with the blood of many cruel persecutions, still, on the whole, unbelievers have enjoyed under Muhammadan rule a measure of toleration, the like of which is not to be found in Europe until quite modern times. Forcible conversion was forbidden, in accordance with the precepts of the Qur'ān :—" Let there be no compulsion in religion " (ii. 257). " Wilt thou compel men to become believers ? No soul can believe but by the permission of God " (x. 99, 100). The very existence of so many Christian sects and communities in countries that have been for centuries under Muhammadan rule is an abiding testimony to the toleration they have enjoyed, and shows that the persecutions they have from time to time been called upon to endure at the hands of bigots and fanatics, have been excited by some special and local circumstances rather than inspired by a settled principle of intolerance.[1]

[1] e. g. The persecution, under al-Mutawakkil, by the orthodox reaction against *all* forms of deviation from the popular creed : in Persia and other parts of Asia about the end of the thirteenth century in revenge for the domineering and insulting behaviour of the Christians in the hour of their advancement and power under the early Mongols. (Maqrīzī (2), Tome i. Première Partie, pp. 98, 106.) Assemani (tom. iii. pars. ii. p.c.), speaking of the causes that have excited the persecution of the Christians under Muhammadan rule, says :—" Non raro persecutionis procellam excitarunt mutuae Christianorum ipsorum simultates, sacerdotum licentia, praesulum fastus, tyrannica magnatum potestas, et medicorum praesertim scribarumque de supremo in gentem suam imperio altercationes." During the crusades the Christians of the East frequently fell under the suspicion of favouring the invasions of their co-religionists from the West, and in modern Turkey the movement for Greek Independence and the religious sympathies it excited in Christian Europe contributed to make the lot of the subject Christian races harder than it would have been, had they not been suspected of disloyalty and disaffection towards their Muhammadan ruler. De Gobineau has expressed himself very strongly on this question of the toleration of Islam : " Si l'on sépare la doctrine religieuse de la nécessité politique qui souvent a parlé et agi en son nom, il n'est pas de religion plus tolérante, on pourrait presque dire plus indifférente sur la foi des hommes que l'Islam. Cette disposition organique est si forte qu'en dehors des cas où la raison d'État mise en jeu a porté les gouvernements musulmans à se faire arme de tout pour tendre a l'unité de foi, la tolérance la plus complète a été la regle fournie par le dogme. . . . Qu'on ne s'arrête pas aux violences, aux cruautés commises dans une occasion ou dans une autre. Si on y regarde de près, on ne tardera pas à y découvrir des causes toutes politiques ou toutes de passion humaine et de tempérament chez le souverain ou dans les populations. Le fait religieux n'y est invoqué que comme prétexte et, en réalité, il reste en dehors." (A. de Gobineau (1), pp. 24–5.)

At such times of persecution, the pressure of circumstances has driven many unbelievers to become—outwardly at least—Muhammadans, and many instances might be given of individuals who, on particular occasions, have been harassed into submission to the religion of the Qur'ān. But such oppression is wholly without the sanction of Muhammadan law, either religious or civil. The passages in the Qur'ān that forbid forced conversion and enjoin preaching as the sole legitimate method of spreading the faith have already been quoted above (Introduction, pp. 5–6), and the same doctrine is upheld by the decisions of the Muhammadan doctors. When Moses Maimonides, who under the fanatical rule of the Almohads had feigned conversion to Islam, fled to Egypt and there openly declared himself to be a Jew, a Muslim jurisconsult from Spain denounced him for his apostasy and demanded that the extreme penalty of the law should be inflicted on him for this offence; but the case was quashed by al-Qāḍī al-Fāḍil, 'Abd al-Raḥīm b. 'Alī,[1] one of the most famous of Muslim judges, and the prime minister of the great Saladin, who authoritatively declared that a man who had been converted to Islam by force could not be rightly considered to be a Muslim.[2] In the same spirit, when Ghāzān (1295–1304) discovered that the Buddhist monks who had become Muhammadans at the beginning of his reign (when their temples had been destroyed) only made a pretence of being converted, he granted permission to all those who so wished to return to Tibet, where among their Buddhist fellow-countrymen they would be free once more to follow their own faith.[3] Tavernier tells us a similar story of some Jews of Ispahan who were so grievously persecuted by the governor "that either by force or cunning he caused them to turn Mahometans; but the king (Shāh 'Abbās II) (1642–1667), understanding that only power and fear had constrained them to turn, suffer'd them to resume their own religion and to live in quiet." [4] A story of a much earlier traveller[5] in Persia, in 1478, shows how even in those turbulent times a Muhammadan governor set himself to

[1] For a biography of him, see Ibn Khallikān, vol. ii. pp. 111–15.
[2] Barhebræus (2), pp. 417–18.
[3] C. d'Ohsson, vol. iv. p. 281.
[4] Tavernier (1), p. 160.
[5] Viaggio di Iosafa Barbero nella Persia. (Ramusio, vol. ii. p. 111.)

severely crush an outburst of fanaticism of the same character. A rich Armenian merchant of the city of Tabrīz was sitting in his shop one day when a Ḥājī,[1] with a reputation for sanctity, coming up to him importuned him to become a Musalman and abandon his Christian faith; when the merchant expressed his intention of remaining steadfast in his religion and offered the fellow alms with the hope of getting rid of him, he replied that what he wanted was not his alms but his conversion; and at length, enraged at the persistent refusal of the merchant, suddenly snatched a sword out of the hand of a bystander and struck the merchant a mortal blow on the head and then ran away. When the Governor of the city heard the news, he was very angry and ordered the murderer to be pursued and captured; the culprit having been brought into his presence, the governor stabbed him to death with his own hand and ordered his body to be cast forth to be devoured by dogs, saying: "What! is this the way in which the religion of Muḥammad spreads?" At nightfall, the common people took up the body and buried it, whereupon the Governor, enraged at this contempt of his order, gave up the place for three or four hours to be sacked by his soldiers and afterwards imposed a fine as a further penalty; also he called the son of the merchant to him and comforted him and caressed him with good and kindly words. Even the mad al-Ḥākim (996–1020), whose persecutions caused many Jews and Christians to abandon their own faith and become Musalmans, afterwards allowed these unwilling converts to return again to their own religion and rebuild their ruined places of worship.[2] Neglected as the Eastern Christians have been by their Christian brethren in the West, unarmed for the most part and utterly defenceless, it would have been easy for any of the powerful rulers of Islam to have utterly rooted out

[1] If indeed by Azi is meant Ḥājī.

[2] Makīn, p. 260. Similarly, about a century before, al-Muqtadir (A.D. 908–932) gave orders for the rebuilding of some churches at Ramlah in Palestine which had been destroyed by Muhammadans during a riot, the cause of which is not recorded. (Eutychius, ii. p. 82.) Abū Ṣāliḥ makes mention of the rebuilding of a great many churches and monasteries in Egypt which had either been destroyed in time of war (e. g. during the invasion of the Ghuzz and the Kurds in 1164) (pp. 91, 96, 112, 120), been wrecked by fanatics (pp. 85–6, 182, and Maqrīzī quoted in the Appendix pp. 327–8), or fallen into decay (pp. 5, 87, 103–4).

their Christian subjects or banished them from their dominions, as the Spaniards did the Moors, or the English the Jews for nearly four centuries. It would have been perfectly possible for Salīm I (in 1514) or Ibrāhīm (in 1646) to have put into execution the barbarous notion they conceived of exterminating their Christian subjects, just as the former had massacred 40,000 Shī'ahs with the aim of establishing uniformity of religious belief among his Muhammadan subjects. The muftis who turned the minds of their masters from such a cruel purpose, did so as the exponents of Muslim law and Muslim tolerance.[1]

Still, though the principle that found so much favour in Germany in the seventeenth century[2]—Cuius regio eius religio,—was never adopted by any Muhammadan potentate, it is obvious that the fact of Islam being the state religion could not fail to have had some influence in increasing the number of its adherents. Persons on whom their religious faith sat lightly would be readily influenced by considerations of worldly advantage, and ambition and self-interest would take the place of more laudable motives for conversion. St. Augustine made a similar complaint in the fifth century, that many entered the Christian Church merely because they hoped to gain some temporal advantage thereby: "Quam multi non quaerunt Iesum, nisi ut illis faciat bene secundum tempus! Alius negotium habet, quaerit intercessionem clericorum; alius premitur a potentiore, fugit ad ecclesiam; alius pro se vult interveniri apud eum apud quem parum valet: ille sic, ille sic; impletur quotidie talibus ecclesia."[3]

Moreover, to the barbarous and uncivilised tribes that saw the glory and majesty of the empire of the Arabs in the heyday of its power, Islam must have appeared as imposing and have exercised as powerful a fascination as the Christian faith when presented to the Barbarians of Northern Europe, when "They found Christianity in the Empire—Christianity refined and complex, imperious and pompous—Christianity

[1] A. de la Jonquière, pp. 203, 213, 312.
[2] E. Charvériat: Histoire de la Guerre de Trente Ans, tome ii. pp. 615, 625. (Paris, 1878.)
[3] In Ioannis Evangelium Tractatus, xxv. § 10.

enthroned by the side of kings, and sometimes paramount above them."[1]

Added to this must often have been the slow, persistent influence of daily contact with Muslim life and thought, such as led even a Nestorian writer of the twelfth century to add words of blessing to the mention of the name of the Prophet and the early caliphs,[2] and to pray for the mercy of God on the caliph 'Umar b. 'Abd al-'Azīz.[3] In modern times Christian missionaries complain that the system of public instruction in Egypt under the British occupation, according to which "Christian boys are often compelled to sit and listen to the Koran and Dîn (religious teaching) being taught to their Moslem companions when there is no room where they can be separated,"[4] tends to give the Muhammadans a preponderating influence over their Christian fellow-students. One of the most active of the followers of the late Muftī Muḥammad 'Abduh was originally a Coptic medical student, who had been won over to Islam through the influence of the religious instruction he had heard given in school hours.[5]

But the recital of such motives as little accounts for all cases of conversion in the one religion as in the other, and they should not make us lose sight of other factors in the missionary life of Islam, whose influence has been of a more distinctly religious character. Foremost among these is the influence of the devout lives of the followers of Islam. Strange as it may appear to a generation accustomed to look upon Islam as a cloak for all kinds of vice, it is nevertheless true that in earlier times many Christians who have come into contact with a living Muslim society have been profoundly impressed by the virtues exhibited therein; if these could so strike the traveller and the stranger, they would no doubt have some influence of attraction on the

[1] C. Merivale: The Conversion of the Northern Nations, p. 102. (London, 1866.)

[2] Mārī b. Sulaymān, p. 62 (ll. 4, 6, 13). The learned Maronite, Yūsuf Sim'ān al-Sim'ānī, in the eighteenth century, thus expressed his horror at such a concession to Muslim sentiment: "Mahometi eiusque sectariorum laudes persequitur, et quod sine horrore dici nequit, illius pseudoprophetae nomen es adiuncto praeconio memorat, quo Mahometani solent, nimirum عليه السّلام." (Assemani, tom. iii, pars. i. p. 585.)

[3] Mārī b. Sulaymān, p. 65 (l. 16).

[4] Methods of Mission Work among Moslems, p. 62.

[5] Id. pp. 61–4.

unbeliever who came in daily contact with them. Ricoldus de Monte Crucis, a Dominican missionary who visited the East at the close of the thirteenth century, thus breaks out in praise of the Muslims among whom he had laboured: "Obstupuimus, quomodo in lege tante perfidie poterant opera tante perfectionis inveniri. Referemus igitur hic breviter opera perfectionis Sarracenorum. . . . Quis enim non obstupescat, si diligenter consideret, quanta in ipsis Sarracenis sollicitudo ad studium, devocio in oratione, misericordia ad pauperes, reverencia ad nomen Dei et prophetas et loca sancta, gravitas in moribus, affabilitas ad extraneos, concordia et amor ad suos?"[1] William Petit of Newburgh in similar manner, towards the end of the twelfth century, praised the sobriety of the Saracens as the outcome of the teaching of their Prophet and as inspiring them with a sense of moral superiority over the Christians: "Gulosos vero atque ebriosos, orbi terrarum graves abominatus, sobrietatem docuit, ciborum delicias sugillavit, vini usum, praeterquam paucis certisque diebus solemnibus, interdixit [Macometus]. Inde est, quod cum Sarraceni in fluxu libidinum de sui, ut dictum est, seductoris indulgentia probentur esse spurcissimi; nostris, proh dolor! in frugalitate superiores esse videntur, nobisque, proh pudor! comessationum et ebrietatum sordes improperant. Denique malleus Christiani nominis Saladinus ante annos aliquot, cum nostrorum mores explorans, audisset quod pluribus in prandio ferculis uterentur, dixisse fertur, 'tales Terra Sancta indignos esse.' Unde constat, quod luxus nostrorum conspectus Agarenos, de frugalitate gloriantes, contra nos incitet animetque tanquam dicentes; 'Deus dereliquit crapulatos istos, persequamur et comprehendamus, quia non est qui eripiat.'"[2]

The literature of the Crusades is rich in such appreciations of Muslim virtues, while the Ottoman Turks in the early days of their rule in Europe received many a tribute of praise from Christian lips, as has already been shown in a former chapter.

At the present day there are two chief factors (beyond such of the above-mentioned as still hold good) that make for

[1] Laurent, p. 131.
[2] Historia Rerum Anglicarum Willelmi Parvi de Newburgh, ed. Hans Claude Hamilton, vol. ii. p. 158. (London, 1856.)

missionary activity in the Muslim world. The first of these is the revival of religious life which dates from the Wahhābī reformation at the end of the eighteenth century; though this new departure has long lost all political significance outside the confines of Najd, as a religious revival its influence is felt throughout Africa, India and the Malay Archipelago even to the present day, and has given birth to numerous movements which take rank among the most powerful influences in the Islamic world. In the preceding pages it has already been shown how closely connected many of the modern Muslim missions are with this wide-spread revival: the fervid zeal it has stirred up, the new life it has infused into existing religious institutions, the impetus it has given to theological study and to the organisation of devotional exercises, have all served to awake and keep alive the innate proselytising spirit of Islam.

Side by side with this reform movement, is another of an entirely different character—for, to mention one point of difference only, while the former is strongly opposed to European civilisation, the latter is rather in sympathy with modern thought and offers a presentment of Islam in accordance therewith,—viz. the Pan-Islamic movement, which seeks to bind all the nations of the Muslim world in a common bond of sympathy. Though in no way so significant as the other, still this trend of thought gives a powerful stimulus to missionary labours; the effort to realise in actual life the Muslim ideal of the brotherhood of all believers reacts on collateral ideals of the faith, and the sense of a vast unity and of a common life running through the nations inspirits the hearts of the faithful and makes them bold to speak in the presence of the unbelievers.

What further influence these two movements will have on the missionary life of Islam, the future only can show. But their very activity at the present day is a proof that Islam is not dead. The spiritual energy of Islam is not, as has been so often maintained, commensurate with its political power.[1] On the contrary, the loss of political power and

[1] Frederick Denison Maurice was giving expression to one of the most commonly received opinions regarding this faith when he said, "It has been proved that Mahometanism can only thrive while it is aiming at conquest." (The Religions of the World, p. 28.) (Cambridge, 1852.)

worldly prosperity has served to bring to the front the finer spiritual qualities which are the truest incentives to missionary work. Islam has learned the uses of adversity, and so far from a decline in worldly prosperity being a presage of the decay of this faith, it is significant that those very Muslim countries that have been longest under Christian rule show themselves most active in the work of proselytising. The Indian and Malay Muhammadans display a zeal and enthusiasm for the spread of the faith, which one looks for in vain in Turkey or Morocco.

APPENDIX I.

LETTER OF AL-HĀSHIMĪ INVITING AL-KINDĪ TO EMBRACE ISLAM.

THE following is the text of al-Hāshimī's letter inviting al-Kindī to embrace Islam :—" In the name of God, the Merciful, the Compassionate. I have begun this letter with the salutation of peace and blessing after the fashion of my lord and the lord of the prophets, Muḥammad, the Apostle of God (may the peace and mercy of God be upon him !). For those trustworthy, righteous and truthful persons who have handed down to us the traditions of our Prophet (peace be upon him !) have related this tradition concerning him that such was his habit and that whenever he began to converse with men he would commence with the salutation of peace and blessing and made no distinction of dhimmīs and illiterate, between Muslims and polytheists, saying ' I am sent to be kind and considerate to all men and not to deal roughly or harshly with them,' and quoting the words of God, ' Verily God is kind and merciful to believers.' Likewise I have observed that those of our Khalīfahs that I have met, followed the footsteps of their Prophet in courtesy, nobility, graciousness and beneficence, and made no distinctions in this matter and preferred none before another. So I have followed this excellent way and have begun my letter with the salutation of peace and blessing, that I be blamed of none who sees my letter.

" I have been guided therein by my affection towards you because my lord and prophet, Muḥammad (may the peace and mercy of God be upon him !) used to say that love of kinsmen is true piety and religion. So I have written this to you in obedience to the Apostle of God (may the peace and mercy of God be upon him !), feeling bound to show gratitude for the services you have done us, and because of the love and affection and inclination that you show towards us, and because of the favour of my lord and cousin the Commander of the Faithful (may God assist him !) towards you and his trust in you and his praise of you. So in all sincerity desiring for you what I desire for myself, my family and my parents, I will set forth the religion that we hold, and that God has approved of for us and for all creatures and for which He has promised a good reward in the end and safety from punishment when unto Him we shall return. . . . So I have sought to gain for you what I would gain for myself; and seeing your high moral life, vast learning, nobility of character, your virtuous behaviour, lofty qualities and your extensive influence over your co-religionists, I have had compassion on you lest you should continue in your present faith. Therefore I have determined to set before you what the favour of God has revealed to us and to expound unto you our faith with good and gentle speech, following the commandment of God, 'Dispute not with the people of the book except in the best way.' (xxix. 45.) So I will discuss with you only in words well-chosen, good and mild; perchance you may be aroused and return to the true path and incline unto the words of the Most High God which He has sent down to the last of the Prophets and lord of the children of Adam, our Prophet Muḥammad (the peace and blessing of God be upon him !). I have not despaired of success, but had hope of it for you from God who showeth the right path to whomsoever He willeth, and I have prayed that He may make me an instrument to this end. God in His perfect book says 'Verily the religion before God is Islam' (iii. 17), and again, confirming His first saying, 'And whoso desireth any other religion than Islam, it shall by no means therefore be accepted from him, and in the next world he shall be among the lost' (iii. 79), and again He confirms it decisively, when He says, 'O believers, fear God as He deserveth to be feared; and die not without having become Muslims.' (iii. 97.)

"And you know—(May God deliver you from the ignorance of unbelief and open your heart to the light of faith !)—

that I am one over whom many years have passed and I have sounded the depths of other faiths and weighed them and studied many of their books especially your books." [Here he enumerates the chief books of the Old and New Testaments, and explains how he has studied the various Christian sects.] "I have met with many monks, famous for their austerities and vast knowledge, have visited many churches and monasteries, and have attended their prayers. . . . I have observed their extraordinary diligence, their kneeling and prostrations and touching the ground with their cheeks and beating it with their foreheads and humble bearing throughout their prayers, especially on Sunday and Friday nights, and on their festivals when they keep watch all night standing on their feet praising and glorifying God and confessing Him, and when they spend the whole day standing in prayer, continually repeating the name of the Father, Son, and Holy Ghost, and in the days of their retreats which they call Holy Week when they stand barefooted in sackcloth and ashes, with much weeping and shedding of tears continually, and wailing with strange cries. I have seen also their sacrifices, with what cleanliness they keep the bread for it, and the long prayers they recite with great humility when they elevate it over the altar in the well-known church at Jerusalem with those cups full of wine, and I have observed also the meditations of the monks in their cells during their six fasts,—i. e. the four greater and the two less, etc. On all such occasions I have been present and observant of the people. Also I have visited their Metropolitans and Bishops, renowned for their learning and their devotion to the Christian faith and extreme austerity in the world, and have discussed with them impartially, seeking for the truth, laying aside all contentiousness, ostentation of learning and imperiousness in altercation and bitterness and pride of race. I have given them opportunity to maintain their arguments and speak out their minds without interruption or browbeating, as is done by the vulgar and illiterate and foolish persons among our co-religionists who have no principle to work up to or reasons on which to rest, or religious feeling or good manners to restrain them from rudeness; their speech is but browbeating and proud altercation and they have no knowledge or arguments except taking advantage of the rule of the government. Whenever I have held discussions with them and asked them to speak freely as their reason, their creed and their conclusion prompted, they have spoken openly and without deception of any kind, and their inward feelings have been laid bare to me as plainly as their outward appearance. So I have written at such length to you (may God show you the better way !) after long consideration and profound inquiry and investigation, so that none may suspect that I am ignorant of the things whereof I write and that all into whose hands this letter may come, may know that I have an accurate knowledge of the Christian faith.

" So, now (may God shower His blessings upon you !) with this knowledge of your religion and so long-standing an affection (for you), I invite you to accept the religion that God has chosen for me and I for myself, assuring you entrance into Paradise and deliverance from Hell. And it is this,—You shall worship the one God, the only God, the Eternal, He begetteth not, neither is He begotten, who hath no consort and no son, and there is none like unto Him. This is the attribute wherewith God has denominated Himself, for none of His creatures could know Him better than He Himself. I have invited you to the worship of this the One God, whose attribute is such, and in this my letter I have added nothing to that wherewith He has denominated Himself (high and exalted be His name above what they associate with Him !). This is the religion of your father and our father, Abraham (may the blessings of God rest upon him !), for he was a Ḥanīf and Muslim.

" Then I invite you (may God have you in His keeping !) to bear witness and acknowledge the prophetic mission of my lord and the lord of the sons of Adam, and the chosen one of the God of all worlds and the seal of the prophets, Muḥammad . . . sent by God with glad tidings and warnings to all mankind. ' He it is who hath sent His Apostle with the guidance and a religion of the truth, that He may make it victorious over every other religion, albeit they who assign partners to God be averse from it.' (ix. 33.) So he invited all men from the East and from the West, from land and sea, from mountain and from plain, with compassion and pity and good words, with kindly manners and gentleness. Then all these people accepted his invitation, bearing witness that he is the apostle of God, the Creator of the worlds, to those who are willing to give heed to admonition. All gave willing assent when they beheld the truth and faithfulness of his words, and sincerity of his purpose, and the clear argument and plain proof that he brought, namely the book that was sent down to him from God, the like of which cannot be produced by men or Jinns. 'Say: Assuredly if mankind and the Jinns should conspire to produce the like of this Qur'ān, they could not produce its like, though the one should help the other.' (xvii. 91.) And this is sufficient proof of his mission. So he invited men to the worship of the One God, the only God, the Self-sufficing, and they entered into his religion and accepted his authority without being forced and without unwillingness, but rather humbly acknowledging him and soliciting the light of his guidance, and in his name becoming victorious over those who denied his divine mission and rejected his message and scornfully entreated him. So God set them up in the cities and subjected to them the necks of the nations of men, except those who hearkened to them and accepted their religion and bore witness to their faith, whereby their blood, their property and their honour were safe and they were exempt from humbly paying jizyah." [He then enumerates the various ordinances of Islam, such as the five daily prayers, the fast of Ramaḍān, Jihād; expounds the doctrine of the resurrection of the dead and the last judgment, and recounts the joys of Paradise and the pains of Hell.] "So I have admonished you: if you believe in this faith and accept whatever is read to you from the revealed Word of God, then you will profit from my admonition and my writing to you. But if you refuse and continue in your unbelief and error and contend against the truth, I shall have my reward, having fulfilled the commandment. And the truth will judge you." [He then enumerates various religious duties and privileges of the Muslim, and concludes.] "So now in this my letter I have read to you the words of the great and high God, which are the words of the Truth, whose promises cannot fail and in whose words there is no deceit. Then give up your unbelief and error, of which God disapproves and which calls for punishment, and speak no more of Father, Son, and Holy Ghost, these words that you yourself admit to be so confusing: and give up the worship of the cross which brings loss and no profit, for I wish you to turn away from it, since your learning and nobility of soul are degraded thereby. For the great and high God says: 'Verily, God will not forgive the union of other gods with Himself; but other than this will He forgive to whom He pleaseth. And whoso uniteth gods with God, hath devised a great wickedness.' (iv. 51.) And again: 'Surely now are they infidels who say, "God is the Messiah, Son of Mary;" for the Messiah said, "O children of Israel! worship God, my Lord and your Lord." Verily, those who join other gods with God, God doth exclude from Paradise, and their abode the Fire; and for the wicked no helpers! They surely are infidels who say, "God is a third of three:" for there is no god but one God; and if they refrain not from what they say, a grievous chastisement shall assuredly befall such of them as believe not. Will they not, therefore, turn unto God, and ask pardon of Him? since God is Forgiving, Merciful! The Messiah, Son of Mary, is but an Apostle; other Apostles have flourished before him; and his mother was a just person; they both ate food.' (v. 76–9.) Then leave this path of error and this long and stubborn clinging to your religion and those burdensome and wearisome fasts which are a constant trouble to you and are of no use or profit and produce nothing but weariness of body and torment of soul. Embrace this faith and take this, the right and easy path, the true faith, the ample law and the way that God has chosen for His favoured ones and to which He has invited the people of all religions, that He may show His kindness and favour to them by guiding them into the true path by means of His guidance, and fill up the measure of His goodness unto men.

"So I have advised you and paid the debt of friendship and sincere love, for I have desired to take you to myself, that you and I may be of the same opinion and the same faith, for I have found my Lord saying in his perfect Book:

'Verily the unbelievers among the people of the Book and among the polytheists, shall go into the fire of Hell to abide therein for ever. Of all creatures they are the worst. But they verily who believe and do the things that are right—these of all creatures are the best. Their recompense with their Lord shall be gardens of Eden, 'neath which the rivers flow, in which they shall abide for evermore. God is well pleased with them, and they with Him. This, for him who feareth his Lord.' (xcviii. 5–8.) 'Ye are the best folk that hath been raised up for mankind. Ye enjoin what is just, and ye forbid what is evil, and ye believe in God: and if the people of the book had believed, it had surely been better for them. Believers there are among them, but most of them are disobedient.' (iii. 106.) So I have had compassion upon you lest you might be among the people of Hell who are the worst of all creatures, and I have hoped that by the grace of God you may become one of the true believers with whom God is well pleased and they with Him, and they are the best of all creatures, and I have hoped that you will join yourself to that religion which is the best of the religions raised up for men. But if you refuse and persist in your obstinacy, contentiousness and ignorance, your infidelity and error, and if you reject my words and refuse the sincere advice I have offered you (without looking for any thanks or reward)—then write whatever you wish to say about your religion, all that you hold to be true and established by strong proof, without any fear or apprehension, without curtailment of your proofs or concealment of your beliefs; for I purpose only to listen patiently to your arguments and to yield to and acknowledge all that is convincing therein, submitting willingly without refusing or rejecting or fear, in order that I may compare your account and mine. You are free to set forth your case; bring forward no plea that fear prevented you from making your arguments complete and that you had to put a bridle on your tongue, so that you could not freely express your arguments. So now you are free to bring forward all your arguments, that you may not accuse me of pride, injustice or partiality: for that is far from me.

"Therefore bring forward all the arguments you wish and

say whatever you please and speak your mind freely. Now that you are safe and free to say whatever you please, appoint some arbitrator who will impartially judge between us and lean only towards the truth and be free from the empery of passion: and that arbitrator shall be Reason, whereby God makes us responsible for our own rewards and punishments. Herein I have dealt justly with you and have given you full security and am ready to accept whatever decision Reason may give for me or against me. For 'there is no compulsion in religion' (ii. 257) and I have only invited you to accept our faith willingly and of your own accord and have pointed out the hideousness of your present belief. Peace be with you and the mercy and blessings of God!"

There can be very little doubt but that this document has come down to us in an imperfect condition and has suffered mutilation at the hands of Christian copyists: the almost entire absence of any refutation of such distinctively Christian doctrines as that of the Blessed Trinity, and the references to such attacks to be found in al-Kindī's reply, certainly indicate the excision of such passages as might have given offence to Christian readers.[1]

[1] Similarly, the Spanish editor of the controversial letters that passed between Alvar and "the transgressor" (a Christian convert to Judaism), adds the following note after Epist. xv.: "Quatuordecim in hac pagina ita abrasae sunt liniae, ut nec verbum unum legi possit. Folium subsequens exsecuit possessor codicis, ne transgressoris deliramenta legerentur." (Migne, Patr. Lat., tom. cxxi. p. 483.)

APPENDIX II.

CONTROVERSIAL LITERATURE BETWEEN MUSLIMS AND THE FOLLOWERS OF OTHER FAITHS.

ALTHOUGH Islam has had no organised system of propaganda, no tract societies or similar agencies of missionary work, there has been no lack of reasoned presentments of the faith to unbelievers, particularly to Christians and Jews. Of these it is not proposed to give a detailed account here, but it is of importance to draw attention to their existence if only to remove the wide-spread misconception that mass conversion is the prevailing characteristic of the spread of Islam and that individual conviction has formed no part of the propagandist schemes of the Muslim missionary. The beginnings of Muhammadan controversy against unbelievers are to be found in the Qur'ān itself, but from the ninth century of the Christian era begins a long series of systematic treatises of Muhammadan Apologetics, which has been actively continued to the present day. The number of such works directed against the Christian faith has been far more numerous than the Christian refutations of Islam, and some of the ablest of Muslim thinkers have employed their pens in their composition, e.g. Abū Yūsuf b. Isḥāq al-Kindī (A.D. 813–873), al-Mas'ūdī (ob. A.D. 958), Ibn Ḥazm (A.D. 994–1064), al-Ghazālī (ob. A.D. 1111), etc. It is interesting also to note that several renegades have written apologies for their change of faith and in defence of the Muslim creed, e.g. Ibn Jazlah in the eleventh century, Yūsuf al-Lubnānī and Shaykh Ziyādah b. Yaḥyā in the thirteenth, 'Abd Allāh b. 'Abd Allāh in the fifteenth, Darwesh 'Alī in the sixteenth, Aḥmad b. 'Abd Allāh, an Englishman born at Cambridge, in the seventeenth century, etc. These latter were all Christians before their conversion, but Jewish renegades also, though fewer in number, have been among the apologists of Islam. In India, besides many Muhammadan books written against the Christian religion, there is an enormous number of controversial works against Hinduism : as to whether the Muhammadans have been equally active in other heathen countries, I have no information.

The reader will find a vast store of information on Muslim controversial literature in the following writings : Moritz Steinschneider : Polemische und apologetische Litteratur in arabischer Sprache, zwischen Muslimen, Christen und Juden. (Leipzig, 1877) ; Ignaz Goldziher : Über Muhammedanische Polemik gegen Ahl al-kitâb (Z.D.M.G., vol. 32, p. 341 ff. 1878) ; Martin Schreiner : Zur Geschichte der Polemik zwischen Juden und Muhammedanern (Z.D.M.G., vol. 42, p. 591 ff. 1888) ; W. A. Shedd : Islam and the Oriental Churches, pp. 252–3 ; Carl Güterbock : Der Islam in Lichte der byzantinischen Polemik. (Berlin, 1912.)

APPENDIX III.

MUSLIM MISSIONARY SOCIETIES.

THE formation of societies for carrying on a propaganda in an organised and systematic manner is a recent development in the missionary history of Islam—as indeed it is comparatively recent in the history of Christian missions. Such Muslim missionary societies would appear to have been formed in conscious imitation of similar organisations in the Christian world, and are not in themselves the most characteristic expressions of the missionary spirit in Islam. In the Western world there is very little to note. No attempt seems to have been made to form such a society before the latter half of the nineteenth century, and the earliest efforts were attended with little success. When H. M. Stanley in 1875 urged in the English Press the sending of a Christian mission to King Mutesa of Uganda, the wide-spread attention paid to his appeal led to the formation of a missionary society in Constantinople for the propagation of Islam in that country, but no Muhammadan missionaries were ever sent to Uganda, and the outbreak of the Russo-Turkish war in 1878 diverted the attention of the Turks from any such enterprise.[1] A similar failure to establish organised missionary effort was manifested when the Anglo-Egyptian Government of the Sudan marked out zones of influence for various Christian missionary societies in districts the natives of which were heathen; some Muslims of Cairo claimed that a part of the territory should be allotted to the followers of Islam; whereupon the Government replied that all they had to do was to send the missionaries and the same facilities would be afforded to them as to the Christian missionaries; but the necessary organisation was lacking and the matter was allowed to drop.[2] In 1910 Shaykh Rashīd, the editor of *al-Manār*, founded a missionary society in Cairo, the object of which is to establish a college (entitled *Dār al-daʿwah*

[1] Richter, pp. 164–5.

[2] Artin, p. 35.

wa'l-irshād) for the training of missionaries and apologists for Islam, who are to be sent primarily into heathen and Christian lands, but also into those Muhammadan countries in which attempts are being made to induce the Muhammadans to abandon their faith.[1]

But it is in India that there has been the greatest expansion of such organisations. One of the best organised of these is probably the Anjuman Ḥimāyat-i-Islām of Lahore, but propagandist work forms only a small part of the wide field of its activities and it cannot therefore be described as a missionary society pure and simple. The original purpose for which the Anjuman Ḥāmī Islām of Ajmer was founded was to answer the objections urged against Islam by the members of the Ārya Samāj, but it included among its objects the preaching of Islam and the providing of food and clothing to new converts.[2] The Anjuman Wa'ẓ-i-Islām, as its name denotes, concentrated its efforts on the preaching of Islam, and, while Mawlavī Baqā Ḥusayn Khān (p. 283) was its Secretary, published lists of the converts gained—as did also the Anjuman-i-Islām and the Anjuman Tablīgh-i-Islām (which aimed at the conversion of the Hindu untouchables) established in Ḥaydarabad (Deccan), but it does not appear that either of these societies continues to exist.[3] Among the societies that have been established in the twentieth century are the Madrasa Ilāhiyyāt at Cawnpore, for the training of missionaries and the publication of tracts in defence of Islam and in refutation of attacks made upon it; and the Anjuman Ishā'at wa Ta'līm-i-Islām at Baṭālah in the Panjab, with similar objects. But the largest of these organisations is the Anjuman Hidāyat al-Islām of Dehlī, to which as many as twenty-four other societies,[4] in various parts of India, are affiliated; this Anjuman sends out missionaries to preach the doctrines of Islam and to hold controversies with non-Muslims, and publishes controversial literature, especially in refutation of the attacks made by the members of the Ārya Samāj.

[1] The Moslem World, vol. i. p. 441.
R. du M. M., vol. xv. p. 374; vol. xviii. pp. 216, 224.
[2] Rajputana Herald, April 17, 1889.
[3] Mohammedan World of To-day, p. 183.
[4] A list of these is given on p. 19 of the Annual Report for the year 1328 H.

TITLES OF WORKS CITED BY ABBREVIATED REFERENCES.

(The Titles, etc., of books quoted once only, are given in full in the foot-notes.)

Aa (P. J. B. Robidé van der): Reizen naar Nederlandsch Nieuw-Guinea, met Geschied- en Aardrijkskundige Toelichtingen. (The Hague, 1879.)

'Abd al-Razzāq al-Samarqandi: Matla' al-sa'dayn wa majma' al-baḥrayn. (India Office MS. No. 2704.)

Abh. f. d. K. d. M. hrsg. v. d. D M G: Abhandlungen für die Kunde des Morgenlandes, herausgegeben von der Deutschen Morgenländischen Gesellschaft. (Leipzig.)

Abu'l-Fidā: Géographie d'Aboulféda, traduite par M. Reinaud. (Paris, 1848.)

Abu'l-Ghāzī: Histoire des Mogols et des Tartares par Aboul-Ghâzi Behâdour Khan, traduite par le Baron Desmaisons. (St. Petersburg, 1871–4.)

Abū Ṣāliḥ: The Churches and Monasteries of Egypt, edited and translated by B. T. A. Evetts. (Oxford, 1895.)

Abū Shāmah: Arabische Quellenbeiträge zur Geschichte der Kreuzzüge übersetzt und herausgegeben von E. P. Goergens und R. Röhricht. Erster Band: Zur Geschichte Ṣalâḥ ad-dîn's. (Berlin, 1879.)

Abū 'Ubayd al-Bakrī: Fragments de géographes et d'historiens Arabes et Persans inédits, relatifs aux anciens peuples du Caucase et de la Russie meridionale, traduits par C. Ḍefrémery. (J. A. ivme série. Tome xiii, 1849.)

Abū Yūsuf: Kitāb al-Kharāj. (Cairo, A.H. 1302.)

Adeney (W. F.): The Greek and Eastern Churches. (Edinburgh, 1908.)

Aḥmad b. Yaḥyā b. al-Murtaḍā: Al-Mu'tazilah, being an extract from the Kitāb al-Milal wa'l-Niḥal, edited by T. W. Arnold. (Leipzig, 1902.)

Allégret (E.): L'Islamisme en Afrique. (Revue Chrétienne, iiime sér., tome xiv. (Paris, 1901.)

Alvar: (1) Alvari Cordubensis Epistolae. (Migne, Patr. Lat. tom. cxxi.)
(2) Indiculus Luminosus. (id. ib.)

Alvarez: Viaggio nella Ethiopia al Prete Ianni fatto par Don Francesco Alvarez Portughese. (1520–27.) (Ramusio. Tom. i.)

Amari (Michele): Storia dei Musulmani di Sicilia. (Florence, 1854–72.)

Amélineau (E.): Étude sur le Christianisme en Égypte au septième siècle. (Paris, 1887.)

'Amr b. Mattai: Maris, Amri et Slibae De Patriarchis Nestorianorum Commentaria, ed. Henricus Gismondi. Pars Altera. (Romae, 1896.)

Anderson (John): Chinese Mohammedans. (Journal of the Anthropological Institute of Great Britain and Ireland, vol. i. London, 1872.)

Andriessen (W. F.): De Islam in Nederlandsch Indië. (Vragen van den Dag. Amsterdam, 1889.)

'Arabfaqīh: Histoire de la conquête de l'Abyssinie (XVI_e siècle) par Chihab ed-did Aḥmed ben 'Abd el-Qâder surnommé Arab-Faqih. Texte arabe publié par René Basset. (Paris, 1897–1909.)

Argensola (B. Leonardo de): Conquista de las Islas Malucas. (Madrid, 1609.)

Arminjon (Pierre): Étrangers et protégés dans l'empire ottoman. (Paris, 1903.)

Artin (Yacoub Pasha): England in the Sudan, translated by George Robb. (London, 1911.)

Asboth (J. de): An official tour through Bosnia and Herzegovina. (London, 1890.)

Assemani (J. S.): Bibliotheca Orientalis Clementino-Vaticana. (Rome, 1719–28.)

Azdī: Futūḥ al-Shām by Muḥammad ibn 'Abd Allāh al-Azdī al-Baṣrī, edited by W. N. Lees. (Calcutta, 1854.)

Bahā al-Dīn: Vita et res gestae Saladini, auctore Bohadino filio Sjeddadi. Edidit A. Schultens. (Lugduni Batavorum, 1732.)

Balādhurī: Liber Expugnationis Regionum, auctore Imámo Ahmed ibn Jahja ibn Djábir al-Beládsorí, ed. M. J. de Goeje. (Leiden, 1866.)

Barbaro: Viaggio di Iosafa Barbaro nella Persia. (Ramusio, Tom. ii.)

Barbier de Meynard (A. C.): Un document turc sur la Circassie. (Centenaire de l'École des Langues Orientales Vivantes. Recueil de Mémoires publié par les Professeurs de l'École. Paris, 1895.)

Barbosa (Odoardo): Libro di Odoardo Barbosa Portoghese dell' Indie Orientali, 1516. (Ramusio, Tom. i.)

Barhebraeus: (1) Gregorii Barhebraei Chronicon Ecclesiasticum, ed. J. B. Abbeloos et T. J. Lamy. (Louvain, 1872–77.)
(2) Abu'l-Faraj, Ta'rīkh Mukhtaṣar al-Duwal, ed. A. Ṣāliḥānī. (Bairut, 1890.)
(3) Gregorii Abulpharagii sive Bar-Hebraei Chronicon Syriacum, ed. et vert. P. J. Bruns et G. G. Kirsch. (Lipsiae, 1789.)

Barros (J. de): Da Asia. (Lisbon, 1777–8.)

Basset (René): Études sur l'Histoire d'Éthiopie. (Paris, 1882.)

Bastian (A.): Die Völker des östlichen Asien. (Leipzig, 1866.)

Baudier (Michel): Histoire Générale de la Religion des Turcs. (Rouen, 1641.)

Baudissin (W. W. Graf von): Eulogius und Alvar. Ein Abschnitt spanischer Kirchengeschichte aus der Zeit der Maurenherrschaft. (Leipzig, 1872.)

Baumgarten (Martin): The travels of. (A Collection of Voyages and Travels. London, 1752.)

Becker (C. H.): (1) Materialien zur Kenntnis des Islam in Deutsch-Ostafrika. (Der Islam, vol. ii. Strassburg, 1911.)
(2) Papyri Schott-Reinhardt I., herausgegeben und erklärt. (Veröffentlichungen aus der Heidelberger Papyrus-Sammlung, iii.) (Heidelberg, 1906.)
(3) Zur Geschichte des östlichen Sūdān. (Der Islam, vol. i. Strassburg, 1910.)

Beke (T. C.): Routes in Abyssinia. (J. R. Ggr. Soc., vol. xiv., 1844.)

Belin: Fetwa relatif à la condition des Zimmis et particulièrement de, Chrétiens, en pays musulmans, depuis l'établissement de l'islamismes jusqu'au milieu du viiie siècle de l'hégire, traduit de l'arabe par M. Belin. (J. A. ivme série, tome xviii., 1851.)

Bell (H. I.): Greek Papyri in the British Museum. Catalogue, with Texts, vol. iv. The Aphrodito Papyri, edited by H. I. Bell. With an appendix of Coptic Papyri, edited by W. E. Crum. (London, 1910.)

Bellew (H. W.): The races of Afghanistan. (Calcutta, 1880.)

Benedict of Peterborough: Gesta Regis Henrici Secundi Benedicti Abbatis. Edited by William Stubbs. (London, 1867.)

Berg (L. W. C. *van den*): (1) De Mohamedaansche geestelijkeid en de geestelijke goederen op Java en Madoera. (Ts. ind. t.- l.- vk. Vol. xxvii., 1881.)
(2) Le Ḥadhramout et les Colonies Arabes dans l'Archipel Indien. (Batavia, 1886.)

Bijdr. t. d. t. l. en vlk: Bijdragen tot de Taal-, Land- en Volkenkunde van Nederlandsch-Indië, uitgegeven door het Koniglijk Instituut voor de Taal-, Land- en Volkenkunde van Nederlandsch-Indië. ('s Gravenhage.)

Bizzi: Relatione della visita fatta da me, Marino Bizzi, Arcivescovo d'Antivari, nelle parti della Turchia, Antivari, Albania e Servia, alla Santità di Nostro Signore Papa Paolo Quinto. 1610. (Bibliotheca Barberina, Rome. N[r.] lxiii. 13.)

Blau: Chronik der Sulṭâne von Bornu, bearbeitet von Otto Blau. (ZDMG., vol. 6. 1852.)

Blochet (E.): Introduction à l'Histoire des Mongols de Fadl Allah Rashid ed-Din. ("E. J. W. Gibb Memorial" Series. xii.) (London, 1910.)

Blount: A voyage into the Levant; a brief relation of a journey lately performed by Master Henry Blount, Gentleman. 1634-36. (A Collection of Voyages and Travels. London, 1745.)

Blunt (W. S.): The Future of Islam. (London, 1883.)

Blyden (E. W.): Christianity, Islam and the Negro Race. (London, 1888.)

Bobrovnikoff (S.): Moslems in Russia. (The Moslem World, vol. i. London, 1911.)

Bokemeyer (H.): Die Molukken. (Leipzig, 1888.)

Bonaventura di S. Antonio: Informatione di Fra Bonaventura di S. Antonio, Reformato di S. Francesco, Miss[rio] d'Albania. (Assisi, li 30 Luglio, 1652.) (Bibliotheca Chigiana, Rome. G. iii., 94.)

Bonet-Maury (G.): L'Islamisme et le Christianisme en Afrique. (Paris, 1906.)

Bouche (Pierre): La Côte des Esclaves et le Dahomey. (Paris, 1885.)

Bretschneider (E.): (1) Mediæval Researches from Eastern Asiatic Sources. (London, 1888.)
(2) On the Knowledge possessed by the Ancient Chinese of the Arabs and Arabian Colonies. (London, 1871.)

Broomhall (Marshall): Islam in China. (London, 1910.)

Brosset (M. F.): Histoire de la Géorgie. (St. Petersburg, 1849-58.)

Brumund (J. F. G.): Bijdragen tot de kennis van het Hindoeïsme op Java. (Verh. Bat. Gen. van K. en W. Deel xxxiii. 1868.)

Budge (E. A. Wallis): The Egyptian Sûdân, its history and monuments. (London, 1907.)

Burchard: Burchardi de Monte Sion Descriptio Terrae Sanctae. (Peregrinatores Medii Aevi Quatuor. Ed. J. C. M. Laurent. Lipsiae, 1864.)
Burckhardt (J. L.): (1) Travels in Nubia. (London, 1819.)
(2) Travels in Syria and the Holy Land. (London, 1822.)
Burton (Richard F.): (1) Abeokuta and the Camaroon Mountains. (London, 1863.)
(2) First Footprints in East Africa. (London, 1856.)
Busbecq (Augier Ghislen de): Omnia quae extant. (Amstelodami, 1660.)
Businello (P.): Historische Nachrichten von der Regierungsart der osmanischen Monarchie. (Leipzig, 1778.)
Caetani (Leone, Principe di Teano): Annali dell' Islām. (Milano, 1905– .)
Cahun (Léon): Introduction à l'histoire de l'Asie. Turcs et Mongols. (Paris, 1896.)
Campen (C. F. H.): Nalezingen op het opstel over de godsdienstbegrippen der Halemaherasche Alfoeren. (Ts. ind. t.- l.- vk. Deel xxviii. 1883.)
Canne (H. D.): Bijdrage tot de Geschiedenis der Lampongs. (Ts. ind. t.- l.- vk. Deel xi. 1862.)
Cantacuzenos: Trattato di Theodoro Spandugino Cantacusino de' costumi de' Turchi. (Venice, 1573.)
Chavannes (E.): Documents sur les Tou-Kiue (Turcs) Occidentaux. (Sbornik Trudov Orchonskoy Expedicii. VI. St. Petersburg, 1903.)
Chirāgh 'Alī: Maulavi Cheragh Ali: A Critical Exposition of the Popular Jihád. (Bombay, 1885.)
Chwolsohn (D.): Die Ssabier und der Ssabismus. (St. Petersburg, 1856.)
Chytraeus (David): Oratio de statu ecclesiarum hoc tempore in Graecia, Asia, Africa, Ungaria, Boëmia, etc. (Wittebergae, 1580.)
Clark (E. L.): The Races of European Turkey. (New York, 1878.)
Comuleo: Instruttioni al Rev^{do} Don Alessandro Comuleo Archiprete di S. Girolamo di Roma mandato da Papa Clemente Ottavo al Gran Duca di Moscovia, et altri Principi, et Potentati delle Parti Settentrionali. Con una Relatione del Medesimo Comuleo fatta à S. Santità sopra le cose del Turco. (Bibliotheca Barberina, Rome. N$^{r.}$ lviii. 33.)
Contenson (L. de): Chrétiens et Musulmans. (Paris, 1901.)
Coolsma (S.): De Zendingeeuw voor Nederlandsch Oost-Indië. (Utrecht, 1901.)
Cornaro (F.): Creta Sacra, authore Flaminio Cornelio. (Venice, 1755.)
Crawfurd (John): (1) A Descriptive Dictionary of the Indian Islands and adjacent Countries. (London, 1856.)
(2) History of the Indian Archipelago. (Edinburgh, 1820.)
Creasy (Sir Edward S.): History of the Ottoman Turks. (London, 1878.)
Crisio: Summario della Relatione della Visita di Albania, fatta per ordine della Sac. Cong^{ne} da Don Marco Crisio Sacerdote Albanese. 1651. (Bibliotheca Chigiana, Rome. G. iii. 94.)
Crusius (Martin): Turcograecia. (Basileae, 1584.)
Dalrymple (A.): Essay towards an account of Sulu. (Journal of the Indian Archipelago and Eastern Asia. Vol. iii. Singapore, 1849.)
Dalton (E. T.): Descriptive Ethnology of Bengal. (Calcutta, 1872.)
Delafosse (Maurice): Les confréries musulmanes et le maraboutisme dans les pays du Sénégal et du Niger. (Renseignements Coloniaux et Documents publiés par le Comité de l'Afrique Française et le Comité du Maroc. No. 4. Paris, 1911.)
Depont (Octave) et *Coppolani* (Octave): Les confréries religieuses musulmanes. (Alger, 1897.)

Devéria (Gabriel): Origine de l'Islamisme en Chine. (Centenaire de l'École des Langues Orientales Vivantes. Recueil de Mémoires publié par les Professeurs de l'École. Paris, 1895.)

Dobschütz (E. von): Die confessionellen Verhältnisse in Edessa unter der Araberherrschaft. (Zeitschrift für wissenschaftliche Theologie. 41er Jahrgang, 1898.)

Döllinger (J. J. T.): Mohammed's Religion nach ihrer inneren Entwicklung und ihrem Einflusse auf das Leben der Völker. (Munich, 1838.)

Dorostamus (Athanasius): Neueste Beschreibung derer Griechischen Christen in der Türckey, aufgesetzt von Jacob Elssner. (Berlin, 1737.)

Doughty (Charles M.): Travels in Arabia Deserta. (Cambridge, 1888.)

Dousa: Georgii Dousae de Itinere suo Constantinopolitano epistola. (Lugduni Batavorum, 1599.)

Doutté (E.): Notes sur l'Islam maghribin. (Revue de l'Histoire des Religions, XL, XLI. Paris, 1899, 1900.)

Dozy (R. P. A.): (1) Essai sur l'histoire de l'Islamisme. (Leyde, 1879.)
(2) Histoire des Musulmans d'Espagne. (Leyde, 1861.)
(3) Recherches sur l'histoire et la littérature de l'Espagne pendant le moyen âge, 3me éd. (Leyde, 1881.)

Driesch (G. C. von den): Historische Nachricht von der Röm. Kayserl. Gross-Botschaft nach Constantinopel, welche . . . der Graf Damian Hugo von Virmondt rühmlichst verrichtet. (Nürnberg, 1723.)

Dulaurier (M. E.): Addition au mémoire intitulé Liste des pays qui relevaient de l'empire javanais de Madjapahit. (J. A. ivme série, tome xiii. 1849.)

Duveyrier (H.): La confrérie musulmane de Sîdi Mohammed Ben 'Alî Es-Senoûsî. (Paris, 1886.)

East (D. J.): Western Africa. (London, 1844.)

Elias of Nisibis: F. Baethgen: Fragmente syrischer und arabischer Historiker. (Abh. f. d. K. d. M. hrsg. v. d. DMG. Vol. iii. No. 3. 1884.)

Elliot (Sir H. M.): The History of India, as told by its own historians. The Muhammadan Period. Edited by Prof. John Dowson. London, 1872–7.)

Encyclopaedie van Nederlandsch-Indië, met medewerking van verschillende ambtenaren, geleerden en officieren, samengesteld door P. A. van der Lith en J. F. Snelleman. (Leiden, 1899–1905.)

Enhueber (J. B.): Dissertatio de haeresi Elipandi et Felicis. (Migne, Patr. Lat. tom. ci.)

Eruslanov (P.): Магометанская пропаганда среди черемисъ Уфимской губерніи. (Moscow, 1895.)

Eulogius: Memoriale Sanctorum. (Migne, Patr. Lat., tom. cxv.)

Eutychius: Eutychii Patriarchae Alexandrini Annales, ed. L. Cheikho, B. Carra de Vaux, H. Zayyat. (Corpus Scriptorum Christianorum Orientalium. Scriptores Arabici. Ser. iii. Tom. vi–vii. Paris, 1906–9.)

Evans (A. J.): Through Bosnia and the Herzegovina. (London, 1876.)

Farlati (Daniel): Illyricum Sacrum. (Venice, 1769–1819.)

Finlay (G.): A History of Greece, from its Conquest by the Romans to the present time. (Oxford, 1877.)

Firishtah: History of the Rise of the Mahomedan Power in India, translated from the Persian of Mahomed Kasim Ferishta by John Briggs. (London, 1829.)

Forget (D. A.) : L'Islam et le Christianisme dans l'Afrique Centrale. (Paris, 1900.)

Forrest (T.) : A Voyage to New Guinea and the Moluccas. (London, 1779.)

Fournel (Henri) : Les Berbers. Étude sur la conquête de l'Afrique par les Arabes. (Paris, 1875.)

Frere (Sir Bartle) : (1) Eastern Africa as a field for Missionary Labour. (London, 1874.)
(2) Indian Missions. 3rd. ed. (London, 1874.)

Gaetan : Relatione di Ivan Gaetan del discoprimento dell' Isole Molucche. (Ramusio. Tom. i.)

Gairdner (W. H. T.) : The Reproach of Islam. (London, 1909.)

Garnett (L. M. J.) : The Women of Turkey and their Folklore. The Jewish and Moslem Women. (London, 1891.)

Gasztowtt (Thadée) : La Pologne et l'Islam. (Paris, 1907.)

Gazetteer of the Bombay Presidency. (Bombay, 1877–1904.)

Gazetteer of the North-Western Provinces of India. (Allahabad, 1874–84.)

Gazetteer of the Province of Oudh. (Lucknow, 1877.)

Gazetteer of Rajputana. (Calcutta, 1879.)

Georgieviẓ (Bartholomaeus) : De Turcarum Moribus Epitome. (1598.)

Georgirenes (Joseph) : A Description of the Present State of Samos, Nicaria, Patmos and Mount Athos. (London, 1678.)

Gerlach (Stephan) : Tage-Buch der von zween . . . Römischen Kaysern . . . an die Ottommanische Pforte . . . abgefertigten . . . Gesandtschaft. (Frankfurt, 1674.)

Gfrörer (A. F.) : Byzantinische Geschichten, hrgs. von J. B. Weiss. (Graz, 1872–7.)

G̲hulām Sarwar : K̲hazīnat al-Aṣfīyā. (Lahore, n. d.)

Gibbon (Edward) : The History of the Decline and Fall of the Roman Empire. (London, 1881.)

Gmelin (M. F.) : Christensclaverei und Renegatenthum unter den Völkern des Islam. (Berlin, 1873.)

Gobineau (A. de) : (1) Les Religions et les Philosophies dans l'Asie Centrale. (Paris, 1865.)
(2) Trois Ans en Asie. (Paris, 1859.)

Goldziher (Ignaz) : Muhammedanische Studien. (Halle, 1889–90.)

Gottheil (R. J. H.) : Dhimmis and Moslems in Egypt. (Old Testament and Semitic Studies in memory of William Rainey Harper. Vol. ii. Chicago, 1908.)

Grenard : J.-L. Dutreuil de Rhins. Mission Scientifique dans La Haute Asie, 1890–1895. IIme Partie. Le Turkestan et le Tibet, étude ethnographique et sociologique, par F. Grenard. IIIme Partie. Histoire, Linguistique, Archeólogie, Géographie, par F. Grenard. (Paris, 1898.)

Grenard : La légende de Satoḳ Boghra Khân et l'histoire, par M. F. Grenard. (Journal Asiatique, ixme série, tome xv. Paris, 1900.)

Groeneveldt (W. P.) : Notes on the Malay Archipelago and Malacca, compiled from Chinese sources. (Verh. Bat. Gen. van K. en W. Deel xxxix. 1880.)

Grosier (J. B. G. A.) : De la Chine, ou description générale de cet empire. (Paris, 1819.)

Guignes (C. L. J. de) : Histoire générale des Huns, des Turcs, des Mogols, (Paris, 1756–8.)

Hackett (J.) : A History of the Orthodox Church of Cyprus. (London, 1901.)

Hageman (J.) : Bijdrage tot de Geschiedenis van Borneo. (Ts. ind. t.- l.- vk. Deel vi. 1856.)

Hammer-Purgstall (Joseph von): (1) Geschichte des osmanischen Reiches. (Pesth, 1827–35.)
(2) Des osmanischen Reichs Staatsverfassung und Staatsverwaltung. (Wien, 1815.)
(3) Geschichte der Goldenen Horde in Kiptschak. (Pesth, 1840.)
(4) Geschichte der Ilchanen. (Darmstadt, 1842–3.)

Haneberg (B.): Das muslimische Kriegsrecht. (Munich, 1871.)

Hasselt (A. L. von): Volksbeschrijving van Midden-Sumatra. (Leiden, 1882).

Hauri (J.): Der Islam in seinem Einfluss auf das Leben seiner Bekenner. (Leiden, 1883.)

Haywood (A. H. W.): Through Timbuctu and across the Great Sahara. (London, 1912.)

Hefele (C. J.): Beiträge zur Kirchengeschichte, Archäologie und Liturgik. (Tübingen, 1864.)

Helfferich (Adolf): Der Westgothische Arianismus und die Spanische Ketzer-Geschichte. (Berlin, 1860.)

Hertzberg (G. F.): Geschichte der Byzantiner und des Osmanischen Reiches. (Berlin, 1882–3.)

Hidāyah: The Hedāya, or Guide: A Commentary on the Mussulman Laws, translated by Charles Hamilton. (London, 1791.)

Hilāl al-Ṣābī: Ta'rīkh al-Wuzarā' ed. H. F. Amedroz. (Beirut, 1904.)

Hill (Aaron): A Full and Just Account of the Present State of the Ottoman Empire. (London, 1709.)

Hoëvell (G. W. W. C. Baron von): De Kei-eilanden. (Ts. ind. t.-l.-en vk. Deel xxxiii. 1890.)

Hollander (J. J. de): Handleiding bij de Beoefening der Land- en Volkenkunde van Nederlandsch Oost-Indië. (Breda, 1884.)

Hoveden: Chronica Magistri Rogeri de Hovedene, edited by William Stubbs. (London, 1868-71.)

Howorth (Sir H. H.): History of the Mongols. (London, 1876-80.)

Hurgronje (C. Snouck): (1) De beteekenis van den Islam voor zijne belijders in Oost-Indië. (Leiden, 1883.)
(2) De Sjattarijjah-secte. (Med. Ned. Zendelinggen. Vol. xxxii. 1888.)
(3) Mekka. (The Hague, 1888–9.)

Ibbetson (D. C. J.): The Musulmans of the Panjab. (Indian Evangelical Review. Vol. x. Calcutta, 1884.)

Ibn abī Usaybi'ah: 'Uyūn al-anbā' fī ṭabaqāt al-aṭibbā'. (Cairo, A. H. 1299.)

Ibn abī Zar': Roudh el-Kartas. Histoire des Souverains du Maghreb, traduit de l'Arabe par A. Beaumier. (Paris, 1860.)

Ibn al-Athīr: Ibn el-Athiri Chronicon quod perfectissimum inscribitur, ed. C. J. Tornberg. (Leiden, 1851-76.)

Ibn Baṭūṭah: Voyages d'Ibn Batoutah, texte arabe, accompagné d'une traduction par C. Defrémery et B. R. Sanguinetti. (Paris, 1853–8.)

Ibn Ḥawqal: Kitāb al-masālik wa'l-mamālik, ed. M. G. De Goeje. (Bibliotheca Geographorum Arabicorum II. Leiden, 1873.)

Ibn Isḥāq: Das Leben Muhammed's nach Muhammed Ibn Ishâk, bearbeitet von Abd el-Malik Ibn Hischam, hrsg. von F. Wüstenfeld. (Göttingen, 1859.)

Ibn Khaldūn: Kitāb al-'ibar wa dīwān al-mubtada' wa'l khabar fī ayyām al-'Arab wa'l Barbar. (Būlāq, 1867.)

Ibn Khallikān: Biographical Dictionary, translated by Baron Mac Guckin de Slane. (Paris, 1843–71.)
Ibn Sa'd: al-Ṭabaqāt. Biographien Muhammeds, seiner Gefährten und der späteren Träger des Islams bis zum Jahre 230 der Flucht, hrsg. von E. Sachau, etc. (Leiden, 1904– .)
Ibn Sa'd: Die Schreiben Muhammads und die Gesandtschaften an ihn. (Skizzen und Vorarbeiten von J. Wellhausen. Viertes Heft. Berlin, 1889.)
Idrīsī: Description de l'Afrique et de l'Espagne, publiée par R. Dozy et M. J. de Goeje. (Leiden, 1866.)
Informatione del Segretario de Propaganda Fide circa la missione d'Albania de fratri Riformati di S. Francesco. (Bibliotheca Chigiana, Rome. G. iii. 94.)
Innes (C. A.): Malabar and Anjengo: by C. A. Innes, edited by F. B. Evans. (Madras District Gazetteers.) (Madras, 1908.)
Isenberg (C. M.): Abessinien. (Bonn, 1844.)
Ishok of Romgla: Chronique de Michel le Grand, traduite sur la version arménienne du prêtre Ischôk par Victor Langlois. (Venise, 1868.)
Isidori Pacensis Chronicon. (Migne, Patr. Lat., tom. xcvi.)
Islam and Missions, being papers read at the second Missionary Conference on behalf of the Mohammedan World at Lucknow, January 23–28, 1911, edited by E. M. Wherry, S. M. Zwemer, C. G. Mylrea. (New York, etc., 1911.)
Iṣṭakhrī: Kitāb Masālik wa'l-Mamālik, ed. M. J. de Goeje. (Bibliotheca Geographorum Arabicorum. I. Leiden, 1870.)
J. A.: Journal Asiatique. (Paris.)
J. A. S. B.; Journal of the Asiatic Society of Bengal. (Calcutta.)
J. R. Ggr. Soc.: Journal of the Royal Geographical Society. (London.)
Jacques de Vitry: Jacobi de Vitriaco Libri Duo. Quorum prior Orientalis, sive Hierosolymitanæ: Alter, Occidentalis Historiæ nomine inscribitur. Operâ D. Francisci Moschi editi. (Duaci, 1597.)
Jadrinzew (N.): Sibiren: Geographische, ethnographische und historische Studien, bearbeitet von Ed. Petri. (Jena, 1886.)
Jessup (H. H.): The Mohammedan Missionary Question. (Philadelphia, 1879.)
John of Gorz: Vita Ioannis Abbatis Gorziensis, auctore Ioanne Abbate S. Arnulfi. (Migne, Patr. Lat., tom cxxxvii.)
John of Nikiu; Chronique de Jean, Évêque de Nikiou. Publié et traduit par H. Zotenberg. (Notices et extraits des Manuscrits de la Bibliothèque Nationale. Tome xxiv. Première Partie. Paris, 1883.)
Joinville: Œuvres de Jean, Sire de Joinville, ed. N. de Wailly. (Paris, 1867.)
Joselian (Plato): A Short History of the Georgian Church, translated by S. C. Malan. (London, 1866.)
Jūzjānī: Minhāj-i-Sirāj al-Jūzjānī, Ṭabaqāt-i-Nāṣirī, ed. W. Nassau Lees. (Calcutta, 1864.)
Kanitz (F.): Die fortschreitende Arnautisirung und Muhamedanisirung Alt-Serbiens. (Oesterreichische Monatsschrift für den Orient. Vienna, March, 1888.)
Karamsin (N. M.): Histoire de l'Empire de Russie. (Paris, 1819–26.)
Keane (A. H.): Asia, edited by Sir Richard Temple. (London, 1882.)
Kern (H.): Over den invloed der Indische, Arabische en Europeesche beschaving op de volken van den Indischen Archipel. (Leiden, 1883.)
Khojā Vṛttānt by Sachedīnā Nānjīāṇī. (Aḥmadābād, 1892.)
Kitāb al-Fihrist, herausgegeben von G. Flügel. (Leipzig, 1871–2.)

Klamroth (M.): Der Islam in Deutschostafrika. (Berlin, 1912.)
Klaproth (J. von): Aperçu des entreprises des Mongols en Géorgie et en Arménie dans le xiii siècle. (J. A. série ii., tome xii. 1833.)
Krehl (Ludolf): Das Leben des Muhammed. (Leipzig, 1884.)
Kremer (A von): (1) Culturgeschichte des Orients unter den Chalifen. (Vienna, 1875.)
(2) Culturgeschichtliche Streifzüge auf dem Gebiete des Islams. (Leipzig, 1873.)
(3) Geschichte der herrschenden Ideen des Islams. (Leipzig, 1868.)
(4) Notizen gesammelt auf einem Ausfluge nach Palmyra. (Sitzb. d. Akad. d. Wiss., Philos.-hist. Cl. Vol. v. 1850.)
Krieger (Maximilian): New Guinea. (Berlin, 1899.)
Kritopoulos (Metrophanes): Metrophanis Critopuli Confessio. (E. J. Kimmel: Monumenta Fidei Ecclesiae Orientalis. Pars. II.) (Jenae, 1850.)
Kumm (H. K. W.): Khont-hon-nofer, the Lands of Ethiopia. (London, 1910.)
Kyriakos (A. Diomedes): Geschichte der orientalischen Kirchen von 1453-1898. (Leipzig, 1902.)
La Jonquière (A. de): Histoire de l'Empire Ottoman. (Paris, 1881.)
La Saussaye (P. D. Chantepie de): Lehrbuch der Religionsgeschichte. (Freiburg I. B., 1887–9.)
Lammens (Henri): Études sur le regne du Calife Omaiyade Moʿawia Ier. (Université Saint-Joseph, Beyrouth (Syrie). Mélanges de la Faculté Orientale, I.) (Beyrouth, 1906.)
Lane (E. W.): The Manners and Customs of the Modern Egyptians. 5th ed. (London, 1860.)
Laurent (J. C. M.): Peregrinatores Medii Aevi Quatuor. (Lipsiae, 1864.)
Lazăr (Victor): Die Südrumänen der Türkei und der angrenzenden Länder. (Bukarest, 1910.)
Le Chatelier (A.): (1) Les Confréries musulmanes du Hedjaz. (Paris, 1887.)
(2) L'Islam au xixe siècle. (Paris, 1888.)
(3) L'Islam dans l'Afrique Occidentale. (Paris, 1899.)
Le Quien (Michael): Oriens Christianus. (Paris, 1740.)
Lea (H. C.): The Moriscos of Spain: their conversion and expulsion. (London, 1901.)
Leake (W. M.): Researches in Greece. (London, 1814.)
Leo Africanus: Della Descrittione dell' Africa, par Giovani Lioni Africano. (Ramusio. Tom. i.)
Leslie (Gaultier de): L'Ambassade à la Porte Ottomane, ordonnée par Sa Majesté Impériale, Léopold I., executée par Gualtier de Leslie, Comte du S. Empire. (1665-66.) (Rycaut, tome ii.)
Liefrinck (F. A.): Bijdrage tot de kennis van het eiland Bali. (Ts. ind. t.- l.- vk. Deel xxxiii. 1890.)
Littmann (Enno): Bemerkungen über den Islam in Nordabessinien. (Der Islam, vol. i. Strassburg, 1910.)
Low (Col. James): A Translation of the Keddah Annals. (Journal of the Indian Archipelago and Eastern Asia. Singapore, 1849.)
Luca (Jean de): Relations des Tartares. (Thevenot.)
Ludolf de Suchem: Ludolphi, Rectoris Ecclesiae Parochialis in Suchem, de Itinere Terrae Sanctae Liber, herausgegeben von F. Deycks. (Stuttgart, 1851.)
Lüttke (Moritz): (1) Aegyptens neue Zeit. (Leipzig, 1873.)
(2) Der Islam und seine Völker. (Gütersloh, 1878.)

Luitprandi (Pseudo-) Chronicon. (Migne, Patr. Lat. tom. cxxxvi.)
Lyall (Sir Alfred C.): Asiatic Studies. (London, 1882.)
MSOS: Mittheilungen des Seminars für Orientalische Sprachen. Berlin.
Macarius (Patriarch of Antioch): Travels of, from the Arabic of the Archdeacon Paul, translated by F. C. Belfour. (London, 1829–34.)
Mackenzie (G. Muir) and *Irby* (A. P.): Travels in the Slavonic Provinces of Turkey-in-Europe. (London, 1867.)
Mackenzie (K. R. H.): Schamyl and Circassia. Chiefly from materials collected by Dr. Friedrich Wagner, edited by. (London, 1854.)
McNair (F.): Perak and the Malays. (London, 1878.)
Maḥbūb al-Manbijī: Agapius Episcopus Mabbugensis, Historia Universalis, ed. P. L. Cheikho. (Corpus Scriptorum Christianorum Orientalium. Scriptores Arabici. Ser. iii., tom. v. Beryti, 1912.)
Makīn: Historia Saracenica, arabice olim exarata a Georgio Elmacino et latine reddita operâ Thomae Erpenii. (Lugduni Batavorum, 1625.)
Makkarī: The History of the Mohammedan Dynasties of Spain, by Ahmed ibn Mohammed Al-Makkarī, translated by Pascual de Gayangos. (London, 1840-43.)
Maqrīzī: (1) A short history of the Copts, translated from the Arabic by S. C. Malan. (London, 1873.)
(2) Histoire des Sultans Mamlouks de l'Égypte, traduite par M. Quatremère. (Paris, 1837–45.)
Mārī b. Sulaymān: Maris, Amri et Slibae De Patriarchis Nestorianorum Commentaria, ed. Henricus Gismondi. Pars Prior. (Romae, 1899.)
Marsden (William): History of Sumatra. (London, 1811.)
Marsigli (L. F.): Stato Militare dell' Imperio Ottomanno. (Amsterdam, 1732.)
Mas Latrie (J. M. J. L. de): (1) Histoire de l'île de Chypre sous le règne des princes de la maison de Lusignan. (Paris, 1852–61.)
(2) Relations et commerce de l'Afrique septentrionale avec les nations chrétiennes au moyen âge. (Paris, 1886.)
Massaja (Guglielmo): I miei trentacinque anni di missione nell' Alta Etiopia. (Roma, 1885-93.)
Massimiliano Transilvano: Epistola di, della ammirabile et stupenda nauvigatione fatta per gli Spagnuoli lo anno MDXIX. attorno il mondo. (Ramusio, tom. i.)
Masʿūdi: Les Prairies d'Or. Texte et traduction par C. Barbier de Meynard et Pavet de Courteille. (Paris, 1861–77.)
Med. Ned. Zendelinggen: Mededeelingen van wege het Nederlandsche Zendelinggenootschap. (Rotterdam.)
Menavino (G. A.): Vita et Legge Turchesca. (Venice, 1573.)
Menzel (Theodor): Das Korps der Janitscharen. (Beiträge zur Kenntnis des Orients. Band i. Jahrbuch der Münchner Orientalischen Gesellschaft, 1902–3. Berlin.)
Merensky (A.): Mohammedanismus und Christentum in Kampfe um die Negerländer Afrikas. (Allgemeine Missions-Zeitschrift, Band xxi. Gütersloh, 1894.)
Methods of Mission Work among Moslems, Being those Papers read at the First Missionary Conference on behalf of the Mohammedon World held at Cairo April 4th–9th, 1906, and the discussions thereon, which by order of the Conference were not to be issued to

the public, but were to be privately printed for the use of missionaries and the friends of missions. (New York, etc., 1906.)
Metzger (E.): Die Baduwis auf Java. (Globus, Band xliii. Braunschweig, 1883.)
Meyer (P. C.): Erforschungsgeschichte und Staatenbildungen des Westsudan. (Ergänzungsheft No. 121 zu "Petermanns Mitteilungen.") (Gotha, 1897.)
Michael the Elder: Chronique de Michael le Syrien, patriarche jacobite d'Antioche (1166–1199), éditée . . . par J. B. Chabot. (Paris, 1899–1901.)
Migne, Patr. Gr.: Patrologia Graeca. (Paris, 1857–66.)
„ *Patr. Lat.:* Patrologia Latina. (Paris, 1844–55.)
Milman (H. H.): History of Latin Christianity. (London, 1872.)
Mischlich und Lippert: Beiträge zur Geschichte der Haussastaaten von A. Mischlich. Mit Einleitung von Julius Lippert. (MSOS VI. (1903), Abtheilung III.)
Mission d'Ollone: Recherches sur les Musulmans Chinois par le commandant D'Ollone, le capitaine De Fleurelle, le capitaine Lepage, le lieutenant De Boyve. Études de A. Vissière. Notes de E. Blochet et de divers savants. (Paris, 1911.)
Mohammedan World: The Mohammedan World of to-day, being papers read at the First Missionary Conference on behalf of the Mohammedan World held at Cairo, April 4th–9th, 1906. (New York, etc., 1906.)
Montero y Vidal (D. José): Historia de la Pirateria Malayo-mahometana en Mindanao, Joló y Borneo. (Madrid, 1888.)
Moor (J. H.): Notices of the Indian Archipelago. (Singapore, 1837.)
Moore (Francis): Travels in the Inland Parts of Africa. (The World displayed; or a curious collection of voyages and travels. London, 1760.)
Morgan (J.): Mahometism explained. (London, 1723–5.)
Morié (L. J.): Histoire de l'Éthiopie. (Paris, 1904.)
Moslem World (The), a quarterly review of current events, literature, and thought among Mohammedans, and the progress of Christian Missions in Moslem lands. (London, 1911– .)
Müller (August): Der Islam im Morgen- und Abendland. (Berlin, 1885–7.)
Müller (G. F.): Sammlung Russischer Geschichte. (St. Petersburg, 1761.)
Muḥammad b. 'Uthmān al-Ḥashā'ishī: Voyage au pays des Senoussia, par le cheikh Mohammed ben Otsmane el-Hachaichi, traduit par V. Serres et Lasram. (Paris, 1903.)
Muḥammad Ḥaydar: The Tarikh-i-Rashidi of Mirza Muhammad Haidar, Dughlát. An English version, . . . by N. Elias and E. Denison Ross. (London, 1895).
Muir (Sir William): (1) The Caliphate; its rise, decline and fall. (London, 1891.)
(2) Life of Mahomet. (London, 1858–61.)
Munzinger (Werner): Abessinien. (Petermann's Mittheilungen. Gotha, 1867.)
Narshakhi: Description de Boukhara par Mohammed Nerchakhy, publié par Charles Schefer. (Paris, 1892.)
Neander (A.): (1) General History of the Christian Religion and Church. (London, 1851–8.)
(2) Memorials of Christian Life. (London, 1852.)
Netscher (E.): Kronijk van Sambas en van Soekadana. (Ts. ind. t.- l.- vk. Deel i. 1852.)

Newbold (T. J.) : Political and Statistical Account of the British Settlements in the Straits of Malacca. (London, 1839.)
Nicholson (Reynold A.) : A Literary History of the Arabs. (London, 1907.)
Niemann (G. K.) : Inleiding tot de kennis van den Islam. (Rotterdam, 1861.)
Ohsson (*C. d'*) : Histoire des Mongols. (The Hague, 1834-5.)
Ohsson (*M. d'*) : Tableau général de l'Empire Othoman. (Paris, 1820.)
Olivier (L.) : La Bosnie et l'Herzégovine, ouvrage publié sous la direction de Louis Olivier. (Paris, n.d.)
Oppel (A.) : Die religiöse Verhältnisse von Afrika. (Zeitschrift der Gesellschaft für Erdkunde zu Berlin. Vol. xxii. 1887.)
Orderici Vitalis Historia Ecclesiastica. (Migne, Patr. Lat. tom. clxxxviii.)
Palmer (H. R.) : The Kano Chronicle, translated with an introduction. (Journal of the Royal Anthropological Institute. Vol. xxxviii. 1908.)
Palmieri (Aurelio) : Die Polemik des Islam. Aus dem Italienischen übersetzt von Prof. Valentin Holzer. (Salzburg, 1902.)
Panciera (B.) : I Musulmani. (Florence, 1877.)
Pashley (Robert) : Travels in Crete. (London, 1837.)
Paulitschke (Philipp) : Harar. Forschungsreise nach den Somâl- und Galla-ländern Ost-Afrikas. (Leipzig, 1888.)
Pavy : Œuvres de Mgr. L.- A.- A. Pavy, Évêque d'Alger. (Paris, 1858.)
Perceval (A. P. Caussin de) : Essai sur l'histoire des Arabes avant l'Islamisme, pendant l'époque de Mahomet, et jusqu'à la réduction de toutes les tribus sous la loi musulmane. (Paris, 1847-8.)
Perrot (Georges) : L'île de Crète. (Paris, 1867.)
Phrantzes (Georgios) : Annales, ed. B. G. Niebuhr. (Bonnae, 1838.)
Pichler (A.) : Geschichte der Protestantismus in der orientalischen Kirche im 17. Jahrhundert, oder Der Patriarch Cyrillus Lucaris und seine Zeit. (Munich, 1862.)
Pigafetta (M. Antonio) : Viaggio atorno il mondo fatto et descritto per. (Ramusio, Tom. i.)
Pitzipios (J. G.) : L'Église orientale. (Rome, 1855.)
Plowden (W. C.) : Travels in Abyssinia and the Galla Country. (London, 1868.)
Poensen (C.) : Brieven over den Islam uit de Binnenlanden van Java. (Leiden, 1886.)
Polo (Marco) : The Book of Ser Marco Polo, the Venetian, concerning the Kingdoms and Marvels of the East, translated and edited by Sir Henry Yule. Third Edition, revised by Henri Cordier. (London, 1903.)
Prutz (H.) : Kulturgeschichte der Kreuzzüge. (Berlin, 1883.)
R. du M.M. : Revue du Monde Musulman, publié par la Mission Scientifique du Maroc. (Paris.)
Rabbath (Antoine) : Documents inédits pour servir à l'Histoire du Christianisme en Orient. Tome premier. (Paris, 1905.)
Radloff (W.) : Aus Siberien. (Leipzig, 1884.)
Raffles (Thomas Stamford) : The History of Java. (London, 1817.)
Ramusio (G. B.) : Navigationi et Viaggi. (Venice, 1559.)
Rashīd al-Dīn : Jāmi' al-Tawārīkh. Tarikh-i Moubarek-i Ghazani, histoire des Mongols, éditée par E. Blochet. (Gibb Memorial Series, vol. xviii.) (London, 1911.)
Raverty : Ṭabakāt-i-Nāṣirī : a general history of the Muḥammadan Dynasties of Asia, by Minhāj-ud-Dīn, Abū-'Umar-i-'Usmān. (London, 1881.)
Reade (W. Winwood) : African Sketch Book. (London, 1873.)

GG 2

Reclus (Elisée) : Nouvelle Géographie Universelle. (Paris, 1876-91.)
Reinaud, see *Abu'l-Fidā*.
Renaudot (E.) : Historia Patriarcharum Alexandrinorum Jacobitarum. (Paris, 1713.)
Report of Centenary Conference on the Protestant Missions of the World, held in London, 1888, edited by Rev. J. J. Johnston. (London, 1889.)
Rev. col. int. : Revue Coloniale Internationale. (Amsterdam.)
Richter (J.) : Die Propaganda des Islam als Wegbestreiterin der modernen Mission. (Missionswissenschaftliche Studien. Festschrift zum 70. Geburtstag des Herrn Prof. Dr. Gustav Warneck.) (Berlin, 1904.)
Riedel (J. G. F.) : (1) De Sluik- en Kroesharige Rassen tusschen Selebes en Papua. (The Hague, 1886.)
(2) The Island of Flores or Pulan Bunga. The Tribes between Sika and Manggaraai. (Rev. col. int., tome ii. 1886.)
Rinn (Louis) : Marabouts et Khouan. (Algiers, 1884.)
Roscoe (John) : The Baganda. (London, 1911.)
Ross (Alexander) : A Needful Caveat, or Admonition, for them who desire to know what Use may be made of, or if there be danger in Reading the Alcoran. (The Alcoran of Mahomet, translated out of Arabick into French, by Sieur de Ryer, ... and newly Englished, for the satisfaction of all that desire to look into the Turkish Vanities.) (London, 1688.)
Rouffaer (G. P.) : Het tijdperk van godsdienstovergang (1400-1600) in den Maleischen Archipel. (Bijdr. t.d.t.l. en vlk., dl. 50.) (1899.)
Rubruck : The Journey of William of Rubruck to the Eastern Parts of the World, 1253-55, as narrated by himself. Translated . . . . by William Woodville Rockhill. (Hakluyt Society. Second Series. No. iv.) (London, 1900.)
Rüppell (Eduard) : Reise in Abyssinien. (Frankfurt am Main, 1838.)
Rycaut (Sir Paul) : Histoire de l'état présent de l'empire ottoman, traduit de l'Anglais de Monsieur Ricaut, par M. Briot. (Amsterdam, 1672.)
Sachau (Eduard) : Über den zweiten Chalifen Omar. Ein Charakterbild aus der ältesten Geschichte des Islams. (Sitzungsberichte der Königlichen Preussischen Akademie der Wissenschaften. Berlin, 1902.)
Sacy (Le Bon Silvestre de) : Exposé de la Religion des Druzes. (Paris, 1838.)
Ṣalībā b. Yūḥannā : Maris, Amri et Slibae De Patriarchis Nestorianorum Commentaria, ed. Henricus Gismondi. Pars Altera. (Romae, 1896.)
Salmon (C. S.) : British Policy in West Africa. (Contemporary Review, 1882.)
Samson : Samsonis Abbatis Cordubensis Apologeticus Liber. (Henrique Florez : España Sagrada, tom. xi.) (Madrid, 1747-74.)
Sansovino (Francesco) : Historia Universale dell' Origine et Imperio de' Turchi. (Venice, 1573.)
Sayyid 'Alī Akbar : Trois chapitres du Khitay Namèh. Texte persan et traduction française par Charles Schefer. (Mélanges Orientaux. Publications de l'École des Langues Orientales Vivantes. IIe série. Vol. ix. Paris, 1883.)
Schack (A. F. Graf von) : Poesie und Kunst der Araber in Spanien und Sicilien. (Stuttgart, 1877.)
Schefer (C.) : Notice sur les relations des peuples musulmans avec les Chinois, depuis l'extension de l'Islamisme jusqu'à la fin de XVe siècle. (Centenaire de l'École des Langues Orientales Vivantes, 1795-1895. Recueil de Mémoires publiés par les Professeurs de l'École. Paris, 1895.)

Scheffler (Johannes): Türcken-Schrifft: von den Ursachen der Türckischen Ueberziehung und der Zertretung des Volckes Gottes. (1664.)
Schiltberger (Hans): Reisebuch, herausgegeben von V. Langmantel. (Tübingen, 1885.)
Semper (C.): Die Philippinen und ihre Bewohner. (Würzburg, 1869.)
Severus: Severus ben el Moqaffa', Historia Patriarcharum Alexandrinorum, ed. C. F. Seybold. (Corpus Scriptorum Christianorum Orientalium. Scriptores Arabici. Ser. iii. Tom. ix.) (Beryti, 1904– .)
Shedd (W. A.): Islam and the Oriental Churches. (Philadelphia, 1904.)
Silbernagl (Isidor): Verfassung und gegenwärtiger Bestand sämtlicher Kirchen des Orients. 2te Auflage. (Regensburg, 1904.)
Simon (G.): Islam und Christentum im Kampf um die Eroberung der animistischen Heidenwelt. Beobachtungen aus der Mohammedanermission in Niederländisch-Indien. (Berlin, 1910.)
Sitz. d. Akad. d. Wiss., Philos.-hist. Cl.: Sitzungberichte der philosophisch-historischen Classe der kaiserlichen Akademie der Wissenschaften. (Vienna.)
Smith (Thomas): Remarks upon the Manners, Religion and Government of the Turks. (London, 1678.)
Smith (W. J.): The Present Phases of the Mohammedan Question. (The Churchman. London, Jan., 1888.)
Spons (Jacob): Reisen durch Italien, Dalmatien, Griechenland und die Morgenländer. (Nürnberg, 1713.)
Sprenger (A.): Das Leben und die Lehre des Mohammad. (Berlin, 1861.)
Steinschneider (Moritz): Polemische und apologetische Litteratur in arabischer Sprache, zwischen Muslimen, Christen und Juden. (Leipzig, 1877.)
Stirling-Maxwell (Sir William): Don John of Austria. (London, 1883.)
Ṭabarī: Annales quos scripsit Abu Djafar Mohammed ibn Djarir At-Ṭabari, ed. M. J. de Goeje et alii. (Leiden, 1885–93.)
Ta'rīkh al-Sūdān: Tarikh es-Soudan par Abderrahman ben Abdallah ben 'Imran ben 'Amir es-Sa'di. Texte arabe edité par O. Houdas. (Paris, 1898.)
Tavernier (J. B.) (1) The six voyages. (London, 1677.)
(2) Travels in India. (London, 1678.)
(3) A New Relation of the Inner-Part of the Grand Seignor's Seraglio. (London, 1677.)
Thevenot (M.): Relations de divers voyages curieux. (Paris, 1696.)
Thiersant (P. Dabry de): Le Mahométisme en Chine. (Paris, 1878.)
Thomas of Margā: The Book of Governors: the Historia Monastica of Thomas, Bishop of Margâ A.D. 840, edited by E. A. Wallis Budge. (London, 1893.)
Thomson (Joseph): (1) Mohammedanism in Central Africa. (Contemporary Review, Dec., 1886.)
(2) Note on the African Tribes of the British Empire. (The Journal of the Anthropological Institute of Great Britain and Ireland. Vol. xvi. London, 1887.)
Tijānī: Voyage du Scheikh Et-Tidjani dans la régence de Tunis, pendant les années 706, 707, et 708 de l'hégire (1306–1309); traduit de l'arabe par M. Alphonse Rousseau. (J. A. ivme série, tome xx., 1852.)
Tournefort (J.P.): A Voyage into the Levant. (London, 1741.)
Ts. ind. t.- l.- vk.: Tijdschrift voor Indische Taal-, Land- en Volkenkunde. (Batavia.)

Turchicae Spurcitiae et Perfidiae Suggillatio et Confutatio. (Paris, 1516.)
'Ubayd Allāh : Tuḥfat al-Hind. (Dihlī, A.H. 1309.)
Usāma b. Munqidh : Kitāb al-I'tibār, ed. H. Derenbourg. ii.me Partie : Texte arabe de l'autobiographie d'Ousâma. (Publications de l'École des Langues Orientales Vivantes. iime ser., tome. xii (iime Partie). (Paris, 1886.)
Vambéry (Arminius) : (1) Geschichte Bochara's. (Stuttgart, 1872.)
„ „ (2) Sketches of Central Asia. (London, 1868.)
Vasil'ev (V. P.) : О движенiи магометанства въ Китаѣ. (St. Petersburg, 1867.)
Veniero ; Descrittione dell' Imperio Turchesco del Revermo Monsre Maffeo Veniero, Arcivescovo di Corfù. (R. D. Marci Bibliotheca, Venice. Classe vii., Cod. 882.)
Verh. Bat. Gen. van K. en W. : Verhandelingen van het Bataviaasch Genootschap van Kunsten en Wetenschappen. (Batavia.)
Veth (P. J.) : (1) Atchin en zijne betrekkingen tot Nederland. (Leiden, 1873.)
(2) Borneo's Wester-Afdeeling. (Zaltbommel, 1854.)
(3) Java, geographisch, ethnologisch, historisch. Tweede Druk bewerkt door J. F. Snelleman en J. F. Niermeyer. (Haarlem, 1896–1907.)
Vivien de Saint-Martin (L.) : Nouveau Dictionnaire de Géographie Universelle. (Paris, 1879–95.)
WZKM : Wiener Zeitschrift für die Kunde des Morgenlandes.
Waitz (Theodor) : Anthropologie der Naturvölker. (Leipzig, 1860.)
Wansleben (J. M.) : Histoire de l'église d'Alexandie. (Paris, 1677.)
Waṣṣāf : Geschichte ; persisch herausgegeben und deutsch übersetzt von Hammer-Purgstall. (Vienna, 1856.)
Weil (Gustav) : Geschichte der Chalifen. (Mannheim, 1846–51.)
Wellhausen (J.) : Skizzen und Vorarbeiten. (Berlin, 1885–99.)
Westermann (D.) : Islam in the West and Central Sudan. (The International Review of Missions, vol. i. Edinburgh, 1912.)
Wetzer und Welte's Kirchenlexicon. Zweite Auflage. (Freiburg im Breisgau, 1885 sqq.)
Whishaw (B. and E. M.) : Arabic Spain. (London, 1912.)
Wilken (N. P.) en *Schwarz* (J. A.) (1) Gedachten over het stichten einer zending in Bolaäng-Mongondou. (Med. Ned. Zendelinggen. Vol. xi., 1867.)
(2) Het Heidendom en de Islam in Bolaäng-Mongondou. (id. id.)
Wise (James) : The Muhammadans of Eastern Bengal. (J. A. S. B. Vol. lxiii., Part iii., 1894.)
Wright (William) : A short History of Syriac Literature. (London, 1894.)
Wüstenfeld (F.) : Die Geschichtschreiber der Araber und ihre Werke. (Göttingen, 1882.)
Yaḥyā b. Ādam : Le livre de l'Impôt Foncier, publié par Th. W. Juynboll. (Leide, 1896.)
Yāqūt : Mu'jam al-Buldān. Jacut's Geographisches Wörterbuch, herausgegeben von F. Wüstenfeld. (Leipzig, 1866–73.)
Yule (H.) : Cathay and the Way thither. (London, 1866.)
ZDMG : Zeitschrift der deutschen morgenländischen Gesellschaft. (Leipzig.)
Zayn al-Dīn : Tuhfaḥ al-mujāhidīn. Historia dos Portugueses no Malabar por Zinadím. Manuscripto Arabe publicado e traduzido por David Lopes. (Lisboa, 1898.)
Zenker (J. T.) : Das chinesische Reich, nach dem türkischen Khatainame. (Z.D.M.G., vol. xv. Leipzig, 1861.)

Zmaievich: Notizie universali dello stato di Albania e dell' operato da Monsig. Vincenzo Zmaievich, arcivescovo di Antivari, esaminate nelle Congregationi Generali di Propaganda Fide di 3 Debr. 1703–12 Febr. 1704. (Bibliotheca Barberina, Rome, Nr L. 126.)

Zollinger (H.): (1) The Island of Lombok. Journal of the Indian Archipelago, vol. v. (Singapore, 1851.)
(2) Verslag van eene reis naar Bima en Soembawa. (Verh. Bat. Gen. van K. en W. Deel xxiii. 1850.)

Zwemer (S. M.): Islam: A Challenge to faith. (New York, 1908.)

INDEX.